MACROECONOMICS

Visit the *Macroeconomics: A European Perspective* Companion Website at **www.pearsoned.co.uk/blanchard** to find valuable **student** learning material including:

- Multiple choice questions to help to test learning.
- Active graphs which allow students to manipulate and interact with key graphs to develop their understanding of macroeconomics.
- Glossary explaining key terms.
- A new **Macroeconomics in the News** blog site, updated monthly with the latest news stories related to chapters in the book.

There is also material for **instructors:**

- Instructor's Manual including a motivating question and summaries section of key material for each chapter.
- PowerPoint slides that can be downloaded and used for presentations, containing diagrams and tables that offer you flexibility in your teaching.
- Testbank of question material providing hundreds of questions grouped by chapter.

D1247423

Refreshingly original for an undergraduate text. Relevant applications to European economies and elsewhere are plentiful, and the breadth of topics covered is truly impressive. Unlike many texts at this level, the authors do not avoid potentially tricky, yet important topics; they do their utmost to relate textbook theory to real-world economics. Relative to competing texts, I think students would find this more engaging.
Paul Scanlon, Trinity College Dublin

Up-to-date material on the euro, especially in light of the current crisis; strong open economy emphasis; and lots of examples from European countries. There is so much new material on the monetary union that there is much less need for supplementary reading.
Pekka Ilmakunnas, Aalto University School of Economics

The European adaptation keeps the structure of the original book, already appreciated by lecturers. It integrates specific analysis of recent economic events (in particular the sub-prime crisis), illustrates study cases with European examples and proposes extended theoretical developments. It is sure to become even more popular than its famous ancestor among European students.
Bertrand Candelon, Maastricht University School of Business and Economics

This edition has clear exposition and keeps the analytical level simple, but still at a detailed level. The chapter on the credit crunch is particularly interesting and well written, and the use of the *IS–LM* model to describe the effects of the crisis is well presented. Given the level of the maths explanation in the text, all students should find it easy to follow the analysis in the book.
Gianluigi Vernasca, University of Essex

This is a truly outstanding textbook that beautifully marries theory, empirics and policy. It is surely destined to become the gold standard against which all other texts must be measured.
Charles Bean, Deputy Governor, Bank of England

This book succeeds in explaining complex economic questions with simple language whilst always referring to the data. The chapters on Europe are a welcome feature and will help students to understand the challenges and potentials of the European project.
Lucrezia Reichlin, London Business School

MACROECONOMICS

A EUROPEAN PERSPECTIVE

Olivier Blanchard, Alessia Amighini
and Francesco Giavazzi

Prentice Hall
is an imprint of

PEARSON

Harlow, England • London • New York • Boston • San Francisco • Toronto
Sydney • Tokyo • Singapore • Hong Kong • Seoul • Taipei • New Delhi
Cape Town • Madrid • Mexico City • Amsterdam • Munich • Paris • Milan

Pearson Education Limited

Edinburgh Gate

Harlow

Essex CM20 2JE

England

and Associated Companies throughout the world

Visit us on the World Wide Web at:

www.pearsoned.co.uk

First published 2010

© Pearson Education Limited 2010

The rights of Olivier Blanchard, Alessia Amighini and Francesco Giavazzi
to be identified as authors of this work have been asserted by them in
accordance with the Copyright, Designs and Patents Act 1988.

All rights reserved. No part of this publication may be reproduced, stored in
a retrieval system, or transmitted in any form or by any means, electronic,
mechanical, photocopying, recording or otherwise, without either the prior
written permission of the publisher or a licence permitting restricted copying
in the United Kingdom issued by the Copyright Licensing Agency Ltd,
Saffron House, 6–10 Kirby Street, London EC1N 8TS.

ISBN: 978-0-273-72800-9

British Library Cataloguing-in-Publication Data

A catalogue record for this book is available from the British Library

Library of Congress Cataloging-in-Publication Data

A catalog record for this book is available from the Library of Congress

10 9 8 7 6 5 4 3
13 12

Typeset in 9.5/12.5 pt Charter by 35

Printed and bound in Malaysia

BRIEF CONTENTS

CONTENTS

EXTENSIONS

Supporting resources

Visit **www.pearsoned.co.uk/blanchard** to find valuable online resources

Companion Website for students
- Multiple choice questions.
- Active graphs.
- Glossary.
- A new **Macroeconomics in the News** blog site, updated monthly with the latest news stories related to chapters in the book

For instructors
- Instructor's Manual.
- PowerPoint slides.
- Testbank.

Also: The Companion Website provides the following features:

- Search tool to help locate specific items of content.
- E-mail results and profile tools to send results of quizzes to instructors.
- Online help and support to assist with website usage and troubleshooting.

For more information please contact your local Pearson Education sales representative or visit **www.pearsoned.co.uk/blanchard**.

LIST OF FIGURES

LIST OF TABLES

LIST OF FOCUS BOXES

ABOUT THE AUTHORS

Olivier Blanchard is the Class of 1941 Professor of Economics at MIT. He did his undergraduate work in France and received a PhD in economics from MIT in 1977. He taught at Harvard from 1977 to 1982, and has taught at MIT since 1983. He has frequently received the award for best teacher in the department for economics.

He has done research on many macroeconomic issues, from the effects of fiscal policy, to the role of expectations, price rigidities, speculative bubbles, unemployment in Western Europe, transition in Eastern Europe, labour market institutions and unemployment, and, most recently, the financial and macroeconomic crisis. He has done work for many governments and many international organisations, including the World Bank, the IMF, the OECD, the European Commission and the EBRD. He has published more than 160 articles and edited or written more than 15 books, including *Lectures on Macroeconomics* with Stanley Fischer.

He is a research associate of the National Bureau of Economic Research, a fellow of the Econometric Society, a member of the American Academy of Arts and Sciences, and a past vice president of the American Economic Association. He is a past member of the French Council of Economic Advisers, and a past editor of the *Quarterly Journal of Economics* and of the *American Economic Journal: Macroeconomics*. He is currently on leave from MIT, working as the chief economist of the IMF.

Olivier Blanchard lives in Washington with his wife, Noelle, and has three daughters, Marie, Serena and Giulia.

Francesco Giavazzi is Professor of Economics at Bocconi University in Milan and has been, for many years, a visiting professor at MIT where he has often taught the basic macroeconomics course for undergraduates. After studying electrical engineering in Milan, he received a PhD in economics from MIT in 1978. He then taught at the University of Essex.

His research has focused on fiscal policy, exchange rates and the creation of the European Monetary Union. His books include *Limiting Exchange Rate Flexibility: the European Monetary System* with Alberto Giovannini and *The Future of Europe: Reform or Decline* with Alberto Alesina.

He has frequently advised governments and central banks: he was the Houblon-Norman Fellow at the Bank of England, evaluated IMF research, assessed Sweden's central bank for the Swedish Parliament with Fredrick Mishkin, and is currently an adviser to the French Treasury. He was also the macroeconomics editor of the *European Economic Review*.

Francesco Giavazzi divides his life between Milan and Cambridge (Massachusetts), although his best days are spent skiing in the Dolomites and rowing along the canals of Venice.

Alessia Amighini is Assistant Professor of Economics at Università del Piemonte Orientale in Novara (Italy) and Adjoint Professor of International Economics at the Catholic University in Milan. After graduating from Bocconi University in 1996, she received a PhD in Development Economics from the University of Florence, and then

worked as an Associate Economist at the Macroeconomics and Development Policies Branch of UNCTAD (Geneva) from 2003 to 2006.

She lives in Milan with her husband and two children.

PUBLISHER'S ACKNOWLEDGEMENTS

We are grateful to the following for permission to reproduce copyright material:

CARTOONS

Cartoons on pages 23 and 40, copyright Universal Press Syndicate; Cartoons on pages 37, 287 and 517, copyright cartoonstock.com; Cartoon on page 279, copyright globecartoon.com; Cartoon on page 476 from *Haitzinger Karikaturen 2004*, Bruckmann (Haitzinger, H. 2004) p. 9, copyright Horst Haitzinger.

FIGURES

Figure 1.1 from *World Economic Outlook*, Spring IMF (2009) p. 1; Figures 2.4, 6.3, 8.2, 8.3, 8.4, 8.5 and 8.7 after Eurostat, European Commission, © European Communities, 2009; Figure 5.16 from *The Monetary Transmission Mechanism in the Euro Area: More evidence from Var Analysis*, Working Paper No. 91, December, European Central Bank (Peersman, G. and Smets, F. 2001), data available free of charge from http://www.ecb. europa.eu/home; Figure 7.1 after UK Office for National Statistics, Crown Copyright material is reproduced with the permission of the Controller, Office of Public Sector Information (OPSI); Figures 8.9 and 8.10 from CESifo DICE database; Figure 9.18 from *Worldwide Trends in Energy Use and Efficiency: Key Insights from IEA Indicator Analysis*, International Energy Agency (2008), © OECD/IEA, 2008; Figure 9.19 from *Macroeconomic Policy in a World Economy*, W.W. Norton and Co. Inc. (Taylor, J. B. 1994); Figure 12.3 from Penn World Tables, Center for International Comparisons at the University of Pennsylvania; Figure 14.4 from Dale Jorgenson, post.economics.harvard.edu/faculty/ jorgenson/papers/aea5.ppt; Figure 18.3 from *The Role of Financial Markets' Openess in the Transmission of Shocks in Europe* (National Institute of Economic and Social Research, Discussion Paper No. 271), National Institute of Economic and Social Research (Al-Eyd, A., Barrell, R. and Holland, D. 2006) p. 18; Figure 20.2 from IMF World Economic Outlook Database, IMF; Figure 20.6 adapted from Bank for International Settlements, 2009 Annual Report; Figures 20.13 and 20.15 from *World Economic Outlook, update,* July, IMF (2009) Figures 2 and 1.14; Figure 20.14 from *A Tale of Two Depressions*, voxeu.org, (Eichengreen, B. and O'Rourke, K. H.); Figure 23.1 from 'Political and monetary institutions and public financial policies in the industrial countries', *Economic Policy*, October, pp. 341–92 (Grilli, V., Masciandaro, D. and Tabellini, G. 1991), Wiley-Blackwell; Figure 25.3 from 'Tenth anniversary of the ECB', *Monthly Bulletin*, June, p. 39 (ECB 2008), European Central Bank, data available free of charge from http://www.ecb.europa. eu/home; Figure 25.4 from Smant, D. J. C. 'ECB Interest Rate and Money Growth Rules', Rotterdam, Erasmus University (mimeo); Figure 25.5 from *Monthly Bulletin*, August (ECB 2009), European Central Bank, data available free of charge from http://www.ecb.europa.eu/home; Figure 25.6 from *Twenty-seven is a Crowd: Preparing the ECB for Enlargement*, CEPR Discussion Paper 09, CEPR (Francesco, G., Baldwin, R., Berglof, E. and Widgrén, M. 2001); Figure 26.1 from *Monthly Bulletin*, April (2007), European Central Bank, data available free of charge from http://www.ecb.europa.eu/home.

TABLES

Table 1.1 from *European Economy, Statistical Annex*, Spring, European Commission (2009), © European Communities, 2009; Table 1.4 after IMF World Economic Outlook Database, IMF; Tables 3.1 and 26.1 after Eurostat, European Commission, © European Communities, 2009; Table 7.2 after UK Office for National Statistics, Crown Copyright material is reproduced with the permission of the Controller, Office of Public Sector Information (OPSI); Table 7.4 after Central Statistics Office, Ireland; Table 8.2 after CESifo database; Table 11.3 from 'Ten years of Mrs T.', *NBER Macroeconomics Annual*, 4, Table 3, p. 23 (Bean, C. R. and Symons, J. 1989), National Bureau of Economic Research; Table 12.3 from Penn Tables, Center for International Comparisons, University of Pennsylvania; Table 13.2 from *Postwar Economic Reconstruction and Lessons for the East Today* (Rudiger Dornbusch, Willem Nolling, and Richard Layard, eds), MIT Press, Cambridge (Saint-Paul, G. 1993) 'Economic Reconstruction in France, 1945–1958', © 1993 Massachusetts Institute of Technology, by permission of The MIT Press; Table 16.1 from *Public Policy Towards Pensions* (Sylvester Schieber and

John B. Shoven, eds), MIT Press (Venti, S. and Wise, D. 1997) Table A.1, 'The Wealth of Cohorts: Retirement and Saving and the Changing Assets of Older Americans', © 1997 Massachusetts Institute of Technology, by permission of The MIT Press; Table 20.2 from *Liquidity and Financial Cycles*, Federal Reserve Bank of New York (Adrian, T. and Shin, H. S. 2006); Tables 22.2 and 22.5 from *Studies in the Quantities of Money* (Friedman, M., ed.), University of Chicago Press (Cagan, P. 1956) Table 1; Tables 23.1 and 23.2 from 'Comparing economic models of the Euro economy', *Economic Modelling*, 21 (Wallis, K. F. 2004), Elsevier, copyright 2004, with permission from Elsevier; Table 26.2 from 'Regional non-adjustment and fiscal policy', *Economic Policy*, 13(26), pp. 205–59 (Obstfeld, M. and Peri, G. 1998), Wiley-Blackwell.

TEXT

Box on p. 4 after 'The History of the European Union', http://europa.eu/abc/history/index_en.htm, © European Communities, 2009; Box on p. 211 from 'The role of monetary policy', *American Economic Review*, 58(1), 1–17 (Friedman, M. 1968), American Economic Association; Box on p. 238 after *Ten Years of Mrs T.*, Discussion Paper 316, CEPR (Bean, C. and Symons, J. 1989); Box on p. 268 after *Postwar Economic Reconstruction and Lessons for the East Today* (Dornbusch, R., Nolling, W. and Layard, R., eds), MIT Press, Cambridge (Saint-Paul, G. 1993) 'Economic reconstruction in France, 1945–58', © 1993 Massachusetts Institute of Technology, by permission of The MIT Press.

In some instances we have been unable to trace the owners of copyright material, and we would appreciate any information that would enable us to do so.

GUIDED TOUR

Chapter **Introductions** include a news story or example to illustrate a macroeconomic concept or theme that is built upon within the chapter.

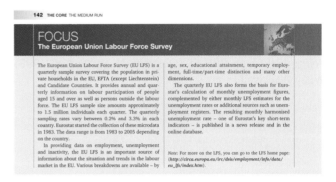

Focus boxes expand on macroeconomic events or examples.

Margin notes create a classroom-like dialogue, remind the student of key terms and issues, and add context to the main text.

At the end of each chapter, a short **Summary** will help consolidate learning, bringing together the key concepts of the chapter to assist with review and revision.

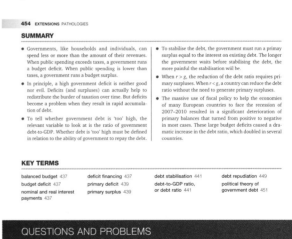

End of chapter questions remind students what they have just read and test that students have understood the chapter.

Chapters new to the European edition include chapters on the financial crisis, European economic and monetary integration, the euro, and high debt.

QUESTIONS AND PROBLEMS

QUICK CHECK

1. *Using the information in this chapter, label each of the following statements true, false or uncertain. Explain briefly.*

a. Changes in the current one-year real interest rate are likely to have a much larger effect on spending than changes in expected future one-year real interest rates.

b. The introduction of expectations in the goods market model makes the *IS* curve flatter, although it is still downward-sloping.

c. Current money demand depends on current and expected future nominal interest rates.

d. The rational expectations assumption implies that consumers take into account the effects of future fiscal policy on output.

e. Expected future fiscal policy affects expected future economic activity but not current economic activity.

f. Depending on its effect on expectations, a fiscal contraction may actually lead to an economic expansion.

g. Ireland's experience with deficit reduction programmes in 1982 and 1987 provides strong evidence against the hypothesis that deficit reduction can lead to an output expansion.

2. *During the late 1990s, many observers claimed that the USA had transformed into a New Economy, and this justified the very high values for stock prices observed at the time.*

a. Discuss how the belief in the New Economy, combined with the increase in stock prices, affected consumption spending.

b. Stock prices subsequently decreased. Discuss how this might have affected consumption.

3. *For each of the changes in expectations in (a) through (d), determine whether there is a shift in the IS curve, the LM curve, both curves or neither. In each case, assume that expected current and future inflation are equal to zero and that no other exogenous variable is changing.*

a. a decrease in the expected future real interest rate

b. an increase in the current money supply

c. an increase in expected future taxes

d. a decrease in expected future income

4. *Consider the following statement.*

'The rational expectations assumption is unrealistic because, essentially, it amounts to the assumption that every consumer has perfect knowledge of the economy.' Discuss.

5. *A new head of state, who promised during the campaign that she would cut taxes, has just been elected. People trust that she will keep her promise, but expect that the tax cuts will be implemented only in the future. Determine the impact of the election on current output, the current interest rate, and current private spending under each of the assumptions in (a) through (c). In each case, indicate what you think will happen to Y"*, *r" and T"*, *and then how these changes in expectations affect output today.*

a. The central bank will not change its policy.

b. The central bank will act to prevent any change in future output.

c. The central bank will act to prevent any change in the future interest rate.

DIG DEEPER

6. The Clinton deficit reduction package

In 1992, the US deficit was $290 billion. During the presidential campaign, the large deficit emerged as a major issue. When President Clinton won the election, deficit reduction was the first item on the new administration's agenda.

a. What does deficit reduction imply for the medium run and the long run? What are the advantages of reducing the deficit?

In the final version passed by Congress in August 1993, the deficit reduction package included a reduction of $20 billion in its first year, increasing gradually to $131 billion four years later.

b. Why was the deficit reduction package back loaded? What are the advantages and disadvantages of this approach to deficit reduction?

In February 1993, President Clinton presented the budget in his State of the Union address. He asked Alan Greenspan, the Fed chairman, to sit next to First Lady Hillary Clinton during the delivery of the address.

c. What was the purpose of this symbolic gesture? How can the Fed's decision to use expansionary monetary policy in the future affect the short-run response of the economy?

7. A new central bank chairman

Suppose, in a hypothetical economy, that the chairman of the central bank unexpectedly announces that he will retire in one year. At the same time, the head of state announces her nominee to replace the retiring central bank chair. Financial market participants expect the nominee to be confirmed by the government. They also believe that the nominee will conduct a more contractionary monetary policy in the future. In other words, market participants expect the money supply to fall in the future.

EUROPE IN PROGRESS

Since 1957, when six European countries (Belgium, the Federal Republic of Germany, France, Italy, Luxembourg and the Netherlands) decided to build a European Economic Community (EEC) based on a common market covering a whole range of goods and services, European economic integration has gone a long way. It now includes 27 countries, 16 of which have also formed a monetary union. Many others have already applied for euro membership, and the few who initially decided to opt out might change their minds in the future.

Chapter 25 European economic and monetary integration

Chapter 25 describes the monetary history of Europe, the early experiments with the system of fixed exchange rates to the European Monetary System (EMS), until the signing of the Maastricht Treaty in 1991, when 12 European countries formally decided to adopt a common currency. It also describes the European Central Bank (ECB), its institutional structure, goals and strategies.

Chapter 26 The euro: the ins and the outs

Chapter 26 discusses the economic reasons for a monetary union and whether the euro area meets them, i.e. whether it is an optimal currency area. It then reviews the first ten years of the euro (1999–2009) and asks why did some European countries decide to opt out of the single currency, and whether the recent financial and economic turmoil has altered the incentives to join EMU.

Source: CartoonStock.com.

Key terms are highlighted in the text when they first appear. These terms are also included in the **Glossary** at the end of the book and on the website.

KEY TERMS

permanent income theory of consumption 327	human wealth 327	inter-temporal budget constraint 329	static expectations 337
life cycle theory of consumption 327	non-human wealth 327	consumption smoothing 330	Tobin's *q* 338
financial wealth 327	total wealth 327	discount rate 330	user cost of capital, or rental cost of capital 338
housing wealth 327	representative consumer 328	panel data set 334	profitability 340
	endowment 328		cash flow 340

QUESTIONS AND PROBLEMS

QUICK CHECK

1. *Using the information in this chapter, label each of the following statements true, false or uncertain. Explain briefly.*

a. For a typical university student, human wealth and non-human wealth are approximately equal.

b. Natural experiments, such as retirement, do not suggest that expectations of future income are a major factor affecting consumption.

c. Buildings and factories depreciate much faster than machines do.

d. A high value for Tobin's *q* indicates that the stock market believes that capital is over-valued, and thus investment should be lower.

e. Economists have found that the effect of current profit on investment can be fully explained by the effect of current profit on expectations of future profits.

f. Data from the past three decades in the USA suggest that corporate profits are closely tied to the business cycle.

g. Changes in consumption and investment typically occur in the same direction and at roughly the same magnitude.

2. *A consumer has non-human wealth equal to €100 000. She earns €40 000 this year and expects her salary to rise by 5% in real terms each year for the following two years. She will then retire. The real interest rate is equal to 0% and is expected to remain at 0% in the future. Labour income is taxed at a rate of 25%.*

a. What is this consumer's human wealth?

b. What is her total wealth?

c. If she expects to live for seven more years after retiring and wants her consumption to remain the same (in real terms) every year from now on, how much can she consume earlier, by how much could this consumer increase consumption now and in the future?

e. Suppose now that at retirement, social security will start paying benefits each year equal to 60% of this consumer's earnings during her last working year. Assume that benefits are not taxed. How much can she consume this year and still maintain constant consumption over her lifetime?

3. *A potato crisp manufacturer is considering buying another crisp-making machine that costs €100 000. The machine will depreciate by 8% per year. It will generate real profits equal to €18 000 next year, €18 000(1 − 8%) two years from now (that is, the same real profits but adjusted for depreciation), €18 000(1 − 8%)² three years from now and so on. Determine whether the manufacturer should buy the machine if the real interest rate is assumed to remain constant at each rate in (a) through (c).*

a. 5%

b. 10%

c. 15%

4. *Suppose that at age 22, you have just finished university and have been offered a job with a starting salary of €40 000. Your salary will remain constant in real terms. However, you have also been accepted onto a post-graduate course. The course can be completed in two years. Upon graduation, you expect your starting salary to be 10% higher in real terms and to remain constant in real terms thereafter. The tax rate on labour income is 40%.*

a. If the real interest rate is zero and you expect to retire at age 60 (i.e. if you do not do the postgraduate course, you expect to work for 38 years total), what is the maximum you should be willing to pay in tuition to do the

PREFACE

This European edition of *Macroeconomics* is based on the well-tested US edition and on the experience of previous European editions in national languages – French, German, Spanish and Italian – some of which have been used in universities around Europe for many years (the Italian edition since 1998).

We had three goals in preparing this edition:

- To provide an integrated view of macroeconomics.

  The book is built on one underlying model, a model that draws the implications of equilibrium conditions in three sets of markets: the goods market, the financial markets, and the labour market. Depending on the issue at hand, the parts of the model relevant to the issue are developed in more detail while the other parts are simplified or lurk in the background. But the underlying model is always the same. This way, you will see macroeconomics as a coherent whole, not a collection of models. And you will be able to make sense not only of past macroeconomic events, but also of those that unfold in the future.
- To make close contact with current macroeconomic events.

  What makes macroeconomics exciting is the light it sheds on what is happening around the world, from the economic impact of the introduction of the euro in Western Europe, to the large US current account deficits, to the economic rise of China and other large emerging economies, and last but not least to the origins of the world crisis that started in 2007. These events – and many more – are described in the book, not in footnotes, but in the text or in detailed boxes. Each box shows how you can use what you have learned to get an understanding of these events. Our belief is that these boxes not only convey the 'life' of macroeconomics, but also reinforce the lessons from the models, making them more concrete and easier to grasp.
- To focus on European events, both from the euro area and from the countries outside the euro, Sweden, Denmark and the UK in particular.

  This edition makes a particular effort to use mainly data, figures and examples taken from the European experience. Two chapters are dedicated to Europe. They describe the long process that led some countries to adopt the euro and others to decide not to adopt it. We have also added many new 'boxes' focusing on Europe – for example, on inflation targeting in

Sweden, on the major macro-econometric models used in the euro area, on Poland's macroeconomic performance during the crisis, on the costs and benefits of a monetary union, on how to measure expected inflation in the euro area, and on the criticisms to the Growth and Stability Pact.

'ORGANISATION'

The book is organised around two central parts: a core, and a set of three major extensions. An introduction precedes the core. The set of extensions is followed by a part on the role of policy and a part dedicated to European Economic and Monetary integration. The flowchart on p. 28 makes it easy to see how the chapters are organised and fit within the book's overall structure.

- Chapters 1 and 2 introduce the basic facts and issues of macroeconomics.

  Chapter 1 offers a tour of the world, from Europe to the United States, to China and the other large emerging economies of Brazil, India and Russia. Some instructors will prefer to cover Chapter 1 later, perhaps after Chapter 2, which introduces basic concepts; articulates the notions of short run, medium run, and long run; and gives the reader a quick tour of the book.
- Chapter 3 through 14 constitute the **core**.

  Chapters 3–6 focus on the **short run**. Chapters 3–5 characterise equilibrium in the goods market and in the financial markets, and they derive the basic model used to study short-run movements in output, the *IS–LM* model. Chapter 6 shows how to extend the basic *IS–LM* model to an open economy.

  Chapters 7–10 focus on the **medium run**. Chapter 7 focuses on equilibrium in the labour market and introduces the notion of the natural rate of unemployment. Chapters 8–10 develop a model based on aggregate demand and aggregate supply, and show how that model can be used to understand movements in activity and movements in inflation, both in the short and in the medium run.

  Chapters 11–13 focus on the **long run**. Chapter 11 describes the facts, showing the evolution of output across countries and over long periods of time. Chapters 12 and 13 develop a model of growth, and describe how capital accumulation and technological progress determine growth. Chapter 13 focuses on the determinants of technological progress, and on its effects not only in the long run, but also in the short run and in the medium run. This topic is typically not covered in textbooks but is important. And the chapter shows how one can integrate the short run, the medium run, and the long run – a clear example of the payoff to an integrated approach to macroeconomics.

- Chapters 14–22 cover the three major **extensions**.

  Chapters 14–17 expand the analysis of **expectations** in the short run and in the medium run. Expectations play a major role in most economic decisions, and, by implication, play a major role in the determination of output.

  Chapters 18 and 19 focus on the implications of **openness** of modern economies. Chapter 19 focuses on the implications of different exchange rate regimes, from flexible exchange rates, to fixed exchange rates, currency boards, and dollarization.

  Chapters 20–22 focus on **pathologies**, times when (macroeconomic) things go very wrong. Chapter 20 looks at the world crisis, and how policymakers have reacted to it. Chapter 21 looks at the implications of high public debt, a major legacy of the current crisis in many countries around the world. Chapter 22 looks at episodes of hyperinflation.

- Chapters 23 and 24 focus on **macroeconomic policy**. Chapter 23 looks at the role and the limits of macroeconomic policy in. Chapters 24 focus on the rationale of having rules that restrain monetary and fiscal policy, such as inflation targeting, interest rate rules and constraints to fiscal policy.

- Chapters 25 and 26 focus on **Europe**. Chapter 25 describes the long process that led a group of European countries to adopt a single currency, the euro. Chapter 26 focuses on the implications of a single currency for the euro members and on the incentives of euro outsiders to join or to keep out.

'A FOCUS ON THE CURRENT CRISIS'

The big macroeconomic event of the last few years is obviously the major crisis affecting the global economy. Particular aspects of it – from the liquidity trap, to the role of fiscal policy, to movements in asset prices – are taken up throughout the book. But, also, the story of the crisis, and the mechanisms behind it, is given in Chapter 20 which explains the origin of the crisis and how fiscal and monetary policies avoided a world depression. It does so by referring back to what you have learned earlier in the book. But, also, by exploring some of the mechanisms that have played a central role in the crisis, the role of banks and liquidity, or the use of unconventional monetary policies such as quantitative easing.

ALTERNATIVE COURSE OUTLINES

Within the book's broad organisation, there is plenty of opportunity for alternative course organisations. We have made the chapters shorter than is standard in textbooks, and, in our experience, most chapters can be covered in an hour and a half. A few (Chapters 5 and 9, for example) might require two lectures to sink in.

- Short courses (15 or fewer lectures).

  A standard short course can be organised around the two introductory chapters and the core, for a total of 13 lectures. This gives the possibility to have a short course by still being able to cover important topics, such as Expectations and Openness in goods and financial market, which are essential for the understanding of European economies, which are extremely open to the rest of the world.

  A very short course can be organised around the two introductory chapters and the core, leaving out Chapters 6 and 6 as well as 10 and 13. This gives a total of 10 lectures, leaving time to cover, for example, Chapter 20 on the recent world crisis (which is explained using the basic *IS–LM* model), for a total of 11 lectures.

  A short course might leave out the study of growth (the long run). In this case, the course can be organised around the introductory chapters, and Chapters 3–10 in the core; this gives a total of 10 lectures, leaving enough time to cover, for example, Chapter 20 on the recent world crisis (which is explained using the basic *IS–LM* model), and Chapter 21 on high debt, for a total of 12 lectures.

  A short course designed to provide an understanding of the implications of openness in Europe might leave out the study of the long run. In this case, the course can be organised around the introductory chapters, and Chapters 3–10 in the core; this gives a total of 10 lectures, leaving enough time to cover Chapters 18 and 19 on exchange rates and policy choices, and Chapters 25 and 26 on Europe, for a total of 14 lectures.

- Longer courses (20–25 lectures).

  A full semester course gives more than enough time to cover the core, plus at least two extensions, and the policy part and or the part on Europe.

  The extensions assume knowledge of the core, but are otherwise mostly self-contained. Given the choice, the order in which they are best taught is probably the order in which they are presented in the book.

  One of the choices facing instructors is likely to be whether or not to teach growth (the long run). If growth is taught, there may not be enough time to cover all three extensions and have a thorough discussion of policy and of European integration. In this case, it may be best to leave out the study of pathologies. If growth is not taught, there should be time to cover most of the other topics in the book.

FEATURES

We have made sure never to present a theoretical result without relating it to the real world. In addition to discussions of facts in the text itself, we have written a large number of **Focus** boxes, which discuss particular macroeconomic events or facts, from around the world and from Europe in particular.

We have tried to recreate some of the student–teacher interactions that take place in the classroom by the use of **Margin notes**, running parallel to the text. The margin notes create a dialogue with the reader, to smooth the more difficult passages, and to give a deeper understanding of the concepts and the results derived along the way.

For students who want to explore macroeconomics further, we have introduced the following two features:

- **Short appendices** to some chapters, which expand on points made within the chapter.
- A **Further readings** section at the end of each chapter, indicating where to find more information, including a number of key internet addresses.

Each chapter ends with three ways of making sure that the material in the chapter has been digested:

- A **summary** of the chapter's main points.
- A list of **key terms**.
- A series of **end-of-chapter exercises**. 'Quick check' exercises are straightforward, 'Dig deeper' exercises are more challenging, and 'Explore further' typically require either access to the internet or the use of a spread-sheet program.
- A list of symbols on pp. 572–3 makes it easy to recall the meaning of the symbols used in the text.

THE TEACHING AND LEARNING PACKAGE

The book comes with a number of supplements to help both students and instructors.

For instructors:

- **Instructor's Manual**. Originally written by Mark Moore, of the University of California-Irvine and adapted to this European edition by Alessia Amighini, Tommaso Colussi and Matteo Duiella, the Instructor's manual discusses pedagogical choices, alternative ways of presenting the material, and ways of reinforcing students' understanding. For each chapter in the book, the manual has seven sections: objectives, in the form of a motivating question; why the answer matters; key tools, concepts, and assumptions; summary; pedagogy; extensions; and observations and additional exercises. The Instructor's Manual also includes the answers to all end-of-chapter questions and exercises.
- **Test Item File**. Originally written by David Findlay, of Colby College, the test bank has been completely revised by Tommaso Colussi.
- **PowerPoint Lecture Slides**. Created by Tommaso Colussi, these electronic slides provide outlines, summaries, equations, and graphs for each chapter, and can be downloaded from www.pearsoned.co.uk/blanchard.

For students:

- **Multiple choice questions**. Originally written by David Findlay, the questions have been completely revised by Tommaso Colussi.
- **Active graphs**. Stephen Peretz, of Washington State University, has created a series of 48 active graphs, corresponding to the most important figures in the book. Each graph allows the student to change the value of some variable or shift a curve, and look at the effects on the equilibrium. Experience indicates that using graphs in this way considerably strengthens the students' intuition and understanding of the mechanisms at work.

For both instructors and students:

Daniele, from Bocconi University, has created an exciting web page dedicated to the book (www.pearsoned.co.uk/ blanchard). This page, which is continually updated, includes articles and references to current events around the world, and connects them to the different chapters of the book. It also provides a chat room, allowing the readers to interact. [. . .]

Olivier Blanchard, Alessia Amighini and Francesco Giavazzi
Cambridge, MA and Milan, December 2009

AUTHOR ACKNOWLEDGMENTS

This book builds on previous US and foreign editions, and the list of people who helped and made comments on them has grown too long to be given here. This particular edition would not have been possible without the dedication and the effort of Tommaso Colussi and Matteo Duiella. The adaptation to Europe of data, charts and examples would not have been possible without their stubbornness: 'These data must exist for Europe!' and they would not give up until those data were found. We are particularly grateful to Ellen Morgan and Shamini Sriskandarajah for their patience and support, to Helen MacFadyen whose work on the final manuscript was invaluable, and to all the team in Pearson who contributed to this project. We are also grateful to the academic staff who reviewed the material: Bertrand Candelon, Maastricht University School of Business and Economics; George Chouliarakis, University of Manchester; Martin Floden, Stockholm School of Economics; Michael Funke, Hamburg University; Pekka Ilmakunnas, School of Economics, Aalto University; Paul Scanlon, Trinity College Dublin; Jennifer Smith, University of Warwick; and Gianluigi Vernasca, University of Essex.

INTRODUCTION

The first two chapters of this book introduce you to the issues and the approach of macroeconomics.

Chapter 1 A tour of the world

Chapter 1 takes you on a macroeconomic tour of the world, from the problem of unemployment in Europe, to the implications of the euro, to the US recession in 2007–2010, to the extraordinary growth in China and three other emerging economies: Brazil, India and Russia.

Chapter 2 A tour of the book

Chapter 2 takes you on a tour of the book. It defines the three central variables of macroeconomics: output, unemployment and inflation. It introduces the three concepts around which the book is organised: the short run, the medium run and the long run.

Chapter 1

A TOUR OF THE WORLD

What is macroeconomics? The best way to answer is not to give you a formal definition, but rather to take you on an economic tour of the world, to describe both the main economic evolutions and the issues that keep macroeconomists and macroeconomic policy makers awake at night.

At the time of writing (early 2010), all attention was focused on the impact of the financial crisis that since the summer of 2007 has shaken first the USA and then Europe before spreading to the rest of the world. In the autumn of 2008 the world economy entered into the deepest recession experienced since the Second World War. Governments and central banks have taken ambitious policy actions to minimise the cost of the recession, but economic growth has continued to decline, at least in advanced countries, in 2009 and early 2010.

However, the current difficulties, albeit very serious, could overshadow the fact that for over two decades the world economy grew more rapidly than ever before, not only in advanced economies, but also (and actually at a higher pace) in emerging and developing countries, as shown in Figure 1.1. Notice two features of Figure 1.1: first, the impressive growth of emerging and developing economies since the 1990s, which largely contributed to the good performance of world output for almost two decades; second, the dramatic decrease of output growth (which actually turned negative in advanced economies) since 2008.

There is no way we can take you on a full tour of the world, so we shall give you a sense of what is happening in Europe, the USA and the so-called BRIC countries (Brazil, the Russian Federation, India and China) – economies that have grown at an extraordinary pace and are now large enough to make a difference for the rest of the world.

- Section 1.1 looks at the European Union.

- Section 1.2 looks at the USA.

- Section 1.3 looks at the BRIC countries.

- Section 1.4 draws some conclusions and introduces some of the questions which will be answered in this book.

Read the chapter as you would read an article in a newspaper. In reading this chapter, do not worry about the exact meaning of the words, or about understanding all the arguments in detail: the words will be defined and the arguments will be developed in later chapters. Regard it as a background, intended to introduce you to the issues involved in studying macroeconomics. If you enjoy reading this chapter, you will probably enjoy reading the whole book. Indeed, once you have read the book, come back to this chapter; see where you stand on the issues, and judge how much progress you have made in your study of macroeconomics.

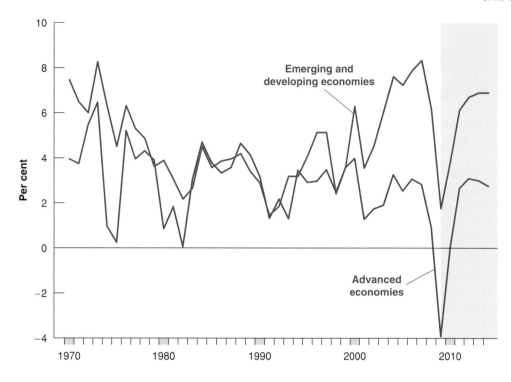

Figure 1.1

Real GDP growth in advanced, emerging and developing economies since 1970

From 2008 until 2010 GDP growth declined all over the world. In advanced economies it turned negative.

Source: IMF, *World Economic Outlook*, Spring 2009, p. 1. (Data from 2010 onwards are forecasts.)

1.1 EUROPE AND THE EURO

In 1957, six European countries decided to form a common market – an economic zone where people and goods could move freely. Since then, 21 more countries have joined, bringing the total to 27. This group is now known as the **European Union**, or **EU27** for short (if you want to know more about the history of European enlargements, read the next Focus box). The group of 27 countries forms a formidable economic power: their combined output (around €12 300 billion in 2009) now exceeds the output of the USA (around €10 000 billion in 2009), and many of them have a standard of living – a level of output per person – not far from that of the USA.

When macroeconomists study an economy, they first look at three variables:

● *Output* – the level of production of the economy as a whole – and its rate of growth.
● The *unemployment rate* – the proportion of workers in the economy who are not employed and are looking for a job.
● The *inflation rate* – the rate at which the average price of the goods in the economy is increasing over time.

Table 1.1 reports these data for the EU27. The first column gives the share of output on the total output of the EU27. Within the EU27, the countries of the euro area account for

Table 1.1 Growth, unemployment and inflation in the EU since 1991

	Share of EU27	Output growth rate[a]		Unemployment rate[b]		Inflation rate[c]	
	2010	1991–2000	2001–2010	1991–2000	2001–2010	1991–2000	2001–2010
EU27	100.0	5.7	3.4	9.2	8.7	2.7	2.2
Euro area	76.1	4.7	3.0	13.0	11.5	2.5	2.0
Germany	20.1	3.8	1.6	7.8	10.4	1.7	1.1
France	16.2	3.4	3.0	10.5	10.7	1.4	2.0
UK	13.2	5.5	3.8	7.9	5.9	2.9	2.3
Italy	13.0	5.4	2.7	10.4	9.4	3.8	2.5
Spain	9.0	7.0	5.6	15.7	11.8	4.1	3.4

[a] Output growth rate: annual rate of growth of output (GDP).
[b] Unemployment rate: average over the year.
[c] Inflation rate: annual rate of change of the price level (GDP deflator).

Source: *Statistical Annex of European Economy*, Spring 2009. Data for 2010 are forecasts.

FOCUS
The history of EU enlargements in a nutshell

The EU begins life in the 1950s as the European Economic Community with six founding members – Belgium, Germany, France, Italy, Luxembourg and the Netherlands. These countries created a new way of coming together to manage their joint interests, based essentially on economic integration. In 1957, the Treaty of Rome created the European Economic Community (EEC), or 'Common Market', among the six member countries.

The first enlargement takes place when Denmark, Ireland and the UK join the EU on 1 January 1973, raising the number of member states to nine. Towards the end of that decade, the European Parliament increases its influence in EU affairs and in 1979 all citizens can, for the first time, elect its members directly.

In 1981, Greece becomes the 10th member of the EU and Spain and Portugal follow in 1986. In 1987 the Single European Act is signed, a treaty establishes the principle of the free-flow of trade across EU borders and thus creates the 'Single Market'. Unification of Germany in 1990 brought in the Länder from Eastern Germany.

In the 1990s, with the collapse of communism across central and Eastern Europe, Europeans become closer

neighbours. In 1993 the Single Market is completed with the 'four freedoms' of movement of goods, services, people and money. The 1990s is also the decade of two treaties, the 'Maastricht' Treaty on European Union in 1993 and the Treaty of Amsterdam in 1999. In 1995, the EU gains three more new members, Austria, Finland and Sweden. A small village in Luxembourg gives its name to the 'Schengen' agreements that gradually allow people to travel within the EU without having their passports checked at the borders.

The 2000s is a decade of further expansion. The euro is the new currency for many Europeans. The political divisions between east and west Europe are finally declared healed in 2004, when the Czech Republic, Estonia, Cyprus, Latvia, Lithuania, Hungary, Malta, Poland, Slovenia and Slovakia join, followed in 2007 by Bulgaria and Romania. Four candidates, Croatia, the Former Yugoslav Republic of Macedonia, Turkey and Iceland have applied for membership.

Source: This box is taken from Eurostat, *EUROPE IN FIGURES – Eurostat Yearbook 2009*.

The euro area now includes 16 countries: Austria, Belgium, Cyprus, Finland, France, Germany, Greece, Ireland, Italy, Luxembourg, Malta, the Netherlands, Portugal, Slovakia, Slovenia and Spain. We will tell the story of how so many European countries decided to adopt a common currency in Chapter 25.

▶ slightly more than three-quarters (76.1%) of this total. The four largest EU economies together (Germany, the UK, France and Italy) account for 62.5% of the EU-27's gross domestic product (GDP) in 2009. The next columns give the average value of the rate of growth of output, the unemployment rate and the inflation rate for the period 1991–2000, and for the period 2001–2010.

The main conclusion to draw from the table is that the economic performance of European countries after the turn of the millennium has not been as good as it was in the 1990s:

● Average annual output growth from 2001–2010 was around 2 percentage points lower than in the previous decade (2.3 and 1.7 in the EU27 and in the euro area, respectively). This reflected a significant slowdown in all of the largest European economies since 2008, and a recession in 2009, when GDP contracted by more than 4%.
● Low output growth was accompanied by persistently high unemployment. Although the average unemployment rate from 2001–2010 has decreased with respect to the 1990s, in the euro area it is still 11.5%, reflecting the high unemployment rate in the largest economies in continental Europe.
● The only good news is about inflation. Average annual inflation was 2.2% in the EU and 2% in the euro area.

At the time of writing (early 2010), all attention was on the economic policies needed to help European economies emerge from the recession that has hit the world economy since 2008. Although short-run problems dominate the debate, European macroeconomists are

Figure 1.2

The unemployment rate in continental Europe and the USA since 1970

Until the beginning of the 1980s, the unemployment rate in the four major European countries was lower than the US rate, but then it rapidly increased.

still also concerned about three main issues that have been at the heart of the economic debate for a long time.

The first is, not surprisingly, high unemployment. Although the unemployment rate has come down from the peak reached in the mid-1990s, it remains very high. High unemployment has not always been the norm in Europe. Figure 1.2 plots the evolution of the unemployment rate in the four largest continental European countries (Germany, France, Italy and Spain) taken as a whole, and in the USA, since 1970. Note how low the unemployment rate was in these European countries in the early 1970s. At that time, Americans used to refer to Europe as the land of the *unemployment miracle*; US macroeconomists travelled to Europe hoping to discover the secrets of that miracle. By the late 1970s, however, the miracle had vanished. Since then, unemployment in the four largest continental European countries has been much higher than in the USA. Despite a decrease since the late 1990s, it stood at 7.5% in 2008 and increased to 12% in 2010. Although the recent increase is due to the recession that hit the world economy since 2008, the unemployment rate in Europe is always nearly 2 percentage points higher than the unemployment rate in the USA. We will study the causes of the high unemployment rate in Europe in Chapter 7.

The second is the growth of income per person (or per capita). Table 1.2 shows income per person in some European countries and in those that have adopted the euro, relative to the USA. Income per person in the USA is set equal to 100 in each year so that, for example, the number 75.3 for the euro area in 1970 means that in that year per capita income in the euro area was 24.7% lower than that in the US. Europe emerged from the Second World War largely destroyed, but in the fifties and sixties the gap with the US shrank rapidly: in 1980, euro area countries had reached almost 80% of US income per capita. However, since then the gap has started to grow. Why? To answer this question, we

Table 1.2 Income per capita in Europe compared to the USA (USA = 100)

	1970	1980	1990	2000	2004	2006
Euro area	75.3	77.8	76.6	72.3	72.8	71.6
Italy	71.2	78.0	76.2	72.6	70.9	65.9
France	80.4	84.7	80.3	76.8	76.1	70.9
Germany	96.7	100.7	98.3	73.9	71.9	72.9

Source: OECD *Economic Outlook* database.

need to understand the factors that contribute to economic growth over time. We will tackle this when discussing the sources of growth in Chapter 11.

The third issue is associated with the introduction, in 1999, of a common currency, the *euro*. After ten years, many questions remain. What has the euro done for Europe? What macroeconomic changes has it brought about? How should macroeconomic policy be conducted in this new environment? Should those European countries that originally decided to opt out of the common currency area now change their minds?

Supporters of the euro point first to its enormous symbolic importance. In light of the many past wars between European countries, what better proof that the page has definitely been turned than the adoption of a common currency? They also point to the economic advantages of having a common currency: no more changes in the relative price of currencies for European firms to worry about, no more need to change currencies when travelling between euro countries. Together with the removal of other obstacles to trade between European countries, which has taken place since 1957, the euro will contribute, they argue, to the creation of a large, if not the largest, economic power in the world. There is little question that the move to the euro is indeed one of the main economic events of the start of the 21st century.

Others worry that the symbolism of the euro may come with some economic costs. They point out that a common currency means a common monetary policy, and that means the same interest rate across the euro countries. What if, they argue, one country plunges into recession while another is in the middle of an economic boom? The first country needs lower interest rates to increase spending and output; the second country needs higher interest rates to slow down its economy. If interest rates have to be the same in both countries, what will happen? Isn't there the risk that one country will remain in recession for a long time or that the other will not be able to slow down its booming economy?

One important benefit has come to those countries that entered the euro with high public debt, such as Italy (where the ratio of debt to gross domestic product is above 100%), and has come in the form of a sharp reduction of interest rates. Before the euro, nominal interest rates in Italy were above 14% and every year the government had to use an amount of tax revenue as high as 12% of GDP to pay the interest bill on the public debt. By 2005, after adopting the euro, nominal interest rates had fallen below 3% and the interest bill on the public debt (whose stock in 2005 was not much smaller than at the time Italy joined the euro) had fallen to 5% of GDP: a saving of 7 percentage points of GDP. Why have interest rates dropped so much? Mainly because interest rates reflect a country's credibility at maintaining low inflation: the European Central Bank enjoys a better reputation than the Bank of Italy and this is reflected in much lower interest rates. Since the cost of debt is the interest that the state pays to holders of public bonds, the lower the interest rate, the lower the cost of debt.

So far, the balance of the arguments for and against the euro is not clear. Who was right? Those EU countries that decided to join from the start, or those, like Denmark, the UK and Sweden, who decided to wait? There is little doubt that highly indebted countries, such as Italy and Greece, benefited enormously from the reduction in the cost of the public debt, but for the rest the jury is still out. We will discuss the first ten years of the euro and how the euro affected member countries in Chapter 26.

1.2 THE ECONOMIC OUTLOOK IN THE USA

At the time of writing (early 2010), the USA is still in the middle of the severe recession triggered by the biggest financial crisis since the Great Depression back in 1929. The economic outlook in the USA is gloomy, as GDP contracted by almost 3% in 2009, after a sharp slowdown the previous year. However, as we saw at the beginning of this chapter, this should not overlook the fact that US economic performance has been remarkable over the past two decades. To put the current numbers in perspective, Table 1.3 gives the same basic

Table 1.3 Growth, unemployment and inflation in the USA since 1991

Output growth rate[a]		Unemployment rate[b]		Inflation rate[c]	
1991–2000	2001–2010	1991–2000	2001–2010	1991–2000	2001–2010
3.3	1.6	4.8	6.2	2.8	2.3

[a] Output growth rate: annual rate of growth of output (GDP).
[b] Unemployment rate: average over the year.
[c] Inflation rate: annual rate of change of the price level (GDP deflator).

Source: OECD *Economic Outlook* database.

numbers for the US economy as Table 1.1 gives for the EU. The columns give the average value of the rate of growth of output, the unemployment rate and the inflation rate for the period 1991–2000, and for the period 2001–2010.

From an economic point of view, there is no question that the 1990s were amongst the best years in recent memory. Look at the column giving the numbers for the period 1991–2000:

- The average rate of growth was 3.3% per year, substantially higher than the average growth rate in the previous two decades.
- The average unemployment rate was 4.8%, again substantially lower than the average unemployment rate in the previous two decades.
- The average inflation rate was 2.8%, slightly higher than in Europe, but lower than the average inflation rate over the previous two decades.

In the recent past, however, the US economy has slowed down. Growth was just 1.1% in 2008; it decreased even further in 2009, when the rate of growth turned negative (−2.8%), and projections for 2010 do not guarantee that the economy will start growing again. As a result, average growth for the current decade more than halved (1.6% per year) compared to the 1990s. What are the reasons for the recent slow down? Between 2007 and 2008, US families were affected by four economic shocks which occurred over a short period of time: an increase in oil prices, though now partially reversed; a fall in the price of their homes; a fall of the stock market; and a restriction of credit.

Let us start with the oil price increase. Figure 1.3 gives an idea of the size of the oil shock which occurred in the summer of 2008, comparing it with the oil price increases that have occurred since the end of the Second World War. (The chart shows the price 'at constant US dollars' that is, taking into account the fact that, in the meantime, all prices went up.) Earlier this decade a barrel of oil cost $20; in the summer of 2008, it reached $145 before returning to around $50: an increase of two and a half times compared to 2000–2001. The easiest way to understand the effects of oil prices on importing countries is the following. If oil imports become more expensive, this means that in order to import the same amount of oil, importing countries will have to transfer a greater share of their income to the oil producing countries. This will contribute to impoverishing importers and to reducing their consumption.

◀ The increase in oil prices has also pushed up inflation. After a long period during which US inflation had ranged between 2 and 3%, by the summer of 2008 the inflation rate had reached 5.6% (the expansionary monetary policy implemented between 2007 and 2008 to avoid the risk of a recession also contributed to increasing inflation).

The second shock that hit the US economy was a fall in house prices. Figure 1.4 shows house prices in the USA at constant prices, that is, adjusted for inflation, from 1890 until 2009. The graph relates house prices (adjusted for inflation) to three explanatory variables: population growth, construction costs and interest rates. The point is that none of these three factors explains the extraordinary rise in the price of homes in the past ten years, which has the characteristics of a 'speculative bubble'.

What is the effect of falling house prices on the economy? To answer this question, consider that the value of the homes in which Americans live is about three-quarters of their total wealth. From the start of the financial crisis (summer 2007) until the end of 2009, the value of US homes fell on average by 30%. This means that the wealth of American households has fallen (again on average) by 22.5% (30 × 0.75). What is the effect on consumption? In Chapter 15 you will learn than in normal circumstances a family spends each year a share

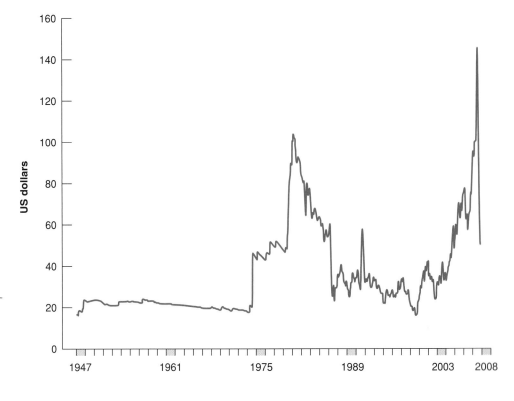

Figure 1.3

Oil prices (in 2008 US dollars): January 1947–December 2008

The price of oil reached a historic high in 2008.

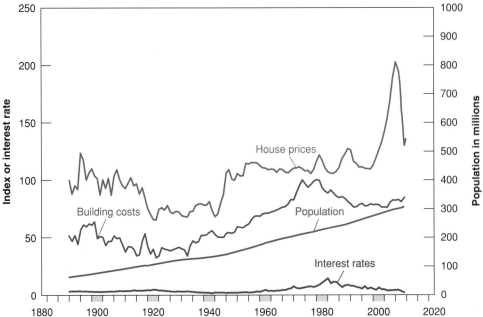

Figure 1.4

US house prices at constant dollars: 1880–2020

House prices in the USA boomed after 2000.

of its wealth equal to the product of the real interest rate multiplied by the value of wealth. Then, with a real interest rate of 2%, this means that the direct effect (we say 'direct' because there are the 'indirect' effects, such as the fall in the stock market induced by the fall in real estate prices) of the real estate crisis on household consumption is to reduce spending by about 0.4% (22.5×0.02).

After the start of the financial crisis in mid-2007, two other shocks contributed to dampening consumption and aggregate demand in the USA. A fall in the stock market reduced the value of households' wealth invested in equities; and a restriction of credit made it more difficult and expensive to access credit. We will describe in detail how the crisis erupted and how it triggered a fully-fledged recession in Chapter 20.

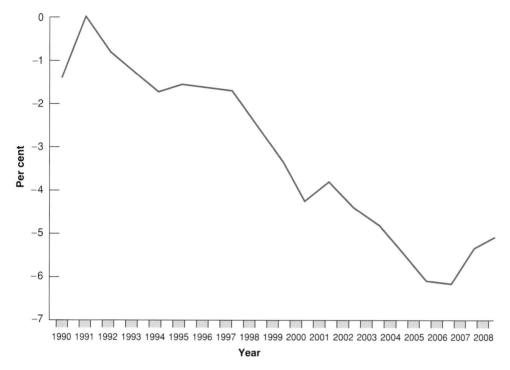

Figure 1.5

The US trade deficit since 1990

The US trade deficit has increased from about 1% of GDP in 1990 to 5% of GDP in 2008.

Here, to complete the outlook for the USA, we should add that, since the mid-1980s, the USA has purchased each year many more goods and services from abroad than those they could sell. In other words, US imports have consistently exceeded US exports to the rest of the world. Moreover, the difference between imports and exports – the trade deficit – has steadily increased and is now very big. Figure 1.5 shows the evolution of the US trade deficit in relation to GDP since 1990.

If you purchase more goods than you are able to sell, it means that your spending exceeds your income, and you must bridge the difference by borrowing. Exactly the same is true for countries. Therefore, to finance the trade deficit, the USA has borrowed from the rest of the world. The increasing trade deficit led to an increase in the amount of money borrowed from abroad. This sounds a little strange: the richest country in the world borrows $720 billion a year from the rest of the world! An obvious question is whether all this can continue. What could happen if the willingness of other nations to lend to the USA stopped?

Think again of your personal situation. As long as people are willing to grant you a loan, you can clearly continue to borrow and thus spend more than your income. However, even if you can borrow, it might not be wise to do so for too long: by borrowing more you will have to repay more and thus spend less in the future. Again, the same logic applies to a country, in this case to the USA.

Can the USA continue to borrow such huge sums of money in the future? So far, foreigners have been prepared – and often eager – to finance the US trade deficit: they have been willing to buy securities issued by the US government or stocks quoted on the US stock exchanges. The question is whether they will be equally willing to do so in the future. In the late 1990s, some Asian countries – Thailand and Indonesia, in particular – were borrowing large amounts from the rest of the world. Suddenly the rest of the world changed its mind, and stopped lending to Asia, forcing those countries to cancel their trade deficits suddenly. This 'sudden stop' caused serious economic crises in countries such as Thailand, Indonesia and South Korea. The USA is not Thailand, but some economists fear that it might become increasingly difficult for the USA to continue to borrow huge amounts of money in the future.

Table 1.4 Output growth and inflation in the BRIC countries since 1991

	Output growth rate[a]		Inflation rate[b]	
	1991–2000	2001–2008	1991–2000	2001–2008
Brazil	2.6	3.6	577.3	8.0
China	10.5	10.2	7.2	4.3
India	5.5	7.6	8.1	4.7
Russia	−3.6	6.7	311.8	16.2

[a] Output growth rate: annual rate of growth of output (GDP).
[b] Inflation rate: annual rate of change of the price level (GDP).

Source: IMF *World Economic Outlook* database.

1.3 BRIC COUNTRIES

Acronyms may change fast when they refer to groups of rapidly growing countries. The BRICs have recently been put side by side, in an **OECD** study, with two other large and rapidly growing economies, Indonesia and South Africa, and therefore the whole group has become the BRIICS.

➤ Brazil, China, India and Russia (which are often called the **BRICs**) have grown rapidly over the past decade and are now the largest economies outside of the group of advanced countries. China, in particular, is in the news every day. It is increasingly seen as one of the major economic powers in the world. China's economy is twice as large as those of the other BRICs combined (and its population is enormous, more than four times that of the USA). China has been growing very fast for more than two decades, and its growth rate is almost twice that of the others.

This is shown in Table 1.4, which gives output growth and inflation for the periods 1991–2000 and 2001–2008 for China and the other three BRIC countries. Note that, compared to the previous tables, this table does not give unemployment rates. Unemployment in poorer countries is much harder to measure, as many workers may decide to stay in agriculture rather than be unemployed. As a result, official unemployment rates are typically not very informative.

Now, focus on the main feature of the table, namely the very high growth rate of output in China since the 1990s, compared to the other three countries considered. Over the past two decades (and also in the 1980s), Chinese output has grown on average at more than 10% a year, and the forecasts are for more of the same. This is a truly astonishing number: compare it to the numbers achieved by Europe or the US economy over the same period. At that rate, output doubles every seven years. . . .

Where does the growth come from? It clearly comes from two sources. The first is very high accumulation of capital. The investment rate (the ratio of investment to output) in China is between 40 and 45% of output, a very high number. For comparison, the investment rate in the USA is only 17%. More capital means higher productivity, and higher output.

The second is very fast technological progress. The strategy followed by the Chinese government has been to encourage foreign firms to come and produce in China. As foreign firms are typically much more productive than Chinese firms, this has increased productivity and output. Another aspect of the strategy has been to encourage joint ventures between foreign and Chinese firms; making Chinese firms work with and learn from foreign firms has made them much more productive. When described in this way, achieving high productivity and high output growth appears easy, with easy recipes that every poor country could and should follow. In fact, things are less obvious.

Although rapidly growing, China's output, expressed in dollars by multiplying the number in yuan (the Chinese currency) by the dollar/yuan exchange rate, is only $2.8 trillion, roughly the same as that of Germany, and less than one-fourth that of the USA. Output per person is only $2100, roughly one-twentieth of output per person in the USA.

➤ China is one of many countries which have made the transition from central planning to a market economy. Most of the other countries, from central Europe to Russia and the other former Soviet republics, have experienced a large *decrease* in output at the time of transition. Look at the rate of growth of output in Russia in the 1990s: on average, it was negative during the whole decade (−3.6%). Most still have growth rates far below that of China. In Brazil and Russia, economic performance over the 1990s was dampened by financial crises and episodes of hyperinflation at the beginning of that decade.

In many countries, widespread corruption and poor property rights make firms unwilling to invest. So why has China fared so much better? Economists are not sure. Some believe that this is the result of a slower, better managed, transition: the first Chinese reforms took place in agriculture in 1980 and, even today, many firms remain owned by the state. Others argue that the fact that the communist party has remained in control has actually helped the economic transition; tight political control has allowed for a better protection of property rights, at least for firms, giving them incentives to invest. What about the comparison between China and India? In 1990, the two countries had the same GDP per person, today GDP per person is twice as high in China as it is in India. What explains this difference, and is the superior performance of the Chinese economy sustainable? Getting the answers to these questions, and thus learning what other poor countries can take from the Chinese experience, can clearly make a huge difference, not only for China but for the rest of the world.

Why have we added the BRIC countries to our tour of the world? After two decades of fast growth, the BRIC share of global output is now 15% (compared to 24% of the USA). Therefore, they start to be large enough to be able to make some difference in the world economy. Take for example the recent recession of 2007–2010. Compared to the negative growth registered by advanced economies in 2009, average weighted real GDP growth in the BRICs was 7–8%.

According to the **IMF**, China added a full percentage point per year to global output growth in 2008–2010 (and thus accounted for 50% of global growth), while the USA 'subtracted' an average of 0.1 percentage points per year from global output during the same period.

1.4 LOOKING AHEAD

This concludes our world tour. There are many other regions of the world we could have looked at:

- Japan, whose growth performance for the 40 years following the Second World War was so impressive that it was referred to as an economic miracle, but is one of the few rich countries which have done very poorly in the past decade. Since a stock market crash in the early 1990s, Japan has been in a prolonged slump, with average output growth of under 1% a year.
- Latin America, which went from very high to low inflation in the 1990s. Some countries, such as Chile, appear to be in good economic shape. Some, such as Argentina, are struggling: a collapse of its exchange rate and a major banking crisis led to a large decline in output in the early 2000s, from which it is now recovering.
- Africa, which has suffered decades of economic stagnation, but where growth has been high since 2000, reaching 6.5% in 2007 (with only a slight decrease to 6% in 2008 and 2009), and reflecting growth in most of the countries of the continent.

There is a limit, however, to how much you can absorb in this first chapter. Think about the questions to which you have been exposed already:

- What determines expansions and recessions? Can monetary policy be used to help the economy out of a recession, as in the USA and in other advanced economies in 2008–2009? How has the euro affected monetary policy in Europe?
- Why is inflation so much lower today than it was in the past? Can Europe reduce its unemployment rate? Should the USA reduce its trade deficit?
- Why do growth rates differ so much across countries, even over long periods? Why is per capita income in Europe lower than in the USA? Can other countries emulate China and grow at the same rate?

The purpose of this book is to give you a way of thinking about these questions. As we develop the tools you need, we shall show you how to use them by returning to these questions and showing you the answers they suggest.

KEY TERMS

European Union (EU27) 3

BRICs 10

Organisation for Economic Cooperation and Development (OECD) 10

International Monetary Fund (IMF) 11

QUESTIONS AND PROBLEMS

QUICK CHECK

1. *Using the information in this chapter, label each of the following statements true, false or uncertain. Explain briefly.*

a. The unemployment rate in the USA increased considerably at the end of the last decade, but it is still substantially lower than the unemployment rate in Europe.

b. In the 1960s and early 1970s, the USA had a higher rate of unemployment than Europe, but at the time of writing it has a much lower rate of unemployment.

c. After the turn of the millennium, European countries experienced a slowdown in output growth.

d. The BRICs all experienced very high growth rates of output in the last two decades and stable inflation.

e. China's growth has contributed to half of world growth during the recession of 2008–2010, and it is likely to become a new engine of world growth in the future.

f. The European 'unemployment miracle' refers to the extremely low rate of unemployment that Europe has been enjoying since the 1980s.

g. Income per capita in the euro area has declined compared to the USA since 1970, and this is true for all the largest member countries.

h. Even though the USA is the richest country in the world, it borrows hundreds of billions of dollars annually from the rest of the world.

2. Macroeconomic policy in Europe

Beware of simplistic answers to complicated macroeconomic questions. Consider each of the following statements and comment on whether there is another side to the story.

a. There is a simple solution to the problem of high European unemployment: reduce labour market rigidities.

b. What can be wrong about joining forces and adopting a common currency? The euro is obviously good for Europe.

3. Productivity growth in China

Productivity growth is at the heart of recent economic developments in China.

a. How has China achieved high rates of productivity growth in recent decades?

b. Has Europe achieved high rates of productivity growth in the past decade?

c. To what degree do you think China's methods of achieving productivity growth are relevant to Europe?

d. Do you think China's experience provides a model for developing countries to follow?

DIG DEEPER

4. Productivity growth in the USA

The average annual growth rate of output per worker in the USA rose from 1.8% during the period 1970–1995 to 2.8% for the years 1996–2006. This has led to talk of a New Economy and of sustained higher growth in the future than in the past.

a. Suppose output per worker grows at 1.8% per year. What will output per worker be – relative to today's level – in 10 years? 20 years? 50 years?

b. Suppose output per worker grows instead at 2.8% per year. What will output per worker be – relative to today's level – in 10 years? 20 years? 50 years?

c. If the USA has really entered a New Economy, and the average annual growth rate of output per worker has increased from 1.8% per year to 2.8%, how much higher will the US standard of living be in 10 years, 20 years and 50 years relative to what it would have been had the USA remained in the Old Economy?

d. Can we be sure the USA has really entered a New Economy, with a permanently higher growth rate? Why or why not?

5. When will Chinese output catch up with US output?

In 2008, US output was $14.3 trillion and Chinese output was $4.4 trillion. Suppose that from now on, the output of China grows at an annual rate of 10% per year (roughly what it has done during the past decade), while the output of the USA grows at an annual rate of 3% per year.

a. Using these assumptions and a spreadsheet, plot US and Chinese output over the next 100 years. How many years will it take for China to have a level of output equal to that of the USA?

b. When China catches the USA in total output, will residents of China have the same standard of living as US residents? Explain.

EXPLORE FURTHER

6. Post-war recessions in Europe

This question looks at the recessions of the past 40 years. To handle this problem, first obtain quarterly data on output growth in your country for the period 1970 to the latest year available from the Eurostat website (go to the Economy and Finance Section under Statistics Databases). Copy the data to your favourite spreadsheet program. Plot the quarterly GDP growth rates from 1970 through the more recent available year. Did any quarters have negative growth? Using the standard definition of recessions as two or more consecutive quarters of negative growth, answer the following questions:

a. How many recessions has the economy undergone since 1970?

b. How many quarters has each recession lasted?

c. In terms of length and magnitude, which two recessions have been the most severe?

7. *From problem 6, write down the quarters during which the economy has experienced negative output growth since 1970. Go to the Eurostat web page. Retrieve the monthly data series on the unemployment rate for the period 1970 to the most recent year available. Make sure all data series are seasonally adjusted.*

a. Look at each recession since 1970. What was the unemployment rate in the first month of the first quarter of negative growth? What was the unemployment rate in the last month of the last quarter of negative growth? By how much did the unemployment rate increase?

b. Which recession had the largest increase in the rate of unemployment?

We invite you to visit the Blanchard page on the Prentice Hall website at **www.prenhall.com/blanchard** for this chapter's World Wide Web exercises.

FURTHER READING

● This book comes with a web page (**www.prenhall.com/ blanchard**), which is updated regularly. For each chapter, the page offers discussions of current events, and includes relevant articles and Internet links. You can also use the page to make comments on the book, and engage in discussions with other readers.

● To understand macroeconomics, it is particularly useful to keep informed about what is happening around the world.

The best way to do this is by reading *The Economist* every week, maybe not all of it, but at least some articles. Get into the habit at the beginning of each week of spending a couple of hours in the library to read it, or occasionally buy it – it is in shops on Friday evening or Saturday morning, depending on the country. You will find that those €5 are among the best you spend in the week.

APPENDIX

Where to find the numbers?

This appendix will help you find the numbers you are looking for, be it inflation in Hungary last year, or consumption in the UK in 1959, or unemployment in Ireland in the 1980s.

For a quick look at current numbers

- The best source for the most recent numbers on output, unemployment, inflation, exchange rates, interest rates and stock prices for a large number of countries is the last four pages of *The Economist*, published each week (*www.economist.com*). This website, like most of the following websites, contains both information available free to anyone and information available only to subscribers. The 12-week subscription to the web version of *the Economist* which comes with this book gives you access to all the numbers and articles.
- A good source for recent numbers about the European economy is *European Economy*, published by the Directorate General on Economic and Financial Affairs of the European Commission (DG ECFIN) in spring and autumn with main economic forecasts, and in between with interim forecasts (*http://ec.europa.eu/economy_finance/publications/specpub_list12526.htm*).

Numbers for other OECD countries

The OECD (*www.oecd.org*) includes most of the rich countries in the world. The OECD puts out three useful publications, all available electronically on the site:

- The first is the *OECD Economic Outlook*, published twice a year. In addition to describing current macroeconomic issues and evolutions, it includes a data appendix, with data for many macroeconomic variables. The data typically go back to the 1980s, and are reported consistently, both across time and across countries. A more complete data set is available in the form of a CD-ROM, which includes most important macroeconomic variables for all OECD countries, typically going back to the 1960s. The data are also available on the OECD site.
- The second is the *OECD Employment Outlook*, published annually. It focuses more specifically on labour-market issues and numbers.

- Occasionally, the OECD puts together current and past data, and publishes the OECD Historical Statistics. At this point in time, the most recent is *Historical Statistics, 1970–2000*, published in 2001.
- The main strength of the publications of the International Monetary Fund (IMF, located in Washington, DC) is that they cover most of the countries of the world (*www.imf.org*). A particularly useful IMF publication is the *World Economic Outlook*, published twice a year, which describes major evolutions in the world and in specific member countries. Selected series associated with the Outlook are available on the IMF site (*http://www.imf.org/external/data.htm*).

For more detail about European economies

- The Directorate General for Economic and Financial Affairs of the European Commission maintains a useful website which offers information on the economies of the Member States, various economic forecasts produced on behalf of the Commission, and several publications on the EU economic situation (*http://ec.europa.eu/economy_finance/index_en.htm*).
- For data on just about everything, including economic data, a precious source is the *Eurostat* website, which offers several statistics, databases and publications, amongst which are *Europe in Figures* and *Principal European Economic Indicators*, both published annually (*http://epp.eurostat.ec.europa.eu/portal/page/portal/eurostat/home/*).

Current macroeconomic issues

A number of websites offer information and commentaries about the macroeconomic issues of the day. In addition to the Economist website mentioned earlier, two useful sites are:

- The Morgan Stanley site, with daily commentaries of macroeconomic events (*www.morganstanley.com/views/index.html*).
- The site maintained by Nouriel Roubini (*www.rgemonitor.com*) offers an extensive set of links to articles and discussions on macroeconomic issues (by subscription).

Chapter 2

A TOUR OF THE BOOK

The words *output*, *unemployment* and *inflation* appear daily in newspapers and on the evening news. So when we used them in Chapter 1, you knew roughly what we were talking about. We now need to define them precisely, and this is what we do in the first two sections of this chapter.

- Section 2.1 focuses on aggregate output and shows how we can look at aggregate output both from the production side and from the income side.

- Section 2.2 looks at the unemployment rate and the inflation rate.

- Section 2.3 introduces the three central concepts around which the book is organised:

  - The *short run* – what happens to the economy from year to year.

  - The *medium run* – what happens to the economy over a decade or so.

  - The *long run* – what happens to the economy over half a century or longer.

- Building on these three concepts, Section 2.4 gives you a road map to the rest of the book.

2.1 AGGREGATE OUTPUT

Economists studying economic activity in the 19th century or during the Great Depression had no measure of aggregate activity (*aggregate* is the word macroeconomists use for *total*) on which to rely. They had to put together bits and pieces of information, such as the shipments of iron ore or sales at some department stores, to try to infer what was happening to the economy as a whole.

Two economists, Simon Kuznets, ➤ from Harvard University, and Richard Stone, from Cambridge University, were awarded the Nobel Prize for their contributions to the development of the national income and product accounts – a gigantic intellectual and empirical achievement.

It was not until the end of the Second World War that the **System of National Accounts (SNA)** was put together in most European countries. (You will find measures of aggregate output for earlier times, but those have been constructed retrospectively.)

Like any other accounting system, the national income accounts first define concepts and then construct measures corresponding to those concepts. You need only to look at statistics from countries that have not yet developed such accounts to realise how crucial such precision and consistency are. Without them, numbers that should add up do not; trying to understand what is going on feels like trying to balance someone else's cheque book. We shall not burden you with the details of national income accounting here. However, because you will occasionally need to know the definition of a variable and how variables relate to each other, we will show you the basic accounting framework used in European countries (and, with minor variations, in most other countries) today.

GDP: production and income

You may come across another term, ➤ **gross national product**, or **GNP**. There is a subtle difference between 'domestic' and 'national,' and thus between GDP and GNP. We examine the distinction in Chapter 6. For now, we will concentrate on GDP.

The measure of **aggregate output** in the national income accounts is called the **gross domestic product** or **GDP** for short. To understand how GDP is constructed, it is best to work with a simple example. Consider an economy composed of just two firms:

- Firm 1 produces steel, employing workers and using machines to do so. It sells the steel for €100 to Firm 2, which produces cars. Firm 1 pays its workers €80, leaving €20 in profit to the firm.
- Firm 2 buys the steel and uses it, together with workers and machines, to produce cars. Revenues from car sales are €200. Of the €200, €100 goes to pay for steel and €70 goes to workers in the firm, leaving €30 in profit to the firm.

We can summarise this information in a table:

€*x* stands for a nominal quantity measured in euros.

Steel company (Firm 1)		
Revenues from sales		€100
Expenses		€80
Wages	€80	
Profit		€20

Car company (Firm 2)		
Revenues from sales		€200
Expenses		€170
Wages	€70	
Steel purchases	€100	
Profit		€30

Would you define aggregate output in this economy as the sum of the values of all goods produced in the economy – the sum of €100 from the production of steel and €200 from the production of cars, so €300? Or would you define aggregate output as just the value of cars, which is equal to €200?

An intermediate good is a good used ➤ in the production of another good. Some goods can be both final goods and intermediate goods. Potatoes sold directly to consumers are final goods. Potatoes used to produce potato chips are intermediate goods. Can you think of other examples?

Some thought suggests that the right answer must be €200. Why? Because steel is an **intermediate good**: it is used up in the production of cars. Once we count the production of cars, we do not want to count the production of the goods that went into the production of those cars.

This motivates the first definition of GDP.

1. *GDP is the value of the final goods and services produced in the economy during a given period.*

The important word here is *final*. We want to count only the production of **final goods**, not intermediate goods. Using our example, we can make this point in another way. Suppose the two firms merged, so that the sale of steel took place inside the new firm and was no longer recorded. The accounts of the new firm would be given by the following table:

Steel and car company	
Revenues from sales	€200
Expenses (wages)	€150
Profit	€50

All we would see would be one firm selling cars for €200, paying workers €80 + €70 = €150, and making €20 + €30 = €50 in profits. The €200 measure would remain unchanged – as it should. We do not want our measure of aggregate output to depend on whether firms decide to merge.

This first definition gives us one way to construct GDP: by recording and adding up the production of all final goods – and this is indeed roughly the way actual GDP numbers are put together. But it also suggests a second way of thinking about and constructing GDP.

2. *GDP is the sum of value added in the economy during a given period.*
The term **value added** means exactly what it suggests. The value added by a firm is defined as the value of its production minus the value of the intermediate goods used in production.

In our two-firm example, the steel company does not use intermediate goods. Its value added is simply equal to the value of the steel it produces, €100. The car company, however, uses steel as an intermediate good. Thus, the value added by the car company is equal to the value of the cars it produces minus the value of the steel it uses in production, €200 – €100 = €100. Total value added in the economy, or GDP, equals €100 (the value added of the steel company) + €100 (the value added of the car company) = €200. (Note that aggregate value added would remain the same if the steel and car firms merged and became a single firm. In this case, we would not observe intermediate goods at all – as steel would be produced and then used to produce cars within the single firm – and the value added in the single firm would simply be equal to the value of cars, €200.)

This definition gives us a second way of thinking about GDP. Put together, the two definitions imply that the value of final goods and services – the first definition of GDP – can also be thought of as the sum of the value added by all the firms in the economy – the second definition of GDP.

So far, we have looked at GDP from the *production side*. The other way of looking at GDP is from the *income side*. Let's return to our example and think about the revenues left to a firm after it has paid for its intermediate goods. Some of the revenues go to pay workers – this component is called *labour income*. The rest goes to the firm – that component is called *capital income*, or *profit income*.

Of the €100 of value added by the steel manufacturer, €80 goes to workers (labour income) and the remaining €20 goes to the firm (capital income). Of the €100 of value added by the car manufacturer, €70 goes to labour income and €30 to capital income. For the economy as a whole, labour income is equal to €150 (€80 + €70), and capital income is equal to €50 (€20 + €30). Value added is equal to the sum of labour income and capital income and is equal to €200 (€150 + €50).

This motivates the third definition of GDP.

3. *GDP is the sum of incomes in the economy during a given period.*
In our example, labour income accounts for 75% of GDP and capital income for 25%. Table 2.1 shows the breakdown of value added among the different types of income in the EU15 (including the 15 member countries prior to the accession of ten candidate countries in 2004) and in the USA in 1970 and 2007. It includes one category of income we did not have in our example, *indirect taxes*, the revenues paid to the government in the form of sales taxes. (In our example, these indirect taxes were equal to zero.) The table shows that the composition of GDP by type of income is very different in the EU (on average) compared to

FOCUS
How is GDP measured?

GDP is measured bringing together various sources of information usually collected by a country's tax authorities.

● Firms report sales: this information is used to build the first definition of GDP:

    GDP = value of final sales of goods and services in the economy in a given period

● Firms pay value added taxes, i.e. taxes on the value added of their activities: this is used to build the second definition of GDP:

GDP = sum of value added in the economy during a given period

● Individuals report income: this is used to build the third definition of GDP:

    GDP = sum of incomes in the economy during a given period.

Of course this raises the issue of the '**underground economy**'. If firms avoid paying taxes, their output goes unrecorded, although sometimes it can be recorded by the taxes paid by their employees, if they pay taxes.

Table 2.1 The composition of GDP by type of income, 1970 and 2007

	EU15*		USA	
	1970	**2007**	**1970**	**2007**
Labour income	52.20%	48.70%	60.40%	56.60%
Capital income	37.00%	39.00%	31.00%	37.40%
Indirect taxes	10.80%	12.30%	8.60%	7.00%

* Was the number of member countries in the EU prior to the accession of ten candidate countries on 1 May 2004. The EU15 comprises the following 15 countries: Austria, Belgium, Denmark, Finland, France, Germany, Greece, Ireland, Italy, Luxembourg, Netherlands, Portugal, Spain, Sweden, UK.

Source: OECD *Economic Outlook* database.

the USA. In fact, the share of labour income on GDP is rather different in the two areas: it accounts for around 49% of GDP in the EU compared to almost 57% of US GDP. This difference is largely explained by indirect taxes: they account for more than 12% in the EU compared to 7% in the USA. Capital income accounts for a similar share of GDP in the EU and the USA (39% and 37.4%, respectively). With respect to 1970, the proportions have slightly changed; the share of labour income has decreased by around 4 percentage points in both areas, whereas capital income has increased (much more in the USA compared to the EU). The major difference comes again from indirect taxes: they have increased a little in the EU, and decreased in the USA.

Two lessons to remember:
1. GDP is the measure of aggregate output, which we can look at from the production side (aggregate production) or the income side (aggregate income).
2. Aggregate production and aggregate income are always equal.

➤ To summarise: You can think about aggregate output – *GDP* – in three different, but equivalent, ways:

● From the *production side* – GDP equals the value of the final goods and services produced in the economy during a given period.
● Also from the *production side* – GDP is the sum of value added in the economy during a given period.
● From the *income side* – GDP is the sum of incomes in the economy during a given period.

Nominal and real GDP

GDP in the EU15 was €10 billion in 2007, compared to €715 million in 1970. Was European output really 14 times higher in 2007 than in 1970? Obviously not: much of the increase reflected an increase in prices rather than an increase in quantities produced. This leads to the distinction between nominal GDP and real GDP.

Nominal GDP is the sum of the quantities of final goods produced multiplied by their current prices. This definition makes clear that nominal GDP increases over time for two reasons:

- The production of most goods increases over time.
- The prices of most goods also increase over time.

If our goal is to measure production and its change over time, we need to eliminate the effect of increasing prices on our measure of GDP. That's why **real GDP** is constructed as the sum of the production of final goods multiplied by *constant* (rather than *current*) prices.

If the economy produced only one final good – say, a particular car model – constructing real GDP would be easy: we would use the price of the car in a given year and then use it to multiply the quantity of cars produced in each year. An example will help here. Consider an economy that produces only cars – and to avoid issues we shall tackle later, assume that the same model is produced every year. Suppose the number and the price of cars in three successive years is given by:

Year	Quantity of cars	Price of cars	Nominal GDP	Real GDP (in 2000 prices)
1999	10	€20 000	€200 000	€240 000
2000	12	€24 000	€288 000	€288 000
2001	13	€26 000	€338 000	€312 000

Nominal GDP, which is equal to the quantity of cars multiplied by their price, goes up from €200 000 in 1999 to €288 000 in 2000 – a 44% increase – and from €288 000 in 2000 to €338 000 in 2001 – a 17% increase.

- To construct real GDP, we need to multiply the number of cars in each year by a *common* price. Suppose we use the price of a car in 2000 as the common price. This approach gives us, in effect, *real GDP in 2000 prices.*
- Using this approach, real GDP in 1999 (in 2000 prices) equals 10 cars × €24 000 per car = €240 000. Real GDP in 2000 (in 2000 prices) equals 12 cars × €24 000 per car = €288 000, the same as nominal GDP in 2000. Real GDP in 2001 (in 2000 prices) is equal to 13 × €24 000 = €312 000. So real GDP goes up from €240 000 in 1999 to €288 000 in 2000 – a 20% increase – and from €288 000 in 2000 to €312 000 in 2001 – an 8% increase.
- How different would our results have been if we had decided to construct real GDP using the price of a car in, say, 2001 rather than 2000? Obviously, the level of real GDP in each year would be different (because the prices are not the same in 2001 as in 2000), but its rate of change from year to year would be the same as above.

The problem in constructing real GDP in practice is that there is obviously more than one final good. Real GDP must be defined as a weighted average of the output of all final goods, and this brings us to what the weights should be.

The *relative prices* of the goods would appear to be the natural weights. If one good costs twice as much per unit as another, then that good should count for twice as much as the other in the construction of real output. However, this raises the question: what if, as is typically the case, relative prices change over time? Should we choose the relative prices of a particular year as weights, or should we change the weights over time? More discussion of these issues, and of the way real GDP is constructed, is left to the appendix to this chapter.

◄ **Warning!** People often use *nominal* to denote small amounts. Economists use *nominal* for variables expressed in current prices. And these do not refer to small amounts: the numbers typically run in the billions or trillions of euros.

◄ To be sure, compute real GDP in 2001 prices and compute the rate of growth from 1999 to 2000 and from 2000 to 2001.

FOCUS
GDP Deflator

Year	Cars		Notebooks	
	Q^C	P^C	Q^N	P^N
2000	12	24 000	10	5000
2001	13	30 000	20	2000

Q = quantity and P = price.

Nominal GDP

$$\text{€}Y_{00} = P^C_{00}Q^C_{00} + P^N_{00}Q^N_{00} = \text{€}338\ 000$$
$$\text{€}Y_{01} = P^C_{01}Q^C_{01} + P^N_{01}Q^N_{01} = \text{€}430\ 000$$

where Y = output.

From 2000 to 2001, nominal GDP has increased by 27.2%. This is due to both increasing production and increasing prices.

Real GDP

$$Y_{00} = \text{€}Y_{00} \qquad\qquad = \text{€}338\ 000$$
$$Y_{01} = P^C_{00}Q^C_{01} + P^N_{00}Q^N_{01} = \text{€}412\ 000$$

From 2000 to 2001, real GDP has increased by 21.9%. This is just due to increasing production, keeping prices constant.

GDP deflator

$$P = \frac{\text{€}Y}{Y}$$

The GDP deflator is defined as the ratio of nominal to real GDP.

2000 In the **base year** $P_{00} = 1$ by assumption (as real GDP is equal to nominal GDP)

2001 [formula] $\dfrac{430000}{412000} = 1.044$

GDP deflator inflation

The GDP deflator inflation is a measure of the increase in the price level of the goods produced in the economy during a given year, Y_t.

π = growth rate of nominal GDP – growth rate of real GDP

$$= \frac{\text{€}Y_t - \text{€}Y_{t-1}}{\text{€}Y_{t-1}} - \frac{Y_t - Y_{t-1}}{Y_{t-1}}$$

$$= \frac{430\ 000 - 338\ 000}{338\ 000} - \frac{412\ 000 - 338\ 000}{338\ 000}$$

$$= 27.2 - 21.9 = 5.3\%$$

Figure 2.1

Nominal and real GDP in the EU15 since 1970

Since 1970, nominal GDP in the EU15 increased by a factor of 14. Real GDP increased by a factor of 2.5.

Source: OECD *Economic Outlook* database.

> Suppose real GDP were measured in 2006 prices rather than 2000 prices. Where would the nominal GDP and real GDP lines on the graph intersect?

Figure 2.1 plots the evolution of both nominal GDP and real GDP in the EU since 1970. By construction, the two are equal in 2000. The figure shows that real GDP in 2007 was about 2.5 times its level of 1970 – a considerable increase, but clearly much less than the 14-fold increase in nominal GDP over the same period. The difference between the two results comes from the increase in prices over the period.

The terms *nominal GDP* and *real GDP* each have many synonyms, and you are likely to encounter them in your readings:

- Nominal GDP is also called **GDP at current prices**.
- Real GDP is also called **GDP in terms of goods, GDP at constant prices, GDP adjusted for inflation** – if the year in which real GDP is set equal to nominal GDP is a base year (currently the year 2000 in EU national accounts).

In the chapters that follow, unless we indicate otherwise:

- GDP will refer to *real GDP*, and Y_t will denote *real GDP in year* t.
- Nominal GDP and variables measured in current prices will be denoted by a euro sign in front of them – for example, $€Y_t$ for nominal GDP in year *t*.

GDP: level versus growth rate

We have focused so far on the level of real GDP. This is an important number, which gives the economic size of a country. A country with twice the GDP of another country is economically twice as big as the other country. Equally important is the level of **real GDP per capita**, the ratio of real GDP to the population of the country. It gives us the average standard of living of the country. In assessing the performance of the economy from year to year, economists focus, however, on the *rate of growth* of real GDP – **GDP growth**. Periods of positive GDP growth are called **expansions**. Periods of negative GDP growth are called **recessions**.

◄ **Warning!** You must be careful about how you do the comparison: recall the discussion in Chapter 1 about the standard of living in China. You'll learn more on this in Chapter 11.

FOCUS
Real GDP, technological progress and the price of computers

A tough problem in computing real GDP is how to deal with changes in quality of existing goods. One of the most difficult cases is computers. It would clearly be absurd to assume that a personal computer in 2010 is the same good as a personal computer produced in 1981 (the year in which the IBM PC was introduced): the same amount of money can clearly buy much more computing in 2010 than it could in 1981. But how much more? Does a 2010 computer provide 10 times 100 times or 1000 times the computing services of a 1981 computer? How should we take into account the improvements in internal speed, the size of the RAM or of the hard disk, the fact that computers can now access the Internet, and so on?

The approach used by economists to adjust for these improvements is to look at the market for computers and how it values computers with different characteristics in a given year. For example, suppose the evidence from prices of different models on the market shows that people are willing to pay 10% more for a computer with a speed of 3 GHz (3000 MHz) rather than 2 GHz. (The first American edition of this book, published in 1996, compared two computers, with speeds of 50 and 16 MHz. This is a good indication of technological progress.) Suppose new computers this year have a speed of 3 GHz compared to a speed of 2 GHz for new computers last year. And suppose the dollar price of new computers this year is the same as the price of new computers last year. Then, economists in charge of computing the adjusted price of computers will conclude that new computers are in fact 10% cheaper than last year.

This approach, which treats goods as providing a collection of characteristics – here speed, memory and so on – each with an implicit price, is called **hedonic pricing** (*hedone* means 'pleasure' in Greek). It is used in several countries to estimate changes in the prices of complex and fast-changing goods, such as automobiles and computers. Using this approach, estimates show that, for given prices, the quality of new computers has increased on average by 18% per year since 1981.

Not only do computers deliver more services, they have become cheaper as well: their price has declined by about 10% per year since 1981. Putting this together with the information in the previous paragraph, this implies that their quality-adjusted price has fallen at an average rate of 18% + 10% = 28% per year.

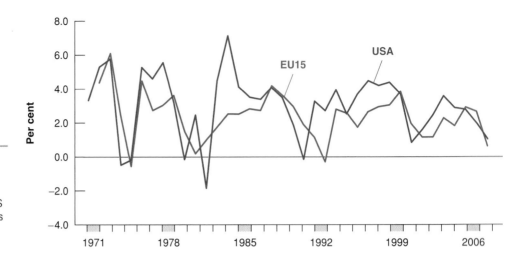

Figure 2.2

Growth rates of GDP in the EU15 and in the USA since 1970

Since 1970, both the EU15 and the US economies have gone through a series of expansions, interrupted by short recessions.

The evolution of GDP growth in the EU15 and the USA since 1970 is given in Figure 2.2. GDP growth in year t is constructed as $(Y_t - Y_{t-1})/Y_{t-1}$. The figure shows how both economies have gone through a series of expansions, interrupted by short recessions. Look in particular at the past 15 years. Note how a recession in the early 1990s gave way to a long expansion from 1992 to 2000. In 2001, growth was positive but very low. It has increased since then, but in 2008 both economies have entered into a severe recession following the financial crisis that has shaken most of the world economy since the summer of 2007. Although there is no official definition of what constitutes a recession, the convention is to refer to a recession if the economy goes through at least two consecutive quarters of negative growth. Sometimes growth is negative in two or more quarters, but positive for a year as a whole. This was the case for the USA in 2001, when growth was negative during each of the first three quarters, but positive for the year as a whole; thus 2001 qualifies as a (mild) recession.

2.2 THE OTHER MAJOR MACROECONOMIC VARIABLES

Because it is a measure of aggregate activity, GDP is obviously the most important macroeconomic variable. However, two other variables, unemployment and inflation, tell us about other important aspects of how an economy is performing.

The unemployment rate

As we will see below, people who do not have a job, but are *not* looking for one are classified as 'out of the labour force'.

Let's start with some definitions: **employment** is the number of people who have a job; **unemployment** is the number of people who do not have a job but are looking for one. The **labour force** is the sum of employment and unemployment:

$$L \quad = \quad N \quad + \quad U$$
Labour force = Employment + Unemployment

The **unemployment rate** is the ratio of the number of people who are unemployed to the number of people in the labour force:

$$u = \frac{U}{L}$$

Constructing the unemployment rate is less obvious than you might think. The cartoon notwithstanding, determining whether somebody is employed is straightforward. Determining whether somebody is unemployed is harder. Recall from the definition that,

Source: from The Gathering of Government Labor Statistics, 119552, Non Sequitur Panel, Universal Uclick.

to be classified as unemployed, a person must meet two conditions: that he or she does not have a job, and that he or she is looking for one; this second condition is harder to assess.

Until recently, in most European countries, the only available source of data on unemployment was the number of people registered at unemployment offices, and so only those workers who were registered in unemployment offices were counted as unemployed. This system led to a poor measure of unemployment. How many of those looking for jobs actually registered at the unemployment office varied both across countries and across time. Those who had no incentive to register – for example, those who had exhausted their unemployment benefits – were unlikely to take the time to go to the unemployment office, so they were not counted. Countries with less generous benefit systems were likely to have fewer unemployed registering and therefore smaller measured unemployment rates.

Today, most rich countries rely on large surveys of households to compute the unemployment rate. In Europe, this survey is called the **Labour Force Survey (LFS)**. It relies on interviews to a representative sample of individuals. Each individual is classified as employed if he or she has worked for at least one hour during the week preceding that of the interview in whatever activity. Estimates based on the LFS show that the average unemployment rate in the European Union (EU15) in 2008 was 7.1%. In the USA, a survey called the Current Population Survey (CPS) relies on interviews of 50 000 households every month. The survey classifies a person as employed if he or she has a job at the time of the interview; it classifies a person as unemployed if he or she does not have a job and has been looking for a job in the past four weeks. Estimates based on the CPS show that, during 2007, an average of 144.4 million people were employed and 7.0 million people were unemployed, so the unemployment rate was $4.6(7.0/(144.4+7.0) \times 100)$.

Note that only those looking for a job are counted as unemployed; those who do not have a job and are not looking for one are counted as **not in the labour force**. When unemployment is high, some of the unemployed give up looking for a job and therefore are no longer counted as unemployed. These people are known as **discouraged workers**. Take an extreme example: if all workers without a job gave up looking for one, the unemployment rate would equal zero. This would make the unemployment rate a very poor indicator of what is happening in the labour market. This example is too extreme; in practice, when the economy slows down, we typically observe both an increase in unemployment and an increase in the number of people who drop out of the labour force. Equivalently, a higher unemployment rate is typically associated with a lower **participation rate**, defined as the ratio of the labour force to the total population of working age.

◀ During the recession of 2008–2009, the number of unemployed people in the US increased by 4 million, raising the unemployment rate from 7% (November 2008) to 10% (November 2009). In the same period the number of discouraged workers increased by 1.3 million.

Figure 2.3 shows the evolution of unemployment in the euro area, the UK and the USA since the early 1990s. At that time, the unemployment rate in the euro area, including the UK, was much higher than in the USA. Since then, it has rapidly gone down in the UK, where now it is similar to the USA, and more slowly in the euro area. In the USA, note in particular how much the unemployment rate decreased during the long expansion of the 1990s,

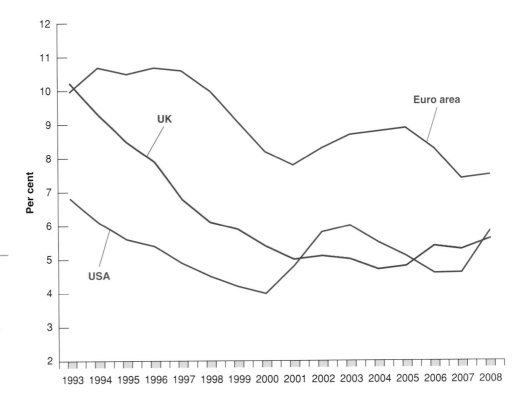

Figure 2.3

Unemployment rates in the euro area, UK and USA since 1993

Since 1993, the unemployment rate has fluctuated between 4% and 11%, going down during expansions and going up during recessions.

Source: OECD *Economic Outlook* database, July 2009.

reaching 3.9% in 2000; and how much it increased during the short recession of 2001 and more recently during the recession which began in 2008.

Why do economists care about unemployment?

Economists care about unemployment for two reasons. They care about unemployment because of its direct effects on the welfare of the unemployed. Although unemployment benefits are more generous today than they were during the Great Depression, unemployment is still often associated with financial and psychological suffering. How much suffering depends on the nature of the unemployment. One image of unemployment is that of a stagnant pool, of people remaining unemployed for long periods of time. As you will see later in this book, this image reflects what happens in many European countries, but things are quite different in some other European countries, as well as in the USA where the unemployed typically remain unemployed for a short time, and the image of a stagnant pool is not appropriate. In the USA, for example, each month, many people become unemployed, and many of the unemployed (on average, 25–30% of them) find jobs. However, even there, some groups (often the young, the ethnic minorities and the unskilled) suffer disproportionately from unemployment, remaining chronically unemployed and being more vulnerable to becoming unemployed when the unemployment rate increases.

Economists also care about the unemployment rate because it provides a signal that the economy may not be using some of its resources efficiently. Many workers who want to work do not find jobs; the economy is not efficiently utilising its human resources. From this viewpoint, can very low unemployment also be a problem? The answer is yes. Like an engine running at too high a speed, an economy in which unemployment is very low may be over-utilising its human resources and may run into labour shortages. How low is 'too low'? This is a difficult question, and one which we will take up later in the book. The question came up in 2000 in the USA. At the end of 2000, some economists worried that the unemployment rate, 4% at the time, was indeed too low. So, while they did not advocate triggering a recession, they favoured lower (but positive) output growth for some time so as to allow the unemployment rate to increase to a somewhat higher level. It turned out that they got more than they had asked for: a recession rather than a slowdown.

The inflation rate

Inflation is a sustained rise in the general level of prices – the **price level**. The **inflation rate** is the rate at which the price level increases. Symmetrically, **deflation** is a sustained decline in the price level. It corresponds to a negative inflation rate.

The practical issue is how to define the price level. Macroeconomists typically look at two measures of the price level, at two *price indexes*: the GDP deflator and the consumer price index.

◄ Deflation is rare, but it happens. Japan has had deflation since the late 1990s. More recently, some countries had deflation during the recession of 2008–2010. We will return to this topic in Chapter 22.

The GDP deflator

We saw earlier how increases in nominal GDP can come either from an increase in real GDP or from an increase in prices. Put another way, if we see nominal GDP increasing faster than real GDP, the difference must come from an increase in prices.

This remark motivates the definition of the GDP deflator. The **GDP deflator** in year t, P_t, is defined as the ratio of nominal GDP to real GDP in year t:

$$P_t = \frac{Nominal\ GDP_t}{Real\ GDP_t} = \frac{€Y_t}{Y_t}$$

Note that in the year in which, by construction, real GDP is equal to nominal GDP (which is currently 2000 in official statistics in the EU, as well as the USA), this definition implies that the price level is equal to 1. This is worth emphasising: the GDP deflator is what is called an **index number**. Its level is chosen arbitrarily – here it is equal to 1 in 2000 – and has no economic interpretation. But its rate of change, $(P_t - P_{t-1})/P_{t-1}$, has a clear economic interpretation: it gives the rate at which the general level of prices increases over time – the rate of inflation.

◄ Compute the GDP deflator and the associated rate of inflation from 1999 to 2000 and from 2000 to 2001 in our car example in Section 2.1, when real GDP is constructed using the 2000 price of cars as the common price.

One advantage to defining the price level as the GDP deflator is that it implies a simple relation between *nominal GDP*, *real GDP* and the *GDP deflator*. To see this, reorganise the previous equation to get:

$$€Y_t = P_t Y_t$$

Nominal GDP is equal to the GDP deflator multiplied by real GDP. Or, putting it in terms of rates of change, the rate of growth of nominal GDP is equal to the rate of inflation plus the rate of growth of real GDP (See Focus on GDP Deflator on page 20).

◄ For a refresher, see Appendix 1, Proposition 7.

The consumer price index

The GDP deflator gives the average price of output – the final goods *produced* in the economy – but consumers care about the average price of consumption – the goods they *consume*. The two prices need not be the same: the set of goods produced in the economy is not the same as the set of goods purchased by consumers, for two reasons:

- Some of the goods in GDP are sold not to consumers but to firms (machine tools, for example), to the government or to foreigners.
- Some of the goods bought by consumers are not produced domestically but are imported from abroad.

To measure the average price of consumption or, equivalently, the **cost of living**, macroeconomists look at another index, the *consumer price index*, or *CPI*. In the USA, the CPI has been in existence since 1917 and is published monthly. In Europe, the price index which is most frequently used is the **harmonised index of consumer prices**, or **HICP**, measured by Eurostat, the Statistical Office of the European Communities. The HICP gives comparable measures of inflation in the euro area, the EU, the European Economic Area (EEA, which includes Norway, Iceland and Liechtenstein, besides the EU) and for other countries including accession and candidate countries. (At the time of writing (early 2010) they are Croatia, Macedonia, Turkey and Iceland.) They provide the official measure of consumer price inflation in the euro area for the purposes of monetary policy and assessing inflation convergence as required under the Maastricht criteria.

◄ Do not confuse the CPI with the PPI, or *producer price index*, which is an index of prices of domestically produced goods in manufacturing, mining, agriculture, fishing, forestry and electric utility industries.

Like the GDP deflator (the price level associated with aggregate output, GDP), the HICP is an index. It is set equal to 100 in the period chosen as the base period, and so its level has

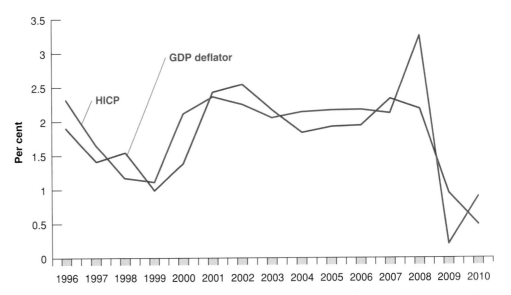

Figure 2.4

Inflation rate, using the HICP and the GDP deflator in the euro area since 1996

The inflation rates, computed using either the HICP or the GDP deflator, are largely similar.

Source: Eurostat, OECD Statistics Database.

no particular significance. The current base period is 2001, so the value for 2001 is equal to 100. In January 2009, the HICP in the euro area was 117.4; thus, it cost 17.4% more in euros to purchase the same consumption basket than in 2001.

You may wonder how the rate of inflation differs depending on whether the GDP deflator or the HICP is used to measure it. The answer is given in Figure 2.4, which plots the two inflation rates since 1996 for the euro area. The figure yields two conclusions:

- The HICP and the GDP deflator move together most of the time. In most years, the two inflation rates differ by less than 0.5%.
- There are clear exceptions to the first conclusion. In 1998, 2002 and 2009, the increase in the HICP was slightly smaller than the increase in the GDP deflator. That means that the price of goods *consumed* in the euro area (measured by the HICP) was lower than the price of goods *produced* in the euro area (measured by the GDP deflator). When the price of imported goods decreases relative to the price of goods produced in the euro area, the HICP increases less than the GDP deflator. This is precisely what happened in these years. The price of oil plummeted: in 1998 it went to a historic low, only slightly above 10 dollars per barrel, and it recorded a second fall in 2002 and a further fall in 2009. As Europe is a major oil importer, the result was a decrease in the HICP compared to the GDP deflator. Look at what happened in 2008, when oil prices went to very high levels (as described in Chapter 1, Figure 1.3): the HICP increased much more than the GDP deflator.

In what follows, we shall typically assume that the two indexes move together, so we do not need to distinguish between them. We shall simply talk about *the price level* and denote it by P_t, without indicating whether we have the consumer price index or the GDP deflator in mind.

Why do economists care about inflation?

If a higher inflation rate meant just a faster but proportional increase in all prices and wages – a case called *pure inflation* – inflation would be only a minor inconvenience for consumers, as relative prices would be unaffected. Take, for example, the workers' *real wage* – the wage measured in terms of goods rather than in euros. In an economy with 10% more inflation, prices would increase by 10% more per year. But wages would also increase by 10% more per year, so real wages would be unaffected by inflation. Inflation would not be entirely irrelevant; people would have to keep track of the increase in prices and wages when making decisions. But this would be a small burden, hardly justifying making control of the inflation rate one of the major goals of macroeconomic policy.

So, why do economists care about inflation? Precisely because there is no such thing as pure inflation:

- During periods of inflation, not all prices and wages rise proportionately. Consequently, inflation affects income distribution, meaning for instance that retirees in many countries receive payments that do not keep up with the price level, so they lose in relation to other groups when inflation is high. For example, during the very high inflation that took place in Russia in the 1990s, retirement pensions did not keep up with inflation, and many retirees were pushed to near starvation.

- Inflation leads to other distortions. Variations in relative prices also lead to more uncertainty, making it harder for firms to make decisions about the future, such as investment decisions. Some prices, which are fixed by law or by regulation, lag behind others, leading to changes in relative prices. Taxation interacts with inflation to create more distortions. If tax brackets are not adjusted for inflation, for example, people move into higher and higher tax brackets as their nominal income increases, even if their real income remains the same.

If inflation is so bad, does this imply that deflation (negative inflation) is good? The answer is no. First, high deflation (a large negative rate of inflation) would create many of the same problems as high inflation, from distortions to increased uncertainty. Second, as we shall see later in the book, even a low rate of deflation limits the ability of monetary policy to affect output. So what is the 'best' rate of inflation? Most macroeconomists believe that the best rate of inflation is a low and stable rate of inflation, somewhere between 0 and 3%. We shall look at the pros and cons of different rates of inflation later in the book.

> ◄ Newspapers sometimes confuse deflation and recession. They may happen together, but they are not the same. Deflation is a decrease in the price level. A recession is a decrease in real output.

We have now looked at the main macroeconomic variables: aggregate output, unemployment and inflation. Clearly, a successful economy is an economy that combines high output growth, low unemployment and low inflation. Can all these objectives be achieved simultaneously? Is low unemployment compatible with low and stable inflation? Do policy makers have the tools to sustain growth, to achieve low unemployment while maintaining low inflation? These are some of the questions we shall take up as we go through the book. The next two sections give you a road map.

2.3 THE SHORT RUN, THE MEDIUM RUN AND THE LONG RUN

What determines the level of aggregate output in an economy?

- Reading newspapers suggests a first answer: movements in output come from movements in the demand for goods. You have probably read news stories that begin like this: 'Production and sales of automobiles were lower last month, due to a fall in consumer confidence.' Stories like this highlight the role demand plays in determining aggregate output; they point to factors that affect demand, ranging from consumer confidence to interest rates.

- But, surely, no number of Indian consumers rushing to Indian showrooms can increase India's output to the level of output in the USA. This suggests a second answer: what matters when it comes to aggregate output is the supply side – how much the economy can produce. How much can be produced depends on how advanced the technology of the country is, how much capital it is using and the size and the skills of its labour force. These factors – not consumer confidence – are the fundamental determinants of a country's level of output.

- The previous argument can be taken one step further: neither technology, nor capital nor skills are given. The technological sophistication of a country depends on its ability to innovate and introduce new technologies. The size of its capital stock depends on how much people save. The skills of workers depend on the quality of the country's education system. Other factors are also important: if firms are to operate efficiently, for example, they need a clear system of laws under which to operate and an honest government to enforce those laws. This suggests a third answer: the true determinants of output are factors such as a country's education system, its saving rate and the quality of its government. If we want to understand what determines the level of output, we must look at these factors.

You might be wondering at this point which of the three answers is right. All three are right. But each applies over a different time frame:

- In the **short run**, say, a few years, the first answer is the right one. Year-to-year movements in output are primarily driven by movements in demand. Changes in demand, perhaps due to changes in consumer confidence or other factors, can lead to a decrease in output (a recession) or an increase in output (an expansion).
- In the **medium run**, say, a decade, the second answer is the right one. Over the medium run, the economy tends to return to the level of output determined by supply factors: the capital stock, the level of technology and the size of the labour force. And, over a decade or so, these factors move sufficiently slowly that we can take them as given.
- In the **long run**, say, a few decades or more, the third answer is the right one. To understand why China has been able to achieve such a high growth rate since 1980, we must understand why both capital and the level of technology in China are increasing so fast. To do so, we must look at factors such as the education system, the saving rate, and the role of the government.

This way of thinking about the determinants of output underlies macroeconomics, and it underlies the organisation of this book.

2.4 A TOUR OF THE BOOK

This book is organised in three parts: a core, four extensions and a closer look at the European economic and monetary integration. This organisation is shown in Figure 2.5. Let us describe it in more detail.

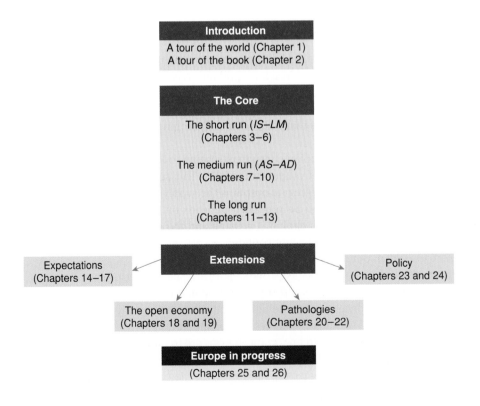

Figure 2.5

The organisation of the book

The core

The core is composed of three parts – the short run, the medium run and the long run:

- Chapters 3–6 look at how output is determined in the short run. To focus on the role of demand, we assume that firms are willing to supply any quantity at a given price. In other words, we ignore supply constraints.

  Chapter 3 looks at the goods market. Chapter 4 focuses on financial markets. Chapter 5 puts the goods and financial markets together. The resulting framework is known as the IS–LM model. Developed in the late 1930s, the IS–LM model still provides a simple way of thinking about the determination of output in the short run, and it remains a basic building block of macroeconomics. It also allows for a first pass at studying the effects of fiscal policy and monetary policy on output. The previous chapters treat the economy as *closed*, ignoring its interactions with the rest of the world. However, in fact economies are increasingly *open*, trading goods and services and financial assets with one another. Chapter 6 discusses the implications of openness in goods and financial markets.

- Chapters 7 to 10 develop the supply side and look at how output is determined in the medium run.

  Chapter 7 introduces the labour market. Chapter 8 puts together goods, financial and labour markets, and shows you how to think about the determination of output both in the short run and in the medium run. The model developed in Chapter 8 is called the aggregate supply–aggregate demand (AS–AD) model of output. Chapters 9 and 10 then show how the AS–AD model can be used to think about many issues, such as the relation between output and inflation and the role of monetary and fiscal policy in both the short run and the medium run.

- Chapters 11–13 focus on the long run.

  Chapter 11 introduces the relevant facts by looking at the growth of output both across countries and over long periods of time. Chapters 12 and 13 then discuss how both capital accumulation and technological progress determine growth.

Extensions

The core chapters give you a way of thinking about how output (and unemployment and inflation) is determined over the short, medium and long run. However, they leave out several elements, which are explored in four extensions:

- The core chapters introduce the role of *expectations*. Expectations play an essential role in macroeconomics. Fiscal and monetary policies affect economic activity not only through their direct effects but also through their effects on people's and firms' expectations. Chapters 14–17 focus on these expectations and their implications for fiscal and monetary policy. Chapter 14 introduces the role of expectations in the economy. In fact, nearly all the economic decisions people and firms make – whether to buy a car, whether to buy bonds or to buy stocks, whether to build a new plant – depend on their expectations about future income, future profits, future interest rates and so on.

- Modern economies are increasingly open to the rest of the world, and therefore increasingly interdependent. The nature of this interdependence is the topics of Chapters 18 and 19. Chapter 18 gives an open economy version of the IS–LM model we saw in the core. Chapter 19 looks at properties of different exchange rate regimes.

- The core chapters on the short run and the medium run focus on fluctuations in output – on expansions and on recessions. Sometimes, however, the word *fluctuations* does not accurately capture what is happening when something goes very wrong such as when, as during the recent recession of 2008–2010, the whole world has gone through a prolonged economic slump, or when government debt becomes very high, or when inflation reaches extremely high rates. These *pathologies* are the topics of Chapters 20–22.

- Monetary policy and fiscal policy are discussed in nearly every chapter of the book. We have seen how economic policy can help a country out of a recession, or slow down an overheating economy, improve its trade position and stimulate capital accumulation. However, there are also arguments in favour of restraining macroeconomic policy. Chapter 23 discusses two possibilities: that policy makers might do more harm than good, and that they might not choose what is the best for the country. Chapter 24 discusses the policy rules that are often introduced by countries to guide or restrain the action of monetary and fiscal policy makers.

Europe in progress

In 1957 some European countries started a process of economic integration which now includes 27 countries. This is now called EU27. More recently, the integration process extended to monetary integration with the adoption of a common currency in 16 countries. This group is called the euro area.

- Chapter 25 focuses on economic and monetary integration in Europe, its history and the functioning of its institutions, and the work of the European Central Bank.
- Chapter 26 focuses on the euro and on its impact on the countries of Europe in the ten years since its introduction in 1999. We will also discuss whether the euro area is an optimal currency area and whether those European countries that have thus far decided not to join should change their minds.

SUMMARY

- We can think of GDP, the measure of aggregate output, in three equivalent ways: (1) GDP is the value of the final goods and services produced in the economy during a given period; (2) GDP is the sum of value added in the economy during a given period; and (3) GDP is the sum of incomes in the economy during a given period.

- Nominal GDP is the sum of the quantities of final goods produced multiplied by their current prices. This implies that changes in nominal GDP reflect both changes in quantities and changes in prices. Real GDP is a measure of output. Changes in real GDP reflect changes in quantities only.

- A person is classified as unemployed if he or she does not have a job and is looking for one. The unemployment rate is the ratio of the number of people unemployed to the number of people in the labour force. The labour force is the sum of those employed and those unemployed.

- Economists care about unemployment because of the human cost it represents. They also look at unemployment because it sends a signal about how efficiently the economy is using its resources. High unemployment indicates that the economy is not utilising its human resources efficiently.

- Inflation is a rise in the general level of prices – the price level. The inflation rate is the rate at which the price level increases. Macroeconomists look at two measures of the price level. The first is the GDP deflator, which is the average price of the goods produced in the economy. The second is the consumer price index, which is the average price of goods consumed in the economy.

- Inflation leads to changes in income distribution. It also leads to distortions and increased uncertainty.

- Macroeconomists distinguish between the short run (a few years), the medium run (a decade) and the long run (a few decades or more). They think of output as being determined by demand in the short run. They also think of output as being determined by the level of technology, the capital stock and the labour force in the medium run. Finally, they think of output as being determined by factors such as education, research, saving and the quality of government in the long run.

KEY TERMS

System of National Accounts (SNA) 16

aggregate output 16

gross domestic product (GDP) 16

gross national product (GNP) 16

intermediate good 16

final good 16

value added 17

underground economy 18

nominal GDP 19

real GDP 19

base year 20

GDP at current prices 21

GDP in terms of goods, GDP at constant prices, GDP adjusted for inflation 21

real GDP per capita 21

GDP growth 21

expansion 21

recession 21

hedonic pricing 21

employment 22

unemployment 22

labour force 22

unemployment rate 22

Labour Force Survey (LFS) 23

not in the labour force 23

discouraged worker 23

participation rate 23

inflation 25

price level 25

inflation rate 25

deflation 25

GDP deflator 25

index number 25

cost of living 25

Harmonised Index of Consumer Prices (HICP) 25

short run 28

medium run 28

long run 28

QUESTIONS AND PROBLEMS

QUICK CHECK

1. *Using the information in this chapter, label each of the following statements true, false or uncertain. Explain briefly.*

a. The share of labour income in GDP is much larger than the share of capital income.

b. GDP in the EU15 was 14 times higher in 2008 than it was in 1970.

c. When the unemployment rate is high, the participation rate is also likely to be high.

d. The rate of unemployment tends to fall during expansions and rise during recessions.

e. If the Japanese CPI is currently at 108 and the EU15 HICP is at 104, then the Japanese rate of inflation is higher than the EU15 rate of inflation.

f. The rate of inflation computed using the CPI is a better index of inflation than the rate of inflation computed using the GDP deflator.

2. *Suppose you are measuring annual GDP by adding up the final value of all goods and services produced in the economy. Determine the effect on GDP of each of the following transactions.*

a. A seafood restaurant buys €100 worth of fish from a fisherman.

b. A family spends €100 on a fish dinner at a seafood restaurant.

c. The Greek national airline buys a new jet from Boeing for €200 million.

d. Airbus sells one of its jets to Denzel Washington for €100 million.

3. *During a given year, the following activities occur:*

i. A silver mining company pays its workers €200 000 to mine 75 pounds of silver. The silver is then sold to a jewellery manufacturer for €300 000.

ii. The jewellery manufacturer pays its workers €250 000 to make silver necklaces, which the manufacturer sells directly to consumers for €1 000 000.

a. Using the 'production-of-final-goods' approach, what is GDP in this economy?

b. What is the value added at each stage of production? Using the 'value-added' approach, what is GDP?

c. What are the total wages and profits earned? Using the income approach, what is GDP?

4. *An economy produces three goods: cars, computers and oranges. Quantities and prices per unit for years 2006 and 2007 are as follows:*

	2006		2007	
	Quantity	**Price**	**Quantity**	**Price**
Cars	10	€2000	12	€3000
Computers	4	€1000	6	€500
Oranges	1000	€1	1000	€1

a. What is nominal GDP in 2006 and in 2007? By what percentage does nominal GDP change from 2006 to 2007?

b. Using the prices for 2006 as the set of common prices, what is real GDP in 2006 and in 2007? By what percentage does real GDP change from 2006 to 2007?

c. Using the prices for 2007 as the set of common prices, what is real GDP in 2006 and in 2007? By what percentage does real GDP change from 2006 to 2007?

d. Why are the two output growth rates constructed in (b) and (c) different? Which one is correct? Explain your answer.

5. *Consider the economy described in problem 4.*

a. Use the prices for 2006 as the set of common prices to compute real GDP in 2006 and in 2007. Compute the GDP deflator for 2006 and for 2007 and compute the rate of inflation from 2006 to 2007.

b. Use the prices for 2007 as the set of common prices to compute real GDP in 2006 and in 2007. Compute the GDP deflator for 2006 and for 2007 and compute the rate of inflation from 2006 to 2007.

c. Why are the two rates of inflation different? Which one is correct? Explain your answer.

6. *Consider the economy described in problem 4.*

a. Construct real GDP for years 2006 and 2007 by using the average price of each good over the two years.

b. By what percentage does real GDP change from 2006 to 2007?

c. What is the GDP deflator in 2006 and 2007? Using the GDP deflator, what is the rate of inflation from 2006 to 2007?

d. Is this an attractive solution to the problems pointed out in problems 4 and 5 (i.e., two different growth rates and two different inflation rates, depending on which set of prices is used)? (The answer is yes and is the basis for the construction of chained-type deflators. See the appendix to this chapter for more discussion.)

DIG DEEPER

7. Hedonic pricing

As the third Focus box in this chapter explains, it is difficult to measure the true increase in prices of goods whose characteristics change over time. For such goods, part of any price increase can be attributed to an increase in quality. Hedonic pricing offers a method to compute the quality-adjusted increase in prices.

a. Consider the case of a routine medical check-up. Name some reasons you might want to use hedonic pricing to measure the change in the price of this service.

Now consider the case of a medical check-up for a pregnant woman. Suppose that a new ultrasound method is introduced. In the first year that this method is available, half of doctors offer the new method, and half offer the old method. A check-up using the new method costs 10% more than a check-up using the old method.

b. In percentage terms, how much of a quality increase does the new method represent over the old method? (*Hint:* Consider the fact that some women choose to see a doctor offering the new method, when they could have chosen to see a doctor offering the old method.)

Now, in addition, suppose that in the first year the new ultrasound method is available, the price of check-ups using the new method is 15% higher than the price of check-ups in the previous year (when everyone used the old method).

c. How much of the higher price for check-ups using the new method (as compared to check-ups in the previous year) reflects a true price increase of check-ups and how much represents a quality increase? In other words, how much higher is the quality-adjusted price of check-ups using the new method as compared to the price of check-ups in the previous year?

In many cases, the kind of information we used in parts (b) and (c) is not available. For example, suppose that in the year the new ultrasound method is introduced, all doctors adopt the new method, so the old method is no longer used. In addition, continue to assume that the price of check-ups in the year the new method is introduced is 15% higher than the price of check-ups in the previous year (when everyone used the old method). Thus, we observe a 15% price increase in check-ups, but we realise that the quality of check-ups has increased.

d. Under these assumptions, what information required to compute the quality-adjusted price increase of check-ups is lacking? Even without this information, can we say anything about the quality-adjusted price increase of check-ups? Is it more than 15%? Less than 15%? Explain.

8. Measured and true GDP

Suppose that instead of cooking dinner for an hour, you decide to work an extra hour, earning an additional €12. You then purchase some (takeout) Chinese food, which costs you €10.

a. By how much does measured GDP increase?

b. Do you think the increase in measured GDP accurately reflects the effect on output of your decision to work? Explain.

EXPLORE FURTHER

9. The labour market and the recession of 2007–2010

Go to the Eurostat web page and retrieve the quarterly data at constant prices for your country and for the EU27.

a. Plot the quarterly GDP growth rates from 2005 to 2010. Did any quarters have negative growth? How did your country differ from the average EU27?

Now retrieve the monthly data series on the participation rate, employment, the employment-to-population ratio and the unemployment rate for the period 2007–2010. Make sure all data series are seasonally adjusted.

a. How did the unemployment rate change in 2007 and after? Do you think the unemployment rate tells the whole story about the labour market? How did the participation rate evolve? What might explain the change in the participation rate?

b. Some economists prefer to look at employment as opposed to unemployment. How did the growth of employment after 2007 compare to the growth of employment before 2001? How did the employment-to-population ratio change?

c. How did the economic performance in your country compare with the EU27's?

---

*We invite you to visit the Blanchard page on the Prentice Hall website, at **www.prenhall.com/blanchard** for this chapter's World Wide Web exercises.*

FURTHER READING

- If you want to learn more about the definitions and the construction of the many economic indicators that are regularly reported on the news – from the help-wanted index to the retail sales index – an easy-to-read reference is: *The Economist Guide to Economic Indicators*, 6th ed., by the staff of *The Economist*, Bloomberg, New York, 2007.

- For a discussion of some of the problems involved in measuring activity, read 'What We Don't Know Could Hurt Us; Some Reflections on the Measurement of Economic Activity', by Katherine Abraham, *Journal of Economic Perspectives*, 2008, 19 (3), 3–18.

- To see why it is hard to measure the price level and output correctly, read 'Viagra and the Wealth of Nations', by Paul Krugman, 1998 (*www.pkarchive.org/theory/viagra.html*). (Paul Krugman is an economist at Princeton University and a columnist for the *New York Times*.) He was awarded the Nobel prize for Economics in 2009.

APPENDIX

The construction of real GDP and chain-type indexes

The example we used in the chapter had only one final good – car – so constructing real GDP was easy. But how do we construct real GDP when there is more than one final good? This appendix gives the answer. To understand how real GDP in an economy with many final goods is constructed, all you need to do is look at an economy where there are just two final goods. What works for two goods works just as well for millions of goods. Suppose that an economy produces two final goods, say wine and potatoes:

- In year 0, it produces 10 pounds of potatoes at a price of €1 per pound and five bottles of wine at a price of €2 per bottle.
- In year 1, it produces 15 pounds of potatoes at a price of €1 per pound and five bottles of wine at a price of €3 per bottle.
- Nominal GDP in year 0 is therefore equal to €20. Nominal GDP in year 1 is equal to €30.

This information is summarised in the following table:

Nominal GDP in Year 0 and in Year 1

	Year 0		
	Quantity	Price (€)	Value (€)
Potatoes (pounds)	10	1	10
Wine (bottles)	5	2	10
Nominal GDP			20

	Year 1		
	Quantity	Price (€)	Value (€)
Potatoes (pounds)	15	1	15
Wine (bottles)	5	3	15
Nominal GDP			30

The rate of growth of nominal GDP from year 0 to year 1 is equal to (€30 − €20)/€20 = 50%. But what is the rate of growth of real GDP?

Answering this question requires constructing real GDP for each of the two years. The basic idea behind constructing real GDP is to evaluate the quantities in each year, using the *same set of prices*.

Suppose we choose, for example, the prices in year 0. Year 0 is then called the *base year*. In this case, the computation is as follows:

- Real GDP in year 0 is the sum of the quantity in year 0 multiplied by the price in year 0 for both goods: (10 × €1 + 5 × €2) = €20.
- Real GDP in year 1 is the sum of the quantity in year 1 multiplied by the price in year 0 for both goods: (15 × €1 + 5 × €2) = €25.
- The rate of growth of real GDP from year 0 to year 1 is then (€25 − €20)/€20, or 25%.

This answer raises an obvious issue: instead of using year 0 as the base year, we could have used year 1, or any other year. If, for example, we had used year 1 as the base year, then:

- Real GDP in year 0 would be equal to (10 × €1 + 5 × €3) = €25.
- Real GDP in year 1 would be equal to (15 × €1 + 5 × €3) = €30.
- The rate of growth of real GDP from year 0 to year 1 would be equal to €5/€25, or 20%.

The answer using year 1 as the base year would therefore be different from the answer using year 0 as the base year. So, if the choice of the base year affects the constructed percentage rate of change in output, which base year should one choose?

In most countries today the practice is to choose a base year and change it infrequently, say, every five years or so. This practice is logically unappealing. Every time the base year is changed and a new set of prices was used, all past real GDP numbers – and all past real GDP growth rates – are recomputed. Economic history is, in effect, rewritten every five years! In Europe, Eurostat – the Statistical Office of the European Union – established specific recommendations about the way in which growth rates should be calculated in the System of National Accounts 1993 (SNS 93).

The method requires four steps:

1. Construct the rate of change of real GDP from year *t* to year *t* + 1 in two different ways. First, use the prices from year *t* as the set of common prices. Then, use the prices from year *t* + 1 as the set of common prices. For example, the rate of change of GDP from 2006 to 2007 is computed by:

a. Constructing real GDP for 2006 and real GDP for 2007 using 2006 prices as the set of common prices, and computing a first measure of the rate of growth of GDP from 2006 to 2007.

b. Constructing real GDP for 2006 and real GDP for 2007 using 2007 prices as the set of common prices, and computing a second measure of the rate of growth of GDP from 2006 to 2007.

2. Construct the rate of change of real GDP as the average of these two rates of change.

3. Construct an index for the level of real GDP by *linking* – or *chaining* – the constructed rates of change for each year.

The index is set equal to 1 in some arbitrary year. At the time this book was written, the arbitrary year is 2000.

Given that the constructed rate of change from 2000 to 2001 by Eurostat is 0.7%, the index for 2001 equals

$(1 + 0.07\%) = 1.007$. The index for 2002 is then obtained by multiplying the index for 2001 by the rate of change from 2001 to 2002, and so on.

4. Multiply this index by nominal GDP in 2000 to derive *chain-linked GDP at constant prices*. As the index is 1 in 2000, this implies that real GDP in 2000 equals nominal GDP in 2000.

Chained refers to the chaining of rates of change described above. (2000) refers to the year where, by construction, real GDP is equal to nominal GDP.

This index is more complicated to construct than the indexes used before 1995. (To make sure you understand the steps, construct real GDP in chained (year 0) dollars for year 1 in our example.) But it is clearly better conceptually:

- The prices used to evaluate real GDP in two adjacent years are the right prices, namely the average prices for those two years.
- Because the rate of change from one year to the next is constructed using the prices in those two years rather than the set of prices in an arbitrary base year, history will not be rewritten every five years – as it used to be when, under the previous method for constructing real GDP, the base year was changed.

THE CORE

"HOW AM I GOING TO LEARN THE VALUE OF A DOLLAR
IF I'M ONLY GETTING 50¢ ALLOWANCE?"

Source: from Dispute Over Pocket Money, dcr 0631, Dave Carpenter,
www.cartoonstock.com.

THE SHORT RUN

In the short run, demand determines output. Many factors affect demand, from consumer confidence to fiscal and monetary policy.

Chapter 3 The goods market

Chapter 3 looks at equilibrium in the goods market and the determination of output. It focuses on the interaction between demand, production and income. It shows how fiscal policy affects output.

Chapter 4 Financial markets

Chapter 4 looks at equilibrium in financial markets and the determination of the interest rate. It shows how monetary policy affects the interest rate.

Chapter 5 Goods and financial markets: the *IS–LM* model

Chapter 5 looks at the goods market and financial markets together. It shows what determines output and the interest rate in the short run. It looks at the roles of fiscal and monetary policies. The model developed in Chapter 5, called the *IS–LM* model, is one of the workhorses of macroeconomics.

Chapter 6 The *IS–LM* model in an open economy

Chapter 6 discusses the implications of openness in goods markets and financial markets. Openness in goods markets allows people to choose between domestic goods and foreign goods. Openness in financial markets allows people to choose between domestic assets and foreign assets.

Chapter 3

THE GOODS MARKET

When economists think about year-to-year movements in economic activity, they focus on the interactions between production, income and demand:

- Changes in the demand for goods lead to changes in production.

- Changes in production lead to changes in income.

- Changes in income lead to changes in the demand for goods.

Nothing makes the point better than the following cartoon:

Source: from Data shows you consumers aren't spending enough, 1776–78, Toles, Universal Uclick.

This chapter looks at these interactions and their implications:

- Section 3.1 looks at the composition of GDP and the different sources of the demand for goods.

- Section 3.2 looks at the determinants of the demand for goods.

- Section 3.3 shows how equilibrium output is determined by the condition that the production of goods must be equal to the demand for goods.

- Section 3.4 gives an alternative way of thinking about the equilibrium, based on the equality of investment and saving.

- Section 3.5 takes a first pass at the effects of fiscal policy on equilibrium output.

3.1 THE COMPOSITION OF GDP

The purchase of a machine by a firm, the decision to go to a restaurant by a consumer and the purchase of school desks by the national government are clearly very different decisions and depend on very different factors. So, if we want to understand what determines the demand for goods, it makes sense to decompose aggregate output (GDP) from the point of view of the different goods being produced, and from the point of view of the different buyers for these goods.

◄ *Output* and *production* are synonymous. There is no rule for using one or the other. Use the one that sounds better.

The decomposition of GDP typically used by macroeconomists is shown in Table 3.1:

1. First comes **consumption** (which we will denote by the letter C when we use algebra throughout this book). These are the goods and services purchased by consumers, ranging from food to airline tickets, to holidays, to new cars and so on. Consumption is by far the largest component of GDP. In 2008, it accounted, on average, for 57.3% of GDP in the EU (EU15), ranging from 46.2% in the Netherlands to 71.2% in Greece. In general, consumption is close to 60% or more of national income in the largest European economies (56.3% in Germany, 57.2% in Spain, 56.7% in France, 59.1% in Italy and up to 64.7% in the UK), whereas in smaller countries consumption tends to be closer to 50% of GDP (46.2% in the Netherlands, 46.5% in Sweden, 48.9% in Denmark, 51.4% in Finland and 52.9% in Austria).

2. Second comes **investment** (I), sometimes called **fixed investment** to distinguish it from inventory investment (which we will discuss shortly). Investment is the sum of **non-residential investment**, the purchase by firms of new plants or new machines (from turbines to computers), and **residential investment**, the purchase by people of new houses or apartments.

   Non-residential investment and residential investment, and the decisions behind them, have more in common than might first appear. Firms buy machines or plants to produce output in the future. People buy houses or apartments to get *housing services* in the future. In both cases, the decision to buy depends on the services these goods will yield in the future. Consequently, it makes sense to treat them together. Together, non-residential and residential investment accounted, on average, for 20.8% of GDP in EU15 in 2008, ranging from 16.6% in the UK and 19.6% in Sweden to 29.4% in Spain.

◄ **Warning!** To most people, *investment* refers to the purchase of assets such as gold or shares. Economists use *investment* to refer to the purchase of new capital goods, such as (new) machines, (new) buildings or (new) houses. When economists refer to the purchase of gold, or shares, or other financial assets, they use the term *financial investment*.

Table 3.1 The Composition of GDP, EU15, 2008

	Billion euros	Percentage of GDP
GDP (Y)	11.5	100.0
1 Consumption (C)	6.6	57.3
2 Investment (I)	2.4	20.8
3 Government spending (G)	2.4	20.9
4 Net exports	0.7	0.6
Exports (X)	4.6	40.0
Imports (IM)	−4.5	−39.4
5 Inventory investment	0.4	0.4

Source: Eurostat.

3. Third comes **government spending** (**G**). This represents the purchases of goods and services by the national, regional and local governments. The goods range from aeroplanes to office equipment. The services include services provided by government employees: in effect, the national income accounts treat the government as buying the services provided by government employees – and then providing these services to the public, free of charge.

Note that G does not include **government transfers** (for instance, unemployment benefits and pensions), or interest payments on the government debt. Although these are clearly government expenditures, they are not purchases of goods and services. In 2008, government spending accounted on average for 20.9% of GDP in EU15. With the notable exception of Germany, where government expenditure is relatively lower, the largest European countries are all close to the average (the UK slightly above with 21.9%), whereas government spending accounts for particularly high shares of GDP in northern European countries (22.1% in Finland, 23.0% in Belgium, 25.0% in the Netherlands, 26.4% in Sweden and 26.5% in Denmark).

4. The sum of points 1, 2, and 3 gives the *purchases of goods and services by resident consumers, resident firms and the government*. To determine the *purchases of domestic goods and services*, two more steps are needed:

First, we must subtract **imports** (**IM**), the purchases of foreign goods and services by domestic consumers, domestic firms, and the government.

Second, we must add **exports** (**X**), the purchases of domestic goods and services by foreigners.

The difference between exports and imports (**X – IM**) is called **net exports**, or the **trade balance**. If exports exceed imports, the country is said to run a **trade surplus**. If exports are less than imports, the country is said to run a **trade deficit**. In 2008, exports from EU15 accounted for 40.0% of GDP and imports were equal to 39.4% of GDP, so EU15 had a trade surplus equal to 0.6% of GDP. Again, this average hides substantial differences across countries: Belgium, Italy, Spain and the UK were running trade deficits, while most northern European countries, as well as Germany, Denmark and the Netherlands, had considerable trade surpluses.

> Exports > Imports ⇔ Trade surplus
>
> Exports < Imports ⇔ Trade deficit

5. So far we have looked at various sources of purchases (sales) of domestic goods and services in 2008. To determine national production in 2008, we need to take one last step.

In any given year, production and sales need not be equal. Some of the goods produced in a given year are not sold in that year, but in later years. And some of the goods sold in a given year may have been produced in an earlier year. The difference between goods produced and goods sold in a given year – the difference between production and sales, in other words – is called **inventory investment**. If production exceeds sales and firms accumulate inventories as a result, then inventory investment is said to be positive. If production is less than sales, and firms inventories fall, then inventory investment is said to be negative. Inventory investment is typically small – positive in some years and negative in others. In 2008, inventory investment was positive, equal to just €43 billion, or 0.4% of GDP. Put another way, production was higher than sales by an amount equal to €43 billion.

> Make sure you understand each of these three equivalent ways of stating the relation between production, sales and inventory investment:
>
> - Inventory investment = Production – Sales
> - Production = Sales + Inventory investment
> - Sales = Production – Inventory investment

We now have what we need to develop our first model of output determination.

3.2 THE DEMAND FOR GOODS

Denote the total demand for goods by Z. Using the decomposition of GDP we saw in Section 3.1, we can write Z as:

$$Z \equiv C + I + G + X - IM$$

> Recall that inventory investment is not part of demand.

This equation is an **identity** (which is why it is written using the symbol ≡ rather than an equals sign). It *defines* Z as the sum of consumption, plus investment, plus government spending, plus exports, minus imports.

We now need to think about the determinants of Z. To make the task easier, let's first make a number of simplifications:

- Assume that all firms produce the same good, which can then be used by consumers for consumption, by firms for investment or by the government. With this (big) simplification, we need to look at only one market – the market for 'the' good – and think about what determines supply and demand in that market.

- Assume that firms are willing to supply any amount of the good at a given price, P. This assumption allows us to focus on the role demand plays in the determination of output. As we shall see later in the book, this assumption is valid only in the short run. When we move to the study of the medium run (starting in Chapter 7), we will abandon it but, for the moment, it will simplify our discussion.

- Assume that the economy is *closed* – that it does not trade with the rest of the world: both exports and imports are zero. This assumption clearly goes against the facts: modern economies trade with the rest of the world. Later on (starting in Chapter 6), we will abandon this assumption as well and look at what happens when the economy is open but, for the moment, this assumption will also simplify our discussion because we won't have to think about what determines exports and imports.

◀ A model nearly always starts with *assume* (or *suppose*). This is an indication that reality is about to be simplified to focus on the issue at hand.

Under the assumption that the economy is closed, $X = IM = 0$, so the demand for goods, Z, is simply the sum of consumption, investment, and government spending:

$$Z = C + I + G$$

Let's discuss each of these three components in turn.

Consumption (C)

Consumption decisions depend on many factors. The main one is surely income or, more precisely, **disposable income** (Y_D), the income that remains after consumers have received transfers from the government and paid their taxes. When their disposable income goes up, people buy more goods; when it goes down, they buy fewer goods.

Let C denote consumption and Y_D denote disposable income. We can then write:

$$C = C(Y_D) \qquad [3.1]$$
$$(+)$$

This is a formal way of stating that consumption, C, is a function of disposable income, Y_D. The function $C(Y_D)$ is called the **consumption function**. The positive sign below Y_D reflects the fact that when disposable income increases, so does consumption. Economists call such an equation a **behavioural equation** to indicate that the equation captures some aspect of behaviour – in this case, the behaviour of consumers.

We will use functions in this book as a way of representing relations between variables. What you need to know about functions – which is very little – is described in Appendix 1 at the end of the book. That appendix develops the mathematics you need to go through this book. Not to worry: we shall always describe a function in words when we introduce it for the first time.

It is often useful to be more specific about the form of the function. Here is such a case. It is reasonable to assume that the relation between consumption and disposable income is given by the simpler relation:

$$C = c_0 + c_1(Y_D) \qquad [3.2]$$

In other words, it is reasonable to assume that the function is a **linear relation**. The relation between consumption and disposable income is then characterised by two **parameters**, c_0 and c_1:

- The parameter c_1 is called the **marginal propensity to consume**. It gives the effect an additional euro of disposable income has on consumption. If c_1 is equal to 0.6, then an additional euro of disposable income increases consumption by €1 × 0.6 = 60 cents.

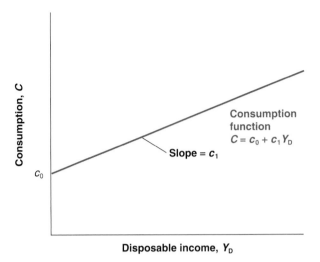

Figure 3.1

Consumption and disposable income

Consumption increases with disposable income, but less than one for one.

A natural restriction on c_1 is that it must be positive: an increase in disposable income is likely to lead to an increase in consumption. Another natural restriction is that c_1 must be less than 1: People are likely to consume only part of any increase in disposable income and save the rest.

- The parameter c_0 has a simple interpretation. It is what people would consume if their disposable income in the current year were equal to zero: if Y_D equals zero in equation (3.2), $C = c_0$.

> Think about your own consumption behaviour. What are your values of c_0 and c_1?

A natural restriction is that, if current income were equal to zero, consumption would still be positive: with or without income, people still need to eat! This implies that c_0 is positive. How can people have positive consumption if their income is equal to zero? Answer: they dissave. They consume either by selling some of their assets, or by borrowing.

The relation between consumption and disposable income shown in equation (3.2) is drawn in Figure 3.1. Because it is a linear relation, it is represented by a straight line. Its intercept with the vertical axis is c_0; its slope is c_1. Because c_1 is less than 1, the slope of the line is less than 1: equivalently, the line is flatter than a 45° line. (A refresher on graphs, slopes and intercepts is given in Appendix 1.)

Next, we need to define disposable income, Y_D. Disposable income is given by

$$Y_D \equiv Y - T$$

where Y is income and T is taxes paid minus government transfers received by consumers. For short, we will refer to T simply as taxes: but remember that it is equal to taxes minus transfers. Note that the equation is an identity, indicated by $\equiv$.

Replacing Y_D in equation (3.2) gives

$$C = c_0 + c_1(Y - T) \qquad [3.3]$$

Equation (3.3) tells us that consumption, C, is a function of income, Y, and taxes, T. Higher income increases consumption, but less than one for one. Higher taxes decrease consumption, also less than one for one.

Investment (*I*)

Models have two types of variables. Some variables depend on other variables in the model and are therefore explained within the model. Variables like these are called **endogenous**. This was the case for consumption above. Other variables are not explained within the model but are instead taken as given. Variables like these are called **exogenous**. This is how we will treat investment here. We will take investment as given and write:

$$I = \bar{I} \qquad [3.4]$$

Putting a bar on investment is a simple typographical way to remind us that we take investment as given.

◄ ● Endogenous variables – explained within the model.
● Exogenous variables – taken as given.

We take investment as given to keep our model simple, but the assumption is not innocu-
ous. It implies that, when we later look at the effects of changes in production, we will
assume that investment does not respond to changes in production. It is not hard to see that
this implication may be a bad description of reality: firms that experience an increase in
production might well decide they need more machines and increase their investment as a
result. For now, though, we will leave this mechanism out of the model. In Chapter 5 we will
introduce a more realistic treatment of investment.

Government spending (G)

The third component of demand in our model is government spending, G. Together with
taxes, T, G describes **fiscal policy** – the choice of taxes and spending by the government.
Just as we did for investment, we will take G and T as exogenous. However, the reason why
we assume G and T are exogenous is different from the reason we assumed investment is
exogenous. It is based on two distinct arguments:

◄ Recall, that 'taxes' stands for taxes minus government transfers.

- First, governments do not behave with the same regularity as consumers or firms, so
there is no reliable rule we could write for G or T corresponding to the rule we wrote, for
example, for consumption. (This argument is not airtight, though. Even if governments
do not follow simple behavioural rules as consumers do, a good part of their behaviour
is predictable. We will look at these issues later, in particular in Chapter 23. Until then,
we will set them aside.)
- Second, and more importantly, one of the tasks of macroeconomists is to think about
the implications of alternative spending and tax decisions. We want to be able to say,
'If the government were to choose these values for G and T, this is what would happen.'
The approach in this book will typically treat G and T as variables chosen by the government and will not try to explain them within the model.

◄ Because we will (nearly always) take G and T as exogenous, we won't use a bar to denote their values. This will keep the notation lighter.

3.3 THE DETERMINATION OF EQUILIBRIUM OUTPUT

Let's put together the pieces we have introduced so far.

Assuming that exports and imports are both zero, the demand for goods is the sum of
consumption, investment and government spending:

$$Z = C + I + G$$

Replacing C and I from equations (3.3) and (3.4), we get

$$Z = c_0 + c_1(Y - T) + \bar{I} + G \qquad [3.5]$$

The demand for goods, Z, depends on income, Y, taxes, T, investment, $\bar{I}$, and government
spending, G.

Let's now turn to **equilibrium** in the goods market and the relation between production
and demand. If firms hold inventories, then production need not be equal to demand. For
example, firms can satisfy an increase in demand by drawing upon their inventories – by
having negative inventory investment. They can respond to a decrease in demand by continuing to produce and accumulating inventories – by having positive inventory investment.
Let us first ignore this complication, though, and begin by assuming that firms do not hold
inventories. In this case, inventory investment is always equal to zero, and **equilibrium in
the goods market** requires that production, Y, be equal to the demand for goods, Z:

◄ Think of an economy that produces only haircuts. There cannot be inventories of haircuts – haircuts produced but not sold – so production must always be equal to demand.

$$Y = Z \qquad [3.6]$$

There are three types of equations:
- identities
- behavioural equations
- equilibrium conditions.

This equation is called an **equilibrium condition**. Models include three types of equations: identities, behavioural equations and equilibrium conditions. You have seen examples of each: the equation defining disposable income is an identity, the consumption function is a behavioural equation and the condition that production equals demand is an equilibrium condition.

Replacing demand, Z, in equation (3.6) by its expression from equation (3.5) gives

$$Y = c_0 + c_1(Y - T) + \bar{I} + G \qquad [3.7]$$

Equation (3.7) represents algebraically what we stated informally at the beginning of this chapter:

> *In equilibrium, production, Y (the left side of the equation), is equal to demand (the right side). Demand in turn depends on income, Y, which is itself equal to production.*

Note that we are using the same symbol Y for production and income. This is no accident! As you saw in Chapter 2, we can look at GDP either from the production side or from the income side. Production and income are identically equal.

Having constructed a model, we can solve it to look at what determines the level of output – how output changes in response to, say, a change in government spending. Solving a model means not only solving it algebraically but also understanding why the results are what they are. In this book, solving a model also means characterising the results using graphs – sometimes skipping the algebra altogether – and describing the results and the mechanisms in words. Macroeconomists always use these three tools:

- *algebra* to make sure that the logic is correct
- *graphs* to build the intuition
- *words* to explain the results.

Make it a habit to do the same.

Using algebra

Rewrite the equilibrium equation (3.7):

$$Y = c_0 + c_1 Y - c_1 T + \bar{I} + G$$

Move $c_1 Y$ to the left side and reorganise the right side:

$$(1 - c_1)Y = c_0 + \bar{I} + G - c_1 T$$

Divide both sides by $(1 - c_1)$:

$$Y = \frac{1}{1 - c_1}[c_0 + \bar{I} + G - c_1 T] \qquad [3.8]$$

Equation (3.8) characterises equilibrium output, the level of output such that production equals demand. Let's look at both terms on the right, beginning with the second term:

Autonomous means independent – in this case, independent of output.

- The term $[c_0 + \bar{I} + G - c_1 T]$ is that part of the demand for goods that does not depend on output. For this reason, it is called **autonomous spending**.

  Can we be sure that autonomous spending is positive? We cannot, but it is very likely to be. The first two terms in brackets, c_0 and $\bar{I}$, are positive. What about the last two, $G - c_1 T$? Suppose the government is running a **balanced budget** – taxes equal government spending. If $T = G$, and the propensity to consume (c_1) is less than 1 (as we have assumed), then $(G - c_1 T)$ is positive, and so is autonomous spending. Only if the government were running a very large budget surplus – if taxes were much larger than government spending – could autonomous spending be negative. We can safely ignore that case here.

If $T = G$, then
$(G - c_1 T) = (T - c_1 T) = (1 - c_1)T > 0$

- Turn to the first term, $1/(1 - c_1)$. Because the propensity to consume (c_1) is between 0 and 1, $1/(1 - c_1)$ is a number greater than 1. For this reason, this number, which *multiplies* autonomous spending, is called the **multiplier**. The closer c_1 is to 1, the larger the multiplier.

  What does the multiplier imply? Suppose that, for a given level of income, consumers decide to consume more. More precisely, assume that c_0 in equation (3.3) increases by €1 billion. Equation (3.8) tells us that output will increase by more than €1 billion. For example, if c_1 equals 0.6, the multiplier equals $1/(1 - 0.6) = 1/0.4 = 2.5$, so that output increases by $2.5 \times$ €1 billion = €2.5 billion.

  We have looked at an increase in consumption, but equation (3.8) makes it clear that any change in autonomous spending – from a change in investment, to a change in government spending, to a change in taxes – will have the same qualitative effect: it will change output by more than its direct effect on autonomous spending.

Where does the multiplier effect come from? Looking back at equation (3.7) gives us a clue: an increase in c_0 increases demand. The increase in demand then leads to an increase in production. The increase in production leads to an equivalent increase in income (remember that the two are identically equal). The increase in income further increases consumption, which further increases demand, and so on. The best way to describe this mechanism is to represent the equilibrium using a graph. Let's do that.

Using a graph

Let's characterise the equilibrium graphically:

- First, plot production as a function of income.

  In Figure 3.2, measure production on the vertical axis. Measure income on the horizontal axis. Plotting production as a function of income is straightforward: recall that production and income are identically equal. Thus, the relation between them is the 45° line, the line with a slope equal to 1.

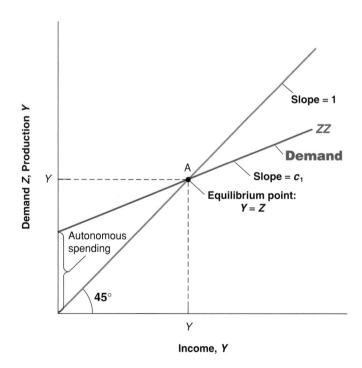

Figure 3.2

Equilibrium in the goods market

Equilibrium output is determined by the condition that production be equal to demand

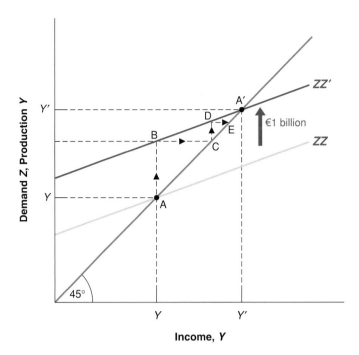

Figure 3.3

The effects of an increase in autonomous spending on output

An increase in autonomous spending has a more than one-for-one effect on equilibrium output.

● Second, plot demand as a function of income.

The relation between demand and income is given by equation (3.5). Let's rewrite it here for convenience, regrouping the terms for autonomous spending together in the term in parentheses:

$$Z = (c_0 + \bar{I} + G - c_1 T) + c_1 Y \qquad [3.9]$$

Demand depends on autonomous spending and on income – via its effect on consumption. The relation between demand and income is drawn as ZZ in the graph. The intercept with the vertical axis – the value of demand when income is equal to zero – equals autonomous spending. The slope of the line is the propensity to consume, c_1: when income increases by 1, demand increases by c_1. Under the restriction that c_1 is positive but less than 1, the line is upward sloping but has a slope of less than 1.

● In equilibrium, production equals demand.

Equilibrium output, Y, therefore occurs at the intersection of the 45° line and the demand function. This is at point A. To the left of A, demand exceeds production; to the right of A, production exceeds demand. Only at A are demand and production equal.

Suppose that the economy is at the initial equilibrium, represented by point A in the graph, with production equal to Y. Now suppose c_0 increases by €1 billion. At the initial level of income (the level of income associated with point A), consumers increase their consumption by €1 billion. What happens is shown in Figure 3.3, which builds on Figure 3.2.

> Look at the vertical axis. The distance between Y and Y' on the vertical axis is larger than the distance between A and B – which is equal to €1 billion.

Equation (3.9) tells us that, for any value of income, demand is higher by €1 billion. Before the increase in c_0, the relation between demand and income was given by the line ZZ. After the increase in c_0 by €1 billion, the relation between demand and income is given by the line ZZ', which is parallel to ZZ but higher by €1 billion. In other words, the demand curve shifts up by €1 billion. The new equilibrium is at the intersection of the 45° line and the new demand relation, at point A'.

Equilibrium output increases from Y not Y'. The increase in output, $(Y' - Y)$, which we can measure either on the horizontal or the vertical axis, is larger than the initial increase in consumption of €1 billion. This is the multiplier effect.

With the help of the graph, it becomes easier to tell how and why the economy moves from A to A'. The initial increase in consumption leads to an increase in demand of €1 billion. At the initial level of income, Y, the level of demand is shown by point B: demand is

€1 billion higher. To satisfy this higher level of demand, firms increase production by €1 billion. This increase in production of €1 billion implies that income increases by €1 billion (recall that income = production), so the economy moves to point C. (In other words, both production and income are higher by €1 billion.) But this is not the end of the story. The increase in income leads to a further increase in demand. Demand is now shown by point D. Point D leads to a higher level of production, and so on, until the economy is at A′, where production and demand are again equal. This is therefore the new equilibrium.

We can pursue this line of explanation a bit more, which will give us another way to think about the multiplier:

- The first-round increase in demand, shown by the distance AB in Figure 3.3 equals €1 billion.
- This first-round increase in demand leads to an equal increase in production, or €1 billion, which is also shown by the distance AB.
- This first-round increase in production leads to an equal increase in income, shown by the distance BC, also equal to €1 billion.
- The second-round increase in demand, shown by the distance CD, equals €1 billion (the increase in income in the first round) multiplied by the marginal propensity to consume, c_1 – hence, €c_1 billion.
- This second-round increase in demand leads to an equal increase in production, also shown by the distance CD, and thus an equal increase in income, shown by the distance DE.
- The third-round increase in demand equals €c_1 billion (the increase in income in the second round), multiplied by c_1, the marginal propensity to consume; it is equal to €$c_1 \times c_1 = $ €c_1^2 billion, and so on.

Following this logic, the total increase in production after, say, $n + 1$ rounds is equal to €1 billion multiplied by the sum:

$$1 + c_1 + c_1^2 + \ldots + c_1^n$$

Such a sum is called a **geometric series**. Geometric series frequently appear in this book. A refresher is given in Appendix 1 at the end of the book. One property of geometric series is that, when c_1 is less than 1 (as it is here) and as n gets larger and larger, the sum keeps increasing but approaches a limit. That limit is $1/(1 - c_1)$, making the eventual increase in output €$1/(1 - c_1)$ billion.

The expression $1/(1 - c_1)$ should be familiar: it is the multiplier, derived another way. This gives us an equivalent but more intuitive way of thinking about the multiplier. We can think of the original increase in demand as triggering successive increases in production, with each increase in production leading to an increase in income, which leads to an increase in demand, which leads to a further increase in production, which leads . . . and so on. The multiplier is the sum of all these successive increases in production.

◀ **Trick question:** think about the multiplier as the result of these successive rounds. What would happen in each successive round if c_1, the propensity to consume, were larger than 1?

Using words

How can we summarise our findings in words?

Production depends on demand, which depends on income, which is itself equal to production. An increase in demand, such as an increase in government spending, leads to an increase in production and a corresponding increase in income. This increase in income leads to a further increase in demand, which leads to a further increase in production, and so on. The end result is an increase in output that is larger than the initial shift in demand, by a factor equal to the multiplier.

The size of the multiplier is directly related to the value of the propensity to consume: the higher the propensity to consume, the higher the multiplier. For example, with a propensity to consume equal to 60% or 0.6, and additional euro of income leads on average to an increase in consumption of 60 cents. This implies that the multiplier is equal to $1/(1 - c_1) = 1/(1 - 0.6) = 2.5$.

How long does it take for output to adjust?

Let's return to our example one last time. Suppose that c_0 increases by €1 billion. We know that output will increase by an amount equal to $1/(1 - c_1)$ multiplied by €1 billion, but how long will it take for output to reach this higher value?

Under the assumptions we have made so far, the answer is: right away! In writing the equilibrium condition (3.6), we have assumed that production is always equal to demand. In other words, we have assumed that production responds to demand instantaneously. In writing the consumption function (3.2), we have assumed that consumption responds to changes in disposable income instantaneously. Under these two assumptions, the economy goes instantaneously from point A to point A′ in Figure 3.3: the increase in demand leads to an immediate increase in production, the increase in income associated with the increase in production leads to an immediate increase in demand, and so on. There is nothing wrong in thinking about the adjustment in terms of successive rounds as we did earlier, even though the equations indicate that all these rounds happen at once.

> In the model we saw earlier, we ruled out this possibility by assuming that firms did not hold inventories and so could not rely on drawing down inventories to satisfy an increase in demand.

This instantaneous adjustment isn't really plausible: a firm that faces an increase in demand might well decide to wait before adjusting its production, meanwhile drawing down its inventories to satisfy demand. A worker who gets a pay raise might not adjust her consumption right away. Delays like these imply that the adjustment of output will take time.

Formally describing this adjustment of output over time – that is, writing the equations for what economists call the **dynamics** of adjustment, and solving this more complicated model – would be too hard to do here, but it is easy to do it in words:

- Suppose, for example, that firms make decisions about their production levels at the beginning of each quarter. Once their decisions are made, production cannot be adjusted for the rest of the quarter. If purchases by consumers are higher than production, firms will draw down their inventories to satisfy the purchases. On the other hand, if purchases are lower than production, firms will accumulate inventories.
- Now suppose that consumers decide to spend more, that they increase c_0. During the quarter in which this happens, demand increases, but production – because we assumed it was set at the beginning of the quarter – does not yet change. Therefore, income does not change either.
- Having observed an increase in demand, firms are likely to set a higher level of production in the following quarter. This increase in production leads to a corresponding increase in income and a further increase in demand. If purchases still exceed production, firms further increase production in the following quarter, and so on.
- In short, in response to an increase in consumer spending, output does not jump to the new equilibrium but rather increases over time from Y to Y'.

How long this adjustment takes depends on how and how often firms revise their production schedules. If firms adjust their production schedules more frequently in response to past increases in purchases, the adjustment will occur more quickly.

We will often do in this book what we just did here: after we have looked at changes in equilibrium output, we will then describe informally how the economy moves from one equilibrium to the other. This will not only make the description of what happens in the economy feel more realistic, but it will often reinforce your intuition about why the equilibrium changes.

We have focused in this section on increases in demand, but the mechanism, of course, works both ways: decreases in demand lead to decreases in output. The 2002–2003 recession in Germany was largely the result of a sudden drop in consumer confidence, leading to a sharp decrease in consumption, which led, in turn, to a sharp decline in output. The origins of this recession are discussed in the Focus box 'Savings and the German Recession of 2002–2003.'

FOCUS
Savings and the German recession of 2002–2003

In 1997, Chancellor Kohl proposed a major pension reform and pushed the law through Parliament explaining that the German system had become unsustainable. The year after, in 1998, Kohl lost the elections and was replaced by Gerhard Shroeder. One of the first decisions of the new Chancellor was to revoke the 1997 pension reform. Such an event produced an increase in uncertainty about future income. As a consequence, German households started saving more. The saving rate went up from 9.8% of disposable income in 1997 to 15.8% in 2000. The increase in the saving rate was due to a shift in consumer confidence: the government's inability to reform the German welfare system – which most people considered unsustainable – resulted in widespread pessimism about the country's future. Consumption fell (from a growth rate of 2% per annum before the election to just above 7%) and the growth rate of output also slowed down.

Note: For a discussion of this episode read F. Giavazzi and H. McMahon, *Policy Uncertainty and Precautionary Savings*, NBER working paper No. 13911, NBER, Cambridge, MA, 2008.

3.4 INVESTMENT EQUALS SAVING: AN ALTERNATIVE WAY OF THINKING ABOUT THE GOODS–MARKET EQUILIBRIUM

Thus far, we have been thinking of equilibrium in the goods market in terms of the equality of the production and the demand for goods. An alternative – but equivalent – way of thinking about equilibrium focuses instead on investment and saving. This is how John Maynard Keynes first articulated this model in 1936, in *The General Theory of Employment, Interest and Money*.

Let's start by looking at saving. **Saving** is the sum of private saving and public saving:

- By definition, **private saving** (S), saving by consumers, is equal to their disposable income minus their consumption:

$$S = Y_D - C$$

Using the definition of disposable income, we can rewrite private saving as income minus taxes minus consumption:

$$S = Y - T - C$$

- By definition, **public saving** is equal to taxes (net of transfers) minus government spending, $T - G$. If taxes exceed government spending, the government is running a **budget surplus**, so public saving is positive. If taxes are less than government spending, the government is running a **budget deficit**, so public saving is negative.
- Now return to the equation for equilibrium in the goods market that we derived earlier. ◄ Saving: Private saving + Public saving
Production must be equal to demand, which in turn is the sum of consumption, investment and government spending:

$$Y = C + \bar{I} + G$$

Subtract taxes (T) from both sides and move consumption to the left side:

$$Y - T - C = \bar{I} + G - T$$

Public saving ⇔ Budget surplus. ➤

The left side of this equation is simply private saving, (S), so

$$S = \bar{I} + G - T$$

Or, equivalently,

$$\bar{I} = S + (T - G) \qquad [3.10]$$

- On the left is investment. On the right is saving, the sum of *private saving* and *public saving*.

Equation (3.10) gives us another way of thinking about equilibrium in the goods market. It says that equilibrium in the goods market requires that investment is equal to saving – the sum of private and public saving. This way of looking at equilibrium explains why the equilibrium condition for the goods market is called the **IS relation**, which stands for 'investment equals saving': what firms want to invest must be equal to what people and the government want to save.

To understand equation (3.10), imagine an economy with only one person who has to decide how much to consume, invest and save – a 'Robinson Crusoe' economy, for example. For Robinson Crusoe, the saving and the investment decisions are one and the same: what he invests (say, by keeping rabbits for breeding rather than having them for dinner), he automatically saves. In a modern economy, however, investment decisions are made by firms, whereas saving decisions are made by consumers and the government. In equilibrium, equation (3.10) tells us all these decisions have to be consistent: investment (the left side) must equal saving (the right side).

To summarise: there are two equivalent ways of stating the condition for equilibrium in the goods market:

$$\text{production} = \text{demand}$$
$$\text{investment} = \text{saving}$$

Earlier, we characterised the equilibrium using the first condition, equation (3.6). We now do the same using the second condition, equation (3.10). The results will be the same, but the derivation will give you another way of thinking about the equilibrium. Note first that *consumption and saving decisions are one and the same*. Given their disposable income, once consumers have chosen consumption, their saving is determined, and vice versa. The way we specified consumption behaviour implies that private saving is given by:

$$S = Y - T - C$$
$$= Y - T - c_0 - c_1(Y - T)$$

Rearranging, we get

$$S = -c_0 + (1 - c_1)(Y - T) \qquad [3.11]$$

In the same way that we called c_1 the marginal propensity to consume, we can call $(1 - c_1)$ the **marginal propensity to save**. The propensity to save tells us how much of an additional unit of income people save. The assumption we made earlier – that the propensity to consume (c_1) is between 0 and 1 implies that the propensity to save $(1 - c_1)$ is also between 0

Consumption and saving decisions are ➤ one and the same.

and 1. Private saving increases with disposable income, but by less than €1 for each additional euro of disposable income.

In equilibrium, investment must be equal to saving, the sum of private and public saving. Replacing private saving in equation (3.10) by its expression from above:

$$\bar{I} = -c_0 + (1 - c_1)(Y - T) + (T - G)$$

Solving for output:

$$Y = \frac{1}{1 - c_1}[c_0 + I + G - c_1 T] \qquad [3.12]$$

FOCUS
The paradox of saving

As we grow up, we are told about the virtues of thrift. Those who spend all their income are condemned to end up poor. Those who save are promised a happy life. Similarly, governments tell us, an economy that saves is an economy that will grow strong and prosper. The model we have seen in this chapter, however, tells a different and surprising story.

Suppose that, at a given level of disposable income, consumers decide to save more. In other words, suppose consumers decrease c_0, therefore decreasing consumption and increasing saving at a given level of disposable income. What happens to output and to saving?

Equation (3.12) makes it clear that equilibrium output decreases: as people save more at their initial level of income, they decrease their consumption, but this decreased consumption decreases demand, which decreases production.

Can we tell what happens to saving? Let's return to the equation for private saving, equation (3.11) (recall that we assume no change in public saving, so saving and private saving move together):

$$S = -c_0 + (1 - c_1)(Y - T)$$

On the one hand, $-c_0$ is higher (less negative): consumers are saving more at any level of income; this tends to increase saving. On the other hand, their income, Y, is lower: this decreases saving. The net effect would seem to be ambiguous. In fact, we can tell which way it goes.

To see how, go back to equation (3.10), the equilibrium condition that investment and saving must be equal:

$$\bar{I} = S + (T - G)$$

By assumption, investment does not change: $I = \bar{I}$. Nor do T or G. So the equilibrium condition tells us that in equilibrium, private saving, S, cannot change either. Although people want to save more at a given level of income, their income decreases by an amount such that their saving is unchanged.

This means that as people attempt to save more, the result is both a decline in output and unchanged saving. This surprising pair of results is known as the paradox of saving (or the paradox of thrift).

So should you forget the old wisdom? Should the government tell people to be less thrifty? No. The results of this simple model are of much relevance in the short run. The desire of consumers to save more led for example to the German recession of 2002–2003. However, as we will see later in this book, when we look at the medium run and the long run, other mechanisms come into play over time, and an increase in the saving rate is likely to lead over time to higher saving and higher income. A warning remains, however: policies that encourage saving might be good in the medium run and in the long run, but they can lead to a recession in the short run.

Equation (3.12) is exactly the same as equation (3.8). This should come as no surprise. We are looking at the same equilibrium condition, just in a different way. This alternative way will prove useful in various applications later in the book. The Focus box looks at such an application, which was first emphasised by Keynes and is often called the **paradox of saving**.

3.5 IS THE GOVERNMENT OMNIPOTENT? A WARNING

Equation (3.8) implies that the government, by choosing the level of spending, G, or the level of taxes, T, can choose the level of output it wants. If it wants output to be higher by, say, €1 billion, all it needs to do is to increase G by €$(1 - c_1)$ billion; this increase in government spending, in theory, will lead to an output increase of €$(1 - c_1)$ billion multiplied by $1/(1 - c_1)$, or €1 billion.

Can governments really choose the level of output they want? Obviously not. There are many aspects of reality that we have not yet incorporated into our model, and all these complicate the government's task. We shall incorporate them in due time. But it is useful to list them briefly here:

- Changing government spending or taxes is not always easy. Getting national parliaments to pass bills always takes time and often becomes a premier's nightmare.
- We have assumed that investment remained constant, but investment is also likely to respond, and so too are imports: some of the increased demand by consumers and firms will not be for domestic goods but for foreign goods. All these responses are likely to be associated with complex, dynamic effects, making it hard for governments to assess them with much certainty.
- Anticipation is likely to matter. For example, the reaction of consumers to a tax cut is likely to depend very much on whether they think of the tax cut as transitory or permanent. The more they perceive the tax cut as permanent, the larger will be their consumption response.
- Achieving a given level of output can come with unpleasant side effects. Trying to achieve too high a level of output can, for example, lead to increasing inflation and, for that reason, be unsustainable in the medium run.
- Cutting taxes or increasing government spending can lead to large budget deficits and an accumulation of public debt. A large debt can have adverse effects in the long run. This is a hot issue in a certain number of countries today, including some highly indebted European countries such as Belgium, Greece and Italy, Japan (the country with the world's highest debt to GDP ratio, well above 150%) and also the USA, where the tax cuts implemented by the Bush administration, together with President Obama's 'stimulus program' designed to respond to the 2007–2010 crisis, have led to large deficits and to increasing public debt.

In short, the proposition that, by using fiscal policy, the government can affect demand and output in the short run is an important and correct one. However, as we refine our analysis, we will see that the role of the government in general, and the successful use of fiscal policy in particular, become increasingly difficult: governments will never again have it as good as they had it in this chapter.

SUMMARY

Here's what you should remember about the components of GDP:

- GDP is the sum of consumption, investment, government spending, inventory investment and exports minus imports.
- Consumption (C) is the purchase of goods and services by consumers. Consumption is the largest component of demand.
- Investment (I) is the sum of non-residential investment (the purchase of new plants and new machines by firms) and of residential investment (the purchase of new houses or apartments by people).
- Government spending (G) is the purchase of goods and services by national, regional and local governments.
- Exports (X) are purchases of domestic goods by foreigners. Imports (IM) are purchases of foreign goods by resident consumers, resident firms and the national government.
- Inventory investment is the difference between production and sales. It can be positive or negative.

Here's what you should remember about our first model of output determination:

- In the short run, demand determines production. Production is equal to income. Income in turn affects demand.
- The consumption function shows how consumption depends on disposable income. The propensity to consume describes how much consumption increases for a given increase in disposable income.
- Equilibrium output is the level of output at which production equals demand. In equilibrium, output equals autonomous spending times the multiplier. Autonomous spending is the part of demand that does not depend on income. The multiplier is equal to $1/(1 - c_1)$, where c_1 is the propensity to consume.
- Increases in consumer confidence, investment demand and government spending, as well as decreases in taxes, all increase equilibrium output in the short run.
- An alternative way of stating the goods market equilibrium condition is that investment must be equal to saving: the sum of private and public saving. For this reason, the equilibrium condition is called the IS relation (I for investment, S for saving).

KEY TERMS

QUESTIONS AND PROBLEMS

QUICK CHECK

1. *Using the information in this chapter, label each of the following statements true, false or uncertain. Explain briefly.*

a. The largest component of GDP is consumption.

b. Government spending, including transfers, was equal, on average, to 20.9% of GDP in EU15 in 2008.

c. The propensity to consume has to be positive, but otherwise it can take on any positive value.

d. *Fiscal policy* describes the choice of government spending and taxes and is treated as exogenous in our goods market model.

e. The equilibrium condition for the goods market states that consumption equals output.

f. An increase of one unit in government spending leads to an increase of one unit in equilibrium output.

g. An increase in the propensity to consume leads to a decrease in output.

2. *Suppose that the economy is characterised by the following behavioural equations:*

$$C = 180 + 0.8Y_D$$
$$I = 160$$
$$G = 160$$
$$T = 120$$

Solve for the following variables.

a. Equilibrium GDP (Y)

b. Disposable income (Y_D)

c. Consumption spending (C)

3. *Use the economy described in problem 2.*

a. Solve for equilibrium output. Compute total demand. Is it equal to production? Explain.

b. Assume that G is now equal to 110. Solve for equilibrium output. Compute total demand. Is it equal to production? Explain.

c. Assume that G is equal to 110, so output is given by your answer to (b). Compute private plus public saving. Is the sum of private and public saving equal to investment? Explain.

DIG DEEPER

4. The balanced budget multiplier

For both political and macroeconomic reasons, governments are often reluctant to run budget deficits. Here, we examine whether policy changes in G and T that maintain a balanced budget are macroeconomically neutral. Put another way, we examine whether it is possible to affect output through changes in G and T so that the government budget remains balanced.

Start from equation (3.8).

a. By how much does Y increase when G increases by one unit?

b. By how much does Y decrease when T increases by one unit?

c. Why are your answers to (a) and (b) different?

Suppose that the economy starts with a balanced budget: G = T. If the increase in G is equal to the increase in T, then the budget remains in balance. Let us now compute the balanced budget multiplier.

d. Suppose that G and T increase by one unit each. Using your answers to (a) and (b), what is the change in equilibrium GDP? Are balanced budget changes in G and T macroeconomically neutral?

e. How does the specific value of the propensity to consume affect your answer to (a)? Why?

5. Automatic stabilisers

So far in this chapter, we have assumed that the fiscal policy variables G and T are independent of the level of income. In the real world, however, this is not the case. Taxes typically depend on the level of income and so tend to be higher when income is higher. In this problem, we examine how this automatic response of taxes can help reduce the impact of changes in autonomous spending on output.

Consider the following behavioural equations:

$$C = c_0 + c_1 Y_D$$
$$T = t_0 + t_1 Y$$
$$Y_D = Y - T$$

G and I are both constant. Assume that t_1 is between 0 and 1.

a. Solve for equilibrium output.

b. What is the multiplier? Does the economy respond more to changes in autonomous spending when t_1 is 0 or when t_1 is positive? Explain.

c. Why is fiscal policy in this case called an automatic stabiliser?

6. Balanced budget versus automatic stabilisers

It is often argued that a balanced budget amendment would actually be destabilising. To understand this argument, consider the economy of problem 5.

a. Solve for equilibrium output.

b. Solve for taxes in equilibrium.

Suppose that the government starts with a balanced budget and that there is a drop in c_0.

c. What happens to Y? What happens to taxes?

d. Suppose that the government cuts spending in order to keep the budget balanced. What will be the effect on Y? Does the cut in spending required to balance the budget counteract or reinforce the effect of the drop in c_0 on output? (Don't do the algebra. Use your intuition and give the answer in words.)

7. Taxes and transfers

Recall that we define taxes, T, as net of transfers. In other words,

$$T = taxes - transfer\ payments$$

a. Suppose that the government increases transfer payments to private households, but these transfer payments are not financed by tax increases. Instead, the government borrows to pay for the transfer payments. Show in

a diagram (similar to Figure 3.2) how this policy affects equilibrium output. Explain.

b. Suppose instead that the government pays for the increase in transfer payments with an equivalent increase in taxes. How does the increase in transfer payments affect equilibrium output in this case?

c. Now suppose that the population includes two kinds of people: those with high propensity to consume and those with low propensity to consume. Suppose the transfer policy increases taxes on those with low propensity to consume to pay for transfers to people with high propensity to consume. How does this policy affect equilibrium output?

d. How do you think the propensity to consume might vary across individuals according to income? In other words, how do you think the propensity to consume compares for people with high incomes and people with low incomes? Explain. Given your answer, do you think tax cuts will be more effective at stimulating output when they are directed toward high-income or toward low-income taxpayers?

8. Investment and income

This problem examines the implications of allowing investment to depend on output. Chapter 5 carries this analysis much further and introduces an essential relation – the effect of the interest rate on investment – not examined in this problem.

a. Suppose the economy is characterised by the following behavioural equations:

$$C = c_0 + c_1 Y_D$$
$$Y_D = Y - T$$
$$I = b_0 + b_1 Y$$

Government spending and taxes are constant. Note that investment now increases with output. (Chapter 5 discusses the reasons for this relation.) Solve for equilibrium output.

b. What is the value of the multiplier? How does the relation between investment and output affect the value of the multiplier? For the multiplier to be positive, what condition must $(c_1 + b_1)$ satisfy? Explain your answers.

c. Suppose that the parameter b_0, sometimes called *business confidence*, increases. How will equilibrium output be affected? Will investment change by more or less than the change in b_0? Why? What will happen to national saving?

EXPLORE FURTHER

9. The paradox of saving revisited

You should be able to complete this question without doing any algebra, although you may find making a diagram helpful for part (a). For this problem, you do not need to calculate the magnitudes of changes in economic variables – only the direction of change.

a. Consider the economy described in problem 8. Suppose that consumers decide to consume less (and therefore to save more) for any given amount of disposable income. Specifically, assume that consumer confidence (c_0) falls. What will happen to output?

b. *As* a result of the effect on output you determined in part (a), what will happen to investment? What will happen to public saving? What will happen to private saving? Explain. (*Hint*: Consider the saving-equals-investment characterisation of equilibrium.) What is the effect on consumption?

c. *Suppose* that consumers had decided to increase consumption expenditure, so that c_0 had increased. What would have been the effect on output, investment and private saving in this case? Explain. What would have been the effect on consumption?

d. Comment on the following logic: 'When output is too low, what is needed is an increase in demand for goods and services. Investment is one component of demand, and saving equals investment. Therefore, if the government could just convince households to attempt to save more then investment, and output, would increase.'

Output is not the only variable that affects investment. As we develop our model of the economy, we will revisit the paradox of saving in future chapter problems.

We invite you to visit the Blanchard page on the Prentice Hall website, at **www.prenhall.com/blanchard** for this chapter's *World Wide Web* exercises.

Chapter 4

FINANCIAL MARKETS

During the recent financial crisis that hit the USA and most of the world starting in 2007, central banks around the world had a particularly hard time. They were asked to design measures to help economies out of the recession and to enable the financial sector to recover and strengthen in the future. Over these years, central banks were often in the headlines explaining what their strategies and priorities were.

However in tranquil times too, barely a day goes by without the media speculating as to whether the central bank – either the ECB (short for European Central Bank) in the euro area, the Bank of England in the UK, Sweden's Central Bank or the Fed (short for the Federal Reserve Bank) in the USA – is going to introduce some monetary policy measure, e.g. to change the interest rate, and how that change is likely to affect the economy. The chairmen of these central banks are very influential policy makers in their countries and among them the chairman of the Fed – Ben Bernanke and his predecessor, Alan Greenspan, chairman of the Fed during 1987–2006 – is widely perceived as the most powerful policy maker in the USA, if not in the world.

The model of economic activity we developed in Chapter 3 did not include the interest rate, so there was no role for Ben Bernanke, Jean-Claude Trichet (Chairman of the ECB) or Mervyn King (Governor of the Bank of England) there. That was an oversimplification which it is now time to correct. This requires that we take two steps.

First, we must look at what determines the interest rate and how the central bank (in particular, the ECB) can affect it – the topic of this chapter. Second, we must look at how the interest rate affects demand and output – the topic of the next chapter.

This chapter has four sections:

- Section 4.1 looks at the demand for money.

- Section 4.2 assumes that the central bank directly controls the supply of money and shows how the interest rate is determined by the condition that the demand for money must be equal to its supply.

- Section 4.3 introduces banks as suppliers of money, revisits interest rates and how they are determined and describes the role of the central bank in this process.

- Section 4.4 presents two alternative ways of looking at equilibrium. One focuses on the inter-bank market. The other focuses on the money multiplier.

4.1 THE DEMAND FOR MONEY

This section looks at the determinants of *the demand for money*. A warning before we start: words such as *money* or *wealth* have very specific meanings in economics, often not the same meanings as in everyday conversations. The purpose of the Focus box 'Semantic traps: money, income and wealth' is to help you avoid some of these traps. Read it carefully and come back to it once in a while.

Suppose, as a result of having steadily saved part of your income in the past, your financial wealth today is €50 000. You may intend to keep saving in the future and increase your wealth further, but its value today is given. Suppose also that you only have the choice between two assets, money and bonds:

- **Money**, which you can use for transactions, pays no interest. In the real world, there are two types of money: **currency**, coins and bills, and **deposit accounts**, the bank deposits on which you can write cheques. The distinction between the two will be important when we look at the supply of money. For the moment, however, the distinction does not matter, and we can ignore it.
- **Bonds** pay a positive interest rate, i, but they cannot be used for transactions. In the real world, there are many types of bonds, each associated with a specific interest rate. For the time being, we will also ignore this aspect of reality and assume that there is just one type of bond and that it pays, i, the rate of interest.

Assume that buying or selling bonds implies some cost – for example, a phone call to a broker and the payment of a transaction fee. How much of your €50 000 should you hold in money and how much in bonds? On the one hand, holding all your wealth in the form of money is clearly very convenient – you won't ever need to call a broker or pay transaction fees – but it also means you will receive no income from interest. On the other hand, if you hold all your wealth in the form of bonds, you will earn interest on the full amount, but you will have to call your broker frequently – whenever you need money to take a bus, pay for a cup of coffee and so on. This is a rather inconvenient way of going through life.

Therefore, it is clear that you should hold both money and bonds, but in what proportions? This depends mainly on two variables:

- Your *level of transactions* – you will want to have enough money on hand to avoid having to sell bonds too often. Say, for example, that you typically spend €3000 per month. In this case, you might want to have, on average, say, two months' worth of spending on hand, or €6000 in money, and the rest, €50 000 – €6000 = €44 000 in bonds. If, instead, you typically spend €8000 per month, you might want to have, say, €16 000 in money and only €34 000 in bonds.
- The *interest rate on bonds* – the only reason to hold any of your wealth in bonds is that they pay interest. If bonds paid zero interest, you would want to hold all your wealth in the form of money because it's more convenient.

  The higher the interest rate, the more you will be willing to deal with the hassle and the costs associated with buying and selling bonds. If the interest rate is very high, you might even decide to squeeze your money holdings to an average of only two weeks' worth of spending, or €1500 (assuming that your monthly spending is €3000). This way, you will be able to keep, on average, €48 500 in bonds and earn more interest as a result.

Let's make this last point more concrete. Many of you probably do not hold bonds; few of you have a broker. However, many of you probably hold bonds indirectly if you have a money market account with a financial institution. **Money market funds** (the full name is *money market mutual funds*) pool together the funds of many people. The funds are then used to buy bonds – typically government bonds. Money market funds pay an interest rate close to but slightly below the interest rate on the bonds they hold – the difference coming from the administrative costs of running the funds and from their profit margins.

Make sure you see the difference between the decision about how much to save (a decision that determines how wealth changes over time) and the decision about how to allocate a given stock of wealth between money and bonds.

We will abandon this assumption and look at a larger menu of interest rates when we focus on the role of expectations, beginning in Chapter 14.

FOCUS
Semantic traps: money, income and wealth

In everyday conversation, we use money to denote many different things. We use it as a synonym for income: 'making money.' We use it as a synonym for wealth: 'She has a lot of money.' In economics, you must be more careful. Here is a basic guide to some terms and their precise meanings in economics.

Income is what you earn from working plus what you receive in interest and dividends. It is a **flow** – something expressed in units of time: weekly income, monthly income or yearly income, for example. J. Paul Getty was once asked what his income was. Getty answered: '$1000.' He meant, but did not say, $1000 per minute!

Saving is the part of after-tax income that you do not spend. It is also a flow. If you save 10% of your income, and your income is €3000 per month, then you save €300 per month. **Savings** (plural) is sometimes used as a synonym for wealth – the value of what you have accumulated over time. To avoid confusion, we will not use *savings* in this book.

Your **financial wealth**, or simply **wealth**, is the value of all your financial assets minus all your financial liabilities. In contrast to income or saving, which are flow variables, financial wealth is a **stock** variable. It is the value of wealth at a given moment in time.

At a given moment in time, you cannot change the total amount of your financial wealth. You can change it only over time as you save or dissave (i.e. spend and therefore reduce your savings), or as the values of your assets and liabilities change. However, you can change the composition of your wealth; you can, for example, decide to pay back part of your mortgage by writing a cheque against your current account. This leads to a decrease in your liabilities (a smaller mortgage) and a corresponding decrease in your assets (a smaller deposit account balance); but, at that moment, it does not change your wealth.

Financial assets that can be used directly to buy goods are called *money*. Money includes currency and deposit accounts – deposits against which you can write cheques. Money is also a stock. Someone who is wealthy might have only small money holdings – say, €1 000 000 in stocks but only €500 in deposit accounts. It is also possible for a person to have a large income, but only small money holdings – say, an income of €10 000 monthly but only €1000 on deposit accounts.

Investment is a term economists reserve for the purchase of new capital goods, from machines to plants to office buildings. When you want to talk about the purchase of shares or other financial assets, you should refer to them as a **financial investment**.

Learn how to be economically correct:

- Do not say 'Mary is making a lot of money'; say 'Mary has a high income.'
- Do not say 'Joe has a lot of money'; say 'Joe is very wealthy.'

When the interest rate on these funds reached 14% per year in the early 1980s (a very high interest rate by today's standards), many people who had previously kept their wealth in deposit accounts (which paid little or no interest) realised how much interest they could earn by moving some of it into money market accounts instead. As a result, accounts like these became very popular. Since then, however, interest rates have fallen. In 2006, the average interest rate paid by money market funds was only 4.7% and it went down to slightly more than 1% during the crisis of 2007–2010. This is better than zero – the rate paid on many deposit accounts – but is much less attractive than the rate in the early 1980s. As a result, people are now less careful about putting as much as they can in their money market funds. Put another way, for a given level of transactions, people now keep more of their wealth in money than they did in the early 1980s.

Deriving the demand for money

Let's go from this discussion to an equation describing the demand for money.

Denote the amount of money people want to hold – their *demand for money* – by M^d. (The superscript d stands for *demand*.) The demand for money in the economy as a whole is just the sum of all the individual demands for money by the people in the economy. Therefore, it depends on the overall level of transactions in the economy and on the interest rate. The overall level of transactions in the economy is hard to measure, but it is likely to be roughly proportional to nominal income (income measured in euros). If nominal income were to increase by 10%, it is reasonable to think that the value of transactions in the economy would also increase by roughly 10%. We can write the relation between the demand for money, nominal income and the interest rate as

$$M^{\mathrm{d}} = \text{€}YL(i) \qquad\qquad [4.1]$$
$$(-)$$

where €Y denotes nominal income. Read this equation in the following way: the demand for money, M^{d}, is equal to nominal income, €Y, times a function of the interest rate, i, with the function denoted by $L(i)$. The minus sign under i in $L(i)$ captures the fact that the interest rate has a negative effect on money demand: an increase in the interest rate *decreases* the demand for money, as people put more of their wealth into bonds.

Equation (4.1) summarises what we have discussed so far:

- First, the demand for money increases in proportion to nominal income. If nominal income doubles, increasing from €Y to €$2Y$, then the demand for money also doubles, increasing from €$YL(i)$ to 2€$YL(i)$.
- Second, the demand for money depends negatively on the interest rate. This is captured by the function $L(i)$ and the negative sign underneath: an increase in the interest rate decreases the demand for money.

The relation between the demand for money, nominal income and the interest rate implied by equation (4.1) is shown in Figure 4.1. The interest rate, i, is measured on the vertical axis. Money, M, is measured on the horizontal axis.

The relation between the demand for money and the interest rate *for a given level of nominal income,* €Y, is represented by the M^{d} curve. The curve is downward sloping: the lower the interest rate (the lower i), the higher the amount of money people want to hold (the higher M).

For a given interest rate, an increase in nominal income increases the demand for money. In other words, an increase in nominal income shifts the demand for money to the right,

> ◀ Revisit Chapter 2's example of an economy composed of a steel company and a car company. Calculate the total value of transactions in that economy. If the steel and the car companies doubled in size, what would happen to transactions and to GDP?

> ◀ What matters here is nominal income – income in euros, not real income. If real income does not change but prices double, leading to a doubling of nominal income, people will need to hold twice as much money to buy the same consumption basket.

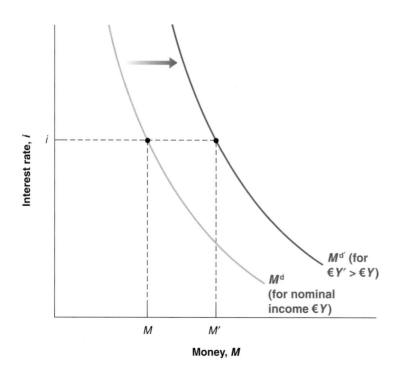

Figure 4.1

The demand for money

For a given level of nominal income, a lower interest rate increases the demand for money. At a given interest rate, an increase in nominal income shifts the demand for money to the right.

FOCUS
Euro vs US dollar as the leading international reserve currency

Of the total amount of US currency in circulation, $750 billion in 2006, around $170 billion was held by US households and around $80 billion by firms (this figure includes an estimate of the amount held by those involved in the underground economy or in illegal activities, such as drug dealers, who often use dollars for their transactions). The remaining $500 billion, or 66% of the total, was held by foreigners.

The dollar is adopted in some countries as a currency for transactions, for example Ecuador and El Salvador. Moreover, in a number of countries that have suffered from high inflation in the past, people have learned that their domestic currency may quickly become worthless, and they see dollars as a safe and convenient asset. This is the case, for example, in Argentina and Russia. Estimates by the US Treasury suggest that Argentina holds more than $50 billion in dollar bills, Russia more than $80 billion – so together they have more than the holdings of US firms.

Besides the private sector's use of the dollar outside of the USA, there is also an important official sector's use of the dollar; central banks and monetary authorities around the world hold foreign exchange reserves in US dollars to safekeep wealth and to intervene in foreign exchange markets. The fact that foreigners hold such a high proportion of the dollar bills in circulation has a major macroeconomic implication. The rest of the world, by holding US currency, is in fact making an interest-free loan to the USA of about $500 billion.

The US dollar has been the leading international reserve currency for more than a century. A leading international currency must have some important features, all of which the USA, unlike any other country in the world, has. The major ones are the following: it must be used as a currency in a large transaction area; it must be the currency of a (strong central) country with stable monetary policy (and therefore stable inflation, otherwise it would not be used as a store of value); it must be free of controls on the part of the government.

Since the turn of the millenium, the birth of the euro has inspired a debate on whether it would ever rival and eventually replace the dollar as the leading international reserve currency. The debate has recently become more lively following an increased willingness of central banks to hold foreign exchange reserves in euros (compared to dollars). Table 4.1 shows how the currency composition of foreign exchange holdings changed since 2001, in both advanced and emerging economies. The euro's share of reserves is higher today than it was prior to monetary union, but it is still well below the US dollar's

from M^d to $M^{d'}$. For example, at interest rate i, an increase in nominal income from €Y to €Y' increases the demand for money from M to M'.

4.2 DETERMINING THE INTEREST RATE: PART 1

Having looked at the demand for money, we now look at the supply of money and then at the equilibrium.

In the real world, there are two types of money: deposit accounts, which are supplied by banks, and currency, which is supplied by the central bank. In this section, we will assume that deposit accounts do not exist – that the only money in the economy is currency. In the next section, we will reintroduce deposit accounts and look at the role banks play. Introducing banks makes the discussion more realistic, but it also makes the mechanics of money supply more complicated. It is better to build up the discussion in two steps.

Money demand, money supply and the equilibrium interest rate

Like a normal commercial bank, a central bank charges interest on the loans made to borrowers, primarily the government, and to other commercial banks, typically as a 'lender of last resort'. However, a central bank is distinguished from a normal commercial bank because it has a monopoly on creating the currency of that nation, which is loaned to the government in the form of legal tender.

Throughout this section, 'money' stands for 'central bank money' or 'currency'.

Suppose the central bank decides to supply an amount of money equal to M, so

$$M^s = M$$

Table 4.1 Currency composition of foreign exchange holdings 2001–2008: dollars vs euros

	2001	2002	2003	2004	2005	2006	2007	2008
World	100	100	100	100	100	100	100	100
US dollars	71.5	67.1	65.9	65.9	66.9	65.5	64.1	64.2
Euros	19.2	23.8	25.2	24.8	24.0	25.1	26.3	26.4
Pound sterling	2.7	2.8	2.8	3.4	3.6	4.4	4.7	4.1
Advanced economies	100	100	100	100	100	100	100	100
US dollars	71.1	67.3	67.8	67.8	69.7	68.6	66.5	68.0
Euros	18.3	22.4	22.5	22.3	20.7	21.6	23.5	22.7
Pound sterling	2.7	2.9	2.4	2.7	2.8	3.3	3.6	2.8
Emerging economies	100	100	100	100	100	100	100	100
US dollars	72.5	66.6	61.9	62.0	62.1	61.0	61.6	60.3
Euros	21.3	26.9	31.1	30.0	29.7	30.1	29.2	30.6
Pound sterling	2.7	2.7	3.6	4.8	5.0	5.9	5.8	5.3

Source: IMF Currency Composition of Official Foreign Exchange Reserves (COFER).

share. The dollar's share declined since the beginning of the decade (by 7.3 percentage points) largely in favour of the euro (whose share increased by 7.2 percentage points).

So, will the euro ever become a reserve currency? For a currency to achieve international status, it is not enough to be perceived as a store of value by central banks; it must also be used by non-residents as a medium of exchange and unit of account. On these grounds, the euro is lagging behind the dollar. As a medium of exchange, the euro is used in 37% of foreign exchange transactions all over the world compared to 86% for the US dollar. As a unit of account, the euro is still well below the dollar as a currency of choice for invoicing, and also as an exchange rate to which other currencies are pegged (as we will learn in Chapter 19). Even if the euro were ever to challenge the dollar in its role as a store of value, it is unlikely that the same would happen in its roles as a unit of account and medium of exchange.

That being said, we should also remind ourselves that a currency's international status depends on others' use of it as such. Therefore, the more it is used as a medium of exchange, the more convenient and attractive it becomes for new users. That is why international currencies tend to be just a few (or even just one) and also why they tend to change slowly. With the birth of the euro, the dollar now has a potential competitor, but it is still – and is likely to be for a long time – dominant.

The superscript s stands for *supply*. (Let's disregard, for the moment, the issue of how exactly the central bank supplies this amount of money. We shall return to it in a few paragraphs.)

Equilibrium in financial markets requires that money supply be equal to money demand, that $M^s = M^d$. Then, using $M^s = M$ and equation (4.1) for money demand, the equilibrium condition is

$$\text{Money supply} = \text{Money demand} \qquad [4.2]$$
$$M = €YL(i)$$

This equation tells us that the interest rate, i, must be such that, given their income, $€Y$, people are willing to hold an amount of money equal to the existing money supply, M. This equilibrium relation is called the **LM relation**.

This equilibrium condition is represented graphically in Figure 4.2. As in Figure 4.1, money is measured on the horizontal axis, and the interest rate is measured on the vertical axis. The demand for money, M^d, drawn for a given level of nominal income, $€Y$, is downward sloping: a higher interest rate implies a lower demand for money. The supply of money is drawn as the vertical line denoted M^s: the money supply equals M and is independent of the interest rate. Equilibrium occurs at point A, and the equilibrium interest rate is given by i.

Now that we have characterised the equilibrium, we can look at how changes in nominal income or changes in the money supply by the central bank affect the equilibrium interest rate:

◄ In the same way as for the *IS* relation, the name of the *LM* relation is more than 50 years old. The letter *L* stands for *liquidity*: economists use liquidity as a measure of how easily an asset can be exchanged for money. Money is *fully liquid*; other assets less so. We can think of the demand for money as a demand for liquidity. The letter *M* stands for *money*. The demand for liquidity must equal the supply of money.

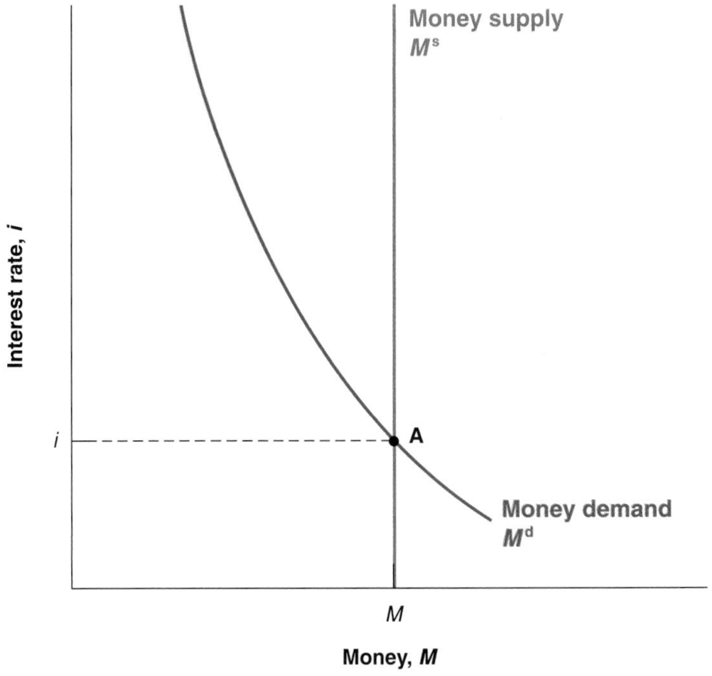

Figure 4.2

The determination of the interest rate

The interest rate must be such that the supply of money (which is independent of the interest rate) is equal to the demand for money (which does depend on the interest rate).

Money supply
M^s

i — — — — — — — — — — — • A

Money demand
M^d

Interest rate, i

M

Money, M

● Figure 4.3 shows the effects of an increase in nominal income on the interest rate.

Figure 4.3 replicates Figure 4.2, and the initial equilibrium is at point A. An increase in nominal income from €Y to €Y' increases the level of transactions, which increases the demand for money at any interest rate. The money demand curve *shifts* to the right, from M^d to $M^{d'}$. The equilibrium moves from A up to A′, and the equilibrium interest rate increases from i to i'.

In words: *an increase in nominal income leads to an increase in the interest rate*. The reason: at the initial interest rate, the demand for money exceeds the supply. An increase in the interest rate is needed to decrease the amount of money people want to hold and to re-establish equilibrium.

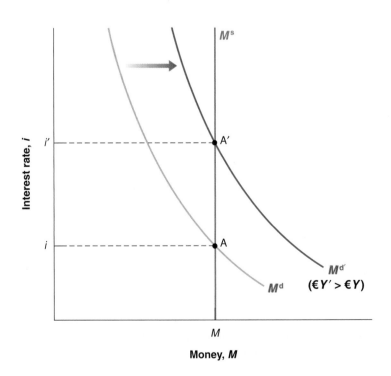

Figure 4.3

The effects of an increase in nominal income on the interest rate

An increase in nominal income leads to an increase in the interest rate.

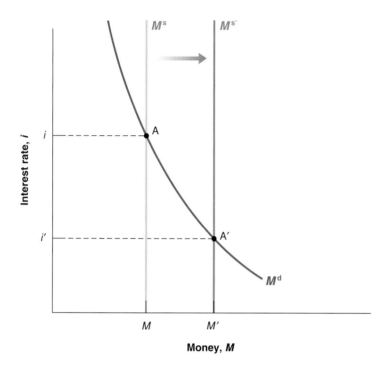

Figure 4.4

The effects of an increase in the money supply on the interest rate

An increase in the supply of money leads to a decrease in the interest rate.

● Figure 4.4 shows the effects of an increase in the money supply on the interest rate.

The initial equilibrium is at point A, with interest rate, i. An increase in the money supply, from $M^s = M$ to $M^{s'} = M'$, leads to a shift of the money supply curve to the right, from M^s to $M^s = M^{s'}$. The equilibrium moves from A down to A'; the interest rate decreases from i to i'.

In words: *an increase in the supply of money by the central bank leads to a decrease in the interest rate.* The decrease in the interest rate increases the demand for money, so it equals the now larger money supply.

Monetary policy and open market operations

We can get a better understanding of the results in Figures 4.3 and 4.4 by looking more closely at how the central bank actually changes the money supply and what happens when it does so.

Open market operations

In modern economies, the way that central banks change the supply of money is by buying or selling bonds in the bond market. If a central bank wants to increase the amount of money in the economy, it buys bonds and pays for them by creating money. If it wants to decrease the amount of money in the economy, it sells bonds and removes from circulation the money it receives in exchange for the bonds. These actions are called **open market operations** because they take place in the 'open market' for bonds.

The balance sheet of the central bank is given in Figure 4.5a. The assets of the central bank are the bonds it holds in its portfolio. Its liabilities are the stock of money in the economy. Open market operations (Figure 4.5b) lead to equal changes in assets and liabilities.

If the central bank buys, say, €1 million worth of bonds, the amount of bonds it holds is higher by €1 million, and so is the amount of money in the economy. Such an operation is called an **expansionary open market operation** because the central bank increases (*expands*) the supply of money.

If the central bank sells €1 million worth of bonds, both the amount of bonds held by the central bank and the amount of money in the economy are lower by €1 million. Such an operation is called a **contractionary open market operation** because the central bank decreases (*contracts*) the supply of money.

◄ The balance sheet of a bank (or a firm or an individual) is a list of its assets and liabilities at a point in time. The assets are the sum of what the bank owns and what is owed to it by others. The liabilities are what the bank owes to others.

Figure 4.5

The balance sheet of the central bank and the effects of an expansionary open market operation

The assets of the central bank are the bonds it holds. The liabilities are the stock of money in the economy. An open market operation in which the central bank buys bonds and issues money increases both assets and liabilities by the same amount.

(a) **Balance sheet**

Assets	Liabilities
Bonds	Money (currency)

(b) **The effects of an expansionary open market operation**

Assets	Liabilities
Change in bond holdings: +€1 million	Change in money stock: +€1 million

Bond prices and bond yields

We have focused so far on the interest rate on bonds. In fact, what is determined in bond markets is not interest rates but bond *prices*; the interest rate on a bond can then be inferred from the price of the bond. Understanding this relation between the interest rate and bond prices will prove useful both here and later in the book:

● Suppose the bonds in our economy are one-year bonds – bonds that promise a payment of a given number of euros, say €100, one year from now. Let the price of a bond today be €P_B, where the subscript B stands for *bond*. If you buy the bond today and hold it for a year, the rate of return on holding the bond for a year is (€100 – €P_B)/€P_B. Therefore, the interest rate on the bond is given by:

> The interest rate is what you get for the bond a year from now (€100) minus what you pay for the bond today (€P_B), divided by the price of the bond today (€P_B).

$$i = \frac{€100 - €P_B}{€P_B}$$

If €P_B is €95, the interest rate equals €5/€95 = 0.053, or 5.3% per year. If €P_B is €90, the interest rate is 11.1% per year. *The higher the price of the bond, the lower the interest rate.*

● If we are given the interest rate, we can figure out the price of the bond using the same formula. Reorganising the formula above, the price today of a one-year bond paying €100 a year from today is given by:

$$€P_B = \frac{€100}{1 + i}$$

> In Japan today, the one-year interest rate is (nearly) equal to zero. If a one-year Japanese government bond promises 100 yen in one year, for what price will it sell today?

The price of the bond today is equal to the final payment divided by 1 plus the interest rate. If the interest rate is positive, the price of the bond is less than the final payment. The higher the interest rate, the lower the price today. When newspapers write that 'bond markets went up today,' they mean that *the prices of bonds went up* and therefore that *interest rates went down*.

We are now ready to return to the effects of an open market operation.

Consider first an expansionary open market operation, in which the central bank buys bonds in the bond market and pays for them by creating money. As the central bank buys bonds, the demand for bonds goes up, increasing their price. Conversely, the interest rate on bonds goes down.

Consider instead a contractionary open market operation, in which the central bank decreases the supply of money. It sells bonds in the bond market. This leads to a decrease in their price and an increase in the interest rate.

Let's summarise what we have learned so far in this chapter:

● The interest rate is determined by the equality of the supply of money and the demand for money.
● By changing the supply of money, the central bank can affect the interest rate.
● The central bank changes the supply of money through open market operations, which are purchases or sales of bonds for money.

- Open market operations in which the central bank increases the money supply by buying bonds lead to an increase in the price of bonds and a decrease in the interest rate.
- Open market operations in which the central bank decreases the money supply by selling bonds lead to a decrease in the price of bonds and an increase in the interest rate.

Let us take up three more issues before moving on.

The liquidity trap

In the previous section, we assumed that the central bank could always affect the interest rate, by changing the money supply. However, there is a limit to what the central bank can do: it cannot decrease the interest rate below zero.

Go back first to our characterisation of the demand and the supply of money in Section 4.1. There we drew the demand for money, for a given level of income, as a decreasing function of the interest rate. The lower the interest rate, the larger the demand for money – equivalently, the smaller the demand for bonds. What we did not ask is what happens when the interest rate goes down to zero. The answer: once people hold enough money for transaction purposes, they are then indifferent between holding the rest of their financial wealth in the form of money or in the form of bonds. The reason they are indifferent: both money and bonds pay the same interest rate: zero. Thus, the demand for money is as shown in Figure 4.6:

◀ Look at Figure 4.1. Note how we avoided the issue by not drawing the demand for money for interest rates close to zero.

- As the interest rate decreases, people want to hold more money (and thus fewer bonds): the demand for money therefore increases.
- As the interest rate becomes equal to zero, people want to hold an amount of money at least equal to the distance OB. This is what they need for transaction purposes, but they are willing to hold even more money (and therefore hold fewer bonds) because they are indifferent between money and bonds. Therefore, the demand for money beyond point B becomes horizontal.

Now consider the effects of an increase in the money supply:

- Consider a case in which the money supply is M^s, so the interest rate consistent with financial market equilibrium is positive and equal to i. (This is the case we considered in Section 4.1.) Starting from that equilibrium in Figure 4.6, an increase in the money supply – a shift of the M^s line to the right – leads to a decrease in the interest rate.
- Now consider a case in which the money supply is $M^{s'}$, so the equilibrium is at point B; or the case where the money supply is $M^{s''}$, so the equilibrium is given at point C. In either

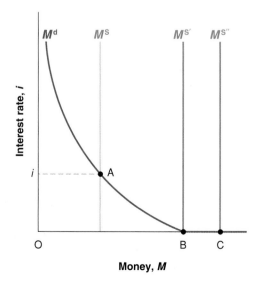

Figure 4.6

Money demand, money supply and the liquidity trap

When the interest rate is equal to zero, and once people have enough money for transaction purposes, they become indifferent between holding money and holding bonds. The demand for money becomes horizontal. This implies that, when the interest rate is equal to zero, further increases in the money supply have no effect on the interest rate.

case, the initial interest rate is zero; and, in either case, an increase in the money supply has no effect on the interest rate. Think of it this way. Suppose the central bank increases the money supply. It does so through an open market operation in which it buys bonds and pays for them by creating money. Because the interest rate is zero, people are indifferent to how much money or how many bonds they hold, so they are willing to hold fewer bonds and more money at the same interest rate: zero. The money supply increases but with no effect on the nominal interest rate – which remains equal to zero.

In short: once the interest rate is equal to zero, expansionary monetary policy becomes powerless. Or, to use the words of Keynes, who was the first to point out the problem, the increase in money falls into a **liquidity trap**: people are willing to hold more money (*more liquidity*) at the same interest rate.

What can a central bank do to expand the money supply if the economy is stuck in a liquidity trap? How can the central bank put more money into the economy in order to boost spending and increase output? And, most importantly, does it make sense to increase the money supply, if such an increase has no effect on the interest rate because it is stuck at zero? These questions have become central to monetary policy during the 2007–2010 crisis because interest rates have fallen to zero. We shall discuss this in Chapter 20. For the time being, remember what happens when the interest rate reaches zero.

Choosing money or choosing the interest rate?

We have described the central bank as choosing the money supply and letting the interest rate be determined at the point where money supply equals money demand. Instead, we could have described the central bank as choosing the interest rate and then adjusting the money supply so as to achieve that interest rate.

To see this, return to Figure 4.4. Figure 4.4 shows the effect of a decision by the central bank to increase the money supply from M^s to $M^{s'}$, causing the interest rate to fall from i to i'. However, we could have described the figure in terms of the central bank's decision to lower the interest rate from i to i' by increasing the money supply from M^s to $M^{s'}$.

> Suppose nominal income increases, as in Figure 4.3, and that the central bank wants to keep the interest rate unchanged. How does it need to adjust the money supply?

Why is it useful to think about the central bank as choosing the interest rate? Because this is what modern central banks, including the ECB, the Bank of England and the Fed, typically do. They typically think about the interest rate they want to achieve and then move the money supply in order to achieve it. This is why, when you listen to the news, you do not hear: 'The central bank decided to increase the money supply today.' Instead you hear: 'The central bank decided to decrease the interest rate today.' The way the central bank did it was by increasing the money supply appropriately.

Money, bonds and other assets

> The complication: the short-term interest rate – the rate directly controlled by the central bank – is not the only interest rate that affects spending. The determination of other interest rates and asset prices (such as stock prices) is the topic of Chapter 14.

We have been looking at an economy with only two assets: money and bonds. This is obviously a much simplified version of actual economies, with their many financial assets and many financial markets but, as you will see in later chapters, the basic lessons we have just learned apply very generally. The only change we will have to make is to replace 'interest rate' in our conclusions with 'short-term interest rate'. You will see that the short-term interest rate is determined by the condition we just discussed – the equilibrium between money supply and money demand. The central bank can, through open market operations, change the short-term interest rate; and open market operations are indeed the basic tool used by most modern central banks to affect interest rates.

> You can skip the next two sections and still go through most of the arguments in the rest of the book. If you do, let us give you the bottom line: even in this more complicated case, the central bank can, by changing the amount of central bank money, control the interest rate.

There is one dimension, however, in which our model must be extended. We have assumed that all money in the economy consists of currency supplied by the central bank. In the real world, money includes not only currency but also deposit accounts. Deposit accounts are supplied not by the central bank but by (private) banks. How the presence of banks and deposit accounts changes our conclusions is the topic of the next section.

4.3 DETERMINING THE INTEREST RATE: PART 2

To understand what determines the interest rate in an economy with both currency and deposit accounts, we must first look at what banks do.

What banks do

Modern economies are characterised by the existence of many types of **financial intermediaries** – institutions that receive funds from people and firms and use those funds to buy financial assets or to make loans to other people and firms. The assets of these institutions are the financial assets they own and the loans they have made. Their liabilities are what they owe to the people and firms from whom they have received funds.

Banks are one type of financial intermediary. What makes banks special – and the reason we focus on banks here rather than on financial intermediaries in general – is that their liabilities are money: people can pay for transactions by writing cheques up to the amount of their account balance. Let's look more closely at what banks do.

The balance sheet of *banks* is shown in Figure 4.7(b):

- Banks receive funds from people and firms who either deposit funds directly or have funds sent to their deposit accounts (via direct deposit of their paycheques, for example). At any point in time, people and firms can write cheques or withdraw up to the full amount of their account balances. The liabilities of the banks are therefore equal to the value of these *deposit accounts*.
- Banks keep as **reserves** some of the funds they receive. The reserves are held partly in cash and partly in an account the banks have at the central bank, which they can draw on when they need to. Banks hold reserves for three reasons:

  1. On any given day, some depositors withdraw cash from their deposit accounts, while others deposit cash into their accounts. There is no reason for the inflows and outflows of cash to be equal, so the bank must keep some cash on hand.
  2. In the same way, on any given day, people with accounts at the bank write cheques to people with accounts at other banks, and people with accounts at other banks write cheques to people with accounts at the bank. What the bank, as a result of these transactions, owes the other banks can be larger or smaller than what the other banks owe to it. For this reason, also, the bank needs to keep reserves.

     The first two reasons imply that the banks would want to keep some reserves even if they were not required to do so. In addition, banks are subject to reserve requirements, which say that they must hold reserves in some proportion of their deposit accounts.
  3. In Europe, there are special reserve requirements applied to banks in the euro area according to which each institution must keep reserves in relation to the composition of their budgets. In particular, the **reserve ratio** is equal to 2% on sight and overnight deposits, on term deposits up to two years and on debt securities with short maturity

◀ This balance sheet is a much-simplified version of the actual balance sheets of banks. Banks have other types of liabilities in addition to deposit accounts and they are engaged in more activities than just holding bonds or making loans. But these complications are not relevant here, so we ignore them.

(a) **Central Bank**

Assets	Liabilities
Bonds	Central bank money = Reserves + Currency

(b) **Banks**

Assets	Liabilities
Reserves Loans Bonds	Deposit accounts

Figure 4.7

The balance sheet of banks and the balance sheet of the central bank, revisited

up to two years (during the 2007–2010 crisis, this limit has been temporarily raised to $250,000 per depositor while on other deposits and securities with longer maturity reserve requirements are 0%; in the USA, reserve requirements are set by the Fed. The actual reserve ratio – the ratio of bank reserves to bank deposit accounts – is about 10% in the USA today. Banks can use the other 90% to make loans or buy bonds).

● Loans represent most of banks' non-reserve assets. Bonds account for the rest. The distinction between bonds and loans is unimportant for our purpose – which is to understand

FOCUS
Bank runs

Is bank money (deposit accounts) just as good as central bank money (currency)? To answer this question, we must look at what banks do with the funds they receive from depositors and at the distinction between making loans and holding bonds.

Making a loan to a firm or buying a government bond are more similar than they may seem. In one case, the bank lends to a firm. In the other, the bank lends to the government. This is why, for simplicity, we have assumed in the text that banks hold only bonds.

In one respect, however, making a loan is very different from buying a bond. Bonds, especially government bonds, are very liquid: if need be, they can be sold easily in the bond market. Loans, on the other hand, are often not liquid at all. Calling them back may be impossible. Firms have probably already used their loans to buy inventories or new machines, so they no longer have the cash on hand. Likewise, individuals are likely to have used their loans to purchase cars, houses or other things. The bank could in principle sell the loans to a third party to get cash. However, selling them might be very difficult because potential buyers would know little about how reliable the borrowers are.

This fact has one important implication: take a healthy bank, a bank with a portfolio of good loans. Suppose rumours start that the bank is not doing well and some loans will not be repaid. Believing that the bank may fail, people with deposits at the bank will want to close their accounts and withdraw cash. If enough people do so, the bank will run out of reserves. Given that the loans cannot be called back, the bank will not be able to satisfy the demand for cash, and it will have to close.

Conclusion: fear that a bank will close can actually cause it to close – even if all its loans are good. The financial history of the USA up to the 1930s is full of such **bank runs**. One bank fails for the right reason (because it has made bad loans). This, then, causes depositors at other banks to panic and withdraw money from their banks, forcing them to close. In an old movie with James Stewart, *It's a Wonderful Life*, after another bank in Stewart's town

fails, depositors at the savings and loan he manages get scared and want to withdraw their money, too. Stewart successfully persuades them this is not a good idea. *It's a Wonderful Life* has a happy ending but, in real life, most bank runs didn't.

What can be done to avoid bank runs? The USA has dealt with this problem since 1934 with **deposit insurance**. The US government insures each account up to a ceiling of $100 000 (where prior to the crisis bank deposits were not guaranteed). As a result, there is no reason for depositors to run and withdraw their money.

In the EU, Directive 94/19/EC of the European Parliament and of the Council of 30 May 1994 on deposit-guarantee schemes, requires all member states to have a deposit guarantee scheme for at least 90% of the deposited amount, up to at least €20 000 per person. On 7 October 2008, the Ecofin (the Economic and Financial Affairs Council comprising the Economics and Financial Affairs Ministers of the 27 EU member states) agreed to increase the minimum amount to €50 000. The increased amount followed Ireland's move, in September 2008, to increase its deposit insurance to an unlimited amount. Many other EU countries, starting with the UK reacted by increasing their own limits to avoid discouraging people from transferring deposits to Irish banks.

Deposit insurance leads, however, to problems of its own. Depositors, who do not have to worry about their deposits, no longer care about the soundness of the banks in which they have their accounts. Banks may then misbehave, by making loans they wouldn't have made in the absence of deposit insurance. (There will be more on this when we discuss the recent recession of 2007–2010 in Chapter 20.)

An alternative to government insurance, which has been often discussed but never implemented, is called **narrow banking**. Narrow banking would restrict banks to holding liquid and safe government securities. Loans would have to be made by financial intermediaries other than banks. This would eliminate bank runs as well as the need for deposit insurance.

how the money supply is determined. For this reason, to keep the discussion simple, we will assume that banks do not make loans and that they hold only reserves and bonds as assets. However, the distinction between loans and bonds is important for other purposes, from the possibility of 'bank runs' to the role of deposit insurance. These topics are explored in the Focus box 'Bank runs.'

Figure 4.7(a) returns to the balance sheet of the central bank, in an economy in which there are banks. It is very similar to the balance sheet of the central bank we saw in Figure 4.5. The asset side is the same as before: the assets of the central bank are the bonds it holds. The liabilities of the central bank are the money it has issued, **central bank money**. The new feature is that not all of central bank money is held as currency by the public. Some of it is held as reserves by banks.

The supply and the demand for central bank money

The easiest way to think about how the interest rate in this economy is determined is by thinking in terms of the supply and the demand for *central bank money*:

- The demand for central bank money is equal to the demand for currency by people plus the demand for reserves by banks.
- The supply of central bank money is under the direct control of the central bank.
- The equilibrium interest rate is such that the demand and the supply for central bank money are equal.

Figure 4.8 shows the structure of the demand and the supply of central bank money in more detail. (Ignore the equations for the time being. Just look at the boxes in the upper part of the figure.) Start on the left side: the demand for money by people is for both deposit accounts and currency. Because banks have to hold reserves against deposit accounts, the demand for deposit accounts leads to a demand for reserves by banks. Consequently, the demand for central bank money is equal to the demand for reserves by banks plus the demand for currency. Go to the right side: the supply of central bank money is determined

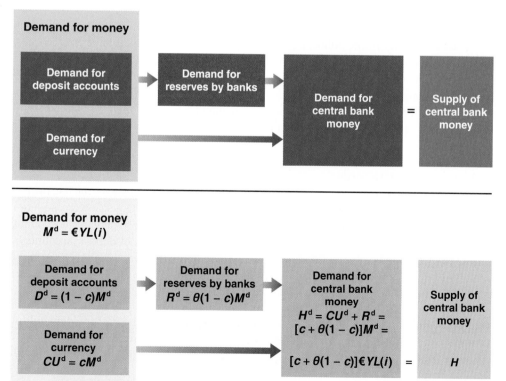

Figure 4.8

Determinants of the demand and supply of central bank money

by the central bank. Look at the equal sign: the interest rate must be such that the demand and the supply of central bank money are equal.

We now go through each of the boxes in Figure 4.8 and ask:

Be careful to distinguish among:

- demand for money (demand for currency and deposit accounts)
- demand for bank money (demand for deposit accounts)
- demand for central bank money (demand for currency by people and demand for reserves by banks).

- What determines the demand for deposit accounts and the demand for currency?
- What determines the demand for reserves by banks?
- What determines the demand for central bank money?
- How does the condition that the demand and the supply of central money be equal determine the interest rate?

The demand for money

When people can hold both currency and deposit accounts, the demand for money involves *two* decisions. First, people must decide how much money to hold. Second, they must decide how much of this money to hold in currency and how much to hold in deposit accounts.

It is reasonable to assume that the overall demand for money (currency plus deposit accounts) is given by the same factors as before. People will hold more money the higher the level of transactions and the lower the interest rate on bonds. We can assume that overall money demand is given by the same equation as before (equation (4.1)):

$$M^d = €YL(i) \qquad [4.3]$$
$$(-)$$

That brings us to the second decision: how do people decide how much to hold in currency and how much in deposit accounts? Currency is more convenient for small transactions and also more convenient for illegal transactions. Cheques are more convenient for large transactions. Holding money in your deposit accounts is safer than holding cash.

Let's assume that people hold a fixed proportion of their money in currency – call this proportion c – and, by implication, hold a fixed proportion $(1 - c)$ in deposit accounts. Call the demand for currency CU^d (CU for currency and d for demand). Call the demand for deposit accounts D^d (D for deposits and d for demand). The two demands are given by

$$CU^d = cM^d \qquad [4.4]$$

$$D^d = (1 - c)M^d \qquad [4.5]$$

Equation (4.4) shows the first component of the demand for central bank money – the demand for currency by the public. Equation (4.5) shows the demand for deposit accounts.

We now have a description of the first box, 'Demand for money', on the left side of Figure 4.8. Equation (4.3) shows the overall demand for money. Equations (4.4) and (4.5) show the demand for currency and the demand for deposit accounts, respectively.

The demand for deposit accounts leads to a demand by banks for reserves, the second component of the demand for central bank money. To see how, let's turn to the behaviour of banks.

The demand for reserves

The larger the amount of deposit accounts, the larger the amount of reserves the banks must hold, for both precautionary and regulatory reasons. Let θ (the Greek lowercase letter theta) be the reserve ratio, the amount of reserves banks hold per euro of deposit accounts. Let R denote the reserves of banks. Let D denote the euro amount of deposit accounts in euros. Then, by the definition of θ, the following relation holds between R and D:

$$R = \theta D \qquad [4.6]$$

If people want to hold D^d in deposits, then, from equation (4.6), banks must hold θD^d in reserves. Combining equations (4.5) and (4.6), the second component of the demand for central bank money – the demand for reserves by banks – is given by:

$$R^d = \theta(1 - c)M^d \qquad [4.7]$$

We now have the equation corresponding to the second box, 'Demand for reserves by banks', on the left side of Figure 4.8.

The demand for central bank money

Call H^d the demand for central bank money. This demand is equal to the sum of the demand for currency and the demand for reserves:

$$H^d = CU^d + R^d \qquad [4.8]$$

Replace CU^d and R^d with their expressions from equations (4.4) and (4.7) to get:

$$H^d = cM^d + \theta(1-c)M^d = [c + \theta(1-c)]M^d$$

Finally, replace the overall demand for money, M^d, with its expression from equation (4.3) to get:

$$H^d = [c + \theta(1-c)] \text{€} YL(i) \qquad [4.9]$$

This gives us the equation corresponding to the third box, 'Demand for central bank money,' in Figure 4.8.

◀ Suppose banks doubled the number of locations of ATMs, making them more convenient to use for their customers. What would happen to the demand for central bank money?

The determination of the interest rate

We are now ready to characterise the equilibrium. Let H be the supply of central bank money. H is directly controlled by the central bank; just like in the previous section, the central bank can change the amount of H through open market operations. The equilibrium condition is that the supply of central bank money be equal to the demand for central bank money:

$$H = H^d \qquad [4.10]$$

or, using equation (4.9):

$$H = [c + \theta(1-c)] \text{€} YL(i) \qquad [4.11]$$

The supply of central bank money (the left side of equation (4.11)) is equal to the demand for central bank money (the right side of equation (4.11)), which is equal to the term in square brackets multiplied by the overall demand for money.

Look at the term in square brackets more closely. Suppose that people held only currency, so $c = 1$. Then, the term in square brackets would be equal to 1, and the equation would be exactly the same as equation (4.2) in Section 4.2 (with the letter H replacing the letter M on the left side, but H and M both stand for the supply of central bank money). In this case, people would hold only currency, and banks would play no role in the supply of money. We would be back to the case we looked at in Section 4.2.

Assume instead that people did not hold currency at all, but held only deposit accounts, so $c = 0$. Then, the term in square brackets would be equal to θ. Suppose, for example, that $\theta = 0.1$, so that the term in square brackets was equal to 0.1. Then, the demand for central bank money would be equal to one-tenth of the overall demand for money. This is easy to understand: people would hold only deposit accounts. For every euro people wanted to hold, banks would need to have 10 cents in reserves. In other words, the demand for reserves would be one-tenth of the overall demand for money.

Leaving aside these two extreme cases, note that as long as people hold some deposit accounts (so that $c < 1$), the term in square brackets is less than 1. This means the demand for central bank money is less than the overall demand for money. This is due to the fact that the demand for reserves by banks is only a fraction of the demand for deposit accounts.

We can represent the equilibrium condition, equation (4.11), graphically, and we do this in Figure 4.9. The figure looks the same as Figure 4.2, but with central bank money rather than money on the horizontal axis. The interest rate is measured on the vertical axis. The demand for central bank money, $CU^d + R^d$, is drawn for a given level of nominal income. A higher interest rate implies a lower demand for central bank money for two reasons:

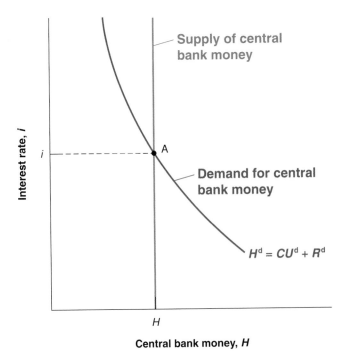

Figure 4.9

Equilibrium in the market for central bank money and the determination of the interest rate

The equilibrium interest rate is such that the supply of central bank money is equal to the demand for central bank money.

(1) the demand for currency by people goes down; (2) the demand for deposit accounts by people also goes down. This leads to lower demand for reserves by banks. The supply of money is fixed and is represented by a vertical line at H. Equilibrium is at point A, with interest rate, i.

The effects of either changes in nominal income or changes in the supply of central bank money are qualitatively the same as in the previous section. In particular, an increase in the supply of central bank money leads to a shift in the vertical supply line to the right. This leads to a lower interest rate. As before, an increase in central bank money leads to a decrease in the interest rate. Conversely, a decrease in central bank money leads to an increase in the interest rate.

Suppose people get worried about the possibility of bank runs and decide to hold a higher proportion of money in the form of currency. If the central bank keeps the money supply constant, what will happen to the interest rate? ➤

4.4 TWO ALTERNATIVE WAYS OF LOOKING AT THE EQUILIBRIUM

In Section 4.3, we looked at the equilibrium through the condition that the supply and the demand of central bank money be equal. There are two other ways of looking at the equilibrium. While they are all equivalent, each provides a different way of thinking about the equilibrium, and going through each one will strengthen your understanding of how monetary policy affects the interest rate.

The interbank market and the overnight interest rate

Instead of thinking in terms of the supply and the demand for central bank money, we can think in terms of the supply and the demand for bank reserves.

The supply of reserves is equal to the supply of central bank money, H, minus the demand for currency by the public, CU^d. The demand for reserves by banks is R^d. So the equilibrium condition that the supply and the demand for bank reserves be equal is given by

$$H - CU^d = R^d$$

Notice that if we move CU^d from the left side to the right side and use the fact that the demand for central bank money, H^d, is given by $H^d = CU^d + R^d$, then this equation is equivalent to $H = H^d$. In other words, looking at the equilibrium in terms of the supply and the demand for reserves is equivalent to looking at the equilibrium in terms of the supply and the demand for central bank money – the approach we followed in Section 4.3.

The market for bank reserves, where the interest rate moves up and down to balance the supply and demand for reserves, is not free: most central banks intervene to influence the interest rate, because all interest rates in the economy are linked to the interest rate on reserves. The central bank can influence the **interbank market**, and thus the interest rate, in different ways. By conducting open market operations, it can influence the supply of reserves. For example, it can buy bonds from banks, thereby increasing their reserves, which (other things being equal) should push the interbank interest rate down.

In the USA and Europe, the central bank (the Fed and the ECB, respectively) controls the interest rate on bank reserves in slightly different ways. The Fed controls the interest rate on bank reserves (which is called the Federal Funds Rate) trying to keep it close to the target (the Federal Funds Target). The ECB keeps the interest rate on bank reserves in the euro area (which is called **EONIA**, short for Euro Overnight Index Average, the rate at which banks lend reserves to one another within a corridor.

Whether banks buy reserves from one another or from the central bank normally makes little difference: the rate at which banks lend money to each other (LIBOR, London Interbank Offered Rate) is usually very close to the EONIA rate (LIBOR typically exceeds the EONIA by around 20 basis points or 0.2%). This slightly higher cost reflects an important difference. When a bank borrows reserves from the central bank, it must post securities as a guarantee; however, no guarantee is required for loans between commercial banks. From 9 August 2007 (the outbreak of the recent financial crisis), the difference between LIBOR and EONIA has literally exploded, reaching, in 2008, 350 basis points. This reflects a situation in which the risk that a bank fails is much increased. In fact, only the offer of guarantees on banks' balance sheets by national governments has reduced the spread between LIBOR and EONIA to 50 basis points.

The supply of money, the demand for money and the money multiplier

We have seen how we can think of the equilibrium in terms of the equality of the supply of and demand for central bank money, or in terms of the equality of the supply of and demand for reserves. There is yet another way of thinking about the equilibrium, which is sometimes very useful. We can think about the equilibrium in terms of the equality of the overall supply and the overall demand for money (currency and deposit accounts).

To derive an equilibrium condition in terms of the overall supply and the overall demand for money, start with the equilibrium condition (4.11) (which states that the supply of central bank money must equal the demand for central bank money) and divide both sides by $[c + \theta(1 - c)]$:

> Remember: all three ways are equivalent in the sense that they yield the same answer, but each gives us a different way of thinking about the answer and strengthens our intuition.

$$\frac{1}{[c + \theta(1 - c)]} H = €YL(i) \qquad [4.12]$$

Supply of money = Demand for money

The right side of equation (4.12) is the overall demand for money (currency plus deposit accounts). The left side is the overall supply of money (currency plus deposit accounts). Basically the equation says that, in equilibrium, the overall supply of and the overall demand for money must be equal:

- If you compare equation (4.12) with equation (4.2), the equation characterising the equilibrium in an economy without banks, you will see that the only difference is that the overall supply of money is not equal just to central bank money but to central bank money multiplied by a constant term $1/[c + \theta(1 - c)]$.

  Notice also that because $[c + \theta(1 - c)]$ is less than 1, its inverse – the constant term on the left of the equation – is greater than 1. For this reason, this constant term is called the **money multiplier**. The overall supply of money is therefore equal to central bank money multiplied by the money multiplier. If the money multiplier is 4, for example, then the overall supply of money is equal to four times the supply of central bank money.

- To reflect the fact that the overall supply of money depends in the end on the amount of central bank money, central bank money is sometimes called **high-powered money** (this is where the letter H we used to denote central bank money comes from), or the **monetary base**. The term *high-powered* reflects the fact that increases in H lead to more than one-for-one increases in the overall money supply and are therefore high-powered. In the same way, the term *monetary base* reflects the fact that the overall money supply depends ultimately on a 'base' – the amount of central bank money in the economy.

The presence of a multiplier in equation (4.12) implies that a given change in central bank money has a larger effect on the money supply – and, in turn, a larger effect on the interest rate – in an economy with banks than in an economy without banks. To understand why, it is useful to return to the description of open market operations, this time in an economy with banks.

Understanding the money multiplier

To make things easier, let's consider a special case where people hold only deposit accounts, so $c = 0$. In this case, the multiplier is $1/\theta$. In other words, an increase of a euro of high-powered money leads to an increase of $1/\theta$ euros in the money supply. Assume further that $\theta = 0.1$, so that the multiplier equals $1/0.1 = 10$. The purpose of what follows is to help you understand where this multiplier comes from and, more generally, how the initial increase in central bank money leads to a ten-fold increase in the overall money supply.

Suppose the central bank buys €100 worth of bonds in an open market operation. It pays the seller – call him seller 1 – €100. To pay the seller, the central bank creates €100 in central bank money. The increase in central bank money is €100. When we looked earlier at the effects of an open market operation in an economy in which there were no banks, this was the end of the story. Here, it is just the beginning:

- Seller 1 (who, we have assumed, does not want to hold any currency) deposits the €100 in a deposit accounts at this bank – call it bank A. This leads to an increase in deposit accounts of €100.
- Bank A keeps €100 times 0.1 = €10 in reserves and buys bonds with the rest, €100 times 0.9 = €90. It pays €90 to the seller of those bonds – call her seller 2.
- Seller 2 deposits €90 in a deposit account in her bank – call it bank B. This leads to an increase in deposit accounts of €90.
- Bank B keeps €90 times 0.1 = €9 in reserves and buys bonds with the rest, €90 times 0.9 = €81. It pays €81 to the seller of those bonds – call him seller 3.
- Sellers 3 deposits €81 in a deposit account in his bank – call it bank C.
- And so on.

By now, the chain of events should be clear. What is the eventual increase in the money supply? The increase in deposit accounts is €100 when seller 1 deposits the proceeds of his sale of bonds in bank A, plus €90 when seller 2 deposits the proceeds of her sale of bonds in bank B, plus €81 when seller 3 does the same, and so on. Let's write the sum as:

$$€100(1 + 0.9 + 0.9^2 + \ldots)$$

Although we here measure quantities in euros for multiplicity, this example equally applies to central banks in countries outside the euro area.

The series in parentheses is a geometric series, so its sum is equal to $1/(1-0.9) = 10$. (See Appendix 1 at the end of this book for a refresher on geometric series.) The money supply increases by €1000 – 10 times the initial increase in central bank money.

This derivation gives us another way of thinking about the money multiplier: we can think of the ultimate increase in the money supply as the result of *successive rounds of purchases of bonds* – the first started by the central bank in its open market operation, and the following rounds by banks. Each successive round leads to an increase in the money supply, and eventually the increase in the money supply is equal to ten times the initial increase in the central bank money. Note the parallel between our interpretation of the money multiplier as the result of successive purchases of bonds and the interpretation of the goods market multiplier (Chapter 3) as the result of successive rounds of spending. Multipliers can often be derived as the sum of a geometric series and interpreted as the result of successive rounds of decisions. This interpretation often gives a better understanding of how the process works.

SUMMARY

- The demand for money depends positively on the level of transactions in the economy and negatively on the interest rate.

- The interest rate is determined by the equilibrium condition that the supply of money be equal to the demand for money.

- For a given supply of money, an increase in income leads to an increase in the demand for money and an increase in the interest rate. An increase in the supply of money leads to a decrease in the interest rate.

- The central bank changes the supply of money through open market operations.

- Expansionary open market operations, in which the central bank increases the money supply by buying bonds, lead to an increase in the price of bonds and a decrease in the interest rate.

- Contractionary open market operations, in which the central bank decreases the money supply by selling bonds, lead to a decrease in the price of bonds and an increase in the interest rate.

- When money includes both currency and deposit accounts, we can think of the interest rate as being determined by the condition that the supply of central bank money be equal to the demand for central bank money.

- The supply of central bank money is under the control of the central bank. The demand for central bank money depends on the overall demand for money, the proportion of money people keep in currency, and the ratio of reserves to deposit accounts chosen by banks.

- Another, but equivalent, way to think about the determination of the interest rate is in terms of the equality of the supply and demand for bank reserves. The market for bank reserves is called the interbank market. The interest rate determined in that market is called the overnight interest rate, EONIA in the euro area.

- Yet another way to think about the determination of the interest rate is in terms of the equality of the overall supply and the overall demand of money. The overall supply of money is equal to central bank money times the money multiplier.

KEY TERMS

money 59	savings 60	expansionary, or contractionary, open market operation 65	deposit insurance 70
currency 59	financial wealth, wealth 60		narrow banking 70
deposit accounts 59			central bank money 71
bond 59	stock 60	liquidity trap 68	interbank market 75
money market funds 59	investment 60	financial intermediary 69	EONIA 75
income 60	financial investment 60	(bank) reserves 69	money multiplier 76
flow 60	*LM* relation 63	reserve ratio 69	high-powered money 76
saving 60	open market operation 65	bank run 70	monetary base 76

QUESTIONS AND PROBLEMS

QUICK CHECK

1. *Using the information in this chapter, label each of the following statements true, false or uncertain. Explain briefly.*

a. Income and financial wealth are both examples of stock variables.

b. The term *investment*, as used by economists, refers to the purchase of bonds and shares of stock.

c. The demand for money does not depend on the interest rate because only bonds earn interest.

d. About two-thirds of US currency is held outside the USA.

e. The central bank can increase the supply of money by selling bonds in the bonds market.

f. The central bank can determine the money supply, but it cannot determine interest rates because interest rates are determined in the private sector.

g. Bond prices and interest rates always move in opposite directions.

h. Since the Great Depression, the USA has used federal deposit insurance to deal with bank runs.

2. *Suppose that a person's yearly income is €60 000. Also suppose that this person's money demand function is given by*

$$M^d = €Y(0.30 - i)$$

a. What is this person's demand for money when the interest rate is 5%? 10%?

b. Explain how the interest rate affects money demand.

c. Suppose that the interest rate is 10%. In percentage terms, what happens to this person's demand for money if her yearly income is reduced by 50%?

d. Suppose that the interest rate is 5%. In percentage terms, what happens to this person's demand for money if her yearly income is reduced by 50%?

e. Summarise the effect of income on money demand. In percentage terms, how does this effect depend on the interest rate?

3. *Consider a bond that promises to pay €100 in one year.*

a. What is the interest rate on the bond if its price today is €75? €85? €95?

b. What is the relation between the price of the bond and the interest rate?

c. If the interest rate is 8%, what is the price of the bond today?

4. *Suppose that money demand is given by*

$$M^d = €Y(0.25 - i)$$

where €Y is €100. Also, suppose that the supply of money is €20.

a. What is the equilibrium interest rate?

b. If the central bank wants to increase i by 10 percentage points (e.g., from 2% to 12%), at what level should it set the supply of money?

DIG DEEPER

5. *Suppose that a person's wealth is €50 000 and that her yearly income is €60 000. Also suppose that her money demand function is given by*

$$M^d = €Y(0.35 - i)$$

a. Derive the demand for bonds. Suppose the interest rate increases by 10 percentage points. What is the effect on the demand for bonds?

b. What are the effects of an increase in wealth on the demand for money and the demand for bonds? Explain in words.

c. What are the effects of an increase in income on the demand for money and the demand for bonds? Explain in words.

d. Consider the statement 'When people earn more money, they obviously will hold more bonds.' What is wrong with this statement?

6. The demand for bonds

In this chapter, you learned that an increase in the interest rate makes bonds more attractive, so it leads people to hold more of their wealth in bonds, as opposed to money. However, you also learned that an increase in the interest rate reduces the price of bonds.

How can an increase in the interest rate make bonds more attractive and reduce their price?

7. ATMs and credit cards

This problem examines the effect of the introduction of ATMs and credit cards on money demand. For simplicity, let's examine a person's demand for money over a period of four days.

Suppose that before ATMs and credit cards, this person goes to the bank once at the beginning of each four-day period and withdraws from her savings account all the money she needs for four days. Assume that she spends €4 per day.

a. How much does this person withdraw each time she goes to the bank? Compute this person's money holdings for days 1 through 4 (in the morning, before she spends any of the money she withdraws).

b. What is the amount of money this person holds, on average?

Suppose now that with the advent of ATMs, this person withdraws money once every two days.

c. Recompute your answer to part (a).

d. Recompute your answer to part (b).

Finally, with the advent of credit cards, this person pays for all her purchases using her card. She withdraws no money until the fourth day, when she withdraws the whole amount necessary to pay for her credit card purchases over the previous four days.

e. Recompute your answer to part (a).

f. Recompute your answer to part (b).

g. Based on your previous answers, what do you think has been the effect of ATMs and credit cards on money demand?

8. The money multiplier

The money multiplier is described in Section 4.4. Assume the following:

i. The public holds no currency.

ii. The ratio of reserves to deposits is 0.1.

iii. The demand for money is given by

$$M^d = €Y(0.8 - 4i)$$

Initially, the monetary base is €100 billion, and nominal income is €5 trillion.

a. What is the demand for central bank money?

b. Find the equilibrium interest rate by setting the demand for central bank money equal to the supply of central bank money.

c. What is the overall supply of money? Is it equal to the overall demand for money at the interest rate you found in part (b)?

d. What is the impact on the interest rate if central bank money is increased to €300 billion?

e. If the overall money supply increases to €3000 billion, what will be the impact on *i*? [*Hint*: Use what you learned in part (c).]

9. Bank runs and the money multiplier

During the Great Depression, the US economy experienced many bank runs, to the point where people became unwilling to keep their money in banks, preferring to keep it in cash.

How would you expect such a shift away from deposit accounts toward currency to affect the size of the money multiplier?

EXPLORE FURTHER

10. Current monetary policy

Go to the website of the European Central Bank (http://www.ecb.int/home/html/index.en.html) and download the most recent monetary policy decisions press release of the Governing Council. Make sure you get the most recent GC press release and not simply the most recent ECB press release.

a. What is the current stance of monetary policy? (Note that policy will be described in terms of increasing or decreasing interest rates as opposed to increasing or decreasing the money supply.)

b. If the interest rate on the main refinancing operations has changed recently, what does the change imply about the bond holdings of the ECB? Has the ECB been increasing or decreasing its bond holdings?

We invite you to visit the Blanchard page on the Prentice Hall website, at **www.prenhall.com/blanchard** for this chapter's World Wide Web exercises.

FURTHER READING

- For more on financial markets and institutions, read a textbook on money and banking. An excellent one is **Money, the Financial System and the Economy**, by R. Glenn Hubbard, Addison-Wesley, Reading, MA, 2007.

- The ECB maintains a useful website that contains not only data on financial markets but also information on what the ECB does (**www.ecb.int/**).

Chapter 5

GOODS AND FINANCIAL MARKETS: THE *IS–LM* MODEL

In Chapter 3, we looked at the goods market. In Chapter 4, we looked at financial markets. We now look at goods and financial markets together. By the end of this chapter, you will have a framework to think about how output and the interest rate are determined in the short run.

In developing this framework, we follow a path first traced by two economists, John Hicks and Alvin Hansen, in the late 1930s and the early 1940s. When the economist John Maynard Keynes published his *General Theory* in 1936, there was much agreement that his book was both fundamental and nearly impenetrable. (Try to read it, and you will agree.) There were many debates about what Keynes 'really meant'. In 1937, John Hicks summarised what he saw as one of Keynes's main contributions: the joint description of goods and financial markets. His analysis was later extended by Alvin Hansen. Hicks and Hansen called their formalisation the *IS–LM* model.

Macroeconomics has made substantial progress since the early 1940s. This is why the *IS–LM* model is treated in this chapter rather than in the final chapter of this book. (If you had taken this course 40 years ago, you would be nearly done!) However, to most economists, the *IS–LM* model still represents an essential building block – one that, despite its simplicity, captures much of what happens in the economy in *the short run.* This is why the *IS–LM* model is still taught and used today.

This chapter has seven sections:

- Section 5.1 looks at equilibrium in the goods market and derives the *IS* relation.

- Section 5.2 looks at equilibrium in financial markets and derives the *LM* relation.

- Sections 5.3 and 5.4 put the *IS* and the *LM* relations together and use the resulting *IS–LM* model to study the effects of fiscal and monetary policy – first separately and then together.

- Section 5.5 shows how the *IS–LM* model must be modified to take into account the liquidity trap introduced in the previous chapter.

- Section 5.6 shows an analytical version of the *IS–LM* model, which is very useful to assess the impact of policy measures on the equilibrium levels of output and the interest rate.

- Section 5.7 introduces dynamics and explores how the *IS–LM* model captures what happens in the economy in the short run.

5.1 THE GOODS MARKET AND THE *IS* RELATION

Let's first summarise what we learned in Chapter 3:

- We characterised equilibrium in the goods market as the condition that production, Y, be equal to the demand for goods, Z. We called this condition the *IS* relation.
- We defined demand as the sum of consumption, investment and government spending. We assumed that consumption was a function of disposable income Y_D (income minus taxes) and took investment spending, government spending and taxes as given:

$$Z = C(Y - T) + \bar{I} + G$$

  In Chapter 3, we assumed, to simplify the algebra, that the relation between consumption, C, and disposable income, $Y - T$, was linear. Here, we do not make that assumption but use the more general form $C = C(Y - T)$ instead.
- The equilibrium condition was thus given by

$$Y = C(Y - T) + \bar{I} + G$$

- Using this equilibrium condition, we then looked at the factors that moved equilibrium output. We looked in particular at the effects of changes in government spending and of shifts in consumption demand.

The main simplification of this first model was that the interest rate did not affect the demand for goods. Our first task in this chapter is to abandon this simplification and introduce the interest rate in our model of equilibrium in the goods market. For the time being, we focus only on the effect of the interest rate on investment and leave a discussion of its effects on the other components of demand until later.

> ◄ We cover much more on the effects of interest rates on both consumption and investment in Chapter 16.

Investment, sales and the interest rate

In Chapter 3, investment was assumed to be constant. This was for simplicity. Investment is in fact far from constant and depends primarily on two factors:

- *The level of sales* – Consider a firm facing an increase in sales and needing to increase production. To do so, it may need to buy additional machines or build an additional plant. In other words, it needs to invest. A firm facing low sales will feel no such need and will spend little, if anything, on investment.
- *The interest rate* – Consider a firm deciding whether to buy a new machine. Suppose that to buy the new machine, the firm must borrow. The higher the interest rate, the less attractive it is to borrow and buy the machine. At a high enough interest rate, the additional profits from using the new machine will not cover interest payments, and the new machine will not be worth buying.

> ◄ The argument still holds if the firm uses its own funds: the higher the interest rate, the more attractive it is to lend the funds rather than to use them to buy the new machine.

To capture these two effects, we write the investment relation as follows:

$$I = I(Y, i) \qquad\qquad [5.1]$$
$$(+, -)$$

Equation (5.1) states that investment, I, depends on production, Y, and the interest rate, i. (We continue to assume that inventory investment is equal to zero, so sales and production are always equal. As a result, Y denotes sales, and it also denotes production.) The positive sign under Y indicates that an increase in production (equivalently, an increase in sales) leads to an increase in investment. The negative sign under the interest rate, i, indicates that an increase in the interest rate leads to a decrease in investment.

> ◄ An increase in output leads to an increase in investment. An increase in the interest rate leads to a decrease in investment.

Determining output

Taking into account the investment relation (5.1), the condition for equilibrium in the goods market becomes

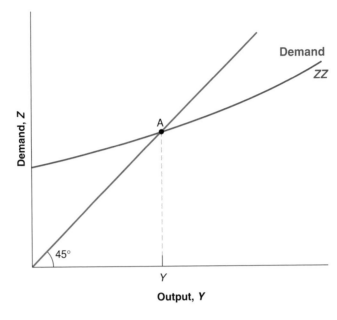

Figure 5.1

Equilibrium in the goods market

The demand for goods is an increasing function of output. Equilibrium requires that the demand for goods be equal to output.

$$Y = C(Y - T) + I(Y, i) + G \qquad [5.2]$$

Production (the left side of the equation) must be equal to the demand for goods (the right side). Equation (5.2) is our expanded *IS* relation. We can now look at what happens to output when the interest rate changes.

Start with Figure 5.1. Measure the demand for goods on the vertical axis. Measure output on the horizontal axis. For a given value of the interest rate, i, demand is an increasing function of output, for two reasons:

- An increase in output leads to an increase in income and thus to an increase in disposable income. The increase in disposable income leads to an increase in consumption. We studied this relation in Chapter 3.
- An increase in output also leads to an increase in investment. This is the relation between investment and production that we have introduced in this chapter.

In short, an increase in output leads, through its effects on both consumption and investment, to an increase in the demand for goods. This relation between demand and output, for a given interest rate, is represented by the upward-sloping curve, *ZZ*.

Note two characteristics of *ZZ* in Figure 5.1:

- Since we have not assumed that the consumption and investment relations in equation (5.2) are linear, *ZZ* is in general a curve rather than a line. Thus, we have drawn it as a curve in Figure 5.1. All the arguments that follow would apply if we assumed that the consumption and investment relations were linear and that *ZZ* were a straight line.
- We have drawn *ZZ* so that it is flatter than the 45° line. Put another way, we have assumed that an increase in output leads to a less than one-for-one increase in demand.

Make sure you understand why the two ➤ statements mean the same thing.

In Chapter 3, where investment was constant, this restriction naturally followed from the assumption that consumers spend only part of their additional income on consumption. However, now that we allow investment to respond to production, this restriction may no longer hold. When output increases, the sum of the increase in consumption and the increase in investment could exceed the initial increase in output. Although this is a theoretical possibility, the empirical evidence suggests that it is not the case in reality. That's why we will assume that the response of demand to output is less than one-for-one and draw *ZZ* flatter than the 45° line.

Equilibrium in the goods market is reached at the point where the demand for goods equals output – that is, at point A, the intersection of *ZZ* and the 45° line. The equilibrium level of output is given by *Y*.

So far, what we have done is extend, in straightforward fashion, the analysis of Chapter 3, but we are now ready to derive the *IS* curve.

Deriving the *IS* curve

We have drawn the demand relation, *ZZ*, in Figure 5.1 for a given value of the interest rate. Let's now derive in Figure 5.2 what happens if the interest rate changes.

Suppose that, in Figure 5.2(a), the demand curve is given by *ZZ*, and the initial equilibrium is at point A. Suppose now that the interest rate increases from its initial value, *i*, to a new higher value, *i'*. At any level of output, the higher interest rate leads to lower investment and lower demand. The demand curve *ZZ* shifts down to *ZZ'*: at a given level of output, demand is lower. The new equilibrium is at the intersection of the lower demand curve, *ZZ'*, and the 45° line, at point A'. The equilibrium level of output is now equal to *Y'*.

In words: the increase in the interest rate decreases investment; the decrease in investment leads to a decrease in output, which further decreases consumption and investment, through the multiplier effect.

Can you show graphically what the size of the multiplier is? (*Hint*: Look at the ratio of the decrease in equilibrium output to the initial decrease in investment.)

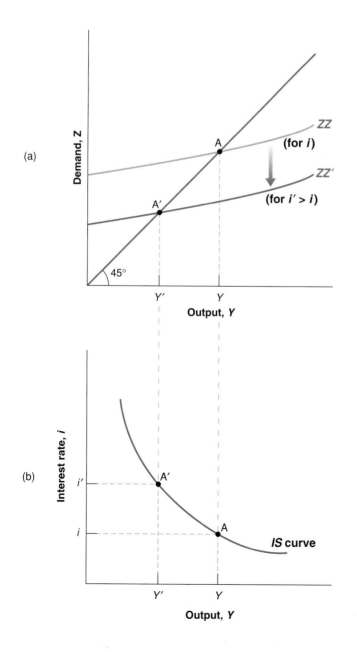

Figure 5.2

The derivation of the *IS* curve

(a) An increase in the interest rate decreases the demand for goods at any level of output, leading to a decrease in the equilibrium level of output.

(b) Equilibrium in the goods market implies that an increase in the interest rate leads to a decrease in output. The *IS* curve is therefore downward sloping.

Using Figure 5.2(a), we can find the equilibrium value of output associated with *any* value of the interest rate. The resulting relation between equilibrium output and the interest rate is drawn in Figure 5.2(b).

Figure 5.2(b) plots equilibrium output, Y, on the horizontal axis against the interest rate on the vertical axis. Point A in Figure 5.2(b) corresponds to point A in Figure 5.2(a), and point A′ in Figure 5.2(b) corresponds to A′ in Figure 5.2(a). The higher interest rate is associated with a lower level of output.

> Equilibrium in the goods market implies that an increase in the interest rate leads to a decrease in output. This relation is represented by the downward-sloping *IS* curve.

This relation between the interest rate and output is represented by the downward-sloping curve in Figure 5.2(b). This curve is called the **IS curve**.

Shifts of the *IS* curve

> For a given interest rate, an increase in taxes leads to a decrease in output. In other words, an increase in taxes shifts the *IS* curve to the left.

We have drawn the *IS* curve in Figure 5.2, taking as given the values of taxes, T, and government spending, G. Changes in either T or G will shift the *IS* curve. To see how, consider Figure 5.3. In Figure 5.3, the *IS* curve gives the equilibrium level of output as a function of the interest rate. It is drawn for given values of taxes and spending. Now consider an increase in taxes, from T to T'. At a given interest rate, say i, disposable income decreases, leading to a decrease in consumption, leading in turn to a decrease in the demand for goods and a decrease in equilibrium output. The equilibrium level of output decreases from Y to Y'. Put another way, the *IS* curve shifts to the left: at a given interest rate, the equilibrium level of output is lower than it was before the increase in taxes.

> Suppose the government announces that the social security system is in trouble, and it may have to cut retirement benefits in the future. How are consumers likely to react? What is then likely to happen to demand and output today?

More generally, any factor that, for a given interest rate, decreases the equilibrium level of output causes the *IS* curve to shift to the left. We have looked at an increase in taxes, but the same would hold for a decrease in government spending or a decrease in consumer confidence (which decreases consumption, given disposable income). Symmetrically, any factor that, for a given interest rate, increases the equilibrium level of output – a decrease in taxes, an increase in government spending, an increase in consumer confidence – causes the *IS* curve to shift to the right.

Let's summarise:

- Equilibrium in the goods market implies that an increase in the interest rate leads to a decrease in output. This relation is represented by the downward-sloping *IS* curve.
- Changes in factors that decrease the demand for goods, given the interest rate, shift the *IS* curve to the left. Changes in factors that increase the demand for goods, given the interest rate, shift the *IS* curve to the right.

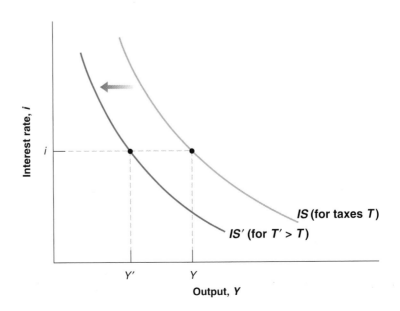

Figure 5.3

Shifts in the *IS* curve

An increase in taxes shifts the *IS* curve to the left.

5.2 FINANCIAL MARKETS AND THE *LM* RELATION

Let's now turn to financial markets. We saw in Chapter 4 that the interest rate is determined by the equality of the supply of and the demand for money:

$$M = €YL(i)$$

The variable M on the left side is the nominal money stock. We will ignore here the details of the money supply process that we saw in Sections 4.3 and 4.4 and simply think of the central bank as controlling M directly.

The right side gives the demand for money, which is a function of nominal income, $€Y$, and of the nominal interest rate, i. As we saw in Section 4.1, an increase in nominal income increases the demand for money; an increase in the interest rate decreases the demand for money. Equilibrium requires that money supply (the left side of the equation) be equal to money demand (the right side of the equation).

Real money, real income and the interest rate

The equation $M = €YL(i)$ gives a relation between money, nominal income and the interest rate. It will be more convenient here to rewrite it as a relation between real money (that is, money in terms of goods), real income (that is, income in terms of goods) and the interest rate.

Recall that nominal income divided by the price level equals real income, Y. Dividing both sides of the equation by the price level, P, gives

$$\frac{M}{P} = YL(i) \qquad\qquad [5.3]$$

Hence, we can restate our equilibrium condition as the condition that the *real money supply* – that is, the money stock in terms of goods, not euros – be equal to the *real money demand*, which depends on real income, Y, and the interest rate, i.

The notion of a 'real' demand for money may feel a bit abstract, so an example will help. ◄ From Chapter 2:
Think not of your demand for money in general but just of your demand for coins. Suppose
you like to have coins in your pocket to buy two cups of coffee during the day. If a cup costs
€1.20, you will want to keep €2.40 in coins: this is your nominal demand for coins.
Equivalently, you want to keep enough coins in your pocket to buy two cups of coffee. This
is your demand for coins in terms of goods – here in terms of cups of coffee.

From Chapter 2:

Nominal GDP = Real GDP multiplied by the GDP deflator: $€Y = Y \times P$.

Equivalently: Real GDP = Nominal GDP divided by the GDP deflator: $Y = €Y/P$.

From now on, we shall refer to equation (5.3) as the *LM relation*. The advantage of writing things this way is that *real income, Y*, appears on the right side of the equation instead of *nominal income, €Y*. And real income (equivalently real output) is the variable we focus on when looking at equilibrium in the goods market. To make the reading lighter, we will refer to the left and right sides of equation (5.3) simply as 'money supply' and 'money demand' rather than the more accurate but heavier 'real money supply' and 'real money demand'. Similarly, we will refer to income rather than 'real income'.

Deriving the *LM* curve

To see the relation between output and the interest rate implied by equation (5.3), let's use Figure 5.4. Look first at Figure 5.4(a). Let the interest rate be measured on the vertical axis and (real) money be measured on the horizontal axis. (Real) money supply is given by the vertical line at M/P and is denoted M^s. For a given level of (real) income, Y, (real) money demand is a decreasing function of the interest rate. It is drawn as the downward-sloping curve denoted M^d. Except for the fact that we measure real rather than nominal money on the horizontal axis, the figure is similar to Figure 4.3 in Chapter 4. The equilibrium is at point A, where money supply is equal to money demand, and the interest rate is equal to i.

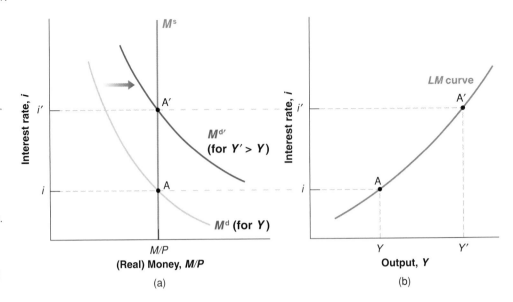

Figure 5.4

The derivation of the *LM* curve

(a) An increase in income leads, at a given interest rate, to an increase in the demand for money. Given the money supply, this increase in the demand for money leads to an increase in the equilibrium interest rate.

(b) Equilibrium in the financial markets implies that an increase in income leads to an increase in the interest rate. The *LM* curve is therefore upward sloping.

Why do we think about shifts of the *IS* ➤ curve to the left or to the right, but about shifts of the *LM* curve up or down? The reason:

- We think of the goods market as determining *Y* given *i*, so we want to know what happens to *Y* when an exogenous variable changes. *Y* is on the horizontal axis and moves right or left.

- We think of financial markets as determining *i* given *Y*, so we want to know what happens to *i* when an exogenous variable changes. *i* is on the vertical axis and moves up or down.

Now consider an increase in income from Y to Y', which leads people to increase their demand for money at any given interest rate. Money demand shifts to the right, to $M^{d'}$. The new equilibrium is at A', with a higher interest rate, i'. Why does an increase in income lead to an increase in the interest rate? When income increases, money demand increases; but the money supply is given. Thus, the interest rate must go up until the two opposite effects on the demand for money – the increase in income that leads people to want to hold more money (instead of bonds) and the increase in the interest rate that leads people to want to hold less money (and more bonds) – cancel each other out. At that point, the demand for money is equal to the unchanged money supply, and financial markets are again in equilibrium.

Using Figure 5.4(a), we can find the value of the interest rate associated with *any* value of income for a given money stock. The relation is derived in Figure 5.4(b).

Figure 5.4(b) plots the equilibrium interest rate, i, on the vertical axis against income on the horizontal axis. Point A in Figure 5.4(b) corresponds to point A in Figure 5.4(a), and point A' in Figure 5.4(b) corresponds to point A' in Figure 5.4(a). More generally, equilibrium in financial markets implies that the higher the level of output, the higher the demand for money and, therefore, the higher the equilibrium interest rate.

This relation between output and the interest rate is represented by the upward-sloping curve in Figure 5.4(b). This curve is called the **LM curve**. Economists sometimes characterise this relation by saying 'higher economic activity puts pressure on interest rates'. Make sure you understand the steps behind this statement.

Shifts of the *LM* curve

Equilibrium in financial markets implies ➤ that, for a given money stock, the interest rate is an increasing function of the level of income. This relation is represented by the upward-sloping *LM* curve.

For a given level of output, an increase ➤ in the money supply leads to a decrease in the interest rate. In other words, an increase in the money supply shifts the *LM* curve down.

We have derived the *LM* curve in Figure 5.4, taking both the nominal money stock, M, and the price level, P – and, by implication, their ratio, the real money stock, M/P – as given. Changes in M/P, whether they come from changes in the nominal money stock, M, or from changes in the price level, P, will shift the *LM* curve.

To see how, let us look at Figure 5.5 and consider an increase in the nominal money supply, from M to M'. Given the fixed price level, the real money supply increases from M/P to M'/P. Then, at any level of income, say Y, the interest rate consistent with equilibrium in financial markets is lower, going down from i to, say, i'. The *LM* curve shifts down, from *LM* to *LM'*. By the same reasoning, at any level of income, a decrease in the money supply leads to an increase in the interest rate. It causes the *LM* curve to shift up.

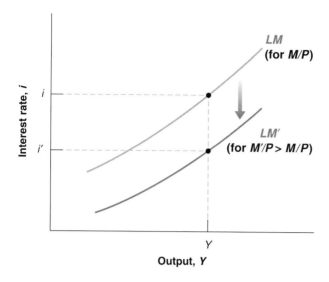

Figure 5.5

Shifts in the *LM* curve

An increase in money causes the *LM* curve to shift down.

Let's summarise:

- Equilibrium in financial markets implies that, for a given real money supply, an increase in the level of income, which increases the demand for money, leads to an increase in the interest rate. This relation is represented by the upward-sloping *LM* curve.
- An increase in the money supply shifts the *LM* curve down; a decrease in the money supply shifts the *LM* curve up.

An alternative derivation of the *LM* curve is given in the Focus box 'An alternative derivation of the *LM* curve as an interest rate rule'.

FOCUS

An alternative derivation of the *LM* relation as an interest rate rule

We have derived the *LM* relation under the assumption that *the money stock remained constant*. This gave us the positive relation between the interest rate and income shown, for example, in Figure 5.4(b).

As we discussed in Chapter 4, however, the assumption that the central bank keeps the money stock constant and lets the interest rate adjust when income changes is not a good description of what modern central banks do. Most central banks think instead in terms of setting the interest rate and adjusting the money stock so as to achieve the interest rate they want. In this case, central banks are said to follow an **interest rate rule**. Thus, we may want to derive the *LM* relation under the alternative assumption that the central bank sets the interest rate and adjusts the money supply as needed to achieve that goal.

To see what this implies, turn to Figure 5.6(a). Like Figure 5.4(a), it plots money supply and money demand,

with the interest rate on the vertical axis, and money on the horizontal axis. The money supply is given by the vertical line M^s, and money demand is given by the downward-sloping curve M^d. The initial equilibrium is at point A, with the interest rate, i_A.

Now consider an increase in income that shifts money demand from M^d to $M^{d'}$. If the central bank does not change the money supply, then the equilibrium will move from A to B, and the interest rate will increase from i_A to i_B. The implied *LM* curve, *LM*, the relation between the interest rate and income, is drawn in Figure 5.6(b). It is exactly the same as in Figure 5.4(a).

Suppose, however, that the central bank wants to keep the interest rate constant in the face of the increase in income. Can it do it? Yes. How can it do it? By increasing the money supply in response to the increase in income, from M^s to $M^{s'}$. If it does so, the interest rate will remain

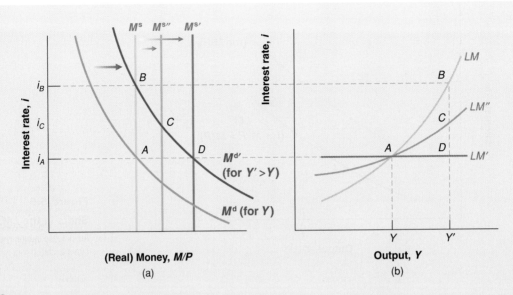

Figure 5.6

The *LM* relation as an interest rate rule

(a) Depending on whether and by how much the central bank increases the money supply in response to a shift in money demand coming from changes in income, the interest rate may remain constant, increase a little or increase a lot.

(b) We can think of the *LM* curve as showing whether and by how much the central bank allows the interest rate to increase in response to increases in income.

constant. The equilibrium will move from A to D, and the interest rate will remain constant, at i_A. The resulting *LM* curve, denoted by *LM'* in Figure 5.6(b), will be horizontal: in response to the increase in income, and thus in money demand, the central bank will adjust the money supply so as to keep the interest rate constant.

This may be too extreme a policy. Perhaps the central bank wants to allow the interest rate to increase, but by less than it would if the central bank kept the money supply constant. For example, in response to the increase in income, the central bank may choose to increase the money supply by $M^{s''} < M^{s'}$. In this case, the equilibrium will move from A to C, and the interest rate will increase from i_A to i_C. The resulting *LM* curve, denoted by *LM''* in Figure 5.6(b), will be upward-sloping but flatter than *LM*.

To summarise: the *LM* relation we derived in the previous section gave us the relation between the interest rate and income for a *given money supply*. The *LM* relation

derived here gives us the relation between the interest rate and income when the central bank follows a *given interest rule* and lets the money supply adjust as needed. Its slope then depends on how much the central bank increases the interest rate in response to increases in income.

Which *LM* relation should you use? It depends on the question at hand. Take, for example, the case of an increase in the deficit, shifting the *IS* curve to the right. You might want to know what would happen to output and the interest rate if the central bank money supply remained constant, in which case you would use the *LM* relation derived in the text. However, you might know, for example, that the central bank is likely to keep the interest rate constant, in which case you would use the *LM* relation derived here – in this particular case, a horizontal *LM* curve. (Under which of the two assumptions will fiscal policy have the strongest effect on output?)

5.3 PUTTING THE *IS* AND THE *LM* RELATIONS TOGETHER

The *IS* relation follows from the condition that the supply of goods must be equal to the demand for goods. It tells us how the interest rate affects output. The *LM* relation follows from the condition that the supply of money must be equal to the demand for money. It tells us how output, in turn, affects the interest rate. We now put the *IS* and *LM* relations together. At any point in time, the supply of goods must be equal to the demand for goods,

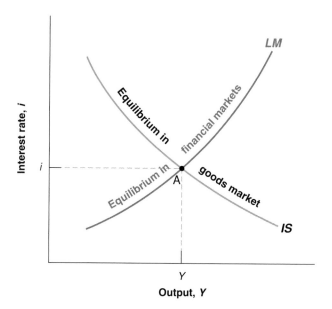

Figure 5.7

The *IS–LM* model

Equilibrium in the goods market implies that an increase in the interest rate leads to a decrease in output. This is represented by the *IS* curve. Equilibrium in financial markets implies that an increase in output leads to an increase in the interest rate. This is represented by the *LM* curve. Only at point A, which is on both curves, are both goods and financial markets in equilibrium.

and the supply of money must be equal to the demand for money. Both the *IS* and *LM* relations must hold. Together, they determine both output and the interest rate.

$$IS \text{ relation: } Y = C(Y - T) + I(Y, i) + G$$

$$LM \text{ relation: } \frac{M}{P} = YL(i)$$

Figure 5.7 plots both the *IS* curve and the *LM* curve on one graph. Output – equivalently, production or income – is measured on the horizontal axis. The interest rate is measured on the vertical axis. *Any point* on the downward-sloping *IS* curve corresponds to equilibrium in the goods market. *Any point* on the upward-sloping *LM* curve corresponds to equilibrium in financial markets. *Only at point* A are both equilibrium conditions satisfied. This means that point A, with the associated level of output, *Y*, and interest rate, *i*, is the overall equilibrium – the point at which there is equilibrium in both the goods market and financial markets.

The *IS* and *LM* relations that underlie Figure 5.7 contain a lot of information about consumption, investment, money demand and equilibrium conditions, but you may ask: so what if the equilibrium is at point A? How does this fact translate into anything directly useful about the world? Don't despair: Figure 5.7 holds the answers to many questions in macroeconomics. Used properly, it allows us to study what happens to output and the interest rate when the central bank decides to increase the money stock, or when the government decides to increase taxes, or when consumers become pessimistic about the future and so on.

Let's now see what the *IS–LM* model can do.

Fiscal policy, activity and the interest rate

Suppose the government decides to reduce the budget deficit and does so by increasing taxes while keeping government spending unchanged. Such a change in fiscal policy is often called a **fiscal contraction**, or a **fiscal consolidation**. (An *increase* in the deficit, due either to an increase in government spending or to a decrease in taxes, is called a **fiscal expansion**.) What are the effects of this fiscal contraction on output, on its composition and on the interest rate?

◀ Decrease in *G* – *T* ⇔ Fiscal contraction ⇔ Fiscal consolidation.

Increase in *G* – *T* ⇔ Fiscal expansion.

When you answer this or any other question about the effects of changes in policy, always go through the following three steps:

1. Ask how the change affects equilibrium in the goods market and how it affects equilibrium in financial markets. Put another way: how does it shift the *IS* and/or the *LM* curve?

2. Characterise the effects of these shifts on the intersection of the *IS* and *LM* curves. What does this do to equilibrium output and the equilibrium interest rate?

3. Describe the effects in words.

With time and experience, you will often be able to go directly to step 3. By then, you will be ready to give an instant commentary on the economic events of the day. However, until you get to that level of expertise, go step by step:

- Start with step 1. The first question is how the increase in taxes affects equilibrium in the goods market – that is, how it affects the *IS* curve.

  Let's draw, in Figure 5.8(a), the *IS* curve corresponding to equilibrium in the goods market before the increase in taxes. Now take an arbitrary point, B, on this *IS* curve. By construction of the *IS* curve, output, Y_B, and the corresponding interest rate, i_B, are such that the supply of goods is equal to the demand for goods.

  At the interest rate, i_B, ask what happens to output if taxes increase from T to T'. We saw the answer in Section 5.1. Because people have less disposable income, the increase in taxes decreases consumption and, through the multiplier, decreases output. At interest rate i_B, output decreases from Y_B to Y_C. More generally, at *any* interest rate, higher taxes lead to lower output. Consequently, the *IS* curve shifts to the left, from *IS* to *IS'*.

  Next, let's see if anything happens to the *LM* curve. Figure 5.8(b) draws the *LM* curve corresponding to equilibrium in financial markets before the increase in taxes. Take an arbitrary point, F, on this *LM* curve. By construction of the *LM* curve, the interest rate, i_F, and income, Y_F, are such that the supply of money is equal to the demand for money.

  > Taxes do not appear in the *LM* relation ⇔ Taxes do not shift the *LM* curve.

  What happens to the *LM* curve when taxes are increased? Nothing. At the given level of income, Y_F, the interest rate at which the supply of money is equal to the demand for money is the same as before, namely i_F. In other words, because taxes do not appear in the *LM* relation, they do not affect the equilibrium condition. They do not affect the *LM* curve.

  > A reminder: an exogenous variable is a variable we take as given, unexplained within the model. Here, taxes are an exogenous variable.
  >
  > Taxes appear in the *IS* relation ⇔ Taxes shift the *IS* curve.

  Note the general principle here: a curve shifts in response to a change in an exogenous variable only if this variable appears directly in the equation represented by that curve. Taxes enter in equation (5.2), so, when they change, the *IS* curve shifts, but taxes do not enter in equation (5.3), so the *LM* curve does not shift.

- Now consider step 2, the determination of the equilibrium. Let the initial equilibrium in Figure 5.8(c) be at point A, at the intersection between the initial *IS* curve and the *LM* curve. The *IS* curve is the same as the *IS* curve in Figure 5.8(a), and the *LM* curve is the same as the *LM* curve in Figure 5.8(b).

  > The increase in taxes shifts the *IS* curve. The *LM* curve does not shift. The economy moves along the *LM* curve.

  After the increase in taxes, the *IS* curve shifts to the left – from *IS* to *IS'*. The new equilibrium is at the intersection of the new *IS* curve and the unchanged *LM* curve, or point A'. Output decreases from Y to Y'. The interest rate decreases from i to i'. Thus, as the *IS* curve *shifts*, the economy *moves along* the *LM* curve, from A to A'. The reason these words are italicised is that it is important to always distinguish between the *shift of* a curve (here the shift of the *IS* curve) and the *movement along* a curve (here the movement along the *LM* curve). Many mistakes come from not distinguishing between the two.

  > If the interest rate did not decline, the economy would go from point A to point D in Figure 5.8(c), and output would be directly below point D. Because of the decline in the interest rate – which stimulates investment – the decline in activity is only to point A'.

- Step 3 is to tell the story in words. The increase in taxes leads to lower disposable income, which causes people to decrease their consumption. This decrease in demand leads, in turn, to a decrease in output and income. At the same time, the decrease in income reduces the demand for money, leading to a decrease in the interest rate. The decline in the interest rate reduces but does not completely offset the effect of higher taxes on the demand for goods.

What happens to the components of demand? By assumption, government spending remains unchanged (We have assumed that the reduction in the budget deficit takes place through an increase in taxes.) Consumption surely goes down, taxes go up and income goes down – so disposable income goes down on both counts. What happens to investment? On the one hand, lower output means lower sales and lower investment. On the other, a lower

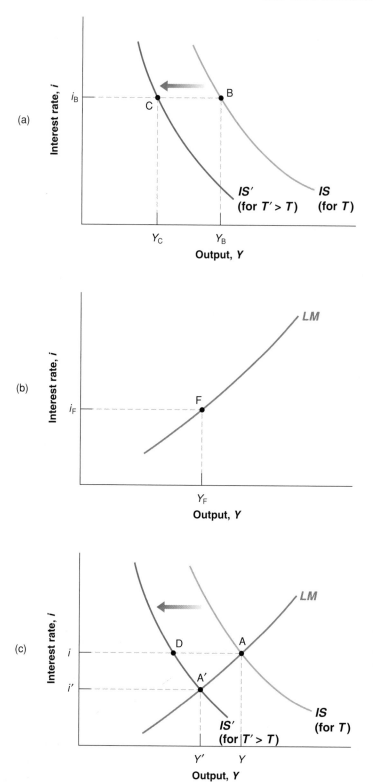

Figure 5.8

The effects of an increase in taxes

An increase in taxes shifts the *IS* curve to the left and leads to a decrease in the equilibrium level of output and the equilibrium interest rate.

interest rate leads to higher investment. Without knowing more about the exact form of the investment relation, equation (5.1), we cannot tell which effect dominates. If investment depended only on the interest rate, then investment would surely increase; if investment depended only on sales, then investment would surely decrease. In general, investment depends on both the interest rate and on sales, so we cannot tell. Contrary to what is often stated by politicians, a reduction in the budget deficit does not necessarily lead to an increase in investment. (The Focus box 'Deficit reduction: good or bad for investment?' discusses this in more detail.)

We shall return to the relation between fiscal policy and investment many times in this book, and we shall qualify this first answer in many ways. However, the result that *in the short run, a reduction of the budget deficit may decrease investment* will remain.

Monetary policy, activity and the interest rate

Increase in M ⇔ Monetary expansion. Decrease in M ⇔ Monetary contraction ⇔ Monetary tightening.

▶ An increase in the money supply is called a **monetary expansion**. A decrease in the money supply is called a **monetary contraction** or **monetary tightening**.

Let's take the case of a monetary expansion. Suppose that the central bank increases nominal money, M, through an open market operation. Given our assumption that the price level is fixed, this increase in nominal money leads to a one-for-one increase in real money, M/P. Let's denote the initial real money supply by M/P and the new higher one by

For a given price level P, M increases ▶ by 10% ⇒ M/P increases by 10%.

M'/P, and let's trace in Figure 5.9 the effects of the money supply increase on output and the interest rate:

- Again, step 1 is to see whether and how the *IS* and *LM* curves shift.

    Let's look at the *IS* curve first. The money supply does not *directly* affect either the supply of or the demand for goods. In other words, M does not appear in the *IS* relation.

Money does not appear in the *IS* relation ▶ ⇔ Money does not shift the *IS* curve.

Money appears in the *LM* relation ⇔ ▶ Money shifts the *LM* curve.

Thus, a change in M does not shift the *IS* curve.

    Money enters the *LM* relation, however, so the *LM* curve shifts when the money supply changes. As we saw in Section 5.2, an increase in the money supply shifts the *LM* curve down, from *LM* to *LM'*: at a given level of income, an increase in money leads to a decrease in the interest rate.

- Step 2 is to see how these shifts affect the equilibrium. The monetary expansion shifts the *LM* curve. It does not shift the *IS* curve. The economy moves along the *IS* curve, and the

The increase in M shifts the *LM* curve ▶ down. It does not shift the *IS* curve. The economy moves along the *IS* curve.

equilibrium moves from point A to point A'. Output increases from Y to Y', and the interest rate decreases from i to i'.

- Step 3 is to say it in words. The increase in money leads to a lower interest rate. The lower interest rate leads to an increase in investment and, in turn, to an increase in demand and output.

    In contrast to the case of fiscal contraction, we can tell exactly what happens to the different components of demand after a monetary expansion. Because income is higher

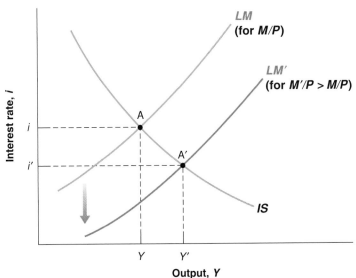

Figure 5.9

The effects of a monetary expansion

A monetary expansion leads to higher output and a lower interest rate.

FOCUS
Deficit reduction: good or bad for investment?

You may have heard the argument before: 'Private saving goes either towards financing the budget deficit or financing investment. It does not take a genius to conclude that reducing the budget deficit leaves more saving available for investment, so investment increases.'

This argument sounds simple and convincing. How do we reconcile it with what we just saw – that a deficit reduction may decrease rather than increase investment?

First go back to Chapter 3, equation (3.10). There we learned that we can also think of the goods market equilibrium condition as

$$Investment = Private\ saving + Public\ saving$$
$$I \quad = \quad S \quad + \quad (T - G)$$

In equilibrium, investment is equal to private saving plus public saving. If public saving is positive, the government is said to be running a budget surplus; if public saving is negative, the government is said to be running a budget deficit. So it is true that, given private saving, if the government reduces its deficit (either by increasing taxes or reducing government spending so that $T - G$ goes up) investment must go up: given S, $T - G$ going up implies that I goes up.

The crucial part of this statement, however, is 'given private saving'. The point is that a fiscal contraction affects private saving as well. The contraction leads to lower output and therefore to lower income. As consumption goes down by less than income, private saving also goes down. And it may go down by more than the reduction in the budget deficit, leading to a decrease rather than an increase in investment. In terms of the equation: if S decreases by more than $T - G$ increases, then I will decrease, not increase.

To sum up, a fiscal contraction may decrease investment. Or, looking at the reverse policy, a fiscal expansion – a decrease in taxes or an increase in spending – may actually increase investment.

and taxes are unchanged, disposable income goes up, and so does consumption. Because sales are higher and the interest rate is lower, investment also unambiguously goes up. So a monetary expansion is more investment friendly than a fiscal expansion.

Let's summarise:

- You should remember the three-step approach we have developed in this section (characterise the shifts, show the effect on the equilibrium, tell the story in words) to look at the effects of changes in policy on activity and the interest rate. We will use it throughout the book.
- Table 5.1 summarises what we have learned about the effects of fiscal and monetary policy. Use the same method to look at changes other than changes in policy. For example, trace the effects of a decrease in consumer confidence through its effect on consumption demand or, say, the introduction of new, more convenient credit cards through their effect on the demand for money.

Table 5.1 The effects of fiscal and monetary policy

	Shift of *IS*	Shift of *LM*	Movement in output	Movement in interest rate
Increase in taxes	Left	None	Down	Down
Decrease in taxes	Right	None	Up	Up
Increase in spending	Right	None	Up	Up
Decrease in spending	Left	None	Down	Down
Increase in money	None	Down	Up	Down
Decrease in money	None	Up	Down	Up

5.4 USING A POLICY MIX

We have looked so far at fiscal policy and monetary policy in isolation. Our purpose was to show how each worked. In practice, the two are often used together. The combination of monetary and fiscal policies is known as the **monetary–fiscal policy mix**, or simply the **policy mix**.

Sometimes, the right mix is to use fiscal and monetary policy in the same direction. This was the case, for example, during the recession of 2007–2010 in Europe and in the USA, as well as in many other countries, when both monetary and fiscal policies were used to fight the recession.

Make sure you can tell the story using the *IS–LM* diagram. Which curves shifted? What was the effect on the equilibrium?

Sometimes, the right mix is to use the two policies in opposite directions – for example, combining a fiscal contraction with a monetary expansion. This was the case in the early 1990s in the USA. When Bill Clinton was elected president in 1992, one of his priorities was to reduce the budget deficit using a combination of cuts in spending and increases in taxes. However, Clinton was worried, that, by itself, such a fiscal contraction would lead to a decrease in demand and trigger another recession. The right strategy was to combine a fiscal contraction (to get rid of the deficit) with a monetary expansion (to make sure that demand and output remained high). This was the strategy adopted and carried out by Bill Clinton (who was in charge of fiscal policy) and Alan Greenspan (who was in charge of monetary policy). The result of this strategy – and a bit of economic luck – was a steady reduction of the budget deficit (which turned into a budget surplus at the end of the 1990s) and a steady increase in output throughout the rest of the decade.

5.5 *IS–LM* AND THE LIQUIDITY TRAP

Let's now turn to the *IS–LM* model and see how it must be modified to take into account the liquidity trap.

When deriving the *LM* curve as shown in the two panels of Figure 5.4, we have shown that the *LM* curve gives, for a given real money stock, the relation between the interest rate and the level of income implied by equilibrium in financial markets. Figure 5.10(a) looks at

Figure 5.10

The derivation of the *LM* curve in the presence of a liquidity trap

For low levels of output, the *LM* curve is a flat segment, with an interest rate equal to zero. For higher levels of output, it is upward sloping: an increase in income leads to an increase in the interest rate.

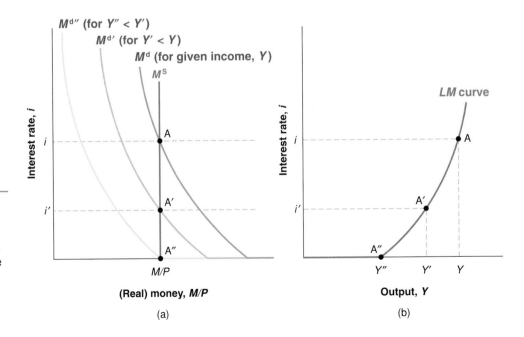

(a)

(b)

equilibrium in financial markets for a given value of the real money stock, M^s, and draws three money demand curves, each corresponding to a different level of income:

- M^d shows the demand for money for a given level of income, Y. The equilibrium is given by point A, with interest rate equal to i. This combination of income, Y, and interest rate, i, gives us the first point on the *LM* curve, point A in Figure 5.10(b).
- $M^{d'}$ shows the demand for money for a lower level of income, $Y' < Y$. Lower income means fewer transactions and, therefore, a lower demand for money at any interest rate. In this case, the equilibrium is given by point A′, with interest rate equal to i'. This combination of income, Y', and interest rate, i', gives us the second point on the *LM* curve, point A′ in Figure 5.10(b).
- $M^{d''}$ gives the demand for money for a still lower level of income, $Y'' < Y'$. In this case, the equilibrium is given by point A″ in Figure 5.10(a), with interest rate equal to zero. Point A″ in Figure 5.10(b) corresponds to A″ in Figure 5.10(a).

What happens if income decreases below Y'', shifting the demand for money further to the left in Figure 5.10(a)? The intersection between the money supply curve and the money demand curve takes place on the horizontal portion of the money demand curve. The equilibrium remains at A″, and the interest rate remains equal to zero.

Let's summarise: in the presence of a liquidity trap, the *LM* curve looks as drawn in Figure 5.10(b). For values of income greater than Y'', it is upward sloping – just as it was in Figure 5.4, when we first characterised the *LM* curve. For values of income less than Y'', it is flat at $i = 0$. Intuitively: the interest rate cannot go below zero.

Having derived the *LM* curve in the presence of a liquidity trap, we can look at the properties of the *IS–LM* model modified in this situation. Suppose the economy is initially at point A in Figure 5.11. Equilibrium is at point A, at the intersection of the *IS* curve and the *LM* curve, with output Y and interest rate i. And suppose that this level of output is far below the natural level of output, Y_n. The question is: can monetary policy help the economy return to Y_n?

Suppose the central bank increases the money supply, shifting the *LM* curve from *LM* to *LM′*. The equilibrium moves from point A down to point B. The interest rate decreases from i to zero, and output increases from Y to Y'. Thus, to this extent, expansionary monetary policy can indeed increase output.

What happens, however, if starting from point B, the central bank increases the money supply further, shifting the *LM* curve from *LM′* to, say, *LM″*? The intersection of *IS* and *LM″* remains at point B, and output remains equal to Y'. Expansionary monetary policy no longer has an effect on output.

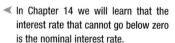
◄ In Chapter 14 we will learn that the interest rate that cannot go below zero is the nominal interest rate.

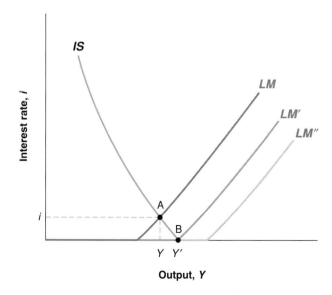

Figure 5.11

The *IS–LM* model and the liquidity trap

In the presence of a liquidity trap, there is a limit to how much monetary policy can increase output. Monetary policy may not be able to increase output back to its natural level.

In words: when the interest rate is equal to zero, the economy falls in a *liquidity trap*. The central bank can increase *liquidity* – that is, increase the money supply. But this *liquidity* falls into a *trap*: the additional money is willingly held by financial investors at an unchanged interest rate, namely zero. If, at this zero interest rate, the demand for goods is still too low, then there is nothing further monetary policy can do to increase output.

5.6 AN ANALYTICAL VERSION OF THE *IS–LM* MODEL*

In this section we present a formal version of the *IS–LM* model. We derive equations for the *IS* and *LM* curves, and use them to derive and discuss equilibrium in goods and financial markets as well as monetary and fiscal policy multipliers.

The *IS* curve

The *IS* curve graphically represents all the combinations of output and interest rate for which the goods market is in equilibrium, that is, the demand for goods equals the supply of goods. To derive explicitly the *IS* curve, we must choose a functional form for the relation [5.2] that we rewrite for convenience:

$$Y = C(Y - T) + I(Y, i) + G \qquad [5.4]$$

More precisely, we must choose a functional form for consumption, $C(Y - T)$, and for investment demand, $I(Y, i)$. For consumption we use the linear function used in Chapter 3:

$$C = c_0 + c_1(Y - T) \quad c_0 > 0, \, 0 < c_1 < 1 \qquad [5.5]$$

For investment we use a *linear* function of the type:

$$I = \bar{I} + d_1 Y - d_2 i \quad d_1, d_2 > 0 \qquad [5.6]$$

where $\bar{I}$ is the independent (or exogenous) component of investment, while d_1 and d_2 measure, respectively, the sensitivity of investment to income and to the interest rate.

According to equation (5.6), investment depends positively on the level of production and negatively on the interest rate. The positive relationship between investment and income is due to the fact that, faced with an increase in sales, companies increase production and then buy new machinery thereby increasing investment. The negative relationship between investment and the interest rate is determined by the fact that the higher the interest rate, the lower the incentive for a company to borrow to make new investment.

To derive the *IS* curve, just replace the consumption function (5.5) and the investment function (5.6) in equation (5.4):

$$Y = [c_0 + c_1(Y - T)] + \bar{I} + d_1 Y - d_2 i + G \qquad [5.7]$$

and solve this equation for Y in order to derive the equilibrium level of output as a function of the interest rate:

$$Y = \frac{1}{1 - c_1 - d_1} A - \frac{d_2}{1 - c_1 - d_1} i \qquad [5.8]$$

where $A = [c_0 + \bar{I} + G - c_1 T]$ is autonomous spending and $c_1 + d_1 < 1$ is the marginal propensity to spend (consumption *plus* investment). To represent the *IS* curve in a graph (Y, i), we rewrite equation (5.8) as:

$$i = \frac{1}{d_2} A - \frac{1 - c_1 - d_1}{d_2} Y \qquad [5.9]$$

Equation (5.9) is a straight line with intercept $(1/d_2)A$ and slope $-(1 - c_1 - d_1)/d_2$.

---

* This section is entirely optional.

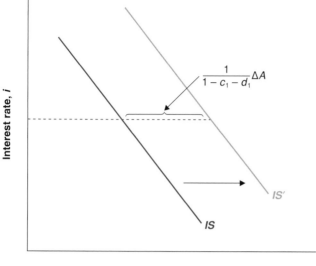

Figure 5.12

Shifts of the *IS* curve

An increase in autonomous spending by ΔA shifts the *IS* curve horizontally to the right by $1/(1 - c_1 - d_1)\Delta A$.

The position of the *IS* curve

The position of the *IS* curve is determined by the intercept $(1/d_2)A$, i.e. the level of the autonomous component of aggregate demand. This means that changes in autonomous spending cause *movements* of the *IS* curve. In other words, the *IS* moves when one of the following varies: (1) the exogenous component of consumption demand, Δc_0; (2) the autonomous investment spending, $\Delta \bar{I}$; (3) public spending, ΔG; or (4) taxes which, by changing the disposable income, change aggregate demand by $-c_1\Delta T$. Given equation (5.8), and *for a given interest rate*, i, a variation of ΔA in autonomous spending increases production by:

$$\Delta Y = \frac{1}{1 - c_1 - d_1}\Delta A \qquad [5.10]$$

In equation (5.10), the term $1/(1 - c_1 - d_1)$ is the multiplier of autonomous demand in the case that investment and not only consumption depends on income.

Graphically, as shown in Figure 5.12, a ΔA increase in autonomous spending moves the *IS* curve horizontally to the right, and the size of displacement is given by $1/(1 - c_1 - d_1)\Delta A$. Conversely, a reduction in autonomous spending by ΔA moves the *IS* curve horizontally to the left. It is important to note that following a change in autonomous demand only a shift in the *IS* curve occurs and not a movement along the curve itself. Furthermore, since changes in autonomous spending will not change the slope of the *IS* curve, the shift of the latter occurs parallel to itself.

Slope of the *IS* curve

At the beginning of this chapter we saw that the *IS* curve is downward sloping because a higher interest rate reduces investment and consumption and thus the equilibrium level of output. But what determines the slope of the IS curve? Intuitively, the slope of the curve depends on the extent to which the equilibrium level of production varies following a change in the interest rate. If, following a small change in the interest rate, production has to change much to restore equilibrium in the goods market, the *IS* curve will be slightly sloped. This result is illustrated in Figure 5.13.

To give a more rigorous answer to our question, we can use equation (5.8). *Given A*, a Δi change in the interest rate changes income by:

$$\Delta Y = -\frac{d_2}{1 - c_1 - d_1}\Delta i \qquad [5.11]$$

The larger d_2 – the sensitivity of investment demand to the interest rate – the greater ΔY. Graphically, if d_2 is high and the multiplier is large, the *IS* curve is flat, and the greater the

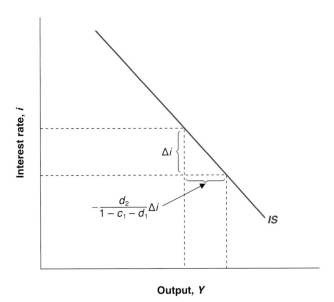

Figure 5.13

Movements along the *IS* curve

The *IS* curve is flat if, following a small change in the interest rate, output has to change a lot to restore equilibrium in the goods market, that is if $d_2/(1 - c_1 - d_1)$ is high.

response of output to changes in the interest rate. Conversely, if d_2 is small and the multiplier is low, the *IS* curve will have a greater slope. Similarly, the variation of Y is large if c_1 and d_1 are high, that is to say the multiplier $1/(1 - c_1 - d_1)$ is large. From an economic point of view, the greater the sensitivity of investment to the interest rate $- d_2$ is high $-$ the greater will be the direct effect of the interest rate on demand. This direct effect is then amplified through the multiplier. The total effect of a change in the interest rate on production depends, therefore, on the sensitivity of investment to the interest rate and on the demand multiplier.

The *LM* curve

Graphically the *LM* curve represents all the combinations of output and interest rate for which the money market is in equilibrium, i.e. the demand for money equals the supply of money (or demand for bonds equals the supply of bonds). To develop the analytical version of the *LM* curve we have to choose a functional form for equation (5.3) which we rewrite for convenience:

$$\frac{M}{P} = L(Y, i) \qquad [5.12]$$

Similarly to the derivation of the *IS* curve, we consider the following *linear* relationship between money, output and the interest rate:

$$\frac{M}{P} = f_1 Y - f_2 i \qquad f_1, f_2 > 0 \qquad [5.13]$$

In equation (5.13), parameters f_1 and f_2 measure, respectively, the response of demand for (real) money to changes in income and interest rate. An increase in income raises the demand for money; an increase in the interest rate decreases the demand for money. Solving for Y, we derive the equilibrium level of Y as a function of i:

$$Y = \frac{1}{f_1} \frac{M}{P} + \frac{f_2}{f_1} i \qquad [5.14]$$

This equation, with intercept $(1/f_1)(M/P)$ and slope f_2/f_1, is the *LM* curve in the space (Y, i).

The position of the *LM* curve

The position of the *LM* curve depends on the intercept $(1/f_1)(M/P)$, that is on the real money supply. What happens if the central bank varies the nominal supply of money ΔM?

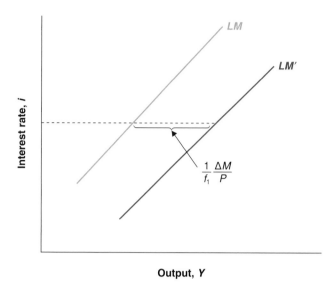

Figure 5.14

Shifts of the *LM* curve

An increase in the nominal money supply by ΔM shifts the *LM* curve horizontally to the right by $(1/f_1)\Delta M/P$.

Given the assumption of constant prices, real money supply will also change by $\Delta M/P$. So, according to equation (5.14), and *for a given interest rate i*, the change in M/P will change production by:

$$\Delta Y = \frac{1}{f_1} \frac{\Delta M}{P} \qquad [5.15]$$

In other words, if the nominal money supply increases by ΔM, the *LM* curve *moves horizontally to the right* by $(1/f_1) \Delta M/P$ (see Figure 5.14). Indeed, for a given interest rate, the level of income must increase in order to raise the demand for money to the new (increased) level of money supply. Conversely, if the nominal money supply decreases by ΔM, the *LM* curve *moves horizontally to the left*. Notice that the lower the sensitivity of money demand to income – f_1 is small – the larger must be the change in income for any given change in M. The reason is simple. If f_1 is small, the response of money demand to a change in income is low. Then income must grow enough to increase the demand for money and balance the money market.

Slope of the *LM* curve

Now consider the slope of the *LM* curve. Figure 5.15 shows that when the *LM* curve is flat, a small change in the interest rate implies that output must grow enough to restore

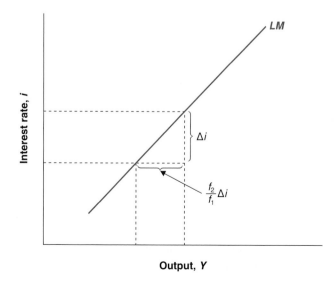

Figure 5.15

Movements along the *LM* curve

The *LM* curve is flat if, following a small change in the interest rate, output has to increase a lot to restore equilibrium in the money market, that is if f_2/f_1 is high.

equilibrium in the money market. According to equation (5.14), the relationship between the change in output and the change in the interest rate is given by:

$$\Delta Y = \frac{f_2}{f_1} \Delta i \qquad [5.16]$$

Therefore the total effect of a change in the interest rate on output depends on the ratio f_2/f_1. If this ratio is high, the curve will flatten. For example, if the demand for money is very sensitive to the interest rate – f_2 is high – a small increase in the interest rate is sufficient to cause a sharp drop in demand for money. In turn, if the demand for money is not very sensitive to changes in income – f_1 is small – production must increase enough to ensure sufficient growth in demand for money necessary to balance the money market.

Equilibrium

In Section 5.3 we said that the simultaneous equilibrium in goods and financial markets is represented by the intersection of *IS* and *LM* curves (see Figure 5.7). The intersection corresponds to the unique combination of production and interest rate that ensures equilibrium in *both* markets. To compute the values of Y and i we have to jointly solve the equations *IS* and *LM*, which we rewrite for convenience:

$$Y = [c_0 + c_1(Y - T)] + [\bar{I} + d_1Y - d_2i] + G \qquad [5.7]$$

$$\frac{M}{P} = f_1Y - f_2i \qquad [5.13]$$

In practice, we have to solve for the interest rate in equation (5.13) and replace it in equation (5.7) in order to derive the equilibrium value of output:

$$Y = \frac{1}{(1 - c_1 - d_1)\dfrac{f_2}{d_2} + f_1} \frac{M}{P} + \frac{1}{(1 - c_1 - d_1) + d_2\dfrac{f_1}{f_2}} A \qquad [5.17]$$

Subsequently, to calculate the equilibrium value of the interest rate we should replace the equilibrium value of Y in equation (5.13), which is the *LM* curve:

$$i = -\frac{1}{f_2 + \dfrac{d_2f_1}{1 - c_1 - d_1}} \frac{M}{P} + \frac{1}{(1 - c_1 - d_1)\dfrac{f_2}{f_1} + d_2} A \qquad [5.18]$$

Both equations show that:

- Both Y and i are *functions of exogenous variables*: the real money supply M/P and autonomous spending A. An increase in autonomous spending increases both production and the interest rate. Instead, an increase in real money supply raises output, but decreases the interest rate.
- Both Y and i are linear functions of exogenous variables. This result derives from the assumption of linearity of *IS* and *LM* functions.
- The coefficients of money supply and autonomous spending are complex functions of all the parameters that appear in the *IS* and *LM* equations. These expressions are the result of the interaction between the goods market and the money market and allow us to derive the so-called multiplier of fiscal policy and monetary policy.

Fiscal policy multiplier

From equations (5.17) and (5.18) we can calculate the effect on the equilibrium levels of income and interest rate of a change in autonomous spending, where the real money supply is given:

$$\Delta Y = \frac{1}{(1 - c_1 - d_1) + d_2 \dfrac{f_1}{f_2}} \Delta A \qquad [5.19]$$

$$\Delta i = \frac{1}{(1 - c_1 - d_1)\dfrac{f_2}{f_1} + d_2} \Delta A \qquad [5.20]$$

Since we assumed that $c_1 + d_1 < 1$, the effect on output and the interest rate of an increase in autonomous spending is unambiguously positive. An increase in autonomous spending moves the *IS* curve up and to the right, along the *LM* curve, causing an increase in both the interest rate and production.

If we use equation (5.19) and divide ΔY for ΔA, we obtain the **fiscal policy multiplier**

$$\frac{\Delta Y}{\Delta A} = \frac{1}{(1 - c_1 - d_1) + d_2 \dfrac{f_1}{f_2}} \qquad [5.21]$$

that measures how much the equilibrium level of output changes following a change in autonomous spending. It should be noted that the fiscal policy multiplier resembles the demand multiplier $1/(1 - c_1 - d_1)$. However the latter was obtained by looking only at the goods market, while the fiscal policy multiplier has been obtained taking into account the interactions between the goods market and the money market. The fiscal policy multiplier allows us to make the following observations:

- The higher is the demand multiplier, that is, the smaller $(1 - c_1 - d_1)$, the greater ΔY, given the other parameters. A high value of $1/(1 - c_1 - d_1)$ has a stronger multiplicative effect on demand and thus on ΔY. In turn, the stronger the response of production to an increase in autonomous spending, the greater the effect of income on the demand for money and the greater will be the increase in the interest rate to restore equilibrium in the money market (see equation (5.19)).
- The response of Y to A is strong if d_2 and f_1 are small and f_2 is big. Although the sensitivity of investment demand to interest rate is relatively low – d_2 is small – the negative effect of a higher interest rate on investment demand is limited. Therefore it is the lower crowding out effect in the interest rate that compensates, although only partially, for the positive effect of an increase of A on Y. Also, if the sensitivity of money demand to income is low – f_1 is small – the demand for money grows to a limited extent with increasing production. Consequently, the increase in the interest rate needed to reduce money demand is small and so is the crowding out effect on investment. Finally, if the demand for money is very sensitive to the interest rate – f_2 is high – just a small adjustment of the interest rate is needed to restore equilibrium in the money market.

It should be noted, confirming what we have said, that calculating $\Delta i/\Delta A$:

$$\frac{\Delta i}{\Delta A} = \frac{1}{(1 - c_1 - d_1)\dfrac{f_2}{f_1} + d_2} \qquad [5.22]$$

the interest rate varies little when f_2 is large and/or f_1 is small. Also, if d_2 is high, the change in the interest rate for any given change in A will be lower.

Monetary policy multiplier

Consider now what happens to Y and i when the real money supply changes. From equation (5.15), we can calculate the size of Δi following a change in $\Delta M/P$ for a given level of A:

$$\frac{\Delta i}{\Delta M/P} = -\frac{1}{f_2 + \dfrac{d_2 f_1}{1 - c_1 - d_1}} \qquad [5.23]$$

Moreover, from equation (5.14), we can calculate the **monetary policy multiplier**, namely the response of production *to a change in the money supply*:

$$\frac{\Delta Y}{\Delta M/P} = -\frac{1}{(1 - c_1 - d_1)\frac{f_2}{d_2} + f_1} \qquad [5.24]$$

Notice that in both cases, changes in Y and i depend on $(1 - c_1 - d_1), f_1, f_2$ and d_2. We leave it up to you to figure out the interpretation of equations (5.23) and (5.24) following a change in these parameters.

5.7 HOW DOES THE *IS–LM* MODEL FIT THE FACTS?

We have so far ignored dynamics. For example, when looking at the effects of an increase in taxes in Figure 5.7 – or the effects of a monetary expansion in Figure 5.8 – we made it look as if the economy moved instantaneously from A to A′ and as if output went instantaneously from Y to $Y′$. This is clearly not realistic: the adjustment of output clearly takes time. To capture this time dimension, we need to reintroduce dynamics.

Introducing dynamics formally would be difficult but, as we did in Chapter 3, we can describe the basic mechanisms in words. Some of the mechanisms will be familiar from Chapter 3, and some are new:

- Consumers are likely to take some time to adjust their consumption following a change in disposable income.
- Firms are likely to take some time to adjust investment spending following a change in their sales.
- Firms are likely to take some time to adjust investment spending following a change in the interest rate.
- Firms are likely to take some time to adjust production following a change in their sales.

So, with an increase in taxes, it takes some time for consumption to respond to the decrease in disposable income, some more time for production to decrease in response to the decrease in consumption, yet more time for investment to decrease in response to lower sales, for consumption to decrease in response to the decrease in income and so on.

> The size of a change in the interest rate is equal to a typical monetary policy shock in the two areas under consideration, measured as one standard deviation (equal to 30 basis points in the euro area and 45 basis points in the USA).

With a monetary expansion, it takes some time for investment to respond to the decrease in the interest rate, some more time for production to increase in response to the increase in demand, yet more time for consumption and investment to increase in response to the induced change in output and so on.

Describing precisely the adjustment process implied by all these sources of dynamics is obviously complicated, but the basic implication is straightforward: time is needed for output to adjust to changes in fiscal and monetary policy. How much time? This question can only be answered by looking at the data and using econometrics. Figure 5.16 shows the results of such an econometric study, which uses data for the euro area and the USA from 1980 to 1998. The study compares the effects of an increase in the interest rate in the euro area and in the USA. It describes the typical effects of such an increase on macroeconomic variables.

> There is no such thing in econometrics as learning the exact value of a coefficient or the exact effect of one variable on another. Rather, what econometrics does is to provide a best estimate – here, the purple line – and a measure of confidence we can have in the estimate – here, the confidence band.

Each box in Figure 5.16 represents the effects of a change in the interest rate on a given variable. Each box contains three lines. The purple line at the centre represents the best estimate of the effect of a change in the interest rate on the variable considered in that frame. The green and blue lines and the space between them represent a confidence interval, an interval within which the true value lies with a probability of 90%.

- Figure 5.16 (a) shows the effects of an increase in the interest rate, respectively on production and prices in the euro area (the last box at the bottom shows the evolution of the interest rate itself). The percentage change of variables is shown on the vertical axis and the time, measured in quarters, is shown on the horizontal axis.

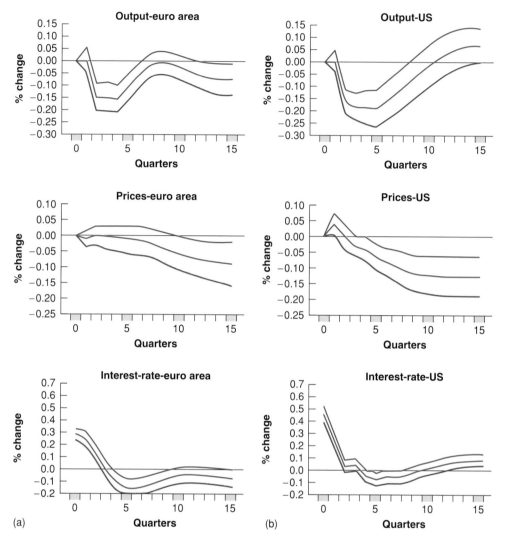

Figure 5.16

The empirical effects of an increase in the interest rate in (a) the euro area and (b) the USA

In the short run, an increase in the interest rate leads to a decrease in output and to an increase in unemployment, but it also has little effect on the price level.

Source: G. Peersman and F. Smets, *The Monetary Transmission Mechanism in the Euro Area: More Evidence from Var Analysis*, European Central Bank, working paper No. 91, December 2001.

Looking the best estimate – the purple line – we can see that increasing the interest rate leads to a reduction in output. In the euro area, the greatest decline in production is reached in the second and third quarters after the increase in the interest rate, compared to five quarters in the USA.

The second panel from top shows the evolution of the price level. Remember that one of the assumptions of the *IS–LM* model is that the price level is given, and thus does not vary with changes in demand. The figure shows that this assumption is not a bad representation of reality in the short term. In the euro area the price level remains almost unchanged approximately for the first five quarters (compared to two quarters in the USA). It is only after the first five quarters that the price level begins to decline. This suggests that the *IS–LM* model becomes less reliable when we look at the medium term: in the medium term we can no longer assume that the price level is given, and changes in prices become significant.

Comparing the euro area and the USA we observe that prices react more rapidly in the USA, although the size of the responses are the same.

Figure 5.16 illustrates two important lessons:

1. It gives us a sense of the dynamics of adjustment in output and other variables in response to monetary policy.
2. It shows that what we observe in the economy is consistent with the implications of the *IS–LM* model. This does not prove that that model is the right model. It could also be that

what we observe is the result of a completely different mechanism, and that the fact that the *IS–LM* model works well is just a coincidence, but this seems unlikely.

The *IS–LM* model seems to be a good starting point for the analysis of economic trends in the short term. In the following chapter we will extend the model, considering the effects of openness on goods and financial markets (Chapter 6). Then we will see what determines output in the medium and long run.

SUMMARY

- The *IS–LM* model characterises the implications of equilibrium in both the goods and financial markets.

- The *IS* relation and the *IS* curve show the combinations of the interest rate and the level of output that are consistent with equilibrium in the goods market. An increase in the interest rate leads to a decline in output. Consequently, the *IS* curve is downward-sloping.

- The *LM* relation and the *LM* curve show the combinations of the interest rate and the level of output consistent with equilibrium in financial markets. Given the real money supply, an increase in output leads to an increase in the interest rate. Consequently, the *LM* curve is upward-sloping.

- A fiscal expansion shifts the *IS* curve to the right, leading to an increase in output and an increase in the interest rate. A fiscal contraction shifts the *IS* curve to the left, leading to a decrease in output and a decrease in the interest rate.

- A monetary expansion shifts the *LM* curve down, leading to an increase in output and a decrease in the interest rate. A monetary contraction shifts the *LM* curve up, leading to a decrease in output and an increase in the interest rate.

- The combination of monetary and fiscal policies is known as the monetary–fiscal policy mix, or simply the policy mix. Sometimes monetary and fiscal policy are used in the same direction. Sometimes, they are used in opposite directions. Fiscal contraction and monetary expansion can, for example, achieve a decrease in the budget deficit while avoiding a decrease in output.

- The *IS–LM* model appears to describe well the behaviour of the economy in the short run. In particular, the effects of monetary policy appear to be similar to those implied by the *IS–LM* model once dynamics is introduced in the model. An increase in the interest rate due to a monetary contraction leads to a steady decrease in output, with the maximum effect taking place after about two quarters in the euro area and after about five quarters in the USA.

KEY TERMS

IS curve 84

LM curve 86

interest rate rule 87

fiscal contraction, fiscal consolidation 89

fiscal expansion 89

monetary expansion 92

monetary contraction, monetary tightening 92

monetary–fiscal policy mix, policy mix 94

fiscal policy multiplier 101

monetary policy multiplier 102

QUESTIONS AND PROBLEMS

QUICK CHECK

1. *Using the information in this chapter, label each of the following statements true, false or uncertain. Explain briefly.*

a. The main determinants of investment are the level of sales and the interest rate.

b. If all the exogenous variables in the *IS* relation are constant, then a higher level of output can be achieved only by lowering the interest rate.

c. The *IS* curve is downward-sloping because goods market equilibrium implies that an increase in taxes leads to a lower level of output.

d. If government spending and taxes increase by the same amount, the *IS* curve does not shift.

e. The *LM* curve is upward-sloping because a higher level of the money supply is needed to increase output.

f. An increase in government spending leads to a decrease in investment.

g. Government policy can increase output without changing the interest rate only if both monetary and fiscal policy variables change.

2. *Consider first the goods market model with constant investment that we saw in Chapter 3. Consumption is given by*

$$C = c_0 + c_1(Y - T)$$

and I, G and T are given.

a. Solve for equilibrium output. What is the value of the multiplier?

Now let investment depend on both sales and the interest rate:

$$I = b_0 + b_1 Y - b_2 i$$

b. Solve for equilibrium output. At a given interest rate, is the effect of a change in autonomous spending bigger than what it was in part (a)? Why? (Assume $c_1 + b_1 < 1$.)

Next, write the LM relation as

$$M/P = d_1 Y - d_2 i$$

c. Solve for equilibrium output. (*Hint*: Eliminate the interest rate from the *IS* and *LM* relations.) Derive the multiplier (the effect of a change of one unit in autonomous spending on output).

d. Is the multiplier you obtained in part (c) smaller or larger than the multiplier you derived in part (a)? Explain how your answer depends on the parameters in the behavioural equations for consumption, investment and money demand.

3. The response of investment to fiscal policy

a. Using the *IS–LM* diagram, show the effects on output and the interest rate of a decrease in government spending. Can you tell what happens to investment? Why?

Now consider the following IS–LM model:

$$C = c_0 + c_1(Y - T)$$
$$I = b_0 + b_1 Y - b_2 i$$
$$M/P = d_1 Y - d_2 i$$

b. Solve for equilibrium output. Assume $c_1 + b_1 < 1$. (*Hint*: You may want to work through problem 2 if you are having trouble with this step.)

c. Solve for the equilibrium interest rate. (*Hint*: Use the *LM* relation.)

d. Solve for investment.

e. Under what conditions on the parameters of the model (i.e., c_0, c_1, and so on) will investment increase when G decreases? (*Hint*: If G decreases by one unit, by how much does I increase? Be careful; you want the change in I to be positive when the change in G is negative.)

f. Explain the condition you derived in part (e).

4. *Consider the following IS–LM model:*

$$C = 400 + 0.25Y_D$$
$$I = 300 + 0.25Y - 1500i$$
$$G = 600$$
$$T = 400$$
$$(M/P)^d = 2Y - 12\,000i$$
$$M/P = 3000$$

a. Derive the *IS* relation. (*Hint*: You want an equation with Y on the left side and everything else on the right.)

b. Derive the *LM* relation. (*Hint*: It will be convenient for later use to rewrite this equation with i on the left side and everything else on the right.)

c. Solve for equilibrium real output. (*Hint*: Substitute the expression for the interest rate given by the *LM* equation into the *IS* equation and solve for output.)

d. Solve for the equilibrium interest rate. (*Hint*: Substitute the value you obtained for Y in part (c) into either the *IS* or *LM* equations and solve for i. If your algebra is correct, you should get the same answer from both equations.)

e. Solve for the equilibrium values of C and I, and verify the value you obtained for Y by adding C, I and G.

f. Now suppose that the money supply increases to $M/P = 4320$. Solve for Y, i, C and I, and describe in words the effects of an expansionary monetary policy.

g. Set M/P equal to its initial value of 1600. Now suppose that government spending increases to $G = 840$. Summarise the effects of an expansionary fiscal policy on Y, i and C.

DIG DEEPER

5. Investment and the interest rate

The chapter argues that investment depends negatively on the interest rate because an increase in the cost of borrowing discourages investment. However, firms often finance their investment projects using their own funds.

If a firm is considering using its own funds (rather than borrowing) to finance investment projects, will higher interest rates discourage the firm from undertaking these projects? Explain.

(*Hint: Think of yourself as the owner of a firm that has earned profits and imagine that you are going to use the profits either to finance new investment projects or to buy bonds. Will your decision to invest in new projects in your firm be affected by the interest rate?*)

6. The liquidity trap

a. Suppose the interest rate on bonds is negative. Will people want to hold bonds or to hold money? Explain.

b. Draw the demand for money as a function of the interest rate for a given level of real income. How does your answer to part (a) affect your answer? (*Hint*: Show that the demand for money becomes very flat as the interest rate gets very close to zero.)

c. Derive the *LM* curve. What happens to the *LM* curve as the interest rate gets very close to zero? (*Hint*: It becomes very flat.)

d. Consider your *LM* curve. Suppose that the interest rate is very close to zero, and the central bank increases the supply of money. What happens to the interest rate at a given level of income?

e. Can an expansionary monetary policy increase output when the interest rate is already very close to zero?

The inability of the central bank to reduce the interest rate when it is already very close to zero is known as the liquidity trap and was first mentioned by Keynes in 1936 in his General Theory – which laid the foundations of the IS–LM model.

7. Policy mixes

Suggest a policy mix to achieve each of the following objectives.

a. Increase *Y* while keeping *i* constant.

b. Decrease the fiscal deficit while keeping *Y* constant. What happens to *i*? to investment?

8. The (less paradoxical) paradox of saving

A chapter problem at the end of Chapter 3 considered the effect of a drop in consumer confidence on private saving and investment, when investment depended on output but not the interest rate. Here, we consider the same experiment in the context of the IS–LM framework, in which investment depends on the interest rate and output.

a. Suppose households attempt to save more, so that consumer confidence falls. In an *IS–LM* diagram, show the effect of the fall in consumer confidence on output and the interest rate.

b. How will the fall in consumer confidence affect consumption, investment and private saving? Will the attempt to save more necessarily lead to more saving? Will this attempt necessarily lead to less saving?

EXPLORE FURTHER

9. Consumption, investment and the recession of 2007–2010

*This question asks you to examine the movements of investment and consumption before, during and after the recession of 2007–2010. Go to the Eurostat website (**http://epp.eurostat.ec.europa.eu/portal/page/portal/eurostat/home/**). Find the data on the percentage change in real GDP and its components and on the contribution of the components of GDP to the overall percentage change in GDP. Investment is more variable than consumption, but consumption is much bigger than investment, so smaller percentage changes in consumption can have the same impact on GDP as much larger percentage changes in investment. Note that the quarterly percentage changes are annualised (i.e. expressed as annual rates). Get quarterly data on real GDP, consumption, gross private domestic investment and non-residential fixed investment for the years 2005–2010.*

a. Identify the quarters of negative growth in 2009 and 2010.

b. Track consumption and investment around 2009 and 2010. Which variable had the bigger percentage change around this time? Compare non-residential fixed investment with overall investment. Which variable had the bigger percentage change?

c. Get the contribution to GDP growth of consumption and investment for 2008–2010. Calculate the average of the quarterly contributions for each variable for each year. Now calculate the change in the contribution of each variable for 2009 and 2010 (i.e., subtract the average contribution of consumption in 2009 from the average contribution of consumption in 2010, subtract the average contribution of consumption in 2009 from the average contribution of consumption in 2010, and do the same for investment for both years). Which variable had the bigger fall in contribution to growth? What do you think was the proximate cause of the recession of 2007–2010? (Was it a fall in investment demand or a fall in consumption demand?)

We invite you to visit the Blanchard page on the Prentice Hall website, at **www.prenhall.com/blanchard** for this chapter's World Wide Web exercises.

FURTHER READING

- A description of the US economy, from the period of 'irrational exuberance' to the 2001 recession and the role of fiscal and monetary policy is given by **Paul Krugman, in** *The Great Unraveling*, **W.W. Norton, New York, 2003.** (Warning: Krugman does not like the Bush administration or its policies!)

Chapter 6

THE *IS–LM* MODEL IN AN OPEN ECONOMY

We have assumed until now that the economy was *closed* – that it did not interact with the rest of the world. We started this way to keep things simple and build up your intuition for the basic macroeconomic mechanisms. In fact, most economies, and most European economies in particular, are very *open* – they trade both goods and assets with the rest of the world (and also, actually mostly, with each other).

'Openness' has three distinct dimensions:

1. **Openness in goods markets** – The ability of consumers and firms to choose between domestic goods and foreign goods.

2. **Openness in financial markets** – The ability of financial investors to choose between domestic assets and foreign assets.

3. **Openness in factor markets** – The ability of firms to choose where to locate production, and of workers to choose where to work.

The EU is the biggest ever common market among sovereign countries, with 27 member states. Within the EU, goods, services and factors are free to circulate without **tariffs** or impediments. Since the Schengen Agreement in 1995, citizens from any member states can freely circulate inside the EU.

However, in most other countries the choice between domestic and foreign goods is not completely free of restrictions: even the countries with the strongest commitment to free trade have tariffs – taxes on imported goods – and **quotas** – restrictions on the quantity of goods that can be imported – on at least some foreign goods. At the same time, in most countries, average tariffs are low and getting lower.

In financial markets, openness is much higher than in goods markets. Most world financial markets are closely integrated, although some countries still forbid the free movement of financial assets. China for example prohibits its citizens from buying foreign financial assets.

Factors markets are also increasingly integrated. Multinational companies operate plants in many countries and move their operations around the world to take advantage of lower production costs. Much of the debate about the accession to the EU of countries in central and Eastern Europe centred on the extent to which this would induce European firms to relocate abroad. And immigration from low-wage countries is a hot political issue in France, Germany and Italy.

In this chapter, we study the main macroeconomic implications of openness in goods and financial markets. This chapter has five sections:

● Section 6.1 looks at openness in goods markets, the determinants of the choice between domestic goods and foreign goods and the role of the real exchange rate.

● Section 6.2 looks at openness in financial markets, the determinants of the choice between domestic goods and foreign goods and the role of the real exchange rate.

● Section 6.3 characterises equilibrium in the goods market for an open economy.

● Section 6.4 looks at equilibrium in financial markets, including the foreign exchange market.

● Section 6.5 puts the two equilibrium conditions together and looks at the determination of output, the interest rate and the exchange rate.

6.1 OPENNESS IN GOODS MARKETS

Let's start by looking at how much an open economy, such as the UK, sells to and buys from the rest of the world. Then we will be better able to think about the choice between domestic goods and foreign goods and the role of the relative price of domestic goods in terms of foreign goods – the real exchange rate.

Exports and imports

Figure 6.1 plots the evolution of UK exports and UK imports, as ratios to GDP, since 1960. ('UK exports' means exports *from* the UK; 'UK imports' means imports *into* the UK.) The figure suggests two main conclusions:

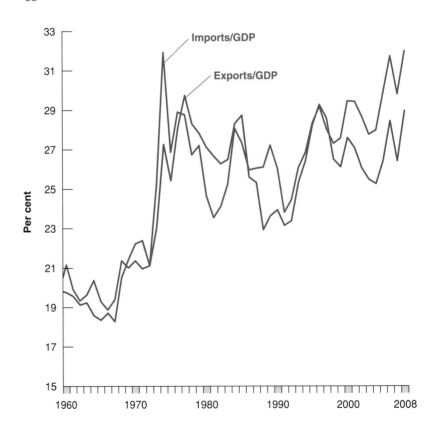

Figure 6.1

UK exports and imports as ratios of GDP since 1960

Since 1948, exports and imports have increased by around 10 percentage points in relation to GDP.

Source: UK Office for National Statistics.

- The UK economy has become more open over time. Exports and imports, which were around 20% of GDP in 1960 are now equal to about 30% of GDP (29% for exports, 32% for imports). In other words, the UK trades much more (relative to its GDP) with the rest of the world than it did just 50 years ago. Notice the large increase in both exports and imports in the early 1970s, which corresponds to the time the UK joined the European Union.

  ◄ From Chapter 3: the trade balance is the difference between exports and imports. If exports exceed imports, there is a trade surplus (equivalently, a positive trade balance). If imports exceed exports, there is a trade deficit (equivalently, a negative trade balance).

- Although imports and exports have broadly followed the same upward trend, they have also diverged for long periods of time, generating sustained trade surpluses and trade deficits. Three episodes stand out:
  - The large surplus in the early 1980s – The ratio of the trade surplus to GDP reached 3.1% in 1981.
  - The large trade deficits at the end of the 1980s – The ratio of the trade deficit to GDP reached 3.6% in 1989 and then decreased to less than 1% in the early 1990s.
  - The large and increasing trade deficits since the mid-1990s – The ratio of the trade deficit to GDP reached 3.4% in 2005 and remained relatively high in the following years.

Understanding the sources and implications of these trade imbalances (especially the case of trade deficits) is a central issue in macroeconomics today, and one to which we shall return later.

Given all the talk in the media about *globalisation*, a volume of trade (measured by the average of the ratios of exports and imports to GDP) around 30% of GDP might strike you as small. However, the volume of trade is not necessarily a good measure of openness. Many firms are exposed to foreign competition but, by being competitive and keeping their prices low enough, these firms are able to retain their domestic market share and limit imports. This suggests that a better index of openness than export or import ratios is the proportion of aggregate output composed of **tradable goods** – goods that compete with foreign goods in either domestic markets or foreign markets.

◄ • Tradable goods: cars, computers, and so on.
• Non-tradable goods: housing, most medical services, haircuts, restaurants, and so on.

With exports around 26% of GDP, it is true that the UK has one of the smallest ratios of exports to GDP among the rich countries of the world. Table 6.1 gives ratios for a number of OECD countries.

The USA is at the low end of the range of export ratios, with 12%, followed by Japan with 18%. In Europe, most of the largest economies have export ratios around 50%, including Germany, Switzerland, Denmark, Finland, Norway and Sweden. In this picture, the UK stands out as having the smallest export ratio within Europe. Finally, the smaller European countries have the highest ratios (89% in Belgium, 79% in Ireland and 75% in the Netherlands). (Belgium's 89% ratio of exports to GDP raises an odd possibility: can a country have exports larger than its GDP? In other words, can a country have an export ratio greater than 1? The answer is yes. The reason is given in the Focus box 'Can exports exceed GDP?')

Do these numbers indicate that the UK has more trade barriers than, say, Germany or Belgium? No. The main factors behind these differences are geography and size. Distance from other markets explains a good part of the low Japanese ratio. Size also matters: the smaller the country, the more it must specialise in producing and exporting only a few

◄ Iceland is both isolated and small. What would you expect its export ratio to be? (Answer: 44% in 2008.)

Table 6.1 Ratios of exports to GDP for selected OECD countries, 2007

Country	Export ratio (%)	Country	Export ratio (%)
Belgium	89	Netherlands	75
Denmark	52	Norway	46
Finland	46	Sweden	53
Germany	47	Switzerland	56
Ireland	79	UK	26
Japan	18	USA	12

Source: OECD *Economic Outlook* database.

products and rely on imports for other products. Belgium can hardly afford to produce the range of goods produced by Germany, a country roughly seven times bigger.

The choice between domestic goods and foreign goods

How does openness in goods markets force us to rethink the way we look at equilibrium in the *goods market*?

In a closed economy, people face one ➤ decision:

● Save or buy (consume).

In an open economy, they face two decisions:

● Save or buy.
● Buy domestic or buy foreign.

Until now, when we were thinking about consumers' decisions in the goods market we focused on their decision to save or to consume. When goods markets are open, domestic consumers face a second decision: whether to buy domestic goods or to buy foreign goods. Indeed, all buyers – including domestic and foreign firms and governments – face a similar decision. This decision has a direct effect on domestic output: if buyers decide to buy more domestic goods, the demand for domestic goods increases, and so does domestic output. If they decide to buy more foreign goods, then foreign output increases instead of domestic output.

FOCUS
Can exports exceed GDP?

Can a country have exports larger than its GDP – that is, can it have an export ratio greater than 1?

It would seem that the answer must be no: a country cannot export more than it produces, so the export ratio must be less than 1. Not so. The key to the answer is to realise that exports and imports may include exports and imports of intermediate goods.

Take, for example, a country that imports intermediate goods for €1 billion. Suppose it then transforms them into final goods using only labour. Say labour is paid €200 million and that there are no profits. The value of these final goods is thus equal to €1200 million. Assume that €1 billion worth of final goods is exported and the rest, €200 million, is consumed domestically.

Exports and imports therefore both equal €1 billion. What is GDP in this economy? Remember that GDP is value added in the economy (see Chapter 2). So, in this example, GDP equals €200 million, and the ratio of exports to GDP equals €1000/€200 = 5.

Hence, exports can exceed GDP. This is actually the case for a number of small countries where most economic activity is organised around a harbour and import–export activities, such as the Netherlands, where the ratio of exports to GDP in 2008 was 75%. This is even the case for small countries such as Malaysia, where the ratio of exports to GDP exceeded 100%. In 2007, the ratio of exports to GDP in Singapore was 229%!

Central to the decision of whether to buy domestic goods or foreign goods is the price of domestic goods relative to foreign goods. We call this relative price the **real exchange rate**. The real exchange rate is not directly observable, and you will not find it in newspapers. What you will find in newspapers are *nominal exchange rates*, the relative prices of currencies. We start by looking at nominal exchange rates and then see how we can use them to construct real exchange rates.

Nominal exchange rates

Nominal exchange rates between two currencies can be quoted in one of two ways:

● As the price of the domestic currency in terms of the foreign currency – If, for example, we look at the UK and the euro area and think of the pound as the domestic currency and the euro as the foreign currency, we can express the nominal exchange rate as the price of a pound in terms of euros. In June 2009, the exchange rate defined this way was 1.15. In other words, £1 was worth €1.15.

● As the price of the foreign currency in terms of the domestic currency – Continuing with the same example, we can express the nominal exchange rate as the price of a euro in terms of pounds. In June 2009, the exchange rate defined this way was 0.86. In other words, €1 was worth £0.86.

Either definition is fine; the important thing is to remain consistent. In this book, we adopt the first definition: we define the **nominal exchange rate** as *the price of the domestic currency in terms of foreign currency* and denote it by *E*. When looking, for example, at the exchange rate between the UK and the euro area (from the viewpoint of the UK, so the pound is the domestic currency), *E* denotes the price of a pound in terms of euros (so, for example, *E* was 1.15 in June 2009).

Exchange rates between most foreign currencies change every day and every minute of the day. These changes are called *nominal appreciations* or *nominal depreciations* – *appreciations* or *depreciations* for short:

● An **appreciation** of the domestic currency is an increase in the price of the domestic currency in terms of a foreign currency. Given our definition of the exchange rate, an appreciation corresponds to an *increase* in the exchange rate.

● A **depreciation** of the domestic currency is a decrease in the price of the domestic currency in terms of a foreign currency. So, given our definition of the exchange rate, a depreciation of the domestic currency corresponds to a decrease in the exchange rate, *E*.

You may have encountered two other words to denote movements in exchange rates: 'revaluations' and 'devaluations.' These two terms are used when countries operate under **fixed exchange rates** – a system in which two or more countries maintain a constant exchange rate between their currencies. Under such a system, increases in the exchange rate – which are infrequent by definition – are called **revaluations** (rather than appreciations). Decreases in the exchange rate are called **devaluations** (rather than depreciations).

Figure 6.2 plots the nominal exchange rate between the pound and the euro since 1999. Note the two main characteristics of the figure:

> ◄ **Warning:** There is no agreed-upon rule among economists or among newspapers as to which of the two definitions to use. You will encounter both. Usually, the first definition is preferred in the UK, the second definition is preferred in the rest of Europe. Always check which definition is used.

> ◄ *E*: Nominal exchange rate – price of domestic currency in terms of foreign currency. (From the point of view of the UK looking at the USA, the price of a pound in terms of dollars.)

> Appreciation of the domestic currency
> ◄ ⇔ Increase in the price of the domestic currency in terms of foreign currency
> ⇔ Increase in the exchange rate.

> ◄ Depreciation of the domestic currency ⇔ Decrease in the price of the domestic currency in terms of foreign currency ⇔ Decrease in the exchange rate.

> ◄ We shall discuss fixed exchange rates in Chapter 19.

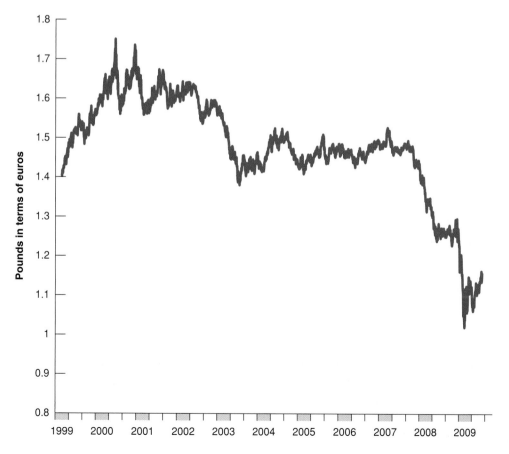

Figure 6.2

The nominal exchange rate between the British pound and the euro since 1999

Source: European Central Bank.

- *The trend decrease in the exchange rate* – In 1999, £1 was worth €1.4. In 2009, £1 was worth €1.15. Put another way, there was a depreciation of the pound vis-à-vis the euro over the period.
- *The large fluctuations in the exchange rate* – In the space of a few years, from 1999 to 2003, the value of the pound increased from £1.4 in 1999 to £1.75 in 2000, back down to £1.5 in mid-2001 and to £1.3 in mid-2003. Put another way, there was a very large appreciation of the pound at the end of the 1990s, followed by a large depreciation in the following decade.

If we are interested, however, in the choice between domestic goods and foreign goods, the nominal exchange rate gives us only part of the information we need. Figure 6.2, for example, tells us only about movements in the relative price of the two currencies, the pound and the euro. To British tourists thinking of visiting Italy, France or Greece the question is not only how many euros they will get in exchange for their pounds, but how much goods will cost in the euro area relative to how much they cost in the UK. This takes us to our next step – the construction of real exchange rates.

From nominal to real exchange rates

How can we construct the real exchange rate between the UK and the euro area – the price of UK goods in terms of European goods?

Suppose the UK produced only one good, a Jaguar, and the euro area also produced only one good, a Mercedes. (This is one of those 'suppose' statements that run completely against the facts, but we shall become more realistic shortly.) Constructing the real exchange rate, the price of the UK goods (Jaguars) in terms of European goods (Mercedes), would be straightforward. We would express both goods in terms of the same currency and then compute their relative price.

Suppose, for example, we expressed both goods in terms of pounds. Then:

If we expressed both in terms of euros instead, we would get the same result for the real exchange rate. ▶

- The first step would be to take the price of a Mercedes in euros and convert it to a price in pounds. The price of a Mercedes in the euro area is €50 000. A pound is worth €1.15, so the price of a Mercedes in pounds is €50 000/1.15 = £43 000.
- The second step would be to compute the ratio of the price of the Mercedes in pounds to the price of the Jaguar in pounds. The price of a Jaguar in the UK is £30 000. So the price of a Mercedes in terms of Jaguars – that is, the real exchange rate between the UK and the euro area – would be £43 000/£30 000 = 1.4. In other words, a Mercedes is 40% more expensive relative to a Jaguar in the UK.

The example is straightforward, but how do we generalise it? The UK and the euro area produce more than Jaguars and Mercedes, and we want to construct a real exchange rate that reflects the relative price of *all* the goods produced in the UK in terms of *all* the goods produced in the euro area.

The computation we just went through tells us how to proceed. Rather than use the price of a Jaguar and the price of a Mercedes, we must use a price index for all goods produced in the UK and a price index for all goods produced in the euro area. This is exactly what the GDP deflators we introduced in Chapter 2 do: they are, by definition, price indexes for the set of final goods and services produced in the economy.

Let P be the GDP deflator for the UK, $P*$ be the GDP deflator for the euro area (as a rule, we shall denote foreign variables with an asterisk) and E be the pound–euro nominal exchange rate. Figure 6.3 goes through the steps needed to construct the real exchange rate:

$ε$: real exchange rate – price of domestic goods in terms of foreign goods. (For example, from the point of view of the UK looking at the euro area, the price of UK goods in terms of European goods.) ▶

1. The price of UK goods in pounds is P. Multiplying it by the exchange rate, E – the price of pounds in terms of euros – gives us the price of UK goods in euros, EP.
2. The price of European goods in euros is $P*$. The *real exchange rate*, the price of UK goods in terms of European goods, which we shall call $ε$ (the Greek lowercase epsilon), is thus given by

$$ε = \frac{EP}{P*}$$

[6.1]

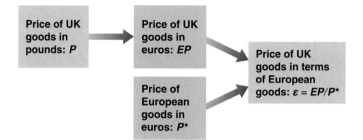

Figure 6.3

**The construction of
the real exchange rate**

The real exchange rate is constructed by multiplying the domestic price level by the nominal exchange rate and then dividing by the foreign price level – a straightforward extension of the computation we made in our Jaguar/Mercedes example.

Note, however, an important difference between our Jaguar/Mercedes example and this more general computation. Unlike the price of Jaguars in terms of Mercedes, the real exchange rate is an index number: that is, its level is arbitrary and, therefore, uninformative. It is uninformative because the GDP deflators used to construct the real exchange rate are themselves index numbers; as we saw in Chapter 2, they are equal to 1 (or 100) in whatever year is chosen as the base year.

But all is not lost. Although the level of the real exchange rate is uninformative, the rate of change of the real exchange rate is informative. If, for example, the real exchange rate between the UK and the euro area increases by 10%, this tells us UK goods are now 10% more expensive relative to European goods than they were before.

Like nominal exchange rates, real exchange rates move over time. These changes are called *real appreciations* or *real depreciations*:

- An increase in the real exchange rate – that is, an increase in the relative price of domestic goods in terms of foreign goods – is called a **real appreciation**.
- A decrease in the real exchange rate – that is, a decrease in the relative price of domestic goods in terms of foreign goods – is called a **real depreciation**.

Figure 6.4 plots the evolution of the real exchange rate between the UK and the euro area since 1999, constructed using equation (6.1). For convenience, it also reproduces the evolution of the nominal exchange rate from Figure 6.2.

Two aspects stand out in Figure 6.4. The large nominal and real appreciation of the pound at the end of the 1990s and the collapse of the pound in 2008–2009.

The large fluctuations in the nominal exchange rate we saw in Figure 6.2 also show up in the real exchange rate. This not surprising: year-to-year movements in the price ratio, P/P^*, are typically small compared to the often-sharp movements in the nominal exchange rate, E. Thus, from year to year, or even over the course of a few years, movements in the real exchange rate, ε, tend to be driven mostly by movements in the nominal exchange rate, E. Note that, since 1999, the nominal exchange rate and the real exchange rate have moved nearly together. This reflects the fact that, since then, inflation rates have been very similar – and low – in both areas.

◄ If inflation rates were exactly equal, P/P^* would be constant, and ε and E would move together exactly.

From bilateral to multilateral exchange rates

We need to take one last step. We have so far concentrated on the exchange rate between the UK and the euro area, but the euro area is just one of many partners the UK trades with.

Table 6.2 shows the geographic composition of UK trade for both exports and imports. The main message of the table is that the UK does most of its trade with two countries: the USA and Germany (which together account for 25% of UK exports and 21% of UK imports). The second largest group of export partners includes the closest countries of Western Europe, such as Ireland, the Netherlands, France and Belgium.

How do we go from **bilateral exchange rates**, like the real exchange rate between the UK and the euro area we focused on earlier, to **multilateral exchange rates** that reflect this

These are all equivalent names for the relative price of domestic goods in terms of foreign goods:

- The real multilateral exchange rate.
- The **trade-weighted real exchange rate**.
- The **effective real exchange rate**.

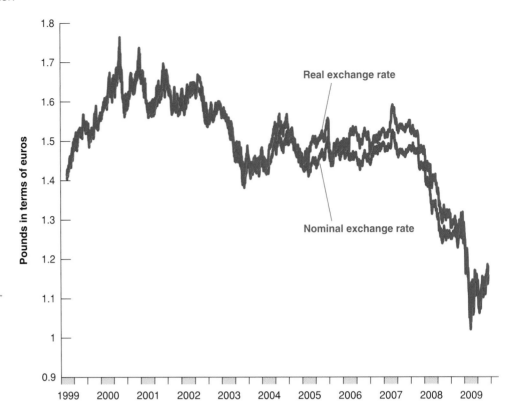

Source: ECB, Eurostat, Bank of England.

Figure 6.4

Real and nominal exchange rates in the UK since 1999

The nominal and the real exchange rates in the UK have moved largely together since 1999.

Table 6.2 The country composition of UK exports and imports, 2008

	Proportion of exports to (%)	Proportion of imports from (%)
USA	14	8
Germany	11	13
Netherlands	8	8
Ireland	8	4
France	7	7
Belgium	5	5
Spain	4	3
Italy	4	4
Sweden	2	2
China	2	7
Russia	2	2
India	2	1
Japan	2	3
Hong Kong	2	2
Norway	1	6
TOTAL	74	75

Source: UK Office for National Statistics.

composition of trade? The principle we want to use is simple, even if the details of construction are complicated: we weigh each country by how much each country trades with the UK and how much it competes with the UK in other countries. The variable constructed in this way is called the **multilateral real exchange rate**, or the real exchange rate for short.

Figure 6.5 shows the evolution of this multilateral real exchange rate, the price of domestic goods in terms of foreign goods for the UK, since 1980. Like the bilateral real exchange rate we saw in Figure 6.4, it is an index number. So its level is also arbitrary; here it is set equal to 1 in January 2005. The most striking aspect of the figure is the large swing in the real exchange rate in the 1980s and 1990s, compared to the relative stability between the

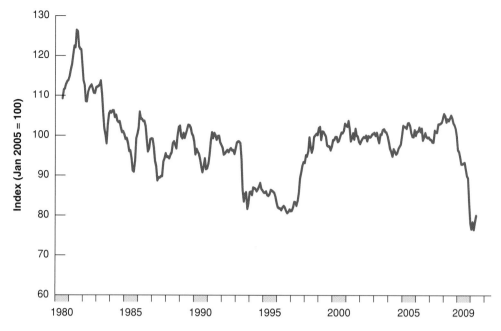

Figure 6.5

The UK multilateral real exchange rate since 1980

The 1980s and 1990s were characterised by large swings in the real exchange rate. The real exchange rate was much more stable since the end of the 1990s, until the large real depreciation in 2009.

Source: Bank of England.

mid-1990s and 2007. The second remarkable aspect of the figure is the collapse of the real exchange rate in 2009.

6.2 OPENNESS IN FINANCIAL MARKETS

Openness in financial markets allows financial investors to hold both domestic assets and foreign assets, to diversify their portfolios, to speculate on movements in foreign interest rates versus domestic interest rates, to speculate on movements in exchange rates, and so on.

Diversify and speculate they do. Given that buying or selling foreign assets implies buying or selling foreign currency – sometimes called **foreign exchange** – the volume of transactions in foreign exchange markets gives us a sense of the importance of international financial transactions. In 2005, for example, the recorded *daily* volume of foreign exchange transactions in the world was €4 trillion, of which 37% – about €1.6 trillion – involved euros on one side of the transaction (and 86% involved dollars on one side of the transation).

To get a sense of the magnitude of these numbers, the sum of exports and imports of the euro area with the rest of the world in 2007 totalled €3 trillion *for the year*, or about €8 billion per day. Suppose the only euro transactions in foreign exchange markets had been, on one side, by euro area exporters selling their foreign currency earnings, and on the other side by euro area importers buying the foreign currency they needed to buy foreign goods. Then, the volume of transactions involving euros in foreign exchange markets would have been €8 billion per day, or about 0.5% of the actual daily total volume of transactions (€1.6 trillion) involving euros in foreign exchange markets. This computation tells us that most of the transactions are associated not with trade but with purchases and sales of financial assets. Moreover, the volume of transactions in foreign exchange markets is not only high but also rapidly increasing. The volume of foreign exchange transactions has more than doubled since 2001. Again, this increase in activity reflects mostly an increase in financial transactions rather than an increase in trade.

For a country as a whole, openness in financial markets has another important implication. It allows the country to run trade surpluses and trade deficits. Recall that a country running a trade deficit is buying more from the rest of the world than it is selling to the rest of the world. In order to pay for the difference between what it buys and what it sells, the country must borrow from the rest of the world. It borrows by making it attractive for foreign financial investors to increase their holdings of domestic assets – in effect, to lend to the country.

Table 6.3 The UK balance of payments, 2008 (in billions of pounds)

Current account		
Exports	422	
Inports	459	
Trade balance (deficit = –) (1)		–37
Investment income received	263	
Investment income paid	236	
Net investment income (2)		27
Net transfers received (3)		–14
Current account balance (deficit = –) (1) + (2) + (3)		–24
Capital account		
Increase in foreign holdings of UK assets (4)	650	
Increase in UK holdings of foreign assets (5)	620	
Capital account balance (deficit = –) (4) – (5)		30
Statistical discrepancy		–6

Source: UK Office of National Statistics (*http://www.statistics.gov.uk/pdfdir/bop0909.pdf*).

Let's start by looking more closely at the relation between trade flows and financial flows. When this is done, we shall look at the determinants of these financial flows.

The balance of payments

A country's transactions with the rest of the world, including both trade flows and financial flows, are summarised by a set of accounts called the **balance of payments**. Table 6.3 presents the UK balance of payments for 2008. The table has two parts, separated by a line. Transactions are referred to as being either **above the line** or **below the line**.

The current account

The transactions above the line record payments to and from the rest of the world. They are called **current account** transactions:

- The first two lines record the exports and imports of goods and services. Exports lead to payments from the rest of the world, and imports lead to payments to the rest of the world. In 2008, imports exceeded exports, leading to a UK trade deficit of £37 billion – roughly 8.4% of UK GDP.
- Exports and imports are not the only sources of payments to and from the rest of the world. UK residents receive **investment income** on their holdings of foreign assets, and foreign residents receive UK investment income on their holdings of UK assets. In 2008, UK investment income received from the rest of the world was £263 billion, and investment income paid to foreigners was £236 billion, for a net balance of £27 billion.
- Finally, countries give and receive foreign aid; the net value of these payments is recorded as **net transfers received**. These net transfers amounted in 2008 to –£14 billion. This negative amount reflects the fact that, in 2008, the UK was – as it has traditionally been – a net donor of foreign aid.

Can a country have:

- A trade deficit and no current account deficit?
- A current account deficit and no trade deficit?

(The answer to both questions: Yes.)

The sum of net payments to and from the rest of the world is called the **current account balance**. If net payments from the rest of the world are positive, the country is running a **current account surplus**; if they are negative, the country is running a **current account deficit**. Adding all payments to and from the rest of the world, net payments from the UK to the rest of the world were equal in 2008 to £37 – £27 + £14 = £24 billion. Put another way, in 2008, the UK ran a current account deficit of £24 billion – roughly 5.4% of its GDP.

The capital account

The fact that the UK had a current account deficit of £24 billion in 2008 implies that it had to borrow £24 billion from the rest of the world – or, equivalently, that net foreign holdings of UK assets had to increase by £24 billion. The numbers below the line describe how this was achieved. Transactions below the line are called **capital account** transactions.

The decrease in foreign holdings of UK assets was £620 billion: foreign investors, be they foreign private investors, foreign governments or foreign central banks, sold £620 billion worth of UK stocks, UK bonds and other UK assets. At the same time, there was a decrease in UK holdings of foreign assets of £650 billion: UK investors, private and public, sold £650 billion worth of foreign stocks, bonds and other assets. The result was an increase in net UK foreign indebtedness (the increase in foreign holdings of UK assets minus the decrease in UK holdings of foreign assets), also called **net capital flows**, to the UK of £(−620) − £(−650) = £30 billion. Another name for net capital flows is the **capital account balance**: positive net capital flows are called a **capital account surplus**; negative net capital flows are called a **capital account deficit**. So, put another way, in 2008, the UK ran a capital account surplus of £30 billion.

> ◄ A country that runs a current account deficit must finance it through positive net capital flows. Equivalently, it must run a capital account surplus.

Shouldn't net capital flows (equivalently, the capital account surplus) be exactly equal to the current account deficit (which we saw earlier was equal to £24 billion in 2008)? In principle, yes; in practice, no.

The numbers for current and capital account transactions are constructed using different sources; although they should give the same answers, typically they do not. In 2008, the difference between the two – the **statistical discrepancy** – was £6 billion, about 25% of the current account balance. This is yet another reminder that, even for a rich country such as the UK, economic data are far from perfect. (This problem of measurement manifests itself in another way as well. The sum of the current account deficits of all the countries in the world should be equal to 0: one country's deficit should show up as a surplus for the other countries taken as a whole. However, this is not the case in the data: if we just add the published current account deficits of all the countries in the world, it would appear that the world is running a large current account deficit and the answer cannot be that we are exporting to Mars less than we are importing!)

Now that we have looked at the current account, we can return to an issue we touched on in Chapter 2: the difference between GDP, the measure of output we have used so far, and GNP, another measure of aggregate output. This is done in the following Focus box 'GDP versus GNP: the example of Ireland.'

The choice between domestic and foreign assets

Openness in financial markets implies that people (or financial institutions, for example investment trusts, that act on their behalf) face a new financial decision: whether to hold domestic assets or foreign assets.

Remembering what we learned in Chapter 5, it would appear that we actually have to think about at least *two* new decisions. The choice of holding domestic *money* versus foreign *money*, and the choice of holding domestic *interest-paying assets* versus foreign *interest-paying assets*. But remember why people hold money: to engage in transactions. For someone who lives in the UK and whose transactions are mostly or fully in pounds, there is little point in holding foreign currency: foreign currency cannot be used for transactions in the UK and, if the goal is to hold foreign assets, holding foreign currency is clearly less desirable than holding foreign bonds, which pay interest. This leaves us with only one new choice to think about, the choice between domestic interest-paying assets and foreign interest-paying assets.

Let's think of these assets for now as domestic one-year bonds and foreign one-year bonds. Consider, for example, the choice between US one-year bonds and UK one-year bonds, from your point of view, as a UK investor:

● Suppose you decide to hold UK bonds.

Let i_t be the one-year UK nominal interest rate in year t (the subscript t refers to the year). Then, as Figure 6.6 shows, for every £1 you put in UK bonds, you will get £$(1 + i_t)$ next year. (This is represented by the arrow pointing to the right at the top of the figure.)

FOCUS
GDP versus GNP: the example of Ireland

Should value added in an open economy be defined as:

- the value added domestically (that is, within the country), or
- the value added by domestically owned factors of production?

The two definitions are not the same: some domestic output is produced with capital owned by foreigners, while some foreign output is produced with capital owned by domestic residents.

The answer is that either definition is fine, and economists use both. **Gross domestic product (GDP)**, the measure we have used so far, corresponds to value added domestically. **Gross national product (GNP)** corresponds to the value added by domestically owned factors of production. To go from GDP to GNP, one must start from GDP, add factor payments received from the rest of the world, and subtract factor payments paid to the rest of the world. Put another way, GNP is equal to GDP plus net factor payments from the rest of the world. While GDP is now the measure most commonly mentioned, GNP was widely used until the early 1990s, and you will still encounter it in newspapers and academic publications.

For most countries, the difference between GNP and GDP is typically small because factor payments to and from the rest of the world roughly cancel one another. There are a few exceptions. Among them is Ireland. Ireland has received a great amount of foreign direct investment during the last two decades. Therefore, the country now pays substantial factor income to the rest of the world. Table 6.4 gives GDP, GNP and net factor payments for Ireland from 2002 to 2008. Note how much larger GDP is compared to GNP throughout the period. Net factor payment now exceed 15% of GDP.

Table 6.4 GDP, GNP and net factor income in Ireland, 2002–2008

Year	GDP	GNP	Net factor income
2002	130 258	106 562	−23 696
2003	139 763	118 039	−21 724
2004	149 098	126 219	−22 879
2005	162 091	137 188	−24 903
2006	176 759	152 529	−24 230
2007	189 751	161 244	−28 507
2008	181 815	154 596	−27 218

Note: numbers are in millions of euros.

Source: Central Statistics Office Ireland.

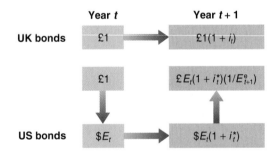

Figure 6.6

Expected returns from holding one-year UK bonds or one-year US bonds

The decision about whether to invest abroad or at home depends on more than interest rates. It also depends on the expected movements in the exchange rate in the future.

- Suppose you decide instead to hold US bonds.

   To buy US bonds, you must first buy dollars. Let E_t be the nominal exchange rate between the pound and the dollar at the start of year t. For every £1, you get $\$E_t$. (This is represented by the arrow pointing downward in the figure.)

   Let i_t^* denote the one-year nominal interest rate on US bonds (in dollars) in year t. When next year comes, you will have $\$E_t(1 + i_t^*)$. (This is represented by the arrow pointing to the right at the bottom of the figure.)

   You will then have to convert your dollars back into pounds. If you expect the nominal exchange rate next year to be E_{t+1}^e (the superscript e indicates that it is an expectation: you do not yet know what the pound/dollar exchange rate will be in year $t + 1$), each dollar will be worth £$(1/E_{t+1}^e)$. So you can expect to have £$E_t(1 + i_t^*)(1/E_{t+1}^e)$ next year for every £1 you invest now. (This is represented by the arrow pointing upward in the figure.) We shall look at the expression we just derived in more detail soon, but note its basic implication already: In assessing the attractiveness of US versus UK bonds, you cannot look just at the US interest rate and the UK interest rate; you must also assess what you think will happen to the pound/dollar exchange rate between this year and next.

Let's now assume that you and other financial investors care only about the expected rate of return and therefore want to hold only the asset with the highest expected rate of return. In that case, if both US bonds and UK bonds are to be held, they must have the same expected rate of return. In other words the following relation must hold:

$$(1 + i_t) = (E_t)(1 + i_t^*)\left(\frac{1}{E_{t+1}^e}\right)$$

Reorganising, we have

$$(1 + i_t) = (1 + i_t^*)\left(\frac{E_t}{E_{t+1}^e}\right) \tag{6.2}$$

Equation (6.2) is called the **uncovered interest parity** relation, or simply the **interest parity condition**.

The assumption that financial investors will hold only the bonds with the highest expected rate of return is obviously too strong, for two reasons:

- It ignores transaction costs. Going into and out of US bonds requires three separate transactions, each with a transaction cost.
- It ignores risk. The exchange rate a year from now is uncertain; holding US bonds is therefore more risky, in terms of pounds, than holding UK bonds.

However, as a characterisation of capital movements among the major world financial markets (New York, Frankfurt, London and Tokyo), the assumption is not far off. Small changes in interest rates and rumours of impending appreciation or depreciation can lead to movements of billions of dollars within minutes. For the rich countries of the world, the assumption in equation (6.2) is a good approximation of reality. Other countries whose capital markets are smaller and less developed, or countries that have various forms of **capital controls**, have more leeway in choosing their domestic interest rate than is implied by equation (6.2). We shall return to this issue at the end of Chapter 18.

Interest rates and exchange rates

Let's get a better sense of what the interest parity condition implies. First, rewrite E_t/E_{t+1}^e as $1/[1 + (E_{t+1}^e - E_t)/E_t]$. Replacing in equation (6.2) gives

$$(1 + i_t) = \frac{(1 + i_t^*)}{[1 + (E_{t+1}^e - E_t)/E_t]} \tag{6.3}$$

This gives us a relation between the domestic nominal interest rate, i_t, the foreign nominal interest rate, i_t^*, and the expected rate of appreciation of the domestic currency, $(E_{t+1}^e - E_t)/E_t$. As long as interest rates and the expected rate of depreciation are not too large – say below 20% per year – a good approximation to this equation is given by

$$i_t \approx i_t^* - \frac{E_{t+1}^e - E_t}{E_t} \tag{6.4}$$

This is the form of the interest parity condition you must remember: *arbitrage by investors implies that the domestic interest rate must be equal to the foreign interest rate minus the expected appreciation rate of the domestic currency.*

> The word *uncovered* is to distinguish this relation from another relation called the *covered interest parity* condition. The covered interest parity condition is derived by looking at the following choice:
>
> Buy and hold UK bonds for one year. Or buy dollars today, buy one-year US bonds with the proceeds and agree to sell the dollars for pounds a year ahead at a predetermined price, called the *forward exchange rate*. The rate of return on these two alternatives, which can both be realised at *no risk today*, must be the same. The covered interest parity condition is a *riskless arbitrage* condition.

> Whether holding US bonds or UK bonds is more risky actually depends on which investors we are looking at. Holding UK bonds is more risky from the point of view of US investors. Holding US bonds is more risky from the point of view of UK investors. (Why?)

If the pound is expected to depreciate by 3% vis-à-vis the dollar, then the dollar is expected to appreciate by 3% vis-à-vis the pound.

Note that the expected appreciation rate of the domestic currency is also the expected depreciation rate of the foreign currency. So equation (6.4) can be equivalently stated as saying that *the domestic interest rate must be equal to the foreign interest rate minus the expected depreciation rate of the foreign currency.*

Let's apply this equation to US bonds versus UK bonds. Suppose the one-year nominal interest rate is 1.0% in the USA, and it is 2.0% in the UK. Should you hold UK bonds or US bonds? The answer:

- It depends whether you expect the pound to depreciate vis-à-vis the dollar over the coming year by more or less than the difference between the US interest rate and the UK interest rate, 1.0% in this case (2.0% − 1.0%).
- If you expect the pound to depreciate by more than 1.0%, then, despite the fact that the interest rate is higher in the UK than in the USA, investing in UK bonds is less attractive than investing in US bonds. By holding UK bonds, you will get higher interest payments next year, but the pound will be worth less in terms of dollars next year, making investing in UK bonds less attractive than investing in US bonds.
- If you expect the pound to depreciate by less than 1.0% or even to appreciate, then the reverse holds, and UK bonds are more attractive than US bonds.

Looking at it another way: if the uncovered interest parity condition holds, and the US one-year interest rate is 1% lower than the UK interest rate, it must be that financial investors are expecting on average an appreciation of the dollar vis-à-vis the pound over the coming year of about 1%, and this is why they are willing to hold US bonds despite their lower interest rate. (Another application of the uncovered interest parity condition is provided in the Focus box 'Buying Brazilian bonds.')

FOCUS
Buying Brazilian bonds

Let's go back to September 1993 because the very high interest rate in Brazil at the time helps make the point we want to get across here. Brazilian bonds are paying a *monthly* interest rate of 36.9%. This seems very attractive compared to the *annual* rate of 3% on US bonds – corresponding to a monthly interest rate of about 0.2%. Shouldn't you buy Brazilian bonds?

The discussion in this chapter tells you that, in order to decide, you need one more crucial element: the expected rate of depreciation of the *cruzeiro* (the name of the Brazilian currency at the time; the currency is now called the *real*) in terms of dollars.

You need this information because, as we saw in equation (6.3), the return in dollars from investing in Brazilian bonds for a month is equal to 1 plus the Brazilian interest rate, divided by 1 plus the expected rate of depreciation of the *cruzeiro* relative to the *dollar*:

$$\frac{1 + i_1^*}{[1 + (E_{t+1}^e - E_t)/E_t]}$$

What rate of depreciation of the cruzeiro should you expect over the coming month? A reasonable assumption is to expect the rate of depreciation during the coming month to be equal to the rate of depreciation during last month. The dollar was worth 100 000 cruzeiros at the end of July 1993, and it was worth 134 600 cruzeiros at the end of August 1993, so the rate of appreciation of the dollar vis-à-vis the cruzeiro – equivalently, the rate of depreciation of the cruzeiro vis-à-vis the dollar – in August was 34.6%. If depreciation is expected to continue at the same rate in September as it did in August, the expected return from investing in Brazilian bonds for a month is

$$\frac{1.369}{1.346} = 1.017$$

The expected rate of return in dollars from holding Brazilian bonds is only (1.017 − 1) = 1.7% per month, not the 36.9% per month that initially looked so attractive. Note that 1.7% per month is still much higher than the monthly interest rate on US bonds (about 0.2%). But think of the risk and the transaction costs – all the elements we ignored when we wrote the arbitrage condition. When these are taken into account, you may well decide to keep your funds out of Brazil.

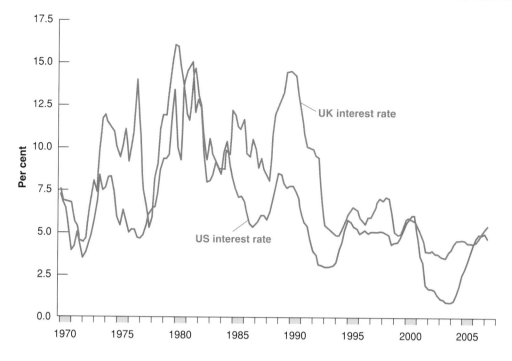

Figure 6.7

Three-months nominal interest rates in the USA and in the UK since 1970

UK and US nominal interest rates have largely moved together over the past 40 years

The arbitrage relation between interest rates and exchange rates, either in the form of equation (6.2) or equation (6.4), will play a central role in the following chapters. It suggests that, unless countries are willing to tolerate large movements in their exchange rates, domestic and foreign interest rates are likely to move very much together. Take the extreme case of two countries that commit to maintaining their bilateral exchange rates at a fixed value. If markets have faith in this commitment, they will expect the exchange rate to remain constant: the expected depreciation will then be equal to zero. In this case, the arbitrage condition implies that interest rates in the two countries will have to move exactly together. Most of the time, as we shall see, governments do not make such absolute commitments to maintain the exchange rate, but they often do try to avoid large movements in the exchange rate. This puts sharp limits on how much they can allow their interest rates to deviate from interest rates elsewhere in the world.

◄ If $E_{t+1}^e = E_t$, then the interest parity condition implies that $i_t = i_t^*$.

How much do nominal interest rates actually move together in major countries? Figure 6.7 plots the three-month nominal interest rate in the USA and the three-month nominal interest rate in the UK (both expressed at annual rates) since 1970. The figure shows that the movements are related but not identical. Interest rates were very high in both countries in the early 1980s, and they were high again – although much more so in the UK than in the USA – in the late 1990s. They have been low in both countries since the mid-1990s. At the same time, differences between the two have sometimes been quite large: in 1990, for example, the UK interest rate was nearly 7% higher than the US interest rate. In the coming chapters, we shall return to why such differences emerge and what their implications may be. For the time being all you have studied so far in this chapter allows us to describe equilibrium in the goods market in an open economy.

◄ Meanwhile, do the following. Look at the back pages of a recent issue of *The Economist* for short-term interest rates in different countries relative to the currency of your country. Assume that uncovered interest parity holds. Which currencies are expected to appreciate against your currency?

6.3 THE *IS* RELATION IN AN OPEN ECONOMY

When we were assuming that the economy was closed to trade, there was no need to distinguish between the *domestic demand for goods* and the *demand for domestic goods*: they were clearly the same thing. Now, we must distinguish between the two. Some domestic demand falls on foreign goods, and some of the demand for domestic goods comes from foreigners. Let's look at this distinction more closely.

◄ 'The domestic demand for goods' and 'the demand for domestic goods' sound close but are not the same. Part of domestic demand falls on foreign goods. Part of foreign demand falls on domestic goods.

The demand for domestic goods

In an open economy, the **demand for domestic goods** is given by

$$Z = C + I + G - \frac{IM}{\varepsilon} + X \qquad [6.5]$$

The first three terms – consumption, C, investment, I, and government spending, G – constitute the **domestic demand for goods**. If the economy were closed, $C + I + G$ would also be the demand for domestic goods. This is why, until now, we have only looked at $C + I + G$, but now we have to make two adjustments:

In Chapter 3, we ignored the real exchange rate and subtracted *IM*, not *IM/ε*. But that was a cheat; we did not want to have to talk about the real exchange rate – and complicate matters – so early in the book.

Domestic demand for goods, $C + I + G$
Minus domestic demand for foreign goods (imports), IM/ε
Plus foreign demand for domestic goods (exports), X.
Equals demand for domestic goods,
$$C + I + G - IM/\varepsilon + X$$

- First, we must subtract imports – that part of the domestic demand that falls on foreign goods rather than on domestic goods.
  We must be careful here: foreign goods are different from domestic goods, so we cannot just subtract the quantity of imports, IM. If we were to do so, we would be subtracting apples (foreign goods) from oranges (domestic goods). We must first express the value of imports in terms of domestic goods. This is what IM/ε in equation (6.5) stands for: recall from Section 6.1 that ε, the real exchange rate, is defined as the price of domestic goods in terms of foreign goods. Equivalently, $1/\varepsilon$ is the price of foreign goods in terms of domestic goods. So $IM\ (1/\varepsilon)$ – or, equivalently, IM/ε – is the value of imports in terms of domestic goods.
- Second, we must add exports – that part of the demand for domestic goods that comes from abroad. This is captured by the term X in equation (6.5).

The determinants of *C*, *I* and *G*

Having listed the five components of demand, our next task is to specify their determinants. Let's start with the first three: C, I and G. Now that we are assuming that the economy is open, how should we modify our earlier descriptions of consumption, investment and government spending? The answer: not very much, if at all. How much consumers decide to spend still depends on their income and their wealth. While the real exchange rate surely affects the *composition* of consumption spending between domestic goods and foreign goods, there is no obvious reason why it should affect the overall *level* of consumption. The same is true of investment: the real exchange rate may affect whether firms buy domestic machines or foreign machines, but it should not affect total investment.

This is good news because it implies that we can use the descriptions of consumption, investment and government spending that we developed earlier. Therefore,

$$\text{Domestic demand: } C + I + G = C(Y - T) + I(Y, i) + G$$
$$(+) \qquad (+, -)$$

We assume that consumption depends positively on disposable income, $Y - T$, and that investment depends positively on production, Y, and negatively on the interest rate, i. We continue to take government spending, G, as given.

The determinants of imports

Imports are the part of domestic demand that falls on foreign goods. What do they depend on? They clearly depend on domestic income: higher domestic income leads to a higher domestic demand for all goods, both domestic and foreign. So a higher domestic income leads to higher imports. Imports also clearly depend on the real exchange rate – the price of domestic goods in terms of foreign goods. The more expensive domestic goods are relative to foreign goods – equivalently, the cheaper foreign goods are relative to domestic goods – the higher the domestic demand for foreign goods. So a higher real exchange rate leads to higher imports. Thus, we write imports as

$$IM = IM(Y, \varepsilon) \qquad\qquad [6.6]$$
$$(+, +)$$

- An increase in domestic income, Y (equivalently, an increase in domestic output – income and output are still equal in an open economy), leads to an increase in imports. This positive effect of income on imports is captured by the positive sign under Y in equation (6.6).
- An increase in the real exchange rate, ε, leads to an increase in imports, IM. This positive effect of the real exchange rate on imports is captured by the positive sign under ε in equation (6.6). (As ε goes up, note that IM goes up, but $1/\varepsilon$ goes down, so what happens to IM/ε, the *value* of imports in terms of domestic goods, is ambiguous. We will return to this point shortly.)

The determinants of exports

Exports are the part of foreign demand that falls on domestic goods. What do they depend on? They depend on foreign income: higher foreign income means higher foreign demand for all goods, both foreign and domestic. So higher foreign income leads to higher exports. Exports also depend on the real exchange rate: the higher the price of domestic goods in terms of foreign goods, the lower the foreign demand for domestic goods. In other words, the higher the real exchange rate, the lower the exports.

Let Y^* denote foreign income (equivalently, foreign output). We therefore write exports as

$$X = X(Y^*, \varepsilon) \qquad\qquad [6.7]$$
$$(+, -)$$

◀ Recall that asterisks refer to foreign variables.

- An increase in foreign income, Y^*, leads to an increase in exports.
- An increase in the real exchange rate, ε, leads to a decrease in exports.

Putting the components together

Figure 6.8 puts together what we have learned so far. It plots the various components of demand against output, keeping constant all other variables (the interest rate, taxes, government spending, foreign output and the real exchange rate) that affect demand.

In Figure 6.8(a), the line DD plots domestic demand, $C + I + G$, as a function of output, Y. ◀ For a given real exchange rate ε, IM/ε – the value of imports in terms of domestic goods – moves exactly with IM – the quantity of imports. This relation between demand and output is familiar from Chapter 3. Under our standard assumptions, the slope of the relation between demand and output is positive but less than 1. An increase in output – equivalently, an increase in income – increases demand but less than one-for-one. (In the absence of good reasons to the contrary, we draw the relation between demand and output, and the other relations in this chapter, as lines rather than curves. This is purely for convenience, and none of the discussions that follow depends on this assumption.)

To arrive at the demand for domestic goods, we must first *subtract imports*. This is done in Figure 6.8(b), and it gives us the line AA. The line AA represents the domestic demand for domestic goods. The distance between DD and AA equals the value of imports, IM/ε. Because the quantity of imports increases with income, the distance between the two lines increases with income. We can establish two facts about line AA, which will be useful later in the chapter:

- AA is flatter than DD: as income increases, some of the additional domestic demand falls on foreign goods rather than on domestic goods. In other words, as income increases, the domestic demand for domestic goods increases less than total domestic demand.
- As long as some of the additional demand falls on domestic goods, AA has a positive slope: an increase in income leads to some increase in the demand for domestic goods.

Finally, we must *add exports*. This is done in Figure 6.8(c), and it gives us the line ZZ, which is above AA. The line ZZ represents the demand for domestic goods. The distance

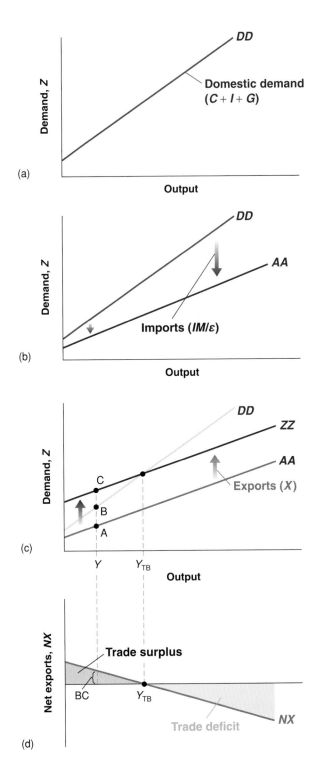

Figure 6.8

The demand for domestic goods and net exports

Panel (a): The domestic demand for goods is an increasing function of income (output).

Panels (b) and (c): The demand for domestic goods is obtained by subtracting the value of imports from domestic demand and then adding exports.

Panel (d): The trade balance is a decreasing function of output.

Recall that net exports is synonymous with trade balance. Positive net exports correspond to a trade surplus, whereas negative net exports correspond to a trade deficit.

between ZZ and AA equals exports. Because exports do not depend on domestic income (they depend on foreign income), the distance between ZZ and AA is constant, which is why the two lines are parallel. Because AA is flatter than DD, ZZ is also flatter than DD.

From the information in Figure 6.8(c), we can characterise the behaviour of net exports – the difference between exports and imports – as a function of output. At output level Y, for example, exports are given by the distance AC and imports $(X - IM/\varepsilon)$ by the distance AB, so net exports are given by the distance BC.

This relation between net exports and output is represented as the line NX (for Net Exports) in Figure 6.8(d). Net exports are a decreasing function of output: as output increases, imports increase, and exports are unaffected, so net exports decrease. Call Y_{TB} (TB for trade balance) the level of output at which the value of imports equals the value of exports, so that net exports are equal to 0. Levels of output above Y_{TB} lead to higher imports and to a trade deficit. Levels of output below Y_{TB} lead to lower imports and to a trade surplus.

To determine the equilibrium output in an open economy, you just have to recall what you learned in Chapter 5. The goods market is in equilibrium when domestic output equals the demand – both domestic and foreign – for domestic goods:

$$Y = Z$$

Collecting the relations we derived for the components of the demand for domestic goods, Z, we get

$$Y = C(Y - T) + I(Y, i) + G - IM(Y, \varepsilon)/\varepsilon + X(Y^*, \varepsilon) \qquad [6.8]$$
$$\quad\;\; (+) \qquad (+, -) \qquad\quad (+, +) \qquad (+, -)$$

For the goods market to be in equilibrium, output (the left side of the equation) must be equal to the demand for domestic goods (the right side of the equation). The demand for domestic goods is equal to consumption, C, plus investment, I, plus government spending, G, minus the value of imports, IM/ε, plus exports, X:

- Consumption, C, depends positively on disposable income, $Y - T$.
- Investment, I, depends positively on output, Y, and negatively on the interest rate, i.
- Government spending, G, is taken as given.
- The quantity of imports, IM, depends positively on both output, Y, and the real exchange rate, ε. The value of imports in terms of domestic goods is equal to the quantity of imports divided by the real exchange rate.
- Exports, X, depend positively on foreign output, $Y,^*$ and negatively on the real exchange rate, ε.

This equilibrium condition determines output as a function of all the variables we take as given, from taxes to the real exchange rate to foreign output. This is not a simple relation; Figure 6.9 represents it graphically, in a more user-friendly way.

In Figure 6.9(a), demand is measured on the vertical axis, and output (equivalently production or income) is measured on the horizontal axis. The line ZZ plots demand as a function of output; this line simply replicates the line ZZ in Figure 6.8; ZZ is upward-sloping but with slope less than 1.

Equilibrium output is at the point where demand equals output, at the intersection of the line ZZ and the 45° line: point A in the figure, with associated output level Y.

Figure 6.9(b) replicates Figure 6.8(d), drawing net exports as a decreasing function of output. There is, in general, no reason why the equilibrium level of output, Y, should be the same as the level of output at which trade is balanced, Y_{TB}. As we have drawn the figure, equilibrium output is associated with a trade deficit, equal to the distance BC. Note that we could have drawn it differently, so equilibrium output was associated instead with a trade surplus.

> ◀ The equilibrium level of output is given by the condition $Y = Z$. The level of output at which there is trade balance is given by the condition $X = IM/\varepsilon$. These are two different conditions.

It will be convenient in what follows to regroup the last two terms under 'net exports,' defined as exports minus the value of imports:

$$NX(Y, Y^*, \varepsilon) \equiv X(Y^*, \varepsilon) - IM(Y, \varepsilon)/\varepsilon$$

It follows from our assumptions about imports and exports that net exports, NX, depend on domestic output, Y, foreign output, Y^*, and the real exchange rate, ε. An increase in domestic output increases imports, thus decreasing net exports. An increase in foreign output increases exports, thus increasing net exports. An increase in the real exchange rate leads to a decrease in net exports.

> ◀ We shall assume, throughout the chapter, that an increase in the real exchange rate – a real appreciation – leads to a decrease in net exports (this condition is called the Marshall–Lerner condition, as we will learn in Chapter 18).

Using this definition of net exports, we can rewrite the equilibrium condition as

$$Y = C(Y - T) + I(Y, i) + G + NX(Y, Y^*, \varepsilon) \qquad [6.9]$$
$$\quad\;\; (+) \qquad (+, -) \qquad\quad (-, +, -)$$

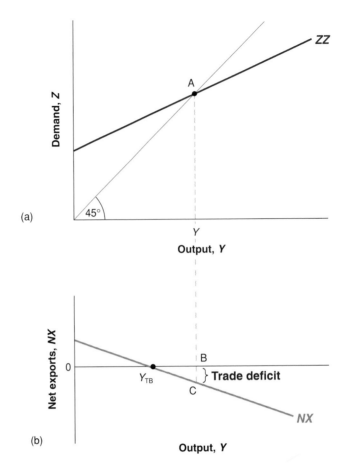

Figure 6.9

Equilibrium output and net exports

The goods market is in equilibrium when domestic output is equal to the demand for domestic goods. At the equilibrium level of output, the trade balance may show a deficit or a surplus.

For our purposes, the main implication of equation (6.9) is that both the interest rate and the real exchange rate affect demand and, in turn, equilibrium output:

- An increase in the interest rate leads to a decrease in investment spending and, as a result, to a decrease in the demand for domestic goods. This leads, through the multiplier, to a decrease in output.
- An increase in the exchange rate leads to a shift in demand toward foreign goods and, as a result, to a decrease in net exports. The decrease in net exports decreases the demand for domestic goods. This leads, through the multiplier, to a decrease in output.

For the remainder of the chapter, we shall make a simplification to equation (6.9):

$P = P^*$, so $\varepsilon = E$

- As we are still studying the short run, when prices are assumed to be constant, the real exchange rate, $\varepsilon \equiv EP/P^*$, and the nominal exchange rate, E, move together. A decrease in the nominal exchange rate – a nominal depreciation – leads, one-for-one, to a decrease in the real exchange rate – a real depreciation. Conversely, an increase in the nominal exchange rate – a nominal appreciation – leads, one-for-one, to an increase in the real exchange rate – a real appreciation. If, for notational convenience, we choose P and P^* so that $P/P^* = 1$ (and we can do so because both are index numbers), then $\varepsilon = E$, and we can replace ε by E in equation (6.9).

With these two simplifications, equation (6.9) becomes

$$Y = C(Y - T) + I(Y, i) + G + NX(Y, Y^*, E)$$
$$ (+) \quad\ \ (+, -) (-, +, -)$$

In words: Goods market equilibrium implies that output depends negatively on both the nominal interest rate and the exchange rate.

6.4 EQUILIBRIUM IN FINANCIAL MARKETS

When we looked at financial markets in the *IS–LM* model for a closed economy, we assumed that people chose between only two financial assets, money and bonds. Now that we are looking at a financially open economy, we must also take into account the fact that people have a choice between domestic bonds and foreign bonds. Let's consider each choice in turn.

Money versus bonds

When we looked at the determination of the interest rate in the *IS–LM* model in Chapter 5, we wrote the condition that the supply of money be equal to the demand for money as

$$\frac{M}{P} = YL(i) \qquad\qquad [6.10]$$

We took the real supply of money [the left side of equation (6.10)] as given. We assumed that the real demand for money [the right side of equation (6.10)] depended on the level of transactions in the economy, measured by real output, Y, and on the opportunity cost of holding money rather than bonds – that is, the interest rate on bonds, i.

How should we change this characterisation now that the economy is open? You will like the answer: not very much, if at all.

In an open economy, the demand for domestic money is still mostly a demand by domestic residents. There is not much reason for, say, the residents of the UK to hold euro currency or demand deposits. Transactions in the UK require payment in pounds, not in euros. If residents of the UK want to hold euro-denominated assets, they are better off holding euro bonds, which at least pay a positive interest rate. And the demand for money by domestic residents in any country still depends on the same factors as before: their level of transactions, which we measure by domestic real output, and the opportunity cost of holding money, the interest rate on bonds.

Therefore, we can still use equation (6.10) to think about the determination of the interest rate in an open economy. The interest rate must be such that the supply of money and the demand for money are equal. An increase in the money supply leads to a decrease in the interest rate. An increase in money demand, say as a result of an increase in output, leads to an increase in the interest rate.

Domestic bonds versus foreign bonds

As we look at the choice between domestic bonds and foreign bonds, we shall rely on the assumption we introduced in Section 6.2: financial investors, domestic or foreign, go for the highest expected rate of return. This implies that, in equilibrium, both domestic bonds and foreign bonds must have the same expected rate of return; otherwise, investors would be willing to hold only one or the other, but not both, and this could not be an equilibrium. (Like most other economic relations, this relation is only an approximation to reality and does not always hold. More on this in the Focus box 'Sudden stops, the strong dollar and limits to the interest parity condition' in Section 6.5.)

As we saw earlier [equation (6.2)], this assumption implies that the following arbitrage relation – the *interest parity condition* – must hold:

$$(1 + i_t) = (1 + i_t^*)\left(\frac{E_t}{E_{t+1}^e}\right)$$

where i_t is the domestic interest rate, i_t^* is the foreign interest rate, E_t is the current exchange rate and E_{t+1}^e is the future expected exchange rate. The left side gives the return, in terms of domestic currency, from holding domestic bonds. The right side gives the expected return, also in terms of domestic currency, from holding foreign bonds. In equilibrium, the two expected returns must be equal.

The presence of E_t comes from the fact that, in order to buy the foreign bond, you must first exchange domestic currency for foreign currency. The presence of E_{t+1}^e comes from the fact that, in order to bring the funds back next period, you will have to exchange foreign currency for domestic currency.

Multiply both sides by E_{t+1}^e and reorganise, to get

$$E_t = \frac{1 + i_t}{1 + i_t^*} E_{t+1}^e \qquad [6.11]$$

For now, we shall take the expected future exchange rate as given and denote it as $\bar{E}^e$ (we shall relax this assumption in Chapter 18). Under this assumption, and dropping time indexes, the interest parity condition becomes

$$E = \frac{1 + i}{1 + i^*} \bar{E}^e \qquad [6.12]$$

This relation tells us that the current exchange rate depends on the domestic interest rate, on the foreign interest rate and on the expected future exchange rate:

- An increase in the domestic interest rate leads to an increase in the exchange rate.
- An increase in the foreign interest rate leads to a decrease in the exchange rate.
- An increase in the expected future exchange rate leads to an increase in the current exchange rate.

This relation plays a central role in the real world and will play a central role in this chapter. To understand the relation further, consider the following example.

Consider financial investors – investors, for short – choosing between UK bonds and Japanese bonds. Suppose that the one-year interest rate on UK bonds is 5% and the one-year interest rate on Japanese bonds is also 5%. Suppose that the current exchange rate is 100 (1 pound is worth 100 yen), and the expected exchange rate a year from now is also 100. Under these assumptions, both UK and Japanese bonds have the same expected return in pounds, and the interest parity condition holds.

Suppose that investors now expect the exchange rate to be 10% higher a year from now, so E^e is now equal to 110. At an unchanged current exchange rate, UK bonds are now much more attractive than Japanese bonds: UK bonds offer an interest rate of 5% in pounds. Japanese bonds still offer an interest rate of 5% in yen, but yen a year from today are now expected to be worth 10% less in terms of pounds. In terms of pounds, the return on Japanese bonds is therefore 5% (the interest rate) – 10% (the expected depreciation of the yen relative to the pound), or –5%.

So what will happen? At the initial exchange rate of 100, investors want to shift out of Japanese bonds into UK bonds. To do so, they must first sell Japanese bonds for yen, then sell yen for pounds, and then use the pounds to buy UK bonds. As investors sell yen and buy pounds, the pound appreciates. By how much? Equation (6.12) gives us the answer: $E = (1.05/1.05)\ 110 = 110$. The current exchange rate must increase in the same proportion as the expected future exchange rate. Put another way, the pound must appreciate today by 10%. When it has appreciated by 10%, so, $E = \bar{E}^e = 110$, the expected returns on UK and Japanese bonds are again equal, and there is equilibrium in the foreign exchange market.

Suppose instead that, as a result of a UK monetary contraction, the UK interest rate increases from 5% to 8%. Assume that the Japanese interest rate remains unchanged at 5%, and that the expected future exchange rate remains unchanged at 100. At an unchanged current exchange rate, UK bonds are now again much more attractive than Japanese bonds. UK bonds yield a return of 8% in pounds. Japanese bonds give a return of 5% in yen and – because the exchange rate is expected to be the same next year as it is today – an expected return of 5% in pounds as well.

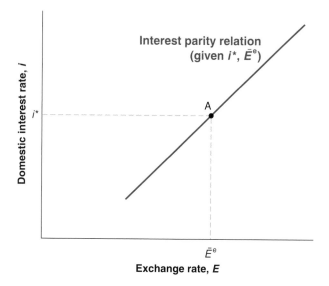

Figure 6.10

The relation between the interest rate and exchange rate implied by interest parity

A higher domestic interest rate leads to a higher exchange rate – an appreciation.

So what will happen? Again, at the initial exchange rate of 100, investors want to shift out of Japanese bonds into UK bonds. As they do so, they sell yen for pounds, and the pound appreciates. By how much? Equation (6.12) gives the answer: $E = (1.08/1.05)100 \approx 103$. The current exchange rate increases by approximately 3%. Why 3%? Think of what happens when the pound appreciates. If, as we have assumed, investors do not change their expectation of the future exchange rate, then the more the pound appreciates today, the more investors expect it to depreciate in the future (as it is expected to return to the same value in the future). When the pound has appreciated by 3% today, investors expect it to depreciate by 3% during the coming year. Equivalently, they expect the yen to appreciate vis-à-vis the pound by 3% over the coming year. The expected rate of return in pounds from holding Japanese bonds is therefore 5% (the yen interest rate) + 3% (the expected yen appreciation), or 8%. This expected rate of return is the same as the rate of return on holding UK bonds, so there is equilibrium in the foreign exchange market.

Note that our argument relies heavily on the assumption that, when the interest rate changes, the expected exchange rate remains unchanged. This implies that an appreciation today leads to an expected depreciation in the future – because the exchange rate is expected to return to the same, unchanged, value. We shall relax the assumption that the future exchange rate is fixed in Chapter 18. But the basic conclusion will remain: *an increase in the domestic interest rate relative to the foreign interest rate leads to an appreciation.*

◀ Make sure you understand the argument. Why doesn't the pound appreciate by, say, 20%?

Figure 6.10 plots the relation between the domestic interest rate, i, and the exchange rate, E, implied by equation (6.12) – the interest parity relation. The relation is drawn for a given expected future exchange rate, $\bar{E}^e$, and a given foreign interest rate, i^*, and is represented by an upward-sloping line: the higher the domestic interest rate, the higher the exchange rate. Equation (6.12) also implies that when the domestic interest rate is equal to the foreign interest rate ($i = i^*$), the exchange rate is equal to the expected future exchange rate ($E = \bar{E}^e$). This implies that the line corresponding to the interest parity condition goes through point A in the figure.

◀ What happens to the line if i^* increases? What happens to the line if $\bar{E}^e$ increases?

6.5 PUTTING GOODS AND FINANCIAL MARKETS TOGETHER

We now have the elements we need to understand the movements of output, the interest rate, and the exchange rate.

Goods market equilibrium implies that output depends, among other factors, on the interest rate and the exchange rate:

$$Y = C(Y - T) + I(Y, i) + G + NX(Y, Y^*, E)$$

The interest rate, in turn, is determined by the equality of money supply and money demand:

$$\frac{M}{P} = YL(i)$$

And the interest parity condition implies a positive relation between the domestic interest rate and the exchange rate:

$$E = \frac{1+i}{1+i^*}\bar{E}^e$$

Together, these three relations determine output, the interest rate and the exchange rate. Working with three relations is not very easy, but we can easily reduce them to two by using the interest parity condition to eliminate the exchange rate in the goods market equilibrium relation. Doing this gives us the following two equations, the open-economy versions of our familiar *IS* and *LM* relations:

$$IS: \quad Y = C(Y - T) + I(Y, i) + G + NX\left(Y, Y^*, \frac{1+i}{1+i^*}\bar{E}^e\right)$$

$$LM: \frac{M}{P} = YL(i)$$

Take the *IS* relation first and consider the effects of an increase in the interest rate on output. An increase in the interest rate now has two effects:

- The first effect, which was already present in a closed economy, is the direct effect on investment: a higher interest rate leads to a decrease in investment, a decrease in the demand for domestic goods and a decrease in output.
- The second effect, which is present only in the open economy, is the effect through the exchange rate: an increase in the domestic interest rate leads to an increase in the exchange rate – an appreciation. The appreciation, which makes domestic goods more expensive relative to foreign goods, leads to a decrease in net exports and, therefore, to a decrease in the demand for domestic goods and a decrease in output.

Both effects work in the same direction: an increase in the interest rate decreases demand directly and indirectly – through the adverse effect of the appreciation on demand.

> An increase in the interest rate leads, both directly and indirectly (through the exchange rate), to a decrease in output.

The *IS* relation between the interest rate and output is drawn in Figure 6.11(a), for given values of all the other variables in the relation – namely *T*, *G*, *Y**, *i** and *Ē*^e. The *IS* curve is downward-sloping: an increase in the interest rate leads to lower output. The curve looks very much the same in an open economy as in a closed economy, but it hides a more complex relation than before: the interest rate affects output not only directly but also indirectly through the exchange rate.

The *LM* relation is exactly the same in an open economy as in a closed economy. The *LM* curve is upward-sloping. For a given value of the real money stock, *M/P*, an increase in output leads to an increase in the demand for money and to an increase in the equilibrium interest rate.

Equilibrium in the goods and financial markets is attained at point A in Figure 6.11(a), with output level *Y* and interest rate *i*. The equilibrium value of the exchange rate cannot be read directly from the graph, but it is easily obtained from Figure 6.11(b), which replicates Figure 6.10, and gives the exchange rate associated with a given interest rate. The exchange rate associated with the equilibrium interest rate, *i*, is equal to *E*.

Let's summarise: we have derived the *IS* and the *LM* relations for an open economy.

- The *IS* curve is downward-sloping – An increase in the interest rate leads directly and indirectly (through the exchange rate) to a decrease in demand and a decrease in output.
- The *LM* curve is upward-sloping – An increase in income increases the demand for money, leading to an increase in the equilibrium interest rate.

FOCUS
Sudden stops, the strong dollar and the limits to the interest parity condition

The interest parity condition assumes that financial investors care only about expected returns. As we discussed in Section 6.2, investors care not only about returns but also about risk and about liquidity – how easy it is to buy or sell an asset.

Much of the time, we can ignore these other factors. Sometimes, however, these factors play a big role in investors' decisions and in determining exchange rate movements.

Perceptions of risk often play an important role in the decisions of large financial investors – for example, pension funds – to invest or not to invest at all in a country. Sometimes the perception that risk has decreased leads many foreign investors to simultaneously buy assets in a country, leading to a large increase in demand for the assets of that country. Sometimes the perception that risk has increased leads the same investors to want to sell all the assets they have in that country, no matter what the interest rate. These episodes, which have affected many Latin American and Asian emerging economies, are known as sudden stops. During these episodes, the interest parity condition fails, and the exchange rate may decrease a lot, without any change in domestic or foreign interest rates.

Large countries can also be affected. For example, the appreciation of the dollar in the 1990s came not so much from an increase in US interest rates over foreign interest rates, as from an increased foreign demand for dollar assets at a given interest rate. Many private foreign investors wanted to have some proportion of their wealth in US assets: they perceived US assets as being relatively safe. Many foreign central banks wanted to hold a large proportion of their reserves in US T-bills. The reason they did so is because the T-bill market is very liquid, so they could buy and sell T-bills without affecting the price. This very high demand for US assets, at a given interest rate, was behind the 'strong dollar' in the 1990s. Even while US interest rates are relatively low, foreign investors are still eager to increase their holdings of US assets, and thus to finance the large US trade deficit. How long they are willing to do so will determine what happens to the dollar and to the US trade balance.

Equilibrium output and the equilibrium interest rate are given by the intersection of the *IS* and the *LM* curves. Given the foreign interest rate and the expected future exchange rate, the equilibrium interest rate determines the equilibrium exchange rate.

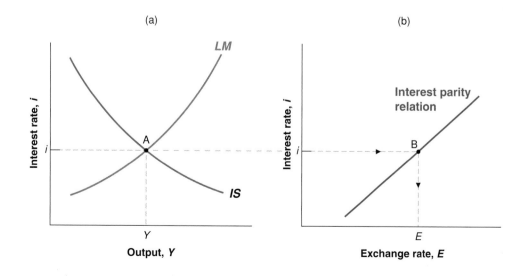

Figure 6.11

The *IS–LM* model in an open economy

An increase in the interest rate reduces output both directly and indirectly (through the exchange rate): the *IS* curve is downward-sloping. Given the real money stock, an increase in output increases the interest rate: the *LM* curve is upward-sloping.

SUMMARY

- Openness in goods markets allows people and firms to choose between domestic goods and foreign goods. Openness in financial markets allows financial investors to hold domestic financial assets or foreign financial assets.

- The nominal exchange rate is the price of the domestic currency in terms of foreign currency. From the viewpoint of the UK, the nominal exchange rate between the UK and the USA is the price of a pound in terms of dollars.

- A nominal appreciation (an appreciation, for short) is an increase in the price of the domestic currency in terms of foreign currency. In other words, it corresponds to an increase in the exchange rate. A nominal depreciation (a depreciation, for short) is a decrease in the price of the domestic currency in terms of foreign currency. It corresponds to a decrease in the exchange rate.

- The real exchange rate is the relative price of domestic goods in terms of foreign goods. It is equal to the nominal exchange rate times the domestic price level divided by the foreign price level.

- A real appreciation is an increase in the relative price of domestic goods in terms of foreign goods – i.e. an increase in the real exchange rate. A real depreciation is a decrease in the relative price of domestic goods in terms of foreign goods – i.e. a decrease in the real exchange rate.

- The multilateral real exchange rate, or real exchange rate for short, is a weighted average of bilateral real exchange rates, with the weight for each foreign country equal to its share in trade.

- In an open economy, the demand for domestic goods is equal to the domestic demand for goods (consumption plus investment plus government spending) minus the value of imports (in terms of domestic goods) plus exports.

- In an open economy, an increase in domestic demand leads to a smaller increase in output than it would in a closed economy because some of the additional demand falls on imports. For the same reason, an increase in domestic demand also leads to a deterioration of the trade balance.

KEY TERMS

QUESTIONS AND PROBLEMS

QUICK CHECK

1. *Using the information in this chapter, label each of the following statements true, false or uncertain. Explain briefly.*

a. The national income identity implies that budget deficits cause trade deficits.

b. Opening the economy to trade tends to increase the multiplier because an increase in expenditure leads to more exports.

c. If the trade deficit is equal to zero, then the domestic demand for goods and the demand for domestic goods are equal.

d. A real depreciation leads to an immediate improvement in the trade balance.

e. A small open economy can reduce its trade deficit through fiscal contraction at a smaller cost in output than can a large open economy.

f. While the export ratio can be larger than one – as it is in Singapore – the same cannot be true of the ratio of imports to GDP.

g. That a rich country like Japan has such a small ratio of imports to GDP is clear evidence of an unfair playing field for European exporters to Japan.

h. Given the definition of the exchange rate adopted in this chapter, if the euro is the domestic currency and the dollar the foreign currency, a nominal exchange rate of 0.75 means that €1 is worth $0.75.

i. A real appreciation means that domestic goods become less expensive relative to foreign goods.

2. Real and nominal exchange rates and inflation

Using the definition of the real exchange rate (and Propositions 7 and 8 in Appendix 1 at the end of the book), you can show that

$$\frac{(\varepsilon_t - \varepsilon_{t-1})}{\varepsilon_{t-1}} = \frac{(E_t - E_{t-1})}{E_{t-1}} + \pi_t - \pi_t^*$$

In words: the percentage real appreciation equals the percentage nominal appreciation plus the difference between domestic and foreign inflation.

a. If domestic inflation is higher than foreign inflation, but the domestic country has a fixed exchange rate, what happens to the real exchange rate over time? Assume that the Marshall–Lerner condition holds. What happens to the trade balance over time? Explain in words.

b. Suppose the real exchange rate is constant – say, at the level required for net exports (or the current account) to equal zero. In this case, if domestic inflation is higher than foreign inflation, what must happen to the nominal exchange rate over time?

DIG DEEPER

3. *Consider a world with three equal-sized economies (A, B and C) and three goods (clothes, cars and computers). Assume that consumers in all three economies want to spend an equal amount on all three goods.*

The value of production of each good in the three economies is given below.

	A	B	C
Clothes	10	0	5
Cars	5	10	0
Computers	0	5	10

a. What is GDP in each economy? If the total value of GDP is consumed and no country borrows from abroad, how much will consumers in each economy spend on each of the goods?

b. If no country borrows from abroad, what will be the trade balance in each country? What will be the pattern of trade in this world (i.e., which good will each country export and to whom)?

c. Given your answer to part (b), will country A have a zero trade balance with country B? With country C? Will any country have a zero trade balance with any other country?

d. The USA has a large trade deficit. It has a trade deficit with each of its major trading partners, but the deficit is much larger with some countries (e.g. China) than with others. Suppose the USA eliminates its overall trade deficit (with the world as a whole). Do you expect it to have a zero trade balance with every one of its trading partners? Does the especially large trade deficit with China necessarily indicate that China does not allow US goods to compete on an equal basis with Chinese goods?

4. Net exports and foreign demand

a. Suppose there is an increase in foreign output. Show the effect on the domestic economy (i.e. replicate Figure 6.4). What is the effect on domestic output? On domestic net exports?

b. If the interest rate remains constant, what will happen to domestic investment? If taxes are fixed, what will happen to the domestic budget deficit?

c. Using equation (6.5), what must happen to private saving? Explain.

d. Foreign output does not appear in equation (6.5), yet it evidently affects net exports. Explain how this is possible.

5. Eliminating a trade deficit

a. Consider an economy with a trade deficit ($NX < 0$) and with output equal to its natural level. Suppose that, even though output may deviate from its natural level in the short run, it returns to its natural level in the medium run. Assume that the natural level is unaffected by the real exchange rate. What must happen to the real exchange rate over the medium run to eliminate the trade deficit (i.e., to increase NX to 0)?

b. Now write down the national income identity. Assume again that output returns to its natural level in the medium run. If NX increases to 0, what must happen to domestic demand ($C + I + G$) in the medium run? What government policies are available to reduce domestic demand in the medium run? Identify which components of domestic demand each of these policies affect.

EXPLORE FURTHER

6. *Retrieve the nominal exchange rates between Japan and the USA from the Internet. A useful and free Canadian site that allows you to construct graphs online is the Pacific Exchange Rate Service (fx.sauder.ubc.ca), provided by Werner Antweiler at the Sauder School of Business, University of British Columbia.*

a. Plot the yen versus the dollar since 1979. During which times period(s) did the yen appreciate? During which period(s) did the yen depreciate?

b. Given the current Japanese slump (although there are some encouraging signs at the time of writing), one way of increasing demand would be to make Japanese goods more attractive. Does this require an appreciation or a depreciation of the yen?

c. What has happened to the yen during the past few years? Has it appreciated or depreciated? Is this good or bad for Japan?

7. Saving and investment throughout the world

Retrieve the most recent World Economic Outlook (WEO) from the website of the International Monetary Fund (www.imf.org). In the Statistical Appendix, find the table titled 'Summary of Sources and Uses of World Saving', which lists saving and investment (as a percentage of GDP) around the world. Use the data for the most recent year available to answer parts (a) and (b).

a. Does world saving equal investment? (You may ignore small statistical discrepancies.) Offer some intuition for your answer.

b. How does US saving compare to US investment? How is the USA able to finance its investment? (*We explain this explicitly in the next chapter, but your intuition should help you figure it out now.*)

We invite you to visit the Blanchard page on the Prentice Hall website, at **www.prenhall.com/blanchard** for this chapter's World Wide Web exercises.

FURTHER READING

- If you want to learn more about international trade and international economics, read the very good textbook by **Paul Krugman and Maurice Obstfeld**, *International Economics, Theory and Policy*, 7th ed., Pearson Addison-Wesley, New York, 2007.

- If you want to know current exchange rates between nearly any pair of currencies in the world, look at the currency converter at *www.oanda.com*.

- A good discussion of the relation among trade deficits, budget deficits, private saving and investment is given in **Barry Bosworth**, *Saving and Investment in a Global Economy*, Brookings Institution, Washington, DC, 1993.

- A good discussion of the US trade deficit and its implications for the future is given in **William Cline**, *The United States as a Debtor Nation*, Peterson Institute, Washington, DC, 2005.

THE MEDIUM RUN

In the medium run, the economy returns to a level of output associated with the natural rate of unemployment.

Chapter 7 The labour market

Chapter 7 looks at equilibrium in the labour market. It derives the natural rate of unemployment – the unemployment rate to which the economy tends to return in the medium run. Associated with the natural rate of unemployment is a natural level of output.

Chapter 8 Putting all markets together: the *AS–AD* model

Chapter 8 looks at equilibrium in all three markets – goods, financial and labour – together. It shows that, while output typically deviates from the natural level of output in the short run, it returns to the natural level in the medium run. The model developed in Chapter 8 is called the *AS–AD* model and, together with the *IS–LM* model, it is one of the workhorses of macroeconomics.

Chapter 9 The natural rate of unemployment and the Phillips curve

Chapter 9 looks more closely at the relation between inflation and unemployment, a relation known as the Phillips curve. It shows that low unemployment leads to an increase in inflation; high unemployment leads to a decrease in inflation.

Chapter 10 Inflation, activity and the nominal money growth

Chapter 10 looks at the determination of output, unemployment and inflation and the effects of money growth. In the short run, decreases in money growth can trigger a recession. In the medium run, however, they are neutral; they have no effect on unemployment or output but are reflected one-for-one in changes in the rate of inflation.

Chapter 7

THE LABOUR MARKET

Think about what happens when firms respond to an increase in demand by increasing production. Higher production leads to higher employment. Higher employment leads to lower unemployment. Lower unemployment leads to higher wages. Higher wages increase production costs, leading firms to increase prices. Higher prices lead workers to ask for higher wages. Higher wages lead to further increases in prices, and so on.

So far, we have simply ignored this sequence of events: by assuming a constant price level, we have in effect assumed that firms were able and willing to supply any amount of output at a given price level. So long as our focus was on the *short run*, this assumption was acceptable. But as our attention turns to the *medium run*, we must now abandon this assumption, explore how prices and wages adjust over time, and explore how this, in turn, affects output. This will be our task in this and the next three chapters.

At the centre of the sequence of events described here is the *labour market*, the market in which wages are determined. This chapter focuses on the labour market. It has five sections:

- Section 7.1 provides an overview of the labour market in Europe.

- Sections 7.2 and 7.3 look at wage and price determination.

- Section 7.4 looks at equilibrium in the labour market. It characterises the *natural rate of unemployment*, the rate of unemployment to which the economy tends to return in the medium run.

- Section 7.5 gives a map of where we will be going next.

7.1 A TOUR OF THE LABOUR MARKET

The total EU27 population in 2008 was 490 million (Figure 7.1). Excluding those who were either under working age (under 15), or above the retirement age (65), the number of people potentially available for employment, the **population in working age**, was 330 million.

The **labour force** – the sum of those either working or looking for work – was only 238 million. The other 92 million people were **out of the labour force**, neither working in the marketplace nor looking for work. The **participation rate**, defined as the ratio of the labour force to the population in working age, was therefore 238/330, or 72%. Conversely, the non-participation rate, defined as the number of people out of the labour force divided by the population in working age, was 92/330, or 28%. In Europe, as in most of the other OECD countries, the participation rate has steadily increased over time, reflecting mostly the increasing participation rate of women: in Western Europe, like in the USA, in 1950, one woman out of three was in the labour force; now the number is close to two out of three and not far from the participation rate of men (three out of four). However, this is not true in all European countries. Figure 7.2 shows the participation rates of men and women in Europe

◀ Work in the home, such as cooking or raising children, is not classified as work in the official statistics. This is a reflection of the difficulty of measuring these activities – not a value judgement about what constitutes work and what doesn't.

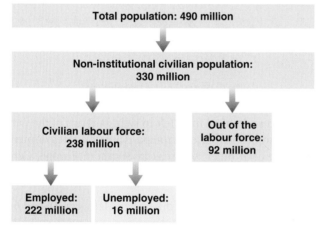

Figure 7.1

Population, labour force, employment and unemployment in the EU27 (in millions), 2008

Source: Eurostat.

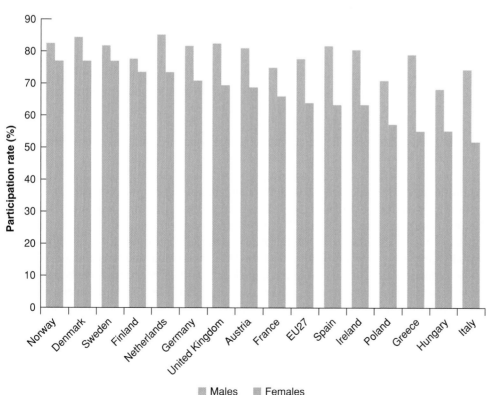

Figure 7.2

The participation rate of men and women in Europe, 2008

Source: Eurostat.

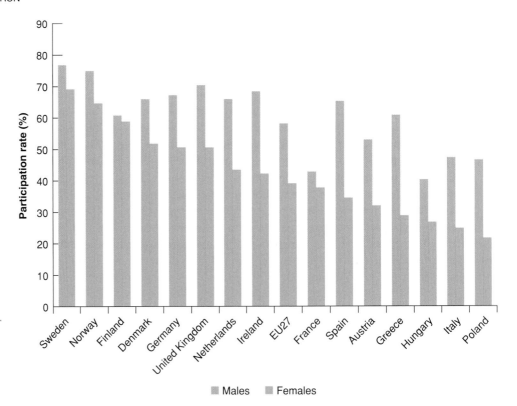

Figure 7.3

The participation rate of men and women between 55 and 64 years in Europe, 2008

Source: Eurostat.

in 2008 (where countries are ranked from left to right in terms of the participation rate of women): in Northern European countries, the participation rates of men and women are pretty high and close to each other, whereas in Southern Europe, Central and Eastern Europe, and also in Ireland, the participation rate of women is much lower, down to just around 50%.

Moreover, if we look at older workers, workers aged between 55 and 64, the differences among the participation rates of men and women are even more striking: the average for the EU27 is 39% for women and 58% for men. As shown in Figure 7.3, the ranking is pretty much the same as the one shown in Figure 7.2, but participation rates for both genders are much lower and the gap between men and women is even more pronounced. This in part reflects the differences in the retirement ages across European countries, many of which are still below 65 years, as in France, and the differences in the retirement ages between men and women, the latter often allowed to retire earlier (usually at 60 years) than men, as in Austria, Greece, Italy, Poland and the UK.

Of those in the labour force, 222 million were employed, and 16 million were unemployed – looking for work. The **unemployment rate**, defined as the ratio of the unemployed to the labour force, was therefore $16/238 = 6.7\%$.

Unemployment in Europe has not always been so high. Between the end of the Second World War and the end of the 1970s, European unemployment was very low, around 2%. It started to rise during the 1970s; it hit 8% in the 1980s and reached a peak of 10% in the 1990s. Today it is still rather high (6.7% in 2008), but the average unemployment rate actually hides a lot of differences among European countries. Figure 7.4 shows unemployment rates in European countries together with the EU27 as a whole and the USA and Japan in 2008. In many of them unemployment is quite low: Austria, Denmark, the Netherlands and Norway have unemployment rates lower than the USA (5.8%). The high average unemployment rate in Europe reflects high unemployment rates in the four largest European economies: France, Germany, Italy and Spain. Among the latter there are yet big differences: the unemployment rate in Germany has increased from the very low pre-unification rates and now hides huge regional differences between East and West Germany; in Spain, the unemployment rate went well above 20% in the early 1990s, then it decreased, and then it increased again in the last few year following the financial crisis which began in 2007.

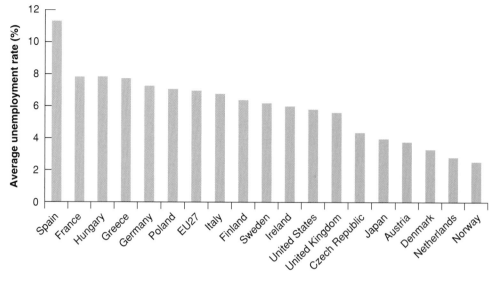

Figure 7.4

The average unemployment rate in European countries, 2008(a)

The average unemployment rate in Europe hides big differences among countries.

Source: Eurostat.

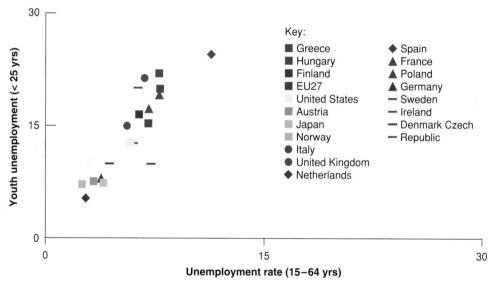

Figure 7.5

The average unemployment rate in European countries, 2008(b)

The incidence of unemployment is usually higher among young workers (< 25 years).

Source: Eurostat.

The average unemployment rate also hides large differences among different groups of workers within the same country. The most notable one is the higher incidence of unemployment among young workers. Figure 7.5 shows the total unemployment rate (i.e. the unemployment rate computed for the total labour force) and the youth unemployment rate (i.e. the unemployment rate among worker younger than 25 years). The figure shows a dramatic incidence of unemployment among young workers compared to the average incidence of unemployment, and this is true in all European countries, especially in countries with higher-than-average unemployment rates (such as Greece, Italy and Spain), but also where the total unemployment rate is very low (such as the Netherlands and Norway).

Flows of workers between employment, unemployment and non-participation

To get a sense of what a given unemployment rate implies for individual workers, consider the following analogy. Take an airport full of passengers. It may be crowded because many planes are coming and going, and many passengers are quickly moving in and out of the airport. Or it may be crowded because bad weather is delaying flights and passengers are stuck, waiting for the weather to improve. The number of passengers in the airport will be high in both cases, but their plights are quite different. Passengers in the second scenario are likely to be much less happy.

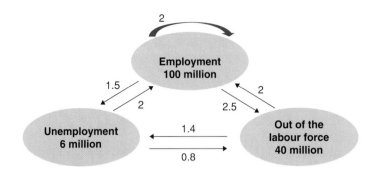

Figure 7.6

Average flows between employment, unemployment and non-participation in a hypothetical country

Sclerosis, a medical term, means ➤ hardening of tissue. By analogy, it is used in economics to describe markets that function poorly and have few transactions.

In the same way, a given unemployment rate may reflect two very different realities. It may reflect an active labour market, with many **separations** and many **hires**, and so with many workers entering and exiting unemployment; or it may reflect a sclerotic labour market, with few separations, few hires and a stagnant unemployment pool.

Finding out which reality hides behind the aggregate unemployment rate requires data on the movements of workers. These data are available in Europe from a quarterly survey called the **Labour Force Survey (LFS)**. If you want to know more about how the LFS is conducted, see the Focus box 'The European Union Labour Force Survey' later in this chapter. Here, to see how these data can be used to study the labour market, let us imagine – to keep things simple – a hypothetical country whose flows are reported in Figure 7.6.

Imagine that, out of an employment pool of 100 million, in a given month 2 million workers move directly from one job to another (shown by the circular arrow at the top of the figure). Another 1.5 million move from employment to unemployment (shown by the arrow from employment to unemployment). And 2.5 million move from employment out of the labour force (shown by the arrow from employment to out of the labour force). This means that, on average, there are 6 (2 + 1.5 + 2.5) million separations each month in this country.

One third (2 out of 6 million) of all separations are **leavers** – workers leaving their jobs for a better alternative. The remaining two-thirds are **layoffs**. Layoffs may come from changes in employment levels across firms. At any given time, some firms are suffering decreases in demand and decreasing their employment; other firms are enjoying increases in demand and increasing employment. If aggregate employment numbers are stable, this does not mean nothing happens in the labour market, a high number of layoffs suggests a reality of continual job destruction and job creation across firms.

In our hypothetical country, the flows in and out of the labour force are large: each month, 4 million workers drop out of the labour force (2.5 plus 1.5), and the same number join the labour force (2 plus 2).

This fact has another important implication. The sharp focus on the unemployment rate by economists, policy makers and the news media is partly misdirected. Some of the people classified as 'out of the labour force' are very much like the unemployed. They are in effect **discouraged workers**. And while they are not actively looking for a job, they will take one

Working in the opposite direction: ➤ Some of the unemployed may be unwilling to accept any job offered to them and should probably not be counted as unemployed because they are not really looking for a job.

if they find one. This is why economists sometimes focus on the **non-employment rate**, the ratio of population minus employment to population, rather than the unemployment rate. We will follow tradition in this book and focus on the unemployment rate, but you should keep in mind that the unemployment rate is not the best estimate of the number of people available for work.

Going back to our hypothetical country, the average flow out of unemployment each month is 2.8 million: 2 million people get a job and 0.8 million stop searching for one and drop out of the labour force. Put another way, the proportion of unemployed leaving unemployment equals 2.8/6 or about 47% each month.

The proportion of unemployed leaving unemployment each month is a very useful piece of information, as it allows computing the average **duration of unemployment**, which is the average length of time people spend unemployed. To see why, consider an example. Suppose the number of unemployed is constant and equal to 100, and each unemployed person remains unemployed for two months. So, at any given time, there are 50 people who have been unemployed for one month and 50 who have been unemployed for two months. Each month, the 50 unemployed who have been unemployed for two months leave unemployment. In this example, the proportion of unemployed leaving unemployment each month is 50/100, or 50%. The duration of unemployment is two months – the inverse of 1/50%. The average duration of unemployment equals the inverse of the proportion of unemployed leaving unemployment each month. Now, suppose that each unemployed person remains unemployed for five months. In this case, at any given time, there are 20 people who have been unemployed for one month, 20 who have been unemployed for two months, 20 who have been unemployed for three months, 20 who have been unemployed for four months and 20 who have been unemployed for five months. Each month, the 20 unemployed who have been unemployed for five months leave unemployment. In this case, the proportion of unemployed leaving unemployment each month is 20/100, or 20%. The duration of unemployment is five months – the inverse of 1/20%. In our hypothetical country, where the proportion of the unemployed leaving unemployment each month is 47%, the average duration of unemployment is 2.1 month – the inverse of 1/47%.

The longer it takes for unemployed people to find a job, the higher is the average duration of unemployment. Countries with a high percentage of long-term unemployment (usually defined as unemployment for more than 12 months) have high average duration, and vice versa.

The average duration of unemployment has an important implication. In a country where the average duration is high, unemployment can be described as a stagnant pool of workers waiting indefinitely for jobs. In a country where the average duration is low, as in our example, for most (but obviously not all) of the unemployed, being unemployed is more a quick transition than a long wait between jobs. Among rich countries, the USA has one of the lowest average duration of unemployment of all (and one of the lowest percentage of long-term unemployment on total unemployment, 9.9% in 2007). The average duration of unemployment is much longer in Western Europe (where the incidence of long-term unemployment is much higher than in the USA, ranging from 12.9% in Sweden to 27.3% in the UK, to 40.3% in France, up to a dramatic 70.8% in the Slovak Republic). Figure 7.7 shows the average duration of unemployment in some European countries, compared to the USA, since 2000.

The most striking feature of Figure 7.7 is the large difference between Europe and the USA: the average duration of unemployment is now slightly more than one year in Europe compared to around four months in the USA. Unemployment is still a very different phenomenon in Europe, on average, than in the USA: being unemployed in Europe is often not a transitory condition as it is, on average, in the USA.

The second feature of Figure 7.7 is the divergent trends between Western and Northern Europe, where the average duration has decreased since 2000, and Central and Eastern Europe, where it has increased since then.

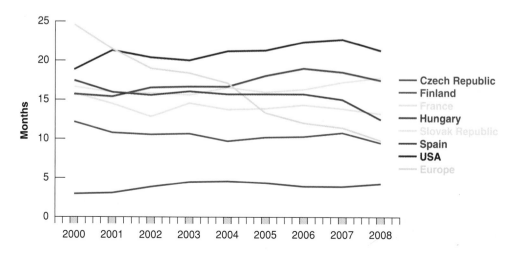

Figure 7.7

Average duration of unemployment in Europe and the USA

Source: Eurostat.

FOCUS
The European Union Labour Force Survey

The European Union Labour Force Survey (EU LFS) is a quarterly sample survey covering the population in private households in the EU, EFTA (except Liechtenstein) and Candidate Countries. It provides annual and quarterly information on labour participation of people aged 15 and over as well as persons outside the labour force. The EU LFS sample size amounts approximately to 1.5 million individuals each quarter. The quarterly sampling rates vary between 0.2% and 3.3% in each country. Eurostat started the collection of these microdata in 1983. The data range is from 1983 to 2005 depending on the country.

In providing data on employment, unemployment and inactivity, the EU LFS is an important source of information about the situation and trends in the labour market in the EU. Various breakdowns are available – by age, sex, educational attainment, temporary employment, full-time/part-time distinction and many other dimensions.

The quarterly EU LFS also forms the basis for Eurostat's calculation of monthly unemployment figures, complemented by either monthly LFS estimates for the unemployment rates or additional sources such as unemployment registers. The resulting monthly harmonised unemployment rate – one of Eurostat's key short-term indicators – is published in a news release and in the online database.

Note: For more on the LFS, you can go to the LFS home page: (*http://circa.europa.eu/irc/dsis/employment/info/data/ eu_lfs/index.htm*).

7.2 WAGE DETERMINATION

Having looked at unemployment, let's turn to wage determination and to the relation between wages and unemployment.

Wages are set in many ways. Sometimes they are set through **collective bargaining** – that is, bargaining between firms and unions. Negotiations may take place at the firm level, at the industry level or at the national level. Sometimes contract agreements apply only to firms that have signed the agreement. Sometimes they are automatically extended to all firms and all workers in the sector or the economy.

In most of the countries in Europe, collective bargaining is the predominant mean by which wages are agreed. The percentage of workers covered by collective bargaining is as high as 98% in Austria, 95% in Finland and higher than 90% in Belgium, Germany and France. In the rest of Europe, it is slightly lower, generally between 60 and 80%, but still much higher than in the USA or in Japan, where the percentage of workers covered by collective bargaining is around 20%. In Europe, however, the UK stands out as an exception, as collective bargaining plays a limited role, especially outside the manufacturing sector. Today, just around one third of UK workers have their wages set by collective bargaining agreements. For the rest, wages are either set by employers or by bargaining between the employer and individual employees. The higher the skills needed to do the job, the more likely there is to be bargaining. Wages offered for entry-level jobs at McDonald's are on a take-it-or-leave-it basis. New college graduates, on the other hand, can typically negotiate a few aspects of their compensation. CEOs and football stars can negotiate a lot more.

Given these differences across workers and across countries, can we hope to formulate anything like a general theory of wage determination? Yes. Although institutional differences influence wage determination, there are common forces at work in all countries. Two sets of facts stand out:

- Workers are typically paid a wage that exceeds their **reservation wage**, the wage that would make them indifferent between working or being unemployed. In other words, most workers are paid a high enough wage that they prefer being employed to being unemployed.
- Wages typically depend on labour market conditions. The lower the unemployment rate, the higher the wages. (We will state this more precisely in the next section.)

To think about these facts, economists have focused on two broad lines of explanation. The first is that even in the absence of collective bargaining, workers have some bargaining power, which they can and do use to obtain wages above their reservation wages. The second is that firms themselves may, for a number of reasons, want to pay wages higher than the reservation wage. Let's look at each explanation in turn.

Bargaining

How much **bargaining power** a worker has depends on two factors. The first is how costly it would be for the firm to replace him or her, were he or she to leave the firm. The second is how hard it would be for him or her to find another job, were he or she to leave the firm. The more costly it is for the firm to replace the worker, and the easier it is for him or her to find another job, the more bargaining power he or she will have. This has two implications:

- How much bargaining power a worker has depends first on the nature of the job. Replacing a worker at McDonald's is not very costly: the required skills can be taught quickly, and typically a large number of willing applicants have already filled out job application forms. In this situation, the worker is unlikely to have much bargaining power. If he or she asks for a higher wage, the firm can lay him or her off and find a replacement at minimum cost. In contrast, a highly skilled worker who knows in detail how the firm operates may be very difficult and costly to replace. This gives him or her more bargaining power. If he or she asks for a higher wage, the firm may decide that it is best to give it to him or her.
- How much bargaining power a worker has also depends on labour market conditions. When the unemployment rate is low, it is more difficult for firms to find acceptable replacement workers. At the same time, it is easier for workers to find other jobs. Under these conditions, workers are in a stronger bargaining position and may be able to obtain a higher wage. Conversely, when the unemployment rate is high, finding good replacement workers is easier for firms, while finding another job is harder for workers. Being in a weak bargaining position, workers may have no choice but to accept a lower wage.

Efficiency wages

Regardless of workers' bargaining power, firms may want to pay more than the reservation wage. They may want their workers to be productive, and a higher wage can help them achieve that goal. If, for example, it takes a while for workers to learn how to do a job correctly, firms will want their workers to stay for some time. But if workers are paid only their reservation wage, they will be indifferent between staying or leaving. In this case, many of them will quit, and the turnover rate will be high. Paying a wage above the reservation wage makes it financially attractive for workers to stay. It decreases turnover and increases productivity.

Behind this example lies a more general proposition: most firms want their workers to feel good about their jobs. Feeling good promotes good work, which leads to higher productivity. Paying a high wage is one instrument a firm can use to achieve these goals. (See the Focus box 'Henry Ford and Efficiency Wages'.) Economists call the theories that link the *productivity* or the *efficiency* of workers to the wage they are paid **efficiency wage theories**.

Like theories based on bargaining, efficiency wage theories suggest that wages depend on both the nature of a job and on labour market conditions:

- Firms – such as high-tech firms – that see employee morale and commitment as essential to the quality of their work will pay more than firms in sectors where workers' activities are more routine.

◀ Before 11 September 2001, the approach to airport security was to hire workers at low wages and accept the resulting high turnover. Now that airport security has become a much higher priority, the approach is to make the jobs more attractive and better paying so as to get more motivated and more competent workers, and reduce turnover.

FOCUS
Henry Ford and efficiency wages

In 1914, Henry Ford – the builder of the most popular car in the world at the time, the Model T – made a stunning announcement. His company would pay every qualified employee a minimum of $5 per day for an eight-hour day. This was a very large salary increase for most employees, who had been earning an average of $2.30 for a nine-hour day. From the point of view of the Ford company, this increase in pay was far from negligible – it represented about half of the company's profits at the time.

What Ford's motivations were is not entirely clear. Ford himself gave too many reasons for us to know which ones he actually believed. The reason was not that the company had a hard time finding workers at the previous wage. But the company clearly had a hard time retaining workers. There was a very high turnover rate, and there was much dissatisfaction among workers.

Whatever the reasons behind Ford's decision, the results of the wage increase were astounding, as Table 7.1 shows.

The annual turnover rate (the ratio of separations to employment) plunged from a high of 370% in 1913 to a low of 16% in 1915. (An annual turnover rate of 370% means that, on average, 31% of the company's workers left each month, so that over the course of a year, the ratio of separations to employment was 31% × 12 = 370%.) The layoff rate collapsed from 62% to nearly 0%. The average rate of absenteeism (not shown in the table), which ran at close to 10% in 1913, was down to 2.5% one year later. There is little question that higher wages were the main source of these changes.

Did productivity at the Ford plant increase enough to offset the cost of increased wages? The answer to this question is less clear. Productivity was much higher in 1914 than in 1913. Estimates of the productivity increases range from 30% to 50%. Despite higher wages, profits were also higher in 1914 than in 1913. But how much of this increase in profits was due to changes in workers' behaviour and how much was due to the increasing success of Model T cars is harder to establish.

While the effects support efficiency wage theories, it may be that the increase in wages to $5 per day was excessive, at least from the point of view of profit maximisation. But Henry Ford probably had other objectives as well, from keeping the unions out – which he did – to generating publicity for himself and the company – which he also surely did.

Table 7.1 Annual turnover and layoff rates (%) at Ford, 1913–1915

	1913	1914	1915
Turnover rate	370	54	16
Layoff rate	62	7	0.1

Source: Dan Raff and Lawrence Summers, 'Did Henry Ford Pay Efficiency Wages?' *Journal of Labour Economics*, 1987, **5**(4), 557–586.

- Labour market conditions will affect the wage. A low unemployment rate makes it more attractive for employed workers to leave: when unemployment is low, it is easy to find another job. This means that when unemployment decreases, a firm that wants to avoid an increase in leavers will have to increase wages to induce workers to stay with the firm. When this happens, lower unemployment will again lead to higher wages. Conversely, higher unemployment will lead to lower wages.

Wages, prices and unemployment

We capture our discussion of wage determination by using the following equation:

$$W = P^e F(u, z) \qquad [7.1]$$
$$(-, +)$$

The aggregate nominal wage, W, depends on three factors:

- The expected price level, P^e.
- The unemployment rate, u.
- A catchall variable, z, that stands for all other variables that may affect the outcome of wage setting.

Let's look at each factor.

The expected price level

First, ignore the difference between the expected and the actual price levels and ask: why does the price level affect nominal wages? Because both workers and firms care about *real wages*, not nominal wages:

- Workers do not care about how much money they receive but about how many goods they can buy with that money. In other words, they do not care about the nominal wages they receive but about the nominal wages, W, they receive relative to the price of the goods they buy, P. They care about W/P.
- In the same way, firms do not care about the nominal wages they pay but about the nominal wages, W, they pay relative to the price of the goods they sell, P. So they also care about W/P.

Think of it another way: if workers expect the price level – the price of the goods they buy – to double, they will ask for a doubling of their nominal wage. If firms expect the price level – the price of the goods they sell – to double, they will be willing to double the nominal wage. So, if both workers and firms expect the price level to double, they will agree to double the nominal wage, keeping the real wage constant. This is captured in equation (7.1): a doubling in the expected price level leads to a doubling of the nominal wage chosen when wages are set.

◄ An increase in the expected price level leads to an increase in the nominal wage, in the same proportion.

Return now to the distinction we set aside earlier: why do wages depend on the *expected price level*, P^e, rather than the *actual price level*, P? Because wages are set in nominal (say, euro) terms, and when they are set, the relevant price level is not yet known. For example, in many union contracts in Europe, nominal wages are set in advance for a few years. Unions and firms have to decide what nominal wages will be over the following years based on what they expect the price level to be over those years. Even when wages are set by firms or by bargaining between the firm and each worker, nominal wages are typically set for a year. If the price level goes up unexpectedly during the year, nominal wages are typically not readjusted. (How workers and firms form expectations of the price level will occupy us for much of the next three chapters; we will leave this issue aside for the moment.)

The unemployment rate

Also affecting the aggregate wage in equation (7.1) is the unemployment rate, u. The minus sign under u indicates that an increase in the unemployment rate *decreases* wages.

The fact that wages depend on the unemployment rate was one of the main conclusions of our earlier discussion. If we think of wages as being determined by bargaining, then higher unemployment weakens workers' bargaining power, forcing them to accept lower wages. If we think of wages as being determined by efficiency wage considerations, then higher unemployment allows firms to pay lower wages and still keep workers willing to work.

◄ An increase in unemployment leads to a decrease in the nominal wage.

The other factors

The third variable in equation (7.1), z, is a catchall variable that stands for all the factors that affect wages, given the expected price level and the unemployment rate. By convention, we will define z so that an increase in z implies an increase in the wage (hence the positive sign under z in the equation). Our earlier discussion suggests a long list of potential factors here.

◄ By definition of z, an increase in z leads to an increase in the nominal wage.

Take, for example, **unemployment insurance** – the payment of unemployment benefits to workers who lose their jobs. There are very good reasons why society should provide some insurance to workers who lose their jobs and have a hard time finding new ones. But there is little question that, by making the prospects of unemployment less distressing, more generous unemployment benefits do increase wages at a given unemployment rate. To take an extreme example, suppose unemployment insurance did not exist. Some workers would have little to live on and would be willing to accept very low wages to avoid remaining unemployed. But unemployment insurance does exist, and it allows unemployed workers to hold out for higher wages. In this case, we can think of z as representing the level of

Table 7.2 Net replacement rates in Europe, 2002

	Initial phase of unemployment		Long-term unemployment	
	Single person	One earner married couple with 2 children	Single person	One earner married couple with 2 children
Austria	55	73	51	78
Belgium	66	61	55	61
Czech Republic	50	54	31	71
Denmark	59	76	50	78
Finland	64	82	51	85
France	71	76	41	70
Germany	61	78	61	68
Greece	46	50	0	3
Hungary	44	54	24	30
Ireland	29	55	51	73
Italy	52	60	0	0
Netherlands	71	78	58	72
Norway	66	73	42	64
Poland	44	51	30	73
Slovak Republic	62	72	42	91
Spain	70	75	27	41
Sweden	81	83	51	78
UK	45	46	45	73
USA	56	53	7	41

Source: CESifo DICE database, based on data from EU Commission and MISSOC 2009.

unemployment benefits: at a given unemployment rate, higher unemployment benefits increase the wage.

In Europe, unemployment benefits – which are computed as the fraction of the last wage which the social security system provides to a person if he or she no longer works (and are called 'net replacement rates') – vary across countries and, within each country, vary basically according to the type of household (single person or couple with children) and the sector of industry. Table 7.2 shows the net replacement rates for an average production worker in the initial phase of unemployment and at the end of the fifth year of benefit receipt (the data refer to the year 2002). In practically all countries, the net replacement rate at the beginning of a spell of unemployment is usually higher for a couple with two children than for someone who is single. For instance in Finland, where the initial replacement rate is 82%, the unemployed have little incentive to seek regular work. The net replacement rates for long-term unemployed are lowest in Italy, Greece and the USA and highest in the Scandinavian countries (except Norway), the Slovak Republic, the Netherlands, Austria and Germany.

Another aspect of unemployment insurance that is likely to affect wages is the duration of unemployment insurance, that is the number of months it is provided for by the social security system. At a given unemployment rate, a longer duration of unemployment benefits increases the wage. In Europe, the duration of unemployment insurance varies a lot across countries, much more than the level of the benefits provided. Figure 7.8 shows the duration of unemployment insurance in European countries in 2008. In most of the countries, unemployment benefits are granted for less than one year, with the noteworthy exceptions of Belgium, where the benefits are unlimited, and of Denmark and the Netherlands where the benefits are paid for four to five years. In the other European countries, there are a few cases of extended provision of unemployment benefits to long-term unemployed people depending on age, employment record or insurance payment.

Another factor that affects wages, given the expected price level and the unemployment rate, is the level of **employment protection**. The higher State protection for workers is, the more expensive it is for firms to lay off workers. Higher employment protection is likely to lead to higher wages. This is because high employment protection is likely to increase the

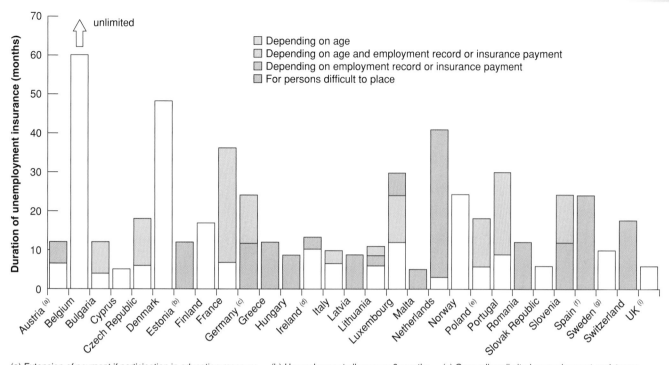

(a) Extension of payment if participation in education measure. – (b) Unemployment allowance: 9 months. – (c) Generally unlimited unemployment assistance, the entitlement must be proven every 6 months. – (d) Unlimited unemployment assistance. – (e) Depends also on regional unemployment rate. – (f) Unemployment assistance is available with the same periods. If it is granted after exhaustion of unemployment benefit it is restricted to the half of the period. – (g) Unemployment assistance: 6 to 18 months. – (h) Additional 5 months for applicants who have a child aged under 18 years. – (i) Income-based jobseekers' allowance: unlimited.

Figure 7.8

Duration of unemployment insurance in Europe, 2008 (in months)

Source: CESifo DICE database, based on data from EU Commission and MISSOC 2009.

bargaining power of workers covered by this protection (laying them off and hiring other workers is now more costly for firms), increasing the wage for a given unemployment rate.

In Europe, the level of State protection for workers is on average higher than in the USA. However, there are also wide variations within Europe itself: most notably, the UK has significantly reduced the level employment protection since the 1980s and is now rather different from the so-called European social model which prevails in continental Europe. Figure 7.9 shows the level of employment protection in Europe, compared to other OECD countries. The indicator of employment protection ranges between 0 and 2 and it increases with strictness of employment protection (that is, the higher the indicator, the higher employment protection). In Europe, the UK ranks very low, followed by Ireland and the Scandinavian countries, while countries in Southern Europe – France, Spain, Italy and Portugal – have the highest level of employment protection of all.

A further factor that is likely to affect wages, given the expected price level and unemployment, is the presence of a **minimum wage** set by the law. The presence of a minimum wage can cause wage rigidity, as it prevents wages from falling below the legal minimum to restore equilibrium in the labour market. Although most workers earn well above the minimum wage, for some groups of workers, especially for the unskilled, the presence of a minimum wage is likely to reduce firms' demand for unskilled labour. This is the reason why many economists argue that the presence of a minimum wage is largely responsible for higher than average youth unemployment. In fact, an increase in the minimum wage may increase not only the minimum wage itself but also wages just above the minimum wage, leading to an increase in the average wage, W, at a given unemployment rate.

Europe, including the UK since April 1999, as well as the USA, has had a mandatory minimum wage. Figure 7.10 shows the gross minimum wage in euro per month in each European country in 2009. The striking feature of Figure 7.10 is the very low level of

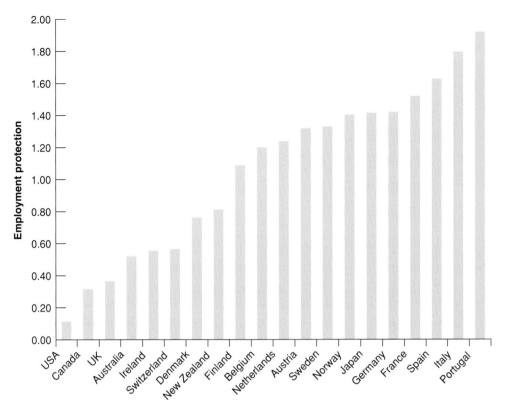

Figure 7.9

Employment protection across European countries, 1995

Source: CESifo DICE database, based on data from EU Commission and MISSOC 2009.

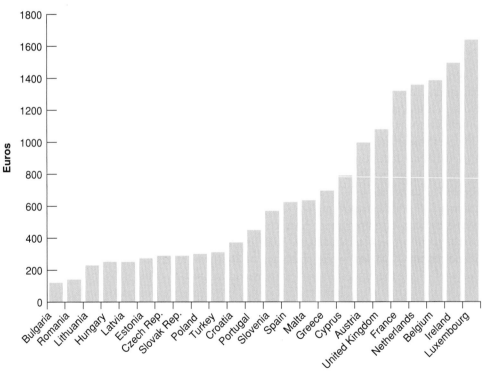

Figure 7.10

Gross minimum wages,ᵃ euro per month, 2009

Source: CESifo DICE database, based on data from EU Commission and MISSOC 2009.

Note: (a) Full-time adult employees, aged 23+. The amounts for countries outside the euro zone have been converted using the average exchange rate for 01/2009 (see Eurostat, http://epp.eurostat.ec.europa.eu/).

minimum wages in Eastern and Central European countries, where the statutory gross minimum wage per month is around €200. The size of the minimum wage in absolute terms varies a lot across countries, ranging from very low levels such as in Portugal and Spain (where the minimum wage is significantly lower than in the USA), to high levels such as in the Netherlands or in Ireland. (In the USA, the Federal minimum wage is $7.25 per hour. Individual states can and often do apply different minimum wages.)

It has been widely debated whether the European social model should be considered one of the sources of the higher unemployment rates in continental Europe compared to the UK or the USA. According to some labour economists, there is no doubt that high levels of unemployment insurance, employment protection and high minimum wages are partly responsible for the high unemployment rates in many European countries. Yet, it has also been argued that high employment protection need not necessarily be associated with high unemployment. Indeed, if it is true, on average, that countries with higher employment protection have higher unemployment rates, it is also true that some countries with low unemployment rates do have high level of State protection of workers. The most notable case in Europe is Denmark. The Danish system, since the early 1980s, combines high levels of social welfare and unemployment protection with an effective system of job search assistance: the result is a low unemployment rate, one of the lowest in Europe.

7.3 PRICE DETERMINATION

Having looked at wage determination, let's now turn to price determination.

The prices set by firms depend on the costs they face. These costs depend, in turn, on the nature of the **production function** – the relation between the inputs used in production and the quantity of output produced and on the prices of these inputs.

For the moment, we will assume that firms produce goods using labour as the only factor of production. We will write the production function as follows:

$$Y = AN$$

where Y is output, N is employment and A is labour productivity. This way of writing the production function implies that **labour productivity** – output per worker – is constant and equal to A.

It should be clear that this is very much simplified. In reality, firms use other factors of production in addition to labour. They use capital – machines and factories. They use raw materials – oil, for example. Moreover, there is technological progress, so that labour productivity, A, is not constant but steadily increases over time. We shall introduce these complications later. We will introduce raw materials in Chapter 8, when we discuss changes in the price of oil. We will focus on the role of capital and technological progress when we turn to the determination of output in the *long run* in Chapters 11–13. For the moment, though, this simple relation between output and employment will make our lives easier and still serve our purposes.

Given the assumption that labour productivity, A, is constant, we can make one further simplification. We can choose the units of output so that one worker produces one unit of output – in other words, so that $A = 1$. (This way, we do not have to carry the letter A around, and this will simplify notation.) With this assumption, the production function becomes

$$Y = N \qquad [7.2]$$

The production function, $Y = N$, implies that the cost of producing one more unit of output is the cost of employing one more worker, at wage W. Using the terminology introduced in your microeconomics course: the *marginal cost of production* – the cost of producing one more unit of output – is equal to W.

If there were perfect competition in the goods market, the price of a unit of output would be equal to marginal cost: P would be equal to W. But many goods markets are not competitive, and firms charge a price higher than their marginal cost. A simple way of capturing this fact is to assume that firms set their prices according to

$$P = (1 + \mu)W \qquad [7.3]$$

where μ is the **mark-up** of the price over the cost. If goods markets were perfectly competitive, μ would be equal to zero, and the price, P, would simply equal the cost, W. To the extent that they are not competitive, and firms have market power (that is, they can set

◄ We can use a term from microeconomics here: this assumption implies *constant returns to labour* in production. If firms double the number of workers they employ, they double the amount of output they produce.

a price higher than the marginal cost, which would be the case in perfectly competitive markets), μ is positive, and the price, P, will exceed the cost, W, by a factor equal to $(1 + \mu)]$.

We can think of the mark-up as depending on the degree of competition in the product market. The higher the degree of competition, the lower the mark-up and, vice versa, the lower the degree of competition, the higher the mark-up. To keep things simple, we can assume that the degree of competition is higher the higher the number of competing products in a market. In fact, a high number of competing products in a market forces producers to keep prices down in order not to lose market share. Moreover, the mark-up also depends on the degree of regulation of the product market. To see this, imagine a highly regulated product market with a lot of trade barriers: trade barriers will limit the number of foreign products that can be sold in that market, and therefore will reduce the degree of market competition. Therefore, the higher the degree of product market regulation, the lower the degree of competition. We can express this by writing the mark-up as a positive function of product market regulation (*PMR*):

$$\mu = f(PMR) \tag{1}$$
$$(+)$$

Equation (1) tells us that the mark-up μ depends positively on product market regulation, thus it depends negatively on the level of competition in the market.

In the context of European integration, for example, decreases in *PMR* may reflect the elimination of tariff barriers, or standardisation measures making it easier to sell domestic products in other EU countries. Suppose the government increases competition in the product market, for a given number of firms. Higher competition means that firms face a more elastic demand for their products (as consumers can more easily switch to other suppliers if they want to). Hence, to maintain their market share, they have to decrease their mark-up, leading in turn to both an increase in real wages and a decrease in unemployment. Therefore, a lower product market regulation should be associated with higher real wages (as we shall see in Section 7.4).

This is exactly what we observe in Europe, where the completion of the internal market has increased both competition and real wages. Figure 7.11 shows the evolution of product market regulation and real wages in Europe from 1998–2008. Since 1998, product market regulation has decreased everywhere, even more so in countries which started from higher levels, such as France, Italy and Spain. Today, the differences in the levels of product market regulation across European countries are very small compared to the end of the 1990s. Scandinavian countries show slightly lower levels – that is, higher internal competition.

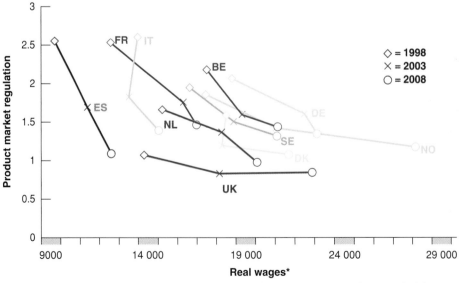

Figure 7.11

Relationship between trends in product market regulation and wages in Europe (1998, 2003, 2008)

Source: OECD, Eurostat.

*Real wages are computed net of income taxes and corrected for the change in labour productivity over the period considered.

Over the same decade, increased competition has been associated with higher wages. Wages increased all over Europe, more so in Scandinavian countries, Germany and the UK and much less in Southern Europe.

An interesting question is to what extent a lower product market regulation leads to higher wages. Does a similar decrease in product market regulation, as one can deem must have happened in all the Europeans countries that joined the EU since the beginning, lead to similar increase in wages across Europe? Figure 7.11 shows the negative relation between product market regulation and wages. The figure has two interesting features. First, countries that started out with higher degree of product market regulation at the end of the 1990s, i.e. France, Italy and Spain, registered the largest improvement, and are now comparable to the rest of Western Europe.

The second feature is the large difference among European countries in terms of the real wage increase associated with a given decrease in product market regulation. A decrease in regulation of the same size had very different impacts in different countries. In the UK, a small decrease in the PMR was associated with a large increase in wages, while in the rest of Europe the increase in wages was much less pronounced, as in Italy and Spain, where PMR decreased much more than in the rest of Europe, but real wages increased much less than elsewhere.

7.4 THE NATURAL RATE OF UNEMPLOYMENT

Let's now look at the implications of wage and price determination for unemployment.

> ◄ The rest of the chapter is based on the assumption that $P^e = P$.

For the rest of this chapter, let's do so under the assumption that nominal wages depend on the actual price level, P, rather than on the expected price level, P^e. (Why we make this assumption will become clear soon.) Under this additional assumption, wage setting and price setting determine the equilibrium rate of unemployment. Let's see how.

The wage-setting relation

Given the assumption that nominal wages depend on the actual price level, P, rather than on the expected price level, P^e, equation (7.1), which characterises wage determination, becomes

$$W = PF(u, z)$$

We can divide both sides by the price level:

$$\frac{W}{P} = F(u, z)$$
$$(-, +) \qquad\qquad [7.4]$$

Wage determination implies a negative relation between the real wage, W/P, and the unemployment rate, u: *the higher the unemployment rate, the lower the real wage chosen by wage setters*. The intuition is straightforward: the higher the unemployment rate, the weaker the position of workers in bargaining and the lower the real wage will be.

This relation between the real wage and the rate of unemployment – let's call it the **wage-setting relation** – is drawn in Figure 7.12. The real wage is measured on the vertical axis. The unemployment rate is measured on the horizontal axis. The wage-setting relation is drawn as the downward-sloping curve WS (for wage setting): the higher the unemployment rate, the lower the real wage.

> ◄ Wage setters are unions and firms if wages are set by collective bargaining, individual workers and firms if wages are set on a case-by-case basis, and firms if wages are set on a take-it-or-leave-it basis.

The price-setting relation

Let's now look at the implications of price determination. If we divide both sides of the price-determination equation (7.3), by the nominal wage, we get

$$\frac{P}{W} = 1 + \mu \qquad\qquad [7.5]$$

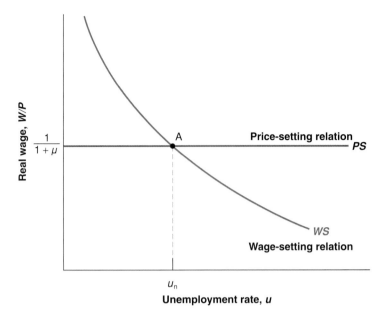

Figure 7.12

Wages, prices and the natural rate of unemployment

The ratio of the price level to the wage implied by the price-setting behaviour of firms equals 1 plus the mark-up. Now invert both sides of this equation to get the implied real wage:

$$\frac{W}{P} = \frac{1}{1 + \mu} \qquad\qquad [7.6]$$

Note what this equation says: *price-setting decisions determine the real wage paid by firms*. An increase in the mark-up leads firms to increase their prices, given the wage they have to pay; equivalently, it leads to a decrease in the real wage.

The step from equation (7.5) to equation (7.6) is algebraically straightforward. But how price setting actually determines the real wage paid by firms may not be intuitively obvious. Think of it this way: suppose the firm you work for increases its mark-up and therefore increases the price of its product. Your real wage does not change very much: you are still paid the same nominal wage, and the product produced by the firm you work for is at most a small part of your consumption basket.

Now suppose that not only the firm you work for but all the firms in the economy increase their mark-up. All prices go up. If you are paid the same nominal wage, your real wage goes down. So, the higher the mark-up set by firms, the lower your (and everyone else's) real wage will be.

The **price-setting relation** in equation (7.6) is drawn as the horizontal line *PS* (for price setting) in Figure 7.12. The real wage implied by price setting is $1/(1 + \mu)$; it does not depend on the unemployment rate.

Equilibrium real wages and unemployment

Equilibrium in the labour market requires that the real wage chosen in wage setting be equal to the real wage implied by price setting. (This way of stating equilibrium may sound strange if you learned to think in terms of labour supply and labour demand in your microeconomics course. The relation between wage setting and price setting on the one hand and labour supply and labour demand on the other is closer than it looks at first and is explored further in the appendix at the end of this chapter.) In Figure 7.12, equilibrium is therefore given by point A, and the equilibrium unemployment rate is given by u_n.

We can also characterise the equilibrium unemployment rate algebraically; eliminating W/P between equations (7.4) and (7.6) gives

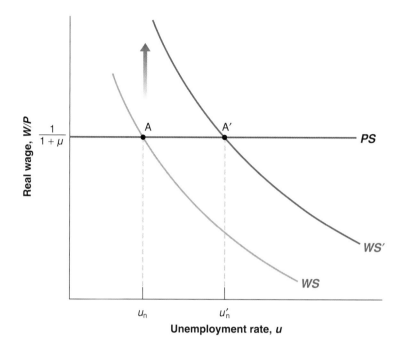

Figure 7.13

Unemployment benefits and the natural rate of unemployment

$$F(u_n, z) = \frac{1}{1+\mu} \qquad [7.7]$$

The equilibrium unemployment rate, u_n, is such that the real wage chosen in wage setting – the left side of equation (7.8) – is equal to the real wage implied by price setting – the right side of equation (7.7).

The equilibrium unemployment rate (u_n) is called the **natural rate of unemployment** (which is why we have used the subscript n to denote it). The terminology has become standard, so we will adopt it, but this is actually a bad choice of words. The word *natural* suggests a constant of nature, one that is unaffected by institutions and policy. As its derivation makes clear, however, the 'natural' rate of unemployment is anything but natural. The positions of the wage-setting and price-setting curves, and thus the equilibrium unemployment rate, depend on both z and μ. Consider two examples:

> *Natural*, in Webster's dictionary, means 'in a state provided by nature, without man-made changes'.

- An increase in unemployment benefits – An increase in unemployment benefits can be represented by an increase in z: because an increase in benefits makes the prospect of unemployment less painful, it increases the wage set by wage setters at a given unemployment rate. So it shifts the wage-setting relation up, from WS to WS' in Figure 7.13. The economy moves along the PS line, from A to A'. The natural rate of unemployment increases from u_n to u'_n.

  In words: at a given unemployment rate, higher unemployment benefits lead to a higher real wage. A higher unemployment rate is needed to bring the real wage back to what firms are willing to pay.

  > An increase in unemployment benefits shifts the wage-setting curve up. The economy moves along the price-setting curve. Equilibrium unemployment increases.

- A less stringent enforcement of existing competition law – To the extent that this allows firms to collude more easily and increase their market power, it leads to an increase in their mark-up – an increase in μ. The increase in μ implies a decrease in the real wage paid by firms, and so it shifts the price-setting relation down, from PS to PS' in Figure 7.14. The economy moves along WS. The equilibrium moves from A to A', and the natural rate of unemployment increases from u_n to u'_n.

  In words: by letting firms increase their prices given the wage, less stringent enforcement of competition law leads to a decrease in the real wage. Higher unemployment is required to make workers accept this lower real wage, leading to an increase in the natural rate of unemployment.

  > An increase in the mark-up shifts the price-setting line down. The economy moves along the wage-setting curve. Equilibrium unemployment increases.

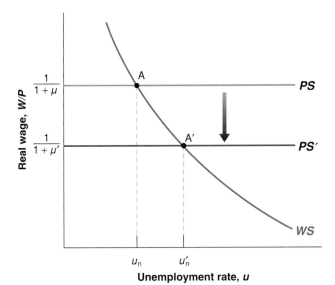

Figure 7.14

Mark-ups and the natural rate of unemployment

An increase in mark-ups decreases the real wage and leads to an increase in the natural rate of unemployment.

This name has been suggested by ➤ Edmund Phelps from Columbia University. Phelps was awarded the Nobel Prize in 2006. For more on some of his contributions, see Chapter 9.

Factors such as the generosity of unemployment benefits or competition law can hardly be thought of as the result of nature. Rather, they reflect various characteristics of the structure of the economy. For that reason, a better name for the equilibrium rate of unemployment would be the **structural rate of unemployment**, but so far the name has not caught on.

From unemployment to employment

Associated with the natural rate of unemployment is a **natural level of employment**, the level of employment that prevails when unemployment is equal to its natural rate.

Let's review the relation between unemployment/employment and the labour force. Let U denote unemployment, N denote employment and L the labour force. Then:

$$u = \frac{U}{L} = \frac{L-N}{L} = 1 - \frac{N}{L}$$

The first step follows from the definition of the unemployment rate, u. The second follows from the fact that, from the definition of the labour force, the level of unemployment, U, equals the labour force, L, minus employment, N. The third step follows from simplifying the fraction. Putting all three steps together: the unemployment rate, u, equals 1 minus the ratio of employment, N, to the labour force, L.

Rearranging to get employment in terms of the labour force and the unemployment rate gives:

$$N = L(1-u)$$

Employment, N, is equal to the labour force, L, times 1 minus the unemployment rate, u.

So, if the natural rate of unemployment is u_n, and the labour force is equal to L, the natural level of employment, N_n, is given by

$$N_n = L(1 - u_n)$$

For example, if the labour force is 150 million and the natural rate of unemployment is 5%, then the natural level of employment is $150 \times (1 - 0.05) = 142.5$ million.

From employment to output

Finally, associated with the natural level of employment is the **natural level of output**, the level of production when employment is equal to the natural level of employment. Given the production function we have used in this chapter ($Y = N$), the natural level of output, Y_n, is easy to derive. It is given by

$$Y_n = N_n = L(1 - u_n)$$

Using equation (7.6) and the relations between the unemployment rate, employment and the output we just derived, the natural level of output satisfies the following equation:

$$F\left(1 - \frac{Y_n}{L}, z\right) = \frac{1}{1 + \mu} \qquad [7.8]$$

The natural level of output, Y_n, is such that, at the associated rate of unemployment ($u_n = 1 - Y_n/L$), the real wage chosen in wage setting – the left side of equation (7.8) – is equal to the real wage implied by price setting – the right side of equation (7.8). As you will see, equation (7.8) will turn out to be very useful in Chapter 8. Make sure you understand it.

We have gone through many steps in this section. Let's summarise: assume that the expected price level is equal to the actual price level. Then:

- The real wage chosen in wage setting is a decreasing function of the unemployment rate.
- The real wage implied by price setting is constant.
- Equilibrium in the labour market requires that the real wage chosen in wage setting be equal to the real wage implied by price setting.
- This determines the equilibrium unemployment rate.
- This equilibrium unemployment rate is known as the natural rate of unemployment.
- Associated with the natural rate of unemployment are a natural level of employment and a natural level of output.

7.5 WHERE WE GO FROM HERE

We have just seen how equilibrium in the labour market determines the equilibrium unemployment rate (which we have called the natural rate of unemployment), which in turn determines the level of output (which we have called the natural level of output).

So, you may ask, what did we do in Chapters 3–5? If equilibrium in the labour market determines the unemployment rate and, by implication, the level of output, why did we spend so much time looking at the goods and financial markets? What about our earlier conclusions that the level of output was determined by factors such as monetary policy, fiscal policy, consumer confidence and so on – all factors that do not enter equation (7.8) and therefore do not affect the natural level of output?

The key to the answer is simple:

- We have derived the natural rate of unemployment and the associated levels of employment and output under two assumptions. First, we have assumed equilibrium in the labour market. Second, we have assumed that the price level was equal to the expected price level.
- However, there is no reason for the second assumption to be true in the *short run*. The price level may well turn out to be different from what was expected when nominal wages were set. Hence, in the short run, there is no reason for unemployment to be equal to the natural rate, or for output to be equal to its natural level. ◄ In the short run, the factors that determine movements in output are the factors we focused on in Chapters 3–5: monetary policy, fiscal policy, and so on.

  As we will see in Chapter 8, the factors that determine movements in output *in the short run* are indeed the factors we focused on in Chapters 3–5: monetary policy, fiscal policy, and so on. Your time (and ours) was not wasted.
- Expectations are unlikely to be systematically wrong (say, too high or too low) forever. That is why, in the medium run, unemployment tends to return to the natural rate, and output tends to return to the natural level. *In the medium run*, the factors that determine unemployment and output are the factors that appear in equations (7.7) and (7.8). ◄ In the medium run, output tends to return to the natural level, and the factors that determine output are the factors we have focused on in this chapter.

Developing these answers in detail will be our task in the next three chapters.

SUMMARY

- The labour force consists of those who are working (employed) and looking for work (unemployed). The unemployment rate is equal to the ratio of the number of unemployed to the number in the labour force. The participation rate is equal to the ratio of the labour force to the working-age population.

- The European labour market is characterised by large differences across countries, in terms of employment, of participation rate among men and women and the incidence of unemployment across different groups of workers.

- Wages are set unilaterally by firms or through bargaining between workers and firms. They depend negatively on the unemployment rate and positively on the expected price level. The reason wages depend on the expected price level is that they are typically set in nominal terms for some period of time. During that time, even if the price level turns out to be different from what was expected, wages are typically not readjusted.

- The price set by firms depends on the wage and on the mark-up of prices over wages. The higher the mark-up chosen by firms, the higher the price, given the wage, and

thus the lower the real wage implied by price-setting decisions.

- Real wages increased in most European countries over the past decade, as a result of a decrease in the degree of product market regulation.

- Equilibrium in the labour market requires that the real wage chosen in wage setting be equal to the real wage implied by price setting. Under the additional assumption that the expected price level is equal to the actual price level, equilibrium in the labour market determines the unemployment rate. This unemployment rate is known as the *natural rate of unemployment*.

- In general, the actual price level may turn out to be different from the price level expected by wage setters. Therefore, the unemployment rate need not be equal to the natural rate.

- The coming chapters will show that, in the short run, unemployment and output are determined by the factors we focused on in Chapters 3–5, but, in the medium run, unemployment tends to return to the natural rate, and output tends to return to its natural level.

KEY TERMS

population in working age 137

labour force; out of the labour force 137

participation rate 137

unemployment rate 138

separations 140

hires 140

Labour Force Survey (LFS) 140

leavers 140

layoffs 140

discouraged worker 140

non-employment rate 140

duration of unemployment 140

collective bargaining 142

reservation wage 143

bargaining power 143

efficiency wage theories 143

unemployment insurance 145

employment protection 146

minimum wage 147

production function 149

labour productivity 149

mark-up 149

wage-setting relation 151

price-setting relation 152

natural rate of unemployment 153

structural rate of unemployment 154

natural level of employment 154

natural level of output 154

QUESTIONS AND PROBLEMS

QUICK CHECK

1. *Using the information in this chapter, label each of the following statements true, false or uncertain. Explain briefly.*

a. Since 1950, the participation rate in the Europe has remained roughly constant at 60%.

b. In Europe, the average duration of unemployment is small compared to the USA.

c. The incidence of unemployment among different groups of workers is similar.

d. The unemployment rate tends to be high in recessions and low in expansions.

e. Most workers are typically paid their reservation wage.

f. Workers who do not belong to unions have no bargaining power.

g. It may be in the best interest of employers to pay wages higher than their workers' reservation wage.

h. The natural rate of unemployment is unaffected by policy changes.

2. *Answer the following questions using the information provided in this chapter.*

a. Is it true that European countries have very different participation rates, regardless of the gender of workers?

b. Is it true that countries with lower participation rates among women also have lower participation rates among men?

c. Is it true that countries with lower participation rates (on the total population in working age) also have lower participation rates of older workers?

d. Which are the countries with the lowest and the highest total unemployment?

e. Which are the countries with the lowest and the highest youth unemployment? Are they the same countries in your answer at part (d)?

3. The natural rate of unemployment

Suppose that the mark-up of goods prices over marginal cost is 5%, and that the wage-setting equation is $W = P(1 - u)$, where u is the unemployment rate.

a. What is the real wage, as determined by the price-setting equation?

b. What is the natural rate of unemployment?

c. Suppose that the mark-up of prices over costs increases to 10%. What happens to the natural rate of unemployment? Explain the logic behind your answer.

DIG DEEPER

4. Reservation wages

In the mid-1980s, a famous supermodel once said that she would not get out of bed for less than $10 000 (presumably per day).

a. What is your own reservation wage?

b. Did your first job pay more than your reservation wage at the time?

c. Relative to your reservation wage at the time you accept each job, which job pays more: your first one or the one you expect to have in ten years' time?

d. Explain your answers to parts (a) through (c) in terms of the efficiency wage theory.

5. Bargaining power and wage determination

Even in the absence of collective bargaining, workers do have some bargaining power that allows them to receive wages higher than their reservation wage. Each worker's bargaining power depends both on the nature of the job and on the economy-wide labour market conditions. Let's consider each factor in turn.

a. Compare the job of a delivery person and a computer network administrator. In which of these jobs does a worker have more bargaining power? Why?

b. For any given job, how do labour market conditions affect a worker's bargaining power? Which labour market variable would you look at to assess labour market conditions?

c. Suppose that for given labour market conditions [the variable you identified in part (b)], worker bargaining power throughout the economy increases. What effect would this have on the real wage in the medium run? In the short run? What determines the real wage in the model described in this chapter?

6. The existence of unemployment

a. Suppose the unemployment rate is very low. How easy is it for firms to find workers to hire? How easy is it for workers to find jobs? What do your answers imply about the relative bargaining power of workers and firms when the unemployment rate is very low? What do your answers imply about what happens to the wage as the unemployment rate gets very low?

b. Given your answer to part (a), why is there unemployment in the economy? (What would happen to real wages if the unemployment rate were equal to zero?)

7. The informal labour market

You learned in Chapter 2 that informal work at home (e.g. preparing meals, taking care of children) is not counted as part of GDP. Such work also does not constitute employment in labour market statistics. With these observations in mind, consider two economies, each with 100 people, divided into 25 households, each composed of four people. In each household, one person stays at home and prepares the food, two people work in the non-food sector, and one person is unemployed. Assume that the workers outside food preparation produce the same actual and measured output in both economies.

In the first economy, EatIn, the 25 food-preparation workers (one per household) cook for their families at home and do not work outside the house. All meals are prepared and eaten at home. The 25 food preparation workers in this economy do not seek work in the formal labour market (and, when asked, they say they are not looking for work). In the second economy, EatOut, the 25 food preparation workers are employed by restaurants. All meals are purchased in restaurants.

a. Calculate measured employment and unemployment and the measured labour force for each economy. Calculate the measured unemployment rate and participation rate for each economy. In which economy is measured GDP higher?

b. Suppose now that EatIn's economy changes. A few restaurants open, and the food-preparation workers in ten households take jobs in the restaurants. The members of these ten households now eat all of their meals in restaurants. The food preparation workers in the remaining 15 households continue to work at home and do not seek jobs in the formal sector. The members of these 15 households continue to eat all of their meals at home. Without calculating the numbers, what will happen to measured employment and unemployment and to the measured labour force, unemployment rate and participation rate in EatIn? What will happen to measured GDP in EatIn?

c. Suppose that you want to include work at home in GDP and the employment statistics. How would you measure the value of work at home in GDP? How would you alter the definitions of *employment, unemployment* and *out of the labour force*?

d. Given your new definitions in part (c), would the labour market statistics differ for EatIn and EatOut? Assuming that the food produced by these economies has the same value, would measured GDP in these economies differ? Under your new definitions, would the experiment in part (b) have any effect on the labour market or GDP statistics for EatIn?

EXPLORE FURTHER

8. Unemployment spells and long-term unemployment

In the example presented in this chapter, about 47% of unemployed workers leave unemployment each month.

a. What is the probability that an unemployed worker will still be unemployed after one month? Two months? Six months?

Now consider the composition of the unemployment pool. We will use a simple experiment to determine the proportion of the unemployed who have been unemployed for six months or more. Suppose the number of unemployed workers is constant and equal to x (where x is some constant). Each month, 47% of the unemployed find jobs, and an equivalent number of previously employed workers become unemployed.

b. Consider the group of x workers who are unemployed this month. After a month, what percentage of this group

will still be unemployed? (*Hint:* if 47% of unemployed workers find jobs every month, what percentage of the original x unemployed workers did not find jobs in the first month?)

c. After a second month, what percentage of the original x unemployed workers has been unemployed for at least two months? [*Hint:* given your answer to part (b), what percentage of those unemployed for at least one month do not find jobs in the second month?] After the sixth month, what percentage of the original x unemployed workers has been unemployed for at least six months? *This percentage applies to the economy at any time (remember that we started with an arbitrary month). Under our assumptions, the percentage of the unemployed who have been unemployed six months or more is constant.*

9. *Go to the Eurostat website (http://epp.eurostat.ec. europa.eu/portal/page/portal/eurostat/home/). Find the labour market data for your country.*

a. What are the latest monthly data on the size of the labour force, on the number of unemployed and on the unemployment rate in your country?

b. How many people are employed?

c. Compute the change in the number of unemployed from the first number in the table to the most recent month in the table. Do the same for the number of employed workers. Is the decline in unemployment equal to the increase in employment? Explain in words.

10. *Go to the Eurostat website (http://epp.eurostat.ec. europa.eu/portal/page/portal/eurostat/home/). Find the data on harmonised unemployment in the statistics portal.*

a. What are the latest monthly data on the unemployment rate in your country, by gender?

b. What are the latest monthly data on the unemployment rate in your country, by age groups?

c. Compute the change in the unemployment rate from the first number in the table to the most recent month in the table. Do the same for men, women and different age groups. Is the change in unemployment equal for all groups of workers? Explain in words.

We invite you to visit the Blanchard page on the Prentice Hall website, at **www.prenhall.com/blanchard** for this chapter's World Wide Web exercises.

FURTHER READING

- A further discussion of unemployment along the lines of this chapter is given by **Richard Layard, Stephen Nickell and** **Richard Jackman**, in *The Unemployment Crisis*, Oxford University Press, Oxford, UK, 1994.

APPENDIX

Wage and price setting relations versus labour supply and labour demand

If you have taken a microeconomics course, you have probably seen a representation of labour market equilibrium in terms of labour supply and labour demand. You may therefore be asking: how does the representation in terms of wage setting and price setting relate to the representation of the labour market I saw in that course?

In an important sense, the two representations are similar. To see why, let's redraw Figure 7.8 in terms of the real wage on the vertical axis and the level of *employment* (rather than the unemployment rate) on the horizontal axis. We do this in Figure 7.15.

Employment, N, is measured on the horizontal axis. The level of employment must be somewhere between zero and L, the labour force: employment cannot exceed the number of people available for work – that is, the labour force. For any employment level, N, unemployment is given by $U = L - N$. Knowing that, we can measure unemployment by starting from L and *moving to the left* on the horizontal axis: unemployment is given by the distance between L and N. The lower is employment, N, the higher is unemployment and, by implication, the higher is the unemployment rate, u.

Let's now draw the wage-setting and price-setting relations and characterise the equilibrium:

- An increase in employment (a movement to the right along the horizontal axis) implies a decrease in unemployment and therefore an increase in the real wage chosen in wage setting. Thus, the wage-setting relation is now *upward-sloping:* higher employment implies a higher real wage.

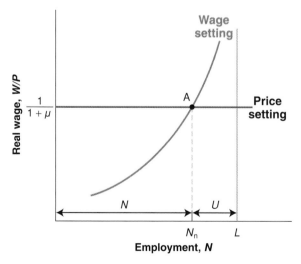

Figure 7.15

Wage and price setting and the natural level of employment

- The price-setting relation is still a horizontal line, at $W/P = 1/(1 + m)$.
- The equilibrium is given by point A, with natural employment level, N_n, and an implied natural unemployment rate equal to $u_n = (L - N_n)/L$.

In Figure 7.15, the wage-setting relation looks like a labour supply relation. As the level of employment increases, the real wage paid to workers increases as well. For that reason, the wage-setting relation is sometimes called the 'labour supply' relation (in quotes).

What we have called the price-setting relation looks like a flat labour demand relation. The reason it is flat rather than downward-sloping has to do with our simplifying assumption of constant returns to labour in production. Had we assumed, more conventionally, that there were decreasing returns to labour in production, our price-setting curve would, like the standard labour demand curve, be downward-sloping: as employment increased, the marginal cost of production would increase, forcing firms to increase their prices, given the wages they pay. In other words, the real wage implied by price setting would decrease as employment increased.

In a number of ways, however, the two approaches are different:

- The standard labour supply relation gives the wage at which a given number of workers are willing to work: the higher the wage, the larger the number of workers who are willing to work.

  In contrast, the wage corresponding to a given level of employment in the wage-setting relation is the result of a process of bargaining between workers and firms, or unilateral wage setting by firms. Factors such as the structure of collective bargaining or the use of wages to deter leavers affect the wage-setting relation. In the real world, they seem to play an important role. Yet they play no role in the standard labour supply relation.
- The standard labour demand relation gives the level of employment chosen by firms at a given real wage. It is derived under the assumption that firms operate in competitive goods and labour markets and therefore take wages and prices – and, by implication, the real wage – as given.

  In contrast, the price-setting relation takes into account the fact that in most markets, firms actually set prices. Factors such as the degree of competition in the goods market affect the price-setting relation by affecting the mark-up, but these factors aren't considered in the standard labour demand relation.

● In the labour supply–labour demand framework, those unemployed are *willingly unemployed*: at the equilibrium real wage, they prefer to be unemployed rather than work.

In contrast, in the wage setting–price setting framework, unemployment is likely to be involuntary. For example, if firms pay an efficiency wage – a wage above the reservation wage – workers would rather be employed than unemployed. Yet, in equilibrium, there is still involuntary unemployment. This also seems to capture reality better than does the labour supply–labour demand framework.

These are the three reasons we have relied on the wage-setting and price-setting relations rather than on the labour supply–labour demand approach to characterise equilibrium in this chapter.

Chapter 8

PUTTING ALL MARKETS TOGETHER: THE *AS–AD* MODEL

In Chapter 5, we looked at the determination of output in a closed economy in the short run. In Chapter 7, we looked at the determination of output in a closed economy in the medium run. We now put the two together and look at the determination of output in a closed economy in both the short run and the medium run.

To do so, we use the equilibrium conditions for *all* the markets we have looked at so far – the goods and financial markets in Chapter 5 and the labour market in Chapter 7. Then, using these equilibrium conditions, we derive two relations:

The first relation, which we call the *aggregate supply relation*, captures the implications of equilibrium in the labour market; it builds on what you saw in Chapter 7.

The second relation, which we call the *aggregate demand relation*, captures the implications of equilibrium in both the goods market and financial markets; it builds on what you saw in Chapter 5.

Combining these two relations gives us the *AS–AD* model (for aggregate supply–aggregate demand). This chapter presents the basic version of the model. When confronted with a macroeconomic question, this is the version we typically use to organise our thoughts. For some questions, however (in particular, for the study of inflation), the basic *AS–AD* model must be extended. That is what we will do in the next two chapters.

This chapter is organised as follows:

- Section 8.1 derives the aggregate supply relation, and Section 8.2 derives the aggregate demand relation.

- Section 8.3 combines the two relations to characterise equilibrium output in the short run and in the medium run.

- Sections 8.4–8.6 show how we can use the model to look at the dynamic effects of monetary policy, of fiscal policy and of changes in the price of oil.

- Section 8.7 summarises.

8.1 AGGREGATE SUPPLY

The **aggregate supply relation** captures the effects of output on the price level. It is derived from the behaviour of wages and prices we described in Chapter 7.

In Chapter 7, we derived the following equation for wage determination [equation (7.1)]:

$$W = P^e F(u, z)$$

The nominal wage, W, set by wage setters, depends on the expected price level, P^e; on the unemployment rate, u; and on the catchall variable, z, for all the other factors that affect wage determination, from unemployment benefits to the form of collective bargaining.

Also in Chapter 7, we derived the following equation for price determination [equation (7.3)]:

$$P = (1 + \mu)W$$

The price, P, set by firms (equivalently, the price level) is equal to the nominal wage, W, multiplied by 1 plus the mark-up, μ.

We then used these two relations together with the additional assumption that the actual price level was equal to the expected price level. Under this additional assumption, we derived the natural rate of unemployment and, by implication, the natural level of output.

The difference in this chapter is that we will not impose this additional assumption. (It will turn out that the price level is equal to the expected price level in the medium run but will typically not be equal to the expected price level in the short run.) Without this additional assumption, the price-setting relation and the wage-setting relation give us a relation, which we now derive, between the price level, the output level and the expected price level.

The first step is to eliminate the nominal wage, W, between the two equations. Replacing the nominal wage in the second equation above by its expression from the first gives

$$P = P^e(1 + \mu)F(u, z) \qquad [8.1]$$

The price level, P, depends on the expected price level, P^e, on the unemployment rate, u (as well as on the mark-up, μ, and on the catchall variable, z; but we will assume that both μ and z are constant here).

The second step is to replace the unemployment rate, u, with its expression in terms of output. To replace u, recall the relation between the unemployment rate, employment and output we derived in Chapter 7:

$$u = \frac{U}{L} = \frac{L - N}{L} = 1 - \frac{N}{L} = 1 - \frac{Y}{L}$$

The first equality follows from the definition of the unemployment rate. The second equality follows from the definition of unemployment ($U = L - N$). The third equality just simplifies the fraction. The fourth equality follows from the specification of the production function, which says that to produce one unit of output requires one worker, so that $Y = N$. What we get then is

$$u = 1 - \frac{Y}{L}$$

In words: for a given labour force, the higher the output, the lower the unemployment rate.

A better name would be the 'labour market relation'. But, because the relation looks graphically like a supply curve (there is a positive relation between output and the price), it is called the 'aggregate supply relation'. We will follow tradition.

Replacing u with $1 - Y/L$ in equation (8.1) gives us the *aggregate supply relation, or AS relation*:

$$P = P^e(1 + \mu)F\left(1 - \frac{Y}{L}, z\right) \qquad [8.2]$$

The price level, P, depends on the expected price level, P^e, and the level of output, Y (and also on the mark-up, μ; the catchall variable, z; and the labour force, L, which we take as constant here). The AS relation has two important properties.

The first property of the *AS* relation is that *an increase in output leads to an increase in the price level*. This is the result of four underlying steps:

1. An increase in output leads to an increase in employment.
2. The increase in employment leads to a decrease in unemployment and therefore to a decrease in the unemployment rate.
3. The lower unemployment rate leads to an increase in the nominal wage.
4. The increase in the nominal wage leads to an increase in the prices set by firms and therefore to an increase in the price level.

◀ An increase in Y leads to an increase in P.

The second property of the *AS* relation is that *an increase in the expected price level leads, one-for-one, to an increase in the actual price level*. For example, if the expected price level doubles, the price level will also double. This effect works through wages:

◀ An increase in P^e leads to an increase in P.

1. If wage setters expect the price level to be higher, they set a higher nominal wage.
2. The increase in the nominal wage leads to an increase in costs, which leads to an increase in the prices set by firms and a higher price level.

The relation between the price level, P, and output, Y, for a given value of the expected price level, P^e, is represented by the *AS* curve in Figure 8.1. The *AS* curve has three properties that will prove useful in what follows:

- The aggregate supply curve is upward-sloping. Put another way, an increase in output, Y, leads to an increase in the price level, P. You saw why earlier.

◀ Put informally: high economic activity puts pressure on prices.

- The aggregate supply curve goes through point A, where $Y = Y_n$ and $P = P^e$. Put another way: when output, Y, is equal to the natural level of output, Y_n, the price level, P, turns out to be exactly equal to the expected price level, P^e.

    How do we know this? From the definition of the natural level of output in Chapter 7. Recall that we defined the natural rate of unemployment (and, by implication, the natural level of output) as the rate of unemployment (and, by implication, the level of output) that prevails if the price level and the expected price level are equal. This property – that the price level equals the expected price level when output is equal to the natural level of output – has two straightforward implications:

    When output is above the natural level of output, the price level is higher than expected. In Figure 8.1, if Y is to the right of Y_n, P is higher than P^e. Conversely, when output is below the natural level of output, the price level is lower than expected. In Figure 8.1, if Y is to the left of Y_n, P is lower than P^e.

- An increase in the expected price level, P^e, shifts the aggregate supply curve up. Conversely, a decrease in the expected price level shifts the aggregate supply curve down.

    This third property is shown in Figure 8.2. Suppose the expected price level increases from P^e to P'^e. At a given level of output and, correspondingly, at a given unemployment

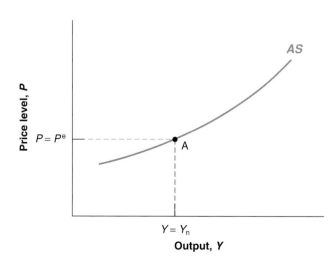

Figure 8.1

The aggregate supply curve

Given the expected price level, an increase in output leads to an increase in the price level. If output is equal to the natural level of output, the price level is equal to the expected price level.

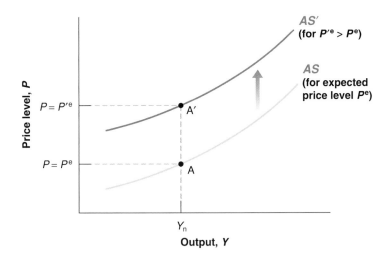

Figure 8.2

The effect of an increase in the expected price level on the aggregate supply curve

An increase in the expected price level shifts the aggregate supply curve up.

Recall that when output equals the ➤ natural level of output, the price level turns out to be equal to the expected price level.

rate, the increase in the expected price level leads to an increase in wages, which leads in turn to an increase in prices. So, at any level of output, the price level is higher: the aggregate supply curve shifts up. In particular, instead of going through point A (where $Y = Y_n$ and $P = P^e$), the aggregate supply curve now goes through point A′ (where $Y = Y_n$, $P = P'^e$).

Let's summarise:

- Starting from wage determination and price determination in the labour market, we have derived the *aggregate supply relation*.
- This relation implies that, for a given expected price level, the price level is an increasing function of the level of output. It is represented by an upward-sloping curve, called the *aggregate supply curve*.
- Increases in the expected price level shift the aggregate supply curve up; decreases in the expected price level shift the aggregate supply curve down.

8.2 AGGREGATE DEMAND

The **aggregate demand relation** captures the effect of the price level on output. It is derived from the equilibrium conditions in the goods and financial markets described in Chapter 5.

In Chapter 5, we derived the following equation for goods market equilibrium [equation (5.2)]:

$$Y = C(Y - T) + I(Y, i) + G$$

Equilibrium in the goods market requires that output equal the demand for goods – the sum of consumption, investment and government spending. This is the *IS* relation.

Also in Chapter 5, we derived the following equation for equilibrium in financial markets [equation (5.3)]:

$$\frac{M}{P} = YL(i)$$

Equilibrium in financial markets requires that the supply of money equal the demand for money. This is the *LM* relation.

Recall that what appears on the left side of the *LM* equation is the real money stock, M/P. We focused in Chapter 5 on changes in the real money stock that came from changes in nominal money, M, made by the central bank, but changes in the real money stock, M/P, can also come from changes in the price level, P. A 10% increase in the price level, P, has the same effect on the real money stock as a 10% decrease in the stock of nominal money, M: either leads to a 10% decrease in the real money stock.

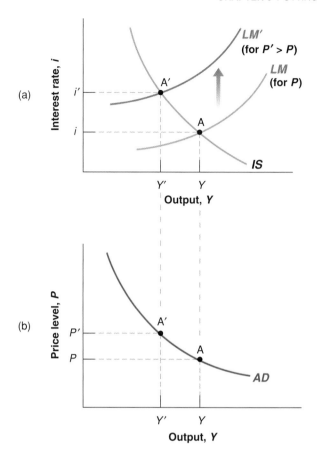

(a)

(b)

Figure 8.3

The derivation of the aggregate demand curve

An increase in the price level leads to a decrease in output.

Using the *IS* and *LM* relations, we can derive the relation between the price level and the level of output implied by equilibrium in the goods and financial markets. We do this in Figure 8.3:

● Figure 8.3(a) draws the *IS* curve and the *LM* curve. The *IS* curve is drawn for given values of G and T. It is downward-sloping: an increase in the interest rate leads to a decrease in output. The *LM* curve is drawn for a given value of M/P. It is upward-sloping: an increase in output increases the demand for money, and the interest rate increases so as to maintain equality of money demand and the (unchanged) money supply. The point at which the goods market and the financial market are both in equilibrium is at the intersection of the *IS* curve and the *LM* curve, at point A.

   Now consider the effects of an increase in the price level from P to P'. Given the stock of nominal money, M, the increase in the price level, P, decreases the real money stock, M/P. This implies that the *LM* curve shifts up: at a given level of output, the lower real ◀ A better name would be the 'goods money stock leads to an increase in the interest rate. The economy moves along the *IS*   market and financial markets relation'. curve, and the equilibrium moves from A to A′. The interest rate increases from i to i', and   But, because it is a long name, and output decreases from Y to Y'. In short: the increase in the price level leads to a decrease   because the relation looks graphically in output.   like a demand curve (that is, a negative relation between output and the price),

   In words: the increase in the price level leads to a decrease in the real money stock.   it is called the 'aggregate demand rela-This monetary contraction leads to an increase in the interest rate which leads, in turn,   tion'. We will, again, follow tradition. to a lower demand for goods and lower output.

● This negative relation between output and the price level is drawn as the downward-sloping curve *AD* in Figure 8.3(b). Points A and A′ in Figure 8.3(b) correspond to points A and A′ in Figure 8.3(a). An increase in the price level from P to P' leads to a decrease in ◀ Recall that open-market operations are output from Y to Y'. This curve is called the *aggregate demand curve*. The underlying nega-   the means through which the central tive relation between output and the price level is called the *aggregate demand relation*.   banks changes the nominal money stock.

Any variable other than the price level that shifts either the IS curve or the LM curve also shifts the aggregate demand relation.

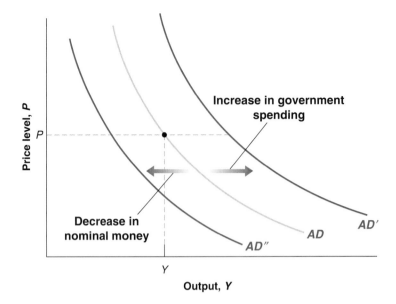

Price level, *P*

P

Increase in government spending

Decrease in nominal money

AD″

AD

AD′

Y

Output, Y

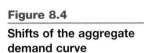

Figure 8.4

Shifts of the aggregate demand curve

At a given price level, an increase in government spending increases output, shifting the aggregate demand curve to the right. At a given price level, a decrease in nominal money decreases output, shifting the aggregate demand curve to the left.

Take, for example, an increase in government spending, *G*. At a given price level, the level of output implied by equilibrium in the goods and the financial markets is higher: in Figure 8.4, the aggregate demand curve shifts to the right, from *AD* to *AD′*.

Or take a contractionary, open market operation – a decrease in *M*. At a given price level, the level of output implied by equilibrium in the goods and the financial markets is lower. In Figure 8.4, the aggregate demand curve shifts to the left, from *AD* to *AD″*.

We can represent what we have just discussed by the following aggregate demand relation:

$$Y = Y\left(\frac{M}{P}, G, T\right)$$ [8.3]

$$(\,+,\ \ +,\ -)$$

Output, *Y*, is an increasing function of the real money stock, *M/P*; an increasing function of government spending, *G*; and a decreasing function of taxes, *T*.

Given monetary and fiscal policy – that is, given *M*, *G* and *T* – an increase in the price level, *P*, leads to a decrease in the real money stock, *M/P*, which leads to a decrease in output. This is the relation captured by the *AD* curve in Figure 8.3(b).

Let's summarise:

- Starting from the equilibrium conditions for the goods and financial markets, we have derived the *aggregate demand relation*.
- This relation implies that the level of output is a decreasing function of the price level. It is represented by a downward-sloping curve, called the *aggregate demand curve*.
- Changes in monetary or fiscal policy – or, more generally, in any variable other than the price level that shifts the *IS* or the *LM* curves – shift the aggregate demand curve.

8.3 EQUILIBRIUM IN THE SHORT RUN AND IN THE MEDIUM RUN

The next step is to put the *AS* and the *AD* relations together. From Sections 8.1 and 8.2, the two relations are given by

$$AS\ \text{relation:}\quad P = P^{e}(1 + \mu)F\left(1 - \frac{Y}{L}, z\right)$$

$$AD\ \text{relation:}\quad Y = Y\left(\frac{M}{P}, G, T\right)$$

For a given value of the expected price level, P^e (which enters the aggregate supply relation), and for given values of the monetary and fiscal policy variables M, G and T (which enter the aggregate demand relation), these two relations determine the equilibrium value of output, Y, and the price level, P.

Note that the equilibrium depends on the value of P^e. The value of P^e determines the position of the aggregate supply curve (go back to Figure 8.2), and the position of the aggregate supply curve affects the equilibrium. In the short run, we can take P^e, the price level expected by wage setters when they last set wages, as given. But over time, P^e is likely to change, shifting the aggregate supply curve and changing the equilibrium. With this in mind, we first characterise equilibrium in the short run – that is, taking P^e as given. We then look at how P^e changes over time and how that change affects the equilibrium.

Equilibrium in the short run

The short-run equilibrium is characterised in Figure 8.5:

- The aggregate supply curve, *AS*, is drawn for a given value of P^e. It is upward-sloping: the higher the level of output, the higher the price level. The position of the curve depends on P^e. Recall from Section 8.1 that, when output is equal to the natural level of output, the price level is equal to the expected price level. This means that, in Figure 8.5, the aggregate supply curve goes through point B: if $Y = Y_n$, then $P = P^e$.
- The aggregate demand curve, *AD*, is drawn for given values of M, G and T. It is downward-sloping: the higher the price level, the lower the level of output.

The equilibrium is given by the intersection of the *AS* and *AD* curves at point A. By construction, at point A, the goods market, the financial markets and the labour market are *all* in equilibrium. The fact that the labour market is in equilibrium is because point A is on the aggregate supply curve. The goods and financial markets are in equilibrium because point A is on the aggregate demand curve. The equilibrium level of output and price level are given by Y and P.

There is no reason, in general, why equilibrium output, Y, should be equal to the natural level of output, Y_n. Equilibrium output depends both on the position of the aggregate supply curve (and therefore on the value of P^e) and on the position of the aggregate demand curve (and therefore on the values of M, G and T). As we have drawn the two curves, Y is greater than Y_n: in other words, the equilibrium level of output exceeds the natural level of output, but we could clearly have drawn the *AS* and the *AD* curves so that equilibrium output, Y, was smaller than the natural level of output, Y_n.

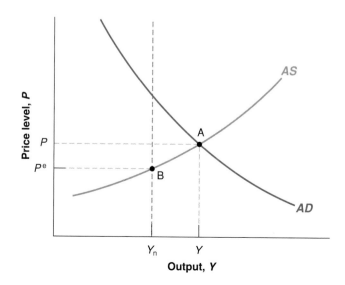

Figure 8.5

The short-run equilibrium

The equilibrium is given by the intersection of the aggregate supply curve and the aggregate demand curve. At point A, the labour market, the goods market and financial markets are all in equilibrium.

If you live in an economy where the ▶ inflation rate is typically positive then, even if the price level this year turns out to be equal to what you expected, you may still take into account the presence of inflation and expect the price level to be higher next year. In this chapter, we look at an economy in which there is no steady inflation. We will focus on the dynamics of output and inflation in the next two chapters.

Figure 8.5 gives us our first important conclusion: in the *short run*, there is no reason output should equal the natural level of output. Whether it does depends on the specific values of the expected price level and the values of the variables affecting the position of aggregate demand.

We must now ask: what happens over time? More precisely, suppose that in the short run, output is above the natural level of output – as is the case in Figure 8.5. What will happen over time? Will output eventually return to the natural level of output? If so, how? These are the questions we take up in the rest of the section.

From the short run to the medium run

To think about what happens over time, consider Figure 8.6. The curves denoted *AS* and *AD* are the same as in Figure 8.5, and so the short-run equilibrium is at point A – which corresponds to point A in Figure 8.5. Output is equal to Y and is higher than the natural level of output, Y_n.

At point A, output exceeds the natural level of output. So we know from Section 8.1 that the price level is higher than the expected price level – higher than the price level wage setters expected when they set nominal wages.

The fact that the price level is higher than wage setters expected is likely to lead them to revise upward their expectations of what the price level will be in the future. So, next time they set nominal wages, they are likely to make their decision based on a higher expected price level, say based on P'^e, where $P'^e > P^e$.

This increase in the expected price level implies that in the next period the aggregate supply curve shifts up, from *AS* to *AS'*: at a given level of output, wage setters expect a higher price level. They set a higher nominal wage which, in turn, leads firms to set a higher price. The price level therefore increases.

This upward shift in the *AS* curve implies that the economy moves up along the *AD* curve. The equilibrium moves from A to A'. Equilibrium output decreases from Y to Y'.

The adjustment does not end at point A'. At A', output, Y', still exceeds the natural level of output, Y_n, so the price level is still higher than the expected price level. Because of this, wage setters are likely to continue to revise upward their expectation of the price level.

This means that as long as equilibrium output exceeds the natural level of output, Y_n, the expected price level increases, shifting the *AS* curve upward. As the *AS* curve shifts upward and the economy moves up along the *AD* curve, equilibrium output continues to decrease.

Does this adjustment eventually come to an end? Yes. It ends when the *AS* curve has shifted all the way to *AS"*, when the equilibrium has moved all the way to A", and the equilibrium level of output is equal to Y_n. At A", equilibrium output is equal to the natural level of output, so the price level is equal to the expected price level. At this point, wage setters have no reason to change their expectations; the *AS* curve no longer shifts, and the economy stays at A".

Figure 8.6

The adjustment of output over time

If output is above the natural level of output, the *AS* curve shifts up over time until output has fallen back to the natural level of output.

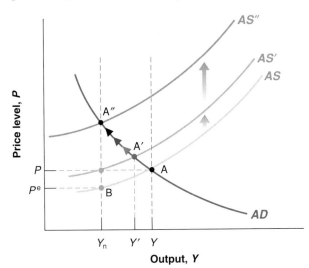

In words: as long as output exceeds the natural level of output, the price level turns out to be higher than expected. This leads wage setters to revise their expectations of the price level upward, leading to an increase in the price level. The increase in the price level leads to a decrease in the real money stock, which leads to an increase in the interest rate, which leads to a decrease in output. The adjustment stops when output is equal to the natural level of output. At that point, the price level is equal to the expected price level, expectations no longer change and output remains at the natural level of output. Put another way, in the *medium run*, output returns to the natural level of output.

We have looked at the dynamics of adjustment, starting from a case in which initial output was higher than the natural level of output. Clearly, a symmetric argument holds when initial output is below the natural level of output. In this case, the price level is lower than the expected price level, leading wage setters to lower their expectations of the price level. Lower expectations of the price level cause the *AS* curve to shift down and the economy to move down the *AD* curve until output has increased back to the natural level of output.

Let's summarise:

- In the *short run*, output can be above or below the natural level of output. Changes in any of the variables that enter either the aggregate supply relation or the aggregate demand relation lead to changes in output and to changes in the price level.

- In the *medium run*, output eventually returns to the natural level of output. The adjust- ◄ Short run: $Y \neq Y_n$
  ment works through changes in the price level. When output is above the natural level of output, the price level increases. The higher price level decreases demand and output. When output is below the natural level of output, the price level decreases, increasing demand and output.

- The best way to more fully understand the *AS–AD* model is to use it to look at the ◄ Medium run: $Y = Y_n$
  dynamic effects of changes in policy or in the economic environment. In the next three sections, we focus on three such changes: the first two – a change in the stock of nominal money and a change in the budget deficit – are old favourites by now. The third, which we could not examine until we had developed a theory of wage and price determination, is an increase in the price of oil.

8.4 THE EFFECTS OF A MONETARY EXPANSION

What are the short-run and medium-run effects of an expansionary monetary policy, say of an increase in the level of nominal money from M to M'?

◄ We will take up the more difficult question of the effects of a change in the rate of money growth – rather than a change in the level of money – in the next two chapters.

The dynamics of adjustment

Look at Figure 8.7. Assume that before the change in nominal money, output is at its natural level. Aggregate demand and aggregate supply cross at point A, the level of output at A equals Y_n and the price level equals P.

Now consider an increase in nominal money. Recall the specification of aggregate demand from equation (8.3):

$$Y = Y\left(\frac{M}{P}, G, T\right)$$

For a given price level, P, the increase in nominal money, M, leads to an increase in the real money stock, M/P, leading to an increase in output. The aggregate demand curve shifts to the right, from AD to AD'. In the short run, the economy goes from point A to A'. Output increases from Y_n to Y', and the price level increases from P to P'.

Over time, the adjustment of price expectations comes into play. As output is higher ◄ than the natural level of output, the price level is higher than wage setters expected. They then revise their expectations, which causes the aggregate supply curve to shift up over time. The economy moves up along the aggregate demand curve, AD'. The adjustment

We think of shifts in the *AD* curve as shifts to the right or to the left because we think of the *AD* relation as telling us what output is for a given price level. We then ask: at a given price level, does output increase (a shift to the right) or decrease (a shift to the left)? We think of shifts in the *AS* curve as shifts up or down because we think of the *AS* relation as telling us what the price level is for a given level of output. We then ask: at a given output level, does the price level increase (a shift up) or decrease (a shift down)?

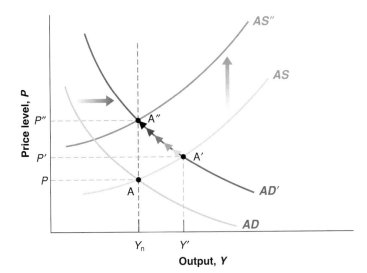

Figure 8.7

The dynamic effects of a monetary expansion

A monetary expansion leads to an increase in output in the short run but has no effect on output in the medium run.

Go back to equation (8.3): if Y is unchanged (and G and T are also unchanged), then M/P must also be unchanged.

If M/P is unchanged, it must be that M and P both increase in the same proportion.

process stops when output has returned to the natural level of output. At that point, the price level is equal to the expected price level. In the medium run, the aggregate supply curve is given by AS'', and the economy is at point A'': output is back to Y_n, and the price level is equal to P''.

We can actually pin down the exact size of the eventual increase in the price level. If output is back to the natural level of output, the real money stock must also be back to its initial value. In other words, the proportional increase in prices must be equal to the proportional increase in the nominal money stock: if the initial increase in nominal money is equal to 10%, then the price level ends up 10% higher.

Going behind the scenes

To get a better sense of what is going on, it is useful to go behind the scenes to see what happens not only to output and to the price level but also to the interest rate. We can do this by looking at what happens in terms of the *IS–LM* model.

Figure 8.8(a) reproduces Figure 8.7 (leaving out the AS'' curve to keep things simple) and shows the adjustment of output and the price level in response to the increase in nominal money. Figure 8.8(b) shows the adjustment of output and the interest rate by looking at the same adjustment process but in terms of the *IS–LM* model.

Look first at Figure 8.8(b). Before the change in nominal money, the equilibrium is given by the intersection of the *IS* and *LM* curves – that is, at point A, which corresponds to point A in Figure 8.8(a). Output is equal to the natural level of output, Y_n, and the interest rate is given by i.

The short-run effect of the monetary expansion is to shift the *LM* curve down from *LM* to *LM'*, moving the equilibrium from point A to point A', which corresponds to point A' in Figure 8.8(a). The interest rate is lower and output is higher.

Note that there are two effects at work behind the shift from *LM* to *LM'*: one is due to the increase in nominal money. The other, which partly offsets the first, is due to the increase in the price level. Let's look at these two effects more closely:

Why only partially? Suppose the price level increased in the same proportion as the increase in nominal money, leaving the real money stock unchanged. If the real money stock were unchanged, output would remain unchanged as well. But if output were unchanged, the price level would not increase, contradicting our premise.

- If the price level did not change, the increase in nominal money would shift the *LM* curve down to *LM''*. So, if the price level did not change – as was our assumption in Chapter 5 – the equilibrium would be at the intersection of *IS* and *LM''*, or point B.
- However, even in the short run, the price level increases – from P to P' in Figure 8.8(a). This increase in the price level shifts the *LM* curve upward from *LM''* to *LM'*, partially offsetting the effect of the increase in nominal money.
- The net effect of these two shifts – down from *LM* to *LM''* in response to the increase in nominal money, and up from *LM''* to *LM'* in response to the increase in the price level – is a shift of the *LM* curve from *LM* to *LM'*, and the equilibrium is given by A'.

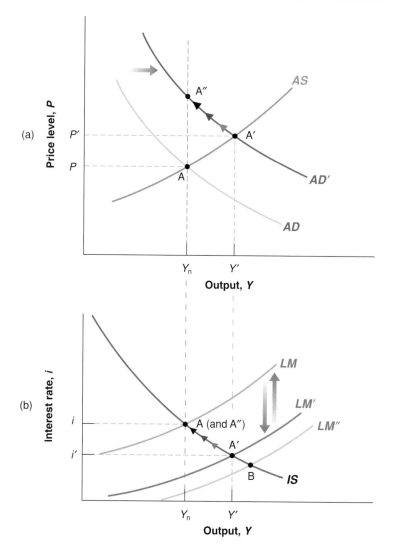

Figure 8.8

The dynamic effects of a monetary expansion on output and the interest rate

The increase in nominal money initially shifts the *LM* curve down, decreasing the interest rate and increasing output. Over time, the price level increases, shifting the *LM* curve back up until output is back at the natural level of output.

Over time, the fact that output is above its natural level implies that the price level continues to increase. As the price level increases, it further reduces the real money stock and shifts the *LM* curve back up. The economy moves along the *IS* curve: the interest rate increases, and output declines. Eventually, the *LM* curve returns to where it was before the increase in nominal money.

The economy ends up at point A, which corresponds to point A″ in Figure 8.8(a): the increase in nominal money is exactly offset by a proportional increase in the price level. The real money stock is therefore unchanged. With the real money stock unchanged, output is back to its initial value, Y_n, which is the natural level of output, and the interest rate is also back to its initial value, i.

The neutrality of money

Let's summarise what we have just discussed about the effects of monetary policy:

- In the *short run*, a monetary expansion leads to an increase in output, a decrease in the interest rate and an increase in the price level.

    How much of the effect of a monetary expansion falls initially on output and how much on the price level depends on the slope of the aggregate supply curve. In Chapter 5, we assumed that the price level did not respond at all to an increase in output; we assumed in effect that the aggregate supply curve was flat. Although we intended this as a simplification, empirical evidence does show that the initial effect of changes in output on the price level is quite small. We saw this when we looked at estimated responses to changes in the interest rate in Figure 5.16: despite the change in output, the price level remained practically unchanged for quite a long time (around two quarters in the USA and five quarters in the euro area).

Actually, the way the proposition is typically stated is that money is neutral in the *long run*. This is because many economists use 'long run' to refer to what we call in this book the 'medium run'.

● Over time, the price level increases, and the effects of the monetary expansion on output and on the interest rate disappear. In the medium run, the increase in nominal money is reflected entirely in a proportional increase in the price level. The increase in nominal money has no effect on output or on the interest rate. (How long it takes in reality for the effects of money on output to disappear is the topic of the Focus box 'How long lasting are the real effects of money?') Economists refer to the absence of a medium-run effect of money on output and on the interest rate by saying that money is neutral in the medium run.

The **neutrality of money** in the medium run does not mean that monetary policy cannot or should not be used to affect output. An expansionary monetary policy can, for example, help the economy move out of a recession and return more quickly to the natural level of output. As we saw in Chapter 5, this is exactly the way monetary policy was used to fight the 2001 recession, but it is a warning that monetary policy cannot sustain higher output forever.

8.5 A DECREASE IN THE BUDGET DEFICIT

Recall from Chapter 5 that a reduction in the budget deficit is also called a fiscal contraction, or a fiscal consolidation.

The policy we just looked at – a monetary expansion – led to a shift in aggregate demand coming from a shift in the *LM* curve. Let's now look at the effects of a shift in aggregate demand coming from a shift in the *IS* curve.

Suppose the government is running a budget deficit and decides to reduce it by decreasing its spending from G to G' while leaving taxes, T, unchanged. How will this affect the economy in the short run and in the medium run?

Assume that output is initially at the natural level of output so that the economy is at point A in Figure 8.9: output equals Y_n. The decrease in government spending from G to G' shifts the aggregate demand curve to the left, from AD to AD': for a given price level, output is lower. In the short run, the equilibrium moves from A to A'; output decreases from Y_n to Y', and the price level decreases from P to P'.

The initial effect of the deficit reduction triggers lower output. We first derived this result in Chapter 3, and it holds here as well.

What happens over time? As long as output is below the natural level of output, we know that the aggregate supply curve keeps shifting down. The economy moves down along the aggregate demand curve, AD', until the aggregate supply curve is given by AS'' and the economy reaches point A''. By then, the recession is over, and output is back at Y_n.

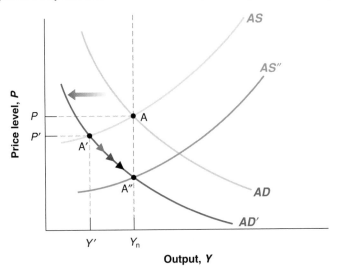

Figure 8.9

The dynamic effects of a decrease in the budget deficit

A decrease in the budget deficit leads initially to a decrease in output. Over time, however, output returns to the natural level of output.

FOCUS
How long lasting are the real effects of money?

To determine how long lasting the real effects of money are, economists use **macroeconometric models**. These models are larger-scale versions of the aggregate supply and aggregate demand model in this chapter.

The model we examine in this box was built in the early 1990s by John Taylor at Stanford University.

The Taylor model is substantially larger than the model we studied in this chapter. On the aggregate supply side, it has separate equations for price and for wage setting. On the demand side, it has separate equations for consumption, for investment, for exports and for imports. (Recall that, so far, we have assumed that the economy is closed, so we have ignored exports and imports altogether.) In addition, instead of looking at just one country, as we have done here, it looks at eight countries (the USA and seven major OECD countries) and solves for equilibrium in all eight countries simultaneously. Each equation, for each country, is estimated using econometrics and allows for a richer dynamic structure than the equations we have relied on in this chapter.

The implications of the model for the effects of money on output are shown in Figure 8.10. The simulation looks at the effects of an increase in nominal money of 3%, taking place over four quarters – 0.1% in the first quarter, another 0.6% in the second, another 1.2% in the third and another 1.1% in the fourth. After these four step increases, nominal money remains at its new higher level forever.

The effects of money on output reach a maximum after three quarters. By then, output is 1.8% higher than it would have been without the increase in nominal money. Over time, however, the price level increases, and output returns to the natural level of output. In year 4, the price level is up by 2.5%, while output is up by only 0.3%. Therefore, the Taylor model suggests that it takes roughly four years for output to return to its natural level or, put another way, four years for changes in nominal money to become neutral.

Do all macroeconometric models give the same answer? No. Because they differ in the way they are constructed, in the way variables are chosen and in the way equations are estimated, their answers are different. But most of them have the following implications in common: the effects of an increase in money on output build up for one to two years and then decline over time. (For a sense of how the answers differ across models, see the Focus box 'Four macroeconometric models' in Chapter 23.)

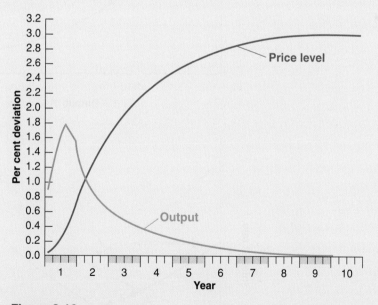

Figure 8.10

The effects of an expansion in nominal money in the Taylor model

Source: Figure 8.10 is reproduced from John Taylor, *Macroeconomic Policy in a World Economy*, W. W. Norton, New York, 1993, Figure 5-1A, p. 138.

The fact that the price level decreases ➤ along the way may seem strange: we rarely observe deflation (although recall the case of Japan, from Chapter 2). This result comes from the fact that we are looking at an economy in which money growth is zero (we are assuming that M is constant, not growing), and so there is no inflation in the medium run. When we introduce money growth in the next chapter, we will see that a recession typically leads to a decrease in inflation, not to a decrease in price level.

Like an increase in nominal money, a reduction in the budget deficit does not affect output forever. Eventually, output returns to its natural level. But there is an important difference between the effects of a change in money and the effects of a change in the deficit. At point A″, not everything is the same as before: output is back to the natural level of output, but the price level and the interest rate are lower than before the shift. The best way to see why is to look at the adjustment in terms of the underlying IS–LM model.

Deficit reduction, output and the interest rate

Figure 8.11(a) reproduces Figure 8.10, showing the adjustment of output and the price level in response to the increase in the budget deficit (but leaving out AS″ to keep things visually simple). Figure 8.11(b) shows the adjustment of output and the interest rate by looking at the same adjustment process, but in terms of the IS–LM model.

Look first at Figure 8.11(b). Before the change in fiscal policy, the equilibrium is given by the intersection of the IS curve and the LM curve, at point A – which corresponds to point A in Figure 8.11(a). Output is equal to the natural level of output, Y_n, and the interest rate is given by i.

As the government reduces the budget deficit, the IS curve shifts to the left, to IS′. If the price level did not change (the assumption we made in Chapter 5), the economy would move from point A to point B. But because the price level declines in response to the

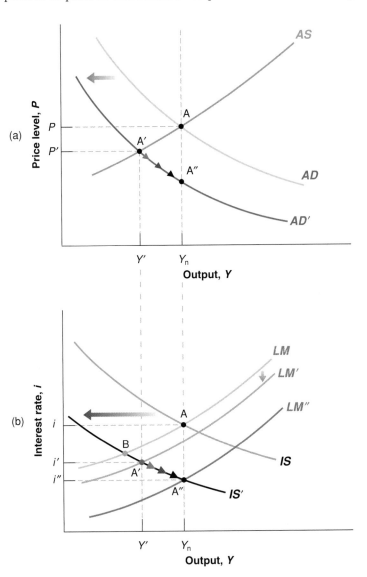

Figure 8.11

The dynamic effects of a decrease in the budget deficit on output and the interest rate

A deficit reduction leads in the short run to a decrease in output and to a decrease in the interest rate. In the medium run, output returns to its natural level, while the interest rate declines further.

decrease in output, the real money stock increases, leading to a partially offsetting shift of the *LM* curve, down to *LM′*. So the initial effect of deficit reduction is to move the economy from point A to point A′ – which corresponds to point A′ in Figure 8.11(a). Both output and the interest rate are lower than before the fiscal contraction. Note that, just as was the case in Chapter 5, we cannot tell whether investment increases or decreases in the short run: lower output decreases investment, but the lower interest rate increases investment.

So long as output remains below the natural level of output, the price level continues to decline, leading to a further increase in the real money stock. The *LM* curve continues to shift down. In Figure 8.11(b), the economy moves down from point A′ along *IS′* and eventually reaches A″ – which corresponds to A″ in Figure 8.11(a). At A″, the *LM* curve is given by *LM″*.

At A″, output is back at the natural level of output, but the interest rate is lower than it was before deficit reduction, down from *i* to *i″*. The composition of output is also different: to see how and why, let's rewrite the *IS* relation, taking into account that at A″, output is back at the natural level of output, so that $Y = Y_n$:

$$Y_n = C(Y_n - T) + I(Y_n, i) + G$$

Because income, Y_n, and taxes, *T*, are unchanged, consumption, *C*, is the same as before the deficit reduction. By assumption, government spending, *G*, is lower than before. Therefore, investment, *I*, must be higher than before the deficit reduction – higher by an amount exactly equal to the decrease in *G*. Put another way, in the medium run, a reduction in the budget deficit unambiguously leads to a decrease in the interest rate and an increase in investment.

◄ Recall the discussion of the policy mix in Chapter 5.

Budget deficits, output and investment

Let's summarise what we have just discussed about the effects of fiscal policy:

- In the *short run*, a budget deficit reduction, if implemented alone – that is, without an accompanying change in monetary policy – leads to a decrease in output and may lead to a *decrease* in investment. Note the qualification 'without an accompanying change in monetary policy': in principle, these adverse short-run effects on output can be avoided by using the right monetary–fiscal mix. What is needed is for the central bank to increase the money supply enough to offset the adverse effects of the decrease in government spending on aggregate demand.
- In the *medium run*, output returns to the natural level of output, and the interest rate is lower. In the medium run, a deficit reduction leads unambiguously to an *increase* in investment.
- We have not taken into account so far the effects of investment on capital accumulation and the effects of capital on production (we will do so in Chapter 11 and beyond when we look at the long run). But it is easy to see how our conclusions would be modified if we did take into account the effects on capital accumulation. In the long run, the level of output depends on the capital stock in the economy. So if a lower government budget deficit leads to more investment, it will lead to a higher capital stock, and the higher capital stock will lead to higher output.

Everything we have just said about the effects of deficit reduction would apply equally to measures aimed at increasing private (rather than public) saving. An increase in the saving rate increases output and investment in the medium run and in the long run. But it may also create a recession and a decrease in investment in the short run.

Disagreements among economists about the effects of measures aimed at increasing either public saving or private saving often come from differences in time frames. Those who are concerned with short-run effects worry that measures to increase saving, public or private, might create a recession and decrease saving and investment for some time. Those who look beyond the short run see the eventual increase in saving and investment and emphasise the favourable medium-run and long-run effects on output.

8.6 CHANGES IN THE PRICE OF OIL

Effects of a deficit reduction:

- Short run: *Y* decreases, *I* increases or decreases.
- Medium run: *Y* unchanged, *I* increases.
- Long run: *Y* increases, *I* increases.

➤ We have looked so far at the effects of variables that shift the aggregate demand curve: an increase in the money supply and a reduction in the budget deficit. Now that we have formalised the supply side, we can look at the effects of variables that shift the aggregate supply curve. An obvious candidate is the price of oil. Increases in the price of oil have often made the news in the recent past, and for good reasons: the price of oil, which stood around $7.5 per barrel at the end of 1998, in the summer of 2008 went above $128, and then declined to $45. What effects such an increase is likely to have on the economy is clearly of much current concern to policy makers.

This is not the first time the world economy has experienced a sharp increase in the price of oil. In the 1970s, the formation of OPEC (the Organization of Petroleum Exporting Countries), a cartel of oil producers, together with disruptions due to wars and revolutions in the Middle East, led to two sharp increases in the price of oil, the first one in 1973–1975, the second in 1979–1981. Figure 8.12 plots the real price of oil, defined as the ratio of the price of crude petroleum to the CPI, since 1970 (the ratio is set to 100 in 1970). As the figure shows, by 1981, the real price of oil reached 2.5 times its level in 1970. This high price did not last very long. From 1982 until the late 1990s, the OPEC cartel became steadily weaker, unable to enforce the production quotas it had set for its members. By 1998, the real price of oil was less than half its 1970 level. Since then, however, the combination of the Iraq war and a steady increase in the demand for oil by fast-growing countries such as China and India, has led to large increases in prices, to levels higher than those of the early 1980s. Note that the recent hike in oil prices led the nominal price of oil to levels that are almost triple compared to 1981 (around $94 per barrel in 2008 compared to $32 per barrel in 1981) but, in real terms, the price today is not three times higher than 1981 (around $87 per barrel in 2008 compared to $71 per barrel in 1981). This is due to the fact that, since 1981, the general price level also increased.

Moreover, in real terms, oil price in Europe increased less than in the USA. Figure 8.13 compares the real price of oil in Europe and in the USA since 1996. Until 2002, the real price of oil was similar in the two areas but, beginning in 2003, the depreciation of the dollar vis-à-vis the euro led to a much more limited increase in the real price of oil in Europe: in 2008 the real price of oil stood around $70 in Europe, while it exceeded $100 in the USA.

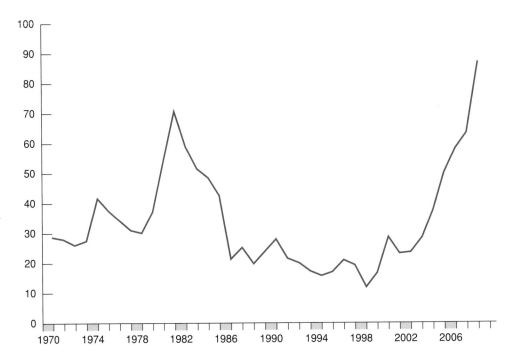

Figure 8.12

The real price of oil since 1970

There were two sharp increases in the relative price of oil in the 1970s, followed by a decrease until the 1990s, and a large increase since then.

Source: Energy Information Administration (EIA) Official Energy Statistics from the US Government. Eurostat.

Figure 8.13

The real price of oil in Europe and in the USA

Since 2003, the real price of oil in Europe increased less rapidly than in the USA.

Source: Dow Jones & Company and US Department of Labor: Bureau of Labor Statistics for the USA, Eurostat for Europe.

Each of the two large price increases of the 1970s was associated with a sharp recession and a large increase in inflation – a combination macroeconomists call **stagflation**, to capture the combination of *stag*nation and in*flation* that characterised these episodes. The obvious worry is that the recent price of oil may trigger another such episode. So far, it has not happened, and we shall re-examine the issue shortly. First, we must understand the effects of the price of oil in our model.

Note that we face a serious problem in using the model to think about the macroeconomic effects of an increase in the price of oil: the price of oil appears neither in our aggregate supply relation nor in our aggregate demand relation! The reason is that, until now, we have assumed that output was produced using only labour. One way to extend our model would be to recognise explicitly that output is produced using labour and other inputs (including energy) and then figure out what effect an increase in the price of oil has on the price set by firms and on the relation between output and employment. An easier way, and the way we will go, is simply to capture the increase in the price of oil by an increase in μ – the mark-up of the price over the nominal wage. The justification is straightforward: given wages, an increase in the price of oil increases the cost of production, forcing firms to increase prices.

We can then track the dynamic effects of an *increase in the mark-up* on output and the price level. It will be easiest here to work backward in time, first asking what happens in the medium run and then working out the dynamics of adjustment from the short run to the medium run.

Effects on the natural rate of unemployment

What happens to the natural rate of unemployment when the price of oil increases? Figure 8.14 reproduces the characterisation of labour market equilibrium from Chapter 7. The wage-setting curve is downward sloping. The price-setting relation is represented by the horizontal line at $W/P = 1/(1 + \mu)$. The initial equilibrium is at point A, and the initial natural unemployment rate is u_n. An increase in the mark-up leads to a downward shift of the price-setting line, from PS to PS': the higher the mark-up, the lower the real wage implied by price setting. The equilibrium moves from A to A'. The real wage is lower. The natural unemployment rate is higher: getting workers to accept the lower real wage requires an increase in unemployment.

The increase in the natural rate of unemployment leads to a decrease in the natural level of employment. If we assume that the relation between employment and output is

Figure 8.14

The effects of an increase in the price of oil on the natural rate of unemployment

An increase in the price of oil leads to a lower real wage and a higher natural rate of unemployment.

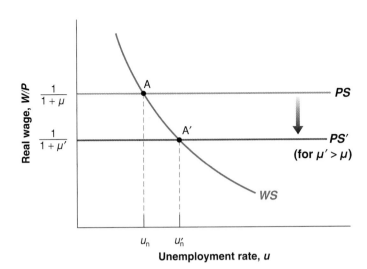

Figure 8.15

The dynamic effects of an increase in the price of oil

An increase in the price of oil leads, in the short run, to a decrease in output and an increase in the price level. Over time, output decreases further and the price level increases further.

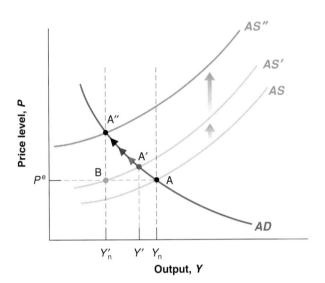

unchanged – that is, that each unit of output still requires one worker in addition to the energy input – then the decrease in the natural level of employment leads to an identical decrease in the natural level of output. Putting things together: an increase in the price of oil leads to a decrease in the natural level of output.

The dynamics of adjustment

> Do not be confused: u and μ are not the same; u is the unemployment rate, and μ is the mark-up.

Let's now turn to dynamics. Suppose that before the increase in the price of oil, the aggregate demand curve and the aggregate supply curve are given by AD and AS, respectively, so the economy is at point A in Figure 8.15, with output at the natural level of output, Y_n, and, by implication, $P = P^e$.

We have just established that the increase in the price of oil decreases the natural level of output. Call this lower level Y'_n. We now want to know what happens in the short run and how the economy moves from Y_n to $P = P^e$.

To think about the short run, recall that the aggregate supply relation is given by

$$P = P^e(1 + \mu)F\left(1 - \frac{Y}{L}, z\right)$$

Recall that we capture the effect of an increase in the price of oil by an increase in the mark-up, μ. So, in the short run (given P^e), the increase in the price of oil shows up as an increase in the mark-up, μ. This increase in the mark-up leads firms to increase their prices, resulting in an increase in the price level, P, at any level of output, Y. The aggregate supply curve shifts up.

We can be more specific about the size of the shift, and knowing the size of this shift will be useful in what follows. We know from Section 8.1 that the aggregate supply curve always goes through the point such that output equals the natural level of output and the price level equals the expected price level. Before the increase in the price of oil, the aggregate supply curve in Figure 8.15 goes through point A, where output equals Y_n and the price level is equal to P^e. After the increase in the price of oil, the new aggregate supply curve goes through point B, where output equals the new lower natural level of output, Y'_n, and the price level equals the expected price level, P^e. The aggregate supply curve shifts from AS to AS'.

Does the aggregate demand curve shift as a result of the increase in the price of oil? Maybe. There are many channels through which demand might be affected at a given price level: the higher price of oil may lead firms to change their investment plans, cancelling some investment projects and/or shifting to less energy-intensive equipment. The increase in the price of oil also redistributes income from oil buyers to oil producers. Oil producers may spend less than oil buyers, leading to a decrease in consumption demand. Let's take the easy way out: because some of the effects shift the aggregate demand curve to the right and others shift the aggregate demand curve to the left, let's simply assume that the effects cancel each other out and that aggregate demand does not shift.

Under this assumption, in the short run, only the AS shifts. The economy therefore moves along the AD curve, from A to A'. Output decreases from Y_n to Y'. The increase in the price of oil leads firms to increase their prices. This increase in the price level then decreases demand and output.

What happens over time? Although output has fallen, the natural level of output has fallen even more: at point A', output, Y', is still above the new natural level of output, Y'_n, the aggregate supply curve continues to shift up. The economy therefore moves over time along the aggregate demand curve, from A' to A''. At point A'', output, Y', is equal to the new lower natural level of output, Y'_n, and the price level is higher than before the oil shock: shifts in aggregate supply affect output not only in the short run but in the medium run as well.

◄ This was the case in the 1970s. The OPEC countries realised that high oil revenues might not last forever. Many of them saved a large proportion of the income from oil revenues.

Do these implications fit what we have observed in response to increases in the price of oil, both in the 1970s and recently? The answer is given by Figure 8.16, which plots the evolution of the real price of oil and inflation – using the CPI – and Figure 8.17, which plots the evolution of the real price of oil and the unemployment rate, in the UK since 1970.

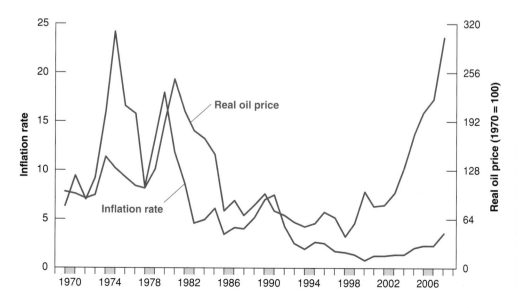

Figure 8.16

Oil price increases and inflation in the UK since 1970

The oil price increases of the 1970s were associated with large increases in inflation, but this has not been the case for the recent oil price increases.

Source: Energy Information Administration (EIA) – Official Energy Statistics from the US Government, Eurostat.

Figure 8.17

Oil price increases and unemployment in the UK since 1970

The oil price increases of the 1970s were associated with large increases in unemployment, but this has not been the case for the recent oil price increases.

Source: Energy Information Administration (EIA) – Official Energy Statistics from the US Government. Eurostat.

FOCUS

Oil price increases: why are the 2000s so different from the 1970s?

The question triggered by Figures 8.16 and 8.17 is an obvious one: why is it that oil price increases were associated with stagflation in the 1970s but have had so little apparent effect on the economy in the 2000s?

A first line of explanation is that other shocks besides just the increase in the price of oil were at work in the 1970s and in the 2000s. In the 1970s, not only did the price of oil increase, so did the prices of many other raw materials. This implies that the aggregate supply relation shifted up by more than implied by just the increase in the price of oil. In the 2000s, many economists believe that, partly because of globalisation and foreign competition, workers in advanced countries became weaker in bargaining. If true, this implies that, while the increase in oil prices shifted the aggregate supply curve up, the decrease in bargaining power of workers shifted it down, dampening or even eliminating the adverse effects of the oil price increase on output and the price level.

Econometric studies suggest, however, that more was at work, and that, even after controlling for the presence of these other factors, the effects of the price of oil have changed since the 1970s. Figure 8.18 shows the effects of a 100% increase in the price of oil on output and the price level, estimated using data from two different periods. The black and brown lines show the effects of an increase in the price of oil on the CPI and on GDP, based on data from 1970:1 to 1986:4; the blue and pink lines do the same, but based on data from 1987:1 to 2006:4 (the time

scale on the horizontal axis is in quarters). The figure suggests two main conclusions. First, in both periods, as predicted by our model, the increase in the price of oil leads to an increase in the CPI and a decrease in GDP. Second, the effects of the increase in the price of oil on both the CPI and GDP have become smaller, roughly half of what they were earlier.

Why have the adverse effects of the increase in price of oil become smaller? This is still very much a topic of research but, at this stage, two hypotheses appear plausible.

The first hypothesis is that, today, US workers are less powerful in bargaining than they were in the 1970s. Thus, as the price of oil has increased, workers have been more willing to accept a reduction in wages, limiting the upward shift in the aggregate supply curve and thus limiting the adverse effect on the price level and on output. (Make sure you understand this statement, using Figure 8.15.)

The second hypothesis concerns monetary policy. When the price of oil increased in the 1970s, people started expecting much higher prices, and P^e increased a lot. The result was a further shift of the aggregate supply curve, leading to a larger increase in the price level and a larger decrease in output. Today, monetary policy is very different from what it was in the 1970s, and expectations are that central banks will not let the increase in the price of oil lead to a higher price level. Thus, P^e has barely increased, leading to a smaller shift of the aggregate

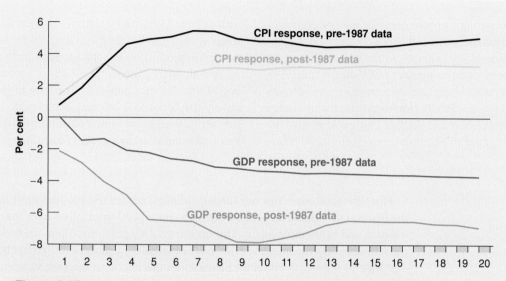

Figure 8.18

The effects of 100% increase in the price of oil on the CPI and on GDP

The effects of an increase in the price of oil on output and the price level are much smaller than they used to be.

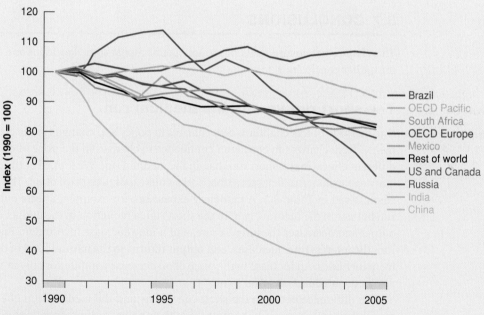

Figure 8.19

Energy intensity of GDP from 1990–2005

From 1990 to 2005 the use of energy per unit of output declined in many countries of the world, both among the OECD countries and among the emerging countries, with the exception of Brazil.

Source: International Energy Agency (2008), Worldwide Trends in Energy Use and Efficiency.

supply curve, and thus a smaller effect on output and the price level, than in the 1970s. (Again, make sure you understand this statement, using Figure 8.15.)

The third hypothesis regards the evolution of energy use in the last three decades. Figure 8.19 shows the trend in energy intensity of GDP (which measures how much energy is needed to produce one unit of product) in a number of countries and regions from 1990 to 2005. All countries have seen a decrease, with the exception of Brazil. This means that for every unit of output, the power requirements have decreased in almost every country in the world and hence the impact of an increase in the price of oil is lower today than it was in the 1970s, when the degree of intensity was much higher. In general, in the OECD countries the reduction was less rapid than in non-OECD countries. In many cases, these reductions can be attributed to strong improvements in energy efficiency following the introduction of technology and modern production processes. For example, in the case of China, the sharp decline in energy intensity of GDP during the 1990s was caused mainly by an improvement in energy efficiency. However, in addition to the degree of energy efficiency, there are other factors that explain why the levels of energy are so different between countries: these are the climate, geographical conditions, the size of the economic system and the productive structure. For example, changes in production structure may decrease or increase the overall energy intensity of GDP of a country. In the case of Brazil, for example, the increase in energy intensity of GDP between 1990 and 2005 is due to the sharp increase of energy in manufacturing and the transport sector, accompanied by a modest economic growth.

First, the good news (for our model, although not for the UK economy): note how both the first and the second large increases in the price of oil were followed by major increases in inflation and in unemployment. This fits our analysis perfectly. Then, the bad news (for our model): note how the increase in the price of oil since the late 1990s has not been associated – at least so far – with either an increase in inflation or an increase in unemployment. In light of what happened in the 1970s, this lack of an effect has come as a surprise to macroeconomists. The state of research and the various hypotheses being explored are discussed in the Focus box 'Oil price increases: why are the 2000s so different from the 1970s?'

8.7 CONCLUSIONS

This chapter has covered a lot of ground. Let us repeat some key ideas and develop some of the earlier conclusions.

The short run versus the medium run

We will return to these issues many times in this book. See the discussion of the recent recession of 2007–2010 in Chapter 20 and see Chapters 23 and 24 on policy.

One message of this chapter is that changes in policy and changes in the economic environment – from changes in consumer confidence to changes in the price of oil – typically have different effects in the short run than in the medium run. We looked at the effects of a monetary expansion, a deficit reduction, and an increase in the price of oil. The main results are summarised in Table 8.1. A monetary expansion, for example, affects output in the short run but not in the medium run. In the short run, a reduction in the budget deficit decreases output and decreases the interest rate, and it may decrease investment. But in the medium run, the interest rate decreases, and output returns to the natural level of output, so investment increases. An increase in the price of oil decreases output not only in the short run but also in the medium run. And so on.

This difference between the short-run effects and the medium-run effects of policies is one of the reasons economists disagree in their policy recommendations. Some economists believe the economy returns quickly to its medium-run equilibrium, so they emphasise medium-run implications of policy. Others believe the adjustment mechanism through which output returns to the natural level of output can be very slow, so they put more emphasis on the short-run effects of policy. They are more willing to use active monetary policy or fiscal policy to get out of a recession, even if money is neutral in the medium run and budget deficits have adverse implications in the long run.

Table 8.1 Short-run effects and medium-run effects of a monetary expansion, a budget deficit reduction, and an increase in the price of oil on output, the interest rate and the price level

	Short run			Medium run		
	Output level	Interest rate	Price level	Output level	Interest rate	Price level
Monetary expansion	Increase	Decrease	Increase (small)	No change	No change	Increase
Deficit reduction	Decrease	Decrease	Decrease (small)	No change	Decrease	Decrease
Increase in oil price	Decrease	Increase	Increase	Decrease	Increase	Increase

Shocks and propagation mechanisms

This chapter also gives you a general way of thinking about **output fluctuations** (some- ◄
times called **business cycles**) – movements in output around its trend (a trend that we have
ignored so far but on which we will focus in Chapters 11–13).

The economy is constantly hit by **shocks** to aggregate supply, or to aggregate demand or
to both. These shocks may be shifts in consumption coming from changes in consumer
confidence, shifts in investment, shifts in the demand for money, changes in oil prices and
so on. Or they may come from changes in policy – from the introduction of a new tax law,
to a new programme of infrastructure investment, to a decision by the central bank to fight
inflation by tightening the money supply.

Each shock has dynamic effects on output and its components. These dynamic effects are
called the **propagation mechanism** of the shock. Propagation mechanisms are different for
different shocks. The effects of a shock on activity may be largest at the beginning of the
shock and then decrease over time. Or the effects may build up for a while and then
decrease and disappear. We saw, for example, that the effects of an increase in money on
output reach a peak after six to nine months and then slowly decline afterward, as the price
level eventually increases in proportion to the increase in nominal money. Some shocks
have effects even in the medium run. This is the case for any shock that has a permanent
effect on aggregate supply, such as a permanent change in the price of oil.

Fluctuations in output come from the continual appearance of new shocks, each with its
propagation mechanism. At times, some shocks are sufficiently bad or come in sufficiently
bad combinations that they create a recession. The two world recessions of the 1970s were
due largely to increases in the price of oil; more recently, as we anticipated in Chapter 1, four
shocks hit the US economy, and caused the most severe recession after the Great Depression
in 1929 (we will explain the origins of the recession of 2007–2010 in Chapter 20). What we
call *economic fluctuations* are the result of these shocks and their dynamic effects on output.

> How to define *shocks* is harder than it looks. Suppose a failed economic programme in an emerging country leads to political chaos in that country, which leads to increased risk of nuclear war in the region, which leads to a fall in consumer confidence in the whole EU which leads to a recession in the USA. What is the 'shock'? The failed programme? The fall of democracy? The increased risk of nuclear war? Or the decrease in consumer confidence? In practice, we have to cut the chain of causation somewhere. Thus, we may refer to the drop in consumer confidence as the shock, ignoring its underlying causes.

Where we go from here: output, unemployment and inflation

In developing the model of this chapter, we assumed that the nominal money stock was
constant. That is, although we considered the effects of a one-time change in the level of
nominal money (in Section 8.4), we did not allow for sustained nominal money growth.
We are now ready to relax this assumption and allow for nominal money growth. Only
by considering positive nominal money growth can we explain why inflation is typically
positive and think about the relation between economic activity and inflation. Movements
in unemployment, output and inflation are the topics of the next two chapters.

SUMMARY

- The model of aggregate supply and aggregate demand describes the movements in output and the price level when account is taken of equilibrium in the goods market, the financial market and the labour market.

- The aggregate supply relation captures the effects of output on the price level. It is derived from equilibrium in the labour market. It is a relation between the price level, the expected price level and the level of output. An increase in output decreases unemployment; the decrease in unemployment increases wages and, in turn, increases the price level. An increase in the expected price level leads, one-for-one, to an increase in the actual price level.

- The aggregate demand relation captures the effects of the price level on output. It is derived from equilibrium in goods and financial markets. An increase in the price

level decreases the real money stock, increasing the interest rate and decreasing output.

- In the short run, movements in output come from shifts in either aggregate demand or aggregate supply. In the medium run, output returns to the natural level of output, which is determined by equilibrium in the labour market.

- An expansionary monetary policy leads in the short run to an increase in the real money stock, a decrease in the interest rate and an increase in output. Over time, the price level increases and the real money stock decreases until output has returned to its natural level. In the medium run, money does not affect output and changes in money are reflected in proportional increases in the price level. Economists refer to this fact by saying that, in the medium run, money is neutral.

- A reduction in the budget deficit leads in the short run to a decrease in the demand for goods and therefore to a decrease in output. Over time, the price level decreases, leading to an increase in the real money stock and a decrease in the interest rate. In the medium run, output increases back to the natural level of output, but the interest rate is lower and investment is higher.

- An increase in the price of oil leads, in both the short run and the medium run, to a decrease in output. In the short run, it leads to an increase in the price level, which decreases the real money stock and leads to a contraction of demand and output. In the medium run, an increase in the price of oil decreases the real wage paid by firms, increases the natural rate of unemployment and, therefore, decreases the natural level of output.

- The difference between short-run effects and medium-run effects of policies is one of the reasons economists disagree in their policy recommendations. Some economists believe the economy adjusts quickly to its medium-run equilibrium, so they emphasise medium-run implications of policy. Others believe the adjustment mechanism through which output returns to the natural level of output is a slow process at best, so they put more emphasis on the short-run effects of policy.

- Economic fluctuations are the result of a continual stream of shocks to aggregate supply or to aggregate demand and of the dynamic effects of each of these shocks on output. Sometimes the shocks are sufficiently adverse, alone or in combination, that they lead to a recession.

KEY TERMS

aggregate supply relation 162

aggregate demand relation 164

neutrality of money 172

macroeconometric models 173

stagflation 177

output fluctuations, business cycles 183

shocks 183

propagation mechanism 183

QUESTIONS AND PROBLEMS

QUICK CHECK

1. *Using the information in this chapter, label each of the following statements true, false or uncertain. Explain briefly.*

a. The aggregate supply relation implies that an increase in output leads to an increase in the price level.

b. The natural level of output can be determined by looking at the aggregate supply relation alone.

c. The aggregate demand relation slopes down because at a higher price level, consumers wish to purchase fewer goods.

d. In the absence of changes in fiscal or monetary policy, the economy will always remain at the natural level of output.

e. Expansionary monetary policy has no effect on the level of output in the medium run.

f. Fiscal policy cannot affect investment in the medium run because output always returns to its natural level.

g. In the medium run, output and the price level always return to the same value.

2. Spending shocks and the medium run

Suppose the economy begins with output equal to its natural level. Then, there is a reduction in income taxes.

a. Using the *AS–AD* model developed in this chapter, show the effects of a reduction in income taxes on the position of the *AD*, *AS*, *IS* and *LM* curves in the medium run.

b. What happens to output, the interest rate, and the price level in the medium run? What happens to consumption and investment in the medium run?

3. Supply shocks and the medium run

Consider an economy with output equal to the natural level of output. Now suppose there is an increase in unemployment benefits.

a. Using the model developed in this chapter, show the effects of an increase in unemployment benefits on the position of the *AD* and *AS* curves in the short run and in the medium run.

b. How will the increase in unemployment benefits affect output and the price level in the short run and in the medium run?

4. The neutrality of money

a. In what sense is money neutral? How is monetary policy useful if money is neutral?

b. Fiscal policy, like monetary policy, cannot change the natural level of output. Why then is monetary policy considered neutral but fiscal policy is not?

c. Discuss the statement: 'Because neither fiscal nor monetary policy can affect the natural level of output, it follows that, in the medium run, the natural level of output is independent of all government policies.'

DIG DEEPER

5. The paradox of saving, one last time

In chapter problems at the end of Chapters 3 and 5, we examined the paradox of saving in the short run, under different assumptions about the response of investment to output and the interest rate. Here we consider the issue one last time in the context of the AS–AD model.

a. Suppose the economy begins with output equal to its natural level. Then there is a decrease in consumer confidence, as households attempt to increase their saving, for a given level of disposable income.

b. In *AS–AD* and *IS–LM* diagrams, show the effects of the decline in consumer confidence in the short run and the medium run. Explain why curves shift in your diagrams.

c. What happens to output, the interest rate and the price level in the short run? What happens to consumption, investment and private saving in the short run? Is it possible that the decline in consumer confidence will actually lead to a fall in private saving in the short run?

d. Repeat part (b) for the medium run. Is there any paradox of saving in the medium run?

6. Suppose that the interest rate has no effect on investment

a. Can you think of a situation in which this may happen?

b. What does this imply for the slope of the *IS* curve?

c. What does this imply for the slope of the *LM* curve?

d. What does this imply for the slope of the *AD* curve?

Continue to assume that the interest rate has no effect on investment. Assume that the economy starts at the natural level of output. Suppose there is a shock to the variable z, so that the AS curve shifts up.

e. What is the short-run effect on output and the price level? Explain in words.

f. What happens to output and the price level over time? Explain in words.

7. *You learned in problem 6 (on the liquidity trap) in Chapter 5 that money demand becomes very flat at low interest rates. For this problem, consider the money demand function to be horizontal at a zero nominal interest rate.*

a. Draw the *LM* curve. How does the slope of the curve change when the interest rate rises above zero?

b. Draw the *IS* curve. Does the shape of the curve change (necessarily) when the interest rate falls below zero?

c. Draw the *AD* curve? (*Hint*: from the *IS–LM* diagram, think about the price level at which the interest rate is zero. How does the *AD* curve look above this price level? How does the *AD* curve look below this price level?)

d. Draw the *AD* and *AS* curves and assume that equilibrium is at a point where output is below the natural level of output and where the interest rate is zero. Suppose the central bank increases the money supply. What will be the effects on output in the short run and in the medium run? Explain in words.

8. Demand shocks and demand management

Assume that the economy starts at the natural level of output. Now suppose there is a decline in business confidence, so that investment demand falls for any interest rate.

a. In an *AD–AS* diagram, show what happens to output and the price level in the short run and the medium run.

b. What happens to the unemployment rate in the short run? in the medium run?

Suppose that the European Central Bank decides to respond immediately to the decline in business confidence in the short run. In particular, suppose that the European Central Bank wants to prevent the unemployment rate from changing in the short run after the decline in business confidence.

c. What should the European Central Bank do? Show how the European Central Bank's action, combined with the decline in business confidence, affects the *AD–AS* diagram in the short run and the medium run.

d. How do short-run output and the short-run price level compare to your answers from part (a)?

e. How do the short-run and medium-run unemployment rates compare to your answers from part (b)?

9. Supply shocks and demand management

Assume that the economy starts at the natural level of output. Now suppose there is an increase in the price of oil.

a. In an *AS–AD* diagram, show what happens to output and the price level in the short run and the medium run.

b. What happens to the unemployment rate in the short run? in the medium run?

Suppose that the European Central Bank decides to respond immediately to the increase in the price of oil. In particular, suppose that the European Central Bank wants to prevent the unemployment rate from changing in the short run, after the increase in the price of oil. Assume that the European Central Bank changes the money supply once – immediately after the increase in the price of oil – and then does not change the money supply again.

c. What should the European Central Bank do to prevent the unemployment rate from changing in the short run? Show how the European Central Bank's action, combined with the decline in business confidence, affects the *AD–AS* diagram in the short run and the medium run.

d. How do output and the price level in the short run and the medium run compare to your answers from part (a)?

e. How do the short-run and medium-run unemployment rates compare to your answers from part (b)?

10. *Based on your answers to problems 8 and 9 and the material from the chapter, comment on the following statement:*

The European Central Bank has the easiest job in the world. All it has to do is conduct expansionary monetary policy when the unemployment rate increases and contractionary monetary policy when the unemployment rate falls.

11. Taxes, oil prices and workers

Everyone in the labour force is concerned with two things: whether they have a job and, if so, their after-tax income from the job (i.e. their after-tax real wage). An unemployed worker may also be concerned with the availability and amount of unemployment benefits, but we will leave that issue aside for this problem.

a. Suppose there is an increase in oil prices. How will this affect the unemployment rate in the short run and the medium run? How about the real wage (W/P)?

b. Suppose there is a reduction in income taxes. How will this affect the unemployment rate in the short run and the medium run? How about the real wage? For a given worker, how will after-tax income be affected?

c. According to our model, what policy tools does the government have available to increase the real wage?

d. During 2003 and 2004, oil prices increased more or less at the same time that income taxes were reduced. A popular joke at the time was that people could use their tax refunds to pay for the higher petrol prices. How do your answers to this problem make sense of this joke?

EXPLORE FURTHER

12. Adding energy prices to the AS curve

In this problem, we incorporate the price of energy inputs (e.g. oil) explicitly into the AS curve.

Suppose the price-setting equation is given by

$$P = (1 + \mu)W^a P_E^{1-a}$$

where P_E is the price of energy resources and $0 < a < 1$. Ignoring a multiplicative constant, $W^a P_E^{1-a}$ is the marginal cost function that would result from the production technology, $Y = N^a E^{1-a}$, where N is employed labour and E represents units of energy resources used in production.

As in the text, the wage-setting relation is given by

$$W = P^e F(u, z)$$

Make sure to distinguish between P_E, the price of energy resources, and P^e, the expected price level for the economy as a whole.

a. Substitute the wage-setting relation into the price-setting relation to obtain the aggregate supply relation.

b. Let $x \equiv P_E/P$, the real price of energy. Observe that $P \times x = P_E$ and substitute for P_E in the AS relation you derived in part (a). Solve for P to obtain

$$P = P^e(1 + \mu)^{1/a}F(u, z)x^{(1-a)/a}$$

c. Graph the AS relation from part (b) for a given P^e and a given x.

d. Suppose that $P = P^e$. How will the natural rate of unemployment change if x, the real price of energy, increases? [*Hint*: you can solve the AS equation for x to obtain the answer, or you can reason it out. If $P = P^e$, how must $F(u, z)$ change when x increases to maintain the equality in part (b)? How must u change to have the required effect on $F(u, z)$?]

e. Suppose that the economy begins with output equal to the natural level of output. Then the real price of energy increases. Show the short-run and medium-run effects of the increase in the real price of energy in an AD–AS diagram.

The text suggests that a change in expectations about monetary policy may help explain why increases in oil prices over the past few years have had less of an adverse effect on the economy than the oil price shocks of the 1970s. Let us examine how such a change in expectations would alter the effect of an oil price shock.

f. Suppose there is an increase in the real price of energy. In addition, despite the increase in the real price of energy, suppose that the expected price level (i.e. P^e) does not change. After the short-run effect of the increase in the real price of energy, will there be any further adjustment of the economy over the medium run? In order for the expected price level not to change, what monetary action must wage setters be expecting after an increase in the real price of energy?

13. Growth and fluctuations: some economic history

When economists think about history, fluctuations often stand out – oil shocks and stagflation in the 1970s, a recession followed by a long expansion in the 1980s, a recession followed by an extraordinary low-unemployment, low-inflation boom in the 1990s. This question puts these fluctuations into some perspective.

Go to the website of the OECD Economic Outlook Database and and retrieve the quarterly data on real GDP at constant prices. Get real GDP for the fourth quarter of 1959, 1969, 1979, 1989 and 1999 and for the fourth quarter of the most recent year available.

a. Using the real GDP numbers for 1959 and 1969, calculate the decadal growth rate of real GDP for the 1960s. Do the same for the 1970s, 1980s and 1990s and for the available years of the most recent decade.

b. How does growth in the 1970s compare to growth in the later decades? How does growth in the 1960s compare to the later decades? Which decade looks most unusual?

---

*We invite you to visit the Blanchard page on the Prentice Hall website, at **www.prenhall.com/blanchard** for this chapter's World Wide Web exercises.*

Chapter 9

THE NATURAL RATE OF UNEMPLOYMENT AND THE PHILLIPS CURVE

In 1958, A. W. Phillips drew a diagram plotting the rate of inflation against the rate of unemployment in the UK for each year from 1861–1957. He found clear evidence of a negative relation between inflation and unemployment: when unemployment was low, inflation was high, and when unemployment was high, inflation was low, often even negative.

◄ William Phillips was an influential New Zealand economist who spent most of his academic career at the London School of Economics (LSE).

Two years later, Paul Samuelson and Robert Solow replicated Phillips exercise for the USA, using data from 1900–1960. Figure 9.1 reproduces their findings, using CPI inflation as a measure of the inflation rate. Apart from the period of very high unemployment during the 1930s (the years from 1931–1939 are denoted by triangles and are clearly to the right of the other points in the figure), there also appeared to be a negative relation between inflation and unemployment in the USA.

◄ Paul Samuelson and Robert Solow are two well-known US economists, both Nobel prize winners, respectively in 1970 and 1987.

This relation, which Samuelson and Solow labelled the **Phillips curve**, rapidly became central to macroeconomic thinking and policy. It appeared to imply that countries could choose between different combinations of unemployment and inflation. A country could achieve low unemployment if it were willing to tolerate higher inflation, or it could achieve price-level stability – zero inflation – if it were willing to tolerate higher unemployment. Much of the discussion about macroeconomic policy became a discussion about which point to choose on the Phillips curve.

In the 1970s, however, the relation broke down. In the USA and most other OECD countries, there was both high inflation *and* high unemployment, clearly contradicting the original Phillips curve. A relation reappeared, but it reappeared as a relation between the unemployment rate and the *change* in the inflation rate. Today, high unemployment leads not to low inflation but to a decrease in inflation over time. Conversely, low unemployment doesn't lead to high inflation but to an increase in inflation over time.

The purpose of this chapter is to explore the mutations of the Phillips curve and, more generally, to understand the relation between inflation and unemployment. You will see that what Phillips discovered was the aggregate supply relation and that the mutations of the Phillips curve came from changes in the way people and firms formed expectations.

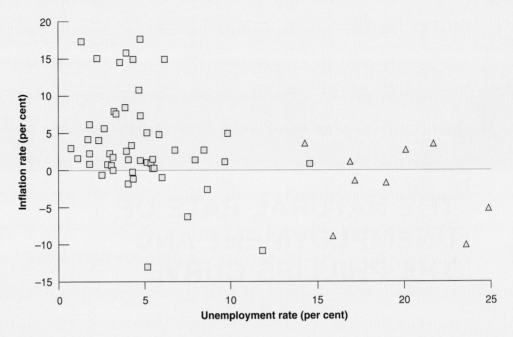

Figure 9.1

Inflation versus unemployment in the USA, 1900–1960

During the period 1900–1960 in the USA, a low unemployment rate was typically associated with a high inflation rate, and a high unemployment rate was typically associated with a low or negative inflation rate.

The chapter has three sections:

- Section 9.1 shows how we can think of the aggregate supply relation as a relation between inflation, expected inflation and unemployment.

- Section 9.2 uses this relation to interpret the mutations in the Phillips curve over time.

- Section 9.3 further discusses the relation between unemployment and inflation across countries and over time.

9.1 INFLATION, EXPECTED INFLATION AND UNEMPLOYMENT

We then replaced the unemployment rate by its expression in terms of output to obtain a relation between the price level, the expected price level and output. We do not need to take that step here.

Our first step will be to show that the aggregate supply relation we derived in Chapter 8 can be rewritten as a relation between *inflation*, *expected inflation* and the *unemployment rate*.

Let's go back to the aggregate supply relation between the price level, the expected price level and the unemployment rate we derived in Chapter 8 [equation (8.1)]:

$$P = P^e(1 + \mu)F(u, z)$$

The function, *F*, comes from the wage-setting relation, equation (7.1):

$$W = P^e F(u, z)$$

Recall that the function, *F*, captures the effects on the wage of the unemployment rate, *u*, and of the other factors that affect wage setting, represented by the catchall variable, *z*. It will be convenient here to assume a specific form for this function. We shall assume that this function *F* is exponential:

$$F(u, z) = e^{-\alpha u + z}$$

This captures the notion that the higher the unemployment rate, the lower the wage; and the higher *z* (for example, the more generous unemployment benefits are), the higher the wage. The parameter α (the Greek lowercase letter alpha) captures the strength of the effect of unemployment on the wage.

Replace the function, *F*, by this specific form in the aggregate supply relation above:

$$P = P^e(1 + \mu)e^{-\alpha u + z} \qquad [9.1]$$

Now, take logarithms of (9.1) to get:

$$\log P = \log P^e + \log(1 + \mu) - \alpha u + z$$

Then, subtract $\log P_{-1}$ from both sides to get:

$$\log P - \log P_{-1} = \log P^e - \log P_{-1} + \log(1 + \mu) - \alpha u + z$$

Then, equation (9.1) can be rewritten as

$$\pi = \pi^e + (\mu + z) - \alpha u \qquad [9.2]$$

where $\pi = \log P - \log P_{-1}$, $\pi^e = \log P^e - \log P_{-1}$ and $\log(1 + \mu) \approx \mu$ because μ is small. Thus equation (9.2) is less and less precise as inflation rises – say in Argentina . . . You should make sure you understand each of the effects at work in equation (9.2):

◀ Note that $\log P - \log P_{-1} = \log(P/P_{-1}) = \log\left(1 + \dfrac{P - P_{-1}}{P_{-1}}\right) = \log(1 + \pi) \approx \pi$, if π is small.

- *An increase in expected inflation, π^e, leads to an increase in actual inflation, π.*

  To see why, start from equation (9.1). An increase in the expected price level, P^e, leads, one for one, to an increase in the actual price level, P: if wage setters expect a higher price level, they set a higher nominal wage, which leads to an increase in the price level.

  ◀ From now on, to lighten your reading, we often refer to the *inflation rate* simply as *inflation* and to the *unemployment rate* simply as *unemployment*.

  Now note that, given last period's price level, a higher price level this period implies a higher rate of increase in the price level from last period to this period – that is, higher inflation. Similarly, given last period's price level, a higher expected price level this period implies a higher expected rate of increase in the price level from last period to this period – that is, higher expected inflation. So the fact that an increase in the expected price level leads to an increase in the actual price level can be restated as: an increase in expected inflation leads to an increase in inflation.

  ◀ Increase in π^e ⇒ Increase in π.

- *Given expected inflation, π^e, an increase in the mark-up, μ, or an increase in the factors that affect wage determination – an increase in z – leads to an increase in inflation, π.*

  From equation (9.1): given the expected price level, P^e, an increase in either μ or z increases the price level, P. Using the same argument as in the previous bullet to restate this proposition in terms of inflation and expected inflation: given expected inflation, π^e, an increase in either μ or z leads to an increase in inflation π.

  ◀ Increase in μ or z ⇒ Increase in π.

- *Given expected inflation, π^e, an increase in the unemployment rate, u, leads to a decrease in inflation, π.*

  From equation (9.1): given the expected price level, P^e, an increase in the unemployment rate, u, leads to a lower nominal wage, which leads to a lower price level, P. Restating this in terms of inflation and expected inflation: given expected inflation, π^e, an increase in the unemployment rate, u, leads to a decrease in inflation, π.

  ◀ Increase in u ⇒ Decrease in π.

We need one more step before we return to a discussion of the Phillips curve: when we look at movements in inflation and unemployment in the rest of the chapter, it will often be convenient to use time indexes so that we can refer to variables such as inflation, or expected inflation or unemployment in a specific year. So we rewrite equation (9.2) as:

$$\pi_t = \pi_t^e + (\mu + z) - \alpha u_t \qquad [9.3]$$

The variables π_t, π_t^e and u_t refer to inflation, expected inflation and unemployment in year t. Be sure you see that there are no time indexes on μ and z. This is because we shall typically think of both μ and z as constant while we look at movements in inflation, expected inflation and unemployment over time.

9.2 THE PHILLIPS CURVE

Now let's look at the relation between unemployment and inflation as it was first discovered by Phillips, Samuelson and Solow around 1960. Unlike Phillips, who worked on UK data from the 19th century, Samuelson and Solow worked on more recent US data. Here we will tell the story of how they discovered that the Phillips curve actually changes over time. This represented a huge progress in macroeconomics.

The early incarnation

Imagine an economy where inflation is positive in some years, negative in others and is on average equal to zero. As we will see later in this chapter, average inflation *was* close to zero during much of the period Phillips, Samuelson and Solow were looking at.

In such an environment, how will wage setters choose nominal wages for the coming year? With the average inflation rate equal to zero in the past, it is reasonable for wage setters to expect that inflation will be equal to zero over the next year as well. So, let's assume that expected inflation is equal to zero – that $\pi_t^e = 0$. Equation (9.3) then becomes

$$\pi_t = (\mu + z) - \alpha u_t \qquad [9.4]$$

This is precisely the negative relation between unemployment and inflation that Phillips found for the UK and that Solow and Samuelson found for the USA. The story behind it is simple: given the expected price level, which workers simply take to be last year's price level, lower unemployment leads to a higher nominal wage. A higher nominal wage leads to a higher price level. Putting the steps together, lower unemployment leads to a higher price level this year relative to last year's price level – that is, to higher inflation. This mechanism has sometimes been called the **wage–price spiral**, an expression that captures well the basic mechanism at work:

- In response to the higher nominal wage, firms increase their prices and the price level increases.
- In response to the higher price level, workers ask for a higher nominal wage the next time the wage is set.
- The higher nominal wage leads firms to further increase their prices. As a result, the price level increases further.
- In response to this further increase in the price level, workers, when they set the wage again, ask for a further increase in the nominal wage.
- Low unemployment leads to a higher nominal wage.

And so the race between prices and wages results in steady wage and price inflation.

Mutations

The combination of an apparently reliable empirical relation together with a plausible story to explain it led to the adoption of the Phillips curve by macroeconomists and policy makers. During the 1960s, US macroeconomic policy was aimed at maintaining unemployment in a range that appeared consistent with moderate inflation. And, throughout the 1960s, the negative relation between unemployment and inflation provided a reliable guide to the joint movements in unemployment and inflation.

Figure 9.2 plots the combinations of the inflation rate and the unemployment rate in the USA for each year from 1948–1969. Note how well the Phillips relation held during the long economic expansion that lasted during most of the 1960s. During the years 1961–1969, denoted by black diamonds in the figure, the unemployment rate declined steadily from 6.8% to 3.4%, and the inflation rate steadily increased from 1.0% to 5.5%. Put informally, from 1961–1969, the US economy moved up along the Phillips curve.

Around 1970, however, the relation between the inflation rate and the unemployment rate, so visible in Figure 9.2, broke down. Figure 9.3 shows the combination of the inflation rate and the unemployment rate in the USA for each year since 1970. The points are scattered in a roughly symmetric cloud: there is no visible relation between the unemployment rate and the inflation rate.

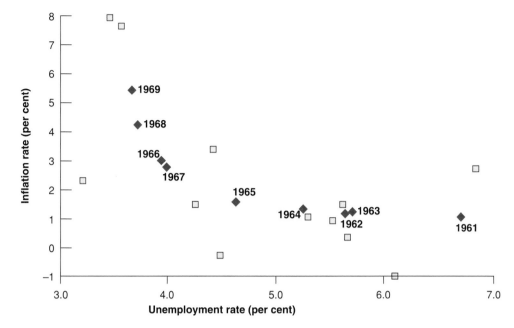

Figure 9.2

Inflation versus unemployment in the USA, 1948–1969

The steady decline in the US unemployment rate throughout the 1960s was associated with a steady increase in the inflation rate.

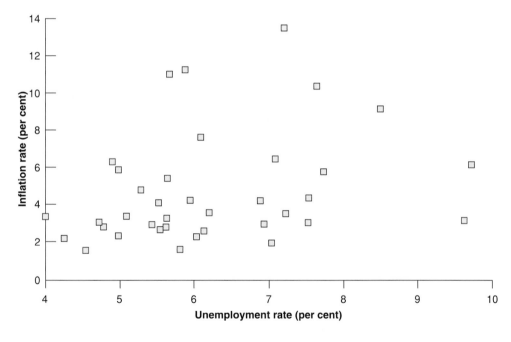

Figure 9.3

Inflation versus unemployment in the USA since 1970

Beginning in 1970, the relation between the unemployment rate and the inflation rate disappeared in the USA.

Why did the original Phillips curve vanish? There are two main reasons:

- The USA was hit twice in the 1970s by large increases in the price of oil (see Chapter 8). The effect of these increases in non-labour costs was to force firms to increase their prices relative to the wages they were paying – in other words, to increase the mark-up, μ. As shown in equation (9.3), an increase in μ leads to an increase in inflation, even at a given rate of unemployment, and this happened twice in the 1970s. But the main reason for the breakdown of the Phillips curve relation was the second reason.
- Wage setters changed the way they formed their expectations. This change came, in turn, from a change in the behaviour of inflation. Look at Figure 9.4, which shows the US inflation rate since 1900. Starting in the 1960s (the decade shaded in the figure), you can see a clear change in the behaviour of the rate of inflation. First, rather than being sometimes positive and sometimes negative, as it had been for the first part of the century, the rate of inflation became consistently positive. Second, inflation became more

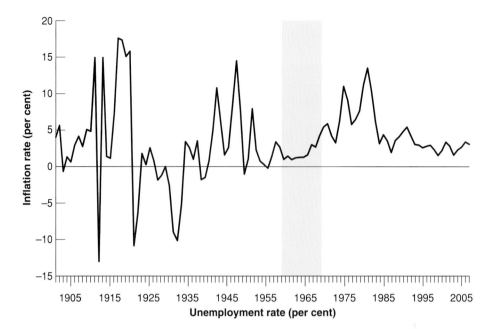

Figure 9.4

US inflation since 1900

Since the 1960s, the US inflation rate has been consistently positive. Inflation has also become more persistent: a high inflation rate this year is more likely to be followed by a high inflation rate next year.

persistent: high inflation in one year became more likely to be followed by high inflation the next year.

The persistence of inflation led workers and firms to revise the way they formed their expectations. When inflation is consistently positive year after year, expecting that the price level this year will be the same as the price level last year – which is the same as expecting zero inflation – becomes systematically incorrect; worse, it becomes foolish. People do not like to make the same mistake repeatedly. So, as inflation became consistently positive and more persistent, when people formed expectations, they started to take into account the presence and the persistence of inflation. This change in expectation formation changed the nature of the relation between unemployment and inflation.

Let's look at the argument in the previous paragraph more closely. First, suppose expectations of inflation are formed according to

$$\pi_t^e = \theta \pi_{t-1} \qquad [9.5]$$

The value of the parameter θ (the Greek lowercase theta) captures the effect of last year's inflation rate, π_{t-1}, on this year's expected inflation rate, π_t^e. The higher the value of θ, the more last year's inflation leads workers and firms to revise their expectations of what inflation will be this year. We can think of what happened in the 1970s as an increase in the value of θ over time:

- As long as inflation was low and not very persistent, it was reasonable for workers and firms to ignore past inflation and to assume that the price level this year would be roughly the same as price level last year. For the period that Samuelson and Solow had looked at, θ was close to zero, and expectations were roughly given by $\pi_t^e = 0$.

Think about how *you* form expectations. What do you expect inflation to be next year? How did you come to this conclusion?

- As inflation became more persistent, workers and firms started changing the way they formed expectations. They started assuming that if inflation was high last year, inflation was likely to be high this year as well. The parameter θ, the effect of last year's inflation rate on this year's expected inflation rate, increased. The evidence suggests that, by the mid-1970s, people formed expectations by expecting this year's inflation rate to be the same as last year's inflation rate – in other words, that θ was now equal to 1.

Now turn to the implications of different values of θ for the relation between inflation and unemployment. To do so, replace equation (9.5) in equation (9.3):

$$\pi_t = \overbrace{\theta \pi_{t-1}}^{\pi_t^e} + (\mu + z) - \alpha u_t$$

- When θ equals 0, we get the original Phillips curve, a relation between the inflation rate and the unemployment rate:

$$\pi_t = (\mu + z) - \alpha u_t$$

- When θ is positive, the inflation rate depends not only on the unemployment rate but also on last year's inflation rate:

$$\pi_t = \theta\pi_{t-1} + (\mu + z) - \alpha u_t$$

- When θ equals 1, the relation becomes (moving last year's inflation rate to the left side of the equation)

$$\pi - \pi_{t-1} = (\mu + z) - \alpha u_t \qquad [9.6]$$

So, when $\theta = 1$, the unemployment rate affects not the *inflation rate* but rather the *change in the inflation rate*: high unemployment leads to decreasing inflation; low unemployment leads to increasing inflation.

This discussion is the key to what happened from 1970 onward. As θ increased from 0 to 1, the simple relation between the unemployment rate and the inflation rate disappeared. This disappearance is what we saw in Figure 9.3. But a new relation emerged, this time between the unemployment rate and the change in the inflation rate – as predicted by equation (9.6). This relation is shown in Figure 9.5, which plots the change in the inflation rate versus the unemployment rate observed for each year since 1970. The figure shows a clear negative relation between the unemployment rate and the change in the inflation rate. The line that best fits the scatter of points for the period 1970–2006 is given by

◄ This line, called a regression line, is obtained using econometrics. (See Appendix 2 at the end of the book.) Note that the line does not fit the cloud of points very tightly. There are years when the change in inflation is much larger than implied by the line, and years when the change in inflation is much smaller than implied by the line. We return to this point later.

$$\pi_t - \pi_{t-1} = 4.4\% - 0.73u_t \qquad [9.7]$$

The line is drawn in Figure 9.5. For low unemployment, the change in inflation is positive. For high unemployment, the change in inflation is negative. This is the form the Phillips curve relation between unemployment and inflation takes today.

To distinguish it from the original Phillips curve [equation (9.4)], equation (9.6) – or its empirical counterpart, equation (9.7) – is often called the **modified Phillips curve**, or the **expectations-augmented Phillips curve** (to indicate that P_{t-1} stands for expected inflation), or the **accelerationist Phillips curve** (to indicate that a low unemployment rate leads to an increase in the inflation rate and thus *an acceleration* of the price level). We will

◄ ● Original Phillips curve: Increase in $u_t \Rightarrow$ Lower inflation
● Modified Phillips curve: Increase in $u_t \Rightarrow$ Lower increase in inflation

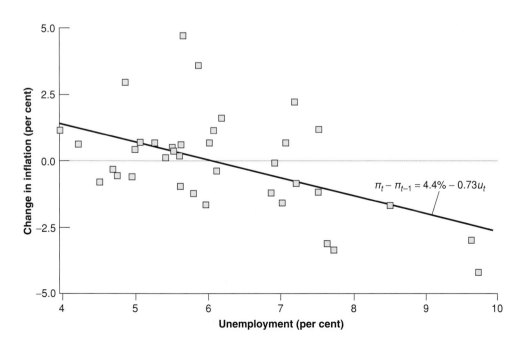

Figure 9.5

Change in inflation versus unemployment in the USA since 1970

Since 1970, there has been a negative relation between the unemployment rate and the change in the inflation rate in the USA.

simply call equation (9.6) the Phillips curve and refer to the earlier incarnation, equation (9.4), as the *original* Phillips curve.

Back to the natural rate of unemployment

The history of the Phillips curve is closely related to the discovery of the concept of the natural unemployment rate that we introduced in Chapter 7.

The original Phillips curve implied that there was no such thing as a natural unemployment rate: if policy makers were willing to tolerate a higher inflation rate, they could maintain a lower unemployment rate forever.

In the late 1960s, while the original Phillips curve still gave a good description of the data, two economists, Milton Friedman and Edmund Phelps, questioned the existence of such a trade-off between unemployment and inflation. They questioned it on logical grounds, arguing that such a trade-off could exist only if wage setters systematically under-predicted inflation and that they were unlikely to make the same mistake forever. Friedman and Phelps also argued that, if the government attempted to sustain lower unemployment by accepting higher inflation, the trade-off would ultimately disappear; the unemployment rate could not be sustained below a certain level, a level they called the 'natural rate of unemployment'. Events proved them right, and the trade-off between the unemployment rate and the inflation rate indeed disappeared. (See the Focus box 'Theory ahead of facts: Milton Friedman and Edmund Phelps'.) Today, most economists accept the notion of a *natural rate of unemployment* – subject to the many caveats we will see in the next section.

► Friedman was awarded the Nobel Prize in 1976. Phelps was awarded the Nobel Prize in 2006.

Let's make explicit the connection between the Phillips curve and the natural rate of unemployment.

By definition (see Chapter 7), the natural rate of unemployment is the unemployment rate such that the actual price level is equal to the expected price level. Equivalently, and more conveniently here, the natural rate of unemployment is the unemployment rate such that the actual inflation rate is equal to the expected inflation rate. Denote the natural unemployment rate by u_n (where the index, n, stands for *natural*). Then, imposing the condition that actual inflation and expected inflation be the same ($\pi_t = \pi_t^e$) in equation (9.3) gives

$$0 = (\mu + z) - \alpha u_n$$

Solving for the natural rate, u_n:

$$u_n = \frac{\mu + z}{\alpha} \qquad [9.8]$$

The higher the mark-up, μ, or the higher the factors that affect wage setting, z, the higher the natural rate of unemployment.

Now rewrite equation (9.3) as

$$\pi_t - \pi_t^e = -\alpha\left(u_t - \frac{\mu + z}{\alpha}\right)$$

Note from equation (9.8) that the fraction on the right side is equal to u_n, so we can rewrite the equation as

$$\pi_t - \pi_t^e = -\alpha(u_t - u_n) \qquad [9.9]$$

If the expected rate of inflation (π_t^e) is well approximated by last year's inflation rate, π_{t-1}, the equation finally becomes

$$\pi_t - \pi_{t-1} = -\alpha(u_t - u_n) \qquad [9.10]$$

Equation (9.10) is an important relation, for two reasons:

● It gives us another way of thinking about the *Phillips curve* as a relation between the actual unemployment rate, u_t, the natural unemployment rate, u_n, and the change in the inflation rate, $\pi_t - \pi_{t-1}$.

The change in the inflation rate depends on the difference between the actual and the natural unemployment rates. When the actual unemployment rate is higher than the natural unemployment rate, the inflation rate decreases; when the actual unemployment rate is lower than the natural unemployment rate, the inflation rate increases.

◄ $u_t < u_n \Rightarrow \pi_t > \pi_{t-1}$
$u_t > u_n \Rightarrow \pi_t < \pi_{t-1}$

- It also gives us another way of thinking about the *natural rate of unemployment*: the natural rate of unemployment is the rate of unemployment required to keep the inflation rate constant. This is why the natural rate is also called the **non-accelerating inflation rate of unemployment (NAIRU)**.

◄ Calling the natural rate 'the non-accelerating–inflation rate of unemployment' is actually wrong. It should be called 'the non-increasing inflation rate of unemployment'. But NAIRU has now become so standard that it is too late to change it.

What has been the natural rate of unemployment in the USA since 1970? Put another way: what has been the unemployment rate that, on average, has led to constant inflation?

To answer this question, all we need to do is to return to equation (9.7), the estimated relation between the change in inflation and the unemployment rate since 1970. Setting the change in inflation equal to zero in that equation implies a value for the natural unemployment rate of 4.4%./0.73 = 6%. In words: the evidence suggests that, since 1970 in the USA, the average rate of unemployment required to keep inflation constant has been equal to 6%.

◄ From 1997–2006, the average unemployment rate was 4.9%. Yet the inflation rate was roughly the same in 2006 as in 1997. This suggests that the US natural rate of unemployment is now lower than 6%. More on this in the next section.

Let's summarise what we have discussed so far:

- The aggregate supply relation is well captured in most industrialised economies today by a relation between the change in the inflation rate and the deviation of the unemployment rate from the natural rate of unemployment [equation (9.8)].
- When the unemployment rate exceeds the natural rate of unemployment, the inflation rate decreases. When the unemployment rate is below the natural rate of unemployment, the inflation rate increases.

FOCUS
Theory ahead of facts: Milton Friedman and Edmund Phelps

Economists are usually not very good at predicting major changes before they happen, and most of their insights are derived after the fact. Here is an exception.

In the late 1960s – precisely as the original Phillips curve relation was working like a charm – two economists, Milton Friedman and Edmund Phelps, argued that the appearance of a trade-off between inflation and unemployment was an illusion.

Here are a few quotes from Milton Friedman. About the Phillips curve, he said:

> Implicitly, Phillips wrote his article for a world in which everyone anticipated that nominal prices would be stable and in which this anticipation remained unshaken and immutable whatever happened to actual prices and wages. Suppose, by contrast, that everyone anticipates that prices will rise at a rate of more than 75% a year – as, for example, Brazilians did a few years ago. Then, wages must rise at that rate simply to keep real wages unchanged. An excess supply of labor [by this, Friedman means high unemployment] will be reflected in a less rapid rise in nominal wages than in anticipated prices, not in an absolute decline in wages.

He went on:

> To state [my] conclusion differently, there is always a temporary trade-off between inflation and unemployment; there is no permanent trade-off. The temporary trade-off comes not from inflation per se, but from a rising rate of inflation.

He then tried to guess how much longer the apparent trade-off between inflation and unemployment would last in the USA:

> But how long, you will say, is 'temporary'? . . . I can at most venture a personal judgment, based on some examination of the historical evidence, that the initial effect of a higher and unanticipated rate of inflation lasts for something like two to five years; that this initial effect then begins to be reversed; and that a full adjustment to the new rate of inflation takes as long for employment as for interest rates, say, a couple of decades.

Friedman could not have been more right. A few years later, the original Phillips curve started to disappear, in exactly the way Friedman had predicted.

Source: Milton Friedman, 'The Role of Monetary Policy', *American Economic Review*, 1968, **58**(1), 1–17. (The article by Phelps, 'Money – Wage Dynamics and Labor–Market Equilibrium', *Journal of Political Economy*, 1968, 76, 678–711, made many of the same points more formally.)

9.3 THE PHILLIPS CURVE AND THE NATURAL RATE OF UNEMPLOYMENT IN EUROPE

In the previous section we showed how the relation between inflation and unemployment has held quite well in the USA since 1970. But evidence from its earlier history, as well as evidence from other countries, suggests that the relation between inflation and unemployment can and does vary across countries and time. What has been the natural rate of unemployment in European countries since 1970? And has it changed over time?

Variations in the natural rate across European countries

To know what the natural rate of unemployment has been in Europe since 1970, we need to return again to equation (9.7), the estimated relation between the change in inflation and the unemployment rate since 1970. By setting the change in inflation equal to zero in that equation we find a value for the natural unemployment rate. Recall from equation (9.8) that the natural rate of unemployment depends on all the factors that affect wage setting, represented by the catchall variable, z; the mark-up set by firms, μ; and the response of inflation to unemployment, represented by α. If these factors differ across countries, there is no reason to expect all countries to have the same natural rate of unemployment. And natural rates indeed differ across countries, sometimes considerably. The first column in Table 9.1 reports the value for the natural rate of unemployment in some European countries since 1970.

Some European countries have unemployment rates that are very low by international standards, even compared to the USA. The Netherlands and Denmark are such cases. Other countries such as Finland, France and Ireland suffer from high unemployment. Because their inflation rates are stable, we can, relying on the argument just developed, reach a stronger conclusion: this high unemployment reflects a high natural rate of unemployment, not a deviation of the unemployment rate from the natural rate. This in turn tells us where we should look for explanations: in the factors determining the wage-setting and the price-setting relations.

Is it easy to identify the relevant factors? One often hears the statement that one of the main problems of Europe is its *labour market rigidities*. These rigidities, the argument goes, are responsible for its high unemployment. While there is some truth to this statement, the reality is more complex.

Table 9.1 The natural rate of unemployment in some European countries

Country	1970–2008	1970–1990	1991–2008
Denmark	6.0%	5.8%	6.5%
Finland	77.0%	4.6%	9.3%
France	7.4%	6.5%	9.4%
Germany	6.0%	4.1%	8.6%
Ireland	7.5%	9.0%	9.0%
Netherlands	5.6%	6.9%	4.7%
Sweden	3.9%	2.6%	7.3%
UK	6.7%	6.7%	6.7%

Source: OECD *Economic Outlook* database.

What explains European unemployment?

What do critics have in mind when they talk about the 'labour market rigidities' afflicting Europe? They have in mind in particular:

● A generous system of unemployment insurance – The replacement rate (that is, the ratio of unemployment benefits to the after-tax wage) is often high in Europe, and the duration of benefits – the period of time for which the unemployed are entitled to receive benefits – often runs in years.

Some unemployment insurance is clearly desirable, but generous benefits may increase unemployment in at least two ways: they decrease the incentives the unemployed have to search for jobs. They may also increase the wage that firms have to pay. Recall our discussion of efficiency wages in Chapter 7: the higher unemployment benefits are, the higher the wages firms have to pay in order to motivate and keep workers.

- A high degree of employment protection – By employment protection, economists have in mind the set of rules that increase the cost of layoffs for firms. These range from high severance payments to the need for firms to justify layoffs, to the possibility for workers to appeal the decision and have it reversed.

  The purpose of employment protection is to decrease layoffs and thus to protect workers from the risk of unemployment. What it does, however, is also increase the cost of labour for firms, thus reducing those hired and making it harder for the unemployed to get jobs. The evidence suggests that, while employment protection does not necessarily increase unemployment, it changes its nature: the flows in and out of unemployment decrease, but the average duration of unemployment increases. Such long duration increases the risk that the unemployed lose skills and morale, decreasing their employability.

- Minimum wages – Most European countries have national minimum wages. In some countries, the ratio of the minimum wage to the median wage can be quite high. As we discussed in Chapter 7, high minimum wages clearly run the risk of decreasing employment for the least skilled workers, thus increasing their unemployment rate.

- Bargaining rules – In most European countries, labour contracts are subject to extension agreements. A contract agreed to by a subset of firms and unions can be automatically extended to all firms in the sector. This considerably reinforces the bargaining power of unions because it reduces the scope for competition by non-unionised firms. As we saw in Chapter 7, stronger bargaining power on the part of the unions may result in higher unemployment: higher unemployment is needed to reconcile the demands of workers with the wages paid by firms.

Do these labour market institutions really explain high unemployment in Europe? Is the case open and shut? Not quite. Here it is important to recall two important facts.

Fact 1: as we saw in Chapter 1, unemployment was not always high in Europe. Recall the evolution of unemployment shown in Figure 1.2: in the 1970s, the unemployment rate in the four major continental European countries was lower than that in the USA, around 2–3% (compared to 5% in the USA). The natural rate in these countries has increased since 1970–1990 and today is around 8–9%. Let us return to Table 9.1. The second and third columns in the table compare the natural unemployment rate in 1970–1990 with the same rate in 1991–2008. In most cases, with the exceptions of the Netherlands and the UK, the natural rate of unemployment increased. How do we explain this increase?

One hypothesis is that institutions were different then and that labour market rigidities have appeared only in the past 40 years. This turns out not to be the case, however. It is true that, in response to the adverse shocks of the 1970s (in particular the two recessions following the increases in the price of oil), many European governments increased the generosity of unemployment insurance and the degree of employment protection. But, even in the 1960s, European labour market institutions looked nothing like US labour market institutions. Social protection was higher in Europe, yet unemployment was lower.

A different line of explanation focuses on the interaction between institutions and shocks. Some labour market institutions may be benign in some environments and very costly in others. Take employment protection. If competition between firms is limited, the need to adjust employment in each firm may be limited as well, and so the cost of employment protection may be low. But if competition, either from other domestic firms or from foreign firms, increases, the cost of employment protection may become very high. Firms

◄ When inflation is stable, then the unemployment rate is roughly equal to the natural rate.

that cannot adjust their labour force quickly may simply be unable to compete and may go out of business. Thus, even if employment protection rules do not change, higher competition can lead to a higher natural rate.

Fact 2: many European countries actually have low unemployment. This is shown in Figure 7.4, which gives the unemployment rate for the EU27. In all these countries, inflation is stable, so the unemployment rate is roughly equal to the natural rate. The unemployment rate is high in the four large continental countries; this is indeed why we focused on them in Chapter 1. But note how low the unemployment rate is in some other countries – in particular, Denmark, Ireland and the Netherlands.

Is it the case that these low-unemployment countries have low benefits, low employment protection and weak unions? Things are unfortunately not so simple: countries such as Ireland and the UK indeed have labour market institutions that resemble those of the USA: limited benefits, low employment protection and weak unions. But countries such as Denmark and the Netherlands have a high degree of social protection – in particular, high unemployment benefits and strong unions.

So what is one to conclude? An emerging consensus among economists is that the devil is in the details: generous social protection is consistent with low unemployment, but it has to be provided efficiently. For example, unemployment benefits can be generous, as long as the unemployed are, at the same time, forced to take jobs if such jobs are available. Some employment protection – for example, in the form of generous severance payments – may not prevent low unemployment as long as firms do not face the prospect of long administrative or judicial uncertainty when they lay off workers. Countries such as Denmark appear to have been more successful in achieving these goals. Creating incentives for the unemployed to take jobs and simplifying the rules of employment protection are on the reform agenda of many European governments. One may hope they will lead to a decrease in the natural rate in the future.

Variations in the natural rate over time

In writing equation (9.6) and estimating equation (9.7), we treated $\mu + z$ as a constant, but there are good reasons to believe that μ and z vary over time. The degree of monopoly power of firms, the structure of wage bargaining, the system of unemployment benefits and so on are likely to change over time, leading to changes in either μ or z and, by implication, changes in the natural rate of unemployment.

Changes in the natural unemployment rate over time are hard to measure. The reason is, again, that we do not observe the natural rate, only the actual rate. But broad evolutions can be established by comparing average unemployment rates, say across decades. Using this approach, we just saw how the natural rate of unemployment had increased in Europe since the 1970s, and discussed some reasons why this might be. In the USA, the natural rate has moved much less than that in Europe. Nevertheless, it is also far from constant. From the 1950s to the 1980s, the US unemployment rate fluctuated around a slowly increasing trend: average unemployment was 4.5% in the 1950s, and it was 7.3% in the 1980s. Since 1990, the trend appears to have been reversed, with an average unemployment rate of 5.7% in the 1990s and (so far) an average unemployment rate of 5.1% in the 2000s. This has led a number of economists to conclude that the US natural rate of unemployment has fallen. It is probably close to 5% today.

High inflation and the Phillips curve relation

Recall how, in the 1970s, the US Phillips curve changed as inflation became more persistent and wage setters changed the way they formed inflation expectations. The lesson is a general one: the relation between unemployment and inflation is likely to change with the level and the persistence of inflation. Evidence from countries with high inflation confirms

FOCUS
The Phillips curve and long-term unemployment

In this chapter we have studied the relation between inflation and unemployment regardless of the duration of unemployment. We made the assumption that the long-term unemployed and the newly unemployed have the same impact on wage and price formation. However, longer unemployment spells can be related to lower probabilities of transition out of unemployment and into employment. Therefore, the long-term unemployed might be less relevant to wage and price formation than the newly unemployed.

How important is the duration of unemployment for the short-run trade-off between inflation and unemployment implied by the Phillips curve? This is a relevant question, given that the inverse short-run relationship between prices and unemployment is widely used by policy-making institutions to assess the desired monetary policy. Yet, in the presence of long-term unemployment, the aggregate rate of unemployment may provide a distorted measure of the true pressures exerted on prices and wages. To take into account the duration of unemployment, one has to include different unemployment lengths in the Phillips curve. This can be done by constructing an index of unemployment that assigns different weights to the unemployed based on the length of their unemployment spell.

By doing this, one can show that unemployment duration does matter in the determination of prices and that a smaller weight ought to be given to the long-term unemployed. Moreover, the impact of the long-term unemployed is not found to be uniform across countries. In some countries, in particular some Western European countries, the long-term unemployed have a negligible effect on prices. This variation across countries can be explained by some of the institutions that characterise labour markets in the OECD, such as employment protection and unionisation levels.

Insofar as the monetary authority employs Phillips curve models and the corresponding NAIRUs derived to asses inflationary pressures and to forecast inflation, the policy maker should look at a breakdown of unemployment in terms of duration to get more accurate information concerning inflationary developments.

Source: *The Phillips curve and long-term unemployment* by Ricardo Llaudes, European Central Bank Working Paper Series No. 441, February 2005.

this lesson. Not only does the way workers and firms form their expectations change, but so do institutional arrangements.

When the inflation rate becomes high, inflation also tends to become more variable. As a result, workers and firms become more reluctant to enter into labour contracts that set nominal wages for a long period of time: if inflation turns out to be higher than expected, real wages may plunge, and workers will suffer a large cut in their living standard. If inflation turns out to be lower than expected, real wages may go up sharply. Firms may not be able to pay their workers. Some may go bankrupt.

For this reason, the terms of wage agreements change with the level of inflation. Nominal wages are set for shorter periods of time, down from a year to a month or even less. **Wage indexation**, a provision that automatically increases wages in line with inflation, becomes more prevalent.

These changes lead in turn to a stronger response of inflation to unemployment. To see this, an example based on wage indexation will help. Imagine an economy that has two types of labour contracts. A proportion, λ (the Greek lowercase letter lambda), of labour contracts is indexed: nominal wages in those contracts move one for one with variations in the actual price level. A proportion, $1 - \lambda$, of labour contracts is not indexed: nominal wages are set on the basis of expected inflation.

Under this assumption, equation (9.9) becomes

$$\pi_t = [\lambda \pi_t + (1 - \lambda) \pi_t^e] - \alpha(u_t - u_n)$$

◄ More concretely: when inflation runs, on average, at 3% per year, wage setters can be confident that inflation will be between 1% and 5%. When inflation runs, on average, at 30% per year, wage setters can be confident inflation will be between 20% and 40%. In the first case, the real wage may end up 2% higher or lower than expected when the wage setters set the nominal wage. In the second case, it may end up 10% higher or lower than expected. There is much more uncertainty in the second case.

The term in brackets on the right reflects the fact that a proportion, λ, of contracts is indexed and thus responds to actual inflation, π_t, and a proportion, $1 - \lambda$, responds to expected inflation, π_t^e. If we assume that this year's expected inflation is equal to last year's actual inflation, $\pi_t^e = \pi_{t-1}$, we get

$$\pi_t = [\lambda\pi_t + (1 - \lambda)\pi_{t-1}] - \alpha(u_t - u_n) \qquad [9.11]$$

When $\lambda = 0$, all wages are set on the basis of expected inflation – which is equal to last year's inflation, π_{t-1} – and the equation reduces to equation (9.10):

$$\pi_t - \pi_{t-1} = -\alpha(u_t - u_n)$$

When λ is positive, however, a proportion, λ, of wages is set on the basis of actual inflation rather than expected inflation. To see what this implies, reorganise equation (9.11): move the term in brackets to the left, factor $(1 - \lambda)$ on the left of the equation and divide both sides by $(1 - \lambda)$, to get

$$\pi_t - \pi_{t-1} = -\frac{\alpha}{1 - \lambda}(u_t - u_n)$$

Wage indexation increases the effect of unemployment on inflation. The higher the proportion of wage contracts that are indexed – the higher λ – the larger the effect the unemployment rate has on the change in inflation – the higher the coefficient $\alpha/(1 - \lambda)$.

The intuition is as follows: without wage indexation, lower unemployment increases wages, which in turn increases prices. But because wages do not respond to prices right away, there is no further increase in prices within the year. With wage indexation, however, an increase in prices leads to a further increase in wages within the year, which leads to a further increase in prices, and so on, so that the effect of unemployment on inflation within the year is higher.

If, and when, λ gets close to 1 – which is when most labour contracts allow for wage indexation – small changes in unemployment can lead to very large changes in inflation. Put another way, there can be large changes in inflation with nearly no change in unemployment. This is what happens in countries where inflation is very high: the relation between inflation and unemployment becomes more and more tenuous and eventually disappears altogether.

High inflation is the topic of Chapter 22. ➤

Deflation and the Phillips curve relation

We have just looked at what happens to the Phillips curve when inflation is very high. Another issue is what happens when inflation is low, and possibly negative – when there is deflation.

The motivation for asking the question is given by an aspect of Figure 9.1 we mentioned at the start of the chapter but then left aside. In that figure, note how the points corresponding to the 1930s (they are denoted by triangles) lie to the right of the others. Not only is unemployment unusually high – this is no surprise because we are looking at the years corresponding to the Great Depression – but, *given the high unemployment rate*, the inflation rate is surprisingly high. In other words, given the very high unemployment rate, we would have expected not merely deflation but a large rate of deflation. In fact, deflation was limited, and from 1934–1937, inflation was actually positive.

How do we interpret this fact? There are two potential explanations.

One explanation is that the Great Depression was associated with an increase not only in the actual unemployment rate but also in the natural unemployment rate. This seems unlikely. Most economic historians see the Depression primarily as the result of a large adverse shift in aggregate demand leading to an increase in the actual unemployment rate over the natural rate of unemployment rather than an increase in the natural rate of unemployment itself.

The other explanation is that, when the economy starts experiencing deflation, the Phillips curve relation breaks down. One possible reason is the reluctance of workers to accept decreases in their nominal wages. Workers will unwittingly accept a cut in their real wages that occurs when their nominal wages increase more slowly than inflation. However, they are likely to fight the same cut in their real wages if it results from an overt cut in their nominal wages. If this argument is correct, this implies that the Phillips curve relation between the change in inflation and unemployment may disappear or at least become weaker when the economy is close to zero inflation.

This issue is a crucial one at this stage because, in many countries, inflation is now very low. Inflation has actually been negative in Japan since the late 1990s. What happens to the Phillips curve relation in this environment of low inflation or even deflation is one of the developments closely watched by macroeconomists today.

◀ Consider two scenarios. In one, inflation is 4%, and your nominal wage goes up by 2%. In the other, inflation is 0%, and your nominal wage is cut by 2%. Which do you dislike most? You should be indifferent between the two: in both cases, your real wage goes down by 2%. There is some evidence, however, that most people find the first scenario less painful. More on this in Chapter 24.

SUMMARY

- The aggregate supply relation can be expressed as a relation between inflation, expected inflation and unemployment. Given unemployment, higher expected inflation leads to higher inflation. Given expected inflation, higher unemployment leads to lower inflation.

- When inflation is not very persistent, expected inflation does not depend very much on past inflation. Thus, the aggregate supply relation becomes a relation between inflation and unemployment. This is what Phillips in the UK and Solow and Samuelson in the USA discovered when they looked, in the late 1950s, at the joint behaviour of unemployment and inflation.

- As inflation became more persistent in the 1970s and 1980s, expectations of inflation became based more and more on past inflation. In the USA today, the aggregate supply relation takes the form of a relation between unemployment and the change in inflation. High unemployment leads to decreasing inflation; low unemployment leads to increasing inflation.

- The natural unemployment rate is the unemployment rate at which the inflation rate remains constant. When the actual unemployment rate exceeds the natural rate of unemployment, the inflation rate decreases; when the

actual unemployment rate is less than the natural unemployment rate, the inflation rate increases.

- The natural rate of unemployment depends on many factors that differ across countries and can change over time. This is why the natural rate of unemployment varies across countries: it is much higher in Europe than in the USA. This is also why the natural unemployment rate varies over time: in Europe, the natural unemployment rate has increased a lot since the 1960s. In the USA, the natural unemployment rate increased by 1–2% from the 1960s to the 1980s, and appears to have decreased since then.

- Changes in the way the inflation rate varies over time affect the way wage setters form expectations and also how much they use wage indexation. When wage indexation is widespread, small changes in unemployment can lead to very large changes in inflation. At high rates of inflation, the relation between inflation and unemployment disappears altogether.

- At very low or negative rates of inflation, the Phillips curve relation appears to become weaker. During the Great Depression, even very high unemployment led only to limited deflation. The issue is important because many countries have low inflation today.

KEY TERMS

Phillips curve 187

wage–price spiral 190

modified, or expectations-augmented, or accelerationist Phillips curve 193

non-accelerating inflation rate of unemployment (NAIRU) 195

wage indexation 199

QUESTIONS AND PROBLEMS

QUICK CHECK

1. *Using the information in this chapter, label each of the following statements true, false or uncertain. Explain briefly.*

a. The original Phillips curve is the negative relation between unemployment and inflation first observed in the UK.

b. The original Phillips curve relation has proven to be very stable across countries and over time.

c. The aggregate supply relation is consistent with the Phillips curve as observed before the 1970s, but not since.

d. Policy makers can exploit the inflation–unemployment trade-off only temporarily.

e. In the late 1960s, the economists Milton Friedman and Edmund Phelps said that policy makers could achieve as low a rate of unemployment as they wanted.

f. The expectations-augmented Phillips curve is consistent with workers and firms adapting their expectations after the macroeconomic experience of the 1960s.

2. *Discuss the following statements.*

a. The Phillips curve implies that when unemployment is high, inflation is low, and vice versa. Therefore, we may experience either high inflation or high unemployment, but we will never experience both together.

b. As long as we do not mind having high inflation, we can achieve as low a level of unemployment as we want. All we have to do is increase the demand for goods and services by using, for example, expansionary fiscal policy.

3. Mutations of the Phillips curve

Suppose that the Phillips curve is given by

$$\pi_t = \pi_t^e + 0.1 - 2u_t$$

a. What is the natural rate of unemployment?

Assume,

$$\pi_t^e = \theta\pi_{t-1}$$

and suppose that θ is initially equal to 0. Suppose that the rate of unemployment is initially equal to the natural rate. In year t, the authorities decide to bring the unemployment rate down to 3% and hold it there forever.

b. Determine the rate of inflation in years t, $t + 1$, $t + 2$ and $t + 5$.

c. Do you believe the answer given in (b)? Why or why not? (*Hint*: think about how people are likely to form expectations of inflation.)

Now suppose that in year $t + 5$, θ increases from 0 to 1. Suppose that the government is still determined to keep u at 3% forever.

d. Why might θ increase in this way?

e. What will the inflation rate be in years $t + 5$, $t + 6$ and $t + 7$?

f. Do you believe the answer given in (e)? Why or why not?

4. Oil shocks, inflation and unemployment

Suppose that the Phillips curve is given by

$$\pi_t - \pi_t^e = 0.08 + 0.1\mu_t - 2u_t$$

where μ is the mark-up of prices over wages. Suppose that μ is initially equal to 20%, but that as a result of a sharp increase in oil prices, μ increases to 40% in year t and after.

a. Why would an increase in oil prices result in an increase in μ?

b. What is the effect of the increase in μ on the natural rate of unemployment? Explain in words.

DIG DEEPER

5. The macroeconomic effects of the indexation of wages

Suppose that the Phillips curve is given by

$$\pi_t - \pi_t^e = 0.1 - 2u_t$$

where

$$\pi_t^e = \pi_{t-1}$$

Suppose that inflation in year $t - 1$ is zero. In year t, the authorities decide to keep the unemployment rate at 4% forever.

a. Compute the rate of inflation for years t, $t + 1$, $t + 2$ and $t + 3$.

Now suppose that half the workers have indexed labour contracts.

b. What is the new equation for the Phillips curve?

c. Re-compute your answer to part (a).

d. What is the effect of wage indexation on the relation between π and u?

6. The price of oil declined substantially in the 1990s

a. Can the fall in the price of oil help explain the evidence (presented in this chapter) on inflation and unemployment in the 1990s?

b. What was the likely effect of the fall in the price of oil on the natural rate of unemployment?

7. Supply shocks and wage flexibility

Suppose that the Phillips curve is given by

$$\pi_t - \pi_{t-1} = -\alpha(u_t - u_n)$$

where

$$u_n = (\mu + z)/\alpha$$

Recall that this Phillips curve was derived in this chapter under the assumption that the wage bargaining equation took the form

$$W = P^e(1 - \alpha u_t + z)$$

We can think of α as a measure of wage flexibility – the higher is α, the greater is the response of the wage to a change in the unemployment rate, αu_t.

a. Suppose $\mu = 0.03$ and $z = 0.03$. What is the natural rate of unemployment if $\alpha = 1$? if $\alpha = 2$? What is the relation between α and the natural rate of unemployment? Interpret your answer.

In Chapter 9, the text suggested that a reduction in the bargaining power of workers may have something to do with the economy's relatively mild response to the increases in oil prices in the past few years as compared to the economy's response to increases in oil prices in the 1970s. One manifestation of a reduction in worker bargaining power could be an overall increase in wage flexibility, i.e., an increase in π.

b. Suppose that as a result of an oil price increase, μ increases to 0.06. What is the new natural rate of unemployment if $\alpha = 1$? if $\alpha = 2$? Would an increase in wage flexibility tend to weaken the adverse effect of an oil price increase?

EXPLORE FURTHER

8. Estimating the natural rate of unemployment

*To answer this question, you will need data on the annual unemployment and inflation rates since 1970, which can be obtained from the website of the Organization for Economic Cooperation and Development (OECD) (**www.oecd.org**).*

Retrieve the data for the unemployment rate. In addition, retrieve the data for the consumer price index (CPI), all urban consumers.

a. Define the inflation rate in year t as the percentage change in the CPI between year $t - 1$ and year t. Compute the inflation rate for each year and the change in the inflation rate from one year to the next.

b. Plot the data for all the years since 1970 on a diagram, with the change in inflation on the vertical axis and the rate of unemployment on the horizontal axis. Is your graph similar to Figure 9.5?

c. Using a ruler, draw the line that appears to fit best the points in the figure. Approximately what is the slope of the line? What is the intercept? Write down the corresponding equation.

d. According to your analysis in (b), what has been the natural rate of unemployment since 1970?

9. Changes in the natural rate of unemployment

a. Repeat problem 8, but now draw separate graphs for the period 1970 to 1990 and the period since 1990.

b. Do you find that the relation between inflation and unemployment is different in the two periods? If so, how has the natural rate of unemployment changed?

---

*We invite you to visit the Blanchard page on the Prentice Hall website, at **www.prenhall.com/blanchard** for this chapter's World Wide Web exercises.*

FURTHER READING

For more, read Olivier Blanchard, 'European unemployment. The evolution of facts and ideas', *Economic Policy*, Volume 1, 2006, 1–54.

APPENDIX

From the aggregate supply relation to a relation between inflation, expected inflation and unemployment

We show here how to go from the relation between the price level, the expected price level and the unemployment rate given by equation (9.1)

$$P = P^e(1 + \mu)(1 - \alpha u + z)$$

to the relation between inflation, expected inflation and the unemployment rate given by equation (9.2)

$$\pi = \pi^e + (\mu + z) - \alpha u$$

First, introduce time subscripts for the price level, the expected price level and the unemployment rate, so P_t, P_t^e and u_t refer to the price level, the expected price level and the unemployment rate in year t, retrospectively. Equation (9.1) becomes

$$P_t = P_t^e(1 + \mu)(1 - \alpha u_t + z)$$

Next, go from an expression in terms of price levels to an expression in terms of inflation rates. Divide both sides by last year's price level, P_{t-1}^e:

$$\frac{P_t}{P_{t-1}} = \frac{P_t^e}{P_{t-1}}(1 + \mu)(1 - \alpha u_t + z) \qquad [9A.1]$$

Take the fraction P_t/P_{t-1} on the left side and rewrite it as

$$\frac{P_t}{P_{t-1}} = \frac{P_t - P_{t-1} + P_{t-1}}{P_{t-1}} = 1 + \frac{P_t - P_{t-1}}{P_{t-1}} = 1 + \pi_t$$

where the first equality follows from adding and subtracting P_{t-1} in the numerator of the fraction, the second equality follows from the fact that $P_{t-1}/P_{t-1} = 1$ and the third follows from the definition of the inflation rate $[\pi_t = (P_t - P_{t-1})/P_{t-1}]$.

Do the same for the fraction P_t^e/P_{t-1} on the right side, using the definition of the expected inflation rate $(\pi_t^e \equiv (P_t^e - P_{t-1})/P_{t-1})$:

$$\frac{P_t^e}{P_{t-1}} = \frac{P_t^e - P_{t-1} + P_{t-1}}{P_{t-1}} = 1 + \frac{P_t^e - P_{t-1}}{P_{t-1}} = 1 + \pi_t^e$$

Replacing P_t/P_{t-1} and P_t^e/P_{t-1} in equation (9A.1) with the expressions we have just derived:

$$(1 + \pi_t) = (1 + \pi_t^e)(1 + \mu)(1 - \alpha u_t + z)$$

This gives us a relation between inflation, π_t, expected inflation, π_t^e, and the unemployment rate (u_t). The remaining steps make the relation look more friendly: divide both sides by $(1 + \pi_t^e)(1 + \mu)$:

$$\frac{(1 + \pi_t)}{(1 + \pi_t^e)(1 + \mu)} = 1 - \alpha u_t + z$$

As long as inflation, expected inflation and the mark-up are not too large, a good approximation to the left side of this equation is given by $1 + \pi_t - \pi_t^e - \mu$ (see Propositions 3 and 6 in Appendix 1 at the end of the book). Replacing in the equation above and rearranging gives

$$\pi_t = \pi_t^e + (\mu + z) - \alpha u_t$$

Dropping the time indexes, this is equation (9.2) in the text. With the time indexes kept, this is equation (9.3) in the text.

The inflation rate, π_t, depends on the expected inflation rate, π_t^e, and the unemployment rate, u_t. The relation also depends on the mark-up, μ, on the factors that affect wage setting, z, and on the effect of the unemployment rate on wages, α.

Chapter 10

INFLATION, ACTIVITY AND NOMINAL MONEY GROWTH

At the end of the 1970s, inflation reached very high levels in most industrialised countries: 14% per year in the USA and over 13% in the UK. In 1979, the Fed in the USA and the first government led by Margaret Thatcher in the UK decided to reduce inflation and, to do so, embarked on a major monetary contraction. Five years later, and after a deep recession, inflation was down to 3% per year in the USA and below 6% in the UK.

Why did the government decide to reduce inflation in both countries? How did it do it? Why was there a recession? More generally, what are the effects of nominal money growth on inflation and output? Our treatment of expectations in Chapter 8 was too simple to allow us to take up these questions. But, with our discussion of expectations and the introduction of the Phillips curve relation in Chapter 9, we now have the tools we need to answer them. This is what we do in this chapter:

● Section 10.1 extends the model of Chapter 9 and looks at the three relations between output, unemployment and inflation: Okun's law, the Phillips curve and the aggregate demand relation.

● Section 10.2 looks at the effects of money growth on output, unemployment and inflation, in both the short and the medium run.

● Section 10.3 revisits disinflation, looking at the trade-off between unemployment and inflation and looking at how credibility of the central bank affects the adjustment of the economy to a decrease in nominal money growth.

10.1 OUTPUT, UNEMPLOYMENT AND INFLATION

In Chapter 9, we examined the behaviour of two variables: output and the price level. We characterised the economy by two relations: an aggregate supply relation and an aggregate demand relation. In this chapter, we extend the model of Chapter 9 to examine three variables: output, unemployment and inflation. We characterise the economy by three relations:

- A relation between *output growth* and the *change in unemployment*, called Okun's law.
- A relation between *unemployment*, *inflation* and *expected inflation*. This is the Phillips curve relation we developed in Chapter 8.
- An aggregate demand relation between *output growth*, *money growth* and *inflation*. This relation follows from the aggregate demand relation we derived in Chapter 9.

In this section, we look at each of these relations on its own. In Section 10.2, we put them together and show their implications for movements in output, unemployment and inflation.

Okun's law

We discussed the relation between output and unemployment in Chapter 7. We did so, however, under two convenient but restrictive assumptions. We assumed that output moved one-for-one with employment, so changes in output led to equal changes in employment. We also assumed that the labour force was constant, so changes in employment were reflected one-for-one in opposite changes in unemployment.

> We assumed that $Y = N$ and that L (the labour force) was constant.

We must now move beyond these assumptions. To see why, let's see what they imply for the relation between the rate of output growth and the unemployment rate. If output and employment moved together, a 1% increase in output would lead to a 1% increase in employment. And if movements in employment were reflected in opposite movements in unemployment, the 1% increase in employment would lead to a decrease of 1% in the unemployment rate. Let u_t denote the unemployment rate in year t, u_{t-1} the unemployment rate in year $t - 1$, and g_{yt} the growth rate of output from year $t - 1$ to year t. Then, under these two assumptions, the following relation would hold:

$$u_t - u_{t-1} = -g_{yt} \qquad [10.1]$$

In words: the change in the unemployment rate would be equal to the negative of the growth rate of output. If output growth is, say, 4% for a year, then the unemployment rate should decline by 4% in that year.

> The relation is named after Arthur Okun, an economist and an adviser to President Kennedy, who first characterised and interpreted this relation.

Contrast this with the actual relation between output growth and the change in the unemployment rate, a relation called **Okun's law**. Figure 10.1 plots the change in the unemployment rate against the rate of output growth in the USA for each year since 1970. It also plots the regression line that best fits the scatter of points. The equation corresponding to the line is given by

$$u_t - u_{t-1} = -0.4(g_{yt} - 3\%) \qquad [10.2]$$

Like equation (10.1), equation (10.2) shows a negative relation between the change in unemployment and output growth. But it differs from equation (10.1) in two ways:

> If $g_{yt} > 3\%$ then $u_t < u_{t-1}$
> If $g_{yt} < 3\%$ then $u_t > u_{t-1}$
> If $g_{yt} = 3\%$ then $u_t = u_{t-1}$

- Annual output growth has to be at least 3% to prevent the unemployment rate from rising. This is because of two factors we have neglected so far: labour force growth and labour productivity growth.

  To maintain a constant unemployment rate, employment must grow at the same rate as the labour force. Suppose the labour force grows at 1.7% per year; then employment must grow at 1.7% per year. If, in addition, labour productivity – output per worker – grows at 1.3% per year, this implies that output must grow at $1.7\% + 1.3\% = 3\%$ per year.

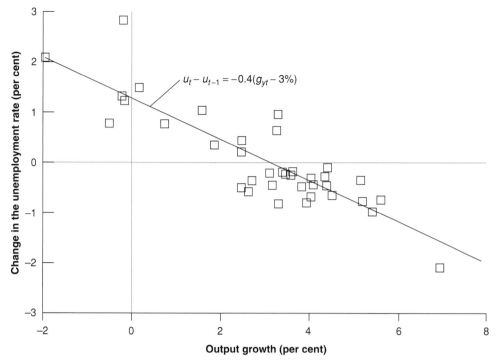

Figure 10.1

Changes in the unemployment rate versus output growth in the USA since 1970

High output growth is associated with a reduction in the unemployment rate; low output growth is associated with an increase in the unemployment rate.

In other words, just to maintain a constant unemployment rate, output growth must be equal to the sum of labour force growth and labour productivity growth.

In the USA, the sum of the rate of labour force growth and of labour productivity growth has been roughly equal to 3% per year on average since 1960, and this is why the number 3% appears on the right side of equation (10.2). We shall call the rate of output growth needed to maintain a constant unemployment rate the **normal growth rate** in the following text.

◄ Suppose productivity growth increases from 1.3% to 2.3%. What is now the growth rate of output required to maintain a constant unemployment rate?

- The coefficient on the right side of equation (10.2) is −0.4, compared to −1.0 in equation (10.1). Put another way, output growth 1% above normal leads only to a 0.4% reduction in the unemployment rate in equation (10.2) rather than a 1% reduction in equation (10.1). There are two reasons:

  1. Firms adjust employment less than one-for-one in response to deviations of output growth from normal. More specifically, output growth 1% above normal for one year leads to only a 0.6% increase in the employment rate.

     ◄ Employment responds less than one-for-one to movements in output.

     One reason is that some workers are needed, no matter what the level of output. The accounting department of a firm, for example, needs roughly the same number of employees whether the firm is selling more or less than normal.

     Another reason is that training new employees is costly; for this reason, firms prefer to keep current employees rather than lay them off when output is lower than normal and to ask them to work overtime rather than hire new employees when output is higher than normal. In bad times, firms in effect hoard labour – the labour they will need when times are better; this behaviour of firms is therefore called **labour hoarding**.

  2. An increase in the employment rate does not lead to a one-for-one decrease in the unemployment rate. More specifically, a 0.6% increase in the employment rate leads to only a 0.4% decrease in the unemployment rate. The reason is that labour force participation increases. When employment increases, not all the new jobs are filled by the unemployed. Some of the jobs go to people who were classified as *out of the labour force*, meaning they were not actively looking for jobs. Also, as labour market prospects improve for the unemployed, some discouraged workers – who were previously classified as out of the labour force – decide to start actively looking for jobs and become classified as unemployed. For both reasons, unemployment decreases less than employment increases.

     ◄ Employment responds less than one-for-one to movements in output. Putting the two steps together: unemployment responds less than one-for-one to movements in employment, which itself responds less than one-for-one to movements in output.

Let's write equation (10.2) using letters rather than numbers. Let $\bar{g}_y$ denote the normal growth rate (about 3% per year for the USA). Let the coefficient β (the Greek lowercase beta) measure the effect of output growth above normal on the change in the unemployment rate. As you saw in equation (10.2), in the USA, β equals 0.4. We will give the evidence for European countries in the next section. We can then write:

$$u_t - u_{t-1} = -\beta(g_{yt} - \bar{g}_y) \qquad [10.3]$$

Okun's law:
$g_{yt} > \bar{g}_y \Rightarrow u_t < u_{t-1}$
$g_{yt} < \bar{g}_y \Rightarrow u_t > u_{t-1}$

➤ Output growth above normal leads to a decrease in the unemployment rate; output growth below normal leads to an increase in the unemployment rate.

The operation of Okun's law in several different countries is described in the Focus box 'Okun's law across European and non-European countries'.

The Phillips curve

We saw in Chapter 10 that the aggregate supply relation can be expressed as a relation between inflation, expected inflation and unemployment [equation (9.10)], the *Phillips curve*:

$$\pi_t = \pi_t^e - \alpha(u_t - u_n) \qquad [10.4]$$

Inflation depends on expected inflation and on the deviation of unemployment from the natural rate of unemployment.

We then argued that in the USA today, expected inflation is well approximated by last year's inflation. This means we can replace π_t^e with π_{t-1}. With this assumption, the relation between inflation and unemployment takes the form

$$\pi_t - \pi_{t-1} = -\alpha(u_t - u_n) \qquad [10.5]$$

Unemployment below the natural rate leads to an increase in inflation; unemployment above the natural rate leads to a decrease in inflation. The parameter α gives the effect of unemployment on the change in inflation. We saw in Chapter 9 that, since 1970 in the USA, the natural unemployment rate has been on average equal to 6%, and α has been equal to 0.73. This value of α means that an unemployment rate of 1% above the natural rate for one year leads to a decrease in the inflation rate of about 0.73%.

Phillips curve
$u_t < u_n \Rightarrow \pi_t > \pi_{t-1}$
$u_t > u_n \Rightarrow \pi_t < \pi_{t-1}$

The aggregate demand relation

The third relation we will need is a relation between output growth, money growth, and inflation. We will now see that it follows from the aggregate demand relation we derived in Chapter 8.

In Chapter 8, we derived the aggregate demand relation as a relation between the level of output and the real money stock, government spending and taxes [equation (8.3)], based on equilibrium in both goods and financial markets:

$$Y_t = Y\left(\frac{M_t}{P_t}, G_t, T_t\right)$$

Note that have added time indexes, which we did not need in Chapter 8 but will need in this chapter. To simplify things, we will make two further assumptions here.

First, to focus on the relation between the real money stock and output, we will ignore changes in factors other than real money here and write the aggregate demand relation simply as

$$Y_t = Y\left(\frac{M_t}{P_t}\right)$$

Second, we shall assume a linear relation between real money balances and output and rewrite the aggregate demand relation further as

$$Y_t = \gamma\left(\frac{M_t}{P_t}\right) \qquad [10.6]$$

where γ (the Greek lowercase gamma) is a positive parameter. This equation states that the demand for goods, and thus output, is proportional to the real money stock. You should keep in mind, however, that behind this simple relation hides the mechanism you saw in the *IS–LM* model:

- An increase in the real money stock leads to a decrease in the interest rate.
- The decrease in the interest rate leads to an increase in the demand for goods and, therefore, to an increase in output.

Equation (10.6) gives a relation between *levels* – the output level, the level of money, and the price level. We need to go from this relation to a relation between *growth rates* – the growth rate of output, the growth rate of money and the inflation rate (the growth rate of the price level). Fortunately, this is easy:

Let g_{yt} be the growth rate of output. Let π_t be the growth rate of the price level – the rate of inflation – and g_{mt} be the growth rate of nominal money. Then, from equation (10.6), it follows that

$$g_{yt} = g_{mt} - \pi_t \qquad\qquad [10.7]$$

If a variable is the ratio of two variables, its growth rate is equal to the difference between the growth rates of these two variables. (See Proposition 8 in Appendix 1 at the end of the book.) So if

$$Y = \gamma M/P$$

and γ is constant,

$$g_y = g_m - \pi.$$

FOCUS
Okun's law across European and non-European countries

The coefficient β in Okun's law gives the effect on the unemployment rate of deviations of output growth from normal. A value of β of 0.4 tells us that output growth 1% above the normal growth rate for one year decreases the unemployment rate by 0.4%.

The coefficient β depends in part on how firms adjust their employment in response to fluctuations in production. This adjustment of employment depends in turn on such factors as the internal organisation of firms and the legal and social constraints on hiring and firing. As these differ across countries, we would therefore expect the coefficient β to differ across countries, and indeed it does. Table 10.1 gives the estimated coefficient β for a number of countries.

The first column gives estimates of β based on data from 1960–1980. Germany has the highest coefficient

Table 10.1 Okun's law coefficients across countries and time

Country	1960–1980	1981–2007
Germany	0.20	0.29
Denmark	0.18	0.72
UK	0.15	0.48
France	0.14	0.41
Netherlands	0.13	0.50
Sweden	0.09	0.49
Italy	0.08	0.11
Non-European countries:		
USA	0.39	0.41
Australia	0.26	0.47
Japan	0.02	0.11

among European countries, 0.20, followed by Denmark, 0.18. The UK, 0.11, France, 0.14 and the Netherlands, 0.13, have slightly lower coefficients. The lowest coefficients are in Italy, 0.08 and Sweden, 0.09. The table also reports Okun's coefficients for three non-European countries, the USA, with the highest coefficient of all, 0.39, Australia, which also has a rather high coefficient, and Japan, with the lowest coefficient of all, 0.02.

The ranking in the 1960–1980 column fits well with what we know about the behavior of firms and the structure of firing/hiring regulations across countries. Italian firms – somehow like Japanese firms, although to a lesser extent – have traditionally offered a high degree of job security to their workers, so variations in Italy's output have little effect on employment and, by implication, little effect on unemployment. So it is no surprise that β is very small in Italy (and is the smallest in Japan). A high degree of employment protection (see Chapter 7) explains why the coefficients estimated for most European countries are in between those of Japan and the USA.

The last column gives estimates based on data from 1981–2007. The coefficient is nearly unchanged for the USA, but it becomes higher for all the other countries. This again fits with what we know about firms and regulations. Increased competition in goods markets since the early 1980s has led firms in these countries to reconsider and reduce their commitment to job security. And, at the urging of firms, legal restrictions on hiring and firing have been weakened in many countries. Both factors have led to a larger response of employment to fluctuations in output, thus to a larger value of β.

Aggregate demand relation:
$g_{mt} > \pi_t \Rightarrow g_{yt} > 0$
$g_{mt} < \pi_t \Rightarrow g_{yt} < 0$

➤ If nominal money growth exceeds inflation, real money growth is positive, and so is output growth. If nominal money growth is less than inflation, real money growth is negative, and so is output growth. In other words, given inflation, expansionary monetary policy (high nominal money growth) leads to high output growth; contractionary monetary policy (low nominal money growth) leads to low, possibly negative, output growth.

10.2 THE EFFECTS OF MONEY GROWTH

Let's collect the three relations between inflation, unemployment and output growth we have just derived:

- Okun's law relates the change in the unemployment rate to the deviation of output growth from normal [equation (10.3)]:

$$u_t - u_{t-1} = -\beta(g_{gt} - \bar{g}_y)$$

- The Phillips curve – equivalently the aggregate supply relation – relates the change in inflation to the deviation of the unemployment rate from the natural rate [equation (10.5)]:

$$\pi_t - \pi_{t-1} = -\alpha(u_t - u_n)$$

- The aggregate demand relation relates output growth to the difference between nominal money growth and inflation [equation (10.7)]:

$$g_{yt} = g_{mt} - \pi_t$$

These three relations are shown in Figure 10.2. Start on the left and follow the arrows. Through aggregate demand, nominal money growth and inflation determine output growth. Through Okun's law, output growth determines the change in unemployment. And through the Phillips curve relation, unemployment determines the change in inflation.

Our task now is to see what these three relations imply for the effects of nominal money growth on output, unemployment and inflation. The easiest way to proceed is to work backward in time – that is, to start by looking at the medium run (by looking at where the economy ends up when all the dynamics have worked themselves out) and then to turn to the dynamics themselves (that is, to see how the economy gets there).

The medium run

Assume that the central bank maintains a constant growth rate of nominal money, call it $\bar{g}_m$. In this case, what will be the values of output growth, unemployment and inflation in the *medium run*?

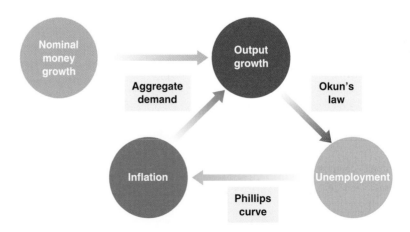

Figure 10.2

Output growth, unemployment, inflation and nominal money growth

- In the medium run, the unemployment rate must be constant: the unemployment rate cannot increase or decrease forever. Putting $u_t = u_{t-1}$ in Okun's law implies that $g_{yt} = \bar{g}_y$. In the medium run, output must grow at its normal rate of growth, $\bar{g}_y$.
- With nominal money growth equal to $\bar{g}_m$ and output growth equal to $\bar{g}_y$, the aggregate demand relation implies that inflation is constant and satisfies

◄ Medium run:

$g_y = \bar{g}_y$

$$\bar{g}_y = \bar{g}_m - \pi$$

Moving π to the left and $\bar{g}_y$ to the right gives an expression for inflation:

$$\pi = \bar{g}_m - \bar{g}_y \qquad [10.8]$$

In the medium run, inflation must be equal to nominal money growth minus normal output growth. If we define **adjusted nominal money growth** as equal to nominal money growth minus normal output growth, equation (10.8) can be stated as: *in the medium run, inflation equals adjusted nominal money growth.*

◄ Medium run:

$\pi = \bar{g}_m - \bar{g}_y$

The way to think about this result is as follows: a growing level of output implies a growing level of transactions and thus a growing demand for real money. So, if output is growing at 3%, the real money stock must also grow at 3% per year. If the nominal money stock grows at a rate different from 3% per year, the difference must show up in inflation (or deflation). For example, if nominal money growth is 8% per year, then inflation must be equal to 5% per year.

- If inflation is constant, then inflation this year is equal to inflation last year: $\pi_t = \pi_{t-1}$. Putting $\pi_t = \pi_{t-1}$ in the Phillips curve implies that $u_t = u_n$. *In the medium run, the unemployment rate must be equal to the natural rate of unemployment.*

◄ Medium run:

$u = u_n$

Let's summarise: in the medium run, output growth is equal to the normal growth rate. Unemployment is equal to the natural rate. And both are independent of nominal money growth. Nominal money growth affects only inflation.

These results are the natural extension of the results we derived in Chapter 8. There, we saw that *changes in the level of nominal money* were neutral in the medium run: they had no effect on either output or unemployment but were reflected one-for-one in changes in the price level. We see here that a similar neutrality result applies to *changes in the growth rate of nominal money*: changes in nominal money growth have no effect on output or unemployment in the medium run but are reflected one-for-one in changes in the rate of inflation.

Another way to state this last result is that the only determinant of inflation in the medium run is nominal money growth. Milton Friedman put it this way: *inflation is always and everywhere a monetary phenomenon.* Unless they lead to higher nominal money growth, factors such as the monopoly power of firms, strong unions, strikes, fiscal deficits, the price of oil and so on have no effect on inflation *in the medium run*.

◄ The word *unless* is important. During episodes of very high inflation (see Chapter 22), fiscal deficits often lead to nominal money creation and to higher nominal money growth.

Nominal and real interest rates in the medium run

What will happen to output and to nominal and real interest rates in the medium run?

To answer that question, we can rely on an important proposition we derived in Chapter 7: in the medium run, output returns to the natural level of output, Y_n.

This has a straightforward implication for what happens to the real interest rate. To see why, return to the *IS* equation:

$$Y = C(Y - T) + I(Y, r) + G$$

One way of thinking about the *IS* relation is that it tells us, for given values of G and T, what real interest rate, r, is needed to sustain a given level of spending and so a given level of output, Y. If, for example, output is equal to the natural level of output, Y_n, then, for given values of G and T, the real interest rate must be such that

$$Y_n = C(Y_n - T) + I(Y_n, r) + G$$

This is what the rate was called by ➤ Wicksell, a Swedish economist, at the turn of the 20th century.

Since we used the word *natural* to denote the level of output in the medium run, let's similarly call this value of the real interest rate the *natural real interest rate* and denote it by r_n. Then, our earlier proposition that, in the medium run, output returns to its natural level, Y_n, has a direct implication for the real interest rate:

In the medium run, the real interest rate returns to the natural interest rate, r_n. It is independent of the rate of money growth.

In this chapter we have learned that the rate of inflation is equal to the rate of money growth minus the rate of growth of output.

In the medium run (if $g_y = 0$), $\pi = g_m$. ➤

If we assume, as we have done here, that output growth, g_y is equal to zero, this proposition takes an even simpler form: in the medium run, the rate of inflation, π, is equal to the rate of nominal money growth, g_m.

This proposition, together with the previous result about the real interest rate, has a straightforward implication for what happens to the nominal interest rate in the medium run. To see why, recall the relation between the nominal interest rate and the real interest rate:

$$i = r + \pi^e$$

We saw that in the medium run, the real interest rate equals the natural interest rate, r_n. Also in the medium run, expected inflation is equal to actual inflation (people cannot have incorrect expectations of inflation forever). It follows that

$$i = r_n + \pi$$

Now, because, in the medium run, inflation is equal to money growth, g_m, we get

$$i = r_n + g_m$$

In the medium run, the nominal interest rate is equal to the natural real interest rate plus the rate of money growth. So an increase in money growth leads to an equal increase in the nominal interest rate.

Let's summarise: in the medium run, money growth does not affect the real interest rate, but it affects both inflation and the nominal interest rate one-for-one.

A permanent increase in nominal money growth of, say, 10%, is eventually reflected in a 10% increase in the inflation rate and a 10% increase in the nominal interest rate – leaving the real interest rate unchanged. This result – that, in the medium run, the nominal interest rate increases one-for-one with inflation – is known as the **Fisher effect**, or the **Fisher hypothesis**, after Irving Fisher, an economist at Yale University who first stated it and its logic at the beginning of the 20th century.

The short run

Let's now turn to dynamics. Suppose that the economy is initially at its medium-run equilibrium: unemployment is equal to the natural rate. Output growth is equal to the normal growth rate. The inflation rate is equal to adjusted nominal money growth.

Suppose that the central bank decides to decrease nominal money growth. We saw earlier that, in the medium run, lower money growth will lead to lower inflation and unchanged output growth and unemployment. The question now is: what will happen in the short run?

Lower g_m ⇒ Lower $g_m - \pi$ ⇒ Lower g_y. ➤

Just by looking at our three relations, we can tell the beginning of the story:

- Look at the aggregate demand relation – Given the initial rate of inflation, lower nominal money growth leads to lower real nominal money growth and thus to a decrease in output growth.

Lower g_y ⇒ Higher u. ➤

- Now, look at Okun's law – Output growth below normal leads to an increase in unemployment.

Higher u ⇒ Lower π. ➤

- Now, look at the Phillips curve relation – Unemployment above the natural rate leads to a decrease in inflation.

Table 10.2 The effects of a monetary tightening

		Year 0	Year 1	Year 2	Year 3
1 Real money growth %	$(g_m - \pi)$	3.0	0.05	5.05	3.0
2 Output growth %	(g_y)	3.0	0.05	5.05	3.0
3 Unemployment rate %	(u)	6.0	7.00	6.00	6.0
4 Inflation rate %	(π)	5.0	4.00	4.00	4.0
5 (Nominal money growth) %	(g_m)	8.0	4.05	9.05	7.0

So we have our first result: tighter monetary policy leads initially to lower output growth and lower inflation. If tight enough, it may lead to negative output growth and thus to a recession. What happens between this initial response and the medium run (when unemployment returns to the natural rate)? The answer depends on the path of monetary policy, and the best way to show what happens is to work out a simple example.

Suppose the economy starts in year 0 in medium-run equilibrium. Assume that normal output growth is 3%, the natural unemployment rate is 6% and nominal money growth is 8%. Inflation is therefore equal to nominal money growth minus output growth, 8% – 3% = 5%. Real money growth is equal to nominal money growth minus inflation, 8% – 5% = 3% .

Suppose that the central bank decides to tighten monetary policy in the following way: it decides to decrease real money growth relative to trend by 2.5% in year 1 and to increase it relative to trend by 2.5% in year 2. (Why 2.5%? To make the arithmetic simple, as will be clear later on.) The path of the relevant macroeconomic variables is given in Table 10.2:

- Row 1 shows the path of real money growth. In year 0 (before the change in policy), real money growth is equal to 3%. Under the assumptions we have just made, the change in monetary policy leads to real money growth of 0.5% (2.5% below normal) in year 1, 5.5% (2.5% above normal) in year 2 and 3% thereafter.

- Row 2 shows the path of output growth. From the aggregate demand relation, real money growth of 0.5% in year 1 leads to output growth of 0.5% (2.5% below normal); real money growth of 5.5% in year 2 leads to output growth of 5.5% (2.5% above normal); thereafter, output growth is equal to the normal growth rate, 3%.

- Row 3 shows the path of the unemployment rate. Okun's law implies that output growth of 2.5% below normal for one year leads to an increase in the unemployment rate of 1 percentage point (2.5% multiplied by 0.4, the coefficient in Okun's law). So, in year 1, the unemployment rate increases from 6% to 7%. In year 2, output growth of 2.5% above normal for one year leads to a decrease in the unemployment rate of 1 percentage point. So, in year 2, the unemployment rate decreases from 7% back to 6%. The unemployment rate remains equal to 6% thereafter.

- Row 4 shows the path of the inflation rate. For this computation, let's assume that α is equal to 1.0 rather than its estimated value of 0.73 that we saw in Chapter 9. This assumption will simplify our computations. From the Phillips curve relation, an unemployment rate of 7%, which is 1% above the natural rate, leads to a decrease in inflation from 5% to 4% in year 1. In year 2 and thereafter, the unemployment rate is equal to the natural rate and, therefore, inflation remains constant at 4%.

- For completeness, row 5 shows the behaviour of nominal money growth consistent with the path of real money growth we assumed in row 1. Nominal money growth is equal to real money growth plus inflation. Adding the numbers for real money growth in row 1 and for inflation in row 4 gives the numbers in row 5. This implies a decrease in the rate of nominal money growth from 8% to 4.5% in year 1, an increase to 9.5% in year 2 and a decrease to 7% thereafter.

In words: in the short run, monetary tightening leads to a slowdown in growth and a temporary increase in unemployment. In the medium run, output growth returns to normal and the unemployment rate returns to the natural rate. Money growth and inflation are both permanently lower.

◄ It would be more natural to describe monetary policy in terms of what happens to nominal money growth. The algebra would get more complicated, however. For our purposes, it is easier to describe it in terms of what happens to real money growth. We can do so without loss of generality: given the inflation rate, the central bank can always choose nominal money growth to achieve the real money growth it wants.

◄ Put less formally: the temporary increase in unemployment buys a permanent decrease in inflation.

From the short run to the medium run

We are now able to explain what happens to nominal and real interest rates from the short run to the medium run. In Chapter 14 you will learn that an increase in monetary growth (a monetary expansion) leads to *a decrease* in nominal interest rates in the short run. In this chapter, we explained that a monetary expansion leads instead to *an increase* in nominal interest rates in the medium run.

What happens, however, between the short run and the medium run? A full characterisation of the movements of the real interest rate and the nominal interest rate over time would take us beyond what we can do here, but the basic features of the adjustment process are easy to describe.

In the short run, the real interest rate and the nominal interest rate both go down. Why don't they stay down forever? Let us first state the answer in short: low interest rates lead to higher demand, which leads to higher output, which eventually leads to higher inflation; higher inflation leads in turn to a decrease in the real money stock and an increase in interest rates.

Now, here is the answer step-by-step:

- As long as the real interest rate is below the natural real interest rate – that is, the value corresponding to the natural level of output – output is higher than the natural level of output, and unemployment is below its natural rate.
- From the Phillips curve relation, we know that, as long as unemployment is below the natural rate of unemployment, inflation increases.
- As inflation increases, it eventually becomes higher than nominal money growth, leading to negative real money growth. When real money growth turns negative, the nominal interest rate starts increasing. And, given expected inflation, so does the real interest rate.
- In the medium run, the real interest rate increases back to its initial value. Output is then back to the natural level of output, unemployment is back to the natural rate of unemployment, and inflation is no longer changing. As the real interest rate converges back to its initial value, the nominal interest rate converges to a new higher value, equal to the real interest rate plus the new, higher, rate of nominal money growth.

Figure 10.3 summarises these results by showing the adjustment over time of the real interest rate and the nominal interest rate to an increase in nominal money growth from,

Negative real money growth ⇔ ➤
Monetary contraction.

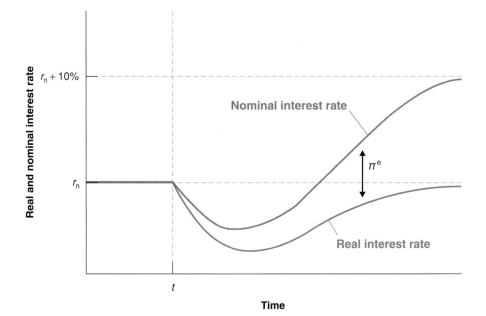

Figure 10.3

The adjustment of the real and the nominal interest rates to an increase in money growth

An increase in money growth leads initially to decreases in both the real and the nominal interest rates. Over time, however, the real interest rate returns to its initial value, and the nominal interest rate converges to a new higher value, equal to the initial value plus the increase in money growth.

FOCUS
Nominal interest rates and inflation across Latin America in the early 1990s

Figure 10.4 plots nominal interest rate–inflation pairs for eight Latin American countries (Argentina, Bolivia, Chile, Ecuador, Mexico, Peru, Uruguay and Venezuela) for 1992 and 1993 – a period of high inflation in Latin America. Because the Brazilian numbers would dwarf those from other countries, they are not included in the figure. (In 1992, Brazil's annual inflation rate was 1008%, and its nominal interest rate was 1560%. In 1993, its inflation was 2140%, and its nominal interest rate was 3240%!) The numbers for inflation refer to the rate of change of the consumer price index. The numbers for nominal interest rates refer to the 'lending rate'. The exact definition of the lending rate varies with each country, but you can think of it as corresponding to the prime interest rate in the USA – the rate charged to borrowers with the best credit rating.

Note the wide range of inflation rates, from 10% to about 100%. This is precisely why we have chosen to present numbers from Latin America in the early 1990s. With this much variation in inflation, we can learn a lot about the relation between nominal interest rates and inflation. And the figure indeed shows a clear relation between inflation and nominal interest rates. The line drawn in the figure plots what the nominal interest rate should be under the Fisher hypothesis, assuming an underlying real interest rate of 5%, so that $i = 5\% + \pi$. The slope of the line is 1: under the Fisher hypothesis, a 1% increase in inflation should be reflected in a 1% increase in the nominal interest rate.

As you can see, the line fits reasonably well, and roughly half of the points are above the line, and the other half are below. The Fisher hypothesis appears roughly consistent with the cross-country evidence from Latin America in the early 1990s.

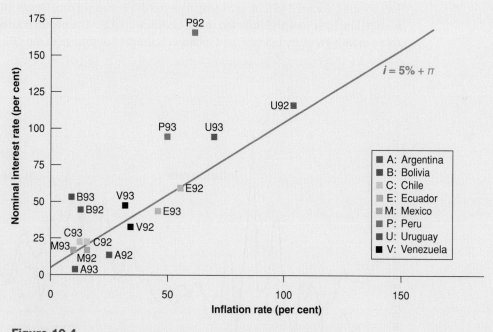

Figure 10.4

Nominal interest rates and inflation in Latin America, 1992–1993

say, 0% to 10%, starting at time t. Before time t, both interest rates are constant and equal to each other. The real interest rate is equal to r_n. The nominal interest rate is also equal to r_n (as inflation and expected inflation are equal to zero).

At time t, the rate of money growth increases from 0% to 10%. The increase in the rate of nominal money growth leads, for some time, to an increase in the real money stock and to a decrease in the nominal interest rate. As expected inflation increases, the decrease in the real interest rate is larger than the decrease of the nominal interest rate.

Eventually, the nominal interest rate and the real interest rate start increasing. In the medium run, the real interest rate returns to its initial value. Inflation and expected inflation converge to the new rate of money growth – in this case, 10%. The result is that the nominal interest rate converges to a value equal to the real interest rate plus 10%.

Evidence for the Fisher hypothesis

There is plenty of evidence that a monetary expansion decreases nominal interest rates in the short run (see, for example, Chapter 5, Section 5.5). But how much evidence is there for the Fisher hypothesis, the proposition that, in the medium run, increases in inflation lead to one-for-one increases in nominal interest rates?

Economists have tried to answer this question by looking at two types of evidence. One is the relation between nominal interest rates and inflation *across countries*. Because the relation holds only in the medium run, we should not expect inflation and nominal interest rates to be close to each other in any one country at any one time, but the relation should hold on average. This approach is explored further in the Focus box 'Nominal interest rates and inflation across Latin America in the early 1990s', which looks at Latin American countries during a period when they had high inflation and finds substantial support for the Fisher hypothesis.

The other type of evidence is the relation between the nominal interest rate and inflation over time in a given country. Again, the Fisher hypothesis does not imply that the two should move together from year to year, but it does suggest that the long swings in inflation should eventually be reflected in similar swings in the nominal interest rate. To see these long swings, we need to look at as long a period of time as we can. Figure 10.5 looks at the nominal interest rate and inflation in the USA since 1927. The nominal interest rate is the three-month Treasury bill rate, and inflation is the rate of change of the CPI.

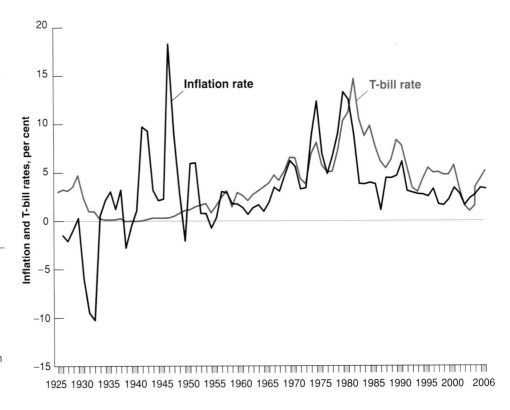

Figure 10.5

The three-month treasury bill rate and inflation since 1927

The increase in inflation from the early 1960s to the early 1980s was associated with an increase in the nominal interest rate. The decrease in inflation since the mid-1980s has been associated with a decrease in the nominal interest rate.

Figure 10.5 has at least three interesting features:

- The steady increase in inflation from the early 1960s to the early 1980s was associated with a roughly parallel increase in the nominal interest rate. The decrease in inflation since the mid-1980s has been associated with a decrease in the nominal interest rate. This evidence supports the Fisher hypothesis.
- Evidence of the short-run effects that we discussed earlier is also easy to see. The nominal interest rate lagged behind the increase in inflation in the 1970s, while the disinflation of the early 1980s was associated with an initial *increase* in the nominal interest rate, followed by a much slower decline in the nominal interest rate than in inflation.
- The other episode of inflation, during and after the Second World War, underscores the importance of the 'medium run' qualifier in the Fisher hypothesis. During that period, inflation was high but short-lived. And it was gone before it had time to be reflected in a higher nominal interest rate. The nominal interest rate remained very low throughout the 1940s.

> ◀ This was the result of a deliberate policy by the Fed to maintain a very low nominal interest rate, to reduce interest payments on the large government debt created during the Second World War.

More careful studies confirm our basic conclusion. The Fisher hypothesis that, in the medium run, increases in inflation are reflected in a higher nominal interest rate, appears to fit the data quite well, but the adjustment takes a long time. The data confirm the conclusion reached by Milton Friedman, which we quoted in the Focus box 'Theory ahead of facts' in Chapter 9, that it typically takes a 'couple of decades' for nominal interest rates to reflect the higher inflation rate.

10.3 DISINFLATION

To better understand the mechanics and the implications of our model, let's imagine a situation in which the economy is in medium-run equilibrium: unemployment is at the natural rate of unemployment; output growth is equal to the normal growth rate. The inflation rate is equal to adjusted nominal money growth. The rate of nominal money growth and, by implication, the inflation rate, are high, however, and there is a consensus among policy makers that inflation must be reduced.

> ◀ At this point, you might ask: what is so bad about high inflation if growth is proceeding at a normal rate and unemployment is at the natural rate of unemployment? To answer, we need to discuss the costs of inflation. We shall do so in Chapter 22.

We know from the previous section that lower inflation requires lower money growth. We also know that lower money growth implies an increase in unemployment for some time. For the central bank, the question now is: having decided to act, at what pace should it proceed?

A first pass

A first pass at the answer can be given by using the Phillips curve relation [equation (10.5)]:

$$\pi_t - \pi_{t-1} = -\alpha(u_t - u_n)$$

The relation makes it clear that **disinflation** – the decrease in inflation – can only be obtained at the cost of higher unemployment: for the left side of the equation to be negative – that is, for inflation to decrease – the term $(u_t - u_n)$ must be positive. In other words, the unemployment rate must exceed the natural rate.

> Make sure to distinguish between:
> - Deflation: decrease in the price level (equivalently, negative inflation).
> - Disinflation: decrease in the inflation rate.

The equation, however, has a stronger and more striking implication: the total amount of unemployment required for a given decrease in inflation does not depend on the speed at which disinflation is achieved. In other words, disinflation can be achieved quickly, at the cost of high unemployment for a few years. Or, alternatively, it can be achieved more slowly, with a smaller increase in unemployment spread over many years. In both cases, the total amount of unemployment, summed over the years, will be the same.

Let's see why. First, define a **point-year of excess unemployment** as the difference between the actual and the natural unemployment rates of 1 percentage point for one year. While the expression may sound a bit strange, the concept is simple: for example, if the natural rate of unemployment is 6%, an unemployment rate of 8% four years in a row corresponds to 4 times $(8 - 6) = 8$ point-years of excess unemployment.

> When should you use *percentage point* rather than *per cent*? Suppose you are told that the unemployment rate, which was equal to 10%, has increased by 5%. Is it 5% of itself, in which case the unemployment rate is (1.05) × 10% = 10.5%? Or is it 5 percentage points, in which case it is 10% + 5% = 15%?
>
> ◀ The use of *percentage point* rather than *per cent* helps avoid the ambiguity. If you are told the unemployment rate has increased by 5 percentage points, this means that the unemployment rate is 10% + 5% = 15%.

Now look at a central bank that wants to reduce inflation by x percentage points. To make things simpler, let's use specific numbers: assume that the central bank wants to reduce inflation from 14% to 4%, so that x is equal to 10. Let's also make the convenient, if not quite correct, assumption that α equals 1; again, this will simplify computations:

- Suppose the central bank wants to achieve the reduction in inflation in one year. Equation (10.5) tells us that what is required is one year of unemployment at 10% above the natural rate. In this case, the right side of the equation is equal to −10%, and the inflation rate decreases by 10% within a year.
- Suppose the central bank wants to achieve the reduction in inflation over two years. Equation (10.5) tells us that what is required is two years of unemployment at 5% above the natural rate. During each of the two years, the right side of the equation is equal to −5%, so the inflation rate decreases by 5% each year, thus by $2 \times 5\% = 10\%$ over two years.
- By the same reasoning, reducing inflation over five years requires five years of unemployment at 2% above the natural rate ($5 \times 2\% = 10$); reducing inflation over ten years requires ten years of unemployment at 1% above the natural rate ($10 \times 1\% = 10\%$); and so on.

Note that in each case the number of point-years of excess unemployment required to decrease inflation is the same, namely ten: one year times 10% excess unemployment in the first scenario, two years times 5% in the second, ten years times 1% in the last. The implication is straightforward: the central bank can choose the distribution of excess unemployment over time, but it cannot change the total number of point-years of excess unemployment.

We can state this conclusion another way: define the **sacrifice ratio** as the number of point-years of excess unemployment needed to achieve a decrease in inflation of 1%:

$$\text{sacrifice ratio} = \frac{\text{point-years of excess unemployment}}{\text{decrease in inflation}}$$

From equation (10.5), excess unemployment of 1% for one year decreases the inflation rate by α times 1%. Put the other way, to reduce the inflation rate by 1%, excess unemployment must be equal to $1/\alpha$ for one year.

Equation (10.5) then implies that this ratio is independent of policy and simply equal to $(1/\alpha)$.

If the sacrifice ratio is constant, does this mean that the speed of disinflation is irrelevant? No. Suppose that the central bank tried to achieve the decrease in inflation in one year. As you have just seen, this would require an unemployment rate of 10% above the natural rate for one year. With a natural unemployment rate of 6%, this would require increasing the actual unemployment rate to 16% for one year. From Okun's law, using a value of 0.4 for β and a normal output growth rate of 3%, output growth would have to satisfy

$$u_t - u_{t-1} = -\beta(g_{yt} - \bar{g}_y)$$

$$16\% - 6\% = -0.4(g_{yt} - 3\%)$$

This implies a value for $g_{yt} = -(10\%)/0.4 + 3\% = -22\%$. In words, output growth would have to equal −22% for a year! In comparison, the largest negative growth rate ever in the USA in the 20th century was −15%. It occurred in 1931, during the Great Depression. During the recent recession of 2007–2010, the worst after the Great Depression, the lowest growth rate registered by the USA was −6.4% in the first quarter of 2009. It is fair to say that macroeconomists do not know with great confidence what would happen if monetary policy were aimed at inducing such a large negative growth rate, but they would surely be unwilling to try. The increase in the overall unemployment rate would lead to extremely high unemployment rates for some groups – specifically the young and the unskilled, whose unemployment typically increases more than the average unemployment rate. The associated sharp drop in output would most probably also lead to a large number of bankruptcies. This suggests that the central bank will want to go more slowly and to achieve disinflation over a number of years rather than do it all in one year.

The analysis we have just developed is close to the type of analysis economists at the Fed were conducting in the late 1970s. The econometric model they used, as well as most econometric models in use at the time, shared our simple model's property that policy could change the timing but not the number of point-years of excess unemployment. We shall call this the *traditional approach* in the following text. The traditional approach was challenged, however, by two separate groups of macroeconomists. The focus of both groups was the role of expectations and how changes in expectation formation might affect the unemployment cost of disinflation but, despite this common focus, they reached quite different conclusions.

Expectations and credibility: the Lucas critique

The conclusions of the first group were based on the work of Robert Lucas and Thomas Sargent, then at the University of Chicago. In what has become known as the **Lucas critique**, Lucas pointed out that when trying to predict the effects of a major policy change – such as the change considered by the Fed at the time – it could be very misleading to take as given the relations estimated from past data.

◄ Robert Lucas was awarded the Nobel Prize in 1995 and is still at the University of Chicago. Thomas Sargent is now at New York.

In the case of the Phillips curve, taking equation (10.5) as given was equivalent to assuming that wage setters would keep expecting inflation in the future to be the same as it was in the past, that the way wage setters formed their expectations would not change in response to the change in policy. This was an unwarranted assumption, Lucas argued: why shouldn't wage setters take policy changes directly into account? If wage setters believed that the Fed was committed to lowering inflation, they might well expect inflation to be lower in the future than in the past. If they lowered their expectations of inflation, then actual inflation would decline without the need for a protracted recession.

The logic of Lucas's argument can be seen by returning to equation (10.4), the Phillips curve with expected inflation on the right:

$$\pi_t = \pi_t^e - \alpha(u_t - u_n)$$

◄ If $\pi_t^e = \pi_{t-1}$, the Phillips curve is given by
$$\pi_t - \pi_{t-1} = -\alpha(u_t - u_n)$$
To achieve $\pi_t < \pi_{t-1}$, it must be that
$$u_t > u_n.$$

If wage setters kept forming expectations of inflation by looking at the previous year's inflation (if $P_t^e = P_{t-1}$), then the only way to decrease inflation would be to accept higher unemployment for some time; we explored the implications of this assumption in the preceding subsection.

But if wage setters could be convinced that inflation was indeed going to be lower than in the past, they would decrease their expectations of inflation. This would in turn reduce actual inflation, without any change in the unemployment rate. For example, if wage setters were convinced that inflation, which had been running at 14% in the past, would be only 4% in the future, and if they formed their expectations accordingly, then inflation would fall to 4% *even if unemployment remained at the natural rate of unemployment*:

$$\pi_t = \pi_t^e - \alpha(u_t - u_n)$$

$$4\% = 4\% - 0\%$$

Nominal money growth, inflation and expected inflation could all be reduced without the need for a recession. Put another way, decreases in nominal money growth could be neutral not only in the medium run but also in the short run.

Lucas and Sargent did not believe that disinflation could really take place without some increase in unemployment. But Sargent, looking at the historical evidence on the end of several very high inflations, concluded that the increase in unemployment could be small. The sacrifice ratio – the amount of excess unemployment needed to achieve disinflation – might be much lower than suggested by the traditional approach. The essential ingredient of successful disinflation, he argued, was **credibility** of monetary policy – the belief by wage setters that the central bank was truly committed to reducing inflation. Only credibility would cause wage setters to change the way they formed their expectations. Furthermore, he

The *credibility* view is that fast disinfla- ➤ tion is likely to be more credible than slow disinflation. Credibility decreases the unemployment cost of disinflation. So the central bank should go for fast disinflation.

argued, a clear and quick disinflation programme was much more likely to be credible than a protracted one that offered plenty of opportunities for reversal and political infighting along the way.

Nominal rigidities and contracts

A contrary view was taken by Stanley Fischer, then from MIT, and John Taylor, then at Columbia University. Both emphasised the presence of **nominal rigidities**, meaning that, in modern economies, many wages and prices are set in nominal terms for some time and are typically not readjusted when there is a change in policy.

Fischer is now the Governor of the ➤ Central Bank of Israel. Taylor was undersecretary for international affairs in the G. W. Bush administration and is now a professor at Stanford University.

Fischer argued that, even with credibility, too rapid a decrease in nominal money growth would lead to higher unemployment. Even if the Fed fully convinced workers and firms that nominal money growth was going to be lower, the wages set before the change in policy would still reflect the expectations of inflation prior to the policy change. In effect, inflation would already be built into existing wage agreements and could not be reduced instantaneously and without cost. At the very least, Fischer said, a policy of disinflation should be announced sufficiently in advance of its actual implementation to allow wage setters to take it into account when setting wages.

Taylor's argument went one step further. An important characteristic of wage contracts, he argued, is that they are not all signed at the same time. Instead, they are staggered over time. He showed that this **staggering of wage decisions** imposed strong limits on how fast disinflation could proceed without triggering higher unemployment, even if the Fed's commitment to inflation was fully credible. Why the limits? If workers cared about their wage relative to the wages of other workers, each wage contract would choose a wage not very different from the wages in the other contracts in force at the time. Too rapid a decrease in nominal money growth would therefore not lead to a proportional decrease in inflation. As a result, the real money stock would decrease, triggering a recession and an increase in the unemployment rate.

Taking into account the time pattern of wage contracts in the USA, Taylor then showed that, under full credibility of monetary policy, there *was* a path of disinflation consistent *with no increase in unemployment*. This path is shown in Figure 10.6.

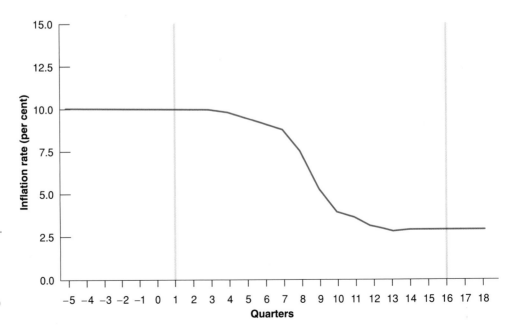

Figure 10.6

Disinflation without unemployment in the Taylor model

If wage decisions are staggered, disinflation must be phased in slowly to avoid an increase in unemployment.

In Figure 10.6, disinflation starts in quarter 1 and lasts for 16 quarters. Once it is achieved, the inflation rate, which started at 10%, is 3%. The striking feature is how slowly disinflation proceeds at the beginning. One year (four quarters) after the announcement of the change in policy, inflation is still 9.9%. But then disinflation proceeds more quickly. By the end of the third year, inflation is down to 4%, and by the end of the fourth year, the desired disinflation is achieved.

The reason for the slow decrease in inflation at the beginning – and, behind the scenes, for the slow decrease in nominal money growth – is straightforward: wages in force at the time of the policy change are the result of decisions made before the policy change occurred. Because of this, the path of inflation in the near future is largely predetermined. If nominal money growth were to decrease sharply, inflation could not fall very much right away, and the result would be a decrease in real money and a recession. So the best policy is for the Fed to proceed slowly at the beginning of the process while announcing it will proceed faster in the future. This announcement leads new wage settlements to take into account the new policy. When most wage decisions in the economy are based on decisions made after the change in policy, disinflation can proceed much more quickly. This is what happens in the third year following the policy change.

Like Lucas and Sargent, Taylor did not believe that disinflation could really be implemented without an increase in unemployment. For one thing, he realised that the path of disinflation drawn in Figure 10.6 might not be credible. Announcing this year that the Fed will decrease nominal money growth two years from now is likely to cause a serious credibility problem. Wage setters are likely to ask: if the decision has been made to disinflate, why does the central bank want to wait two years? Without credibility, inflation expectations might not change, defeating the hope of disinflation without an increase in the unemployment rate. But Taylor's analysis had two clear messages. First, like Lucas and Sargent, Taylor's analysis emphasised the role of expectations. Second, it suggested that a slow but credible disinflation might have a cost lower than the one implied by the traditional approach.

Who turned out to be right? The traditional approach, the Sargent–Lucas approach, or the Fischer–Taylor approach? The answer is given in the Focus box 'Disinflation in the UK, 1979–1985', and is easy to summarise: the disinflation of about 10% triggered a deep recession and about 12 point-years of excess unemployment. In other words, there were no obvious credibility gains, and the sacrifice ratio turned out to be roughly what was predicted by the traditional approach.

> ◄ The *nominal rigidities view* is that many wages are set in nominal terms, sometimes for many years. The way to decrease the unemployment cost of disinflation is to give wage setters time to take into account the change in policy. So the central bank should go for slow disinflation.

Was this outcome due to a lack of credibility of the change in monetary policy or to the fact that credibility is not enough to substantially reduce the cost of disinflation? One way of learning more is to look at other disinflation episodes. This is the approach followed by Laurence Ball, from the Johns Hopkins University in the USA, who estimated sacrifice ratios for 65 disinflation episodes in 19 OECD countries over the past 30 years. He reached three main conclusions:

- Disinflations typically lead to a period of higher unemployment. Put another way, even if a decrease in nominal money growth is neutral in the medium run, unemployment increases for some time before returning to the natural rate of unemployment.
- Faster disinflations are associated with smaller sacrifice ratios. This conclusion provides some evidence to support the expectation and credibility effects emphasised by Lucas and Sargent.
- Sacrifice ratios are smaller in countries that have shorter wage contracts. This provides some evidence to support Fischer and Taylor's emphasis on the structure of wage settlements.

Let's summarise: policy-makers face a trade-off between unemployment and inflation. In particular, to permanently lower inflation requires higher unemployment for some time. One might have hoped that, with credible policies, the trade-off would be much more favourable. The evidence can be read as saying that credibility gains may be present, but they are small.

FOCUS
Disinflation in the UK, 1979–1985

In 1979, at the start of Margaret Thatcher's government, the economic performance of the UK was rather poor. The inflation rate was higher than 13% and the immediate objective was to reduce it using monetary policy. To this end the government instituted a Medium Term Financial Strategy (MTFS) that envisaged a steady reduction in nominal GDP growth through a gradual reduction in the rate of growth of the money stock, accompanied by a reduction in public sector borrowing requirements (PSBR). Targets for the money stock were not new, having been first introduced by the Labour government in 1977. The MTFS, however, was different in providing target ranges for a number of years ahead. The rate of growth of the monetary base slowed from 12.1% in 1979 to 2.6% in 1981. The reduction in inflation is indeed one of the most conspicuous economic successes of the Thatcher years.

The most obvious failure has been the level of unemployment. Let us compare the UK's unemployment experience with those of most industrialised countries that went through a short period of disinflation during the first half of the 1980s. Has disinflation been more costly in the UK than elsewhere? Table 10.3 reports inflation and unemployment rates in 1980 and 1985 in the UK and a number of other countries.

Economic policies in the USA and the UK after 1979 provide good laboratories to test the credibility hypothesis, which states that credible policies to reduce inflation would lead to a more rapid and less costly reduction in inflation than would traditional approaches. Bean and Symons calculate 'sacrifice ratios' for the UK and other countries in Table 10.3.

The 'sacrifice ratio' is the ratio of the cumulated excess of the unemployment rate over its 1980 level during the disinflation period. Compared to Japan, Sweden and the USA – three countries with very different economic and institutional structures – the UK's performance was rather poor. However, its performance is better when compared to the rest of the EU; Germany for instance fared especially badly under the sacrifice ratio criterion. However, the most obvious comparison, in terms of similarity of initial conditions, is with Italy.

The results suggest that there was no credibility miracle. The UK sacrifice ratio ranks third out of seven even though most would agree that the UK had the most draconian anti-inflation policies of any of the countries. It is interesting to note as well that the country with the most deeply embedded hostility to inflation, Germany, has the highest sacrifice ratio.

If one also looks at the evolution of inflation and unemployment in the second half of the 1980s, in the UK as well as continental Europe, one can notice that rising trends in unemployment have gone along with apparent stickiness of wage inflation. The experience is in contrast with the conventional Phillips-curve theory, which cannot explain why inflation does not continue to decline with rates of unemployment that are presumably well above the natural rates.

The Phillips curve theory has great difficulties in explaining wage–price movements over the 1980s in the UK and in much of Europe. Attempts to find stable Phillips curves have proven elusive, except perhaps for Japan and the USA.

Source: Charles Bean and James Symons, 1989 'Ten Years of Mrs T', *NBER Macroeconomics Annual*, Volume 4, NBER, Cambridge, MA, 13–72.

Table 10.3 Comparative inflation and unemployment performance

| | Inflation | | Unemployment | | 'Sacrifice ratio' |
	1980	1985	1980	1985	
Germany	4.9	2.3	3.0	7.2	6.8
France	11.6	5.9	6.3	10.2	2.1
Italy	21.5	9.2	7.5	10.1	0.7
Japan	3.9	1.5	2.0	2.6	1.0
Sweden	11.9	6.9	2.0	2.8	0.4
UK	19.1	5.8	6.4	11.2	1.8
USA	9.1	3.0	7.0	7.1	1.0

Source: Charles Bean and James Symons, 'Ten Years of Mrs T', in *NBER Macroeconomics Annual*, Volume 4, 13–61, Table 3, p. 23. NBER, Cambridge, MA, 1989.

SUMMARY

- Three relations link inflation, output and unemployment:
  1. Okun's law, which relates the change in the unemployment rate to the deviation of the rate of growth of output from the normal growth rate. In the USA today, output growth of 1% above normal for a year leads to a decrease in the unemployment rate of about 0.4%.
  2. The aggregate supply relation – the Phillips curve – which relates the change in the inflation rate to the deviation of the actual unemployment rate from the natural rate of unemployment. In the USA today, an unemployment rate 1% below the natural rate of unemployment for a year leads to an increase in inflation of about 1%.
  3. The aggregate demand relation, which relates the rate of growth of output to the rate of growth of real money. The growth rate of output is equal to the growth rate of nominal money minus the rate of inflation. Given nominal money growth, higher inflation leads to a decrease in output growth.

- In the medium run, the unemployment rate is equal to the natural rate of unemployment, and output grows at its normal growth rate. Nominal money growth determines the inflation rate: a 1% increase in nominal money growth leads to a 1% increase in the inflation rate. As Milton Friedman put it: inflation is always and everywhere a monetary phenomenon.

- In the short run, a decrease in nominal money growth leads to a slowdown in growth and an increase in unemployment for some time.

- The proposition that, in the medium run, changes in inflation are reflected one-for-one in changes in the nominal interest rate is known as the Fisher effect or the Fisher hypothesis. The empirical evidence suggests that, while it takes a long time, changes in inflation are eventually reflected in changes in the nominal interest rate.

- Disinflation (a decrease in the inflation rate) can be achieved only at the cost of more unemployment. How much unemployment is required is a controversial issue. The traditional approach assumes that people do not change the way they form expectations when monetary policy changes, so the relation between inflation and unemployment is unaffected by the change in policy. This approach implies that disinflation can be achieved by a short but large increase in unemployment or by a longer and smaller increase in unemployment. But policy cannot affect the total number of point-years of excess unemployment.

- An alternative view is that, if the change in monetary policy is credible, expectation formation may change, leading to a smaller increase in unemployment than predicted by the traditional approach. In its extreme form, this alternative view implies that if policy is fully credible, it can achieve disinflation at no cost in unemployment. A less extreme form recognises that while expectation formation may change, the presence of nominal rigidities is likely to result in some increase in unemployment, but less than that implied by the traditional approach.

KEY TERMS

Okun's law 206

normal growth rate 207

labour hoarding 207

adjusted nominal money growth 211

Fisher effect, Fisher hypothesis 212

disinflation 217

point-year of excess unemployment 217

sacrifice ratio 218

Lucas critique 219

credibility 219

nominal rigidities 220

staggering of wage decisions 220

QUESTIONS AND PROBLEMS

QUICK CHECK

1. *Using the information in this chapter, label each of the following statements true, false or uncertain. Explain briefly.*

a. The unemployment rate will remain constant as long as there is positive output growth.

b. Many firms prefer to keep workers around when demand is low (rather than lay them off) even if the workers are underutilised.

c. The behaviour of Okun's law across countries and across decades is consistent with our knowledge of firms' behaviour and labour market regulations.

d. There is a reliable negative relation between the rate of inflation and the growth rate of output.

e. In the medium run, the rate of inflation is equal to the rate of nominal money growth.

f. In the medium run, the real interest rate is not affected by money growth.

g. The Fisher effect states that in the medium run, the nominal interest rate is not affected by money growth.

h. The experience of Latin American countries in the early 1990s supports the Fisher hypothesis.

i. According to the Phillips curve relation, the sacrifice ratio is independent of the speed of disinflation.

j. If Lucas and Sargent were right, and if monetary policy was fully credible, there would be no relation between inflation and unemployment – i.e. no Phillips curve relation.

k. Contrary to the traditional Phillips curve analysis, Taylor's analysis of staggered wage contracts makes the case for a slow approach to disinflation.

l. Ball's analysis of disinflation episodes provides some support for both the credibility effects of Lucas and Sargent and the wage-contract effects of Fischer and Taylor.

2. *As shown by equation (10.2), the estimated Okun's law for the USA is given by*

$$u_t - u_{t-1} = -0.4(g_{yt} - 3\%)$$

a. What growth rate of output leads to an increase in the unemployment rate of 1% per year? How can the unemployment rate increase even though the growth rate of output is positive?

b. Suppose output growth is constant for the next four years. What growth rate would reduce the unemployment rate by 2 percentage points over the next four years?

c. How would you expect Okun's law to change if the rate of growth of the labour force was higher by 2 percentage points? How do you expect Okun's law to change if the rate of growth of the labour force increases by 2 percentage points?

3. *Suppose that an economy can be described by the following three equations:*

$$u_t - u_{t-1} = -0.4(g_{yt} - 3\%) \quad \text{Okun's law}$$
$$\pi_t - \pi_{t-1} = -(u_t - 5\%) \quad \text{Phillips curve}$$
$$g_{yt} = g_{mt} - \pi_t \quad \text{Aggregate demand}$$

a. What is the natural rate of unemployment for this economy?

b. Suppose that the unemployment rate is equal to the natural rate and that the inflation rate is 8%. What is the growth rate of output? What is the growth rate of the money supply?

c. Suppose that conditions are as in (b), when, in year *t*, the authorities use monetary policy to reduce the inflation rate to 4% in year *t* and keep it there. Given this inflation rate and using the Phillips curve, what must happen to the unemployment rate in years *t*, *t* + 1, *t* + 2 and so on? Given the unemployment rate and using Okun's law, what must happen to the rate of growth of output in years *t*, *t* + 1, *t* + 2 and so on? Given the rate of growth of output and using the aggregate demand equation, what must be the rate of nominal money growth in years *t*, *t* + 1, *t* + 2 and so on?

4. *Suppose that you are advising a government that wants to reduce the inflation rate. It is considering two options: a gradual reduction over several years or an immediate reduction.*

a. Lay out the arguments for and against each option.

b. Considering only the sacrifice ratio, which option is preferable? Why might you want to consider criteria other than the sacrifice ratio?

c. What particular features of the economy would you want to consider before giving your advice?

5. Mark-ups, unemployment and inflation

Suppose that the Phillips curve is given by

$$\pi_t - \pi_{t-1} = -(u_t - 5\%) + 0.1\mu$$

where μ is the mark-up.

Suppose that unemployment is initially at its natural rate. Suppose now that μ increases as a result of an oil price shock, *but that the monetary authority continues to keep the unemployment rate at its previous value.*

a. What will happen to inflation?

b. What should the monetary authority do instead of trying to keep the unemployment rate at its previous value?

6. The Fisher hypothesis

a. What is the Fisher hypothesis?

b. Does the experience of Latin American countries in the 1990s support or refute the Fisher hypothesis? Explain.

c. Look at the figure in the Focus box on Latin America. Note that the line drawn through the scatter of points does not go through the origin. Does the 'Fisher effect' suggest that it should go through the origin? Explain.

d. Consider this statement: 'If the Fisher hypothesis is true, then changes in the growth rate of the money stock translate one-for-one into changes in i, and the real interest rate is left unchanged. Thus, there is no room for monetary policy to affect real economic activity.' Discuss.

DIG DEEPER

7. Credibility and disinflation

Suppose that the Phillips curve is given by

$$\pi_t = \pi_t^e - (u_t - 5\%)$$

and expected inflation is given by

$$\pi_t^e = \pi_{t-1}$$

a. What is the sacrifice ratio in this economy?

Suppose that unemployment is initially equal to the natural rate and $\pi = 12\%$. The central bank decides that 12% inflation is too high and that, starting in year t, it will maintain the unemployment rate 1 percentage point above the natural rate of unemployment until the inflation rate has decreased to 2%.

b. Compute the rate of inflation for years t, $t + 1$, $t + 2$ and so on.

c. For how many years must the central bank keep the unemployment rate above the natural rate of unemployment? Is the implied sacrifice ratio consistent with your answer to (a)?

Now suppose that people know that the central bank wants to lower inflation to 2%, but they are not sure about the central bank's willingness to accept an unemployment rate above the natural rate of unemployment. As a result, their expectation of inflation is a weighted average of the target of 2% and last year's inflation – i.e.

$$\pi_t^e = \lambda 2\% + (1 - \lambda)\pi_{t-1}$$

where λ is the weight they put on the central bank's target of 2%.

d. Let $\lambda = 0.25$. How long will it take before the inflation rate is equal to 2%? What is the sacrifice ratio? Why is it different from the answer in (c)?

Suppose that after the policy has been in effect for one year, people believe that the central bank is indeed committed to reducing inflation to 2%. As a result, they now set their expectations according to

$$\pi_t^e = 2\%$$

e. From what year onward can the central bank let the unemployment rate return to the natural rate? What is the sacrifice ratio now?

f. What advice would you give to a central bank that wants to lower the rate of inflation by increasing the rate of unemployment as little and for as short a time period as possible?

8. The effects of a permanent decrease in the rate of nominal money growth

Suppose that the economy can be described by the following three equations:

$u_t - u_{t-1} = -0.4(g_{yt} - 3\%)$	*Okun's law*
$\pi_t - \pi_{t-1} = -(u_t - 5\%)$	*Phillips curve*
$g_{yt} = g_{mt} - \pi_t$	*Aggregate demand*

a. Reduce the three equations to two by substituting g_{yt} from the aggregate demand equation into Okun's law.

Assume initially that $u_t = u_{t-1} = 5\%$, $g_{mt} = 13\%$ and $\pi_t = 10\%$. Now suppose that money growth is permanently reduced from 13% to 3%, starting in year t.

b. Compute (using a calculator or a spreadsheet program) unemployment and inflation in year t, $t + 1$, . . . , $t + 10$.

c. Does inflation decline smoothly from 10% to 3%? Why or why not?

d. Compute the values of the unemployment rate and the inflation rate in the medium run.

EXPLORE FURTHER

9. *Go to the Eurostat website and retrieve quarterly data on gross domestic product at constant prices for 2009 and 2010 and on monthly unemployment rates and monthly employment levels for 2009 and 2010, for your country.*

a. Was output growth positive throughout 2009 and 2010?

b. What happened to the unemployment rate over the period January 2009–June 2010?

c. How do you reconcile your answers to parts (a) and (b)?

d. Now consider the employment level. Compare the monthly employment levels from September 2009 and December 2009. What happened to employment over the last quarter of 2009?

e. Was output growth positive in the last quarter of 2009?

f. How do you reconcile your answers to parts (d) and (e)?

10. *Go the Eurostat website and retrieve monthly data on the level of employment and unemployment for 2009. You will* notice that the level of unemployment rose in every month of 2009.

a. Did the level of employment rise in any month(s) in 2009?

b. How is it possible that both employment and unemployment could rise in the same month?

We invite you to visit the Blanchard page on the Prentice Hall website, at **www.prenhall.com/blanchard** for this chapter's World Wide Web exercises.

FURTHER READING

- To learn more about how countries, decided to respond to the 2007–2010 crisis, you can read the speech given by Ben Bernanke, Chairman of the Fed, at the London School of Economics, London, UK, on 13 January 2009, available at: *http://www.federalreserve.gov/newsevents/speech/bernanke20090113a.htm.*

- To find out more about the monetary policy measures introduced to help the economies out of the 2007–2010 recession, you can read 'Fiscal aspects of quantitative easing' by Paul Krugman, Nobel Laureate in Economics in 2008, available at *http://krugman.blogs.nytimes.com/2009/03/20/fiscal-aspects-of-quantitative-easing-wonkish/.*

- The ECB's response to the crisis can be seen in statements made by Jean-Claude Trichet, President of the ECB, in 2009, available at *http://www.ecb.int/press/key/date/2009/html/sp090220.en.html* and *http://www.ecb.int/press/key/date/2009/html/sp090427.en.html.*

- A description of US monetary policy in the 1980s is given by Michael Mussa in Chapter 2 of **Martin Feldstein, ed., American Economic Policy in the 1980s, University of Chicago Press** and **NBER, Chicago, EL, 1994, 81–164.** One of the comments on the chapter is by Paul Volcker, who was Chairman of the Fed from 1979–1987.

THE LONG RUN

The next three chapters focus on the long run. In the long run, what dominates is not fluctuations, but growth. So now we need to ask: what determines growth?

Chapter 11 The facts of growth

Chapter 11 looks at the facts of growth. It first documents the large increase in output that has taken place in rich countries over the past 50 years. Then, taking a wider look, it shows that, on the scale of human history, such growth is a recent phenomenon. And it is not a universal phenomenon: some countries are catching up, but many poor countries are suffering from no or low growth.

Chapter 12 Saving, capital accumulation and output

Chapter 12 focuses on the role of capital accumulation in growth. It shows that capital accumulation cannot by itself sustain growth, but that it does affect the level of output. A higher saving rate typically leads to lower consumption initially but to more consumption in the long run.

Chapter 13 Technological progress and growth

Chapter 13 turns to technological progress. It shows how, in the long run, the growth rate of an economy is determined by the rate of technological progress. It looks at the role of R&D in generating such progress. It returns to the facts of growth presented in Chapter 11 and shows how to interpret those facts in the light of the theory developed in Chapters 11–13.

Chapter 11

THE FACTS OF GROWTH

Our perceptions of how the economy is doing are often dominated by year-to-year fluctuations in economic activity. A recession leads to gloom, and an expansion leads to optimism. But if we step back to take a look at activity over longer periods – say over many decades – the picture changes. Fluctuations fade. *Growth* – the steady increase in aggregate output over time – dominates the picture.

Figure 11.1 shows the evolution of GDP (in million 1990 PPP dollars) in some industrialised European economies (France, Germany and the UK) since 1890, compared to three poorer countries, Greece and Portugal in Europe, and Argentina. Notice how similar, although at different levels, were the evolutions of GDP before 1940, and how rapid was output growth in the first group of countries. In France, Germany and the UK, the years from 1940–1945 correspond to the large decrease in output during the Second World War, and the years 2008–2009 correspond to the largest post-war recession. Note how small these two episodes appear compared to the steady increase in output over the past 100 years.

We now shift our focus from fluctuations to growth. Put another way, we turn from the study of the determination of output in the *short run* and *medium run* – where fluctuations dominate – to the determination of output in the *long run* – where growth dominates. Our goal is to understand what determines growth, why some countries are growing while others are not, and why some countries are rich while many others are still poor.

- Section 11.1 discusses a central measurement issue: how to measure the standard of living.

- Section 11.2 looks at growth in the USA and other rich countries over the past 50 years.

- Section 11.3 takes a broader look at growth across both time and space.

- Section 11.4 gives a primer on growth and introduces the framework that will be developed in the next chapters.

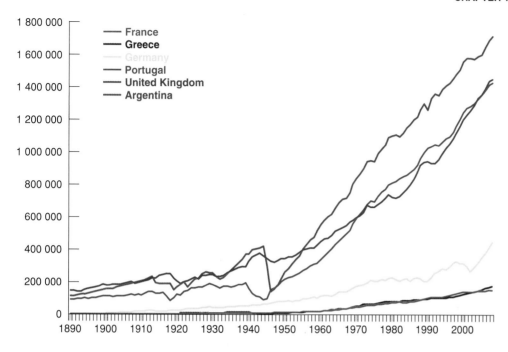

Figure 11.1

GDP in selected economies since 1890

Source: OECD.

11.1 MEASURING THE STANDARD OF LIVING

The reason we care about **growth** is that we care about the **standard of living**. Looking across time, we want to know by how much the standard of living has increased. Looking across countries, we want to know how much higher the standard of living is in one country than in another. Thus, the variable we want to focus on and compare either over time or across countries is **output per person** rather than *output* itself.

A practical problem then arises: how do we compare output per person across countries? Countries use different currencies, so output in each country is expressed in terms of its own currency. A natural solution is to use exchange rates: when comparing, say, the output per person of India to the output per person of the UK, we can compute Indian GDP per person in rupees, use the exchange rate to get Indian GDP per person in pounds, and compare it to UK GDP per person in pounds. This simple approach will not do, however, for two reasons:

- Exchange rates can vary a lot (as we have learned in Chapter 7). For example, the pound decreased since the summer of 2008 by roughly 30% vis-à-vis the US dollar, the euro and other major currencies. But, surely, the standard of living in the UK did not decrease by 30% compared to the standard of living of the USA and of other European countries during the last year. Yet this is the conclusion we would reach if we were to compare GDP per person using exchange rates.

- The second reason goes beyond fluctuations in exchange rates. In 2006, income per person in India, using the current exchange rate, was $820, compared to $40 660 in the UK. Surely no one could live on $820 per year in the UK. But people live on it – admittedly, not very well – in India, where the prices of basic goods – those goods needed for subsistence – are much lower than in the UK. The level of consumption of the average person in India, who consumes mostly basic goods, is not 50 (40 660 divided by 820) times smaller than that of the average person in the UK. This point applies to other countries besides the UK and India: in general, the lower a country's output per person, the lower the prices of food and basic services in that country.

So, when we focus on comparing standards of living, we get more meaningful comparisons by correcting for the two effects we just discussed – variations in exchange rates

> The scale used to measure GDP on the vertical axis in Figure 11.1 is called a **logarithmic scale**. The defining characteristic of a logarithmic scale is that the same proportional increase in a variable is represented by the same distance on the vertical axis. For more discussion, see Appendix 1 at the end of the book.

> Output per person is also called *output per capita* (*capita* means 'head' in Latin). Given that output and income are always equal, it is also called *income per person*, or *income per capita*.

> Recall a similar discussion in Chapter 1, when looking at output per person in China.

and systematic differences in prices across countries. The details of construction are complicated, but the principle is simple: the numbers for GDP – and hence for GDP per person – are constructed using a common set of prices for all countries. Such adjusted real GDP numbers, which you can think of as measures of **purchasing power** across time or across countries, are called **purchasing power parity (PPP)** numbers. Further discussion is given in the Focus box 'The construction of PPP numbers'.

When comparing rich versus poor countries, the differences between PPP numbers and the numbers based on current exchange rates can be very large. Return to the comparison between India and the UK. We saw that, at current exchange rates, the ratio of GDP per person in the UK to GDP per person in India was 50. Using PPP numbers, the ratio is 'only' 14. Although this is still a large difference, it is much smaller than the ratio we obtained using current exchange rates. Differences between PPP numbers and numbers based on current exchange rate are typically smaller when making comparisons among rich countries. Based on the numbers we saw in Chapter 1 – those numbers were constructed using current exchange rates – GDP per person in the USA in 2006 was equal to 125% of the GDP per person in Germany. Based on PPP numbers, GDP per person in the USA is in fact equal to 138% of GDP per person in Germany. More generally, PPP numbers suggest that the USA still has the highest GDP per person among in the world.

> The bottom line: when comparing standard of living across countries, make sure to use PPP numbers.

Let us end this section with three remarks before we move on and look at growth:

- What matters for people's welfare is their consumption rather than their income. One might therefore want to use *consumption per person* rather than output per person as

FOCUS
The construction of PPP numbers

Consider two countries – let's call them the USA and Russia, although we are not attempting to fit the characteristics of those two countries very closely:

In the USA, annual consumption per person equals $20 000. People in the USA each buy two goods: every year, they buy a new car for $10 000 and spend the rest on food. The price of a yearly bundle of food in the USA is $10 000.

In Russia, annual consumption per person equals 60 000 roubles. People there keep their cars for 15 years. The price of a car is 300 000 roubles, so individuals spend on average 20 000 roubles – 300 000/15 – per year on cars. They buy the same yearly bundle of food as their US counterparts, at a price of 40 000 roubles.

Russian and US cars are of identical quality, and so is Russian and US food. (You may dispute the realism of these assumptions. Whether a car in country X is the same as a car in country Y is very much the type of problem confronting economists constructing PPP measures.) The exchange rate is such that $1 is equal to 30 roubles. What is consumption per person in Russia relative to consumption per person in the USA?

One way to answer is by taking consumption per person in Russia and converting it into dollars, using the exchange rate. Using that method, Russian consumption per person in dollars is $2000 (60 000 roubles divided by the exchange rate, 30 roubles to the dollar). According to these numbers, consumption per person in Russia is only 10% of US consumption per person.

Does this answer make sense? True, Russian consumers are poorer than US consumers, but food is much cheaper in Russia. A US consumer spending all of his $20 000 on food would buy two bundles of food ($20 000/$10 000). A Russian consumer spending all of his 60 000 roubles on food would buy 1.5 bundles of food (60 000 roubles/ 40 000 roubles). In terms of food bundles, the difference a measure of the standard of living. (This is indeed what we do in the Focus box 'The construction of PPP numbers'.) Because the ratio of consumption to output is rather similar across countries, the ranking of countries is roughly the same whether we use consumption per person or output per person.

- Thinking about the production side, one may be interested in differences in productivity rather than in differences in the standard of living across countries. In this case, the appropriate measure is *output per worker* – or, even better, *output per hour worked* if the information about total hours worked is available – rather than output per person. Output per person and output per worker (or per hour) will differ to the extent that the ratio of the number of workers (or hours) to population differs across countries. Most of the difference between output per person in the USA and in Germany we noted earlier comes, for example, from differences in hours worked per person rather than from differences in productivity. Put another way, German workers are about as productive as their US counterparts. However, they work fewer hours, so their standard of living is lower.

- The reason we ultimately care about the standard of living is presumably that we care about happiness. One may therefore ask the obvious question: does a higher standard of living lead to greater happiness? The answer is given in the Focus box 'Growth and happiness'. The answer: yes, at least for countries with output per person below $20 000, or roughly half of the US level. The relation appears much weaker, however, for richer countries.

looks much smaller between US and Russian consumption per person. And given that one-half of consumption in the USA and two-thirds of consumption in Russia goes to spending on food, this seems like a relevant computation.

Can we improve on our initial answer? Yes. One way is to use the same set of prices for both countries and then measure the quantities of each good consumed in each country using this common set of prices. Suppose we use US prices. In terms of US prices, annual consumption per person in the USA is obviously still $20 000. What is it in Russia? Every year, the average Russian buys approximately 0.07 car (one car every 15 years) and one bundle of food. Using US prices – specifically, $10 000 for a car and $10 000 for a bundle of food – gives Russian consumption per person as [(0.07 × $10 000) + (1 × $10 000)] = ($700 + $10 000) = $10 700. So, using US prices to compute consumption in both countries puts annual Russian consumption per person at $10 700/ $20 000 = 53.5% of annual US consumption per person, a better estimate of relative standards of living than we obtained using our first method (which put the number at only 10%).

This type of computation – the construction of variables across countries using a common set of prices – underlies PPP estimates. Rather than use US dollar prices, as in our example (why use US rather than Russian or, for that matter, French prices?), these estimates use average prices across countries. These average prices are called *international dollar prices*. Many of the estimates we use in this chapter are the result of an ambitious project known as the 'Penn World Tables'. (Penn stands for the University of Pennsylvania, where the project is taking place.) Led by three economists – Irving Kravis, Robert Summers and Alan Heston – over the course of more than 40 years, researchers working on the project have constructed PPP series not only for consumption (as we just did in our example) but, more generally, for GDP and its components, going back to 1950, for most countries in the world.

Note: For more on the construction of PPP numbers, go to the website ***pwt.econ.upenn.edu***. (In the Penn tables, what is the ratio of Russian PPP GDP per person to US PPP GDP per person?) The IMF and the World Bank also construct their own sets of PPP numbers. The IMF numbers are easily available on the IMF website, ***www.imf.org***.

FOCUS
Growth and happiness

Economists often take for granted that higher output per person means higher welfare and increased happiness. The evidence on direct measures of happiness, however, points to a more complex picture.

Looking at growth and happiness across countries

Figure 11.2 shows the results of a study of happiness in 81 countries in the late 1990s. In each country, a sample of people were asked two questions. The first one was: 'Taking all things together, would you say you are very happy, quite happy, not very happy, not at all happy?' The second was: 'All things considered, how satisfied are you with your life as a whole these days?' with answers on a scale ranging from 1 (dissatisfied) to 10 (satisfied). The measure on the vertical axis in Figure 11.2 is constructed as the average of the percentage of people declaring themselves very happy or happy in answer to the first question and the percentage of people answering 6 or more to the second question. The measure of income per person on the horizontal axis is the level of income per person, measured at PPP prices, in 1999 dollars. (The levels of income per person used in the figure were constructed by the World Bank.) The figure suggests three conclusions.

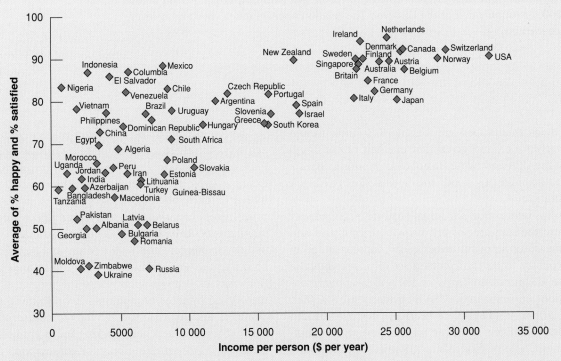

Figure 11.2

Happiness and income per person across countries

Source: World Values Survey, 1999–2000 Wave.

11.2 GROWTH IN RICH COUNTRIES SINCE 1950

In this section, let's start by looking at growth in rich countries since 1950. In the next section, we shall look further back in time and across a wider range of countries.

Table 11.3 shows the evolution of output per person (GDP, measured at PPP prices, divided by population) for France, Ireland, Japan, Sweden, the UK and the USA since 1950. We have chosen these six countries not only because they are some of the world's major

First, most of the countries with very low happiness levels are the Eastern European countries, which in the 1990s were suffering from the collapse of the communist regimes and the difficult transition to capitalism.

Second, and leaving those countries aside, there appears to be a positive relation between happiness and the level of income per person. Happiness is lower in poor countries than in rich ones.

Third, looking at rich countries – the countries with PPP output per person above $20 000 (in 1999 dollars), there appears to be little relation between the level of income per person and happiness. (To see that, cover the left side of the figure, and just look at the right side.) For this set of countries, higher income per person does not seem to be associated with greater happiness.

Looking at growth and happiness over time

One may reasonably argue that comparing happiness across countries is difficult. Different cultures may have different notions of what happiness is. Some countries may be chronically happier or unhappier than others. For this reason, it may be more informative to look at what happens to happiness over time in a given country. This can be done for the USA, where the General Social Survey has asked the following question since the early 1970s: 'Taken all together, how would you say things are these days – would you say you are very happy, pretty happy or not too happy?' Table 11.1 gives the proportion of answers in each category given in 1975 and in 1996.

The numbers in the table are striking. During those 21 years, output per person increased by more than 60%, but there was basically no change in the distribution of happiness. In other words, a higher standard of living was not associated with an increase in self-reported happi-

Table 11.1 Distribution of happiness in the USA over time (per cent)

	1975	1996
Very happy	32	31
Pretty happy	55	58
Not too happy	13	11

Table 11.2 Distribution of happiness in the USA across income groups (per cent)

	Top quarter	Bottom quarter
Very happy	37	16
Pretty happy	57	53
Not too happy	6	31

ness. Evidence from Gallup polls over the past 60 years confirms the finding: the proportion of people defining themselves as 'very happy' is the same as it was in the early 1950s.

Looking at growth and happiness across individuals

Do the conclusions in the preceding section mean that 'money' (more properly 'income') does not bring happiness? The answer is no. If one looks across individuals at any point in time, rich people are likely to report themselves as happier than poor people. This is shown in Table 11.2, which is again constructed using the answers to the General Social Survey and gives the distribution of happiness for different income groups in the USA in 1998.

The results are again striking: the proportion of 'very happy' people is much higher among the rich (the people in the top quarter of the income distribution) than among the poor (the people in the bottom quarter of the income distribution). And the reverse holds for the proportion of 'not too happy' people: the proportion is much lower among the rich than among the poor.

What conclusions can we draw from all this evidence? At low levels of output per person, say up to $20 000 or about half of the current US level, increases in output per person lead to increases in happiness. At higher levels, however, the relation appears to be much weaker. Happiness appears to depend more on people's relative incomes. If this is indeed the case, it has important implications for economic policy, at least in rich countries. Growth, and therefore policies that stimulate growth, may not be the key to happiness.

Source: Richard Layard, *Happiness. Lessons from a New Science*, Penguin Books, New York, 2005.

economic powers but because what has happened to them is broadly representative of what has happened in other advanced countries over the past half century or so.

Table 11.3 yields two main conclusions:

- There has been a large increase in output per person.
- There has been convergence of output per person across countries.

Let's look at each of these points in turn.

Table 11.3 The evolution of output per person in six rich countries since 1950

	Annual growth rate output per person (%)	Real output per person (2000 dollars)		
	1950–2004	1950	2004	2004/1950
France	3.3	5920	26 168	4.4
Ireland	3.6	4422	28 956	6.5
Japan	4.6	2187	24 661	11.3
Sweden	2.2	8507	27 072	3.2
UK	2.7	8091	26 762	3.3
USA	2.6	11 233	36 098	3.2
Average	3.2	6727	28 286	4.2

Note: the average in the last line is a simple (unweighted) average.

Source: Penn World Tables (*pwt.econ.upenn.edu*).

The large increase in the standard of living since 1950

Look at the last column of Table 11.3. Since 1950, output per person has increased by a factor of 3.2 in Sweden and in the USA, by a factor of 3.3 in the UK by a factor of 4.4 in France, by a factor of 6.5 in Ireland and by a factor of 11.3 in Japan.

These numbers show what is sometimes called the *force of compounding*. In a different context, you have probably heard how saving even a little while you are young will build to a large amount by the time you retire. For example, if the interest rate is 4.6% per year, an investment of €1, with the proceeds reinvested every year, will grow to about €11 in 54 years ($[1 + 0.046]^{54} = \$11.3$). The same logic applies to growth rates. The average annual growth rate in Japan over the period 1950–2004 was equal to 4.6%. This high growth rate has led to an 11-fold increase in real output per person in Japan over the period.

$1.01^{40} - 1 = 1.48 - 1 = 48\%$ ➤

Unfortunately, policy measures with ➤ such magical results have proven difficult to discover!

Clearly, a better understanding of growth, if it leads to the design of policies that stimulate growth, can have a very large effect on the standard of living. Suppose we could find a policy measure that permanently increased the growth rate by 1% per year. This would lead, after 40 years, to a standard of living 48% higher than it would have been without the policy – a substantial difference.

The convergence of output per person since 1950

The second and third columns of Table 11.3 show that the levels of output per person have converged (become closer) over time: the numbers for output per person are much more similar in 2004 than they were in 1950. Put another way, those countries that were behind have grown faster, reducing the gap between them and the USA.

In 1950, output per person in the USA was roughly 30% higher than the level of output per person in Sweden and the UK, twice the level of output per person in France and Ireland and more than five times the level of output per person in Japan. From the perspective of Europe or Japan, the USA was seen as the land of plenty, where everything was bigger and better. Today these perceptions have faded, and the numbers explain why. Using PPP numbers, US output per person is still the highest but, in 2004, it was only 40% above the average output per person in Japan and between 20 and 30% in the other European countries; a much smaller difference than in the 1950s.

This **convergence** of levels of output per person across countries is not specific to the four countries we are looking at. It extends to the set of OECD countries. This is shown in Figure 11.3, which plots the average annual growth rate of output per person since 1950 against the initial level of output per person in 1950 for the set of countries that are members of the OECD today. There is a clear negative relation between the initial level of

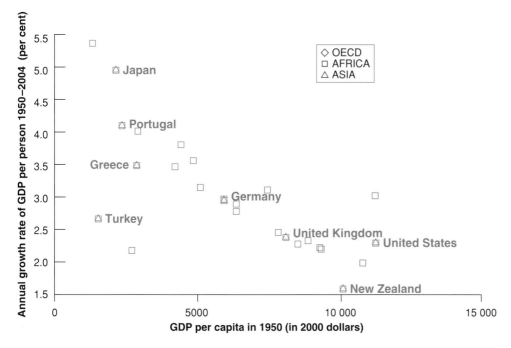

Figure 11.3

Growth rates of GDP per person since 1950 versus GDP per person in 1950 (OECD countries)

Countries with lower levels of output per person in 1950 have typically grown faster.

Source: Penn World Tables. The Czech Republic, Hungary and Poland are not included because of missing data.

output per person and the growth rate since 1950: countries that were behind in 1950 have typically grown faster. The relation is not perfect: Turkey, which had roughly the same low level of output per person as Japan in 1950, has had a growth rate equal to only about half that of Japan. But the relation is clearly there.

Some economists have pointed to a problem in graphs like Figure 11.3. By looking at the set of countries that are members of the OECD today, what we have done in effect is to look at a club of economic winners: OECD membership is not officially based on economic success, but economic success is surely an important determinant of membership. But when you look at a club whose membership is based on economic success, you will find that those who came from behind had the fastest growth: this is precisely why they made it into the club! The finding of convergence could come in part from the way we selected the countries in the first place.

So a better way of looking at convergence is to define the set of countries we look at not on the basis of where they are today – as we did in Figure 11.3 by taking today's OECD members – but on the basis of where they were in, say, 1950. For example, we can look at all countries that had an output per person of at least one-quarter of US output per person in 1950 and then look for convergence within that group. It turns out that most of the countries in that group have indeed converged, and therefore convergence is not solely an OECD phenomenon. However, a few countries – Uruguay, Argentina and Venezuela among them – have not converged. In 1950, those three countries had roughly the same output per person as France. In 2004, they had fallen far behind; their level of output per person stood only between one-quarter and one-half of the French level.

11.3 A BROADER LOOK AT GROWTH ACROSS TIME AND SPACE

In the previous section, we focused on growth over the past 50 years in rich countries. Let's now put this in context by looking at the evidence over both a much longer time span and a wider set of countries.

Looking at growth across two millennia

Has output per person in the currently rich economies always grown at rates similar to the growth rates in Table 11.3? No. Estimates of growth are clearly harder to construct as we look further back in time. But there is agreement among economic historians about the main evolutions over the past 2000 years.

From the end of the Roman Empire to roughly the year 1500, there was essentially no growth of output per person in Europe: most workers were employed in agriculture, in which there was little technological progress. Because agriculture's share of output was so large, inventions with applications outside agriculture could contribute little to overall production and output. Although there was some output growth, a roughly proportional increase in population led to roughly constant output per person.

This period of stagnation of output per person is often called the *Malthusian era*. Thomas Robert Malthus, an English economist, argued at the end of the 18th century that this proportional increase in output and population was not a coincidence. Any increase in output, he argued, would lead to a decrease in mortality, leading to an increase in population until output per person was back to its initial level. Europe was in a **Malthusian trap**, unable to increase its output per person.

Eventually, Europe was able to escape that trap. From about 1500–1700, growth of output per person turned positive, but it was still small – only around 0.1% per year. It then increased to 0.2% per year from 1700–1820. Starting with the Industrial Revolution, growth rates increased, but on the scale of human history, therefore, sustained growth of output per person – especially the high growth rates we have seen since 1950 – is definitely a recent phenomenon.

Looking at growth across many countries

We have seen how output per person has converged among OECD countries. But what about other countries? Are the poorest countries also growing faster? Are they converging toward the USA, even if they are still far behind?

> The numbers for 1950 are missing for too many countries to use 1950 as the initial year, as we did in Figure 11.3.

The answer is given in Figure 11.4, which plots, for 70 countries, the annual growth rate of output per person since 1960 against output per person in 1960.

The striking feature of Figure 11.4 is that there is no clear pattern: it is not the case that, in general, countries that were behind in 1960 have grown faster. Some have, but clearly many have not.

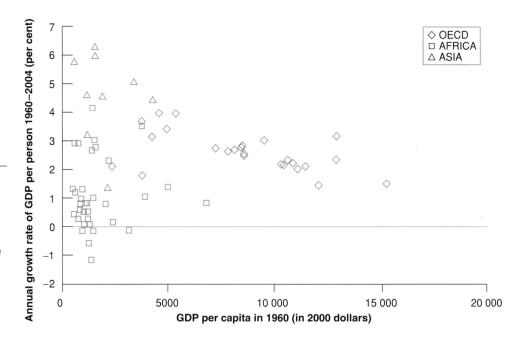

Figure 11.4

Growth rates of GDP per person since 1960 versus GDP per person in 2000 dollars for 70 countries

There is no clear relation between the growth rate of output per person since 1960 and the level of output per person in 1960.

Source: Penn World Tables. The Czech Republic, Hungary and Poland are not included because of missing data.

The cloud of points in Figure 11.4 hides, however, a number of interesting patterns that appear when we put countries into different groups. Note that we have used different symbols in the figure: the diamonds represent OECD countries, the squares represent African countries, and the triangles represent Asian countries. Looking at patterns by groups yields three main conclusions:

1. The picture for the OECD countries (that is, for the rich countries) is much the same as in Figure 11.3, which looks at a slightly longer period of time (from 1950 onward rather than from 1960). Nearly all start at high levels of output per person (say, at least one-third of the US level in 1960), and there is clear evidence of convergence.

2. Convergence is also visible for most Asian countries: all the countries with growth rates above 4% over the period are in Asia. Japan was the first to grow and now has the highest level of output per person in Asia. But a number of other Asian countries (represented by triangles) are trailing it closely. Starting in the 1960s, four countries – Singapore, Taiwan, Hong Kong and South Korea, a group of countries sometimes called the **four tigers** – started catching up quickly. In 1960, their average output per person was about 12% of the US level; by 2004, it had increased to 65% of the US level. More recently, the major story has been China – both because of its very high growth rates and because of its sheer size. Over the period, growth of output per person in China has been 5.6% but, because it started very low, its output per person is still only about 20% of the US level. (Economies with high growth rates but low output per person are often called **emerging economies**, a term we use in the remainder of the book.)

3. The picture is very different, however, for African countries. Convergence is certainly not the rule in Africa. Most African countries (represented by squares) were very poor in 1960, and many have had negative growth of output per person – an absolute decline in their standard of living – since then. Even in the absence of major wars, output per person has declined at 1.1% per year in Madagascar (the lowest square in the figure). Output per person in Niger stands at 60% of its 1960 level.

Looking further back in time, a picture emerges. For much of the first millennium, and until the 15th century, China probably had the world's highest level of output per person. For a couple of centuries, leadership moved to the cities of Northern Italy. But until the 19th century, differences across countries were typically much smaller than they are today. Starting in the 19th century, a number of countries, first in Western Europe and then in North and South America, started growing faster than others. Since then, a number of other countries, most notably in Asia, have started growing fast and are converging. Many others, mainly in Africa, are not.

Our main focus in this chapter and the next is primarily on growth in rich and emerging countries. We do not take on some of the wider challenges raised by the facts we have just seen, such as why growth of output per person started in earnest in the 19th century or why Africa has so far failed to achieve steady growth. Doing so would take us too far into economic history and *development economics*. But these facts put into perspective the two basic facts we discussed earlier when looking at the OECD: neither growth nor convergence is a historical necessity.

As briefly discussed in Chapter 1, in recent years, many African countries have grown at higher rates than they did in the past. It is much too early to conclude that they are on a steady growth path.

The distinction between *growth theory* and *development economics* is fuzzy. A rough distinction: growth theory takes many of the institutions of a country (for example, its legal system, its form of government) as given. Development economics asks what institutions are needed to sustain steady growth and how they can be put in place.

Solow's article 'A Contribution to the Theory of Economic Growth' appeared in 1956. Solow was awarded the Nobel Prize in 1987 for his work on growth.

11.4 THINKING ABOUT GROWTH: A PRIMER

To think about growth, economists use a framework developed originally by Robert Solow, from MIT, in the late 1950s. The framework has proven sturdy and useful, and we will use it here. This section provides an introduction. Chapters 12 and 13 provide a more detailed analysis, first of the role of capital accumulation and then of the role of technological progress in the process of growth.

The aggregate production function

The starting point of any theory of growth must be an **aggregate production function**, a specification of the relation between aggregate output and the inputs in production.

The aggregate production function we introduced in Chapter 7 to study the determination of output in the short run and the medium run took a particularly simple form. Output was simply proportional to the amount of labour used by firms – specifically, it was proportional to the number of workers employed by firms [equation (7.2)]. As long as our focus was on fluctuations in output and employment, the assumption was acceptable. But now that our focus has shifted to growth, that assumption will no longer do: it implies that output per worker is constant, ruling out growth (or at least growth of output per worker) altogether. It is time to relax it. From now on, we will assume that there are two inputs – capital and labour – and that the relation between aggregate output and the two inputs is given by

$$Y = F(K, N) \qquad [11.1]$$

As before, Y is aggregate output. K is capital – the sum of all the machines, plants and office buildings in the economy. N is labour – the number of workers in the economy. The function F, which tells us how much output is produced for given quantities of capital and labour, is the *aggregate production function*.

This way of thinking about aggregate production is an improvement on our treatment in Chapter 7, but it should be clear that it is still a dramatic simplification of reality. Surely, machines and office buildings play very different roles in production and should be treated as separate inputs. Surely, workers with PhDs are different from school leavers; yet by constructing the labour input as simply the *number* of workers in the economy, we treat all workers as identical. We will relax some of these simplifications later. For the time being, equation (11.1), which emphasises the role of both labour and capital in production, will do.

The next step must be to think about where the aggregate production function, F, which relates output to the two inputs, comes from. In other words, what determines how much output can be produced for given quantities of capital and labour? The answer: the **state of technology**. A country with more advanced technology will produce more output from the same quantities of capital and labour than will an economy with primitive technology.

How should we define the *state of technology*? Should we think of it as the list of blueprints defining both the range of products that can be produced in the economy and the techniques available to produce them? Or should we think of it more broadly, including not only the list of blueprints but also the way the economy is organised – from the internal organisation of firms, to the system of laws and the quality of their enforcement, to the political system and so on? In Chapters 12 and 13, we will have in mind the narrower definition – the set of blueprints.

> The aggregate production function is
>
> $Y = F(K, N)$
>
> Aggregate output, Y, depends on the aggregate capital stock, K, and aggregate employment, N.

> The function, F, depends on the state of technology. The higher the state of technology, the higher $F(K, N)$ for a given K and a given N.

Returns to scale and returns to factors

Now that we have introduced the aggregate production function, the next question is: what restrictions can we reasonably impose on this function?

Consider first a thought experiment in which we double both the number of workers and the amount of capital in the economy. What do you expect will happen to output? A reasonable answer is that output will double as well: in effect, we have cloned the original economy, and the clone economy can produce output in the same way as the original economy. This property is called **constant returns to scale**: if the scale of operation is doubled – that is, if the quantities of capital and labour are doubled – then output will also double:

$$2Y = F(2K, 2N)$$

or, more generally, for any number x (this will be useful later on)

$$xY = F(xK, xN) \qquad [11.2]$$

We have just looked at what happens to production when *both* capital and labour are increased. Let's now ask a different question: what should we expect to happen if *only one* of the two inputs in the economy – say capital – is increased?

Surely output will increase. That part is clear. But it is also reasonable to assume that the same increase in capital will lead to smaller and smaller increases in output as the level of capital increases. In other words, if there is little capital to start with, a little more capital will help a lot. If there is a lot of capital to start with, a little more capital may make little difference. Why? Think, for example, of a secretarial pool, composed of a given number of secretaries. Think of capital as computers. The introduction of the first computer will substantially increase the pool's production because some of the most time-consuming tasks can now be done automatically by the computer. As the number of computers increases and more secretaries in the pool get their own computers, production will further increase, although perhaps by less per additional computer than was the case when the first one was introduced. Once each and every secretary has a PC, increasing the number of computers further is unlikely to increase production very much, if at all. Additional computers might simply remain unused and left in their shipping boxes and lead to no increase in output.

We shall refer to the property that increases in capital lead to smaller and smaller increases in output as **decreasing returns to capital** (a property that will be familiar to those who have taken a course in microeconomics).

A similar argument applies to the other input, labour. Increases in labour, given capital, lead to smaller and smaller increases in output. (Return to our example and think of what happens as you increase the number of secretaries for a given number of computers.) There are **decreasing returns to labour** as well.

Output per worker and capital per worker

The production function we have written down, together with the assumption of constant returns to scale, implies that there is a simple relation between *output per worker* and *capital per worker*. To see this, set $x = 1/N$ in equation (11.2), so that

$$\frac{Y}{N} = F\left(\frac{K}{N}, \frac{N}{N}\right) = F\left(\frac{K}{N}, 1\right) \qquad [11.3]$$

Note that Y/N is output per worker and K/N is capital per worker. So equation (11.3) says that the amount of output per worker depends on the amount of capital per worker. This relation between output per worker and capital per worker will play a central role in the following text, so let's look at it more closely.

The relation is drawn in Figure 11.5. Output per worker (Y/N) is measured on the vertical axis, and capital per worker (K/N) is measured on the horizontal axis. The relation

Constant returns to scale:
$F(xK, xN) = xY$

Output here is secretarial services. The two inputs are secretaries and computers. The production function relates secretarial services to the number of secretaries and the number of computers.

Even under constant returns to scale, there are decreasing returns to each factor, keeping the other factor constant:

- There are decreasing returns to capital: given labour, increases in capital lead to smaller and smaller increases in output.
- There are decreasing returns to labour: given capital, increases in labour lead to smaller and smaller increases in output.

Make sure you understand what is behind the algebra. Suppose capital and the number of workers both double. What happens to output per worker?

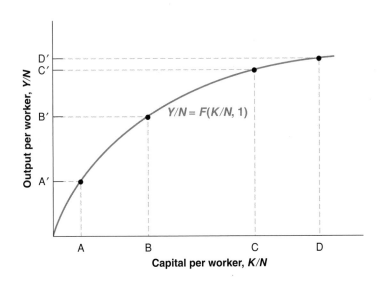

Figure 11.5

Output and capital per worker

Increases in capital per worker lead to smaller and smaller increases in output per worker.

between the two is given by the upward-sloping curve. As capital per worker increases, so does output per worker. Note that the curve is drawn so that increases in capital lead to smaller and smaller increases in output. This follows from the property that there are *decreasing returns to capital:* at point A, where capital per worker is low, an increase in capital per worker, represented by the horizontal distance, AB, leads to an increase in output per worker equal to the vertical distance A′B′. At point C, where capital per worker is larger, the same increase in capital per worker, represented by the horizontal distance, CD (where the distance CD is equal to the distance AB), leads to a much smaller increase in output per worker, only C′D′. This is just like our secretarial pool example, where additional computers had less and less impact on total output.

> Increases in capital per worker lead to smaller and smaller increases in output per worker as the level of capital per worker increases.

The sources of growth

We are now ready to return to our basic question: where does growth come from? Why does output per worker – or output per person, if we assume that the ratio of workers to the population as a whole remains constant – go up over time? Equation (11.3) gives a first answer:

> Increases in capital per worker: movements along the production function.

- Increases in output per worker (Y/N) can come from increases in capital per worker (K/N). This is the relation we just looked at in Figure 11.5. As K/N increases – that is, as we move to the right on the horizontal axis – Y/N increases.
- Increases in output per worker can also come from improvements in the state of technology that shift the production function, F, and lead to more output per worker given capital per worker. This is shown in Figure 11.6. An improvement in the state of technology shifts the production function up, from $F(K/N, 1)$ to $F(K/N, 1)′$. For a given level of capital per worker, the improvement in technology leads to an increase in output per worker. For example, for the level of capital per worker corresponding to point A, output per worker increases from A′ to B′. (To go back to our secretarial pool example, a reallocation of tasks within the pool may lead to better division of labour and an increase in the output per secretary.)

> Improvements in the state of technology shift the production function up.

Hence, we can think of growth as coming from **capital accumulation** and from **technological progress** – the improvement in the state of technology. We will see, however, that these two factors play very different roles in the growth process:

- Capital accumulation *by itself* cannot sustain growth. You can see the intuition behind this from Figure 11.6. Because of decreasing returns to capital, sustaining a steady increase in output per worker will require larger and larger increases in the level of capital per worker. At some stage, the economy will be unwilling or unable to save and invest enough to further increase capital. At that stage, output per worker will stop growing.

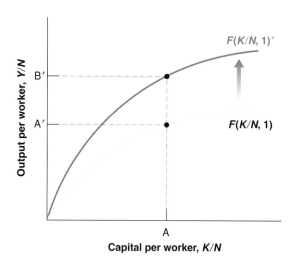

Figure 11.6

The effects of an improvement in the state of technology

An improvement in technology shifts the production function up, leading to an increase in output per worker for a given level of capital per worker.

Does this mean that an economy's **saving rate** — the proportion of income that is saved – is irrelevant? No. It is true that a higher saving rate cannot permanently increase the *growth rate* of output. But a higher saving rate can sustain a higher *level* of output. Let us state this in a slightly different way. Take two economies that differ only in their saving rates. The two economies will grow at the same rate but, at any point in time, the economy with the higher saving rate will have a higher level of output per person than the other. How this happens, how much the saving rate affects the level of output and whether a country such as the USA (which has a very low saving rate) should try to increase its saving rate are topics we take up in Chapter 12.

- Sustained growth requires sustained technological progress. This really follows from the previous proposition: given that the two factors that can lead to an increase in output are capital accumulation and technological progress, if capital accumulation cannot sustain growth forever, then technological progress must be the key to growth. And it is. We will see in Chapter 13 that the economy's rate of growth of output per person is eventually

FOCUS
Why has per capita income in Europe decreased relative to the USA?

In the past two decades income per capita in European countries has decreased relative to the USA. To understand this, we must first understand what determines per capita income. A simple decomposition will help. If a country produces Y with a population of size N, we can decompose per capita income (Y/N) as follows:

$$\frac{Y}{N} = \frac{L}{N} \times \frac{hours}{L} \times \frac{Y}{hours}$$

The first term on the right is the ratio of workers (L) to the working age population, thus labour force participation; the second term measures how many hours (per year) each worker works; and the third term measures productivity per hour: the amount of output produced per hour worked. This decomposition helps understanding why per capita income in any country can increase or decrease over time. There may be three reasons (identified by the three terms on the right side):

- because few people work;
- because those who work work few hours;
- finally, because those who work, when they do, produce little.

Which of these factors explains the low per capita income in Europe relative to the USA? As shown in Table 11.4, the factors differ from country to country. In Italy it is above all the low labour force participation, while in Germany it is mainly a matter of too few hours worked by those who work. Instead hourly productivity is sometimes higher in Europe than in the USA. For example, hourly productivity was 5% higher in Italy than in the USA in 2004.

Understanding this decomposition is clearly the first step to asking which policies are best suited to raising per capita income. For example, in Italy the priority is labour force participation: too few people work or are willing to work. And the problem is not only the participation rate of women – historically very low in Italy as in other Mediterranean countries. Participation is low even among young people, especially in the age group between 24 and 29 years. In France and in Germany, the gap in per capita income with the USA is largely explained by fewer working hours per worker. Ireland was closer to the USA in 2004 than the three largest countries in continental Europe because participation and working hours per head were both higher.

Table 11.4 Decomposition of per capita income in some European countries compared to the USA, 2004

Country (USA = 100)	Output per capita	Participation	Hours worked per capita	Hourly productivity
Italy	75	−19	−11	5
France	77	−11	−15	3
Germany	75	−5	−21	1
Ireland	89	−6	−8	3

determined by its rate of technological progress. This is very important. It means that in the long run, an economy that sustains a higher rate of technological progress will eventually overtake all other economies. This, of course, raises yet another question: what determines the rate of technological progress? Recall the two definitions of the state of technology we discussed earlier: a narrow definition, namely the set of blueprints available to the economy; and a broader definition, which captures how the economy is organised, from the nature of institutions to the role of the government. What we know about the determinants of technological progress narrowly defined – the role of fundamental and applied research, the role of patent laws, the role of education and training – will be taken up in Chapter 13.

SUMMARY

- Over long periods, fluctuations in output are dwarfed by growth – the steady increase of aggregate output over time.

- When looking at growth in six rich countries (France, Ireland, Japan, Sweden, the UK and the USA) since 1950, two main facts emerge:
  1. All six countries have experienced strong growth and a large increase in the standard of living. Growth from 1950–2004 increased real output per person by a factor of 3.2 in Sweden and in the USA up to a factor of 11.3 in Japan.
  2. The levels of output per person across the six countries have converged over time. Put another way, countries that were behind have grown faster, reducing the gap between them and the current leader, the USA.

- When looking at the evidence across a broader set of countries and a longer period, the following facts emerge:
  1. On the scale of human history, sustained output growth is a recent phenomenon.
  2. The convergence of levels of output per person is not a worldwide phenomenon. Many Asian countries are

rapidly catching up, but most African countries have both very low levels of output per person and low growth rates.

- To think about growth, economists start from an aggregate production function, relating aggregate output to two factors of production: capital and labour. How much output is produced, given these inputs, depends on the state of technology.

- Under the assumption of constant returns, the aggregate production function implies that increases in output per worker can come either from increases in capital per worker or from improvements in the state of technology.

- Capital accumulation by itself cannot permanently sustain growth of output per person. Nevertheless, how much a country saves is very important because the saving rate determines the *level* of output per person, if not its growth rate.

- Sustained growth of output per person is ultimately due to technological progress. Perhaps the most important question in growth theory is what determines technological progress.

KEY TERMS

QUESTIONS AND PROBLEMS

QUICK CHECK

1. *Using the information in this chapter, label each of the following statements true, false or uncertain. Explain briefly.*

a. On a logarithmic scale, a variable that increases at 5% per year will move along an upward-sloping line with a slope of 0.05.

b. The price of food is higher in poor countries than it is in rich countries.

c. Evidence suggests that happiness in rich countries increases with output per person.

d. In virtually all the countries of the world, output per person is converging to the level of output per person in the USA.

e. For about 1000 years after the fall of the Roman Empire, there was essentially no growth in output per person in Europe, because any increase in output led to a proportional increase in population.

f. Capital accumulation does not affect the level of output in the long run; only technological progress does.

g. The aggregate production function is a relation between output on one hand and labour and capital on the other.

2. *Assume that the average consumer in Mexico and the average consumer in the UK buy the quantities and pay the prices indicated in the following table:*

	Food		Transportation services	
	Price	Quantity	Price	Quantity
Mexico	5 pesos	400	20 pesos	2000
UK	£1	1000	£2	

a. Compute UK consumption per capita in pounds.

b. Compute Mexican consumption per capita in pounds.

c. Suppose that £1 is worth 10 pesos. Compute Mexico's consumption per capita in pounds.

d. Using the purchasing power parity method and UK prices, compute Mexican consumption per capita in pounds.

e. Under each method, how much lower is the standard of living in Mexico than in the UK? Does the choice of method make a difference?

3. *Consider the production function* $Y = \sqrt{K}\sqrt{N}$.

a. Compute output when $K = 49$ and $N = 81$.

b. If both capital and labour double, what happens to output?

c. Is this production function characterised by constant returns to scale? Explain.

d. Write this production function as a relation between output per worker and capital per worker.

e. Let $K/N = 4$. What is Y/N? Now double K/N to 8. Does Y/N double as a result?

f. Does the relation between output per worker and capital per worker exhibit constant returns to scale?

g. Is your answer in (f) the same as your answer in (c)? Why or why not?

h. Plot the relation between output per worker and capital per worker. Does it have the same general shape as the relation in Figure 11.5? Explain.

DIG DEEPER

4. *The growth rates of capital and output*

Consider the production function given in problem 3. Assume that N is constant and equal to 1. Note that if $z = x^a$, *then* $g_z \approx a g_x$ *where* g_z *and* g_x *are the growth rates of z and x.*

a. Given the growth approximation here, derive the relation between the growth rate of output and the growth rate of capital.

b. Suppose we want to achieve output growth equal to 2% per year. What is the required rate of growth of capital?

c. In (b), what happens to the ratio of capital to output over time?

d. Is it possible to sustain output growth of 2% forever in this economy? Why or why not?

5. *Between 1950 and 1973, France, Germany and Japan all experienced growth rates that were at least 2 percentage points higher than those in the USA. Yet the most important technological advances of that period were made in the USA. How can this be?*

EXPLORE FURTHER

6. *Convergence between Japan and the USA since 1950*

Go to the website containing the Penn World Table (***pwt.econ.upenn.edu***) *and collect data on the annual growth rate of GDP per person for the USA and Japan from 1951 to the most recent year available. In addition, collect the numbers for real GDP per person (chained series) for the USA and Japan in 1973.*

a. Compute the average annual growth rates of GDP per person for the USA and Japan for three time periods: 1951–1973, 1974 to the most recent year available and 1991 to the most recent year available. Did the level of real output per person in Japan tend to converge to the level of real output per person in the USA in each of these three periods? Explain.

b. Suppose that in every year since 1973, Japan and the USA had each achieved their average annual growth rates for the period 1951–1973. How would real GDP per person compare in Japan and the USA today (i.e. in the most recent year available in the Penn World Table)?

7. *Convergence in two sets of countries*

*Go to the website containing the Penn World Table (**pwt.econ.upenn.edu**) and collect data on real GDP per person (chained series) from 1951 to the most recent year available for the USA, France, Belgium, Italy, Argentina, Venezuela, Chad and Madagascar.*

a. Define for each country for each year the ratio of its real GDP to that of the USA for that year (so that this ratio will be equal to 1 for the USA for all years).

b. In one graph, plot the ratios for France, Belgium and Italy over the period for which you have data. Does your graph support the notion of convergence among France, Belgium, Italy and the USA?

c. Draw a graph with the ratios for Argentina, Venezuela, Chad and Madagascar. Does your new graph support the notion of convergence among Argentina, Venezuela, Chad, Madagascar and the USA?

8. *Growth successes and failures*

*Go to the website containing the Penn World Table (**pwt.econ.upenn.edu**) and collect data on real GDP per capita (chained series) for 1970 for all available countries. Do the same for a recent year of data, say one year before the most recent year available in the Penn World Table. (If you choose the most recent year available, the Penn World Table may not have the data for some countries relevant to this question.)*

a. Rank the countries according to GDP per person in 1970. List the countries with the ten highest levels of GDP per person in 1970. Are there any surprises?

b. Carry out the analysis in part (a) for the most recent year for which you collected data. Has the composition of the ten richest countries changed since 1970?

c. For each of the ten countries you listed in part (b), divide the recent level of GDP per capita by the level in 1970. Which of these countries has had the greatest proportional increase in GDP per capita since 1970?

d. Carry out the exercise in part (c) for all the countries for which you have data. Which country has had the highest proportional increase in GDP per capita since 1970? Which country had the smallest proportional increase? What fraction of countries have had negative growth since 1970?

e. Do a brief Internet search on either the country from part (c) with the greatest increase in GDP per capita or the country from part (d) with the smallest increase. Can you ascertain any reasons for the economic success, or lack of it, for this country?

We invite you to visit the Blanchard page on the Prentice Hall website, at **www.prenhall.com/blanchard** for this chapter's World Wide Web exercises.

FURTHER READING

- Brad deLong has a number of fascinating articles on growth on his web page (*http://econ161.berkeley.edu/*). Read, in particular, 'Berkeley Faculty Lunch Talk: Themes of 20th Century Economic History', which covers many of the themes of this chapter.

- A broad presentation of facts about growth is given by Angus Maddison in *The World Economy. A Millenium Perspective*, OECD, Paris, 2001. The associated site **www.theworldeconomy.org** has a large number of facts and data on growth over the past two millennia.

- Chapter 3 in *Productivity and American Leadership* by William Baumol, Sue Anne Batey Blackman and Edward Wolff (MIT Press, Cambridge, MA, 1989) gives a vivid description of how life has been transformed by growth in the USA since the mid-1880s.

- To understand why per capita income is lower in Europe compared with the USA you can read *The Future of Europe: Reform or Decline* by Alberto Alessia and Francesco Giavazzi (MIT Press, Cambridge, MA, 2006).

Chapter 12

SAVING, CAPITAL ACCUMULATION AND OUTPUT

Since 1950, OECD countries have had very different **saving rates** – the ratio of saving to GDP – from one another. Some countries have traditionally high saving rates, such as Japan (30%), Germany (24%) and Italy (30%), some others have much lower savings rate, most notably the USA (17%). Can this explain why growth rates have been different across OECD countries? Can this also explain why growth rates in the USA have been lower than the rates in most other OECD countries in the past 50 years?

We already gave the basic answer to these questions at the end of Chapter 11: the answer is no. Over long periods – an important qualification to which we will return – an economy's growth rate does not depend on its saving rate. However, even if the saving rate does not permanently affect the growth rate, it does affect the level of output and the standard of living.

This chapter focuses on the effects of the saving rate on the level and the growth rate of output:

- Sections 12.1 and 12.2 look at the interactions between output and capital accumulation, and the effects of the saving rate.

- Section 12.3 plugs in numbers to give a better sense of the magnitudes involved.

- Section 12.4 extends the discussion to take into account not only physical, but also human capital.

12.1 INTERACTIONS BETWEEN OUTPUT AND CAPITAL

At the centre of the determination of output in the long run are two relations between output and capital:

- The amount of capital determines the amount of output being produced.
- The amount of output determines the amount of saving and, in turn, the amount of capital accumulated over time.

Together, these two relations, which are represented in Figure 12.1, determine the evolution of output and capital over time. The green arrow captures the first relation, from capital to output. The blue and purple arrows capture the two parts of the second relation, from output to saving and investment, and from investment to the change in the capital stock. Let's look at each relation in turn.

The effects of capital on output

We started discussing the first of these two relations, the effect of capital on output, in Section 11.3. There we introduced the aggregate production function and you saw that, under the assumption of constant returns to scale, we can write the following relation between output and capital per worker:

$$\frac{Y}{N} = F\left(\frac{K}{N}, 1\right)$$

Output per worker, Y/N, is an increasing function of capital per worker, K/N. Under the assumption of decreasing returns to capital, the effect of a given increase in capital per worker on output per worker decreases as the ratio of capital per worker gets larger. When capital per worker is already very high, further increases in capital per worker have only a small effect on output per worker.

To simplify notation, we will rewrite this relation between output and capital per worker simply as

$$\frac{Y}{N} = f\left(\frac{K}{N}\right)$$

where the function f represents the same relation between output and capital per worker as the function F:

$$f\left(\frac{K}{N}\right) \equiv F\left(\frac{K}{N}, 1\right)$$

In this chapter, we make two further assumptions:

- The first assumption is that the size of the population, the participation rate and the unemployment rate are all constant. This implies that employment, N, is also constant. To see why, go back to the relations we saw in Chapter 2 and again in Chapter 7 between population, the labour force, unemployment and employment:

Suppose, for example, that the function F has the 'double square root' form:

$$F(K, N) = \sqrt{K}\sqrt{N}$$
$$\text{so } Y = \sqrt{K}\sqrt{N}.$$

Divide both sides by N, so

$$\frac{Y}{N} = \frac{\sqrt{K}\sqrt{N}}{\sqrt{N}} \longleftarrow N$$

Note that:

$$N \longrightarrow \frac{\sqrt{N}}{\sqrt{N}} = \frac{\sqrt{N}}{\sqrt{N}\sqrt{N}} = \frac{1}{\sqrt{N}}.$$

Replacing in the preceding equation:

$$\frac{Y}{N} = \frac{\sqrt{K}}{\sqrt{N}} = \sqrt{\frac{K}{N}}$$

So, in this case, the function f giving the relation between output per worker and capital per worker is simply the square root function:

$$f\left(\frac{K}{N}\right) = \sqrt{\frac{K}{N}}$$

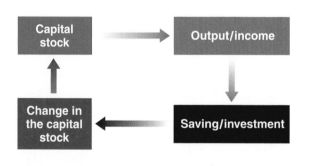

Figure 12.1

Capital, output and saving/investment

The labour force is equal to population times the participation rate. So if population is constant and the participation rate is constant, the labour force is also constant.

Employment, in turn, is equal to the labour force times 1 minus the unemployment rate. If, for example, the size of the labour force is 100 million and the unemployment rate is 5%, then employment is equal to 95 million [100 million times (1 – 0.05)]. So, if the labour force is constant and the unemployment rate is constant, employment is also constant.

Under these assumptions, output per worker, output per person and output itself all move proportionately. Although we usually refer to movements in output or capital *per worker*, to lighten the text, we shall sometimes just talk about movements in output or capital, leaving out the 'per worker' or 'per person' qualification.

The reason for assuming that N is constant is to make it easier to focus on how capital accumulation affects growth: if N is constant, the only factor of production that changes over time is capital. The assumption is not very realistic, however, so we will relax it in Chapter 13, where we will allow for steady population and employment growth.

● The second assumption is that there is no technological progress, so the production function f (or, equivalently, F) does not change over time. Again, the reason for making this assumption – which is obviously contrary to reality – is to focus just on the role of capital accumulation. In Chapter 13, we will introduce technological progress and see that the basic conclusions we derive here about the role of capital in growth also hold when there is technological progress. This step is better left to later.

With these two assumptions, our first relation between output and capital per worker, from the production side, can be written as

$$\frac{Y_t}{N} = f\left(\frac{K_t}{N}\right)$$ [12.1]

where we have introduced time indexes for output and capital – but not for labour, N, which we assume to be constant and so does not need a time index.

In words: higher capital per worker leads to higher output per worker.

◄ From the production side: the level of capital per worker determines the level of output per worker.

The effects of output on capital accumulation

To derive the second relation, between output and capital accumulation, we proceed in two steps:

1. We derive the relation between output and investment.
2. We derive the relation between investment and capital accumulation.

Output and investment

To derive the relation between output and investment, we make three assumptions:

● We continue to assume that the economy is closed. As we saw in Chapter 3 [equation (3.10)], this means that investment, I, is equal to saving – the sum of private saving, S, and public saving, T – G:

$$I - S + (T - G)$$

◄ As we have seen in Chapter 16, saving and investment need not be equal in an open economy. A country can save less than it invests and borrow the difference from the rest of the world. This is the case for the USA today, unlike most European countries.

● To focus on the behaviour of private saving, we assume that public saving, T – G, is equal to zero. (We will relax this assumption later, when we focus on the effects of fiscal policy on growth.) With this assumption, the previous equation becomes

$$I = S$$

Investment is equal to private saving.

- We assume that private saving is proportional to income, so

$$S = sY$$

You have now seen two specifications of saving behaviour (equivalently consumption behaviour): one for the short run in Chapter 3, and one for the long run in this chapter. You may wonder how the two specifications relate to each other and whether they are consistent. The answer is yes. A full discussion is given in Chapter 16.

The parameter s is the saving rate. It has a value between 0 and 1. This assumption captures two basic facts about saving. First, the saving rate does not appear to systematically increase or decrease as a country becomes richer. Second, richer countries do not appear to have systematically higher or lower saving rates than poorer ones.

Combining these two relations, and introducing time indexes, gives a simple relation between investment and output:

$$I_t = sY_t$$

Investment is proportional to output: higher output implies higher saving and, thus, higher investment.

Investment and capital accumulation

Recall: flows are variables that have a time dimension (that is, they are defined per unit of time); stocks are variables that do not have a time dimension (they are defined at a point in time). Output, saving and investment are flows. Employment and capital are stocks.

The second step relates investment, which is a flow (the new machines produced and new plants built during a given period), to capital, which is a stock (the existing machines and plants in the economy at a point in time).

Think of time as measured in years, so t denotes year t, $t + 1$ denotes year $t + 1$, and so on. Think of the capital stock as being measured at the beginning of each year, so K_t refers to the capital stock at the beginning of year t, K_{t+1} to the capital stock at the beginning of year $t + 1$ and so on.

Assume that capital depreciates at rate δ (the lowercase Greek letter delta) per year: that is, from one year to the next, a proportion, δ, of the capital stock breaks down and becomes useless. Equivalently, a proportion $(1 - \delta)$ of the capital stock remains intact from one year to the next.

The evolution of the capital stock is then given by

$$K_{t+1} = (1 - \delta)K_t + I_t$$

The capital stock at the beginning of year $t + 1$, K_{t+1} is equal to the capital stock at the beginning of year t which is still intact in year $t + 1$, $(1 - \delta)K_t$, plus the new capital stock put in place during year t (that is, investment during year t, I_t).

We can now combine the relation between output and investment and the relation between investment and capital accumulation to obtain the second relation we need in order to think about growth: the relation from output to capital accumulation.

Replacing investment by its expression previously and dividing both sides by N (the number of workers in the economy) gives

$$\frac{K_{t+1}}{N} = (1 - \delta)\frac{K_t}{N} + s\frac{Y_t}{N}$$

In words: capital per worker at the beginning of year $t + 1$ is equal to capital per worker at the beginning of year t, adjusted for depreciation, plus investment per worker during year t, which is equal to the saving rate times output per worker during year t.

Expanding the term $(1 - \delta)K_t/N$ to $K_t/N - \delta K_t/N$, moving K_t/N to the left and reorganising the right side, we have

$$\frac{K_{t+1}}{N} - \frac{K_t}{N} = s\frac{Y_t}{N} - \delta\frac{K_t}{N} \qquad [12.2]$$

From the saving side: the level of output per worker determines the change in the level of capital per worker over time.

In words: the change in the capital stock per worker (represented by the difference between the two terms on the left) is equal to saving per worker (represented by the first term on the right) minus depreciation (represented by the second term on the right). This equation gives us the second relation between output and capital per worker.

12.2 THE IMPLICATIONS OF ALTERNATIVE SAVING RATES

We have derived two relations:

- From the production side, we have seen in equation (12.1) how capital determines output.
- From the saving side, we have seen in equation (12.2) how output in turn determines capital accumulation.

We can now put the two relations together and see how they determine the behaviour of output and capital over time.

Dynamics of capital and output

Replacing output per worker, Y_t/N, in equation (12.2) by its expression in terms of capital per worker from equation (12.1) gives

$$\frac{K_{t+1}}{N} - \frac{K_t}{N} = sf\left(\frac{K_t}{N}\right) - \delta\frac{K_t}{N} \qquad [12.3]$$

$$\underbrace{\text{Change in capital}}_{\text{from year } t \text{ to year } t+1} = \underbrace{\text{Investment}}_{\text{during year } t} - \underbrace{\text{Depreciation}}_{\text{during year } t}$$

This relation describes what happens to capital per worker. The change in capital per worker from this year to next year depends on the difference between two terms:

- Investment per worker, the first term on the right – The level of capital per worker this year determines output per worker this year. Given the saving rate, output per worker determines the amount of saving per worker and thus the investment per worker this year. ◄ $K_t/N \Rightarrow f(K_t/N) \Rightarrow sf(K_t/N)$
- Depreciation per worker, the second term on the right – The capital stock per worker determines the amount of depreciation per worker this year. ◄ $K_t/N \Rightarrow \delta K_t/N$

If investment per worker exceeds depreciation per worker, the change in capital per worker is positive: capital per worker increases.

If investment per worker is less than depreciation per worker, the change in capital per worker is negative: capital per worker decreases.

Given capital per worker, output per worker is then given by equation (12.1):

$$\frac{Y_t}{N} = f\left(\frac{K_t}{N}\right)$$

Equations (12.3) and (12.1) contain all the information we need to understand the dynamics of capital and output over time. The easiest way to interpret them is to use a graph. We do this in Figure 12.2, where output per worker is measured on the vertical axis, and capital per worker is measured on the horizontal axis.

In Figure 12.2, look first at the curve representing output per worker, $f(K_t/N)$, as a function of capital per worker. The relation is the same as in Figure 11.5: output per worker increases with capital per worker, but – because of decreasing returns to capital – the effect is smaller the higher the level of capital per worker.

Now look at the two curves representing the two components on the right of equation (12.3):

- The relation representing investment per worker, $sf(K_t/N)$, has the same shape as the production function except that it is lower by the factor s (the saving rate). Suppose the level of capital per worker is equal to K_0/N in Figure 12.2. Output per worker is then given by the vertical distance AB, and investment per worker is given by the vertical ◄ To make the graph easier to read, we have assumed an unrealistically high saving rate. (Can you tell roughly what value we have assumed for s? What would be a plausible value for s?)

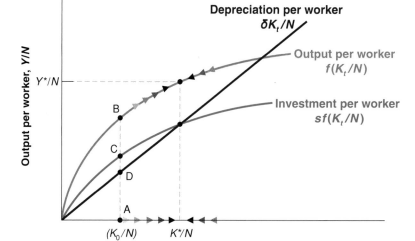

Figure 12.2

Capital and output dynamics

When capital and output are low, investment exceeds depreciation and capital increases. When capital and output are high, investment is less than depreciation and capital decreases.

distance AC, which is equal to s times the vertical distance AB. Thus, just like output per worker, investment per worker increases with capital per worker, but by less and less as capital per worker increases. When capital per worker is already very high, the effect of a further increase in capital per worker on output per worker and, by implication, on investment per worker, is very small.

● The relation representing depreciation per worker, $\delta K_t/N$, is a straight line. Depreciation per worker increases in proportion to capital per worker, so the relation is represented by a straight line with slope equal to δ. At the level of capital per worker K_0/N, depreciation per worker is given by the vertical distance AD.

The change in capital per worker is given by the difference between investment per worker and depreciation per worker. At K_0/N, the difference is positive; investment per worker exceeds depreciation per worker by an amount represented by the vertical distance CD $=$ AC $-$ AD, so capital per worker increases. As we move to the right along the horizontal axis and look at higher and higher levels of capital per worker, investment increases by less and less, while depreciation keeps increasing in proportion to capital. For some level of capital per worker, K^*/N, in Figure 12.2, investment is just enough to cover depreciation, and capital per worker remains constant. To the left of K^*/N, investment exceeds depreciation, and capital per worker increases. This is indicated by the arrows pointing to the right along the curve representing the production function. To the right of K^*/N, depreciation exceeds investment, and capital per worker decreases. This is indicated by the arrows pointing to the left along the curve representing the production function.

> When capital per worker is low, capital per worker and output per worker increase over time. When capital per worker is high, capital per worker and output per worker decrease over time.

Characterising the evolution of capital per worker and output per worker over time is now easy. Consider an economy that starts with a low level of capital per worker – say, K_0/N in Figure 12.2. Because investment exceeds depreciation at this point, capital per worker increases. And because output moves with capital, output per worker increases as well. Capital per worker eventually reaches K^*/N, the level at which investment is equal to depreciation. Once the economy has reached the level of capital per worker K^*/N, output per worker and capital per worker remain constant at Y^*/N and K^*/N, their long-run equilibrium levels.

Think, for example, of a country that loses part of its capital stock, say as a result of bombing during a war. The mechanism we have just seen suggests that, if the country has suffered larger capital losses than population losses, it will come out of the war with a low level of capital per worker – that is, at a point to the left of K^*/N. The country will then experience a large increase in both capital per worker and output per worker for some

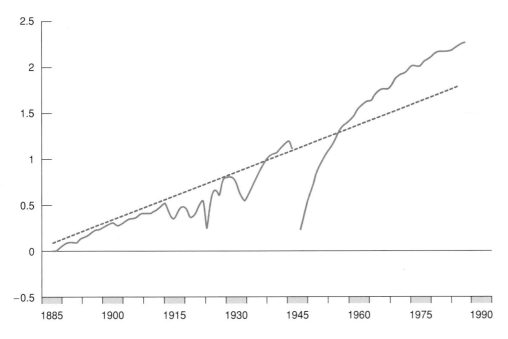

Figure 12.3

German log real GDP, 1885–1990

time. This describes well what happened after the Second World War to countries that had proportionately larger destructions of capital than losses of human lives. Figure 12.3 shows that Germany experienced an extraordinary fast growth of output after 1945 (see also the Focus box 'Capital accumulation and growth in France in the aftermath of the Second World War').

◄ What does the model predict for post-war growth if a country suffers proportional losses in population and in capital? Do you find this answer convincing? What elements may be missing from the model?

If a country starts instead from a high level of capital per worker – that is, from a point to the right of K^*/N – then depreciation will exceed investment, and capital per worker and output per worker will decrease: the initial level of capital per worker is too high to be sustained, given the saving rate. This decrease in capital per worker will continue until the economy again reaches the point where investment is equal to depreciation and capital per worker is equal to K^*/N. From then on, capital per worker and output per worker will remain constant.

Steady-state capital and output

Let's look more closely at the levels of output per worker and capital per worker to which the economy converges in the long run. The state in which output per worker and capital per worker are no longer changing is called the **steady state** of the economy. Setting the left side of equation (12.3) equal to zero (in steady state, by definition, the change in capital per worker is 0), the steady-state value of capital per worker, K^*/N, is given by

$$sf\left(\frac{K^*}{N}\right) = \delta\frac{K^*}{N}$$ [12.4]

◄ K^*/N is the long-run level of capital per worker.

The steady-state value of capital per worker is such that the amount of saving per worker (the left side) is just sufficient to cover depreciation of the capital stock per worker (the right side).

Given steady-state capital per worker, K^*/N, the steady-state value of output per worker, Y^*/N, is given by the production function

$$\frac{Y^*}{N} = f\left(\frac{K^*}{N}\right)$$ [12.5]

We now have all the elements we need to discuss the effects of the saving rate on output per worker, both over time and in steady state.

FOCUS
Capital accumulation and growth in France in the aftermath of the Second World War

When the Second World War ended in 1945, France had suffered some of the heaviest losses of all European countries. The losses in lives were large. More than 550 000 people had died, out of a population of 42 million. Relatively speaking, though, the losses in capital were much larger: it is estimated that the French capital stock in 1945 was about 30% below its pre-war value. A vivid picture of the destruction of capital is provided by the numbers in Table 12.1.

The model of growth we have just seen makes a clear prediction about what will happen to a country that loses a large part of its capital stock: the country will experience high capital accumulation and output growth for some time. In terms of Figure 12.2, a country with capital per worker initially far below K^*/N will grow rapidly as it converges to K^*/N and output per worker converges to Y^*/N.

This prediction fares well in the case of post-war France. There is plenty of anecdotal evidence that small increases in capital led to large increases in output. Minor repairs to a major bridge would lead to the reopening of the bridge. Reopening of the bridge would significantly shorten the travel time between two cities, leading to much lower transport costs. The lower transport costs would then enable a plant to get much-needed inputs, increase its production, and so on.

More convincing evidence, however, comes directly from actual aggregate output numbers. From 1946–1950, the annual growth rate of French real GDP was a very high 9.6% per year. This led to an increase in real GDP of about 60% over the course of five years.

Was all the increase in French GDP due to capital accumulation? The answer is no. There were other forces at work in addition to the mechanism in our model. Much of the remaining capital stock in 1945 was old. Investment had been low in the 1930s (a decade dominated by the Great Depression) and nearly non-existent during the war. A good portion of the post-war capital accumulation was associated with the introduction of more modern capital and the use of more modern production techniques. This was another reason for the high growth rates of the post-war period.

Table 12.1 Proportion of the French capital stock destroyed by the end of the Second World War

Railways	Tracks	6%
	Stations	38%
	Engines	21%
	Hardware	60%
Roads	Cars	31%
	Trucks	40%
Rivers	Waterways	86%
	Canal locks	11%
	Barges	80%
Buildings	(numbers)	
	Dwellings	1 229 000
	Industrial	246

Source: See source note opposite.

Source: Gilles Saint-Paul, 'Economic Reconstruction in France, 1945–1958', in Rudiger Dornbusch, Willem Nolling and Richard Layard, eds, Postwar Economic Reconstruction and Lessons for the East Today, MIT Press, Cambridge, MA, 1993.

The saving rate and output

Let's return to the question asked at the beginning of the chapter: how does the saving rate affect the growth rate of output per worker? Our analysis leads to a three-part answer:

1. *The saving rate has no effect on the long-run growth rate of output per worker, which is equal to zero.* This conclusion is rather obvious: we have seen that, eventually, the economy converges to a constant level of output per worker. In other words, in the long run, the growth rate of output is equal to zero, no matter what the saving rate.

   There is, however, a way of thinking about this conclusion that will be useful when we introduce technological progress in Chapter 13. Think of what would be needed to sustain a constant positive growth rate of output per worker in the long run. Capital per worker would have to increase. Not only that, but, because of decreasing returns to capital, it would have to increase faster than output per worker. This implies that each year, the economy would have to save a larger and larger fraction of its output and

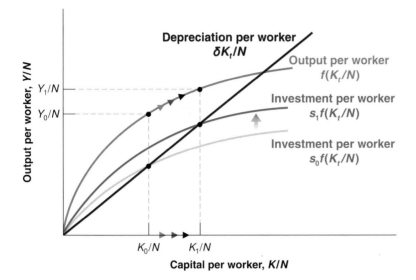

Figure 12.4

The effects of different saving rates

A country with a higher saving rate achieves a higher steady-state level of output per worker.

dedicate it to capital accumulation. At some point, the fraction of output it would need to save would be greater than one – which is clearly impossible. This is why it is impossible to sustain a constant positive growth rate forever. In the long run, capital per worker must be constant, and so output per worker must be constant, too.

2. Nonetheless, *the saving rate determines the level of output per worker in the long run*. Other things equal, countries with a higher saving rate will achieve higher output per worker in the long run.

   Figure 12.4 illustrates this point. Consider two countries with the same production function, the same level of employment and the same depreciation rate, but different saving rates, say s_0 and $s_1 > s_0$. Figure 12.4 draws their common production function, $f(K_t/N)$, and the functions showing saving/investment per worker as a function of capital per worker for each of the two countries, $s_0 f(K_t/N)$ and $s_1 f(K_t/N)$. In the long run, the country with saving rate s_0 will reach the level of capital per worker K_0/N and output per worker Y_0/N. The country with saving rate s_1 will reach the higher levels K_1/N and Y_1/N.

3. *An increase in the saving rate will lead to higher growth of output per worker for some time, but not forever.* This conclusion follows from the two propositions we just discussed. From the first, we know that an increase in the saving rate does not affect the long-run *growth rate of output per worker*, which remains equal to zero. From the second, we know that an increase in the saving rate leads to an increase in the long-run *level of output per worker*. It follows that, as output per worker increases to its new higher level in response to the increase in the saving rate, the economy will go through a period of positive growth. This period of growth will come to an end when the economy reaches its new steady state.

   We can use Figure 12.4 again to illustrate this point. Consider a country that has an initial saving rate of s_0. Assume that capital per worker is initially equal to K_0/N, with associated output per worker Y_0/N. Now consider the effects of an increase in the saving rate from s_0 to s_1. The function giving saving/investment per worker as a function of capital per worker shifts upward from $s_0 f(K_t/N)$ to $s_1 f(K_t/N)$.

   At the initial level of capital per worker, K_0/N, investment exceeds depreciation, so capital per worker increases. As capital per worker increases, so does output per worker, and the economy goes through a period of positive growth. When capital per worker eventually reaches K_1/N, however, investment is again equal to depreciation and growth ends. From then on, the economy remains at K_1/N, with associated output per worker Y_1/N. The movement of output per worker is plotted against time in Figure 12.5. Output per worker is initially constant at level Y_0/N. After the increase in the saving rate, say, at time t, output per worker increases for some time until it reaches the higher level of output per worker, Y_1/N, and the growth rate returns to zero.

◄ Some economists argue that the high output growth achieved by the Soviet Union from 1950–1990 was the result of such a steady increase in the saving rate over time, which could not be sustained forever. Paul Krugman has used the term *Stalinist growth* to denote this type of growth – growth resulting from a higher and higher saving rate over time.

◄ Note that the first proposition is a statement about the growth rate of output per worker. The second proposition is a statement about the level of output per worker.

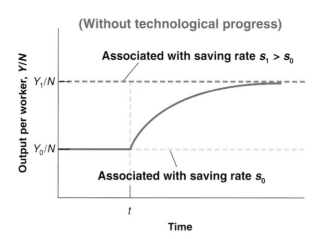

Figure 12.5

The effects of an increase in the saving rate on output per worker

An increase in the saving rate leads to a period of higher growth until output reaches its new, higher steady-state level.

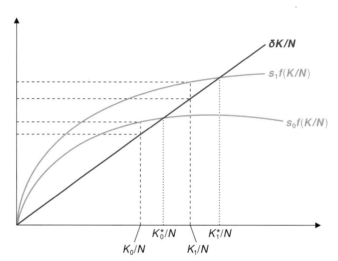

Figure 12.6

Different saving rates and income convergence

A country that is closer to its steady-state level of capital per worker will grow less fast than a country that is more distant to its state level of capital per worker.

Figure 12.4 can also help us to illustrate a further useful point. Consider two economies out of steady state with different saving rates. Country A has a saving rate s_0 and country B has a saving rate s_1, with $s_0 < s_1$. The function giving saving/investment per worker as a function of capital per worker is $s_0 f(K_t/N)$ for country A and $s_1 f(K_t/N)$ for country B. Depreciation per worker is the same in the two countries and is represented by the straight line $\delta K_t/N$. The steady state level of capital per worker in country A is equal to K_0^*/N and in country B is equal to K_1^*/N. Country A is less rich than country B, i.e. has a lower level of capital per worker, $K_0/N < K_1/N$. In Figure 12.6 we replicate Figure 12.4 for these two countries. Note that the distance between each of the two functions giving saving/investment per worker as a function of capital per worker and the depreciation per worker measures the growth rate of capital per worker, $(K_{t-1} - K_t)/K_t$. Country A, although less rich than country B, grows less fast because it is closer to its steady state. This is one reason why we often fail to see convergence in income levels between poor and rich countries: poor countries might grow less than rich countries, if they are closer than the former to their steady-state level of capital per worker.

The saving rate and consumption

Recall that saving is the sum of private plus public saving.

Recall also:

• Public saving ⇔ Budget surplus.
• Public dissaving ⇔ Budget deficit.

Governments can affect the saving rate in various ways. First, they can vary public saving. Given private saving, positive public saving – a budget surplus, in other words – leads to higher overall saving. Conversely, negative public saving – a budget deficit – leads to lower overall saving. Second, governments can use taxes to affect private saving. For example, they can give tax breaks to people who save, making it more attractive to save, thus increasing private saving.

What saving rate should governments aim for? To think about the answer, we must shift our focus from the behaviour of *output* to the behaviour of *consumption*. The reason: what matters to people is not how much is produced but how much they consume.

It is clear that an increase in saving must come initially at the expense of lower con- ◀ sumption (except when we think it helpful, we drop *per worker* in this subsection and just refer to consumption rather than consumption per worker, capital rather than capital per worker and so on): a change in the saving rate this year has no effect on capital this year and, consequently, no effect on output and income *this year*. So an increase in saving comes initially with an equal decrease in consumption.

Because we assume that employment is constant, we are ignoring the short-run effect of an increase in the saving rate on output we focused on in Chapter 3. In the short run, not only does an increase in the saving rate reduce consumption given income, but it may also create a recession and decrease income further. We will return to a discussion of short-run and long-run effects of changes in saving at various points in the book. See, for example, Chapter 17.

Does an increase in saving lead to an increase in consumption in the long run? Not necessarily. Consumption may decrease not only initially but also in the long run. You may find this surprising. After all, we know from Figure 12.4 that an increase in the saving rate always leads to an increase in the level of *output* per worker, but output is not the same as consumption. To see why, consider what happens for two extreme values of the saving rate:

- An economy in which the saving rate is (and has always been) zero is an economy in which capital is equal to zero. In this case, output is also equal to zero, and so is consumption. A saving rate equal to zero implies zero consumption in the long run.

- Now consider an economy in which the saving rate is equal to one: people save all their income. The level of capital, and thus output, in this economy will be very high but, because people save all their income, consumption is equal to zero. What happens is that the economy is carrying an excessive amount of capital: simply maintaining that level of output requires that all output be devoted to replacing depreciation! A saving rate equal to one also implies zero consumption in the long run.

These two extreme cases mean that there must be some value of the saving rate between zero and one that maximises the steady-state level of consumption. Increases in the saving rate below this value lead to a decrease in consumption initially but to an increase in consumption in the long run. Increases in the saving rate beyond this value decrease consumption not only initially but also in the long run. This happens because the increase in capital associated with the increase in the saving rate leads to only a small increase in output – an increase that is too small to cover the increased depreciation: in other words, the economy carries too much capital. The level of capital associated with the value of the saving rate that yields the highest level of consumption in steady state is known as the **golden-rule level of capital**. Increases in capital beyond the golden-rule level reduce consumption.

This argument is illustrated in Figure 12.7, which plots consumption per worker in steady state (on the vertical axis) against the saving rate (on the horizontal axis). A saving rate equal to zero implies a capital stock per worker equal to zero; a level of output per

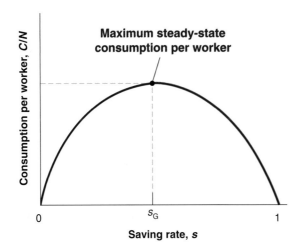

Figure 12.7

The effects of the saving rate on steady-state consumption per worker

An increase in the saving rate leads to an increase and then to a decrease in steady-state consumption per worker.

worker equal to zero and, by implication, a level of consumption per worker equal to zero. For s between zero and s_G (G for golden rule), a higher saving rate leads to higher capital per worker higher output per worker and higher consumption per worker. For s larger than s_G, increases in the saving rate still lead to higher values of capital per worker and output per worker; but they now lead to lower values of consumption per worker. This is because the increase in output is more than offset by the increase in depreciation due to the larger capital stock. For $s = 1$, consumption per worker is equal to zero. Capital per worker and output per worker are high, but all the output is used just to replace depreciation, leaving nothing for consumption.

If an economy already has so much capital that it is operating beyond the golden rule, then increasing saving further will decrease consumption not only now but also later. Is this a relevant worry? Do some countries actually have too much capital? The empirical

FOCUS
Social security, saving and capital accumulation in Europe

Old age pension programmes were introduced across Europe between the end of the 19th and the beginning of the 20th century. The goal of these programmes was to make sure the elderly would have enough to live on. Over time, social security has become the largest government programme in almost every country, amounting to 44% of total expenditure on social protection in the EU (ranging from 25% in Ireland to 58% in Italy), with benefits paid to retirees exceeding 11% of GDP. For the majority of retirees, pension benefits account for most of their income. There is little question that, on their own terms, social security systems have been a great success, decreasing poverty among the elderly. There is also little question that they have led in many countries to a lower saving rate and therefore lower capital accumulation and lower output per person in the long run.

To understand why, we must take a theoretical detour. Think of an economy in which there is no social security system – one where workers have to save to provide for their own retirement. Now, introduce a pension system that collects taxes from workers and distributes benefits to the retirees. It can do so in one of two ways:

● One way is by taxing workers, investing their contributions in financial assets and paying back the principal plus the interest to the workers when they retire. Such a system is called a **fully funded system**: at any time, the system has funds equal to the accumulated contributions of workers, from which it will be able to pay out benefits to these workers when they retire.

● The other way is by taxing workers and redistributing the tax contributions as benefits to the current retirees. Such a system is called a **pay-as-you-go system**: the

system pays benefits out 'as it goes', that is, as it collects them through contributions.

From the point of view of workers, the two systems are broadly similar. In both cases, the workers pay contributions when they work and receive benefits when they retire. What they receive, however, is slightly different in each case:

● What retirees receive in a fully funded system depends on the rate of return on the financial assets held by the fund.

● What retirees receive in a pay-as-you-go system depends on demographics – the ratio of retirees to workers – and on the evolution of the tax rate set by the system.

From the point of view of the economy, however, the two systems have very different implications:

● In the fully funded system, workers save less because they anticipate receiving benefits when they are old. The social security system saves on their behalf, by investing their contributions in financial assets. The presence of a social security system changes the composition of overall saving: private saving goes down and public saving goes up. But, to a first approximation, it has no effect on total saving and therefore no effect on capital accumulation.

● In the pay-as-you-go system, workers also save less because they again anticipate receiving benefits when they are old. But, now, the social security system does not save on their behalf. The decrease in private saving is not compensated by an increase in public saving. Total saving goes down and so does capital accumulation.

evidence indicates that most OECD countries are actually far below their golden-rule level of capital. Increasing their saving rate would lead to higher consumption in the future.

This means that, in practice, governments face a trade-off: an increase in the saving rate leads to lower consumption for some time but higher consumption later. So what should governments do? How close to the golden rule should they try to get? It depends on how much weight they put on the welfare of current generations – who are more likely to lose from policies aimed at increasing the saving rate – versus the welfare of future generations – who are more likely to gain. Enter politics: future generations do not vote. This means that governments are unlikely to ask current generations to make large sacrifices, which in turn means that capital is likely to stay far below its golden-rule level. These intergenerational issues are at the forefront of the current debate on Social Security reform in Europe. The Focus box 'Social security, saving and capital accumulation in Europe' explores this further.

Most actual social security systems are somewhere between pay-as-you-go and fully funded systems. Most European countries have in place public pay-as-you-go pension schemes which are earnings-related. The UK is one exception, as the public pay-as-you-go pension system provides a flat-rate benefit which is aimed at preventing poverty rather than providing income in retirement similar to that in working life. This basic pension is meant to be supplemented by funded private pension, and pension fund assets currently amount to more than 85% of British GDP. Another exception is Denmark, which has a public pension system composed of two elements: a universal, flat-rate scheme financed from general taxation, and a funded scheme financed from contributions from all employed individuals and organised in a separate fund.

In many countries, a shift to a fully funded system has been advocated by many parties, the main argument being that funding the social security systems would increase the saving rate. Such a shift could be achieved by investing, from now on, tax contributions in financial assets rather than distributing them as benefits to retirees. Under such a shift, the social security system would steadily accumulate funds and would eventually become fully funded. Martin Feldstein, an economist at Harvard University and an advocate of such a shift in the USA, has concluded that it could lead to a 34% increase of the capital stock in the long run.

How should we think about such a proposal? It would probably have been a good idea to fully fund the pension systems at the start: each country would have a higher saving rate. The capital stock would be higher, and output and consumption would also be higher. But we cannot rewrite history. The existing systems have promised benefits to retirees, and these promises have to be honoured. This means that, under the proposal we just described, current workers would, in effect, have to contribute twice – once to fund the system and finance their own retirement and then to finance the benefits owed to current retirees. This would impose a disproportionate cost on current workers. The practical implication is that, if it is to happen, the move to a fully funded system will have to be very slow, so that the burden of adjustment does not fall too much on one generation relative to the others. Indeed, some Eastern European countries such as Poland, Slovakia and the Baltic states, are currently implementing a partial shift to a funded system: a share of the contributions paid by workers is now being allocated to individual personal accounts and invested in the financial markets.

What are the potential drawbacks of such reforms? Consider the case in which workers are allowed, from now on, to make contributions to personal accounts instead of to the social security system, and to be able to draw from these accounts when they retire. By itself, this proposal would clearly increase private saving: workers will be saving more. But its ultimate effect on saving depends on how the benefits already promised to current workers and retirees by the social security system are financed. If these benefits are financed not through additional taxes but through debt finance, then the increase in private saving will be offset by an increase in deficits, that is a decrease in public saving: the shift to personal accounts would not increase the total saving rate of the economy. If, instead, these benefits are financed through higher taxes, then the saving rate will increase. But, in that case, current workers will have to both contribute to their personal accounts and pay the higher taxes. They will indeed pay twice.

Note: A detailed overview of the policies and strategies adopted across the EU in the field of social protecion can be found at the website of the European Commission (***http://ec.europa.eu/ employment_social/spsi/social_protection_en.htm***). (We shall return to these issues in Chapter 25.)

12.3 GETTING A SENSE OF MAGNITUDES

How big an impact does a change in the saving rate have on output in the long run? For how long and by how much does an increase in the saving rate affect growth? To get a better sense of the answers to these questions, let's now make more specific assumptions, plug in some numbers and see what we get.

Assume that the production function is

$$Y = \sqrt{K}\sqrt{N} \qquad [12.6]$$

> Check that this production function exhibits both constant returns to scale and decreasing returns to either capital or labour.

Output equals the product of the square root of capital and the square root of labour. (A more general specification of the production function, known as the Cobb–Douglas production function, and its implications for growth are given in the appendix to the chapter.)

Dividing both sides by N (because we are interested in output per worker), we get

$$\frac{Y}{N} = \frac{\sqrt{K}\sqrt{N}}{N} = \frac{\sqrt{K}}{\sqrt{N}} = \sqrt{\frac{K}{N}}$$

Output per worker equals the square root of capital per worker. Put another way, the production function, f, relating output per worker to capital per worker, is given by

> The second equality follows from
>
> $\sqrt{N}/N = \sqrt{N}/(\sqrt{N}\sqrt{N})$
> $= 1/\sqrt{N}$

$$f\left(\frac{K_t}{N}\right) = \sqrt{\frac{K_t}{N}}$$

Replacing $f(K_t/N)$ with $\sqrt{K_t/N}$ in equation (12.3), we have

$$\frac{K_{t+1}}{N} - \frac{K_t}{N} = s\sqrt{\frac{K_t}{N}} - \delta\frac{K_t}{N} \qquad [12.7]$$

This equation describes the evolution of capital per worker over time. Let's look at what it implies.

The effects of the saving rate on steady-state output

How big an impact does an increase in the saving rate have on the steady-state level of output per worker?

Start with equation (12.7). In steady state, the amount of capital per worker is constant, so the left side of the equation equals zero. This implies

$$s\sqrt{\frac{K^*}{N}} = \delta\frac{K^*}{N}$$

(We have dropped time indexes, which are no longer needed because in steady state, K/N is constant. The * is to remind you that we are looking at the steady-state value of capital.) Square both sides:

$$s^2\frac{K^*}{N} = \delta^2\left(\frac{K^*}{N}\right)^2$$

Divide both sides by K/N and change the order of the equality:

$$\frac{K^*}{N} = \left(\frac{s}{\delta}\right)^2 \qquad [12.8]$$

Steady-state capital per worker is equal to the square of the ratio of the saving rate to the depreciation rate.

From equations (12.6) and (12.8), steady-state output per worker is given by

$$\frac{Y^*}{N} = \sqrt{\frac{K^*}{N}} = \sqrt{\left(\frac{s}{\delta}\right)^2} = \frac{s}{\delta} \qquad [12.9]$$

Steady-state output per worker is equal to the ratio of the saving rate to the depreciation rate.

A higher saving rate and a lower depreciation rate both lead to higher steady-state capital per worker [equation (12.8)] and higher steady-state output per worker [equation (12.9)]. To see what this means, let's look at a numerical example. Suppose the depreciation rate is 10% per year, and suppose the saving rate is also 10%. Then, from equations (12.8) and (12.9), steady-state capital per worker and output per worker are both equal to 1. Now suppose that the saving rate doubles, from 10% to 20%. It follows from equation (12.8) that in the new steady state, capital per worker increases from 1 to 4. And from equation (12.9), output per worker doubles, from 1 to 2. Thus, doubling the saving rate leads, in the long run, to doubling the output per worker: this is a large effect.

The dynamic effects of an increase in the saving rate

We have just seen that an increase in the saving rate leads to an increase in the steady-state level of output. But how long does it take for output to reach its new steady-state level? Put another way, by how much and for how long does an increase in the saving rate affect the growth rate?

To answer these questions, we must use equation (12.7) and solve it for capital per worker in year 0, in year 1 and so on.

Suppose that the saving rate, which had always been equal to 10%, increases in year 0 from 10% to 20% and remains at this higher value forever after. In year 0, nothing happens to the capital stock. (Recall that it takes one year for higher saving and higher investment to show up in higher capital.) So, capital per worker remains equal to the steady-state value associated with a saving rate of 0.1. From equation (12.8),

$$\frac{K_0}{N} = (0.1/0.1)^2 = 1^2 = 1$$

In year 1, equation (12.7) gives

$$\frac{K_1}{N} - \frac{K_0}{N} = s\sqrt{\frac{K_0}{N}} - \delta\frac{K_0}{N}$$

With a depreciation rate equal to 0.1 and a saving rate now equal to 0.2, this equation implies

$$\frac{K_1}{N} - 1 = [(0.2)(\sqrt{1})] - [(0.1)1]$$

so

$$\frac{K_1}{N} = 1.1$$

In the same way, we can solve for K_2/N, and so on. When we have determined the values of capital per worker in year 0, year 1 and so on, we can then use equation (12.6) to solve for output per worker in year 0, year 1 and so on. The results of this computation are presented in Figure 12.8. Figure 12.8(a) plots the *level* of output per worker against time. Y/N increases over time from its initial value of 1 in year 0 to its steady-state value of 2 in the long run. Figure 12.8(b) gives the same information in a different way, plotting instead the *growth rate* of output per worker against time. As Figure 12.8(b) shows, growth of output per worker is highest at the beginning and then decreases over time. As the economy reaches its new steady state, growth of output per worker returns to zero.

◄ The difference between investment and depreciation is greatest at the beginning. This is why capital accumulation and, by implication, output growth are highest at the beginning.

Figure 12.8 clearly shows that the adjustment to the new, higher long-run equilibrium takes a long time. It is only 40% complete after ten years, and it is 63% complete after 20 years. Put another way, the increase in the saving rate increases the growth rate of output per worker for a long time. The average annual growth rate is 3.1% for the first ten years, and it is 1.5% for the next ten. Although the changes in the saving rate have no effect on growth in the long run, they do lead to higher growth for a long time.

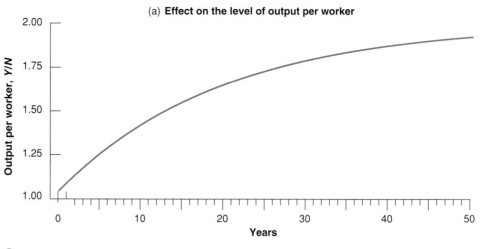

Figure 12.8

The dynamic effects of an increase in the saving rate from 10% to 20% on the level and the growth rate of output per worker

It takes a long time for output to adjust to its new, higher level after an increase in the saving rate. Put another way, an increase in the saving rate leads to a long period of higher growth.

Let's go back to the question raised at the beginning of the chapter: can the low saving/investment rate in the USA explain why the US growth rate has been so low – relative to the rates of other OECD countries – since 1950? The answer would be yes if the USA had a higher saving rate in the past and *if this saving rate had fallen substantially in the past 50 years.* If this were the case, it could explain the period of lower growth in the USA in the past 50 years along the lines of the mechanism in Figure 12.8 (with the sign reversed, as we would be looking at a decrease – not an increase – in the saving rate). But this is not the case: the US saving rate has been low for a long time. Low saving cannot explain the poor US growth performance over the past 50 years.

The saving rate and the golden rule

What is the saving rate that would maximise steady-state consumption per worker? Recall that, in steady state, consumption is equal to what is left after enough is put aside to maintain a constant level of capital. More formally, in steady state, consumption per worker is equal to output per worker minus depreciation per worker:

$$\frac{C}{N} = \frac{Y}{N} - \delta \frac{K}{N}$$

Using equations (12.8) and (12.9) for the steady-state values of output per worker and capital per worker, consumption per worker is thus given by

$$\frac{C}{N} = \frac{s}{\delta} - \delta \left(\frac{s}{\delta}\right)^2 = \frac{s(1-s)}{\delta}$$

Table 12.2 The saving rate and the steady-state levels of capital, output and consumption per worker

Saving rate s	Capital per worker (K/N)	Output per worker (Y/N)	Consumption per worker (C/N)
0.0	0.0	0.0	0.0
0.1	1.0	1.0	0.9
0.2	4.0	2.0	1.6
0.3	9.0	3.0	2.1
0.4	16.0	4.0	2.4
0.5	25.0	5.0	2.5
0.6	36.0	6.0	2.4
–	–	–	–
1.0	100.0	10.0	0.0

Using this equation together with equations (12.8) and (12.9), Table 12.2 gives the steady-state values of capital per worker, output per worker and consumption per worker for different values of the saving rate (and for a depreciation rate equal to 10%).

Steady-state consumption per worker is largest when s equals one-half. In other words, the golden-rule level of capital is associated with a saving rate of 50%. Below that level, increases in the saving rate lead to an increase in long-run consumption per worker. We saw earlier that the average saving rate has been very different across OECD countries since 1950. We can be quite confident that in countries with low saving rates, as in the USA, an increase in the saving rate would increase both output per worker and consumption per worker in the long run. But the same would not happen in countries with very high saving rates, such as Germany or Italy.

◄ Check your understanding of the issues: using the equations in this section, argue the pros and cons of policy measures aimed at increasing the German saving rate.

12.4 PHYSICAL VERSUS HUMAN CAPITAL

We have concentrated so far on physical capital – machines, plants, office buildings and so on. But economies have another type of capital: the set of skills of the workers in the economy, or what economists call **human capital**. An economy with many highly skilled workers is likely to be much more productive than an economy in which most workers cannot read or write.

Over the past two centuries, the increase in human capital has been as large as the increase in physical capital. At the beginning of the Industrial Revolution, only 30% of the population of the countries that constitute the OECD today knew how to read. Today, the literacy rate in OECD countries is above 95%. Schooling was not compulsory prior to the Industrial Revolution. Today it is compulsory, usually until age 16. Still, there are large differences across countries. Today, in OECD countries, nearly 100% of children get a primary education, 90% get a secondary education and 38% get a higher education. The corresponding numbers in poor countries, countries with GDP per person below $400, are 95%, 32% and 4%, respectively.

◄ Even this comparison may be misleading because the quality of education can be quite different across countries.

How should we think about the effect of human capital on output? How does the introduction of human capital change our earlier conclusions? These are the questions we take up in this last section.

Extending the production function

The most natural way of extending our analysis to allow for human capital is to modify the production function relation (12.1) to read

$$\frac{Y}{N} = f\left(\frac{K}{N}, \frac{H}{N}\right)$$

$$(+, +)$$

[12.10]

Note that we are using the same symbol, *H*, to denote the monetary base in Chapter 4 and human capital in this chapter. Both uses are traditional. Do not be confused.

The level of output per worker depends on both the level of physical capital per worker, K/N, and the level of human capital per worker, H/N. As before, an increase in capital per worker, K/N, leads to an increase in output per worker. And an increase in the average level of skill, H/N, also leads to more output per worker. More skilled workers can do more complex tasks; they can deal more easily with unexpected complications. All this leads to higher output per worker.

We assumed earlier that increases in physical capital per worker increased output per worker but that the effect became smaller as the level of capital per worker increased. We can make the same assumption for human capital per worker: think of increases in H/N as coming from increases in the number of years of education. The evidence is that the returns to increasing the proportion of children acquiring a primary education are very large. At the very least, the ability to read and write allows people to use equipment that is more complicated and more productive. For rich countries, however, primary education and secondary education are no longer the relevant margin: most children now get both. The relevant margin is now higher education. We am sure it will come as good news to you that the evidence shows that higher education increases a person's skills, at least as measured by the increase in the wages of those who acquire it. But, to take an extreme example, it is not clear that forcing everyone to acquire a degree would increase aggregate output very much.

We look at this evidence in Chapter 13.

Many people would end up over-qualified and probably more frustrated rather than more productive.

The rationale for using relative wages as weights is that they reflect relative marginal products. A worker who is paid three times as much as another is assumed to have a marginal product that is three times higher.

How should we construct the measure for human capital, H? The answer is: very much the same way we construct the measure for physical capital, K. To construct K, we just add the values of the different pieces of capital, so that a machine that costs \$2000 gets twice the weight of a machine that costs \$1000. Similarly, we construct the measure of H such that workers who are paid twice as much get twice the weight. Take, for example, an economy with 100 workers, half of them unskilled and half of them skilled. Suppose the relative wage of the skilled workers is twice that of the unskilled workers. We can then construct H as $[(50 \times 1) + (50 \times 2)] = 150$. Human capital per worker, H/N, is then equal to $150/100 = 1.5$.

An issue, however, is whether relative wages accurately reflect relative marginal products. To take a controversial example: in the same job, with the same seniority, women still often earn less than men. Is it because their marginal product is lower? Should they be given a lower weight than men in the construction of human capital?

Human capital, physical capital and output

How does the introduction of human capital change the analysis of the previous sections?

Our conclusions about *physical capital accumulation* remain valid: an increase in the saving rate increases steady-state physical capital per worker and therefore increases output per worker. But our conclusions now extend to *human capital accumulation* as well. An increase in how much society 'saves' in the form of human capital – through education and on-the-job training – increases steady-state human capital per worker, which leads to an increase in output per worker. Our extended model gives us a richer picture of how output per worker is determined. In the long run, it tells us that output per worker depends on both how much society saves and how much it spends on education.

What are the relative importance of human capital and physical capital in the determination of output per worker? A place to start is to compare how much is spent on formal education to how much is invested in physical capital. In the USA, spending on formal education is about 6.5% of GDP. This number includes both government expenditures on education and private expenditures by people on education. It is between one-third and one-half of the gross investment rate for physical capital (which is around 16%). But this comparison is only a first pass. Consider the following complications:

- Education, especially higher education, is partly consumption – done for its own sake – and partly investment. We should include only the investment part for our purposes. However, the 6.5% number in the preceding paragraph includes both.
- At least for post-secondary education, the opportunity cost of a person's education is his or her foregone wages while acquiring the education. Spending on education should

include not only the actual cost of education but also this opportunity cost. The 6.5% number does not include this opportunity cost.

- Formal education is only part of education. Much of what we learn comes from on-the-job training, formal or informal. Both the actual costs and the opportunity costs of on-the-job training should also be included. The 6.5% number does not include the costs associated with on-the-job training.

◄ How large is your opportunity cost relative to your tuition?

- We should compare investment rates net of depreciation. Depreciation of physical capital, especially of machines, is likely to be higher than depreciation of human capital. Skills deteriorate, but they generally do so only slowly and, unlike physical capital, they deteriorate less quickly the more they are used.

For all these reasons, it is difficult to come up with reliable numbers for investment in human capital. Recent studies conclude that investment in physical capital and in education play roughly similar roles in the determination of output. This implies that output per worker depends roughly equally on the amount of physical capital and the amount of human capital in the economy. Countries that save more and/or spend more on education can achieve substantially higher steady-state levels of output per worker.

Endogenous growth

Note what the conclusion we just reached said and did not say. It said that a country that saves more or spends more on education will achieve a *higher level* of output per worker in steady state. It did not say that by saving or spending more on education, a country can sustain permanently *higher growth* of output per worker.

This conclusion, however, has been challenged in the past two decades. Following the lead of Robert Lucas and Paul Romer, researchers have explored the possibility that the joint accumulation of physical capital and human capital might actually be enough to sustain growth. Given human capital, increases in physical capital will run into decreasing returns. And given physical capital, increases in human capital will also run into decreasing returns. But, these researchers have asked, what if both physical and human capital increase in tandem? Can't an economy grow forever just by having steadily more capital and more skilled workers?

Models that generate steady growth even without technological progress are called **models of endogenous growth** to reflect the fact that in those models – in contrast to the model we saw in earlier sections of this chapter – the growth rate depends, even in the long run, on variables such as the saving rate and the rate of spending on education. The jury on this class of models is still out, but the indications so far are that the conclusions we drew earlier need to be qualified, not abandoned. The current consensus is as follows:

◄ We have mentioned Lucas once already in connection with the Lucas critique in Chapter 10.

- Output per worker depends on the level of both physical capital per worker and human capital per worker. Both forms of capital can be accumulated – one through physical investment and the other through education and training. Increasing either the saving rate and/or the fraction of output spent on education and training can lead to much higher levels of output per worker in the long run. However, given the rate of technological progress, such measures do not lead to a permanently higher growth rate.
- Note the qualifier in the last proposition: *given the rate of technological progress*. Is technological progress unrelated to the level of human capital in the economy? Won't a better-educated labour force lead to a higher rate of technological progress? These questions take us to the topic of the next chapter: the sources and the effects of technological progress.

SUMMARY

- In the long run, the evolution of output is determined by two relations. (To make the reading of this summary easier, we omit *per worker* in what follows.) First, the level of output depends on the amount of capital. Second, capital accumulation depends on the level of output, which determines saving and investment.

- The interactions between capital and output imply that, starting from any level of capital (and ignoring technological progress, the topic of Chapter 13), an economy converges in the long run to a *steady-state* (constant) level of capital. Associated with this level of capital is a steady-state level of output.

- The steady-state level of capital and, thus, the steady-state level of output depend positively on the saving rate. A higher saving rate leads to a higher steady-state level of output; during the transition to the new steady state, a higher saving rate leads to positive output growth. But (again ignoring technological progress) in the long run, the growth rate of output is equal to zero and so does not depend on the saving rate.

- An increase in the saving rate requires an initial decrease in consumption. In the long run, the increase in the saving rate may lead to an increase or a decrease in consumption, depending on whether the economy is below or above the *golden-rule level of capital*, the level of capital at which steady-state consumption is highest.

- Most countries typically have a level of capital below the golden-rule level. Thus, an increase in the saving rate leads to an initial decrease in consumption followed by an increase in consumption in the long run. When considering whether to adopt policy measures aimed at changing a country's saving rate, policy makers must decide how much weight to put on the welfare of current generations versus the welfare of future generations.

- While most of the analysis of this chapter focuses on the effects of physical capital accumulation, output depends on the levels of both physical *and* human capital. Both forms of capital can be accumulated – one through investment and the other through education and training. Increasing the saving rate and/or the fraction of output spent on education and training can lead to large increases in output in the long run.

KEY TERMS

saving rate 245

steady state 251

golden-rule level of capital 255

fully funded system 256

pay-as-you-go system 256

human capital 261

models of endogenous growth 263

Cobb–Douglas production function 267

QUESTIONS AND PROBLEMS

QUICK CHECK

1. *Using the information in this chapter, label each of the following statements true, false or uncertain. Explain briefly.*

a. The saving rate is always equal to the investment rate.

b. A higher investment rate can sustain higher growth of output forever.

c. If capital never depreciated, growth could go on forever.

d. The higher the saving rate, the higher consumption in steady state.

e. We should transform social security from a pay-as-you-go system to a fully funded system. This would increase consumption both now and in the future.

f. When the capital stock is far below the golden-rule level, the government should give tax breaks for saving.

g. Education increases human capital and thus output. It follows that governments should subsidise education.

2. *Consider the following statement: 'The Solow model shows that the saving rate does not affect the growth rate in the long run, so we should stop worrying about the low saving rate. Increasing the saving rate wouldn't have any important effects on the economy.' Do you agree or disagree?*

3. *In Chapter 3 we saw that an increase in the saving rate can lead to a recession in the short run (i.e. the paradox of saving). We examined the issue in the medium run in a chapter problem at the end of Chapter 8. We can now examine the long-run effects of an increase in saving.*

Using the model presented in this chapter, what is the effect of an increase in the saving rate on output per worker likely to be after one decade? After five decades?

DIG DEEPER

4. *Discuss how the level of output per person in the long run would likely be affected by each of the following changes:*

a. The right to exclude saving from income when paying income taxes.

b. A higher rate of female participation in the labour market (but constant population).

5. *Suppose all European countries moved from the current pay-as-you-go social security system to a fully funded one, and financed the transition without additional government borrowing. How would the shift to a fully funded system affect the level and the rate of growth of output per worker in the long run?*

6. *Suppose that the production function is given by*

$$Y = 0.5\sqrt{K}\sqrt{N}$$

a. Derive the steady-state levels of output per worker and capital per worker in terms of the saving rate, s, and the depreciation rate, δ.

b. Derive the equation for steady-state output per worker and steady-state consumption per worker in terms of s and δ.

c. Suppose that $\delta = 0.05$. With your favourite spreadsheet software, compute steady-state output per worker and steady-state consumption per worker for $s = 0$, $s = 0.1$, $s = 0.2, \ldots , s = 1$. Explain the intuition behind your results.

d. Use your favourite spreadsheet software to graph the steady-state level of output per worker and the steady-state level of consumption per worker as a function of the saving rate (i.e. measure the saving rate on the horizontal axis of your graph and the corresponding values of output per worker and consumption per worker on the vertical axis).

e. Does the graph show that there is a value of s that maximises output per worker? Does the graph show that there is a value of s that maximises consumption per worker? If so, what is this value?

7. *The Cobb–Douglas production function and the steady state. This problem is based on the material in the chapter appendix. Suppose that the economy's production function is given by*

$$Y = K^{\alpha}N^{1-\alpha}$$

and assume that $\alpha = 1/3$.

a. Is this production function characterised by constant returns to scale? Explain.

b. Are there decreasing returns to capital?

c. Are there decreasing returns to labour?

d. Transform the production function into a relation between output per worker and capital per worker.

e. For a given saving rate, s, and depreciation rate, δ, give an expression for capital per worker in the steady state.

f. Give an expression for output per worker in the steady state.

g. Solve for the steady-state level of output per worker when $s = 0.32$ and $\delta = 0.08$.

h. Suppose that the depreciation rate remains constant at $\delta = 0.08$, while the saving rate is reduced by half, to $s = 0.16$. What is the new steady-state output per worker?

8. *Continuing with the logic from problem 7, suppose that the economy's production function is given by $Y = K^{1/3}N^{2/3}$ and that both the saving rate, s, and the depreciation rate, δ, are equal to 0.10.*

a. What is the steady-state level of capital per worker?

b. What is the steady-state level of output per worker?

Suppose that the economy is in steady state and that, in period t, the depreciation rate increases permanently from 0.10 to 0.20.

c. What will be the new steady-state levels of capital per worker and output per worker?

d. Compute the path of capital per worker and output per worker over the first three periods after the change in the depreciation rate.

9. Deficits and the capital stock

For the production function, $Y = \sqrt{K}\sqrt{N}$, equation (12.8) gives the solution for the steady-state capital stock per worker.

a. Retrace the steps in the text that derive equation (12.8).

b. Suppose that the saving rate, s, is initially 15% per year, and the depreciation rate, δ, is 7.5%. What is the steady-state capital stock per worker? What is steady-state output per worker?

c. Suppose that there is a government deficit of 5% of GDP and that the government eliminates this deficit. Assume that private saving is unchanged so that national saving increases to 20%. What is the new steady-state capital stock per worker? What is the new steady-state output per worker? How does this compare to your answer to part (b)?

EXPLORE FURTHER

10. US saving

This question follows the logic of problem 9 to explore the implications of the US budget deficit for the long-run capital stock. The question assumes that the USA will have a budget deficit over the life of this edition of the text.

a. Go to the most recent *Economic Report of the President* (***www.gpoaccess.gov/eop/***). From Table B.32, get the numbers for gross national saving for the most recent year available. From Table B.1, get the number for US GDP for the same year. What is the national saving rate, as a percentage of GDP? Using the depreciation rate and the logic from problem 9, what would be the steady-state capital stock per worker? What would be steady-state output per worker?

b. In Table B.79 of the *Economic Report of the President*, get the number for the federal budget deficit as a percentage of GDP for the year corresponding to the data from part (a). Again using the reasoning from problem 9, suppose that the federal budget deficit was eliminated and there was no change in private saving. What would be the effect on the long-run capital stock per worker? What would be the effect on long-run output per worker?

We invite you to visit the Blanchard page on the Prentice Hall website, at **www.prenhall.com/blanchard** for this chapter's World Wide Web exercises.

FURTHER READING

- The classic treatment of the relation between the saving rate and output is **by Robert Solow**, *Growth Theory: An Exposition*, **Oxford University Press, New York, 1970**.
- An easy-to-read discussion of whether and how to increase saving and improve education in the United States is given in Memoranda 23 to 27 in **Charles Schultze** (the Chairman of the Council of Economic Advisors during the Carter administration), *Memos to the President: A Guide Through Macroeconomics for the Busy Policymaker*, **Brookings Institution, Washington, DC, 1992**.

APPENDIX

The Cobb–Douglas production function and the steady state

In 1928, Charles Cobb (a mathematician) and Paul Douglas (an economist, who went on to become a US senator) concluded that the following production function gave a very good description of the relation between output, physical capital and labour in the USA from 1899–1922:

$$Y = K^\alpha N^{1-\alpha} \qquad [12A.1]$$

with α being a number between 0 and 1. Their findings proved surprisingly robust. Even today, the production function (12A.1), now known as the **Cobb–Douglas production function**, still gives a good description of the relation between output, capital and labour, and it has become a standard tool in the economist's toolbox. (Verify for yourself that it satisfies the two properties we discussed in the text: constant returns to scale and decreasing returns to capital and to labour.)

The purpose of this appendix is to characterise the steady state of an economy when the production function is given by (12A.1). (All you need in order to follow the steps is knowledge of the properties of exponents.)

Recall that, in steady state, saving per worker must be equal to depreciation per worker. Let's see what this implies:

- To derive saving per worker, we must derive first the relation between output per worker and capital per worker implied by equation (12A.1). Divide both sides of equation (12A.1) by N:

$$Y/N = K^\alpha N^{1-\alpha}/N$$

Using the properties of exponents:

$$N^{1-\alpha}/N = N^{1-\alpha}N^{-1} = N^{-\alpha}$$

so, replacing in the preceding equation, we get:

$$Y/N = K^\alpha N^{-\alpha} = (K/N)^\alpha$$

Output per worker, Y/N, is equal to the ratio of capital per worker, K/N, raised to the power α.

Saving per worker is equal to the saving rate times output per worker, so using the previous equation, it is equal to

$$\delta(K^*/N)^\alpha$$

- Depreciation per worker is equal to the depreciation rate times capital per worker:

$$\delta(K^*/N)$$

- The steady-state level of capital, K^*, is determined by the condition that saving per worker be equal to depreciation per worker, so

$$s(K^*/N)^\alpha = \delta(K^*/N)$$

To solve this expression for the steady-state level of capital per worker, K^*/N, divide both sides by $(K^*/N)^\alpha$:

$$s = \delta(K^*/N)^{1-\alpha}$$

Divide both sides by δ and change the order of the equality:

$$(K^*/N)^{1-\alpha} = s/\delta$$

Finally, raise both sides to the power $1/(1 - \alpha)$:

$$(K^*/N) = (s/\delta)^{1/(1-\alpha)}$$

This gives us the steady-state level of capital per worker.

From the production function, the steady-state level of output per worker is then equal to

$$(Y^*/N) = (K/N)^\alpha = (s/\delta)^{\alpha/(1-\alpha)}$$

Let's see what this last equation implies:

- In the text, we actually worked with a special case of equation (12A.1), the case where $\alpha = 0.5$ (Taking a variable to the power 0.5 is the same as taking the square root of the variable.) If $\alpha = 0.5$, the preceding equation means

$$Y^*/N = s/\delta$$

Output per worker is equal to the ratio of the saving rate to the depreciation rate. This is the equation we discussed in the text. A doubling of the saving rate leads to a doubling in steady-state output per worker.

- The empirical evidence suggests, however, that if we think of K as physical capital, α is closer to one-third than to one-half. Assuming that $\alpha = 1/3$, then $\alpha(1 - \alpha) = (1/3)/[1 - (1/3)] = (1/3)/(2/3) = 1/2$, and the equation for output per worker yields

$$Y^*/N = (s/\delta)^{1/2} = \sqrt{s/\alpha}$$

This implies smaller effects of the saving rate on output per worker than was suggested by the computations in the text. A doubling of the saving rate, for example, means that output per worker increases by a factor of $\sqrt{2}$ or only about 1.4 (put another way, a 40% increase in output per worker).

- There is, however, an interpretation of our model in which the appropriate value of α is close to 1/2, so the computations in the text are applicable. If, along the lines of Section 12.4, we take into account human capital as well as physical capital, then a value of α around 1/2 for the contribution of this broader definition of capital to output is, indeed, roughly appropriate. Thus, one interpretation of the numerical results in Section 12.3 is that they show the effects of a given saving rate, but that saving must be interpreted to include saving in both physical capital and human capital (more machines and more education).

Chapter 13

TECHNOLOGICAL PROGRESS AND GROWTH

Our conclusion in Chapter 12 that capital accumulation cannot by itself sustain growth has a straightforward implication: sustained growth *requires* technological progress. This chapter looks at the role of technological progress in growth:

- Section 13.1 looks at the respective role of technological progress and capital accumulation in growth. It shows how, in steady state, the rate of growth of output per person is simply equal to the rate of technological progress. This does not mean, however, that the saving rate is irrelevant. The saving rate affects the level of output per person – but not its rate of growth.

- Section 13.2 turns to the determinants of technological progress, focusing in particular on the role of research and development (R&D).

- Section 13.3 returns to the facts of growth presented in Chapter 11 and interprets them in the light of what we have learned in this and the previous chapter.

13.1 TECHNOLOGICAL PROGRESS AND THE RATE OF GROWTH

In an economy in which there is both capital accumulation and technological progress, at what rate will output grow? To answer this question, we need to extend the model developed in Chapter 12 to allow for technological progress. To introduce technological progress into the picture, we must first revisit the aggregate production function.

Technological progress and the production function

Technological progress has many dimensions:

- It can lead to larger quantities of output for given quantities of capital and labour. Think of a new type of lubricant that allows a machine to run at a higher speed and so produce more.
- It can lead to better products. Think of the steady improvement in car safety and comfort over time.
- It can lead to new products. Think of the introductions of CD players, fax machines, mobile phones and flat-screen monitors.
- It can lead to a larger variety of products. Think of the steady increase in the number of breakfast cereals available at your local supermarket.

> The average number of items carried by a supermarket increased from 2200 in 1950 to 45 500 in 2005 in the USA. To get a sense of what this means, see Robin Williams (who plays an immigrant from the Soviet Union) in the supermarket scene in the movie *Moscow on the Hudson*.

These dimensions are more similar than they appear. If we think of consumers as caring not about the goods themselves but about the services these goods provide, then they all have something in common: in each case, consumers receive more services. A better car provides more safety, a new product such as a fax machine or a new service such as the Internet provides more information services and so on. If we think of output as the set of underlying services provided by the goods produced in the economy, we can think of technological progress as leading to increases in output for given amounts of capital and labour. We can then think of the *state of technology* as a variable that tells us how much output can be produced from given amounts of capital and labour at any time. If we denote the state of technology by A, we can rewrite the production function as

> As you saw in the Focus box 'Real GDP, technological progress and the price of computers' in Chapter 2, thinking of products as providing a number of underlying services is the method used to construct the price index for computers.

$$Y = F(K, N, A)$$
$$(+, +, +)$$

This is our extended production function. Output depends on both capital and labour, K and N, and on the state of technology, A: given capital and labour, an improvement in the state of technology, A, leads to an increase in output.

> For simplicity, we ignore human capital here. We return to it later in the chapter.

It will be convenient to use a more restrictive form of the preceding equation, however, namely

$$Y = F(K, AN) \qquad [13.1]$$

This equation states that production depends on capital and on labour multiplied by the state of technology. Introducing the state of technology in this way makes it easier to think about the effect of technological progress on the relation between output, capital and labour. Equation (13.1) implies that we can think of technological progress in two equivalent ways:

- Technological progress *reduces* the number of workers needed to produce a given amount of output. Doubling A produces the same quantity of output with only half the original number of workers, N.
- Technological progress *increases* the output that can be produced with a given number of workers. We can think of AN as the amount of **effective labour** in the economy. If the state of technology, A, doubles, it is as if the economy had twice as many workers. In other words, we can think of output being produced by two factors: capital, K, and effective labour, AN.

> AN is also sometimes called **labour in efficiency units**. The use of 'efficiency' for 'efficiency units' here and for 'efficiency wages' in Chapter 7 is a coincidence: the two notions are unrelated.

What restrictions should we impose on the extended production function (13.1)? We can build directly here on our discussion in Chapter 11.

Again, it is reasonable to assume constant returns to scale: *for a given state of technology, A,* doubling both the amount of capital, *K,* and the amount of labour, *N,* is likely to lead to a doubling of output:

$$2Y = F(2K, 2AN)$$

More generally, for any number *x,*

$$xY = F(xK, xAN)$$

It is also reasonable to assume decreasing returns to each of the two factors – capital and effective labour. Given effective labour, an increase in capital is likely to increase output, but at a decreasing rate. Symmetrically, given capital, an increase in effective labour is likely to increase output, but at a decreasing rate.

It was convenient in Chapter 11 to think in terms of output *per worker* and capital *per worker.* That was because the steady state of the economy was a state where output *per worker* and capital *per worker* were constant. It is convenient here to look at output *per effective worker* and capital *per effective worker.* The reason is the same: as we shall soon see, in steady state, output *per effective worker* and capital *per effective worker* are constant.

To get a relation between output per effective worker and capital per effective worker, take $x = 1/AN$ in the preceding equation. This gives

$$\frac{Y}{AN} = F\left(\frac{K}{AN}, 1\right)$$

Or, if we define the function *f* so that $f(K/AN) \equiv F(K/AN, 1)$:

$$\frac{Y}{AN} = f\left(\frac{K}{AN}\right)$$

In words: *output per effective worker* (the left side) is a function of *capital per effective worker* (the expression in the function on the right side).

The relation between output per effective worker and capital per effective worker is drawn in Figure 13.1. It looks very much the same as the relation we drew in Figure 11.2 between output per worker and capital per worker in the absence of technological progress. There, increases in K/N led to increases in Y/N, but at a decreasing rate. Here, increases in K/AN lead to increases in Y/AN, but at a decreasing rate.

Interactions between output and capital

We now have the elements we need to think about the determinants of growth. Our analysis will parallel the analysis of Chapter 12. There we looked at the dynamics of *output per*

> Per worker: divided by the number of workers, *N.* Per effective worker: divided by the number of effective workers, *AN* – the number of workers, *N,* times the state of technology, *A.*

> Suppose that *F* has the 'double square root' form:

$$Y = F(K, AN) = \sqrt{K}\sqrt{AN}$$

Then

$$\frac{Y}{AN} = \frac{\sqrt{K}\sqrt{AN}}{AN} = \frac{\sqrt{K}}{\sqrt{AN}}$$

So the function *f* is simply the square root function:

$$F(K/AN) = \sqrt{\frac{K}{AN}}$$

Figure 13.1

Output per effective worker versus capital per effective worker

Because of decreasing returns to capital, increases in capital per effective worker lead to smaller and smaller increases in output per effective worker.

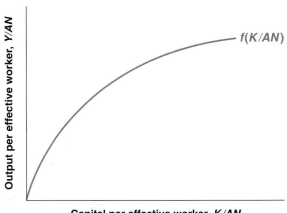

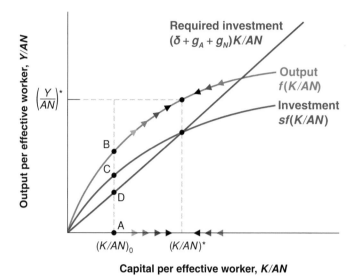

Figure 13.2

The dynamics of capital per effective worker and output per effective worker

Capital per effective worker and output per effective worker converge to constant values in the long run.

worker and *capital per worker*. Here we look at the dynamics of *output per effective worker* and *capital per effective worker*.

In Chapter 12, we characterised the dynamics of output and capital per worker using Figure 12.2. In that figure, we drew three relations:

- The relation between output per worker and capital per worker.
- The relation between investment per worker and capital per worker.
- The relation between depreciation per worker – equivalently, the investment per worker needed to maintain a constant level of capital per worker – and capital per worker.

The dynamics of capital per worker and, by implication, output per worker were determined by the relation between investment per worker and depreciation per worker. Depending on whether investment per worker was greater or smaller than depreciation per worker, capital per worker increased or decreased over time, as did output per worker.

We shall follow the same approach in building Figure 13.2. The difference is that we focus on output, capital and investment *per effective worker* rather than per worker:

- The relation between output per effective worker and capital per effective worker was derived in Figure 13.1. This relation is repeated in Figure 13.2: Output per effective worker increases with capital per effective worker, but at a decreasing rate.
- Under the same assumptions as in Chapter 12 – that investment is equal to private saving, and the private saving rate is constant – investment is given by

$$I = S = sY$$

Divide both sides by the number of effective workers, AN, to get

$$\frac{I}{AN} = s\frac{Y}{AN}$$

Replacing output per effective worker, Y/AN, by its expression from equation (13.2) gives

$$\frac{I}{AN} = sf\left(\frac{K}{AN}\right)$$

The relation between investment per effective worker and capital per effective worker is drawn in Figure 13.2. It is equal to the upper curve – the relation between output per effective worker and capital per effective worker – multiplied by the saving rate, s. This gives us the lower curve.

> ◀ The simple key to understanding the results in this section is that the results we derived for *output per worker* in Chapter 12 still hold in this chapter, but now for *output per effective worker*. For example, in Chapter 12, we saw that output per worker was constant in steady state. In this chapter, we shall see that output per effective worker is constant in steady state. And so on.

- Finally, we need to ask what level of investment per effective worker is needed to maintain a given level of capital per effective worker.

  In Chapter 12, for capital to be constant, investment had to be equal to the depreciation of the existing capital stock. Here, the answer is slightly more complicated: now that we allow for technological progress (so A increases over time), the number of effective workers, AN, increases over time. Thus, maintaining the same ratio of capital to effective workers, K/AN, requires an increase in the capital stock, K, proportional to the increase in the number of effective workers, AN. Let's look at this condition more closely.

In Chapter 12, we assumed $g_A = 0$ and $g_A = 0$. Our focus in this chapter is on the implications of technological progress, $g_A > 0$. But once we allow for technological progress, introducing population growth, $g_N > 0$, is straightforward. Thus, we allow for both $g_A > 0$ and $g_N > 0$.

  Let δ be the depreciation rate of capital. Let the rate of technological progress be equal to g_A. Let the rate of population growth be equal to g_N. If we assume that the ratio of employment to the total population remains constant, the number of workers, N, also grows at annual rate g_N. Together, these assumptions imply that the growth rate of effective labour, AN, equals $g_A + g_N$. For example, if the number of workers is growing at 1% per year and the rate of technological progress is 2% per year, then the growth rate of effective labour is equal to 3% per year.

The growth rate of the product of two variables is the sum of the growth rates of the two variables. See Proposition 7 in Appendix 1 at the end of the book.

  These assumptions imply that the level of investment needed to maintain a given level of capital per effective worker is therefore given by

$$I = \delta K + (g_A + g_N)K$$

or, equivalently,

$$I = (\delta + g_A + g_N)K \qquad [13.3]$$

An amount, δK, is needed just to keep the capital stock constant. If the depreciation rate is 10%, then investment must be equal to 10% of the capital stock just to maintain the same level of capital. And an additional amount, $(g_A + g_N)K$, is needed to ensure that the capital stock increases at the same rate as effective labour. If effective labour increases at 3% per year, for example, then capital must increase by 3% per year to maintain the same level of capital per effective worker. Putting δK and $(g_A + g_N)$ together in this example: if the depreciation rate is 10% and the growth rate of effective labour is 3%, then investment must equal 13% of the capital stock to maintain a constant level of capital per effective worker.

To obtain more precisely the amount of investment per unit of effective worker needed to keep a constant level of capital per unit of effective worker, we need to repeat the steps taken in Section 12.1, where we derived the dynamics of capital per worker over time. Here we derive in a similar way the dynamics of capital per unit of effective worker over time. The dynamics of capital per unit of effective worker can be expressed as:

$$\frac{K_{t+1}}{A_{t+1}N_{t+1}} = \left[(1 - \delta)\frac{K_t}{A_tN_t} + sf\left(\frac{K_t}{A_tN_t}\right) \right]\frac{A_tN_t}{A_{t+1}N_{t+1}} \qquad [13.4]$$

In words: capital per unit of effective worker at the beginning of year $t + 1$ is equal to capital per unit of effective worker at the beginning of year t, taking into account the depreciation rate, plus investment per unit of effective worker in year t, which is equal to the savings rate multiplied by output per unit of effective labour in year t.

If we subtract K_t/A_tN_t from both sides of the equation and rearrange the terms, we can rewrite the previous equation as:

$$\frac{K_{t+1}}{A_{t+1}N_{t+1}} - \frac{K_t}{A_tN_t} = (1 - \delta)\frac{K_t}{A_tN_t}\left(\frac{1}{1 + g_A}\frac{1}{1 + g_N}\right) + sf\left(\frac{K_t}{A_tN_t}\right)\left(\frac{1}{1 + g_A}\frac{1}{1 + g_N}\right) - \frac{K_t}{A_tN_t}$$

If we assume, to keep things simple, that $g_Ag_N \cong 0$ and $(1 + g_A)(1 + g_N) \cong 1$, the previous expression becomes:

$$\frac{K_{t+1}}{A_{t+1}N_{t+1}} - \frac{K_t}{A_tN_t} = sf\left(\frac{K_t}{A_tN_t}\right) - (\delta + g_A + g_N)\frac{K_t}{A_tN_t} \qquad [13.5]$$

In words: the change in the stock of capital per unit of effective worker – given by the difference between the two terms on the left side – is equal to saving per unit of effective worker – given by the first term on the right – minus depreciation per unit of effective worker – given by the second term on the right.

To find the steady-state value of capital per unit of effective worker, let us set the left side of the previous equation to zero to get:

$$sf\left(\frac{K_t}{A_t N_t}\right) = (\delta + g_A + g_N)\frac{K_t}{A_t N_t} \qquad [13.6]$$

The steady-state value of capital per unit of effective labour is such that the amount of saving (the left side) is exactly enough to cover the depreciation of the existing capital stock (the right side).

The level of investment per effective worker needed to maintain a given level of capital per effective worker is represented by the upward-sloping line 'Required investment' in Figure 13.2. The slope of the line equals $(\delta g_A + g_N)$.

Dynamics of capital and output

We can now give a graphical description of the dynamics of capital per effective worker and output per effective worker.

Consider a given level of capital per effective worker, say $(K/AN)_0$ in Figure 13.2. At that level, output per effective worker equals the vertical distance AB. Investment per effective worker is equal to AC. The amount of investment required to maintain that level of capital per effective worker is equal to AD. Because actual investment exceeds the investment level required to maintain the existing level of capital per effective worker, K/AN increases.

Hence, starting from $(K/AN)_0$, the economy moves to the right, with the level of capital per effective worker increasing over time. This goes on until investment per effective worker is just sufficient to maintain the existing level of capital per effective worker, until capital per effective worker equals $(K/AN)^*$.

In the long run, capital per effective worker reaches a constant level, and so does output per effective worker. Put another way, the steady state of this economy is such that *capital per effective worker and output per effective worker are constant and equal to $(K/AN)^*$ and $(Y/AN)^*$*, respectively.

This implies that, in steady state, output, Y, is growing at the same rate as effective labour, AN (so that the ratio of the two is constant). Because effective labour grows at rate $g_A + g_N$ output growth in steady state must also equal $g_A + g_N$. The same reasoning applies to capital: because capital per effective worker is constant in steady state, capital is also growing at rate $g_A + g_N$.

◀ If *Y/AN* is constant, *Y* must grow at the same rate as *AN*. So it must grow at rate $g_A + g_N$.

Stated in terms of capital or output per effective worker, these results seem rather abstract, but it is straightforward to state them in a more intuitive way, and this gives us our first important conclusion:

In steady state, the growth rate of output equals the rate of population growth (g_N) plus the rate of technological progress (g_A). By implication, the growth rate of output is independent of the saving rate.

To strengthen your intuition, let's go back to the argument we used in Chapter 12 to show that, in the absence of technological progress and population growth, the economy could not sustain positive growth forever:

● The argument went as follows: suppose the economy tried to sustain positive output growth. Because of decreasing returns to capital, capital would have to grow faster than output. The economy would have to devote a larger and larger proportion of output to capital accumulation. At some point, there would be no more output to devote to capital accumulation. Growth would come to an end.

Table 13.1 The characteristics of balanced growth

	Rate of growth of:
1 Capital per effective worker	0
2 Output per effective worker	0
3 Capital per worker	g_A
4 Output per worker	g_A
5 Labour	g_N
6 Capital	$g_A + g_N$
7 Output	$g_A + g_N$

● Exactly the same logic is at work here. Effective labour grows at rate $g_A + g_N$. Suppose the economy tried to sustain output growth in excess of $g_A + g_N$. Because of decreasing returns to capital, capital would have to increase faster than output. The economy would have to devote a larger and larger proportion of output to capital accumulation. At some point, this would prove impossible. Thus the economy cannot permanently grow faster than $g_A + g_N$.

> The standard of living is given by output per worker (or, more accurately, output per person), not output per effective worker.

We have focused on the behaviour of aggregate output. To get a sense of what happens not to aggregate output but rather to the standard of living over time, we must look instead at the behaviour of output per worker (not output per *effective* worker). Because output grows at rate $(g_A + g_N)$ and the number of workers grows at rate g_N, output per worker grows at rate g_A. In other words, *when the economy is in steady state, output per worker grows at the rate of technological progress.*

> The growth rate of *Y/N* is equal to the growth rate of *Y* minus the growth rate of *N* (see Proposition 8 in Appendix 1 at the end of the book). So the growth rate of *Y/N* is given by $(g_A - g_N) = (g_A + g_N) - g_N = g_A$.

Because output, capital, and effective labour all grow at the same rate, $g_A + g_N$, in steady state, the steady state of this economy is also called a state of **balanced growth**: in steady state, output and the two inputs, capital and effective labour, grow 'in balance', at the same rate. The characteristics of balanced growth will be helpful later in the chapter and are summarised in Table 13.1.

On the balanced growth path (equivalently: in steady state, or in the long run):

● *Capital per effective worker* and *output per effective worker* are constant; this is the result we derived in Figure 13.2.
● Equivalently, *capital per worker* and *output per worker* are growing at the rate of technological progress, g_A.
● Or, in terms of labour, capital and output: *labour* is growing at the rate of population growth, g_N; *capital* and *output* are growing at a rate equal to the sum of population growth and the rate of technological progress $g_A + g_N$.

The effects of the saving rate

In steady state, the growth rate of output depends *only* on the rate of population growth and the rate of technological progress. Changes in the saving rate do not affect the steady-state growth rate, but changes in the saving rate do increase the steady-state level of output per effective worker.

This result is best seen in Figure 13.3, which shows the effect of an increase in the saving rate from s_0 to s_1. The increase in the saving rate shifts the investment relation up, from $s_0 f(K/AN)$ to $s_1 f(K/AN)$. It follows that the steady-state level of capital per effective worker increases from $(K/AN)_0$ to $(K/AN)_1$, with a corresponding increase in the level of output per effective worker from $(Y/AN)_0$ to $(Y/AN)_1$.

Following the increase in the saving rate, capital per effective worker and output per effective worker increase for some time, as they converge to their new higher level. Figure 13.4 plots output against time. Output is measured on a logarithmic scale. The economy is initially on the balanced growth path AA: output is growing at rate $g_A + g_N$ – so the slope

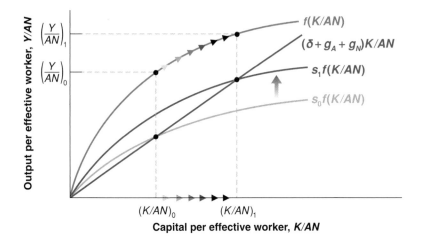

Figure 13.3

The effects of an increase in the saving rate (1)

An increase in the saving rate leads to an increase in the steady-state levels of output per effective worker and capital per effective worker.

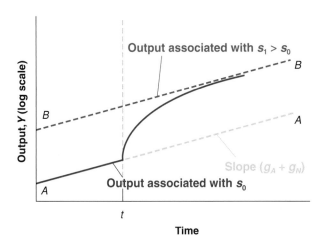

Figure 13.4

The effects of an increase in the saving rate (2)

The increase in the saving rate leads to higher growth until the economy reaches its new, higher, balanced growth path.

of AA is equal to $g_A + g_N$. After the increase in the saving rate at time t, output grows faster for some period of time. Eventually, output ends up at a higher level than it would have been without the increase in saving, but its growth rate returns to $g_A + g_N$. In the new steady state, the economy grows at the same rate, but on a higher growth path, BB. BB, which is parallel to AA, also has a slope equal to $g_A + g_N$.

Let's summarise: in an economy with technological progress and population growth, output grows over time. In steady state, output *per effective worker* and capital *per effective worker* are constant. Put another way, output *per worker* and capital *per worker* grow at the rate of technological progress. Put yet another way, output and capital grow at the same rate as effective labour and, therefore, at a rate equal to the growth rate of the number of workers plus the rate of technological progress. When the economy is in steady state, it is said to be on a *balanced growth path*.

The rate of output growth in steady state is independent of the saving rate. However, the saving rate affects the steady-state level of output per effective worker. Increases in the saving rate lead, for some time, to an increase in the growth rate above the steady-state growth rate.

◀ Figure 13.4 is the same as Figure 12.5, which anticipated the derivation presented here.

For a description of logarithmic scales, see Appendix 1 at the end of the book.

◀ When a logarithmic scale is used, a variable growing at a constant rate moves along a straight line. The slope of the line is equal to the rate of growth of the variable.

13.2 THE DETERMINANTS OF TECHNOLOGICAL PROGRESS

We have just seen that the growth rate of output per worker is ultimately determined by the rate of technological progress. This leads naturally to the next question: what determines the rate of technological progress? We now take up this question.

'Technological progress' brings to mind images of major discoveries: the invention of the microchip, the discovery of the structure of DNA and so on. These discoveries suggest a process driven largely by scientific research and chance rather than by economic forces. But the truth is that most technological progress in modern economies is the result of a humdrum process: the outcome of firms' **research and development (R&D)** activities. Industrial R&D expenditures account for between 2% and 3% of GDP in each of the four major rich countries we looked at in Chapter 11 (the USA, France, Japan and the UK). About 75% of the roughly 1 million US scientists and researchers working in R&D are employed by firms. US firms' R&D spending equals more than 20% of their spending on gross investment and more than 60% of their spending on net investment – gross investment less depreciation.

Firms spend on R&D for the same reason they buy new machines or build new plants: to increase profits. By increasing spending on R&D, a firm increases the probability that it will discover and develop a new product. (We use *product* as a generic term to denote new goods or new techniques of production.) If a new product is successful, the firm's profits will increase. There is, however, an important difference between purchasing a machine and spending more on R&D. The difference is that the outcome of R&D is fundamentally *ideas*. And, unlike a machine, an idea can potentially be used by many firms at the same time. A firm that has just acquired a new machine does not have to worry that another firm will use that particular machine. A firm that has discovered and developed a new product can make no such assumption.

This last point implies that the level of R&D spending depends not only on the **fertility** *of* the *research* process – how spending on R&D translates into new ideas and new products – but also on the **appropriability of research** results – the extent to which firms benefit from the results of their own R&D. Let's look at each aspect in turn.

The fertility of the research process

If research is very fertile – that is, if R&D spending leads to many new products – then, other things being equal, firms will have strong incentives to spend on R&D; R&D spending and, by implication, technological progress will be high. The determinants of the fertility of research lie largely outside the realm of economics. Many factors interact here.

The fertility of research depends on the successful interaction between basic research (the search for general principles and results) and applied research and development (the application of these results to specific uses and the development of new products). Basic research does not lead, by itself, to technological progress, but the success of applied research and development depends ultimately on basic research. Much of the computer industry's development can be traced to a few breakthroughs, from the invention of the transistor to the invention of the microchip. Indeed, the recent increase in productivity growth in the USA, which we discussed in Chapter 1, is widely attributed to the diffusion across the US economy of the breakthroughs in information technology. (This is explored further in the Focus box 'Information technology, the new economy and productivity growth'.)

In Chapter 12, we looked at the role of human capital as an input in production: more educated people can use more complex machines, or handle more complex tasks. Here, we see a second role of human capital: better researchers and scientists and, by implication, a higher rate of technological progress.

Some countries appear to be more successful than others at basic research; other countries are more successful at applied research and development. Studies point to differences in the education system as one of the reasons. For example, it is often argued that the French higher education system, with its strong emphasis on abstract thinking, produces researchers who are better at basic research than at applied research and development. Studies also point to the importance of a 'culture of entrepreneurship,' in which a big part of technological progress comes from the ability of entrepreneurs to organise the successful development and marketing of new products – a dimension where the USA appears to be better than most other countries.

It takes many years, and often many decades, for the full potential of major discoveries to be realised. The usual sequence is that a major discovery leads to the exploration of potential applications, then to the development of new products and, finally, to the adoption

FOCUS

Information technology, the new economy and productivity growth

Average annual productivity growth in the USA from 1996–2006 reached 2.8% – a high number relative to the anaemic 1.8% average achieved from 1970–1995. This has led some to proclaim an **information technology revolution**, announce the dawn of a **New Economy** and forecast a long period of high productivity growth in the future.

What should we make of these claims? Research to date gives reasons both for optimism and for caution. It suggests that the recent high productivity growth is indeed linked to the development of information technologies. It also suggests that a sharp distinction must be drawn between what is happening in the information technology (IT) sector – the sector that produces computers, computer software and software services and communications equipment – and the rest of the economy – which uses this information technology:

● In the IT sector, technological progress has indeed been proceeding at an extraordinary pace.

In 1965, researcher Gordon Moore, who later founded Intel Corporation, predicted that the number of transistors in a chip would double every 18–24 months, allowing for steadily more powerful computers. As shown in Figure 13.5, this relation – now known as **Moore's law** – has held extremely well over time. The first logic chip produced in 1971 had 2300 transistors; the Pentium 4, released in 2000, had 42 million. (The Intel Core 2, released in 2006, and thus not included in the figure, has 291 million.)

Although it has proceeded at a less extreme pace, technological progress in the rest of the IT sector has also been very high. And the share of the IT sector in GDP is steadily increasing, from 3% of GDP in 1980 to 7% today. This combination of high technological progress in the IT sector and of an increasing IT share has led to a steady increase in the economy-wide rate of technological progress. This is one of the factors behind the high productivity growth in the USA since the mid-1990s.

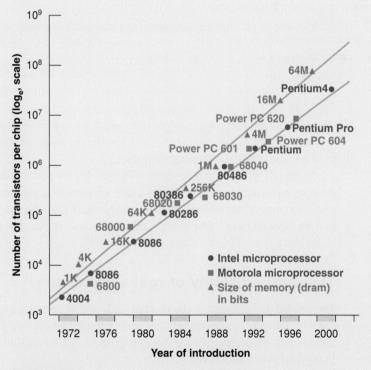

Figure 13.5

Moore's law: number of transistors per chip, 1970–2000

Source: Dale Jorgenson, 'Information Technology and the US Economy', *American Economic Review*, 2001, **91**(1), 1–32.

However, in the non-IT sector – the 'old economy,' which still accounts for more than 90% of the US economy – there is little evidence of a parallel technological revolution:

- On the one hand, the steady decrease in the price of IT equipment (reflecting technological progress in the IT sector) has led firms in the non-IT sector to increase their stock of IT capital. This has led to an increase in the ratio of capital per worker and an increase in productivity growth in the non-IT sector.

  Let's go through this argument a bit more formally. Go back to equation (13.2), which shows the relation of output per effective worker to the ratio of capital per effective worker:

$$Y/AN = f(K/AN)$$

Think of this equation as giving the relation between output per effective worker and capital per effective worker in the non-IT sector. The evidence is that the decrease in the price of IT capital has led firms to increase their stock of IT capital and, by implication, their overall capital stock. In other words, K/AN has increased in the non-IT sector, leading to an increase in Y/AN.

- On the other hand, the IT revolution does not appear to have had a major direct effect on the pace of technological progress in the non-IT sector. You have surely heard claims that the information technology revolution was forcing firms to drastically reorganise, leading to large gains in productivity. Firms may be reorganising but, so far, there is little evidence that this is leading to large gains in productivity: measures of technological progress show only a small rise in the rate of technological progress in the non-IT sector from the post-1970 average.

In terms of the production function relation we just discussed, there is no evidence that the technological revolution has led to a higher rate of growth of A in the non-IT sector.

Are there reasons to expect productivity growth to be higher in the future than in the past 25 years? The answer is yes: the factors we have just discussed are here to stay. Technological progress in the IT sector is likely to remain high, and the share of IT is likely to continue to increase. Moreover, firms in the non-IT sector are likely to further increase their stock of IT capital, leading to further increases in productivity.

How high can we expect productivity growth to be in the future? Probably not as high as it was from 1996–2006 but, according to some estimates, we can expect it to be perhaps 0.5 percentage points higher than its post-1970 average. This may not be the miracle some have claimed but, if sustained, it is an increase that will make a substantial difference to the US standard of living in the future.

Note: For more on these issues, read 'Information Technology and the U.S. Economy', by Dale Jorgenson, *American Economic Review*, 2001, **91**(1), 1–32.

of these new products. An example with which we are all familiar is the personal computer. Twenty years after the commercial introduction of personal computers, it often seems as if we have just begun discovering their uses.

An age-old worry is that research will become less and less fertile – that most major discoveries have already taken place and that technological progress will now slow down. This fear may come from thinking about mining, where higher-grade mines were exploited first, and we have had to exploit lower- and lower-grade mines. But this is only an analogy, and so far there is no evidence that it is correct.

The appropriability of research results

The second determinant of the level of R&D and of technological progress is the degree of *appropriability* of research results. If firms cannot appropriate the profits from the development of new products, they will not engage in R&D, and technological progress will be slow. Many factors are also at work here.

The nature of the research process itself is important. For example, if it is widely believed that the discovery of a new product by one firm will quickly lead to the discovery of an even better product by another firm, there may be little payoff to being first. In other words, a highly fertile field of research may not generate high levels of R&D because no company will find the investment worthwhile. This example is extreme but revealing.

Even more important is the legal protection given to new products. Without such legal protection, profits from developing a new product are likely to be small. Except in rare cases where the product is based on a trade secret (such as Coca-Cola), it will generally not take long for other firms to produce the same product, eliminating any advantage the innovating firm may have had initially. This is why countries have patent laws. A **patent** gives a firm that has discovered a new product – usually a new technique or device – the right to exclude anyone else from the production or use of the new product for some time.

How should governments design patent laws? On the one hand, protection is needed to provide firms with the incentives to spend on R&D. On the other, once firms have discovered new products, it would be best for society if the knowledge embodied in those new products were made available to other firms and to people without restrictions. Take, for example, biogenetic research. Only the prospect of large profits is leading bioengineering firms to embark on expensive research projects. Once a firm has found a new product, and the product can save many lives, it would clearly be best to make it available at cost to all potential users. But if such a policy was systematically followed, it would eliminate incentives for firms to do research in the first place. So, patent law must strike a difficult balance. Too little protection will lead to little R&D. Too much protection will make it difficult for new R&D to build on the results of past R&D and may also lead to little R&D. (The difficulty of designing good patent or copyright laws is illustrated in the cartoon about cloning.)

> This type of dilemma is known as 'time inconsistency.' We shall see other examples and discuss it at length in Chapter 23.
>
> The issues go beyond patent laws. To take two controversial examples: should Microsoft be kept in one piece or broken up to stimulate R&D? Should the government impose caps on the prices of AIDS drugs?

Source: from Let's talk about copyright, Chappatte, www.globalcartoon.com, © Chappatte "L'Hebdo" (Lausanne).

Countries that are less technologically advanced than others often have poorer patent protection. China, for example, is a country with poor enforcement of patent rights. Our discussion helps explain why. These countries are typically users rather than producers of new technologies. Much of their improvement in productivity comes not from inventions within the country but from the adaptation of foreign technologies. In this case, the costs of weak patent protection are small because there would be few domestic inventions anyway. But the benefits of low patent protection are clear: domestic firms can use and adapt foreign technology without having to pay royalties to the foreign firms that developed the technology – which is good for the country.

13.3 THE FACTS OF GROWTH REVISITED

We can now use the theory we have developed in this chapter and Chapter 12 to interpret some of the facts we saw in Chapter 11.

Capital accumulation versus technological progress in rich countries since 1950

Suppose we observe an economy with a high growth rate of output per worker over some period of time. Our theory implies that this fast growth may come from two sources:

- It may reflect a high rate of technological progress under balanced growth.
- It may reflect instead the adjustment of capital per effective worker, K/AN, to a higher level. As we saw in Figure 13.5, such an adjustment leads to a period of higher growth, even if the rate of technological progress has not increased.

Can we tell how much of the growth comes from one source and how much comes from the other? Yes. If high growth reflects high balanced growth, output per worker should be growing at a rate *equal* to the rate of technological progress (see Table 13.1, row 4). If high growth reflects instead the adjustment to a higher level of capital per effective worker, this adjustment should be reflected in a growth rate of output per worker that *exceeds* the rate of technological progress.

In the USA, for example, the ratio of employment to population increased from 38% in 1950 to 51% in 2006. This represents an increase of 0.18% per year. Thus, in the USA, output per person has increased 0.18% more per year than output per worker – a small difference, relative to the numbers in the table.

Let's apply this approach to interpret the facts about growth in rich countries we saw in Table 11.1. This is done in Table 13.2, which gives, in column 1, the average rate of growth of output per worker, $g_Y - g_N$, and, in column 2, the average rate of technological progress, g_A, since 1950, for each of the six countries – France, Ireland, Japan, Sweden, the UK and the USA – we looked at in Table 11.1. (Note one difference between Tables 11.1 and 13.2: as suggested by the theory, Table 13.2 looks at the growth rate of output per worker, while Table 11.1, which focuses on the standard of living, looks at the growth rate of output per person. The differences are small.) The rate of technological progress, g_A, is constructed using a method introduced by Robert Solow; the method and the details of construction are given in the Focus box 'Constructing a measure of technological progress'.

The table leads to two conclusions. First, growth since 1950 has been a result of rapid technological progress, not unusually high capital accumulation. This conclusion follows from the fact that, in all four countries, the growth rate of output per worker (column 1) has been roughly equal to the rate of technological progress (column 2). This is what we would expect when countries are growing along their balanced growth path.

What would have happened to the growth rate of output per worker if these countries had had the same rate of technological progress but no capital accumulation during the period?

Note what this conclusion does not say: it does not say that capital accumulation was irrelevant. Capital accumulation was such as to allow these countries to maintain a roughly constant ratio of output to capital and achieve balanced growth. What it says is that, over

Table 13.2 Average annual rates of growth of output per worker and technological progress in six rich countries since 1950

	Rate of growth of output per worker (%) 1950–2004	Rate of technological progress (%) 1950–2004
France	3.02	3.01
Ireland	–	–
Japan	4.02	3.08
Sweden	–	–
UK	2.04	2.06
USA	1.08	2.00
Average		

Note: 'Average' is a simple average of the growth rates in each column.

Sources: 1950–1970: Angus Maddison, *Dynamic Forces in Capitalist Development*, Oxford University Press, New York, 1991; 1970–2004: OECD *Economic Outlook* database.

the period, growth did not come from an unusual increase in capital accumulation, it came from an increase in the ratio of capital to output.

Second, convergence of output per worker across countries has come from higher technological progress, rather than from faster capital accumulation, in the countries that started behind. This conclusion follows from the ranking of the rates of technological progress across the four countries in the second column, with Japan at the top and the USA at the bottom.

This is an important conclusion. One can think, in general, of two sources of convergence between countries. First, poorer countries are poorer because they have less capital to start with. Over time, they accumulate capital faster than the others, generating convergence. Second, poorer countries are poorer because they are less technologically advanced than the others. Over time, they become more sophisticated, either by importing technology from advanced countries or developing their own. As technological levels converge, so does output per worker. The conclusion we can draw from Table 13.2 is that, in the case of rich countries, the more important source of convergence in this case is clearly the second one.

◄ While the table looks at only four countries, a similar conclusion holds when one looks at the set of all OECD countries. Convergence is mainly due to the fact that countries that were behind in 1950 have had higher rates of technological progress since then.

FOCUS
Constructing a measure of technological progress

In 1957, Robert Solow devised a way of constructing an estimate of technological progress. The method, which is still in use today, relies on one important assumption: that each factor of production is paid its marginal product.

Under this assumption, it is easy to compute the contribution of an increase in any factor of production to the increase in output. For example, if a worker is paid €30 000 a year, the assumption implies that her contribution to output is equal to €30 000. Now suppose that this worker increases the number of hours she works by 10%. The increase in output coming from the increase in her hours will therefore be equal to €30 000 × 10%, or €3000.

Let us write this more formally. Denote output by Y, labour by N and the real wage by W/P. Then, we just established the change in output is equal to the real wage multiplied by the change in labour:

$$\Delta Y = \frac{W}{P} \Delta N$$

Divide both sides of the equation by Y, divide and multiply the right side by N and reorganise:

$$\frac{\Delta Y}{Y} = \frac{WN}{PY} \frac{\Delta N}{N}$$

Note that the first term on the right, WN/PY, is equal to the share of labour in output – the total wage bill in pounds divided by the value of output in pounds. Denote this share by α. Note that $\Delta Y/Y$ is the rate of growth of output and denote it by g_Y. Note similarly that $\Delta N/N$ is the

rate of change of the labour input and denote it by g_N. Then the previous relation can be written as

$$g_Y = \alpha g_N$$

More generally, this reasoning implies that the part of output growth attributable to growth of the labour input is equal to α times g_N. If, for example, employment grows by 2%, and the share of labour is 0.7, then the output growth due to the growth in employment is equal to 1.4% (0.7 × 2%).

Similarly, we can compute the part of output growth attributable to growth of the capital stock. Because there are only two factors of production, labour and capital, and because the share of labour is equal to α, the share of capital in income must be equal to $1 - \alpha$. If the growth rate of capital is equal to g_K, then the part of output growth attributable to growth of capital is equal to $1 - \alpha$ times g_K. If, for example, capital grows by 5%, and the share of capital is 0.3, then the output growth due to the growth of the capital stock is equal to 1.5% (0.3 × 5%).

Putting the contributions of labour and capital together, the growth in output attributable to growth in both labour and capital is equal to $\alpha g_N + (1 - \alpha)g_K$.

We can then measure the effects of technological progress by computing what Solow called the *residual*, the excess of actual growth of output, g_Y, over the growth attributable to growth of labour and the growth of capital, $\alpha g_N + (1 - \alpha)g_K$:

$$\text{Residual} \equiv g_Y - [\alpha g_N + (1 - \alpha)g_K]$$

▷

This measure is called the **Solow residual**. It is easy to compute: all we need to know to compute it are the growth rate of output, g_Y, the growth rate of labour, g_N, and the growth rate of capital, g_K, together with the shares of labour, α and capital, $1 - \alpha$.

To continue with our previous numeric examples, suppose employment grows by 2%, the capital stock grows by 5% and the share of labour is 0.7 (and so the share of capital is 0.3). Then the part of output growth attributable to growth of labour and growth of capital is equal to 2.9% ($0.7 \times 2\% + 0.3 \times 5\%$). If output growth is equal, for example, to 4%, then the Solow residual is equal to 1.1% ($4\% - 2.9\%$).

The Solow residual is sometimes called the **rate of growth of total factor productivity (or the rate of TFP growth**, for short). The use of *total factor productivity* is to distinguish it from the *rate of growth of labour productivity*, which is defined as $g_Y - g_N$, the rate of output growth minus the rate of labour growth.

The Solow residual is related to the rate of technological progress in a simple way. The residual is equal to the share of labour times the rate of technological progress:

$$\text{Residual} = \alpha g_A$$

We shall not derive this result here. But the intuition for this relation comes from the fact that what matters in the production function $Y = F(K, AN)$ [equation (13.1)] is the product of the state of technology and labour, AN.

We saw that to get the contribution of labour growth to output growth, we must multiply the growth rate of labour by its share. Because N and A enter the production function in the same way, it is clear that to get the contribution of technological progress to output growth, we must also multiply it by the share of labour.

If the Solow residual is equal to 0, so is technological progress. To construct an estimate of g_A, we must construct the Solow residual and then divide it by the share of labour. This is how the estimates of g_A presented in the text are constructed.

In the numerical example we saw earlier, the Solow residual is equal to 1.1%, and the share of labour is equal to 0.7. So the rate of technological progress is equal to 1.6% ($1.1\%/0.7$).

Keep straight the definitions of productivity growth you have seen in this chapter:

- Labour productivity growth (equivalently: the rate of growth of output per worker), $g_Y - g_N$.
- The rate of technological progress, g_A.

In steady state, labour productivity growth, $g_Y - g_N$, equals the rate of technological progress, g_A. Outside steady state, they need not be equal: an increase in the ratio of capital per effective worker, due, for example, to an increase in the saving rate, will cause $g_Y - g_N$ to be higher than g_A for some time.

Source: Robert Solow, 'Technical Change and the Aggregate Production Function', *Review of Economics and Statistics*, 1957, **39**(3), 312–320.

Capital accumulation versus technological progress in China since 1980

Going beyond growth in OECD countries, one of the striking facts in Chapter 11 was the high growth rates achieved by a number of Asian countries. This raises again the same questions we just discussed: do these high growth rates reflect fast technological progress, or do they reflect unusually high capital accumulation?

To answer the questions, we shall focus on China because of its size and because of the astonishingly high output growth rate, nearly 10%, it has achieved since the early 1980s. Table 13.3 gives the average rate of growth, g_Y, the average rate of growth of output per worker, $g_Y - g_N$, and the average rate of technological progress, g_A, for the period 1983–2003. The fact that the last two numbers are nearly equal yields a very clear conclusion: growth in China since the early 1980s has been nearly balanced, and the high

Table 13.3 Average annual rate of growth of output per worker and technological progress in China, 1983–2003

Rate of growth of output (%)	Rate of growth of output per worker (%)	Rate of technological progress (%)
9.7	8.0	8.2

Source: *OECD Economic Survey of China*, 2005.

growth of output per worker reflects a high rate of technological progress, 8.2% per year on average.

This is an important conclusion, showing the crucial role of technological progress in explaining China's growth. But, just as in our discussion of OECD countries, it would be wrong to conclude that capital accumulation is irrelevant. To sustain balanced growth at such a high growth rate, the Chinese capital stock has had to increase at the same rate as output. This in turn has required a very high investment rate. To see what investment rate was required, go back to equation (13.3) and divide both sides by output, Y, to get

◄ Recall, from Table 13.1: under balanced growth, $g_K = g_Y = g_A + g_N$.

$$\frac{I}{Y} = (\delta + (g_A + g_N))\frac{K}{Y}$$

Let's plug in numbers for China for the period 1983–2003. The estimate of d, the depreciation rate of capital in China, is 5% a year. As we just saw, the average value of g_A for the period was 8.2%. The average value of g_N, the rate of growth of employment, was 1.7%. The average value of the ratio of capital to output was 2.6. This implies a ratio of investment to output of (5% + 8.2% + 1.7%) × 2.6 = 29%. Thus, to sustain balanced growth, China has had to invest 41% of its output, a very high investment rate in comparison to, say, the US investment rate. So capital accumulation plays an important role in explaining Chinese growth; but it is still the case that sustained growth has come from a high rate of technological progress.

How has China been able to achieve such technological progress? A closer look at the data suggests two main channels. First, China has transferred labour from the countryside, where productivity is very low, to industry and services in the cities, where productivity is much higher. Second, China has imported the technology of more technologically advanced countries. It has, for example, encouraged the development of joint ventures between Chinese firms and foreign firms. Foreign firms have come up with better technologies and, over time, Chinese firms have learned how to use them.

◄ This ratio indeed is very close to the ratio one gets by looking directly at investment and output in the Chinese national income accounts.

This leads to a general point: the nature of technological progress is likely to be different in more and less advanced economies. The more advanced economies, being by definition at the **technological frontier**, need to develop new ideas, new processes and new products. They need to innovate. The countries that are behind can instead improve their level of technology by copying and adapting the new processes and products developed in the more advanced economies. They need to imitate. The further behind a country is, the larger the role of imitation relative to innovation. As imitation is likely to be easier than innovation, this can explain why convergence, both within the OECD and in the case of China and other countries, typically takes the form of **technological catch-up**. It raises, however, yet another question: if imitating is so easy, why is it that so many other countries do not seem to be able to do the same and grow? This points to the broader aspects of technology we discussed earlier in the chapter. Technology is more than just a set of blueprints. How efficiently the blueprints can be used and how productive an economy is depend on its institutions, on the quality of its government and so on.

SUMMARY

- When we think about the implications of technological progress for growth, it is useful to think of technological progress as increasing the amount of effective labour available in the economy (that is, labour multiplied by the state of technology). We can then think of output as being produced with capital and effective labour.

- In steady state, output *per effective worker* and capital *per effective worker* are constant. Put another way, output *per*

worker* and capital *per worker* grow at the rate of technological progress. Put yet another way, output and capital grow at the same rate as effective labour, thus at a rate equal to the growth rate of the number of workers plus the rate of technological progress.

- When the economy is in steady state, it is said to be on a balanced growth path. Output, capital and effective labour are all growing 'in balance' – that is, at the same rate.

- The rate of output growth in steady state is independent of the saving rate. However, the saving rate affects the steady-state level of output per effective worker. And increases in the saving rate will lead, for some time, to an increase in the growth rate above the steady-state growth rate.

- Technological progress depends on both (1) the fertility of research and development – how spending on R&D translates into new ideas and new products – and (2) the appropriability of the results of R&D – the extent to which firms benefit from the results of their R&D.

- When designing patent laws, governments must balance their desire to protect future discoveries and provide incentives for firms to do R&D with their desire to make existing discoveries available to potential users without restrictions.

- France, Japan, the UK and the USA have experienced roughly balanced growth since 1950: growth of output per worker has been roughly equal to the rate of technological progress. The same is true of China. Growth in China is roughly balanced, sustained by a high rate of technological progress and a high investment rate.

KEY TERMS

effective labour, or labour in efficiency units 269

balanced growth 274

research and development (R&D) 276

fertility of research 276

appropriability of research 276

information technology revolution 277

New Economy 277

Moore's law 277

patent 279

Solow residual, or rate of growth of total factor productivity, or rate of TFP growth 282

technology frontier 283

technological catch-up 283

QUESTIONS AND PROBLEMS

QUICK CHECK

1. *Using the information in this chapter, label each of the following statements true, false or uncertain. Explain briefly.*

a. Writing the production function in terms of capital and effective labour implies that as the level of technology increases by 10%, the number of workers required to achieve the same level of output decreases by 10%.

b. If the rate of technological progress increases, the investment rate (the ratio of investment to output) must increase in order to keep capital per effective worker constant.

c. In steady state, output per effective worker grows at the rate of population growth.

d. In steady state, output per worker grows at the rate of technological progress.

e. A higher saving rate implies a higher level of capital per effective worker in the steady state and thus a higher rate of growth of output per effective worker.

f. Even if the potential returns from R&D spending are identical to the potential returns from investing in a new machine, R&D spending is much riskier for firms than investing in new machines.

g. The fact that one cannot patent a theorem implies that private firms will not engage in basic research.

h. Because eventually we will know everything, growth will have to come to an end.

2. R&D and growth

a. Why is the amount of R&D spending important for growth? How do the appropriability and fertility of research affect the amount of R&D spending?

How do each of the policy proposals listed in (b) through (e) affect the appropriability and fertility of research, R&D spending in the long run, and output in the long run?

b. An international treaty that ensures that each country's patents are legally protected all over the world.

c. Tax credits for each euro of R&D spending.

d. A decrease in funding of government-sponsored conferences between universities and corporations.

e. The elimination of patents on breakthrough drugs, so the drugs can be sold at low cost as soon as they are available.

3. Sources of technological progress: economic leaders versus developing countries

a. Where does technological progress come from for the economic leaders of the world?

b. Do developing countries have other alternatives to the sources of technological progress you mentioned in part (a)?

c. Do you see any reasons developing countries may choose to have poor patent protection? Are there any dangers in such a policy (for developing countries)?

DIG DEEPER

4. *For each of the economic changes listed in (a) and (b), assess the likely impact on the growth rate and the level of output over the next five years and over the next five decades.*

a. a permanent reduction in the rate of technological progress.

b. a permanent reduction in the saving rate.

5. Measurement error, inflation and productivity growth

Suppose that there are only two goods produced in an economy: haircuts and banking services. Prices, quantities and the number of workers occupied in the production of each good for year 1 and for year 2 are given below:

	Year 1			Year 2		
	P1	**Q1**	**W1**	**P2**	**Q2**	**W2**
Haircut	10	100	50	12	100	50
Banking	10	200	50	12	230	60

a. What is nominal GDP in each year?

b. Using year 1 prices, what is real GDP in year 2? What is the growth rate of real GDP?

c. What is the rate of inflation using the GDP deflator?

d. Using year 1 prices, what is real GDP per worker in year 1 and year 2? What is labour productivity growth between year 1 and year 2 for the whole economy?

Now suppose that banking services in year 2 are not the same as banking services in year 1. Year 2 banking services include telebanking that year 1 banking services did not include. The technology for telebanking was available in year 1, but the price of banking services with telebanking in year 1 was €13, and no-one chose to purchase this package. However, in year 2, the price of banking services with telebanking was €12, and everyone chose to have this package (i.e. in year 2 no-one chose to have the year 1 banking services package without telebanking). (Hint: assume that there are now two types of banking services: those with telebanking and those without. Rewrite the preceding table but now with three goods: haircuts and the two types of banking services.)

e. Using year 1 prices, what is real GDP for year 2? What is the growth rate of real GDP?

f. What is the rate of inflation using the GDP deflator?

g. What is labour productivity growth between year 1 and year 2 for the whole economy?

h. Consider this statement: 'If banking services are mis-measured – for example, by not taking into account the introduction of telebanking – we will over-estimate inflation and underestimate productivity growth.' Discuss this statement in light of your answers to parts (a) through (g).

6. *Suppose that the economy's production function is*

$$Y = \sqrt{K}\sqrt{AN}$$

that the saving rate, s, is equal to 16%, and that the rate of depreciation, δ, is equal to 10%. Suppose further that the number of workers grows at 2% per year and that the rate of technological progress is 4% per year.

a. Find the steady-state values of the variables listed in (i) through (v).
   i.   The capital stock per effective worker.
   ii. Output per effective worker.
   iii. The growth rate of output per effective worker.
   iv. The growth rate of output per worker.
   v.   The growth rate of output.

b. Suppose that the rate of technological progress doubles to 8% per year. Recompute the answers to part (a). Explain.

c. Now suppose that the rate of technological progress is still equal to 4% per year, but the number of workers now grows at 6% per year. Re-compute the answers to (a). Are people better off in (a) or in (c)? Explain.

7. *Discuss the potential role of each of the factors listed in (a) through (g) on the steady-state level of output per worker. In each case, indicate whether the effect is through A, through K, through H, or through some combination of A, K and H.*

a. geographic location

b. education

c. protection of property rights

d. openness to trade

e. low tax rates

f. good public infrastructure

g. low population growth

EXPLORE FURTHER

8. Growth accounting

The Focus box 'Constructing a measure of technological progress' shows how data on output, capital and labour can be used to construct estimates of the rate of growth of technological progress. We modify that approach in this problem to examine the growth of capital per worker. The function

$$Y = K^{1/3}(AN)^{2/3}$$

gives a good description of production in rich countries. Following the same steps as in the Focus box, you can show that

$$(2/3)g_A = g_Y - (2/3)g_N - (1/3)g_K$$
$$= (g_Y - g_N) - (1/3)(g_K - g_N)$$

where g_x denotes the growth rate of x.

a. What does the quantity $g_Y - g_N$ represent? What does the quantity $g_K - g_N$ represent?

b. Rearrange the preceding equation to solve for the growth rate of capital per worker.

c. Look at Table 13.2 in the chapter. Using your answer to part (b), substitute in the average annual growth rate of output per worker and the average annual rate of technological progress for the USA for the period 1950–2004 to obtain a crude measure of the average annual growth of capital per worker. (Strictly speaking, we should construct these measures individually for every year, but we limit ourselves to readily available data in this problem.) Do the same for the other countries listed in Table 13.2. How does the average growth of capital per worker compare across the countries in Table 13.2? Do the results make sense to you? Explain.

*We invite you to visit the Blanchard page on the Prentice Hall website, at **www.prenhall.com/blanchard** for this chapter's World Wide Web exercises.*

FURTHER READING

- For more on growth, both theory and evidence, read **Charles Jones, *Introduction to Economic Growth*, 2nd ed., Norton, New York, 2002**. Jones's web page, *http://www.stanfard.edu~chadj/*, is a useful portal to the research on growth.

- For more on patents, see the *Economist* survey on *Patents and Technology*, 20 October 2005.

On two issues we have not explored in the text:

- Growth and global warming – Read the *Stern Review on the Economics of Climate Change*, 2006. You can find it at *www.hm-treasury.gov.uk/independent_reviews/stern_review_economics_climate_change/stern_review_report.cfm*. (The report is very long. Read just the executive summary.)

- Growth and the environment – Read the *Economist* survey on *The Global Environment; The Great Race*, 4 July 2002.

EXTENSIONS

Source: from 'I think I see the problem...', efi 0056, Ed Fischer,
www.cartoonstock.com

EXPECTATIONS

The next four chapters represent the first major extension of the core. They look at the role of expectations in output fluctuations.

Chapter 14 Expectations: the basic tools

Chapter 14 introduces the role of expectations. Expectations play an essential role in macroeconomics. Nearly all the economic decisions people and firms make – whether to buy a car, whether to buy bonds or to buy stocks, whether to build a new plant – depend on their expectations about future income, future profits, future interest rates and so on.

Chapter 15 Financial markets and expectations

Chapter 15 focuses on the role of expectations in financial markets. It first looks at the determination of bond prices and bond yields. It shows how we can learn about the course of expected future interest rates by looking at the yield curve. It then turns to stock prices, and shows how they depend on expected future dividends and interest rates. Finally, it discusses whether stock prices always reflect fundamentals, or may instead reflect bubbles or fads.

Chapter 16 Expectations, consumption and investment

Chapter 16 focuses on the role of expectations in consumption and investment decisions. The chapter shows how consumption depends partly on current income, partly on human wealth, and partly on financial wealth. It shows how investment depends partly on current cash flow, and partly on the expected present value of future profits.

Chapter 17 Expectations, output and policy

Chapter 17 looks at the role of expectations in output fluctuations. Starting from the *IS–LM* model, it modifies the description of the goods market equilibrium (the *IS* relation) to reflect the effect of expectations on spending. It revisits the effects of monetary and fiscal policy on output. It shows for example, that, in contrast to the results derived in the core, a fiscal contraction can sometimes increase output, even in the short run.

Chapter 14

EXPECTATIONS: THE BASIC TOOLS

A consumer who considers buying a new car must ask: can I safely take a new car loan? How much of a wage raise can I expect over the next few years? How safe is my job?

A manager who observes an increase in current sales must ask: Is this a temporary boom that I should try to meet with the existing production capacity? Or is it likely to last, in which case should I order new machines?

A pension fund manager who observes a bust in the stock market must ask: are stock prices going to decrease further, or is the bust likely to end? Does the decrease in stock prices reflect expectations of firms' lower profits in the future? Do I share those expectations? Should I move some of my funds into or out of the stock market?

These examples make clear that many economic decisions depend not only on what is happening today but also on expectations of what will happen in the future. Indeed, some decisions should depend very little on what is happening today. For example, why should an increase in sales today – if it is not accompanied by expectations of continued higher sales in the future – cause a firm to alter its investment plans? The new machines may not be in operation before sales have returned to normal. By then, they may sit idle, gathering dust.

Until now, we have not paid systematic attention to the role of expectations in goods and financial markets. We ignored expectations in our construction of both the *IS–LM* model and the aggregate demand component of the *AS–AD* model that builds on the *IS–LM* model. When looking at the goods market, we assumed that consumption depended on current income and that investment depended on current sales. When looking at financial markets, we lumped assets together and called them 'bonds'; we then focused on the choice between bonds and money, and ignored the choice between bonds and stocks, the choice between short-term bonds and long-term bonds and so on. We introduced these simplifications to build the intuition for the basic mechanisms at work. It is now time to think about the role of expectations in economic fluctuations. We shall do so in this and the next three chapters.

This chapter lays the groundwork and introduces two key concepts:

- Section 14.1 examines the distinction between the real interest rate and the nominal interest rate.

- Sections 14.2 and 14.3 build on this distinction to revisit the effects of money growth on interest rates. They lead to a surprising but important result: higher money growth leads to lower nominal interest rates in the short run but to higher nominal interest rates in the medium run.

- Section 14.4 introduces the second concept: the concept of expected present discounted value.

14.1 NOMINAL VERSUS REAL INTEREST RATES

In 1980, the *interest rate* in the UK – the annual average of four UK banks' base rates – was 16.3%. In 2008, the same rate was only 4.7%: the interest rates we face as consumers were also substantially lower in 2008 than in 1980. It was much cheaper to borrow in 2008 than it was in 1980.

Or was it? In 1980, inflation was around 18%. In 2008, inflation was around 3.6%. This would seem relevant: the interest rate tells us how many pounds we shall have to pay in the future in exchange for having £1 more today.

But we do not consume pounds. We consume goods. When we borrow, what we really want to know is how many goods we will have to give up in the future in exchange for the goods we get today. Likewise, when we lend, we want to know how many goods – not how many pounds – we will get in the future for the goods we give up today. The presence of inflation makes the distinction important. What is the point of receiving high interest payments in the future if inflation between now and then is so high that we are unable to buy more goods then?

This is where the distinction between nominal interest rates and real interest rates comes in:

- Interest rates expressed in terms of units of the national currency are called **nominal interest rates**. The interest rates printed in the financial pages of newspapers are nominal interest rates. For example, when we say that the one-year rate on government bonds is 4.36%, we mean that for every euro an individual borrows from a bank, he or she has to pay €1.0436 in one year. More generally, if the nominal interest rate for year t is i_t, borrowing €1 this year requires you to pay €$(1 + i_t)$ next year. (We use interchangeably *this year* for *today* and *next year* for *one year from today*.)   ◁ Nominal interest rate: the interest rate in terms of units of national currency.

- Interest rates expressed *in terms of a basket of goods* are called **real interest rates**. If we denote the real interest rate for year t by r_t, then, by definition, borrowing the equivalent of one basket of goods this year requires you to pay the equivalent of $1 + r_t$ baskets of goods next year.   ◁ Real interest rate: the interest rate in terms of a basket of goods.

What is the relation between nominal and real interest rates? How do we go from nominal interest rates – which we do observe – to real interest rates – which we typically do not observe? The intuitive answer: we must adjust the nominal interest rate to take into account expected inflation.

Let's go through the step-by-step derivation. Assume that there is only one good in the economy, bread (we shall add jam and other goods later). Denote the one-year nominal interest rate, in terms of euros, by i_t: If you borrow €1 this year, you will have to repay €$(1 + i_t)$ next year. But you are not interested in euros. What you really want to know is: if you borrow enough to eat 1 more kilo of bread this year, how much will you have to repay, in terms of kilos of bread, next year?

Figure 14.1 helps us derive the answer. The top part repeats the definition of the one-year real interest rate. The bottom part shows how we can derive the one-year real interest rate from information about the one-year nominal interest rate and the price of bread:

- Start with the arrow pointing down in the lower left of Figure 14.1. Suppose you want to eat 1 more kilo of bread this year. If the price of a kilo of bread this year is €P_t, to eat 1 more kilo of bread, you must borrow €P_t.

- If i_t is the one-year nominal interest rate – the interest rate in terms of euros – and if you borrow €P_t, you will have to repay €$(1 + i_t)P_t$ next year. This is represented by the arrow from left to right at the bottom of Figure 14.1.

- What you care about, however, is not euros but kilos of bread. Thus, the last step involves converting euros back to kilos of bread next year. Let P_{t+1}^e be the price of bread you expect for next year. (The superscript e indicates that this is an expectation: You do not know yet what the price of bread will be next year.) How much you expect to repay next year, in terms of kilos of bread, is therefore equal to $(1 + i)P_t$ (the number of euros you have

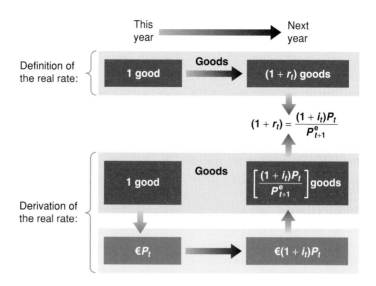

Figure 14.1

Definition and derivation of the real interest rate

If you have to pay €10 next year, and ➤ you expect the price of bread next year to be €2 per kilo, you expect to have to repay the equivalent of 10/2 = 5 kilos of bread next year. This is why we divide the euro amount $(1 + i_t)P_t$ by the expected price of bread next year, P^e_{t+1}.

to repay next year) divided by P^e_{t+1} (the price of bread in terms of euros expected for next year), so $(1 + i_t)P_t/P^e_{t+1}$. This is represented by the arrow pointing up in the lower right of Figure 14.1.

Putting together what you see in the top part and what you see in the bottom part of Figure 14.1, it follows that the one-year real interest rate, r_t, is given by

$$1 + r_t = (1 + i_t)\frac{P_t}{P^e_{t+1}} \quad [14.1]$$

This relation looks intimidating. Two simple manipulations make it look friendlier:

Add 1 to both sides in (14.2): ➤

$$1 + \pi^e_{t+1} = 1 + \frac{(P^e_{t+1} - P_t)}{P_t}$$

Reorganise:

$$1 + \pi^e_{t+1} = \frac{P^e_{t+1}}{P_t}$$

Take the inverse on both sides:

$$\frac{1}{1 + \pi^e_{t+1}} = \frac{P_t}{P^e_{t+1}}$$

Replace in (6.1).

- Denote expected inflation between t and $t + 1$ by p^e_{t+1}. Given that there is only one good – bread – the expected rate of inflation equals the expected change in the euro price of bread between this year and next year, divided by the euro price of bread this year:

$$\pi^e_{t+1} = \frac{(P^e_{t+1} - P_t)}{P_t} \quad [14.2]$$

Using equation (14.2), rewrite P_t/P^e_{t+1} in equation (6.1) as $1/(1 + \pi^e_{t+1})$. Replace in (6.1) to get

$$(1 + r_t) = \frac{1 + i_t}{1 + \pi^e_{t+1}} \quad [14.3]$$

1 plus the real interest rate equals the ratio of 1 plus the nominal interest rate, divided by 1 plus the expected rate of inflation.

- Equation (14.3) gives us the *exact* relation of the real interest rate to the nominal interest rate and expected inflation. However, when the nominal interest rate and expected inflation are not too large – say, less than 20% per year – a close approximation to this equation is given by the simpler relation

See Proposition 6 in Appendix 1 at the ➤ end of the book. Suppose $i = 10\%$ and $\pi^e = 5\%$. The exact relation (6.3) gives $r_t = 4.8\%$. The approximation given by equation (6.4) gives 5% – close enough. The approximation can be quite poor, however, when i and π^e are high. If $I = 100\%$ and $\pi^e = 80\%$, the exact relation gives $\pi^e = 11\%$, but the approximation gives $r = 20\%$, a big difference.

$$r_t \approx i_t - \pi^e_{t+1} \quad [14.4]$$

Equation (14.4) is simple. Remember it. It says that *the real interest rate is (approximately) equal to the nominal interest rate minus expected inflation.* (In the rest of the book, we often treat the relation (14.4) as if it were an equality. Remember, however, that it is only an approximation.)

Note some of the implications of equation (14.4):

1. When expected inflation equals 0, the nominal and the real interest rates are equal.
2. Because expected inflation is typically positive, the real interest rate is typically lower than the nominal interest rate.
3. For a given nominal interest rate, the higher the expected rate of inflation, the lower the real interest rate.

The case where expected inflation happens to be equal to the nominal interest rate is worth looking at more closely. Suppose the nominal interest rate and expected inflation both equal 10%, and you are the borrower. For every euro you borrow this year, you will have to repay €1.10 next year, but euros will be worth 10% less in terms of bread next year. So, if you borrow the equivalent of €1 of bread, you will have to repay the equivalent of €1 of bread next year: the real cost of borrowing – the real interest rate – is equal to 0. Now suppose you are the lender: for every euro you lend this year, you will receive €1.10 next year. This looks attractive, but euros next year will be worth 10% less in terms of bread. If you lend the equivalent of €1 of bread this year, you will get the equivalent of €1 of bread next year: despite the 10% nominal interest rate, the real interest rate is equal to 0.

We have assumed so far that there is only one good – bread. But what we have done generalises easily to many goods. All we need to do is to substitute the *price level* – the price of a basket of goods – for the price of bread in equation (14.1) or equation (14.3). If we use the consumer price index (CPI) to measure the price level, the real interest rate tells us how much consumption we must give up next year to consume more today.

Nominal and real interest rates in the UK since 1980

Let us return to the question at the start of this section. We can now restate it as follows: was the *real interest rate* lower in 2008 than it was in 1985? More generally, what has happened to the real interest rate in the UK since the early 1980s?

The answer is shown in Figure 14.2, which plots both nominal and real interest rates since 1980. For each year, the nominal interest rate is the annual average of four UK banks' base rate. To construct the real interest rate, we need a measure of expected inflation – more precisely, the rate of inflation expected as of the beginning of each year. Figure 14.2 uses, for each year, the forecast of inflation for that year published at the end of the previous year by the OECD. For example, the forecast of inflation used to construct the real interest rate for 2008 is the forecast of inflation published by the OECD in December 2007 – 1.98%. To know more about how inflation expectations can be measured, read the following Focus box.

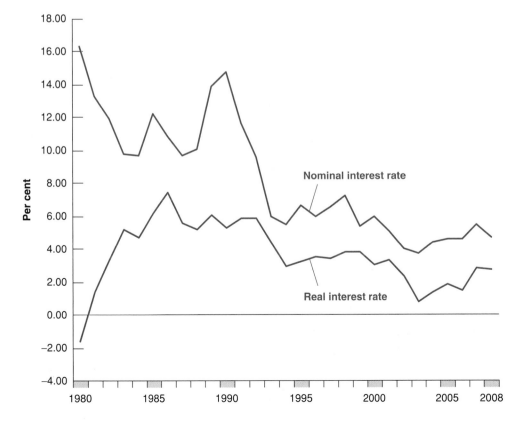

Figure 14.2

Nominal and real interest rates in the UK since 1980

Although the nominal interest rate has declined considerably since the early 1980s, the real interest rate was actually higher in 2008 than in 1980.

Note that the real interest rate $(i - \pi^e)$ is based on *expected* inflation. If actual inflation turns out to be different from expected inflation, the realised real interest rate $(i - \pi)$ will be different from the real interest rate. For this reason, the real interest rate is sometimes called the *ex-ante* real interest rate. (*Ex-ante* means 'before the fact.' Here it means before inflation is known.) The realised real interest rate is called the *ex-post* real interest rate. (*Ex-post* means 'after the fact.' Here it means after inflation is known.)

Real interest rate can be negative when inflation is higher than the nominal interest rate. But remember that the same is not true for the nominal interest rate, which cannot be negative!

Figure 14.2 shows the importance of adjusting for inflation. Although the nominal interest was much lower in 2008 than it was in 1980, the real interest rate was actually *higher* in 2008 than it was in 1980: 2.7% in 2008 versus −1.6% in 1980. Put another way, despite the large decline in nominal interest rates, borrowing was actually more expensive in 2008 than it was 1980. This is due to the fact that inflation (and, with it, expected inflation) was lower in 2008 with respect to 1980.

FOCUS
How can inflation expectations be measured?

Inflation expectations can be measured in two ways:

1. *From surveys of consumers and firms.* In Europe, the forecasts of households and firms are calculated by *The Joint Harmonised EU Programme of Business and Consumer Surveys* (*http://ec.europa.eu/economy_finance/indicators/business_consumer_surveys/userguide_en.pdf*). In particular, household expectations are constructed using the EC survey's question 6, which asks how, by comparison with the past 12 months, the respondents expect that consumer prices will develop in the next 12 months. Note from Figure 14.3 how inflation expectations measured through

surveys tend to go down during recessions, for example in the recent recession started in the summer of 2007.

In the UK, the Bank of England jointly with GfK NOP (a leading market research agency) runs the *Inflation Attitudes Survey*; questions are asked annually that cover perceptions of the relationship between interest rates and inflation and knowledge of who sets rates. In the USA, one such survey is conducted by the Survey Research Center at the University of Michigan.

2. *Comparing the yield on nominal government bonds with that on real government bonds of the same maturity.*

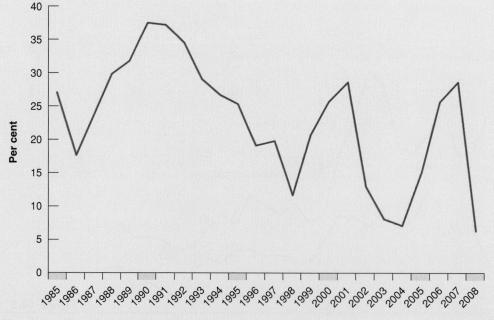

Figure 14.3

Expected inflation from consumers' surveys in the EU

Source: Eurostat.

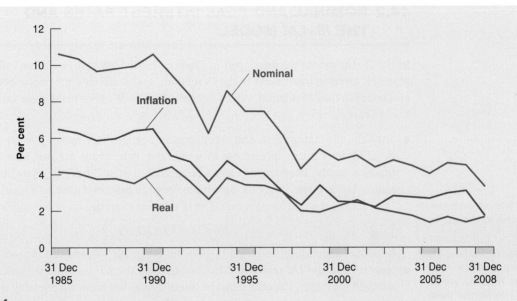

Figure 14.4

Expected inflation in the UK since 1985

Source: Bank of England.

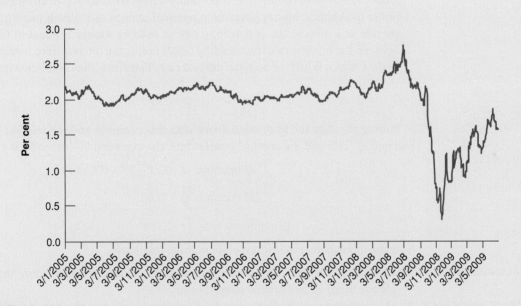

Figure 14.5

Expected inflation calculated on French indexed government bonds (OAT)

Source: Agence France Trésor.

Real bonds or indexed bonds are bonds that promise payments adjusted for inflation rather than fixed nominal payments. The UK was one of the first developed economies to issue index linked bonds in 1981. As an example, Figure 14.4 shows expected inflation calculated as the difference between the nominal annual average yield on ten years' British Government Securities and the real annual average yield on ten years' British Government Securities.

In France the *Agence France Trésor* issues two types of real bonds: the OATi indexed to the French CPI and the OAT€ indexed to the euro area CPI. They also compute the implicit expected inflation rate (called 'point-mort d'inflation'), as shown in Figure 14.5 from January 2005 until June 2009. Note the impressive fall of expected inflation from July 2007 (beginning of the financial crisis) until November 2008 (when some major rescue packages were put in place in the UK and the USA).

14.2 NOMINAL AND REAL INTEREST RATES AND THE *IS–LM* MODEL

In the *IS–LM* model we developed in Chapter 5, 'the' interest rate came into play in two places: it affected investment in the *IS* relation, and it affected the choice between money and bonds in the *LM* relation. Which interest rate – nominal or real – were we talking about in each case?

We shall ignore time subscripts here; they are not needed for this and the next section.

For the time being, we shall focus only on how the interest rate affects investment. In Chapters 16 and 17, you will see how the real interest rate affects both investment and consumption decisions.

- Take the *IS* relation first. Our discussion in Section 14.1 makes it clear that firms, in deciding how much investment to undertake, care about the *real interest rate*: firms produce goods. They want to know how much they will have to repay, not in terms of money but in terms of goods. So what belongs in the *IS* relation is the real interest rate. Let *r* denote the real interest rate. The *IS* relation must therefore be modified as follows:

$$Y = C(Y - T) + I(Y, r) + G$$

Investment spending, and thus the demand for goods, depends on the *real* interest rate.

- Now turn to the *LM* relation. When we derived the *LM* relation, we assumed that the demand for money depended on the interest rate, but were we referring to the nominal interest rate or the real interest rate? The answer is: to the *nominal interest rate.* Remember why the interest rate affects the demand for money. When people decide whether to hold money or bonds, they take into account the opportunity cost of holding money rather than bonds – the opportunity cost is what they give up by holding money rather than bonds. Money pays a zero nominal interest rate. Bonds pay a nominal interest rate of *i*. Hence, the opportunity cost of holding money is equal to the difference between the interest rate from holding bonds minus the interest from holding money, so $i - 0 = i$, which is just the nominal interest rate. Therefore, the *LM* relation is still given by

$$\frac{M}{P} = YL(i)$$

Putting together the IS relation above with this equation and the relation between the real interest rate and the nominal interest rate, the extended *IS–LM* model is given by

$$IS \text{ relation: } Y = C(Y - T) + I(Y, r) + G$$

$$LM \text{ relation: } \frac{M}{P} = YL(i)$$

$$\text{Real interest rate: } r = i - \pi^e$$

Note the immediate implications of these three relations:

Interest rate in the *LM* relation: nominal interest rate, *i*.

Interest rate in the *IS* relation: real interest rate, *r*.

1. The interest rate directly affected by monetary policy (the interest rate that enters the *LM* equation) is the nominal interest rate.
2. The interest rate that affects spending and output (the rate that enters the *IS* relation) is the real interest rate.
3. The effects of monetary policy on output therefore depend on how movements in the nominal interest rate translate into movements in the real interest rate. To explore this question further, the next section looks at how an increase in money growth affects the nominal interest rate and the real interest rate, both in the short run and in the medium run.

14.3 MONEY GROWTH, INFLATION AND NOMINAL AND REAL INTEREST RATES

When reading the economy pages in any newspaper you will find apparently conflicting comments about the reaction of financial markets to possible decisions by the central bank (be it the Bank of England or the European Central Bank or the Riksbank, Sweden's Central

Bank) on the growth rate of money. You might read both that higher money growth will lead to a decline in interest rates and that it will cause higher interest rates in the future. Which one is right? Does higher money growth lead to lower interest rates, or does higher money growth lead to higher interest rates? The answer: Both!

There are two keys to the answer: one is the distinction we just introduced between the real and the nominal interest rate. The other is the distinction we developed in the core between the short run and the medium run. As you will see, the full answer is:

● Higher money growth leads to lower nominal interest rates in the short run but to higher nominal interest rates in the medium run.

● Higher money growth leads to lower real interest rates in the short run but has no effect on real interest rates in the medium run.

The purpose of this section is to develop this answer and explore its implications.

Revisiting the *IS–LM* model

We have derived three equations – the *IS* relation, the *LM* relation and the relation between the real and the nominal interest rates. It will be more convenient to reduce them to two equations. To do so, replace the real interest rate in the *IS* relation with the nominal interest rate minus expected inflation: $r = i - \pi^e$. This gives:

$$IS: \quad Y = C(Y - T) + I(Y, i - \pi^e) + G$$

$$LM: \frac{M}{P} = YL(i)$$

These two equations are the same as in Chapter 5, with just one difference: investment spending in the *IS* relation depends on the real interest rate, which is equal to the nominal interest rate minus expected inflation.

The associated *IS* and *LM* curves are drawn in Figure 14.6, for given values of P, M, G and T, and for a given expected rate of inflation, π^e:

● The *IS* curve is still downward-sloping. For a given expected rate of inflation, π^e, the nominal interest rate and the real interest rate move together. So, a decrease in the nominal interest rate leads to an equal decrease in the real interest rate, leading to an increase in spending and in output.

● The *LM* curve is upward-sloping. Given the money stock, an increase in output, which leads to an increase in the demand for money, requires an increase in the nominal interest rate.

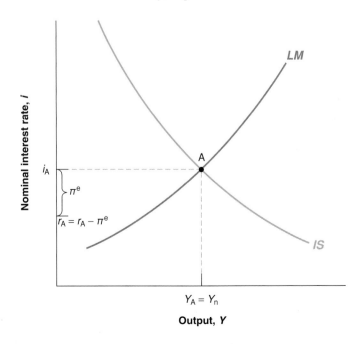

Figure 14.6

Equilibrium output and interest rates

The equilibrium level of output and the equilibrium nominal interest rate are given by the intersection of the *IS* curve and the *LM* curve. The real interest rate equals the nominal interest rate minus expected inflation.

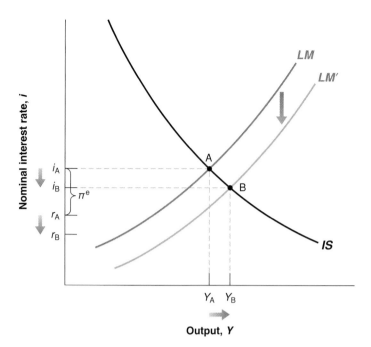

Figure 14.7

The short-run effects of an increase in money growth

An increase in money growth increases the real money stock in the short run. This increase in real money leads to an increase in output and decreases in both the nominal and real interest rates.

● The equilibrium is at the intersection of the *IS* curve and the *LM* curve, point A, with output level, Y_A, and nominal interest rate, i_A. Given the nominal interest rate, the real interest rate, r_A, is given by $r_A = i_A - \pi^e$.

Nominal and real interest rates in the short run

Assume that the economy is initially at the natural rate of output, so $Y_A = Y_n$. Now suppose the central bank increases the rate of growth of money. What happens to output, to the nominal interest rate and to the real interest rate *in the short run*?

One of the lessons from our analysis of monetary policy in the core is that, in the short run, the faster increase in nominal money will not be matched by an equal increase in the price level. In other words, the higher rate of growth of nominal money will lead, in the short run, to an increase in the real money stock, M/P. This is all we need to know for our purposes. What happens to output and to interest rates in the short run is shown in Figure 14.7.

> In the short run, when the rate of money growth increases, *M/P* increases. Both *i* and *r* decrease, and *Y* increases.

The increase in the real money stock causes a shift in the *LM* curve down, from *LM* to *LM'*: for a given level of output, the increase in the real money stock leads to a decrease in the nominal interest rate. If we assume – as seems reasonable – that people and firms do not revise their expectations of inflation immediately, the *IS* curve does not shift: given expected inflation, a given nominal interest rate corresponds to the same real interest rate and to the same level of spending and output.

The economy moves down the *IS* curve, and the equilibrium moves from A to B. Output is higher: the nominal interest rate is lower and, given expected inflation, so is the real interest rate.

Let's summarise: in the short run, the increase in nominal money growth leads to an increase in the real money stock. This increase in real money leads to a decrease in both the nominal and the real interest rates and to an increase in output.

14.4 EXPECTED PRESENT DISCOUNTED VALUES

Let us now turn to the second key concept introduced in this chapter: the concept of expected present discounted value.

Let's return to the example of the manager considering whether to buy a new machine. On the one hand, buying and installing the machine involves a cost today. On the other, the machine allows for higher production, higher sales and higher profits in the future. The question facing the manager is whether the value of these expected profits is higher than the cost of buying and installing the machine. This is where the concept of expected present discounted value comes in handy: the **expected present discounted value** of a sequence of future payments is the value today of this expected sequence of payments. Once the manager has computed the expected present discounted value of the sequence of profits, her problem becomes simple: she compares two numbers, the expected present discounted value and the initial cost. If the value exceeds the cost, she should go ahead and buy the machine. If it does not, she should not.

As for the real interest rate, the practical problem is that expected present discounted values are not directly observable. They must be constructed from information on the sequence of expected payments and expected interest rates. Let's first look at the mechanics of construction.

Computing expected present discounted values

If the one-year nominal interest rate is i_t, lending 1 euro this year implies getting back $1 + i_t$ euros next year. Equivalently, borrowing 1 euro this year implies paying back $1 + i_t$ euros next year. In this sense, 1 euro this year is worth $1 + i_t$ euros next year. This relation is represented graphically in the first line of Figure 14.8.

Turn the argument around and ask: how much is 1 euro *next year* worth this year? The answer, shown in the second line of Figure 14.8, is $1/(1 + i_t)$ euros. Think of it this way: if you lend $1/(1 + i_t)$ euros this year, you will receive times $1/(1 + i_t)$ times $1/(1 + i_t) = 1$ euro next year. Equivalently, if you borrow $1/(1 + i_t)$ euros this year, you will have to repay exactly 1 euro next year. So, 1 euro next year is worth $1/(1 + i_t)$ euros this year.

More formally, we say that $1/(1 + i_t)$ is the *present discounted value* of 1 euro next year. The word *present* comes from the fact that we are looking at the value of a payment next year in terms of euros *today*. The word *discounted* comes from the fact that the value next year is discounted, with $1/(1 + i_t)$ being the **discount factor**. (The one-year nominal interest rate, i_t, is sometimes called the **discount rate**.)

◄ i_t: discount rate.

$1/(1 + i_t)$: discount factor.

If the discount rate goes up, the discount factor goes down.

Because the nominal interest rate is always positive, the discount factor is always less than 1: a euro next year is worth less than 1 euro today. The higher the nominal interest rate, the lower the value today of 1 euro received next year. If $i = 5\%$, the value this year of 1 euro next year is $1/0.5 \approx 95$ cents. If $i = 10\%$, the value today of 1 euro next year is $1/1.10 \approx 91$ cents.

Now apply the same logic to the value today of a euro received *two years from now*. For the moment, assume that current and future one-year nominal interest rates are known with certainty. Let i_t be the nominal interest rate for this year and i_{t+1} be the one-year nominal interest rate next year.

If, today, you lend 1 euro for two years, you will get $1/(1 + i_t) \, 1/(1 + i_{t+1})$ euros two years from now. Put another way, 1 euro today is worth $1/(1 + i_t) \, 1/(1 + i_{t+1})$ euros two years from now. This relation is represented in the third line of Figure 14.8.

What is 1 euro two years from now worth today? By the same logic as before, the answer is $1/(1 + i_t) \, 1/(1 + i_{t+1})$ euros: if you lend $1/[(1 + i_t) \, 1/(1 + i_{t+1})]$ euros this year, you will get exactly 1 euro in two years. So, the *present discounted value of 1 euro two years from now is* equal to $1/[(1 + i_t) \, 1/(1 + i_{t+1})]$ euros. This relation is shown in the last line of Figure 14.8.

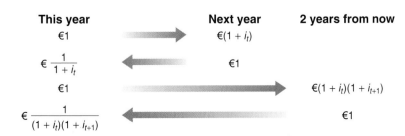

This year	Next year	2 years from now
€1	€(1 + i_t)	
€ $\frac{1}{1 + i_t}$	€1	
€1		€(1 + i_t)(1 + i_{t+1})
€ $\frac{1}{(1 + i_t)(1 + i_{t+1})}$		€1

Figure 14.8

Computing present discounted values

If, for example, the one-year nominal interest rate is the same this year and next, equal to 5% – so $i_t = i_{t+1} = 5\%$ – then the present discounted value of 1 euro in two years is equal to $1/(1.05)$, or about 91 cents today.

The general formula

It is now easy to derive the present discounted value for the case where both payments and interest rates can change over time.

Consider a sequence of payments in euros, starting today and continuing into the future. Assume for the moment that both future payments and future interest rates are known with certainty. Denote today's payment by €z_t, the payment next year by €z_{t+1}, the payment two years from today by €z_{t+2}, and so on.

The present discounted value of this sequence of payments – that is, the value in today's pounds of the sequence of payments – which we shall call €V_t, is given by

$$€V_t = €z_t + \frac{1}{(1+i_t)}€z_{t+1} + \frac{1}{(1+i_t)(1+i_{t+1})}€z_{t+2} + \ldots$$

Each payment in the future is multiplied by its respective discount factor. The more distant the payment, the smaller the discount factor, and thus the smaller today's value of that distant payment. In other words, future payments are discounted more heavily, so their present discounted value is lower.

> This statement ignores an important issue – risk. If people dislike risk, the value of an uncertain (and therefore risky) payment now or in the future will be lower than the value of a riskless payment, even if both have the same expected value. We ignore this effect here but return to it briefly in Chapter 16. For a full treatment, you would have to take a course in finance.

We have assumed that future payments and future interest rates were known with certainty. Actual decisions, however, have to be based on expectations of future payments rather than on actual values for these payments. In our earlier example, the manager cannot be sure how much profit the new machine will actually bring; nor does she know what interest rates will be in the future. The best she can do is get the most accurate forecasts she can and then compute the *expected present discounted value* of profits, based on these forecasts.

How do we compute the expected present discounted value when future payments and interest rates are uncertain? We do this basically in the same way as before but by replacing the *known* future payments and *known* interest rates with *expected* future payments and *expected* interest rates. Formally, we denote expected payments next year by €z^e_{t+1}, expected payments two years from now by €z^e_{t+2}, and so on. Similarly, we denote the expected one-year nominal interest rate next year by €$^e_{t+1}$, and so on (the one-year nominal interest rate this year, i_t, is known today, so it does not need a superscript e). The expected present discounted value of this expected sequence of payments is given by

$$€V_t = €z_t + \frac{1}{(1+i_t)}€z^e_{t+1} + \frac{1}{(1+i_t)(1+i^e_{t+1})}€z^e_{t+2} + \ldots \qquad [14.5]$$

'Expected present discounted value' is a heavy expression. Instead, for short, we will often just use **present discounted value**, or even just **present value**. Also, it is convenient to have a shorthand way of writing expressions like equation (14.5). To denote the present value of an expected sequence for €z, we write $V(€z_t)$, or just $V(€z)$.

Using present values: examples

Equation (14.5) has two important implications:

> €z or future €z^e increase $\Rightarrow$ €V increases.

- The present value depends positively on today's actual payment and expected future payments. An increase in either today's €z or any future €z^e leads to an increase in the present value.

> i or future i^e increase $\Rightarrow$ €V decreases.

- The present value depends negatively on current and expected future interest rates. An increase in either current i or in any future i^e leads to a decrease in the present value.

Equation (14.5) is not simple, however, and so it will help to go through some examples.

Constant interest rates

To focus on the effects of the sequence of payments on the present value, assume that interest rates are expected to be constant over time, so that $i_t = i_{t+1}^e = \ldots$, and denote their common value by i. The present value formula – equation (6.5) – becomes

$$\text{€}V_t = \text{€}z_t + \frac{1}{(1+i_t)}\text{€}z_{t+1}^e + \frac{1}{(1+i)^2}\text{€}z_{t+2}^e + \ldots \qquad [14.6]$$

In this case, the present value is a *weighted sum* of current and expected future payments, with weights that decline *geometrically* through time. The weight on a payment this year is 1, the weight on the payment n years from now is $1/(1+i)^n$. With a positive interest rate, the weights get closer and closer to 0 as we look further and further into the future. For example, with an interest rate equal to 10%, the weight on a payment ten years from today is equal to $1/(1+0.10)^{10} = 0.386$, so that a payment of €1000 in ten years is worth €386 today. The weight on a payment in 30 years is $1/(1+0.10)^{30} = 0.057$, so that a payment of €1000 30 years from today is worth only €57 today!

◀ The weights correspond to the terms of a geometric series. See the discussion of geometric series in Appendix 1 at the end of the book.

Constant interest rates and payments

In some cases, the sequence of payments for which we want to compute the present value is simple. For example, a typical fixed-rate 30-year mortgage requires constant pound payments over 30 years. Consider a sequence of equal payments – call them €z without a time index – over n years, including this year. In this case, the present value formula in equation (14.6) simplifies to

$$\text{€}V_t = \text{€}z_t + \left[1 + \frac{1}{(1+i_t)} + \ldots + \frac{1}{(1+i)^{n-1}}\right]$$

Because the terms in the expression in brackets represent a geometric series, we can compute the sum of the series and get

$$\text{€}V_t = \text{€}z\frac{1 - [1/(1+i)^n]}{1 - [1/(1+i)]}$$

Suppose you have just won €1 million from a lottery and have been presented with a €1 000 000 cheque on TV. Afterward, you are told that, to protect you from your worst spending instincts as well as from your many new 'friends', the state will pay you the million pounds in equal yearly instalments of €50 000 over the next 20 years. What is the present value of your prize today? Taking, for example, an interest rate of 6% per year, the preceding equation gives $V = $ €50 000 $\times (0.688)/(0.057) = $ €608 000. Not bad, but winning the prize did not make you a millionaire.

Constant interest rates and payments, forever

Let's go one step further and assume that payments are not only constant but go on forever. Real-world examples are hard to come by for this case, but one example comes from 19th-century Britain, when the government issued *consols*, bonds paying a fixed yearly amount forever. In euro terms, let €z be the constant payment. Assume that payments start next year rather than right away, as in the previous example (this makes for simpler algebra). From equation (14.6), we have

◀ Most *consols* were bought back by the British government at the end of the 19th century and early 20th century. A few are still around.

$$\text{€}V_t = \frac{1}{(1+i)}\text{€}z + \frac{1}{(1+i)^2}\text{€}z + \ldots$$

$$= \frac{1}{(1+i)}\left[1 + \frac{1}{(1+i)} + \ldots\right]\text{€}z$$

where the second line follows by factoring out $1/(1+i)^n$. The reason for factoring out $1/(1+i)^n$ should be clear from looking at the term in brackets: it is an infinite geometric sum, so we can use the property of geometric sums to rewrite the present value as

$$€V_t = \frac{1}{(1+i)} \times \frac{1}{1 - (1/(1+i))} \times €z$$

Or, simplifying (the steps are given in the application of Proposition 2 in Appendix 1 at the end of the book),

$$€V_t = \frac{€z}{i}$$

The present value of a constant sequence of payments, $€z$, is simply equal to the ratio of $€z$ to the interest rate, i. If, for example, the interest rate is expected to be 5% per year forever, the present value of a consol that promises €10 per year forever equals €10/0.05 = €200. If the interest rate increases and is now expected to be 10% per year forever, the present value of the consol decreases to €10/0.10 = €100.

Zero interest rates

Because of discounting, computing present discounted values typically requires the use of a calculator. There is, however, a case where computations simplify. This is the case where the interest rate is equal to zero: if $I = 0$, then $1/(1 + i)$ equals 1, and so does $[1/(1 + i)^n]$ for any power n. For that reason, the present discounted value of a sequence of expected payments is just the *sum* of those expected payments. Because the interest rate is in fact typically positive, assuming that the interest rate is 0 is only an approximation. But it is a very useful one for back-of-the-envelope computations.

Nominal versus real interest rates and present values

So far, we have computed the present value of a sequence of euro payments by using interest rates in terms of euros – nominal interest rates. Specifically, we have written equation (14.5) as

$$€V_t = €z_t + \frac{1}{(1+i_t)} €z_{t+1}^e + \frac{1}{(1+i)(1+i_{t+1}^e)} €z_{t+2}^e + \dots$$

where $i_t, t_{t+1}^e, \dots$ is the sequence of current and expected future nominal interest rates, and $€z_t, €z_{t+1}^e, €z_{t+2}^e, \dots$ is the sequence of current and expected future euro payments.

Suppose we want to compute instead the present value of a sequence of *real* payments – that is, payments in terms of a basket of goods rather than in terms of euros. Following the same logic as before, we need to use the right interest rates for this case: namely interest rates in terms of the basket of goods – *real interest rates*. Specifically, we can write the present value of a sequence of real payments as

$$V_t = z_t + \frac{1}{(1+r_t)} z_{t+1}^e + \frac{1}{(1+r_t)(1+r_{t+1}^e)} z_{t+2}^e + \dots \qquad [14.7]$$

where $r_t, r_{t+1}^e, \dots$ is the sequence of current and expected future real interest rates, $z_t, z_{t+1}^e, z_{t+2}^e, \dots$ is the sequence of current and expected future real payments and V_t is the real present value of future payments.

These two ways of writing the present value turn out to be equivalent. That is, the real value obtained by constructing $€V_t$ using equation (14.5) and dividing by P_t, the price level, is equal to the real value V_t obtained from equation (14.7), so

$$€V_t/P_t = V_t$$

In words: we can compute the present value of a sequence of payments in two ways. One way is to compute it as the present value of the sequence of payments expressed in euros, discounted using nominal interest rates, and then divided by the price level today. The other way is to compute it as the present value of the sequence of payments expressed in real terms, discounted using real interest rates. The two ways give the same answer.

> The proof is given in the Focus box 'Deriving the present discounted value using nominal and real interest rates'. Go through it to test your understanding of the two tools introduced in this chapter: real interest rates versus nominal interest rates, and expected present values.

Do we need both formulas? Yes. Which one is more helpful depends on the context. Take bonds, for example. Bonds typically are claims to a sequence of nominal payments over a period of years. For example, a ten-year bond might promise to pay €50 each year for ten years, plus a final payment of €1000 in the last year. So when we look at the pricing of bonds in Chapter 16, we shall rely on equation (14.5), which is expressed in terms of euro payments, rather than on equation (14.7), which is expressed in real terms.

However, sometimes, we have a better sense of future expected real values than of future expected euro values. You might not have a good idea of what your euro income will be in 20 years: its value depends very much on what happens to inflation between now and then. But you might be confident that your nominal income will increase by at least as much as inflation – in other words, that your real income will not decrease. In this case, using equation (14.5), which requires you to form expectations of future euro income, will be difficult. However, using equation (14.7), which requires you to form expectations of future real income, may be easier. For this reason, when we discuss consumption and investment decisions in Chapter 16, we shall rely on equation (14.7) rather than equation (14.5).

FOCUS
Deriving the present discounted value using nominal and real interest rates

We show here that the two ways of expressing the present discounted value, represented in equations (14.5) and (14.7), are equivalent. Let us first rewrite the two equations.

Equation (14.5) gives the present value as the sum of current and expected future nominal payments, discounted using the current nominal and expected future interest rates:

$$\text{€}V_t = \text{€}z_t + \frac{1}{1+i_t}\text{€}z_{t+1}^e + \frac{1}{(1+i_t)(1+i_{t+1}^e)}\text{€}z_{t+2}^e + \dots$$

[14.5]

Equation (14.7) gives the present value as the sum of current and expected future real payments, discounted using current and expected future real interest rates:

$$V_t = z_t + \frac{1}{1+r_t}z_{t+1}^e + \frac{1}{(1+r_t)(1+r_{t+1}^e)}z_{t+2}^e + \dots \quad [14.7]$$

We divide both sides of equation (14.5) for the current price level, P_t. The left side becomes $\text{€}V_t/P_t = V_t$, which is the present real discounted value, the same that appearing on the left side of equation (14.7).

Now let us take each term on the right side of equation (14.5) in turn.

The first term becomes $\text{€}z_t/P_t = z_t$, which is the current payment in real terms. This term is equal to the first term on the right side of equation (14.7).

The second term is given by

$$[1/(1+i_t)](\text{€}z_{t+1}^e/P_t)$$

Multiplying numerator and denominator by P_{t+1}^e, the expected price level for the coming year, we get:

$$\frac{1}{1+i_t} \times \frac{P_{t+1}^e}{P_t} \times \frac{\text{€}z_{t+1}^e}{P_{t+1}^e}$$

The third ratio is the real expected payment at time $t + 1$. Now consider the second ratio. Note that

$$(P_{t+1}^e/P_t)$$

can be rewritten as

$$1 + [(P_{t+1}^e - P_t)/P_t]$$

and then, using the definition of expected inflation, as

$$(1 + \pi_t^e)$$

Rewriting all the three ratios of the second term together:

$$\frac{1 + \pi_t^e}{1 + i_t}z_{t+1}^e$$

Finally, using the definition of the real interest rate equation (14.3), we get:

$$\frac{1}{1+r_t}z_{t+1}^e$$

This term is equal to the second term on the right side of equation (14.7).

The same method applies to other terms. Make sure you can derive at least the next one on your own. It follows that equations (14.5) and (14.7) are equivalent ways to define and derive the present discounted value of a sequence of payments.

SUMMARY

- The nominal interest rate tells you how many euros you need to repay in the future in exchange for one euro today.

- The real interest rate tells you how many goods you need to repay in the future in exchange for one good today.

- The real interest rate is approximately equal to the nominal interest rate minus expected inflation.

- Investment decisions depend on the real interest rate. The choice between money and bonds depends on the nominal interest rate. Thus, the real interest rate enters the *IS* relation, while the nominal interest rate enters the *LM* relation.

- In the short run, an increase in money growth decreases both the nominal interest rate and the real interest rate.

- In the medium run, an increase in money growth has no effect on the real interest rate, but it increases the nominal interest rate one-for-one.

- The expected present discounted value of a sequence of payments equals the value this year of the expected sequence of payments. It depends positively on current and future expected payments and negatively on current and future expected interest rates.

- When discounting a sequence of current and expected future nominal payments, one should use current and expected future nominal interest rates. In discounting a sequence of current and expected future real payments, one should use current and expected future real interest rates.

KEY TERMS

nominal interest rate 291

real interest rate 291

expected present discounted value 299

discount factor 299

discount rate 299

present discounted value 300

present value 300

QUESTIONS AND PROBLEMS

QUICK CHECK

1. *Using the information in this chapter, label each of the following statements true, false or uncertain. Explain briefly.*

a. As long as inflation remains roughly constant, the movements in the real interest rate are roughly equal to the movements in the nominal interest rate.

b. If inflation turns out to be higher than expected, the realised real cost of borrowing turns out to be lower than the real interest rate.

c. Looking across countries, the real interest rate is likely to vary much less than the nominal interest rate.

d. The real interest rate is equal to the nominal interest rate divided by the price level.

e. The value today of a nominal payment in the future cannot be greater than the nominal payment itself.

f. The real value today of a real payment in the future cannot be greater than the real payment itself.

2. *For which of the problems listed in (a) through (c) would you want to use real payments and real interest rates, and for which would you want to use nominal payments and nominal interest rates, to compute the expected present discounted value? In each case, explain why.*

a. Estimating the present discounted value of the profits from an investment in a new machine.

b. Estimating the present value of a ten-year British government security.

c. Deciding whether to lease or buy a car.

3. *Compute the real interest rate using the exact formula and the approximation formula for each set of assumptions listed in (a) through (c).*

a. $i = 4\%$; $\pi^e = 2\%$

b. $i = 15\%$; $\pi^e = 11\%$

c. $i = 54\%$; $\pi^e = 46\%$

4. Nominal and real interest rates around the world

a. Can the nominal interest rate ever be negative? Explain.

b. Can the real interest rate ever be negative? Under what circumstances can it be negative? If so, why not just hold cash instead of bonds?

c. What are the effects of a negative real interest rate on borrowing and lending?

d. Find a recent issue of *The Economist* and look at the tables in the back (titled 'Economic Indicators and Financial Indicators'). Use the three-month money market rate as the nominal interest rate and the most recent three-month rate of change in consumer prices as the expected rate of inflation (both are in annual terms). Which countries have the lowest nominal interest rates? Which countries have the lowest real interest rates? Are these real interest rates close to being negative?

5. Choosing between different retirement plans

You want to save €2000 today for retirement in 40 years. You have to choose between two plans listed in (i) and (ii).

(i) Pay no taxes today, put the money in an interest-yielding account and pay taxes equal to 25% of the total amount withdrawn at retirement.

(ii) Pay taxes equivalent to 20% of the investment amount today, put the remainder in an interest-yielding account and pay no taxes when you withdraw your funds at retirement.

a. What is the expected present discounted value of each of these plans if the interest rate is 1%? 10%?

b. Which plan would you choose in each case?

6. Approximating the price of long-term bonds

The present value of an infinite stream of euro payments of €z (that starts next year) is €z/i when the nominal interest rate, i, is constant. This formula gives the price of a consol – a bond paying a fixed nominal payment each year, forever. It is also a good approximation for the present discounted value of a stream of constant payments over long but not infinite periods, as long as i is constant. Let's examine how close the approximation is.

a. Suppose that $i = 10\%$. Let €$z = 100$. What is the present value of the consol?

b. If $i = 10\%$, what is the expected present discounted value of a bond that pays €z over the next ten years? 20 years? 30 years? 60 years? (*Hint*: Use the formula from the chapter but remember to adjust for the first payment.)

c. Repeat the calculations in (a) and (b) for $i = 2\%$ and $i = 5\%$.

DIG DEEPER

7. *When looking at the short run in Section 14.2, we showed how an increase in nominal money growth led to higher output, a lower nominal interest rate and a lower real interest rate.*

The analysis in the text (as summarised in Figure 14.7) assumed that expected inflation, P^e, did not change in the short run. Let us now relax this assumption and assume that, in the short run, both money growth and expected inflation increase.

a. Show the effect on the *IS* curve. Explain in words.

b. Show the effect on the *LM* curve. Explain in words.

c. Show the effect on output and on the nominal interest rate. Could the nominal interest rate end up higher – not lower – than before the change in money growth? Why?

d. Even if what happens to the nominal interest rate is ambiguous, can you tell what happens to the real interest rate? (*Hint*: What happens to output relative to Figure 14.7? What does this imply about what happens to the real interest rate?)

EXPLORE FURTHER

8. Inflation-indexed bonds

Some bonds issued by the British Treasury make payments indexed to inflation. These inflation-indexed bonds compensate investors for inflation. Therefore, the current interest rates on these bonds are real interest rates – interest rates in terms of goods. These interest rates can be used, together with nominal interest rates, to provide a measure of expected inflation. Let's see how.

Go to the website of the Bank of England and get the most recent statistical release listing interest rates (***http://www.bankofengland.co.uk/publications/index.htm***).

Find the current nominal interest rate on British Government Securities with a five-year maturity. Now find the current interest rate on 'inflation-indexed' securities with a five-year maturity. What do you think participants in financial markets think the average inflation rate will be over the next five years?

*We invite you to visit the Blanchard page on the Prentice Hall website, at **www.prenhall.com/blanchard** for this chapter's World Wide Web exercises.*

Chapter 15

FINANCIAL MARKETS AND EXPECTATIONS

In our first pass at financial markets in Chapter 4, we assumed that there were only two assets: money and one type of bond – a one-year bond. We now look at an economy with a richer and more realistic menu of non-money assets: short-term bonds, long-term bonds and stocks.

Our focus throughout this chapter is on the role expectations play in the determination of bond and stock prices. (The reason this belongs in a macroeconomics textbook: as you will see, not only are these prices affected by current and expected future activity, but they in turn affect decisions that affect current activity. Understanding their determination is central to understanding fluctuations.)

- Section 15.1 looks at the determination of bond prices and bond yields. It shows how bond prices and yields depend on current and expected future short-term interest rates. It then shows how we can use the yield curve to learn about the expected course of future short-term interest rates.

- Section 15.2 looks at the determination of stock prices. It shows how stock prices depend on current and expected future profits as well as on current and expected future interest rates. It then discusses how movements in economic activity affect stock prices.

- Section 15.3 discusses fads and bubbles in the stock market – episodes in which stock prices appear to move for reasons unrelated to either profits or interest rates.

15.1 BOND PRICES AND BOND YIELDS

Bonds differ in two basic dimensions:

- **Default risk** – the risk that the issuer of the bond (which could be a government or a company) will not pay back the full amount promised by the bond.
- **Maturity** – the length of time over which the bond promises to make payments to the bondholder. A bond that promises to make one payment of £1000 in six months has a maturity of six months; a bond that promises £100 per year for the next 20 years and a final payment of £1000 at the end of those 20 years has a maturity of 20 years. Maturity is the more important dimension for our purposes, and we shall focus on it here.

Bonds of different maturities each have a price and an associated interest rate, called the *yield to maturity*, or simply the *yield*. Yields on bonds with a short maturity, typically a year or less, are called *short-term interest rates*. Yields on bonds with a longer maturity are called *long-term interest rates*.

◄ Do not worry: we are just introducing the terms here. They will be defined and explained in this section.

On any given day, we observe the yields on bonds of different maturities, and we can trace graphically how the yield depends on the maturity of a bond. This relation between maturity and yield is called the **yield curve**, or the **term structure of interest rates** (where the word *term* is synonymous with maturity). Figure 15.1 gives, for example, two term structures on British Government Securities on 30 June 2007, and on 31 May 2009. The choice of the two dates is not accidental; why we chose them will become clear shortly.

◄ Term structure ≡ yield curve.

Note how, on 30 June 2007, the yield curve was slightly downward-sloping, declining from a one-year interest rate of 5.83% to a five-year interest rate of 5.56%. In other words, long-term interest rates were slightly lower than short-term interest rates. Note how, almost two years later, on 31 May 2009, the yield curve was sharply upward-sloping, increasing from a three-month interest rate of 0.64% to a five-year interest rate of 2.72%. In other words, long-term interest rates were now much higher than short-term interest rates.

Why was the yield curve downward-sloping in June 2007 but upward sloping in May 2009? Put another way, why were long-term interest rates slightly lower than short-term interest rates in June 2007 but higher than short-term interest rates in May 2009? What were financial market participants thinking at each date? To answer these questions and, more generally, to think about the determination of the yield curve and the relation between short-term interest rates and long-term interest rates, we proceed in two steps:

1. We derive *bond prices* for bonds of different maturities.
2. We go from bond prices to *bond yields* and examine the determinants of the yield curve and the relation between short-term and long-term interest rates.

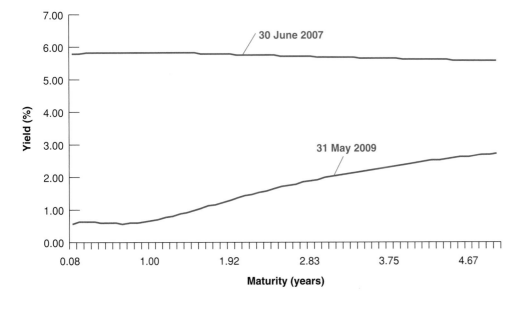

Figure 15.1

UK yield curves: June 2007 and May 2009

The yield curve, which was slightly downward-sloping in June 2007, was sharply upward-sloping in May 2009.

Source: Bank of England.

FOCUS
The vocabulary of bond markets

Understanding the basic vocabulary of financial markets will help make them less mysterious. Here is a basic vocabulary review:

- Bonds are issued by governments or by firms. If issued by the government or government agencies, bonds are called **government bonds**. If issued by firms (corporations), they are called **corporate bonds**.
- In Europe, as in the USA, bonds are rated for their default risk (the risk that they will not be repaid) by two private firms, Standard & Poor's (S&P) and Moody's Investors Service. Moody's **bond ratings** range from Aaa for bonds with nearly no risk of default, such as US government bonds, to C for bonds whose default risk is high. A lower rating typically implies that the bond has to pay a higher interest rate, or else investors will not buy it. The difference between the interest rate paid on a given bond and the interest rate paid on the bond with the highest (best) rating is called the **risk premium** associated with the given bond. Bonds with high default risk are sometimes called **junk bonds**.
- Bonds that promise a single payment at maturity are called **discount bonds**. The single payment is called the **face value** of the bond.
- Bonds that promise multiple payments before maturity and one payment at maturity are called **coupon bonds**. The payments before maturity are called **coupon payments**. The final payment is called the face value of the bond. The ratio of coupon payments to the face value is called the **coupon rate**. The **current yield** is the ratio of the coupon payment to the price of the bond.

  For example, a bond with coupon payments of £5 each year, a face value of £100, and a price of £80 has a coupon rate of 5% and a current yield of 5/80 = 0.0625 = 6.25%. From an economic viewpoint, neither the coupon rate nor the current yield are interesting measures. The correct measure of the interest rate on a bond is its yield to maturity, or simply yield; you can think of it as roughly the average interest rate paid by the bond over its life. (The **life of a bond** is the amount

of time left until the bond matures.) We shall define the yield to maturity more precisely later in this chapter.

- In the UK, the government issues bonds called GILTS – a gilt is a UK government liability in sterling, issued by HM Treasury and listed on the London Stock Exchange. The government has concentrated issuance of conventional gilts around the 5-, 10- and 30-year maturity areas, but in May 2005 the Debt Management Office issued a new 50-year maturity conventional gilt. In Sweden, the government issues different types of nominal bonds. Nominal government bonds are interest-bearing securities with an annual coupon payment. Nominal bonds have maturities from 2 to 15 years. Approximately 45% of all borrowing consists of government bonds. T-bills are securities with short maturities (between three and six months). In all around 20–25% of all borrowing takes place in T-bills.
- Bonds are typically nominal bonds: they promise a sequence of fixed nominal payments – payments in terms of domestic currency. As we already mentioned in this chapter, there are, however, other types of bonds. Among them are **indexed bonds**, bonds that promise payments adjusted for inflation rather than fixed nominal payments. Instead of promising to pay, say, £100 in a year, a one-year indexed bond promises to pay £100 $(1 + \pi)$, whatever π, the rate of inflation that will take place over the coming year, turns out to be. Because they protect bondholders against the risk of inflation, indexed bonds are popular in many countries. In Europe, a certain number of countries issue indexed bonds, including the UK and France. They play a particularly important role in the UK, where, over the past 20 years, people have increasingly used them to save for retirement. By holding long-term indexed bonds, people can make sure that the payments they receive when they retire will be protected from inflation. Indexed bonds (called inflation-indexed bonds) were introduced in the USA in 1997. They account for less than 10% of US government bonds at this point, but their role will surely increase in the future.

Bond prices as present values

In much of this section, we shall look at just two types of bonds: a bond that promises one payment of €100 in one year – a one-year bond – and a bond that promises one payment of €100 in two years – a two-year bond. When you understand how their prices and yields are determined, it will be easy to generalise the results to bonds of any maturity. We shall do so later.

Let's start by deriving the prices of the two bonds:

- Given that the one-year bond promises to pay €100 next year, it follows from Section 14.4 that its price, call it $€P_{1t}$, must be equal to the present value of a payment of €100 next year. Let the current one-year nominal interest rate be i_{1t}. Note that we now denote the one-year interest rate in year t by i_{1t} rather than simply by i_t, as we did in earlier chapters. This is to make it easier for you to remember that it is the *one-year* interest rate. So, ◄ We already saw this relation in Chapter 4, Section 4.2.

$$€P_{1t} = \frac{€100}{1 + i_{1t}} \qquad [15.1]$$

The price of the one-year bond varies inversely with the current one-year nominal interest rate.

- Given that the two-year bond promises to pay €100 in two years, its price, call it $€P_{2t}$, must be equal to the present value of €100 two years from now:

$$€P_{2t} = \frac{€100}{(1 + i_{1t})(1 + i^e_{1t+1})} \qquad [15.2]$$

where i_{1t} denotes the one-year interest rate this year, and i^e_{1t+1} notes the one-year rate expected by financial markets for next year. The price of the two-year bond depends inversely on both the current one-year rate and the one-year rate expected for next year.

Arbitrage and bond prices

Before exploring further the implications of equations (15.1) and (15.2), let us look at an alternative derivation of equation (15.2). This alternative derivation will introduce you to the important concept of *arbitrage*.

Suppose you have a choice between holding one-year bonds or two-year bonds and what you care about is how much you will have one year from today. Which bonds should you hold?

- Suppose you hold one-year bonds. For every euro you put in one-year bonds, you will get $1 + i_{1t}$ euros next year. This relation is represented in the first line of Figure 15.2.
- Suppose you hold two-year bonds. Because the price of a two-year bond is $€P_{2t}$, every euro you put in two-year bonds buys you $€1/€P_{2t}$ bonds today.

    When next year comes, the bond will have only one more year before maturity. Thus, one year from today, the two-year bond will be a one-year bond. Therefore, the price at which you can expect to sell it next year is $€P^e_{1t+1}$, which is the expected price of a one-year bond next year.

    So for every euro you put in two-year bonds, you can expect to receive $€1/€P_{2t}$ times $€P^e_{1t+1}$ or, equivalently, $€P^e_{1t+1}/€P_{2t}$, euros next year. This is represented in the second line of Figure 15.2.

Which bonds should you hold? Suppose you, and other financial investors, care *only* about the expected return. (This assumption is known as the **expectations hypothesis**. It is a strong simplification: you, and other financial investors, are likely to care not only about the expected return but also about the risk associated with holding each bond. If you hold a

Figure 15.2

Returns from holding one-year and two-year bonds for one year

one-year bond, you know with certainty what you will get next year. If you hold a two-year bond, the price at which you will sell it next year is uncertain; holding the two-year bond is risky. We will disregard this for now but briefly discuss it in the appendix to this chapter.)

Under the assumption that you, and other financial investors, care only about expected return, it follows that the two bonds must offer the same expected one-year return. Suppose this condition was not satisfied. Suppose that, for example, the one-year return on one-year bonds was lower than the expected one-year return on two-year bonds. In this case, no one would want to hold the existing supply of one-year bonds, and the market for one-year bonds could not be in equilibrium. Only if the expected one-year return is the same on both bonds will financial investors be willing to hold both one-year bonds and two-year bonds.

If the two bonds offer the same expected one-year return, it follows from Figure 15.2 that

$$1 + i_{1t} = \frac{€P^e_{1t+1}}{€P_{2t}} \qquad [15.3]$$

> We use *arbitrage* to denote the proposition that expected returns on two assets must be equal. Some economists reserve *arbitrage* for the narrower proposition that *riskless* profit opportunities do not go unexploited.

The left side of equation (15.3) gives the return per euro from holding a one-year bond for one year; the right side gives the expected return per euro from holding a two-year bond for one year. We shall call equations such as (15.3) – equations which state that the expected returns on two assets must be equal – **arbitrage** relations. We can rewrite equation (15.3) as

$$€P_{2t} = \frac{€P^e_{1t+1}}{1 + i_{1t}} \qquad [15.4]$$

Arbitrage implies that the price of a two-year bond today is the present value of the expected price of the bond next year. This raises the next question: what does the expected price of one-year bonds next year, $€P^e_{1t+1}$, depend on?

The answer is straightforward: just as the price of a one-year bond this year depends on this year's one-year interest rate, the price of a one-year bond next year will depend on the one-year interest rate next year. Writing equation (15.1) for next year, year $t + 1$, and denoting expectations in the usual way, we get

$$€P^e_{1t-1} = \frac{€100}{(1 + i^e_{1t+1})}$$

The price of the bond next year is expected to equal the final payment, €100, discounted by the one-year interest rate expected for next year.

Replacing $€P^e_{1t+1}$ by $€100/(1 + i^e_{1t+1})$ in equation (15.4) gives

$$€P_{2t} = \frac{€100}{(1 + i_{1t})(1 + i^e_{1t+1})} \qquad [15.5]$$

> The relation between arbitrage and present values: arbitrage between bonds of different maturities implies that bond prices are equal to the expected present values of payments on these bonds.

This expression is the same as equation (15.2). What we have shown is that arbitrage between one- and two-year bonds implies that the price of two-year bonds is the *present value* of the payment in two years, namely €100, discounted using current and next year's expected one-year interest rates.

From bond prices to bond yields

Having looked at bond prices, we now go on to bond yields. The basic point: bond yields contain the same information about future expected interest rates as bond prices. They just do so in a much clearer way.

To begin, we need a definition of the yield to maturity: the **yield to maturity** on an *n*-year bond or, equivalently, the ***n*-year interest rate**, is defined as the constant annual interest rate that makes the bond price today equal to the present value of future payments on the bond.

This definition is simpler than it sounds. Take, for example, the two-year bond we introduced earlier. Denote its yield by i_{2t}, where the subscript 2 reminds us that this is the yield to maturity on a two-year bond or, equivalently, the two-year interest rate. Following the definition of the yield to maturity, this yield is the constant annual interest rate that would make the present value of €100 in two years equal to the price of the bond today. So, it satisfies the following relation:

$$\text{€}P_{2t} = \frac{\text{€}100}{(1 + i_{2t})^2} \qquad [15.6]$$

Suppose the bond sells for €90 today. Then, the two-year interest rate, i_{2t}, is given by $\sqrt{100/90} - 1$, or 5.4%. In other words, holding the bond for two years – until maturity – yields an interest rate of 5.4% per year.

◄ €90 = €100/(1 + i_{2t})² ⇒ (1 + i_{2t})² = €100/€90 ⇒ (1 + i_{2t}) = $\sqrt{\text{€}100/\text{€}90}$ ⇒ i_{2t} = 5.4%

What is the relation of the two-year interest rate to the current one-year interest rate and the expected one-year interest rate? To answer this question, look at equations (15.6) and (15.5). Eliminating €P_{2t} between the two gives

$$\frac{\text{€}100}{(1 + i_{2t})^2} = \frac{\text{€}100}{(1 + i_{1t})(1 + i_{1t+1}^e)}$$

Rearranging, we have

$$(1 + i_{2t})^2 = (1 + i_{1t})(1 + i_{1t+1}^e)$$

◄ We used a similar approximation when we looked at the relation between the nominal interest rate and the real interest rate in Chapter 6. See Proposition 3 in Appendix 1.

This gives us the exact relation between the two-year interest rate, i_{2t}, the current one-year interest rate, i_{1t}, and next year's expected one-year interest rate, i_{1t+1}^e. A useful approximation to this relation is given by

$$i_{2t} \approx \frac{1}{2}(i_{1t} + i_{1t+1}^e) \qquad [15.7]$$

Equation (15.7) simply says that the two-year interest rate is (approximately) the average of the current one-year interest rate and next year's expected one-year interest rate.

We have focused on the relation between the prices and yields of one-year and two-year bonds, but our results can be generalised to bonds of any maturity. For instance, we could look at bonds with maturities shorter than a year. To take an example: the yield on a bond with a maturity of six months is (approximately) equal to the average of the current three-month interest rate and next quarter's expected three-month interest rate. Or, we could look instead at bonds with maturities longer than two years. For example, the yield on a ten-year bond is (approximately) equal to the average of the current one-year interest rate and the one-year interest rates expected for the next nine years.

The general principle is clear: long-term interest rates reflect current and future expected short-term interest rates.

Interpreting the yield curve

The relations we just derived tell us what we need to interpret the slope of the yield curve. By looking at yields for bonds of different maturities, we can infer what financial markets expect short-term interest rates will be in the future.

Suppose we want to find out, for example, what financial markets expect the one-year interest rate to be one year from now. All we need to do is to look at the yield on a two-year bond, i_{2t}, and the yield on a one-year bond, i_{1t}. From equation (15.7), multiplying both sides by 2 and reorganising, we get

$$i_{1t+1}^e = 2i_{2t} - i_{1t} \qquad [15.8]$$

The one-year interest rate expected for next year is equal to twice the yield on a two-year bond minus the current one-year interest rate. Take, for example, the yield curve for 31 May 2009, shown in Figure 15.1.

On 31 May 2009, the one-year interest rate, i_{1t}, was 0.66%, and the two-year interest rate, i_{2t}, was 1.35%. From equation (15.8), it follows that, on 31 May 2009, financial markets expected the one-year interest rate one year later – that is, the one-year interest rate on 31 May 2010 – to equal $2 \times 1.35\% - 0.66\% = 2.04\%$ – that is, 1.4% higher than the one-year interest rate on 31 May 2009. In words: on 31 May 2009, financial markets expected the one-year interest rate to be substantially higher one year later.

More generally: when the yield curve is upward-sloping – that is, when long-term interest rates are higher than short-term interest rates – financial markets expect short-term rates to be higher in the future. When the yield curve is downward-sloping – that is, when long-term interest rates are lower than short-term interest rates as it was, marginally, on 30 June 2007 – financial markets expect short-term interest rates to be lower in the future.

The yield curve and economic activity

We can now return to our earlier question: why did the yield curve go from being downward-sloping in June 2007 to being upward sloping in May 2009? Put another way, why did long-term interest rates go from being lower than short-term interest rates in June 2007 to much higher than short-term interest rates in May 2009?

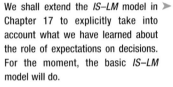
We shall extend the *IS–LM* model in Chapter 17 to explicitly take into account what we have learned about the role of expectations on decisions. For the moment, the basic *IS–LM* model will do.

First, the answer in short: because the financial crisis which started in the summer of 2007 turned into a full-fledged economic crisis in 2008, the Bank of England responded to the crisis by bringing short-term interest rates down. And because, even as the economy was still in recession, financial markets expected output to recover and expected short-term interest rates to return to higher levels in the future, leading long-term interest rates to fall by much less than short-term interest rates.

To go through the answer step-by-step, let's use the *IS–LM* model we developed in Chapter 5. We can think of the interest rate measured on the vertical axis as a short-term nominal interest rate. And to keep things simple, let's assume that expected inflation is equal to 0, so we do not have to worry about the distinction between the nominal and real interest rates we introduced in Chapter 14. This distinction is not central here.

In the summer of 2007, the financial crisis begun in the USA spread rapidly all over the world and, after many years of high growth, the world economy entered in what seemed the most severe recession since the Great Depression. Consumer spending in the UK slowed as the global slowdown gathered pace.

The economic situation at the time is represented in Figure 15.3. The UK economy was at a point such as A, with interest rate, i, and output, Y. The forecasts were that the *IS* curve would gradually shift to the left, from *IS* to *IS'*, leading to a reduction of output, and a decrease in the interest rate, from i to i'. This expected decrease in the interest rate was the reason the yield curve was slightly downward sloping in June 2007.

However, in 2008, the economic situation was worse than had been forecast. What happened is represented in Figure 15.4. There were two major developments:

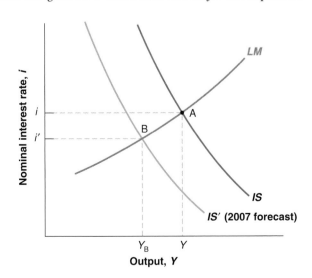

Figure 15.3

The UK economy as of June 2007

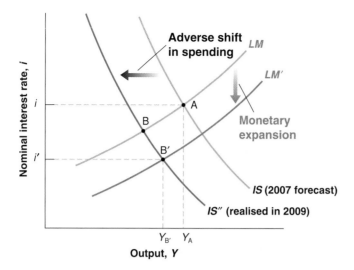

Figure 15.4

The UK economy from June 2007 to May 2009

From June 2007 to May 2009, a sharp reduction in spending, together with a monetary expansion, combined to lead to a decrease in the short-term interest rate.

- The reduction in spending was stronger than had been expected. In late 2008, spending in the UK slowed sharply. Instead of shifting from *IS* to *IS'* as forecast (see Figure 15.3), the *IS* curve shifted by much more, from *IS* to *IS"* in Figure 15.4. Had monetary policy remained unchanged, the economy would have moved along the *LM* curve, and the equilibrium would have moved from A to B, leading to a decrease in output and a decrease in the short-term interest rate.

- There was more at work, however. Realising that the slowdown was stronger than it had anticipated, the Bank of England shifted in early 2009 to a policy of monetary expansion, leading to a downward shift in the *LM* curve. As a result of this shift in the *LM* curve, the economy was, in May 2009, at a point like B' – rather than at a point like B. Output was higher and the interest rate lower than they would have been in the absence of the monetary expansion.

In words: the decline in short-term interest rates – and therefore the decline at the short-term end of the yield curve from 30 June 2007 to 31 May 2009 – was the result of a large adverse shift in spending, combined with a strong response by the central bank aimed at limiting the size of the decrease in output. This still leaves one question: why was the yield curve upward-sloping in May 2009? Equivalently: why were long-term interest rates higher than short-term interest rates?

To answer this question, we must look at what the markets *expected* to happen to the UK economy in the future, as of May 2009. This is represented in Figure 15.5. Although in the UK, GDP fell sharply in the first quarter of 2009, there were promising signs that the pace of

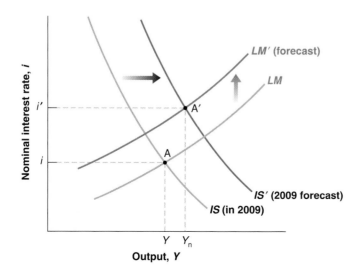

Figure 15.5

The expected path of the UK economy as of May 2009

In May 2009, financial markets expected that the economic stimulus stemming from monetary and fiscal policies would lead to a recovery in economic growth, hence to higher interest rates in the future.

decline had begun to moderate. Financial markets expected a shift of the *IS* curve to the right, from *IS* to *IS'*. The main reasons: a considerable economic stimulus stemming from expansionary monetary policy by the Bank of England and by expansionary fiscal policy at home and abroad.

As a result, financial markets expected the UK economy to move from point A to point A'; they expected both output to recover and short-term interest rates to increase. The anticipation of higher short-term interest rates in the future was the reason long-term interest rates remained high and the reason the yield curve was upward sloping in May 2009.

Note that the yield curve in May 2009 was nearly flat for maturities up to one year. This tells us that financial markets did not expect interest rates to start rising until a year hence – that is, before May 2010. To see if they turned out to be right, you can check what happened to short-term interest rate in 2010.

Let's summarise. We have seen in this section how bond prices and bond yields depend on current and future expected interest rates. By looking at the yield curve, we (and everybody else in the economy, from people to firms) learn what financial markets expect interest rates to be in the future.

15.2 THE STOCK MARKET AND MOVEMENTS IN STOCK PRICES

So far, we have focused on bonds. But while governments finance themselves by issuing bonds, the same is not true of firms. Firms raise funds in two ways: through **debt finance** – bonds and loans; and through **equity finance**, issuing **stocks** – or **shares**, as stocks are also called. Instead of paying predetermined amounts as bonds do, stocks pay **dividends** in an amount decided by the firm. Dividends are paid from the firm's profits. Typically, dividends are less than profits, as firms retain some of their profits to finance their investment. But dividends move with profits: when profits increase, so do dividends.

Our focus in this section is on the determination of stock prices. As a way of introducing the issues, let's look at the behaviour of an index of UK stock prices, the FT30. The FT30 index is based on the share prices of 30 British companies from a wide range of industry. The index, which began on 1 July 1935, is the oldest continuous index in the UK and one of the oldest in the world.

Other indexes are the *Standard & Poor's* and *Dow Jones Industrial*, both indexes of US stock prices. Similar indexes exist for other countries. The *Nikkei index* reflects movements in stock prices in Tokyo, and the *CAC* index reflects stock price movements in Paris.

Figure 15.6 plots the FT30 since 1975 (the index is equal to 100 on 1 July 1935). The striking feature of the figure is obviously the sharp rise of the index during the 1990s, from 1674 in 1990 to 4157 in 1999, followed by a sharp fall in the early 2000s, from 3574 in 2000 down to 1670 in 2002. Then it increased again until 2006 but, in 2008, in the middle of the slowdown caused by the financial crisis of 2007, the index stood below its level in 2002. Why the long rise in the 1990s? Why the sharp fall in the early 2000s and more recently during the economic slowdown in 2007–2008? More generally, what determines the movement in stock prices, and how do stock prices respond to changes in the economic environment and macroeconomic policy? These are the questions we take up in this and the next section.

Stock prices as present values

What determines the price of a stock that promises a sequence of dividends in the future? By now, we are sure the material in Chapter 14 has become second nature, and you already know the answer: the stock price must equal the present value of future expected dividends.

Let $€Q_t$ be the price of the stock. Let $€D_t$ denote the dividend this year, $€D_{t+1}^e$ the expected dividend next year, $€D_{t+2}^e$ the expected dividend two years from now, and so on.

Suppose we look at the price of the stock after the dividend has been paid this year – this price is known as the *ex-dividend price* – so that the first dividend to be paid after the

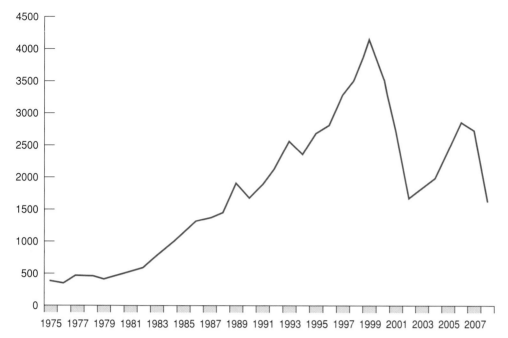

Figure 15.6

FT index: 30 share index (1/7/35 = 100) ordinary shares, since 1975

Note the sharp increase in stock prices in the 1990s, followed by the sharp decrease in the early 2000s. Again an increase until 2007, and then a decrease since 2007.

Source: FTSE.

purchase of the stock is next year's dividend. (This is just a matter of convention; we could alternatively look at the price before this year's dividend has been paid. What term would we have to add?) The price of the stock is then given by

$$€Q_t = \frac{€D^e_{t+1}}{1 + i_{1t}} + \frac{€D^e_{t+1}}{(1 + i_{1t})(1 + i^e_{1t+1})} + \ldots \qquad [15.9]$$

The price of the stock is equal to the present value of the dividend next year, discounted using the current one-year interest rate, plus the present value of the dividend two years from now, discounted using both this year's one-year interest rate and next-year's expected one-year interest rate, and so on.

As in the case of long-term bonds, the present value relation in equation (15.9) can be derived from arbitrage – in this case, the condition that the expected return per pound from holding a stock for one year must be equal to the return from holding a one-year bond. The derivation is given in the appendix to this chapter. (Going through the appendix will improve your understanding of the relation between arbitrage and present values, but it can be skipped without harm.)

Equation (15.9) gives the stock price as the present value of *nominal* dividends, discounted by *nominal* interest rates. From Chapter 14, we know we can rewrite this equation to express the *real* stock price as the present value of *real* dividends, discounted by *real* interest rates. So we can rewrite the real stock price as

$$Q_t = \frac{D^e_{t+1}}{(1 + r_{1t})} + \frac{D^e_{t+2}}{(1 + r_{1t})(1 + r^e_{1t+1})} + \ldots \qquad [15.10]$$

Q_t and D_t, without a euro sign, denote the real price and real dividends at time t. *The real stock price is the present value of future real dividends, discounted by the sequence of one-year real interest rates.*

This relation has two important implications:

- Higher expected future real dividends lead to a higher real stock price.
- Higher current and expected future one-year real interest rates lead to a lower real stock price.

Let's now see what light this relation sheds on movements in the stock market.

Two equivalent ways of writing the stock price:
- The nominal stock price equals the expected present discounted value of future nominal dividends, discounted by current and future nominal interest rates.
- The real stock price equals the expected present discounted value of future real dividends, discounted by current and future real interest rates.

The stock market and economic activity

Figure 15.6 shows the large movements in UK stock prices over the past 30 years. It is not unusual for the price index to go up or down by 20% within a year. In 1997, the stock market went up by 17%; in 2002, it went down by 38%; in 2008 the stock market went down by 40%! Daily movements of 2% or more are not unusual. What causes these movements?

The first point to be made is that these movements should be, and they are for the most part, unpredictable. The reason is best understood by thinking in terms of the choice people have between stocks and bonds. If it were widely believed that, a year from now, the price of a stock was going to be 20% higher than today's price, holding the stock for a year would be unusually attractive, much more attractive than holding short-term bonds. There would be a very large demand for the stock. Its price would increase *today* to the point where the expected return from holding the stock was back in line with the expected return on other assets. In other words, the expectation of a high stock price next year would lead to a high stock price today.

You may have heard the proposition that ➤ stock prices follow a **random walk**. This is a technical term, but with a simple interpretation: something – it can be a molecule or the price of an asset – follows a random walk if each step it takes is as likely to be up as it is to be down. Its movements are therefore unpredictable.

There is indeed a saying in economics that it is a sign of a *well-functioning stock market* that movements in stock prices are unpredictable. The saying is too strong: at any moment, a few financial investors might have better information or simply be better at reading the future. If they are only a few, they may not buy enough of the stock to bid its price all the way up today. Thus, they may get large expected returns. But the basic idea is nevertheless right. The financial market gurus who regularly predict large imminent movements in the stock market are quacks. Major movements in stock prices cannot be predicted.

If movements in the stock market cannot be predicted, if they are the result of news, where does this leave us? We can still do two things:

- We can look back, using the benefit of hindsight to identify the news to which the market reacted.
- We can ask what-if questions. For example: What would happen to the stock market if the central bank were to embark on a more expansionary policy or if consumers were to become more optimistic and increase spending?

Let us look at two what-if questions, using the *IS–LM* model. To simplify, let's assume, as we did earlier, that expected inflation equals 0, so that the real interest rate and the nominal interest rate are equal.

A monetary expansion and the stock market

Suppose the economy is in a recession, and the central bank decides to adopt a more expansionary monetary policy. The increase in money shifts the *LM* curve down in Figure 15.7, and equilibrium output moves from point A to point A'. How will the stock market react?

Figure 15.7

An expansionary monetary policy and the stock market

A monetary expansion decreases the interest rate and increases output. What it does to the stock market depends on whether financial markets anticipated the monetary expansion.

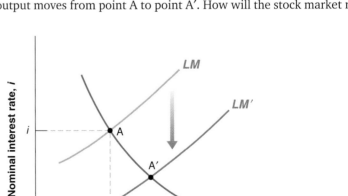

The answer depends on what participants in the stock market expected monetary policy to be before the central bank's move. If they fully anticipated the expansionary policy, then the stock market will not react: neither its expectations of future dividends nor its expectations of future interest rates are affected by a move it had already anticipated. Thus, in equation (15.9), nothing changes, and stock prices will remain the same.

Suppose instead that the central bank's move is at least partly unexpected. In that case, stock prices will increase. They increase for two reasons: first, a more expansionary monetary policy implies lower interest rates for some time. Second, it also implies higher output for some time (until the economy returns to the natural level of output) and, therefore, higher dividends. As equation (15.9) tells us, both lower interest rates and higher dividends – current and expected – will lead to an increase in stock prices.

An increase in consumer spending and the stock market

Now consider an unexpected shift of the *IS* curve to the right, resulting, for example, from stronger-than-expected consumer spending. As a result of the shift, output in Figure 15.8(a) increases from A to A'.

Will stock prices go up? You might be tempted to say yes: a stronger economy means higher profits and higher dividends for some time. But this answer is incomplete, for at least two reasons.

First, the answer ignores the effect of higher activity on interest rates: the movement along the *LM* curve implies an increase in both output and interest rates. Higher output leads to higher profits and, therefore, higher stock prices. Higher interest rates lead to lower stock prices. Which of the two effects – higher profits or higher interest rates – dominates? The answer depends on the slope of the *LM* curve. This is shown in Figure 15.8(b). A very flat *LM* curve leads to a movement from A to A', with small increases in interest rates, large increases in output, and therefore an increase in stock prices. A very steep *LM* curve leads

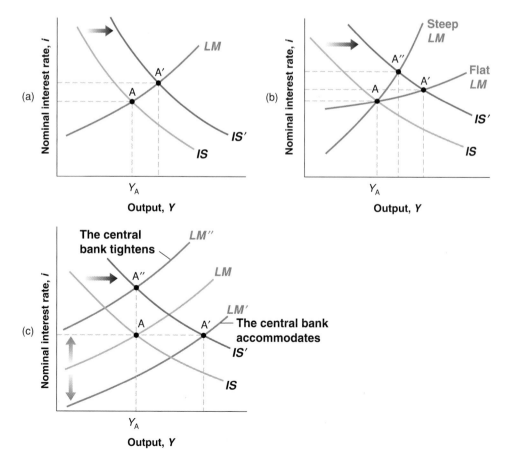

Figure 15.8

An increase in consumption spending and the stock market

(a) The increase in consumption spending leads to a higher interest rate and a higher level of output. What happens to the stock market depends on the slope of the *LM* curve and on the central bank's behaviour.

(b) If the *LM* curve is steep, the interest rate increases a lot, and output increases little. Stock prices go down. If the *LM* curve is flat, the interest rate increases little and output increases a lot. Stock prices go up.

(c) If the central bank increases the amount of money in the economy, the interest rate does not increase, but output does. Stock prices go up. If the central bank decides instead to keep output constant, the interest rate increases, but output does not. Stock prices go down.

to a movement from A to A″, with large increases in interest rates, small increases in output, and therefore a decrease in stock prices.

Second, the answer ignores the effect of the shift in the *IS* curve on the central bank's behaviour. In practice, this is the effect that financial investors often care about the most. After receiving the news of unexpectedly strong economic activity, the main question among financial operators is: how will the central bank react?

- Will the central bank accommodate the shift in the *IS* curve? That is, will the central bank increase the money supply in line with money demand so as to avoid an increase in the interest rate?

  Central bank accommodation corresponds to a downward shift of the *LM* curve, from *LM* to *LM′* in Figure 15.8(c). In this case, the economy will go from point A to point A′. Stock prices will increase, as output is expected to be higher and interest rates are not expected to increase.

- Will the central bank instead keep the same monetary policy, leaving the *LM* curve unchanged? In that case, the economy will move along the *LM* curve. As we saw earlier, what happens to stock prices is ambiguous. Profits will be higher, but so will interest rates.

> Another way of thinking about what happens is to think of the *LM* relation of an interest rate rule, as presented in the appendix to Chapter 5. Depending on how much the central bank decreases the interest rate in response to the decrease in output, the news will lead to an increase or a decrease in the stock market.

- Or will the central bank worry that an increase in output above Y_A may lead to an increase in inflation? This will be the case if the economy is already close to the natural level of output – if, in Figure 15.8(c), Y_A is close to Y_n. In this case, a further increase in output would lead to an increase in inflation, something that the central bank wants to avoid. A decision by the central bank to counteract the rightward shift of the *IS* curve with a monetary contraction causes the *LM* curve to shift up, from *LM* to *LM″*, so the economy goes from A to A″, and output does not change. In that case, stock prices will surely go down: there is no change in expected profits, but the interest rate is now likely to be higher for some time.

Let's summarise. Stock prices depend very much on current and future movements in activity. But this does not imply any simple relation between stock prices and output. How stock prices respond to a change in output depends on (1) what the market expected in the first place, (2) the source of the shocks behind the change in output and (3) how the market expects the central bank to react to the output change.

15.3 BUBBLES, FADS AND STOCK PRICES

Do all movements in stock prices result from news about future dividends or interest rates? Many economists doubt it. They point to Black October in 1929, when the US stock market fell by 23% in two days, and to October 1987 in the UK, when the FT30 index fell by almost 27% in a month. They point to the amazing rise in the Nikkei index (an index of Japanese stock prices) from around 13 000 in 1985 to around 35 000 in 1989, followed by a decline back to 15 000 by 1992. More recently, in October 2008 and again in January 2009 the FT30 fell by almost 17%. In each of these cases, they point to a lack of obvious news, or at least of news important enough to cause such enormous movements.

Instead, they argue that stock prices are not always equal to their **fundamental value**, defined as the present value of expected dividends given in equation (15.10), and that stocks are sometimes under-priced or over-priced. Overpricing eventually comes to an end, sometimes with a crash, as in October 1929, or with a long slide, as in the case of the Nikkei index.

> Recall: arbitrage is the condition that the expected rates of return on two financial assets are equal.

Under what conditions can such mispricing occur? The surprising answer is that it can occur even when investors are rational and when arbitrage holds. To see why, consider the case of a truly worthless stock (that is, the stock of a company that all financial investors know will never make profits and will never pay dividends). Putting D^e_{t+1}, D^e_{t+2} and so on equal to 0 in equation (15.10) yields a simple and unsurprising answer: the fundamental value of such a stock is equal to 0.

FOCUS
Making (some) sense of (apparent) nonsense: why the stock market moved yesterday and other stories

Here are some quotes from the *Wall Street Journal* from April 1997 to August 2001. Try to make sense of them, using what you've just learned.

April 1997. Good news on the economy, leading to an increase in stock prices:

> 'Bullish investors celebrated the release of market-friendly economic data by stampeding back into stock and bond markets, pushing the Dow Jones Industrial Average to its second-largest point gain ever and putting the blue-chip index within shooting distance of a record just weeks after it was reeling.'

December 1999. Good news on the economy, leading to a decrease in stock prices:

> 'Good economic news was bad news for stocks and worse news for bonds. . . . The announcement of stronger-than-expected November retail-sales numbers

wasn't welcome. Economic strength creates inflation fears and sharpens the risk that the Federal Reserve will raise interest rates again.'

September 1998. Bad news on the economy, leading to an decrease in stock prices:

> 'Nasdaq stocks plummeted as worries about the strength of the U.S. economy and the profitability of U.S. corporations prompted widespread selling.'

August 2001. Bad news on the economy, leading to an increase in stock prices:

> 'Investors shrugged off more gloomy economic news, and focused instead on their hope that the worst is now over for both the economy and the stock market. The optimism translated into another 2% gain for the Nasdaq Composite Index.'

FOCUS
Famous bubbles: from Tulipmania in 17th-century Holland to Russia in 1994 and the USA in 2008

Tulipmania in Holland
In the 17th century, tulips became increasingly popular in Western European gardens. A market developed in Holland for both rare and common forms of tulip bulbs.

The episode called the 'tulip bubble' took place from 1634–1637. In 1634, the price of rare bulbs started increasing. The market went into a frenzy, with speculators buying tulip bulbs in anticipation of even higher prices later. For example, the price of a bulb called 'Admiral Van de Eyck' increased from 1500 guineas in 1634 to 7500 guineas in 1637, equal to the price of a house at the time. There are stories about a sailor mistakenly eating bulbs, only to realise the cost of his 'meal' later. In early 1637, prices increased faster. Even the prices of some common bulbs exploded, rising by a factor

of up to 20 in January. But in February 1637, prices collapsed. A few years later, bulbs were trading for roughly 10% of their value at the peak of the bubble.

Source: Taken from Peter Garber, 'Tulipmania', *Journal of Political Economy*, 1989, **97**, 535–560.

The MMM pyramid in Russia
In 1994, a Russian 'financier,' Sergei Mavrody, created a company called MMM and proceeded to sell shares, promising shareholders a rate of return of at least 3000% per year!

The company was an instant success. The price of MMM shares increased from 1600 roubles (then worth £1) in February to 105 000 roubles (then worth £51) in July. And by July, according to the company claims, the number of shareholders had increased to 10 million.

The trouble was that the company was not involved in any type of production and held no assets, except for its 140 offices in Russia. The shares were intrinsically worthless. The company's initial success was based on a standard pyramid scheme, with MMM using the funds from the sale of new shares to pay the promised returns on the old shares. Despite repeated warnings by government officials, including Boris Yeltsin, that MMM was a scam and that the increase in the price of shares was a bubble, the promised returns were just too attractive to many Russian people, especially in the midst of a deep economic recession.

The scheme could work only as long as the number of new shareholders – and thus new funds to be distributed to existing shareholders – increased fast enough. By the end of July 1994, the company could no longer make good on its promises, and the scheme collapsed. The company closed. Mavrody tried to blackmail the government into paying the shareholders, claiming that not doing so would trigger a revolution or a civil war. The government refused, leaving many shareholders angry at the government rather than at Mavrody. Later on in the year, Mavrody actually ran for Parliament, as a self-appointed defender of the shareholders who had lost their savings. He won!

Source: 'More murk in Moscow. MMM pyramid scheme investigation does not harm political ambitions of chairman Sergei Mavrodi', *Economist*, 5 November 1994.

The Madoff scandal of 2008

More recently, the scam perpetrated by Bernie Madoff, a Wall Street veteran, was the biggest financial fraud in history: a hole as big as $50 billion! The scheme was similar to the previous ones. For years, it seems, the returns paid to investors came, in part at least, not from real investment gains but from inflows from new clients. It might still have been going on, were it not for the global financial crisis.

The Madoff scandal of 2008 showed that investors presumed to be sophisticated, such as international bankers, can also be tricked into joining such a scheme by a promoter with a well-established reputation for financial skill. Why were they not suspicious of the unnaturally consistent returns? A former chairman of the NASDAQ stock market, Madoff has served on an advisory committee assembled by the Securities and Exchange Commission (SEC), America's main market watchdog.

Savvy marketing was another factor. Madoff, for example, only permitted one accounting firm, run by his brother-in-law, to perform audits on his hedge fund, claiming the need to keep his strategy secret. Moreover, investors had to be invited, lending his operation an air of exclusivity.

Source: Ponzi squared. Just when Wall Street needs it least, Bernie Madoff's pyramid scheme takes financial fraud to new lows, 15 December 2008, New York, Economist.com.

Might you nevertheless be willing to pay a positive price for this stock? Maybe. You might if you expect the price at which you can sell the stock next year to be higher than this year's price. And the same applies to a buyer next year: he may well be willing to buy at a high price if he expects to sell at an even higher price in the following year. This process suggests that stock prices may increase just because investors expect them to. Such movements in stock prices are called **rational speculative bubbles**: financial investors might well be behaving rationally as the bubble inflates. Even those investors who hold the stock at the time of the crash, and therefore sustain a large loss, may also have been rational. They may have realised there was a chance of a crash, but they thought there was also a chance that the bubble would continue and they could sell at an even higher price.

> In a speculative bubble, the price of a stock is higher than its fundamental value. Investors are willing to pay a high price for the stock, in the anticipation of being able to resell the stock at an even higher price.

To make things simple, our example assumes the stock to be fundamentally worthless. But the argument is general and applies to stocks with a positive fundamental value as well: people might be willing to pay more than the fundamental value of a stock if they expect its price to further increase in the future. And the same argument applies to other assets, such as housing, gold and paintings. Two such bubbles are described in the Focus box 'Famous bubbles: from Tulipmania in seventeenth-century Holland to Russia in 1994 and the USA in 2008'.

Are all deviations from fundamental values in financial markets rational bubbles? Probably not. The fact is that many financial investors are not rational. An increase in stock prices in the past, say due to a succession of good news, often creates excessive optimism. If investors simply extrapolate from past returns to predict future returns, a stock may become 'hot' (high priced) for no reason other than the fact that its price has increased in the past. Such deviations of stock prices from their fundamental value are called **fads**. We are all aware of fads outside the stock market; there are good reasons to believe they exist in the stock market as well.

Let's now go back to the facts we saw in Figure 15.6, and ask: was the large increase in the stock market in the 1990s and in the early 2000s due to fundamentals or to a bubble?

There is no question that there was much good news in the 1990s. After the slowdown in the early 1990s, the UK economy went through a long expansion, from 1992–2007. As Andrew Sentence, Member of the Monetary Policy Committee of the Bank of England, points out, this is in fact the second longest uninterrupted expansion since the mid-19th century, after the 26-year-long expansion immediately after the Second World War (1948–1973). With the long expansion came high profits and high dividends – much higher than had been expected as of 1990. This good news led to higher-than-expected stock prices.

But did this good news justify the tripling of the stock price index that actually occurred? At the time, many economists were – and still are – doubtful.

We have focused in this chapter on how news about economic activity affects bond and stock prices. But bond and stock markets are more than just a sideshow. They affect economic activity by influencing consumption and investment spending. There is little question, for example, that the decline in the stock market was one of the factors behind the 2007 recession. Most economists also believe that the stock market crash of 1929 was one of the sources of the Great Depression and that the large decline in the Nikkei index is one of the causes of the long Japanese slump in the 1990s. These interactions between bond and stock markets, expectations and economic activity are the topics of the next two chapters.

SUMMARY

- Arbitrage between bonds of different maturities implies that the price of a bond is the present value of the payments on the bond, discounted using current and expected short-term interest rates over the life of the bond. Hence, higher current or expected short-term interest rates lead to lower bond prices.

- The yield to maturity on a bond is (approximately) equal to the average of current and expected short-term interest rates over the life of a bond.

- The slope of the yield curve – equivalently, the term structure – tells us what financial markets expect to happen to short-term interest rates in the future. A downward-sloping yield curve (when long-term interest rates are lower than short-term interest rates) implies that the market expects a decrease in short-term interest rates; an upward-sloping yield curve (when long-term interest rates are higher than short-term interest rates) implies that the market expects an increase in short-term rates.

- The fundamental value of a stock is the present value of expected future real dividends, discounted using current and future expected one-year real interest rates. In the absence of bubbles or fads, the price of a stock is equal to its fundamental value.

- An increase in expected dividends leads to an increase in the fundamental value of stocks; an increase in current and expected one-year interest rates leads to a decrease in their fundamental value.

- Changes in output may or may not be associated with changes in stock prices in the same direction. Whether they are depends on (1) what the market expected in the first place, (2) the source of the shocks and (3) how the market expects the central bank to react to the output change.

- Stock prices can be subject to bubbles and fads that cause a stock price to differ from its fundamental value. Bubbles are episodes in which financial investors buy a stock for a price higher than its fundamental value, anticipating reselling it at an even higher price. Fads are episodes in which, for reasons of fashion or over-optimism, financial investors are willing to pay more for a stock than its fundamental value.

KEY TERMS

QUESTIONS AND PROBLEMS

QUICK CHECK

1. *Using the information in this chapter, label each of the following statements true, false or uncertain. Explain briefly.*

a. Junk bonds are bonds nobody wants to hold.

b. The price of a one-year bond decreases when the nominal one-year interest rate increases.

c. Given the Fisher hypothesis, an upward-sloping yield curve may indicate that financial markets are worried about inflation in the future.

d. Long-term interest rates typically move more than short-term interest rates.

e. An equal increase in expected inflation and nominal interest rates at all maturities should have no effect on the stock market.

f. A monetary expansion will lead to an upward-sloping yield curve.

g. A rational investor should never pay a positive price for a stock that will never pay dividends.

2. *Determine the yield to maturity of each of the following bonds:*

a. A discount bond with a face value of €1000, a maturity of three years, and a price of €800.

b. A discount bond with a face value of €1000, a maturity of four years, and a price of €800.

c. A discount bond with a face value of €1000, a maturity of four years, and a price of €850.

3. *Suppose that the annual interest rate this year is 5%, and financial market participants expect the annual interest rate to increase to 5.5% next year, to 6% two years from now and to 6.5% three years from now. Determine the yield to maturity on each of the following bonds.*

a. A one-year bond.

b. A two-year bond.

c. A three-year bond.

4. *Using the IS–LM model, determine the impact on stock prices of each of the policy changes described in (a) through (c). If the effect is ambiguous, explain what additional information would be needed to reach a conclusion.*

a. An unexpected expansionary monetary policy with no change in fiscal policy.

b. A fully expected expansionary monetary policy with no change in fiscal policy.

c. A fully expected expansionary monetary policy together with an unexpected expansionary fiscal policy.

DIG DEEPER

5. Money growth and the yield curve

In Chapter 14, we examined the effects of an increase in the growth rate of money on interest rates and inflation.

a. Draw the path of the nominal interest rate following an increase in the growth rate of money. Suppose that the lowest point in the path is reached after one year and that the long-run values are achieved after three years.

b. Show the yield curve just after the increase in the growth rate of money, one year later and three years later.

6. Interpreting the yield curve

a. What is the current price of the stock if the real interest rate is expected to remain constant at 5%? at 8%?

b. What does a steep yield curve imply about future inflation?

7. Stock prices and the risk premium

This problem is based on the appendix to this chapter.

Suppose a share is expected to pay a dividend of €1000 next year, and the real value of dividend payments is expected to increase by 3% per year forever after.

a. What is the current price of the stock if the real interest rate is expected to remain constant at 5%? at 8%?

Now suppose that people require a risk premium to hold stocks (as described in the appendix).

b. Redo the calculations in part (a) if the required risk premium is 8%.

c. Redo the calculations in part (a) if the required risk premium is 4%.

d. What do you expect would happen to stock prices if the risk premium decreased unexpectedly? Explain in words.

EXPLORE FURTHER

8. UK disinflation in the 1980s and the term structure

At the end of the 1970s, the UK inflation rate reached double digits. On 4 May 1979 Mrs Thatcher won the general election and was appointed Prime Minister. To reduce the inflation rate, the government instituted a Medium Term Financial Strategy (MTFS). In this problem, we will use yield curve data to judge whether the financial markets were indeed expecting the government to succeed in reducing the inflation rate.

Go to the data section of the website of the Bank of England (http://www.statistics.gov.uk/). Go to 'Economy' and download monthly data on the Composite Price Index 1970 to today. Import it into your favourite spreadsheet program.

a. How can the government reduce inflation? How would this policy affect the nominal interest rate?

b. For each month, compute the annual rate of inflation as the percentage change in the Composite Price Index from last year to this year (i.e. over the preceding 12 months). In the same graph, plot the rate of inflation and the one-year interest rate from 1970 to today. When was the rate of inflation at its highest?

Now go to the website of the Bank of England (http://www.bankofengland.uk). Go to 'Statistics', then go to 'Interest rates and exchange rates', then to 'Estimates of UK Yield Curve'. Download the spreadsheet containing Yield Curves. Go to Sheet 4 on the Excel file 'Spot Curve'.

c. For each month, starting in 1970 and until the mid-1980s, draw the yield curve. To do this use the data in the Excel file which shows, for each month, the yield on government bonds with maturities ranging from 6 months, all the way to 20 years. (Doing this for each month is unnecessary and you would not see much with all those curves. Try drawing one yield curve per quarter.)

d. What does a declining yield curve imply about the expectations of financial market participants? As inflation was increasing in the late 1970s, what was happening to the yield curve? Were financial market participants expecting that trend to continue?

e. In 1979, the government announced that they would pursue a gradual reduction in the rate of growth of the money stock. Looking at the yield curves for 1979–1980, do you find any evidence of such an interpretation by financial market participants? Explain.

9. *Go to the website cited in problem 8 and find the most recent observation on the term structure of interest rates ranging from three months to 30 years.*

Is the term structure upward-sloping, downward-sloping or flat? Why?

10. *Do a news search on the Internet about the most recent Governing Council of the ECB.*

a. What did the Governing Council decide about the interest rate?

b. What happened to stock prices on the day of the announcement?

c. To what degree do you think financial market participants were surprised by the Governing Council's announcement? Explain.

---

*We invite you to visit the Blanchard page on the Prentice Hall website, at **www.prenhall.com/blanchard** for this chapter's World Wide Web exercises.*

FURTHER READING

- There are many bad books written about the stock market. A good one, and one that is fun to read, is **Burton Malkiel, *A Random Walk Down Wall Street*, 9th ed.,** Norton, New York, 2006.

- An account of historical bubbles is given by **Peter Garber in 'Famous First Bubbles',** *Journal of Economic Perspectives,* 1990, 4(2) 35–54.

APPENDIX

Arbitrage and stock prices

This appendix has two parts.

The first part of this appendix shows that, in the absence of rational speculative bubbles, arbitrage between stocks and bonds implies that the price of a stock is equal to the expected present value of dividends.

The second part of this appendix shows how to modify the arbitrage relation to take into account the fact that financial investors care about risk. It then shows how the presence of risk modifies the present value relation between stock prices and dividends.

Arbitrage and stock prices

You face the choice of investing either in one-year bonds or in stocks for a year. What should you choose?

- Suppose you decide to hold one-year bonds. Then, for every euro you put in one-year bonds, you will get $1 + i_{1t}$ euros next year. This payoff is represented in the upper line of Figure 15.9.
- Suppose you decide instead to hold stocks for a year. This implies buying a stock today, receiving a dividend next year and then selling the stock. As the price of a stock is $€Q_t$, every euro you put in stocks buys you $€1/€Q_t$ stocks. And for each stock you buy, you expect to receive $€D^e_{t+1} + €Q^e_{t+1}$, the sum of the expected dividend and the stock price next year. Therefore, for every euro you put in stocks, you expect to receive $(€D^e_{t+1} + €Q^e_{t+1})/SQ_t$. This payoff is represented in the lower line of Figure 15.9.

Let's use the same arbitrage argument we used for bonds earlier. Assume that financial investors care only about expected rates of return. Equilibrium then requires that the expected rate of return from holding stocks for one year be the same as the rate of return on one-year bonds:

$$\frac{(€D^e_{t+1} + €Q^e_{t+1})}{€Q_t} = 1 + i_{1t}$$

Rewrite this equation as

$$€Q_t = \frac{€D^e_{t+1}}{(1 + i_{1t})} + \frac{€Q^e_{t+1}}{(1 + i_{1t})} \qquad (15.A1)$$

	Year t	**Year $t + 1$**
1-year bonds	€1	€1$(1 + i_{1t})$
Stocks	€1	€1$\dfrac{€D^e_{t+1} + €Q^e_{t+1}}{€Q_t}$

Figure 15.9

Returns from holding one-year bonds or stocks for one year

Arbitrage implies that the price of the stock today must be equal to the present value of the expected dividend plus the present value of the expected stock price next year.

The next step is to think about what determines $€Q^e_{t+1}$, the expected stock price next year. Next year, financial investors will again face a choice between stocks and one-year bonds. Thus, the same arbitrage relation will hold. Writing the previous equation, but now for time $t + 1$, and taking expectations into account, gives

$$€Q^e_{t+1} = \frac{€D^e_{t+2}}{(1 + i^e_{1t+1})} + \frac{€Q^e_{t+2}}{(1 + i^e_{1t+1})}$$

The expected price next year is simply the present value next year of the sum of the expected dividend and price two years from now. Replacing the expected price $€Q^e_{t+1}$ in equation (15.A1) gives

$$€Q_t = \frac{€D^e_{t+1}}{(1 + i_{1t})} \frac{€D^e_{t+2}}{(1 + i_{1t})(1 + i^e_{1t+1})} + \frac{€Q^e_{t+2}}{(1 + i_{1t})(1 + i^e_{1t+1})}$$

The stock price is the present value of the expected dividend next year, plus the present value of the expected dividend two years from now, plus the expected price two years from now.

If we replace the expected price in two years by the present value of the expected price and dividends in three years, and so on for n years, we get

$$€Q_t = \frac{€D^e_{t+1}}{(1 + i_{1t})} + \cdots + \frac{€D^e_{t+n}}{(1 + i_{1t}) \cdots (1 + i^e_{1t+n-1})} \qquad [15.A2]$$
$$+ \frac{€D^e_{t+n}}{(1 + i_{1t}) \cdots (1 + i^e_{1t+n-1})}$$

Look at the last term in equation (15.A2) – the present value of the expected price in n years. As long as people do not expect the stock price to explode in the future, then, as we keep replacing Q^e_{t+n} and n increases, this term will go to 0. To see why, suppose the interest rate is constant and equal to i. The last term becomes

$$\frac{€Q^e_{t+n}}{(1 + i_{1t}) \cdots (1 + i^e_{1t+n-1})} = \frac{€Q^e_{t+n}}{(1 + i)^n}$$

Suppose further that people expect the price of the stock to converge to some value, call it $€\bar{Q}$, in the far future. Then, the last term becomes

$$\frac{€Q^e_{t+n}}{(1 + i)^n} = \frac{€\bar{Q}}{(1 + i)^n}$$

If the interest rate is positive, this expression goes to 0 as n becomes large. Equation (15.A2) reduces to equation (15.9) in the text: the price today is the present value of expected future dividends.

Can rational bubbles exist?

The condition that people expect the price of the stock to converge to some value over time seems reasonable. And, indeed, most of the time, it is likely to be satisfied. However, imagine instead that all expected future dividends – €D^e_{t+i} – are zero so that the expected present discounted value (EPDV) of future profit is also zero. Assume also that the stock price is still positive, i.e. people are still willing to buy the stock regardless of the EPDV of future profits being zero. Why should people be willing to buy a stock whose EPDV of future profits is zero? Because they are expecting large increases in the stock price in the future. Why should people expect large increases in the stock price in the future? Because they believe they will be able to sell the stock at higher and higher prices in the future. In fact, if the stock price is positive today ($Q_t > 0$), then the expected future prices of the stock are also positive ($Q^e_{t+1} = (1 + r_t) Q_t > 0$; $Q^e_{t+2} = (1 + r_{t+1}) Q_{t+1} > 0$; . . .). And expectations of positive (and increasing) future prices lead to positive current prices. In other words, the belief that prices will be positive and increasing in the future makes current prices also positive. Expected future prices will continue to grow and people to believe that they will grow. In this case – i.e. when people do not expect the price of the stock to converge to some value in the future – the condition that the expected stock price does not explode is not satisfied and the stock price is no longer equal to the present value of expected dividends. In such a case, we say that prices are subject to a bubble.

But are bubbles rational? If the price of the stock today is $Q_t > 0$, then expectations on future prices are rational if they take into account the probability that the future price might be zero, i.e. that the bubble will crash. If the probability that the bubble will continue to grow is p and the probability that it will crash tomorrow is $(1 - p)$, then the future price of the stock is:

$$Q_{t+1} = \frac{1+r}{p}Q_t \quad \text{with probability } p$$

$$= 0 \qquad \text{with probability } (1 - p)$$

Therefore the expected future price of the stock is:

$$Q^e_{t+1} = p\frac{1+r}{p}Q_t + (1-p)0 = (1+r)Q_t$$

Bubbles grow and grow and then eventually crash, but until they grow they are rational!

An extension to the present value formula to account for risk

In this chapter and Chapter 14, we have assumed that people care only about expected return and do not take risk into account. Put another way, we have assumed that people are **risk neutral**. In fact, most people are **risk averse**. They care both about expected return – which they like – and risk – which they dislike.

Most of **finance theory** is indeed concerned with how people make decisions when they are risk averse and what risk aversion implies for asset prices. Exploring these issues would take us too far from our purpose. But we can nevertheless explore a simple extension of our framework that captures the fact that people are risk averse and shows how to modify the arbitrage and the present value relations.

If people perceive stocks to be more risky than bonds, and if people dislike risk, they are likely to require a *risk premium* to hold stocks rather than bonds. In the case of stocks, this risk premium is called the **equity premium**. Denote it by θ (the Greek lowercase letter theta). If θ is, for example, 5%, then people will hold stocks only if the expected rate of return on stocks exceeds the expected rate of return on short-term bonds by 5% per year.

In that case, the arbitrage equation between stocks and bonds becomes

$$\frac{€D^e_{t+1} + €Q^e_{t+1}}{€Q_t} = 1 + i_{1t} + \theta$$

The only change is the presence of θ on the right side of the equation. Going through the same steps as before (replacing Q^e_{t+1} by its expression at time $t + 1$ and so on), the stock price equals

$$€Q_t = \frac{€D^e_{t+1}}{(1 + i_{1t} + \theta)} + \ldots$$

$$+ \frac{€D^e_{t+n}}{(1 + i_{1t} + \theta) \ldots (1 + i^e_{1t+n-1} + \theta)} + \ldots$$

The stock price is still equal to the present value of expected future dividends. But the discount rate here equals the interest rate plus the equity premium. Note that the higher the premium, the lower the stock price.

Chapter 16

EXPECTATIONS, CONSUMPTION AND INVESTMENT

Having looked at the role of expectations in financial markets, we now turn to the role expectations play in determining the two main components of spending – consumption and investment. This description of consumption and investment will be the main building block of the expanded *IS–LM* model we shall develop in Chapter 17.

- Sections 16.1 and 16.2 look at consumption and show how consumption decisions depend not only on a person's current income but also on her expected future income and on financial wealth.

- Section 16.3 turns to investment and shows how investment decisions depend on current and expected profits and on current and expected real interest rates.

- Section 16.4 looks at the movements in consumption and investment over time and shows how to interpret those movements in light of what you learned in this chapter.

16.1 CONSUMPTION THEORY AND THE ROLE OF EXPECTATIONS

How do people decide how much to consume and how much to save? Until now, we have assumed that consumption and saving depended only on current income. By now, you realise that they depend on much more, particularly on expectations about the future. We now explore how those expectations affect the consumption decision.

The theory of consumption on which this section is based was developed independently in the 1950s by Milton Friedman of the University of Chicago, who called it the **permanent income theory of consumption**, and by Franco Modigliani of MIT, who called it the **life cycle theory of consumption**. Each chose his label carefully. Friedman's 'permanent income' emphasised that consumers look beyond current income. Modigliani's 'life cycle' emphasised that consumers' natural planning horizon is their entire lifetime.

The behaviour of aggregate consumption has remained a hot area of research ever since, for two reasons: one is simply the sheer size of consumption as a component of GDP and, therefore, the need to understand movements in consumption. The other is the increasing availability of large surveys of individual consumers, such as British Household Panel Survey in the UK, the Survey of Household Income and Wealth SHIW in Italy, the German Socio Economic Panel Study, the 'Enquête Budget de Famille' in France. These surveys, which were not available when Friedman and Modigliani developed their theories, have allowed economists to steadily improve their understanding of how consumers actually behave. This section summarises what we know today.

◀ Friedman received the Nobel Prize in Economics in 1976; Modigliani received the Nobel Prize in Economics in 1985.

◀ From Chapter 3: consumption spending accounts for 57% of total spending in the EU, 56% in the euro area, 64% in the UK, 49% in Denmark, 47% in Sweden, 46% in Ireland.

The very foresighted consumer

Let's start with an assumption that will surely – and rightly – strike you as extreme but will serve as a convenient benchmark. We'll call it the theory of the *very foresighted consumer*. How would a very foresighted consumer decide how much to consume? He would proceed in two steps:

1. He would add up the value of the stocks and bonds he owns, the value of his banking and savings accounts, the value of the house he owns minus the mortgage still due and so on. This would give him an idea of his **financial wealth** and his **housing wealth**. He would also estimate what his after-tax labour income was likely to be over his working life and compute the present value of expected after-tax labour income. This would give him an estimate of what economists call his **human wealth** – in contrast with his **non-human wealth**, defined as the sum of financial wealth and housing wealth.

◀ With a slight abuse of language, we use *housing wealth* to refer not only to housing but also to the other goods that the consumer may own, from cars to paintings and so on.

2. Adding his human wealth and non-human wealth, he would have an estimate of his **total wealth**. He would then decide how much to spend out of this total wealth. A reasonable assumption is that he would decide to spend a proportion of his total wealth such as to maintain roughly the same level of consumption each year throughout his life. If that level of consumption was higher than his current income, he would then borrow the difference. If it was lower than his current income, he would instead save the difference.

◀ Human wealth + non-human wealth = total wealth.

Let's write this formally. What we have described is a consumption decision of the form

$$C_t = C \text{ (Total wealth}_t) \qquad [16.1]$$

where C_t is consumption at time t, and (Total wealth$_t$) is the sum of non-human wealth (financial plus housing wealth) and human wealth at time t (the expected present value, as of time t, of current and future after-tax labour income).

This description contains much truth: like the foresighted consumer, we surely do think about our wealth and our expected future labour income in deciding how much to consume today. But one cannot help but think that it assumes too much computation and foresight on the part of the typical consumer.

To get a better sense of what that description implies and what is wrong with it, let's apply this decision process to the problem facing a typical student today. Let's assume that you are 19 years old, with three more years of study before you start your first job. You may be in debt today, having taken out a loan to go to university. You may own a car and a few other worldly possessions. For simplicity, let's assume that your debt and your possessions roughly offset each other, so that your non-human wealth is equal to zero. Your only wealth, therefore, is your human wealth, the present value of your expected after-tax labour income.

You expect your starting annual salary in three years to be around €25 000 (measured at 2000 prices) and to increase by an average of 3% per year in real terms, until your retirement at age 60. About 25% of your income will go to taxes.

Building on what you saw in Chapter 15, let's compute the present value of your labour income as the value of *real* expected after-tax labour income, discounted using *real* interest rates [equation (15.7)]. Let Y_{Lt} denote real labour income in year t. Let T_t denote real taxes in year t. Let $V(Y_{Lt}^e - T_t^e)$ denote your human wealth – that is, the expected present value of your after-tax labour income – expected as of year t.

To make the computation simple, assume that the real interest rate equals zero – so the expected present value is simply the sum of expected labour income over your working life and is therefore given by

$$V(Y_{Lt}^e - T_t^e) = (€25\ 000)(0.75)[1 + (1.03) + (1.03)^2 + \ldots + (1.03)^{38}]$$

The first term (€25 000) is your initial level of labour income, measured at 2000 prices.

The second term (0.75) comes from the fact that, because of taxes, you keep only 75% of what you earn.

The computation of the consumption level you can sustain is made easier by our assumption that the real interest rate equals 0. In this case, if you consume one less good today, you can consume exactly one more good next year, and the condition you must satisfy is simply that the sum of consumption over your lifetime is equal to your wealth. So, if you want to consume a constant amount each year, you just need to divide your wealth by the remaining number of years you expect to live.

The third term, $[1 + (1.03) + (1.03)^2 + \ldots + (1.03)^{38}]$, reflects the fact that you expect your real income to increase by 3% per year for 39 years (you will start earning income at age 22 and work until age 60).

Using the properties of geometric series to solve for the sum in brackets gives

$$V(Y_{Lt}^e - T_t^e) = (€25\ 000)(0.75)(72.2) = €1\ 353\ 750$$

Your wealth today, the expected value of your lifetime after-tax labour income, is around €1.3 million.

How much should you consume? You can expect to live about 16 years after you retire, so that your expected remaining life today is 58 years. If you want to consume the same amount every year, the constant level of consumption that you can afford equals your total wealth divided by your expected remaining life, or €1 353 750/ 58 = €23 340 per year. Given that your income until you get your first job is equal to 0, you will have to borrow €23 340 per year for the next three years, and you will begin to save when you get your first job.

The inter-temporal budget constraint

By now you can see that an inter-temporal perspective is crucial to understanding consumption decisions. To better understand the inter-temporal choices of a consumer – i.e. what is 'behind' equation [16.1] – let us start from what you have probably already learned about consumer choices in your microeconomics course.

Let us assume for simplicity that all individuals are identical, namely that in our hypothetical world there is only one individual: the **representative consumer**. Assume that there are only two goods, 1 and 2, and denote by c_1 and c_2, y_1 and y_2, p_1 and p_2, respectively, the quantities of good 1 and good 2 consumed, the amounts of goods 1 and 2 owned by the consumer, called **endowments**, and the prices of goods 1 and 2. The consumer's budget constraint tells us that no one can spend more than he or she has. The value of consumption must be equal to the value of resources:

$$p_1 c_1 + p_2 c_2 = p_1 y_1 + p_2 y_2$$

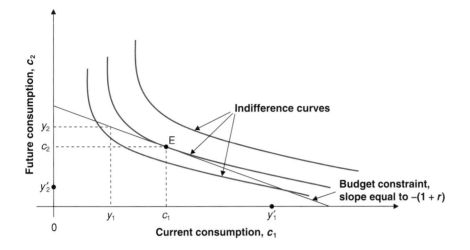

Figure 16.1

The intertemporal budget constraint

or, if we express all in terms of good 1:

$$c_1 + \frac{p_2}{p_1}c_2 = y_1 + \frac{p_2}{p_1}y_2$$

Quantities c_1 and c_2 represent, respectively, consumption at time 1 – today – and at time 2 – tomorrow. The relative price p_1/p_2 is the price of current consumption in terms of future consumption: it corresponds to the real interest rate, r, which measures by how much future consumption can increase by lending one more unit of good today:

$$1 + r = \frac{p_1}{p_2}$$

The budget constraint can therefore be rewritten as follows:

$$c_1 + \frac{1}{1+r}c_2 = y_1 + \frac{1}{1+r}y_2^e = V(y_t^e) \qquad t = 1, 2 \qquad [16.2]$$

where y_t^e is the expected endowment for tomorrow.

The interpretation is straightforward: the present discounted value of each individual's consumption – the sum of present and future consumption measured in terms of goods today – must be equal to the discounted present value of his or her endowments.

We can think of the endowment at time 1 as the sum of financial wealth and housing wealth with which the individual 'comes to the world', plus the net labour income. The expected endowment at time 2 can be thought of as the future labour income net of taxes. The present value of endowments is the total wealth of our consumer, which in turn is the sum of human wealth – the present discounted value of net labour income – plus the non-human wealth – his or her stock of financial wealth and housing wealth at a given time. However, until we consider endowments as exogenous, it is not necessary to distinguish the two components of wealth; let us then assume that y_1 is also labour income.

Let us go back to the budget constraint. It allows us to analyse consumption choices across two subsequent periods: for this reason we call it the **inter-temporal budget constraint**. The inter-temporal budget constraint is drawn in Figure 16.1. It represents all the combinations of current and future consumption (c_1, c_2) that the consumer can choose, given the present value of his or her endowments. Note that endowments (y_1, y_2^e) always satisfy the budget constraint: an individual can always choose to consume $c_1 = y_1$ and $c_2 = y_2^e$.

Intertemporal consumption decisions

Which of the possible intertemporal consumption paths is actually selected? Remember from your microeconomics course that consumer preferences may be represented by a utility function, which associates each basket (c_1, c_2) with a single value $U(c_1, c_2)$. Our representative consumer chooses the basket that maximises his or her utility, provided that it can be bought – that it does not violate the budget constraint.

In Figure 16.1, preferences are represented by a map of indifference curves. Each curve represents the combinations of current and future consumption that provide the same utility level – all the baskets among which the consumer is indifferent. The fact that each indifference curve is negatively-sloped and convex means that, compared to two 'unbalanced' consumption paths (i.e. one with high current consumption and low future consumption, another with low current consumption and high future consumption), the consumer prefers a more balanced path. The preference for a balanced consumption path over time is called **consumption smoothing**.

Graphically, the optimal choice is shown in Figure 16.1. The optimal combination of current and future consumption is the point along the budget constraint that lies on the outermost indifference curve. Except in the case of corner solutions, this corresponds to the point where the budget constraint is tangential to the higher indifference curve. The optimal choice is at point E. In the case represented in Figure 16.1, with endowments (y_1, y_2^e), the consumer borrows $c_1 - y_1$ in the current period and pays $y_2 - c_2$ in the future. Notice that the level of consumption E is also reachable by a consumer with endowments $(y_1', y_2^e)'$: he or she would save in the current period and borrow in the coming years.

To keep things quite simple, let us assume that the inter-temporal utility function $U(c_1, c_2)$ is additive with respect to current and future consumption:

$$U(c_1, c_2) = u(c_1) + \frac{1}{1 + \rho} u(c_2)$$

The function $u(\bullet)$ is sometimes called instantaneous utility function, and can be interpreted as the flow of utility provided by consumption at a certain time, regardless of when the goods are consumed. Let us now assume that utility increases with the level of consumption, but increases in utility get smaller and smaller as consumption increases.

The parameter $\rho \geq 0$ is the **discount rate**. It measures the weight the consumer attaches to the future compared to the present:

- *Case $\rho = 0$*: the consumer attaches the same importance to increases in consumption, irrespective of the time in which they occur. In this case, starting from a perfectly balanced consumption path over time, $c_1 = c_2$, equal increases in c_1 and c_2 have the same impact on total utility.
- *Case $\rho > 0$*: the factor $1/(1 + \rho)$ is less than 1 – an increase of consumption increases total utility to a greater extent if it occurs in the current period rather than in the future. In other words, starting from a balanced consumption path, to maintain the same level of total utility, the consumer requires an increase of $1 + \rho$ units of c_2 to compensate for a reduction in consumption of one unit.

Note that $\rho > 0$ means that individuals are impatient: they prefer to consume today rather than tomorrow. At the point that identifies the optimal combination of present and future consumption, the slope of the indifference curve – the marginal substitution rate (MSR) between the two goods – is equal to slope of the budget constraint $1 + r$. If the utility function is additive, the optimal condition can be written as

$$MRS = \frac{\partial U(c_1, c_2)/\partial c_1}{\partial U(c_1, c_2)} = \frac{\partial u/\partial c_1}{\frac{1}{1 + \rho} \partial u/\partial c_2} = 1 + r$$

and therefore:

$$\frac{\partial U/\partial c_1}{\partial U/\partial c_2} = \frac{1 + r}{1 + \rho} \tag{16.3}$$

This condition tells us that if $r = \rho$ then, along the optimal consumption path, $c_1 = c_2$, the consumer chooses the same level of consumption in both periods because his or her impatience is exactly offset by the interest rate on his or her savings, r. When we explained (in Section 15.1) the problem for a student, we said that probably he or she will choose a constant consumption path during his life. In that example, however, we described the student's preferences in words, without introducing a utility function. In the light of what we have just done – which, as we shall see, could easily be extended to two more periods – and if the preferences of our students are 'regular', then he will choose constant consumption over time only if $\rho = r$.

If instead $r > \rho$, the consumer will choose $c_1 < c_2$ (remember that we have assumed that marginal utility is decreasing). This result is quite intuitive: if the return on savings is sufficiently high, in particular higher than the discount rate, the consumer will find it more convenient to wait and postpone consumption in order to increase future consumption enough to compensate for his impatience. For example, if borrowing €23 340 in each of the three years of study before starting to work entailed paying very high interest, he would probably not borrow and postpone higher levels of consumption to the future.

For the same reason, if $r < \rho$, the consumer will choose a decreasing consumption path, and hence $c_1 > c_2$. These conditions are very important because they allow us to answer the question: how do consumers behave faced with a change in interest rates? The above optimal condition [equation (16.3)], together with the budget constraint [equation (16.2)], gives us a system of two equations in two unknowns, c_1 and c_2. This system can be solved to obtain the optimal values of c_1 and c_2 as functions of exogenous variables – the real interest rate and endowments.

In this section, expectations have not appeared explicitly in our equations. Note, however, that when our consumer, at time 1, chooses the level of his or her current and future consumption under the budget constraint, he or she must have a clue about his or her future labour income y_2, and that is an expectation. The optimal consumption choices for the present and the future are thus functions of $V(y_t^e)$, that is the present value of net current and expected future incomes, which we indicate with y_t^e.

16.2 TOWARD A MORE REALISTIC DESCRIPTION

In this section we give a more realistic description of consumption decisions by answering the question: if it is true that consumption decisions are made on a lifetime horizon, why is it that consumption reacts so much to changes in current income?

Why does consumption react so much to current income?

Let us go back to the computation made on page 328. Your first reaction might be that it is a stark and slightly sinister way of summarising your life prospects. Your second reaction may be that while you agree with most of the elements that went into the computation, you surely do not intend to borrow €23 340 × 3 = €70 020 over the next three years. For example:

● You might not want to plan for constant consumption over your lifetime. Instead you may be quite happy to defer higher consumption until later. Student life usually does not leave much time for expensive activities. You may want to defer trips to the Galápagos Islands to later in life. You also have to think about the additional expenses that will come with having children, sending them to school and college, summer holidays and so on.

● You might find that the amount of maths and foresight involved in the computation we just went through far exceeds the amount you use in your own decisions. You may never have thought until now about exactly how much income you are going to make and for how many years. You might feel that most consumption decisions are made in a simpler, less forward-looking fashion.

- The computation of total wealth is based on forecasts of what is expected to happen. But things can turn out better or worse. What happens if you become unemployed or sick? How will you pay back what you borrowed? You might want to be prudent, making sure that you can adequately survive even the worst outcomes, and thus decide to borrow much less than €70 020.
- Even if you decide to borrow €70 020, you might have a hard time finding a bank willing to lend it to you. Why? The bank may worry that you are taking on a commitment you will not be able to afford if times turn bad and that you may not be able or willing to repay the loan.

These reasons, all good ones, suggest that to characterise consumers' actual behaviour, we must modify the description we gave earlier. The last three reasons in particular suggest that consumption depends not only on total wealth but also on current income.

Take the second reason: you may, because it is a simple rule, decide to let your consumption follow your income and not think about what your wealth might be. In that case, your consumption will depend on your current income, not on your wealth.

Now take the third reason: it implies that a safe rule may be to consume no more than your current income. This way, you do not run the risk of accumulating debt that you cannot repay if times turn bad.

Or take the fourth reason: it implies that you may have little choice anyway. Even if you wanted to consume more than your current income, you might be unable to do so because no bank will give you a loan.

If we want to allow for a direct effect of current income on consumption, what measure of current income should we use? A convenient measure is after-tax labour income, which we introduced when we defined human wealth. This leads to a consumption function of the form

$$C_t = C(W_t, Y_{Lt} - T_t) \qquad [16.4]$$
$$(+, \quad + \quad)$$

where

$$W_t = W_t^F + W_t H + \sum_{i=0}^{T} \frac{Y_{t+i}^e - T_{t+i}^e}{(1+r)^i}$$

with the last element in the sum being the expected present discounted value of net income, EPDV$(Y - T)$.

In words: *consumption is an increasing function of total wealth and of current after-tax labour income. Total wealth is the sum of non-human wealth (financial wealth plus housing wealth) and human wealth (the present value of expected after-tax labour income).*

How much does consumption depend on total wealth (and therefore on expectations of future income), and how much does it depend on current income? The evidence is that most consumers look forward, in the spirit of the theory developed by Modigliani and Friedman. (See the Focus box 'Do people save enough for retirement?') But it is also true that we do observe that consumption reacts a lot to changes in current income. How can we explain this?

One possible explanation: liquidity constraints

Economic theory has given different explanations to justify the fact that consumption is very sensitive, or at least more sensitive than could be expected from the theory of consumptions based on expectations, to temporary changes in current income. As we said in the previous section, one possible explanation is that consumers cannot obtain credit as easily as the theory assumes. This means that consumers may be subject to liquidity constraints. To keep things simple, think of an extreme form of quantitative rationing, such that consumers have no means of getting credit – especially in period 1, when they are young and their

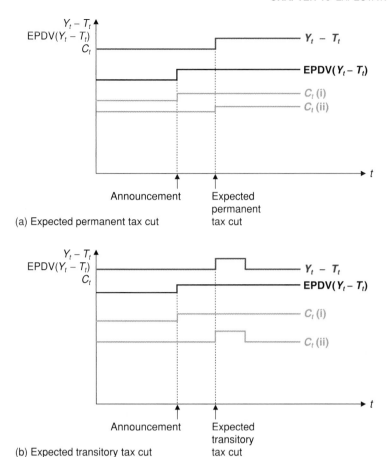

(a) Expected permanent tax cut

(b) Expected transitory tax cut

Figure 16.2

Two types of consumers (a, b)

(i) Consumers with no liquidity constraints can change consumption in line with changes in their EPDV($Y - T$).
(ii) Consumers with liquidity constraints can only consume out of their current disposable income.

endowments are likely to be low. In this case, current consumption cannot be greater than current income. Formally, this implies the presence, in addition to the inter-temporal budget constraint, of an additional constraint

$$c_1 \leq y_1$$

which allows us to better clarify the two results we have obtained in the previous section.

It may not be true that all consumers look forward when taking their consumption decisions. There are indeed two types of consumers. As Figure 16.2 shows, consumers who face no liquidity constraints because they are rich and have easy access to credit are more likely to give more weight to the expected future and to try to maintain roughly constant consumption over time. For example, prior to an announced tax cut in the near future, they can anticipate a future increase in their disposable income and increase the level of consumption accordingly. But some consumers, especially those who have temporarily low income and poor access to credit, are likely to consume their current income, regardless of what they expect will happen to them in the future. This is shown in Figure 16.2. A worker who becomes unemployed and has no financial wealth may have a hard time borrowing to maintain her level of consumption, even if she is fairly confident that she will soon find another job.

Putting things together: current income, expectations and consumption

Let's go back to what motivates this chapter – the importance of expectations in the determination of spending. Note first that, with consumption behaviour described by equation (16.4), expectations affect consumption in two ways:

How expectations of higher output in the future affect consumption today:

Expected future output increases
⇒ Expected future labour income increases
⇒ Human wealth increases
⇒ Consumption increases.

Expected future output increases
⇒ Expected future dividends increase
⇒ Stock prices increase
⇒ Non-human wealth increases
⇒ Consumption increases.

- Expectations affect consumption directly through *human wealth*: to compute their human wealth, consumers have to form their own expectations about future labour income, real interest rates and taxes.

Go back to the two consumption functions we used in the core. ➤

- Expectations affect consumption indirectly, through *non-human wealth* – stocks, bonds and housing. Consumers do not need to do any computation here and can just take the value of these assets as given. As you saw in Chapter 14, the computation is, in effect, done for them by participants in financial markets: the price of their stocks, for example, itself depends on expectations of future dividends and interest rates.

Looking at the short run (Chapter 3), we assumed $C = c_0 + c_1 Y$ (ignoring taxes here). This implied that, when income increased, consumption increased less than proportionately with income (C/Y went down). This was appropriate because our focus was on fluctuations, on transitory movements in income.

Looking at the long run (Chapter 12), we assumed that $S = sY$ or, equivalently, $C = (1 - s)Y$. This implied that when income increased, consumption increased proportionately with income (C/Y remained the same). This was appropriate because our focus was on permanent – long-run – movements in income.

This dependence of consumption on expectations has, in turn, two main implications for the relation between consumption and income:

- *Consumption is likely to respond less than one-for-one to fluctuations in current income.* When deciding how much to consume, a consumer looks at more than his current income. If he concludes that the decrease in his income is permanent, he is likely to decrease consumption one-for-one with the decrease in income. But if he concludes that the decrease in his current income is transitory, he will adjust his consumption by less. In a recession, consumption adjusts less than one-for-one to decreases in income. This is because consumers know that recessions typically do not last for more than a few quarters and that the economy will eventually return to the natural level of output. The same is true in expansions: faced with an unusually rapid increase in income, consumers are unlikely to increase consumption by as much as income. They are likely to assume that the boom is transitory and that things will return to normal.

- *Consumption may move even if current income does not change.* The election of a charismatic president or prime minister who articulates the vision of an exciting future might lead people to become more optimistic about the future in general and about their own

FOCUS
Do people save enough for retirement?

How carefully do people look forward when making consumption and saving decisions? One way to answer this question is to look at how much people save for retirement.

Table 16.1, taken from a study by Steven Venti, from Dartmouth, and David Wise, from Harvard, based on a **panel data set** called the Survey of Income and Program Participation, gives the basic numbers. The table shows the mean level and the composition of (total) wealth for people between 65 and 69 years in 1991 – so, most of them retired.

The first three components of wealth capture the various sources of retirement income. The first is the present value of social security benefits. The second is the value of the retirement plans provided by employers. And the third is the value of personal retirement plans. The last three components include the other assets held by consumers, such as bonds, stocks and housing.

A mean wealth of $314 000 is substantial (for comparison, US per-person personal consumption at the time of

the study, 1991, was $16 000). It gives an image of forward-looking individuals making careful saving decisions and retiring with enough wealth to enjoy a comfortable retirement.

We must be careful, however: the high average may hide important differences across individuals. Some individuals may save a lot, others little. Another study, by

Table 16.1 Mean wealth of people, age 65–69, in 1991 (in thousands of 1991 dollars)

Social security pension	$100
Employer-provided pension	62
Personal retirement assets	11
Other financial assets	42
Home equity	65
Other equity	34
Total	$314

Source: Steven F. Venti and David A. Wise, 'Choice, Chance, and Wealth Dispersion at Retirement', NBER Chapters, in *Aging Issues in the United States and Japan*, NBER, Cambridge, MA, 2001, 25–64.

future income in particular, leading them to increase consumption even if their current income does not change.

One of the main worries macroeconomists had during the financial crisis of 2007 was that consumers would become pessimistic and consumption would drop, leading to a deeper recession. Unfortunately, this was in fact the case. Consumer confidence fell during 2008, and the financial crisis led to a full-fledged economic crisis.

◄ What does this suggest happens to the saving rate in a recession?

16.3 INVESTMENT

How do firms make investment decisions? In our first pass at the answer in Chapter 5, we took investment to depend on the current interest rate and the current level of sales. We refined that answer in Chapter 14 by pointing out that what mattered was the real interest rate, not the nominal interest rate. It should now be clear that investment decisions, just as consumption decisions, depend on more than current sales and the current real interest rate. They also depend very much on expectations of the future. We now explore how those expectations affect investment decisions.

Just like the basic theory of consumption, the basic theory of investment is straightforward. A firm deciding whether to invest – say, whether to buy a new machine – must make a simple comparison. The firm must first compute the present value of profits it can expect from having this additional machine. It must then compare the present value of profits to the cost of buying the machine. If the present value exceeds the cost, the firm should buy the machine – invest; if the present value is less than the cost, then the firm should not buy the machine – not invest. This, in a nutshell, is the theory of investment. Let's look at it in more detail.

Scholz, Seshadri and Khitatrakun, from the University of Wisconsin, sheds light on this aspect. The study is based on another panel data set, called the *Health and Retirement Study*. The panel consists of 7000 households whose heads of household were between 51 and 61 years at the time of the first interview in 1992, and which have been interviewed every two years since. The panel contains information about the level and the composition of wealth for each household, as well as on its labour income (if the individuals in the household have not yet retired). Based on this information, the authors construct a target level of wealth for each household – i.e. the wealth level that each household should have if it wants to maintain a roughly constant level of consumption after retirement. The authors then compare the actual wealth level to the target level for each household.

The first conclusion of their study is similar to the conclusion reached by Venti and Wise: on average, people save enough for retirement. More specifically, the authors find that more than 80% of households have wealth above the target level. Put the other way around, only 20% of households have wealth below the target. But these numbers hide important differences across income levels.

Among those in the top half of the income distribution, more than 90% have wealth that exceeds the target, often by a large amount. This suggests that these households plan to leave bequests and so save more than what is needed for retirement.

Among those in the bottom 20% of the income distribution, however, fewer than 70% have wealth above the target. For the 30% of households below the target, the difference between actual and target wealth is typically small. But the relatively large proportion of individuals with wealth below the target suggests that there are a number of individuals who, through bad planning or bad luck, do not save enough for retirement. For most of these individuals, nearly all their wealth comes from the present value of social security benefits (the first component of wealth in Table 16.1), and it is reasonable to think that the proportion of people with wealth below target would be even larger if social security did not exist. This is indeed what the social security system was designed to do: to make sure that people have enough to live on when they retire. In that regard, it appears to be a success.

Sources: Steven Venti and David Wise, 'The Wealth of Cohorts: Retirement and Saving and the Changing Assets of Older Americans', in Sylvester Schieber and John B. Shoven (eds), *Public Policy Toward Pensions*, MIT Press, Cambridge, MA, 1997; and John Scholz, Ananth Seshadri and Surachai Khitatrakun, 'Are Americans Saving "Optimally" for Retirement?' *Journal of Political Economy*, 2006, **114**, 4, 607–643.

Investment and expected profit

Let's go through the steps a firm must take to determine whether to buy a new machine. (Although we refer to a machine, the same reasoning applies to the other components of investment – the building of a new factory, the renovation of an office complex, and so on.)

Depreciation

If the firm has a large number of machines, we can think of d as the proportion of machines that die every year. (Think of light bulbs – which work perfectly until they die.) If the firm starts the year with K working machines and does not buy new ones, it will have only $K(1 - \delta)$ machines left one year later, and so on.

To compute the present value of expected profits, a firm must first estimate how long a machine will last. Most machines are like cars. They can last nearly forever but, as time passes, they become more and more expensive to maintain and less and less reliable.

Assume that a machine loses its usefulness at rate δ (the Greek lowercase letter delta) per year. A machine that is new this year is worth only $1 - \delta$ machines next year, $(1 - \delta)^2$ machines in two years and so on. The *depreciation rate*, δ, measures how much usefulness the machine loses from one year to the next. What are reasonable values for δ? In the USA, the statisticians in charge of computing how the US capital stock changes over time, based on their studies of depreciation of specific machines and buildings, use numbers between 4% and 15% for machines and between 2% and 4% for buildings and factories.

The present value of expected profits

The firm must then compute the present value of expected profits.

To capture the fact that it takes some time to put machines in place (and even more time to build a factory or an office building), let's assume that a machine bought in year t becomes operational – and starts depreciating – only one year later, in year $t + 1$. Denote profit per machine in real terms by Π.

If the firm buys a machine in year t, the machine will generate its first profit in year $t + 1$. Denote this expected profit by Π^e_{t+1}. The present value, in year t, of this expected profit in year $t + 1$, is given by

$$\frac{1}{1 + r_t} \Pi^e_{t+1}$$

This term is represented by the arrow pointing left in the upper line of Figure 16.3. Because we are measuring profit in real terms, we are using real interest rates to discount future profits. This is one of the lessons we learned in Chapter 14.

Denote expected profit per machine in year $t + 2$ by Π^e_{t+2}. Because of depreciation, only $1 - \delta$ of the machine is left in year $t + 2$, so the expected profit from the machine is equal to $(1 - \delta)\Pi^e_{t+2}$. The present value of this expected profit as of year t is equal to

$$\frac{1}{(1 + r_t)(1 + r^e_{t+1})} (1 - \delta)\Pi^e_{t+2}$$

This computation is represented by the arrow pointing left in the lower line of Figure 16.3.

The same reasoning applies to expected profits in the following years. Putting the pieces together gives us *the present value of expected profits* from buying the machine in year t, which we shall call $V(\Pi^e_t)$

$$V(\Pi^e_t) = \frac{1}{1 + r_t}(\Pi^e_{t+1}) + \frac{1}{(1 + r_t)(1 + r^e_{t+1})}(1 - \delta)\Pi^e_{t+2} + \ldots \qquad [16.5]$$

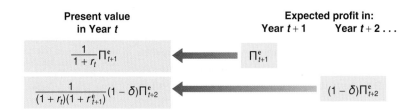

Figure 16.3

Computing the present value of expected profits

The expected present value is equal to the discounted value of expected profit next year, plus the discounted value of expected profit two years from now (taking into account the depreciation of the machine), and so on.

The investment decision

The firm must decide whether to buy the machine. This decision depends on the relation between the present value of expected profits and the price of the machine. To simplify notation, let's assume that the real price of a machine – that is, the machine's price in terms of the basket of goods produced in the economy – equals 1. What the firm must then do is to compare the present value of profits to 1.

If the present value is less than 1, the firm should not buy the machine: if it did, it would be paying more for the machine than it expects to get back in profits later. If the present value exceeds 1, the firm has an incentive to buy the new machine.

Let's now go from this one-firm, one-machine example to investment in the economy as a whole.

Let I_t denote aggregate investment. Denote profit per machine or, more generally, profit per unit of capital (where capital includes machines, factories, office buildings and so on) for the economy as a whole by $\prod_t$ Denote the expected present value of profit per unit of capital by $V(\prod_t^e)$, as defined as in equation (16.3).

Our discussion suggests an investment function of the form

$$I_t = I[V(\prod_t^e)] \qquad [16.6]$$
$$(+)$$

In words: *investment depends positively on the expected present value of future profits (per unit of capital). The higher the current or expected profits, the higher the expected present value and the higher the level of investment. The higher the current or expected real interest rates, the lower the expected present value, and thus the lower the level of investment.*

If the present value computation the firm has to make strikes you as quite similar to the present value computation we saw in Chapter 15 for the fundamental value of a stock, you are right. This relation was first explored by James Tobin, from Yale University, who argued that, for this reason, there should indeed be a tight relation between investment and the value of the stock market. His argument and the evidence for it are presented in the Focus box 'Investment and the stock market'.

◄ Tobin received the Nobel Prize in Economics in 1981.

A convenient special case

Before exploring further implications and extensions of equation (16.6), we'll go through a special case where the relation between investment, profit and interest rates becomes very simple.

Suppose firms expect both future profits (per unit of capital) and future interest rates to remain at the same level as today, so that

$$\prod_{t+1}^e = \prod_{t+2}^e = \ldots = \prod_t$$

and

$$r_{t+1}^e = r_{t+2}^e = \ldots = r_t$$

Economists call such expectations – expectations that the future will be like the present – **static expectations**. Under these two assumptions, equation (16.5) becomes

$$V(\prod_t^e) = \frac{\prod_t}{r_t + \delta} \qquad [16.7]$$

The present value of expected profits is simply the ratio of the profit rate – that is, profit per unit of capital – to the sum of the real interest rate and the depreciation rate. (The derivation is given in the appendix to this chapter.)

FOCUS
Investment and the stock market

Suppose a firm has 100 machines and 100 shares outstanding – 1 share per machine. Suppose the price per share is €2, and the purchase price of a machine is only €1. Obviously, the firm should invest – buy a new machine – and finance it by issuing a share: each machine costs the firm €1 to purchase, but stock market participants are willing to pay €2 for a share corresponding to this machine when it is installed in the firm.

This is an example of a more general argument made by Tobin that there should be a tight relation between the stock market and investment. When deciding whether to invest, he argued, firms might not need to go through the type of complicated computation you saw in the text. In effect, the stock price tells firms how much the stock market values each unit of capital already in place. The firm then has a simple problem: compare the purchase price of an additional unit of capital to the price the stock market is willing to pay for it. If the stock market value exceeds the purchase price, the firm should buy the machine; otherwise, it should not.

Tobin then constructed a variable corresponding to the value of a unit of capital in place relative to its purchase price and looked at how closely it moved with investment. He used the symbol q to denote the variable, and the variable has become known as **Tobin's q**. Its construction is as follows:

1. Take the total value of corporations, as assessed by financial markets. That is, compute the sum of their stock market value (the price of a share times the number of shares). Compute also the total value of their bonds outstanding (firms finance themselves not only through stocks but also through bonds). Add together the values of stocks and bonds.

2. Divide this total value by the value of the capital stock of corporations at replacement cost (the price firms would have to pay to replace their machines, their plants, and so on).

The ratio gives us, in effect, the value of a unit of capital in place relative to its current purchase price. This ratio is Tobin's q. Intuitively, the higher q, the higher the value of capital relative to its current purchase price, and the higher investment should be. (In the example at the start of the box, Tobin's q is equal to 2, so the firm should definitely invest.)

How tight is the relation between Tobin's q and investment? The answer is given in Figure 16.4, which plots two variables for each year from 1960–1999 for the USA.

Measured on the left vertical axis is the change in the ratio of investment to capital.

Measured on the right vertical axis is the change in Tobin's q. This variable has been lagged once. For 1987, for example, the figure shows the change in the ratio of investment to capital for 1987 and the change in Tobin's q for 1986 – that is, a year earlier. The reason for presenting the two variables this way is that the strongest relation in the data appears to be between investment this year and

Replacing (16.7) in equation (16.6), investment is

$$I_t = I\left(\frac{\Pi_t}{r_t + \delta}\right)$$ [16.8]

Investment is a function of the ratio of the profit rate to the sum of the interest rate and the depreciation rate.

The sum of the real interest rate and the depreciation rate is called the **user cost**, or the **rental cost**, **of capital**. To see why, suppose the firm, instead of buying the machine, rented it from a rental agency. How much would the rental agency have to charge per year? Even if the machine did not depreciate, the agency would have to ask for an interest charge equal to r_t times the price of the machine (we have assumed the price of a machine to be 1 in real terms, so r_t times 1 is just r_t): the agency has to get at least as much from buying and then renting the machine out as it would from, say, buying bonds. In addition, the rental agency would have to charge for depreciation, δ times the price of the machine, 1. Therefore:

$$\text{rental cost} = (r_t + \delta)$$

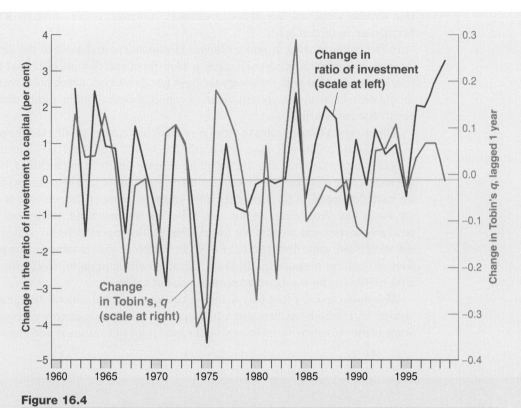

Figure 16.4

Tobin's q versus the ratio of investment to capital: annual rates of change, 1960–1999

Tobin's q last year. Put another way, movements in investment this year are more closely associated with movements in the stock market last year than with movements in the stock market this year; a plausible explanation is that it takes time for firms to make investment decisions, build new factories and so on.

Figure 16.4 shows that there is a clear relation between Tobin's q and investment. This is probably not because firms blindly follow the signals from the stock market, but because investment decisions and stock market prices depend very much on the same factors – expected future profits and expected future interest rates.

Even though firms typically do not rent the machines they use, $r_t + \delta$ still captures the implicit cost – sometimes called the *shadow cost* – to the firm of using the machine for one year.

The investment function given by equation (16.8) then has a simple interpretation: *investment depends on the ratio of profit to the user cost. The higher the profit, the higher the level of investment. The higher the user cost, the lower the level of investment.*

This relation between profit, the real interest rate and investment hinges on a strong assumption: that the future is expected to be the same as the present. It is a useful relation to remember – and one that macroeconomists keep handy in their toolbox. It is time, however, to relax this assumption and return to the role of expectations in determining investment decisions.

Current versus expected profit

The theory we have developed implies that investment should be forward looking and should depend primarily on *expected future profits*. (Under our assumption that it takes a year for investment to generate profits, current profit does not even appear in equation (16.5).)

One striking empirical fact about investment, however, is how strongly it moves with fluctuations in *current profit*.

In fact, when looking at yearly changes in investment and profit in the data, there is a clear positive relation between changes in investment and changes in current profit. Is this relation inconsistent with the theory we have just developed, which holds that investment should be related to the present value of expected future profits rather than to current profit? Not necessarily:

If firms expect future profits to move very much like current profit, then the present value of those future profits will move very much like current profit, and so will investment.

Economists who have looked at the question more closely have concluded, however, that the effect of current profit on investment is stronger than would be predicted by the theory we have developed so far. How they have gathered some of the evidence is described in the Focus box 'Profitability versus cash flow.' On the one hand, some firms with highly profitable investment projects but low current profits appear to be investing too little. On the other hand, some firms that have high current profit appear sometimes to invest in projects of doubtful profitability. In short, current profit appears to affect investment, even after controlling for the expected present value of profits.

Why does current profit play a role in the investment decision? The answer lurks in Section 16.1, where we discussed why consumption depends directly on current income. Some of the reasons we used to explain the behaviour of consumers also apply to firms:

FOCUS
Profitability versus cash flow

How much does investment depend on the expected present value of future profits, and how much does it depend on current profit? In other words, which is more important for investment decisions – **profitability** (the expected present discounted value of future profits) or **cash flow** (current profit, the net flow of cash the firm is receiving now)?

The difficulty in answering this question is that, most of the time, cash flow and profitability move together. Firms that do well typically have both large cash flows and good future prospects. Firms that suffer losses often also have poor future prospects.

The best way to isolate the effects of cash flow and profitability on investment is to identify times or events when cash flow and profitability move in different directions and then to look at what happens to investment. This is the approach taken by Owen Lamont, an economist at Yale University. An example will help you understand Lamont's strategy.

Think of two firms, A and B. Both firms are involved in steel production. Firm B is also involved in oil exploration.

Suppose there is a sharp drop in the price of oil, leading to losses in oil exploration. This shock decreases firm B's cash flow. If the losses in oil exploration are large enough to offset the profits from steel production, firm B might even show an overall loss.

The question we can now ask is: as a result of the fall in the price of oil, will firm B invest less in its steel operation than firm A does? If only the profitability of steel production matters, there is no reason for firm B to invest less in its steel operation than firm A. But if current cash flow also matters, the fact that firm B has a lower cash flow may prevent it from investing as much as firm A in its steel operation. Looking at investment in the steel operations of the two firms can tell us how much investment depends on cash flow versus profitability.

This is the empirical strategy followed by Lamont. He focused on what happened in 1986 when the price of oil in the USA dropped by 50%, leading to large losses in oil-related activities. He then looked at whether firms that had substantial oil activities cut investment in their non-oil activities relatively more than other firms in the same non-oil activities. He concludes that they did. He found that for every $1 decrease in cash flow due to the decrease in the price of oil, investment spending in non-oil activities was reduced by 10 to 20 cents. In short: current cash flow matters.

Source: Owen Lamont, 'Cash Flow and Investment: Evidence from Internal Capital Markets', *Journal of Finance*, 1997, **52**, 83–109.

CHAPTER 16 EXPECTATIONS, CONSUMPTION AND INVESTMENT **341**

- If its current profit is low, a firm that wants to buy new machines can get the funds it needs only by borrowing. It may be reluctant to borrow: although expected profits might look good, things may turn bad, leaving the firm unable to repay the debt. But if current profit is high, the firm might be able to finance its investment just by retaining some of its earnings and without having to borrow. The bottom line is that higher current profit may lead the firm to invest more.

- Even if the firm wants to invest, it might have difficulty borrowing. Potential lenders may not be convinced that the project is as good as the firm says it is, and they may worry that the firm will be unable to repay. If the firm has large current profits, it does not have to borrow and so does not need to convince potential lenders. It can proceed and invest as it pleases, and it is more likely to do so.

In summary, to fit the investment behaviour we observe in practice, the investment equation is better specified as

$$I_t = I[V(\Pi_t^e), \Pi_t] \qquad [16.9]$$
$$(+ , +)$$

In words: *investment depends both on the expected present value of future profits and on the current level of profit.*

Profit and sales

Let's take stock of where we are. We have argued that investment depends on both current and expected profit or, more specifically, current and expected profit per unit of capital. We need to take one last step: what determines profit per unit of capital? Answer: primarily two factors: (1) the level of sales and (2) the existing capital stock. If sales are low relative to the capital stock, profits per unit of capital are likely to be low as well.

Let's write this more formally. Ignore the distinction between sales and output and let Y_t denote output – equivalently, sales. Let K_t denote the capital stock at time t. Our discussion suggests the following relation:

$$\Pi_t = \Pi\left(\frac{Y_t}{K_t}\right) \qquad [16.10]$$
$$(+)$$

Profit per unit of capital is an increasing function of the ratio of sales to the capital stock. For a given capital stock, the higher the sales, the higher the profit per unit of capital. For given sales, the higher the capital stock, the lower the profit per unit of capital.

How well does this relation hold in practice? When looking at the data, there is a tight relation between yearly changes in profit per unit of capital and changes in the ratio of output to capital. Given that most of the year-to-year changes in the ratio of output to capital come from movements in output, and most of the year-to-year changes in profit per unit of capital come from movements in profit (capital moves slowly over time; the reason is that capital is large compared to yearly investment, so even large movements in investment lead to small changes in the capital stock), we can state the relation as follows: profit decreases in recessions and increases in expansions.

Why is this relation between output and profit relevant here? Because it implies a link between *current output and expected future output* on the one hand and *investment* on the other: current output affects current profit, expected future output affects expected future profit and current and expected future profits affect investment. For example, the anticipation of a long, sustained economic expansion leads firms to expect high profits, now and for some time in the future. These expectations in turn lead to higher investment. The effect of current and expected output on investment, together with the effect of investment on demand and output, will play a crucial role when we return to the determination of output in Chapter 17.

◄ High expected output ⇒
High expected profit ⇒
High investment today.

16.4 THE VOLATILITY OF CONSUMPTION AND INVESTMENT

You will surely have noticed the similarities between our treatment of consumption and of investment behaviour in Sections 16.1, 16.2 and 16.3:

- Whether consumers perceive current movements in income to be transitory or permanent affects their consumption decisions. The more transitory consumers expect a current increase in income to be, the less they will increase their consumption.

In the UK, retail sales are 40% higher on average in December than in other months. In France and Italy, sales are 60% higher in December.

- In the same way, whether firms perceive current movements in sales to be transitory or permanent affects their investment decisions. The more transitory firms expect a current increase in sales to be, the less they revise their assessment of the present value of profits, and thus the less likely they are to buy new machines or build new factories. This is why, for example, the boom in sales that happens every year during December in the run-up to Christmas does not lead to a boom in investment every year in December. Firms understand that this boom is transitory.

But there are also important differences between consumption decisions and investment decisions:

- The theory of consumption we developed implies that, when faced with an increase in income consumers perceive as permanent, they respond with at most an equal increase in consumption. The permanent nature of the increase in income implies that they can afford to increase consumption now and in the future by the same amount as the increase in income. Increasing consumption more than one-for-one would require cuts in consumption later, and there is no reason for consumers to want to plan consumption this way.

- Now consider the behaviour of firms faced with an increase in sales they believe to be permanent. The present value of expected profits increases, leading to an increase in investment. In contrast to consumption, however, this does not imply that the increase in investment should be at most equal to the increase in sales. Rather, once a firm has decided that an increase in sales justifies the purchase of a new machine or the building of a new factory, it may want to proceed quickly, leading to a large but short-lived increase in investment spending. This increase in investment spending may exceed the increase in sales.

  More concretely, take a firm that has a ratio of capital to its annual sales of, say, 3. An increase in sales of €10 million this year, if expected to be permanent, requires the firm to spend €30 million on additional capital if it wants to maintain the same ratio of capital to output. If the firm buys the additional capital right away, the increase in investment spending this year will equal *three times* the increase in sales. Once the capital stock has adjusted, the firm will return to its normal pattern of investment. This example is extreme because firms are unlikely to adjust their capital stock right away. But even if they do adjust their capital stock more slowly, say over a few years, the increase in investment might still exceed the increase in sales for a while.

  We can tell the same story in terms of equation (16.10). Because we make no distinction here between output and sales, the initial increase in sales leads to an equal increase in output, Y, so that Y/K – the ratio of the firm's output to its existing capital stock – also increases. The result is higher profit, which leads the firm to undertake more investment. Over time, the higher level of investment leads to a higher capital stock, K, so that Y/K decreases back to normal. Profit per unit of capital returns to normal, and so does investment. Thus, in response to a permanent increase in sales, investment may increase a lot initially and then return to normal over time.

These differences suggest that investment should be more volatile than consumption. How much more? The answer is given in Figure 16.5, which plots yearly rates of change in consumption and investment in the UK since 1960. The shaded areas are years during which the UK economy was in recession. To make the figure easier to interpret, both rates

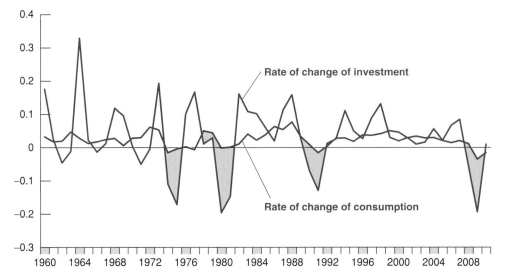

Figure 16.5

Rates of change of consumption and investment in the UK since 1960

Relative movements in investment are much larger than relative movements in consumption.

Source: Eurostat.

of change are plotted as deviations from the average rate of change so that they are, on average, equal to zero.

The figure yields three conclusions:

- Consumption and investment usually move together. Recessions, for example, are typically associated with decreases in *both* investment and consumption. Given our discussion, which has emphasised that consumption and investment depend largely on the same determinants, this should not come as a surprise.

- Investment is much more volatile than consumption. Relative movements in investment range from −20% to 33%, while relative movements in consumption range only from −1% to 8%.

- Because the level of investment is much smaller than the level of consumption (recall ◄ that investment accounts for 16% of GDP versus 64% for consumption), changes in investment from one year to the next end up being of the same overall magnitude as changes in consumption. In other words, both components contribute roughly equally to fluctuations in output over time.

Relative movements in *I* are larger than relative movements in *C*. But, because *I* accounts only for 16% of GDP in the UK (21% in EU27) and *C* accounts for 64% in the UK (57% in EU27), absolute movements in *I* and *C* are of roughly equal magnitude.

SUMMARY

- Consumption depends on both wealth and current income. Wealth is the sum of non-human wealth (financial wealth and housing wealth) and human wealth (the present value of expected after-tax labour income).

- The response of consumption to changes in income depends on whether consumers perceive these changes as transitory or permanent.

- Consumption is likely to respond less than one-for-one to movements in income. Consumption might move even if current income does not change.

- Investment depends on both current profit and the present value of expected future profits.

- Under the simplifying assumption that firms expect profits and interest rates to be the same in the future as

they are today, we can think of investment as depending on the ratio of profit to the user cost of capital, where the user cost is the sum of the real interest rate and the depreciation rate.

- Movements in profit are closely related to movements in output. Hence, we can think of investment as depending indirectly on current and expected future output movements. Firms that anticipate a long output expansion, and thus a long sequence of high profits, will invest. Movements in output that are not expected to last will have a small effect on investment.

- Investment is much more volatile than consumption. But, because investment accounts only for 16% of GDP and consumption accounts for 70%, movements in investment and consumption are of roughly equal magnitude.

KEY TERMS

QUESTIONS AND PROBLEMS

QUICK CHECK

1. *Using the information in this chapter, label each of the following statements true, false or uncertain. Explain briefly.*

a. For a typical university student, human wealth and non-human wealth are approximately equal.

b. Natural experiments, such as retirement, do not suggest that expectations of future income are a major factor affecting consumption.

c. Buildings and factories depreciate much faster than machines do.

d. A high value for Tobin's *q* indicates that the stock market believes that capital is over-valued, and thus investment should be lower.

e. Economists have found that the effect of current profit on investment can be fully explained by the effect of current profit on expectations of future profits.

f. Data from the past three decades in the USA suggest that corporate profits are closely tied to the business cycle.

g. Changes in consumption and investment typically occur in the same direction and at roughly the same magnitude.

2. *A consumer has non-human wealth equal to €100 000. She earns €40 000 this year and expects her salary to rise by 5% in real terms each year for the following two years. She will then retire. The real interest rate is equal to 0% and is expected to remain at 0% in the future. Labour income is taxed at a rate of 25%.*

a. What is this consumer's human wealth?

b. What is her total wealth?

c. If she expects to live for seven more years after retiring and wants her consumption to remain the same (in real terms) every year from now on, how much can she consume this year?

d. If she received a bonus of €20 000 in the current year only, with all future salary payments remaining as stated earlier, by how much could this consumer increase consumption now and in the future?

e. Suppose now that at retirement, social security will start paying benefits each year equal to 60% of this consumer's earnings during her last working year. Assume that benefits are not taxed. How much can she consume this year and still maintain constant consumption over her lifetime?

3. *A potato crisp manufacturer is considering buying another crisp-making machine that costs €100 000. The machine will depreciate by 8% per year. It will generate real profits equal to €18 000 next year, €18 000(1 − 8%) two years from now (that is, the same real profits but adjusted for depreciation), €18 000(1 − 8%)² three years from now and so on. Determine whether the manufacturer should buy the machine if the real interest rate is assumed to remain constant at each rate in (a) through (c).*

a. 5%

b. 10%

c. 15%

4. *Suppose that at age 22, you have just finished university and have been offered a job with a starting salary of €40 000. Your salary will remain constant in real terms. However, you have also been accepted onto a post-graduate course. The course can be completed in two years. Upon graduation, you expect your starting salary to be 10% higher in real terms and to remain constant in real terms thereafter. The tax rate on labour income is 40%.*

a. If the real interest rate is zero and you expect to retire at age 60 (i.e. if you do not do the postgraduate course, you expect to work for 38 years total), what is the maximum you should be willing to pay in tuition to do the course?

b. What is your answer to part (a) if you expect to pay 30% in taxes?

DIG DEEPER

5. Individual saving and aggregate capital accumulation

Suppose that every consumer is born with zero financial wealth and lives for three periods: youth, middle age and old age. Consumers work in the first two periods and retire in the last one. Their income is €5 in the first period, €25 in the second and €0 in the last one. Inflation and expected inflation are equal to zero, and so is the real interest rate.

a. What is the present discounted value of labour income at the beginning of life? What is the highest sustainable level of consumption such that consumption is equal in all three periods?

b. For each age group, what is the amount of saving that allows consumers to maintain the constant level of consumption you found in part (a)? (*Hint:* saving can be a negative number if the consumer needs to borrow in order to maintain a certain level of consumption.)

c. Suppose there are n people born each period. What is total saving in the economy? (*Hint:* add up the saving of each age group. Remember that some age groups may have negative saving.) Explain.

d. What is total financial wealth in the economy? (*Hint:* compute the financial wealth of people at the beginning of the first period of life, the beginning of the second period and the beginning of the third period. Add the three numbers. Remember that people can be in debt, so financial wealth can be negative.)

6. Borrowing constraints and aggregate capital accumulation

Continue with the setup from problem 5, but suppose now that restrictions on borrowing do not allow young consumers to borrow. If we call the sum of income and total financial wealth 'cash on hand', then the borrowing restriction means that consumers cannot consume more than their cash on hand. In each age group, consumers compute their total wealth and then determine their desired level of consumption as the highest level that allows their consumption to be equal in all three periods. However, if at any time, desired consumption exceeds cash on hand, then consumers are constrained to consume exactly their cash on hand.

a. Calculate consumption in each period of life. Compare this answer to your answer to part (a) of problem 5, and explain any differences.

b. Calculate total saving for the economy. Compare this answer to your answer to part (c) of problem 5, and explain any differences.

c. Derive total financial wealth for the economy. Compare this answer to your answer to part (d) of problem 5, and explain any differences.

d. Consider the following statement: 'Financial liberalisation may be good for individual consumers, but it is bad for overall capital accumulation.' Discuss.

7. Saving with uncertain future income

Consider a consumer who lives for three periods: youth, middle age and old age. When young, the consumer earns €20 000 in labour income. Earnings during middle age are uncertain; there is a 50% chance that the consumer will earn €40 000 and a 50% chance that the consumer will earn €100 000. When old, the consumer spends savings accumulated during the previous periods. Assume that inflation, expected inflation and the real interest rate equal zero. Ignore taxes for this problem.

a. What is the expected value of earnings in the middle period of life? Given this number, what is the present discounted value of expected lifetime labour earnings? If the consumer wishes to maintain constant expected consumption over her lifetime, how much will she consume in each period? How much will she save in each period?

b. Now suppose the consumer wishes, above all else, to maintain a minimum consumption level of €20 000 in each period of her life. To do so, she must consider the worst outcome. If earnings during middle age turn out to be €40 000, how much should the consumer spend when she is young to guarantee consumption of at least €20 000 in each period? How does this level of consumption compare to the level you obtained for the young period in part (a)?

c. Given your answer in part (b), suppose that the consumer's earnings during middle age turn out to be €100 000. How much will she spend in each period of life? Will consumption be constant over the consumer's lifetime? (*Hint:* when the consumer reaches middle age, she will try to maintain constant consumption for the last two periods of life, as long as she can consume at least €20 000 in each period.)

d. What effect does uncertainty about future labour income have on saving (or borrowing) by young consumers?

EXPLORE FURTHER

8. The movements of consumption and investment

*Go to the Eurostat website (**www.http://epp.eurostat.ec. europa.eu**) and download data for the years 1980 to the present date for personal consumption expenditures and gross private domestic investment for your country.*

a. On average, how much larger is consumption than investment?

b. Compute the change in the levels of consumption and investment from one year to the next, and graph them for the period 1980 to the present date. Are the year-to-year changes in consumption and investment of similar magnitude?

c. What do your answers in parts (a) and (b) imply about the average annual percentage changes of consumption and investment? Is this implication consistent with Figure 16.6?

9. Consumer confidence and disposable income

*Go to the Eurostat website (**www.http://epp.eurostat.ec. europa.eu**) and download data on the Consumer Confidence Indicator for the latest available years. We will use this data series as our measure of consumer confidence. Now find the percentage change in real personal disposable income. Obtain these data for the latest available years.*

a. Before you look at the data, can you think of any reasons to expect consumer confidence to be related to disposable income? Can you think of reasons why consumer confidence would be unrelated to disposable income?

b. Calculate the average percentage change in personal disposable income over the entire period, and subtract this average from each observation of the percentage change in personal disposable income. Use this new data series as your measure of the change in personal disposable income. Now calculate the change in consumer confidence as the change in the Consumer Confidence Indicator. Plot the change in consumer confidence against the change in personal disposable income (the measure you constructed in this part). Is there a clear relation (positive or negative) between the two variables? If you believe there is a relation, is it very tight? In other words, are there many observations that deviate greatly from the average relation?

c. Look at the data for 2008 and 2009. What happened to personal disposable income during these two years? What happened to consumer confidence? Why do you think consumer confidence behaved differently in these two time periods?

*We invite you to visit the Blanchard page on the Prentice Hall website, at **www.prenhall.com/blanchard** for this chapter's World Wide Web exercises.*

APPENDIX

Derivation of the expected present value of profits under static expectations

You saw in equation (16.5) that the expected present value of profits is given by

$$V(\Pi_t^e) = \frac{1}{1+r_t}\Pi_{t+1}^e + \frac{1}{(1+r_t)(1+r_{t+1}^e)}(1-\delta)\Pi_{t+2}^e + \dots$$

If firms expect both future profits (per unit of capital) and future interest rates to remain at the same level as today, so that $\Pi_{t+1}^e = \Pi_{t+2}^e = \dots = \Pi_t$, and $r_{t+1}^e = r_{t+2}^e = \dots = r_t$, the equation becomes

$$V(\Pi_t^e) = \frac{1}{1+r_t}\Pi_t + \frac{1}{(1+r_t)^2}(1-\delta)\Pi_t + \dots$$

Factoring out $[1/(1+r_t)]\Pi_t$,

$$V(\Pi_t^e) = \frac{1}{1+r_t}\Pi_t\left(1 - \frac{1-\delta}{1+r_t} + \dots\right) \qquad [16.A1]$$

The term in parentheses in this equation is a geometric series, a series of the form $1 + x + x^2 + \dots$. So, from Proposition 2 in Appendix 1 at the end of the book

$$(1 + x + x^2 + \dots) = \frac{1}{1-x}$$

Here x equals $(1-\delta)/(1+r_t)$ so

$$\left(1 + \frac{1-\delta}{1+r_t} + \left(\frac{1-\delta}{1+r_t}\right)^2 + \dots\right) = \frac{1}{1-(1-\delta)/(1+r_t)}$$

$$= \frac{1+r_t}{r_t+\delta}$$

Replacing in equation (16. A1) gives

$$V(\Pi_t^e) = \frac{1}{1+r_t}\frac{1+r_t}{r_t+\delta}\Pi_t$$

Simplifying gives equation (16.5) in the text:

$$V(\Pi_t^e) = \frac{\Pi_t}{(r_t+\delta)}$$

Chapter 17

EXPECTATIONS, OUTPUT AND POLICY

In Chapter 15, we looked at how expectations affect bond and stock prices. In Chapter 16, we examined how expectations affect consumption decisions and investment decisions. In this chapter, we put together the pieces and take another look at the effects of monetary and fiscal policy:

- Section 17.1 draws the major implication of what we have learned, namely that expectations of both future output and future interest rates affect current spending and therefore current output.

- Section 17.2 looks at monetary policy. It shows how the effects of monetary policy depend crucially on how expectations respond to policy: monetary policy directly affects only the short-term interest rate. What happens to spending and output then depends on how changes in the short-term interest rate lead people and firms to change their expectations of future interest rates and future income and, by implication, lead them to change their decisions.

- Section 17.3 turns to fiscal policy. It shows how, in sharp contrast to the simple model you saw in the core, a fiscal contraction may, under some circumstances, lead to an increase in output, even in the short run. Again, how expectations respond to policy is central to the story.

17.1 EXPECTATIONS AND DECISIONS: TAKING STOCK

Let's review what we have learned, and then examine how we should modify the characterisation of goods and financial markets – the *IS–LM* model – we developed in the core.

Expectations, consumption and investment decisions

The theme of Chapter 16 was that both consumption and investment decisions depend very much on expectations of future income and interest rates. The channels through which expectations affect consumption and investment spending are summarised in Figure 17.1.

Note the many channels through which expected future variables affect current decisions, both directly and through asset prices:

- An increase in current and expected future after-tax real labour income and/or a decrease in current and expected future real interest rates increase human wealth (the expected present discounted value of after-tax real labour income), which in turn leads to an increase in consumption.
- An increase in current and expected future real dividends and/or a decrease in current and expected future real interest rates increase stock prices, which leads to an increase in non-human wealth and, in turn, to an increase in consumption.
- A decrease in current and expected future nominal interest rates leads to an increase in bond prices, which leads to an increase in non-human wealth and, in turn, to an increase in consumption.   ◄ Note that in the case of bonds, it is nominal rather than real interest rates which matter because bonds are claims to money rather than goods in the future.
- An increase in current and expected future real after-tax profits and/or a decrease in current and expected future real interest rates increase the present value of real after-tax profits, which leads, in turn, to an increase in investment.

Expectations and the *IS* relation

A model that gave a detailed treatment of consumption and investment along the lines suggested in Figure 17.1 would be very complicated. It can be done – and indeed it is done in the large empirical models that macroeconomists build to understand the economy and analyse policy; but this is not the place for such complication. We want to capture the essence of what you have learned so far, how consumption and investment depend on expectations of the future – without getting lost in the details.

To do so, let's make a major simplification. Let's reduce the present and the future to only ◄ two periods: (1) a *current* period, which you can think of as the current year and (2) a *future*

This way of dividing time between 'today' and 'later' is the way many of us organise our own lives: think of 'things to do today' versus 'things that can wait'.

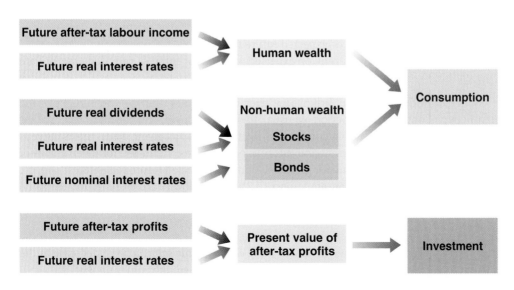

Figure 17.1

Expectations and spending: the channels

Expectations affect consumption and investment decisions, both directly and through asset prices.

period, which you can think of as all future years lumped together. This way, we do not have to keep track of expectations about each future year.

See the equation for the *IS* relation in Chapter 6, which itself extended equation (5.2) in Chapter 5 to allow for a distinction between the real and nominal interest rates.

Having made this assumption, the question becomes: how should we write the *IS* relation for the current period? Earlier, we wrote the following equation for the *IS* relation:

$$Y = C(Y - T) + I(Y, r) + G$$

We assumed that consumption depended only on current income and that investment depended only on current output and the current real interest rate. We now want to modify this to take into account how expectations affect both consumption and investment. We proceed in two steps.

First, we simply rewrite the equation in more compact form, but without changing its content. For that purpose, let's define aggregate private spending as the sum of consumption and investment spending:

$$A(Y, T, r) \equiv C(Y - T) + I(Y, r)$$

The reason for doing this is to group together the two components of demand, *C* and *I*, that both depend on expectations. We continue to treat *G*, government spending, as exogenous – unexplained within our model.

where *A* stands for **aggregate private spending** or, simply, **private spending**. With this notation, we can rewrite the *IS* relation as

$$Y = A(Y, T, r) + G \qquad [17.1]$$
$$(+, -, -)$$

The properties of aggregate private spending, *A*, follow from the properties of consumption and investment that we derived in earlier chapters:

- Aggregate private spending is an increasing function of income, *Y*: higher income (equivalently, output) increases consumption and investment.
- Aggregate private spending is a decreasing function of taxes, *T*: higher taxes decrease consumption.
- Aggregate private spending is a decreasing function of the real interest rate, *r*: a higher real interest rate decreases investment.

The first step only simplified notation. The second step is to extend equation (17.1) to take into account the role of expectations. The natural extension is to allow spending to depend not only on current variables but also on their expected values in the future period:

$$Y = A(Y, T, r, Y'^e, T'^e, r'^e) + G \qquad [17.2]$$
$$(+, -, -, +, -, -)$$

Primes denote future values and the superscript e denotes an expectation, so Y'^e, T'^e and r'^e denote future expected income, future expected taxes and the future expected real interest rate, respectively. The notation is a bit heavy, but what it captures is straightforward:

Y' or Y'^e increases $\Rightarrow$ A increases
T' or T'^e increases $\Rightarrow$ A decreases
r' or r'^e increases $\Rightarrow$ A decreases

- Increases in either current or expected future income increase private spending.
- Increases in either current or expected future taxes decrease private spending.
- Increases in either the current or expected future real interest rate decrease private spending.

With the goods market equilibrium now given by equation (17.2), Figure 17.2 shows the new *IS* curve for the current period. As usual, to draw the curve, we take all variables other than current output, *Y*, and the current real interest rate, *r*, as given. Thus, the *IS* curve is drawn for given values of current and future expected taxes, *T* and T'^e, for given values of expected future output, Y'^e, and for given values of the expected future real interest rate, r'^e.

The new *IS* curve, based on equation (17.2), is still downward-sloping, for the same reason as in Chapter 5: a decrease in the current real interest rate leads to an increase in spending. This increase in spending leads, through a multiplier effect, to an increase in output. We can say more, however: the new *IS* curve is much steeper than the *IS* curve we drew in earlier chapters. Put another way, *everything else being the same*, a large decrease in the current interest rate is likely to have only a small effect on equilibrium output.

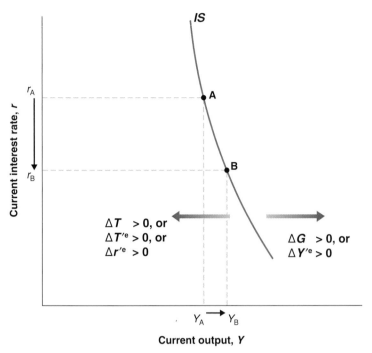

Figure 17.2

The new *IS* curve

Given expectations, a decrease in the real interest rate leads to a small increase in output: the *IS* curve is steeply downward sloping. Increases in government spending or in expected future output shift the *IS* curve to the right. Increases in taxes, in expected future taxes or in the expected future real interest rate shift the *IS* curve to the left.

To see why the effect is small, take point A on the *IS* curve in Figure 17.2, and consider the effects of a decrease in the real interest rate, from r_A to r_B. The effect of the decrease in the real interest rate on output depends on the strength of two effects: the effect of the real interest rate on spending given income and the size of the multiplier. Let's examine each one:

- A decrease in the current real interest rate, *given unchanged expectations of the future real interest rate*, does not have much effect on spending. We saw why in the previous chapters: a change in only the current real interest rate does not lead to large changes in present values and, therefore, does not lead to large changes in spending. For example, firms are not likely to change their investment plans very much in response to a decrease in the current real interest rate if they do not expect future real interest rates to be lower as well.

- The multiplier is likely to be small. Recall that the size of the multiplier depends on the size of the effect a change in current income (output) has on spending. But a change in current income, *given unchanged expectations of future income*, is unlikely to have a large effect on spending. The reason: changes in income that are not expected to last have only a limited effect on either consumption or investment. Consumers who expect their income to be higher only for a year will increase consumption – but by much less than the increase in their income. Firms that expect sales to be higher only for a year are unlikely to change their investment plans much, if at all.

Putting things together, a large decrease in the current real interest rate – from r_A to r_B in Figure 17.2 – leads to only a small increase in output, from Y_A to Y_B. Put another way: the *IS* curve, which goes through points A and B, is steeply downward-sloping.

A change in any variable in equation (17.2) other than Y and r shifts the *IS* curve:

- Changes in current taxes, T, or in current government spending, G, shift the *IS* curve.

    An increase in current government spending increases spending at a given interest rate, shifting the *IS* curve to the right; an increase in taxes shifts the *IS* curve to the left. These shifts are represented in Figure 17.2.

- Changes in expected future variables also shift the *IS* curve.

    An increase in expected future output, Y'^e, shifts the *IS* curve to the right: higher expected future income leads consumers to feel wealthier and spend more; higher

Suppose you have a 30-year loan, and the one-year interest rate goes down from 5% to 2%. All future one-year rates remain the same. By how much will the 30-year interest rate come down? (Answer: from 5% to 4.9%. If you got the answer wrong, go back to the discussion of the relation between short-term interest rates and long-term interest rates in Chapter 15.)

Suppose a firm decides to give all employees a one-time bonus of €10 000. The employees do not expect it to happen again. By how much will they increase their consumption this year? (If you need to, look at the discussion of consumption behaviour in Chapter 16.)

expected future output implies higher expected profits, leading firms to invest more. Higher spending by consumers and firms leads, through the multiplier effect, to higher output. Similarly, an increase in expected future taxes leads consumers to decrease their current spending and shifts the *IS* curve to the left. And an increase in the expected future real interest rate decreases current spending, also leading to a decrease in output, shifting the *IS* curve to the left. These shifts are also represented in Figure 17.2.

The *LM* relation revisited

The *LM* relation we derived in Chapter 4 and have used until now was given by

$$\frac{M}{P} = YL(i) \tag{17.3}$$

where M/P is the supply of money and $YL(i)$ is the demand for money. Equilibrium in financial markets required that the supply of money be equal to the demand for money. The demand for money depended on real income and on the short-term nominal interest rate – the opportunity cost of holding money. We derived this demand for money before thinking about expectations. Now that we have thought about them, the question is whether we should modify equation (17.3). The answer – we are sure this will be good news – is no.

Think of your own demand for money. How much money you want to hold today depends on your *current* level of transactions, not on the level of transactions you expect next year or the year after; there will be ample time for you to adjust your money balances to your transaction level if and when it changes in the future. And the opportunity cost of holding money today depends on the *current* nominal interest rate, not on the expected nominal interest rate next year or the year after. If short-term interest rates were to increase in the future, increasing the opportunity cost of holding money then, the time to reduce your money balances would be then, not now.

So, in contrast to the consumption decision, the decision about how much money to hold is myopic, depending primarily on current income and the current short-term nominal interest rate. We can still think of the demand for money as depending on the current level of output and the current nominal interest rate, and we can use equation (17.3) to describe the determination of the nominal interest rate in the current period.

Let's summarise. We have seen that expectations about the future play a major role in spending decisions. This implies that expectations enter the *IS* relation: private spending depends not only on current output and the current real interest rate but also on expected future output and the expected future real interest rate. In contrast, the decision about how much money to hold is largely myopic: the two variables entering the *LM* relation are still current income and the current nominal interest rate.

17.2 MONETARY POLICY, EXPECTATIONS AND OUTPUT

In the basic *IS–LM* model we developed in Chapter 5, there was only one interest rate, i, which entered both the *IS* relation and the *LM* relation. When the central bank expanded the money supply, 'the' interest rate went down, and spending increased. From the previous three chapters, you have learned that there are in fact many interest rates and that we must keep two distinctions in mind:

1. The distinction between the nominal interest rate and the real interest rate.
2. The distinction between current and expected future interest rates.

The interest rate that enters the *LM* relation, which is the interest rate that the central bank affects directly, is the *current nominal interest rate*. In contrast, spending in the *IS* relation depends on both *current and expected future real interest rates*. Economists sometimes state this distinction even more starkly by saying that, while the central bank controls the *short-term nominal interest rate*, what matters for spending and output is the *long-term real interest rate*. Let's look at this distinction more closely.

From the short nominal rate to current and expected real rates

Recall from Chapter 6 that the real interest rate is approximately equal to the nominal interest rate minus expected current inflation:

$$r = i - \pi^e$$

Expected current inflation: inflation expected, as of today, for the current period (the current year).

Similarly, the expected future real interest rate is approximately equal to the expected future nominal interest rate minus expected future inflation:

$$r'^e = i'^e - \pi'^e$$

Expected future inflation: inflation expected, as of today, for the future period (all future years).

When the central bank increases the money supply – decreasing the current nominal interest rate, i – the effects on the current and the expected future real interest rates depend on two factors:

- Whether the increase in the money supply leads financial markets to revise their expectations of the future nominal interest rate, i'^e.
- Whether the increase in the money supply leads financial markets to revise their expectations of both current and future inflation, π^e and π'^e. If, for example, the change in money leads financial markets to expect more inflation in the future – so π'^e increases – the expected future real interest rate, r'^e, will decrease by more than the expected future nominal interest rate, i'^e.

We explored the role of changing expectations of inflation on the relation between the nominal interest rate and the real interest rate in Chapter 6. Leaving changes in expected inflation aside will keep the analysis simpler here. You have, however, all the elements you need to think through what would happen if we also allowed expectations of current inflation and future inflation to adjust. How would these expectations adjust? Would this lead to a larger or a smaller effect on output in the current period?

To keep things simple, we shall ignore here the second factor – the role of changing expectations of inflation – and focus on the first – the role of changing expectations of the future nominal interest rate. Thus we shall assume that expected current inflation and expected future inflation are both equal to 0. In this case, we do not need to distinguish between the nominal interest rate and the real interest rate, as they are equal, and we can use the same letter to denote both. Let r denote the current real (and nominal) interest rate, and let r'^e denote the expected future real (and nominal) interest rate. With this simplification, we can rewrite the *IS* and *LM* relations in equations (17.2) and (17.3) as

$$IS: \quad Y = A(Y, T, r, Y'^e, T'^e, r'^e) + G \qquad [17.4]$$

$$LM: \quad \frac{M}{P} = YL(r) \qquad [17.5]$$

The *IS* relation is the same as equation (17.2). The *LM* relation is now in terms of the real interest rate – which, here, is equal to the nominal interest rate.

The corresponding *IS* and *LM* curves are drawn in Figure 17.3. The vertical axis measures the current interest rate, r; the horizontal axis measures current output, Y. The *IS* curve is steeply downward-sloping. We saw the reason earlier: for given expectations, a change in the current interest rate has a limited effect on spending, and the multiplier is small. The *LM* is upward-sloping: an increase in income leads to an increase in the demand for money; given the supply of money, the result is an increase in the interest rate. Equilibrium in goods and financial markets implies that the economy is at point A, on both the *IS* and the *LM* curves.

There is no need to distinguish here between the real interest rate and the nominal interest rate: given 0 expected inflation, they are the same.

Monetary policy revisited

Now suppose the economy is in recession, and the central bank decides to increase the money supply.

Assume first that this expansionary monetary policy does not change expectations of either the future interest rate or future output. In Figure 17.4, the *LM* curve shifts down, from *LM* to *LM"*. (Because we have already used primes to denote future values of the

Given expectations, an increase in the money supply leads to a shift in the *LM* curve and a movement down the steep *IS* curve. The result is a large decrease in r and a small increase in Y.

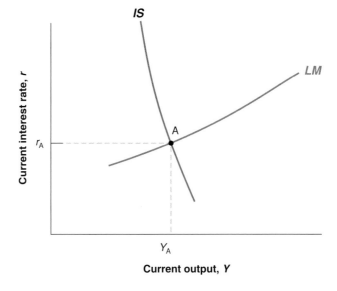

Figure 17.3

The new *IS–LM* curves

The *IS* curve is steeply downward sloping. Other things being equal, a change in the current interest rate has a small effect on output. The *LM* curve is upward sloping. The equilibrium is at the intersection of the *IS* and *LM* curves.

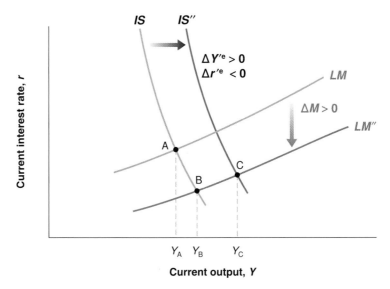

Figure 17.4

The effects of an expansionary monetary policy

The effects of monetary policy on output depend very much on whether and how monetary policy affects expectations.

variables, we use double primes, such as in *LM″*, to denote shifts in curves in this chapter.) The equilibrium moves from point A to point B, with higher output and a lower interest rate. The steep *IS* curve, however, implies that the increase in the money supply has only a small effect on output: changes in the current interest rate, unaccompanied by changes in expectations, have only a small effect on spending and, in turn, a small effect on output.

Is it reasonable, however, to assume that expectations are unaffected by an expansionary monetary policy? Isn't it likely that, as the central bank lowers the current interest rate, financial markets now anticipate lower interest rates in the future as well, along with higher future output stimulated by this lower future interest rate? What happens if they do? At a given current interest rate, prospects of a lower future interest rate and of higher future output both increase spending and output; they shift the *IS* curve to the right, from *IS* to *IS″*. The new equilibrium is given by point C. Thus, while the direct effect of the monetary expansion on output is limited, the full effect, once changes in expectations are taken into account, is much larger.

You have just learned an important lesson: the effects of monetary policy – the effects of any type of macroeconomic policy, for that matter – depend crucially on its effect on expectations:

 If the increase in money leads to an increase in Y'^e and a decrease in r^e, the *IS* curve shifts to the right, leading to a larger increase in *Y*.

- If a monetary expansion leads financial investors, firms and consumers to revise their expectations of future interest rates and output, then the effects of the monetary expansion on output may be very large.
- If expectations remain unchanged, the effects of the monetary expansion on output will be small.

We can link this discussion to our discussion in Chapter 15 about the effects of changes in monetary policy in the stock market. Many of the same issues were present there. If, when the change in monetary policy takes place, it comes as no surprise to investors, firms and consumers, then expectations will not change. The stock market will react only a little, if at all. And demand and output will change only a little, if at all. But if the change comes as a surprise and is expected to last, expectations of future output will go up, expectations of future interest rates will come down, the stock market will boom and output will increase.

At this stage, you may have become very sceptical that macroeconomists can say much about the effects of policy, or the effects of other shocks: if the effects depend so much on what happens to expectations, can macroeconomists have any hope of predicting what will happen? The answer is yes.

Saying that the effect of a particular policy depends on its effect on expectations is not the same as saying that anything can happen. Expectations are not arbitrary. The manager of a mutual fund who must decide whether to invest in stocks or bonds, the firm thinking about whether to build a new plant, the consumer thinking about how much she should save for retirement, all give a lot of thought to what might happen in the future. We can think of each of them as forming expectations about the future by assessing the likely course of future expected policy and then working out the implications for future activity. If they do not do it themselves (surely most of us do not spend our time solving macroeconomic models before making decisions), they do so indirectly by watching TV and reading newsletters and newspapers, which in turn rely on the forecasts of public and private forecasters. Economists refer to expectations formed in this forward-looking manner as **rational expectations**. The introduction of the assumption of rational expectations is one of the most important developments in macroeconomics in the past 35 years. It has largely shaped the way macroeconomists think about policy. It is discussed further in the Focus box 'Rational expectations.'

◄ This is why macroeconomists working on monetary policy often argue that the task of a central bank is not only to adjust the short-term nominal interest rate but also to 'manage expectations' so as to lead to predictable effects of changes in this interest rate on the economy. More on this in Chapter 24.

FOCUS
Rational expectations

Most macroeconomists today routinely solve their models under the assumption of rational expectations. This was not always the case. The past 35 years in macroeconomic research are often called the 'rational expectations revolution'.

The importance of expectations is an old theme in macroeconomics. But until the early 1970s, macroeconomists thought of expectations in one of two ways:

- One was as **animal spirits** (from an expression Keynes introduced in the *General Theory* to refer to movements in investment that could not be explained by movements in current variables). In other words, shifts in

expectations were considered important but were left unexplained.

- The other was as the result of simple, backward-looking rules. For example, people were often assumed to have static expectations – that is, to expect the future to be like the present (we used this assumption when discussing the Phillips curve in Chapter 9 and when exploring investment decisions in Chapter 16). Or people were assumed to have **adaptive expectations**: if, for example, their forecast of a given variable in a given period turned out to be too low, people were assumed to 'adapt' by raising their expectation for the ▶

value of the variable for the following period. For example, seeing an inflation rate higher than they had expected led people to revise upward their forecast of inflation in the future.

In the early 1970s, a group of macroeconomists led by Robert Lucas (at the University of Chicago) and Thomas Sargent (then at the University of Chicago, and now at New York University) argued that these assumptions did not reflect the way people form expectations. (Robert Lucas received the Nobel Prize in 1995 for his work on expectations.) They argued that, in thinking about the effects of alternative policies, economists should assume that people have rational expectations, that people look into the future and do the best job they can in predicting it. This is not the same as assuming that people know the future, but rather that they use the information they have in the best possible way.

Using the popular macroeconomic models of the time, Lucas and Sargent showed how replacing traditional assumptions about expectations formation by the assumption of rational expectations could fundamentally alter the results. We saw, for example, in Chapter 10 how Lucas challenged the notion that disinflation necessarily required an increase in unemployment for some time. Under rational expectations, he argued, a credible disinflation policy might be able to decrease inflation without any increase in unemployment. More generally, Lucas' and Sargent's research showed the need for a complete rethinking of macroeconomic models under the assumption of rational expectations, and this is what happened over the next two decades.

Most macroeconomists today use rational expectations as a working assumption in their models and analyses of policy. This is not because they believe that people always have rational expectations. Surely there are times when people, firms or financial market participants lose sight of reality and become too optimistic or too pessimistic. But these are more the exception than the rule, and it is not clear that economists can say much about those times anyway. When thinking about the likely effects of a particular economic policy, the best assumption to make seems to be that financial markets, people and firms will do the best they can to work out its implications. Designing a policy on the assumption that people will make systematic mistakes in responding to it is unwise.

So why did it take until the 1970s for rational expectations to become a standard assumption in macroeconomics? Largely because of technical problems. Under rational expectations, what happens today depends on expectations of what will happen in the future. But what happens in the future also depends on what happens today. Solving such models is hard. The success of Lucas and Sargent in convincing most macroeconomists to use rational expectations comes not only from the strength of their case but also from showing how it could actually be done. Much progress has been made since in developing solution methods for larger and larger models. Today, a number of large macroeconometric models are solved under the assumption of rational expectations. (The simulation of the Taylor model presented in the Focus box on monetary policy in Chapter 8 was derived under rational expectations. You will see another example in Chapter 24.)

We could go back and think about the implications of rational expectations in the case of a monetary expansion we have just studied. It will be more fun to do this in the context of a change in fiscal policy, and this is what we now turn to.

17.3 DEFICIT REDUCTION, EXPECTATIONS AND OUTPUT

Recall the conclusions we reached in the core about the effects of a budget deficit reduction:

We discussed the short-run and ➤ medium-run effects of changes in fiscal policy in Section 8.5. We discussed the long-run effects of changes in fiscal policy in Section 12.2.

- In the long run, a reduction in the budget deficit is likely to be beneficial for the economy. In the medium run, a lower budget deficit implies higher saving and higher investment. In the long run, higher investment translates into higher capital and thus higher output.
- In the short run, however, a reduction in the budget deficit, unless it is offset by a monetary expansion, leads to lower spending and to a contraction in output.

It is this adverse short-run effect which – in addition to the unpopularity of increases in taxes and reductions in public spending – often deters governments from tackling their budget deficits: why take the risk of a recession now for benefits that will accrue only in the future?

In the recent past, however, a number of economists have argued that a deficit reduction might actually increase output even in the *short run*. Their argument: if people take into account the future beneficial effects of deficit reduction, their expectations about the future might improve enough to lead to an increase – rather than a decrease – in current spending, thereby increasing current output. This section presents their argument more formally. The Focus box 'Can a budget deficit reduction lead to an output expansion? Ireland in the 1980s' reviews some of the supporting evidence.

Assume that the economy is described by equation (17.4) for the *IS* relation and equation (17.5) for the *LM* relation. Now suppose the government announces a program to reduce the deficit, through decreases both in current spending, G, and in future spending, G'^e. What will happen to output *this period*?

The role of expectations about the future

Suppose first that expectations of future output, Y'^e, and of the future interest rate, r'^e, do not change. Then, we get the standard answer: the decrease in government spending in the current period leads to a shift of the *IS* curve to the left and so to a decrease in equilibrium output.

The crucial question, therefore, is what happens to expectations. To answer, let us go back to what we learned in the core about the effects of a deficit reduction in the medium run and the long run.

- In the medium run, a deficit reduction has no effect on output. It leads, however, to a lower interest rate and to higher investment. These were two of the main lessons of Chapter 8. Let's review the logic behind each one.

    Recall that, when we look at the medium run, we ignore the effects of capital accumulation on output. So, in the medium run, the natural level of output depends on the level of productivity (taken as given) and on the natural level of employment. The natural level of employment depends in turn on the natural rate of unemployment. If spending by the government on goods and services does not affect the natural rate of unemployment – and there is no obvious reason why it should – then changes in spending will not affect the natural level of output. Therefore, a deficit reduction has no effect on the level of output in the medium run.

    Now recall that output must be equal to spending and that spending is the sum of public spending and private spending. Given that output is unchanged and that public spending is lower, private spending must therefore be higher. Higher private spending requires a lower equilibrium interest rate. The lower interest rate leads to higher investment and thus to higher private spending, which offsets the decrease in public spending and leaves output unchanged.

    ◄ In the medium run: output, Y, does not change, and investment, I, is higher.

- In the long run – that is, taking into account the effects of capital accumulation on output – higher investment leads to a higher capital stock and, therefore, a higher level of output.

    This was the main lesson of Chapter 12. The higher the proportion of output saved (or invested; investment and saving must be equal for the goods market to be in equilibrium in a closed economy), the higher the capital stock and thus the higher the level of output in the long run.

    ◄ In the long run: I increases
    ⇒ K increases
    ⇒ Y increases.

We can think of our *future period* as including both the medium run and the long run. If people, firms and financial market participants have *rational expectations* then, in response to the announcement of a deficit reduction, they will expect these developments to take place in the future. Thus, they will revise their expectation of future output, Y'^e, up, and their expectation of the future interest rate, r'^e, down.

◄ The way this is likely to happen: forecasts by economists will show that these lower deficits are likely to lead to higher output and lower interest rates in the future. In response to these forecasts, long-term interest rates will decrease, and the stock market will increase. People and firms, reading these forecasts and looking at bond and stock prices, will revise their spending plans and increase spending.

Back to the current period

We can now return to the question of what happens *this period* in response to the announcement and start of the deficit reduction program. Figure 17.5 draws the *IS* and *LM* curves for

FOCUS
Can a budget deficit reduction lead to an output expansion? Ireland in the 1980s

Ireland went through two major deficit reduction programs in the 1980s:

1. The first programme was started in 1982. In 1981, the budget deficit had reached a very high 13.0% of GDP. Government debt, the result of the accumulation of current and past deficits, was 77% of GDP, also a very high level. The Irish government clearly had to regain control of its finances. Over the next three years, it embarked on a programme of deficit reduction, based mostly on tax increases. This was an ambitious programme: had output continued to grow at its normal growth rate, the programme would have reduced the deficit by 5% of GDP.

   The results, however, were dismal. As shown in row 2 of Table 17.1, output growth was low in 1982 and negative in 1983. Low output growth was associated with a major increase in unemployment, from 9.5% in 1981 to 15% in 1984 (row 3). Because of low output growth, tax revenues – which depend on the level of economic activity – were lower than anticipated. The actual deficit reduction, shown in row 1, was only

3.5% of GDP. And the result of continuing high deficits and low GDP growth was a further increase in the ratio of debt to GDP to 97% in 1984.

2. A second attempt to reduce budget deficits was made starting in February 1987. At the time, things were still very bad. The 1986 deficit was 10.7% of GDP; debt stood at 116% of GDP, a record high in Europe at the time. This new programme of deficit reduction was different from the first. It was focused more on reducing the role of government and cutting government spending than on increasing taxes. The tax increases in the programme were achieved through a tax reform widening the tax base – increasing the number of households paying taxes – rather than through an increase in the marginal tax rate. The programme was again very ambitious: had output grown at its normal rate, the reduction in the deficit would have been 6.4% of GDP.

   The results of the second programme could not have been more different from the results of the first. 1987 to 1989 were years of strong growth, with average

Table 17.1 Fiscal and other macroeconomic indicators, Ireland, 1981–1984 and 1986–1989

	1981	1982	1983	1984	1986	1987	1988	1989
1 Budget deficit (% of GDP)	−13.0	−13.4	−11.4	−9.5	−10.7	−8.6	−4.5	−1.8
2 Output growth rate (%)	3.03	2.03	−0.2	4.04	−0.4	4.07	5.02	5.08
3 Unemployment rate (%)	9.05	11.00	13.05	15.00	17.01	16.09	16.03	15.01
4 Household saving rate (% of disposable income)	17.09	19.06	18.01	18.04	15.07	12.09	11.00	12.06

Source: OECD *Economic Outlook* database, June 1998.

Figure 17.5

The effects of a deficit reduction on current output

When account is taken of its effect on expectations, the decrease in government spending need not lead to a decrease in output.

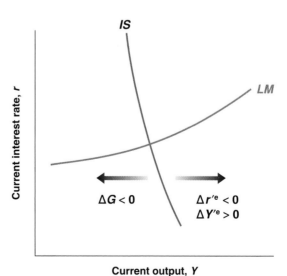

GDP growth exceeding 5%. The unemployment rate was reduced by 2%. Because of strong output growth, tax revenues were higher than anticipated, and the deficit was reduced by nearly 9% of GDP.

A number of economists have argued that the striking difference between the results of the two programmes can be traced to the different reaction of expectations in each case. The first programme, they argue, focused on tax increases and did not change what many people saw as too large a role of government in the economy. The second programme, with its focus on cuts in spending and on tax reform, had a much more positive impact on expectations and, therefore, a positive impact on spending and output.

Are these economists right? One variable, the household saving rate – defined as disposable income minus consumption, divided by disposable income – strongly suggests that expectations are an important part of the story. To interpret the behaviour of the saving rate, recall the lessons from Chapter 16 about consumption behaviour. When disposable income grows unusually slowly or goes down – as it does in a recession – consumption typically slows down or declines by less than disposable income because people expect things to improve in the future. Put another way, when the growth of disposable income is unusually low, the saving rate typically comes down. Now look (in row 4) at what happened from 1981–1984: despite low growth throughout the period and a recession in 1983, the household saving rate actually increased slightly during that period. Put another way, people reduced their consumption by more than the reduction in their disposable income. The reason must be that they were very pessimistic about the future.

Now turn to the period 1986–1989. During that period, economic growth was unusually strong. By the same argument as in the previous paragraph, we would have expected consumption to increase less strongly, and thus the saving rate to increase. Instead, the saving rate dropped sharply, from 15.7% in 1986 to 12.6% in 1989. Consumers must have become much more optimistic about the future to increase their consumption by more than the increase in their disposable income.

The next question is whether this difference in the adjustment of expectations over the two episodes can be attributed fully to the differences in the two fiscal programmes. The answer is surely no. Ireland was changing in many ways at the time of the second fiscal programme. Productivity was increasing much faster than real wages, reducing the cost of labour for firms. Attracted by tax breaks, low labour costs and an educated labour force, many foreign firms were relocating to Ireland and building new plants. These factors played a major role in the expansion of the late 1980s. Irish growth has been very strong ever since, with average output growth exceeding 6% since 1990. Surely, this long expansion is due to many factors. Nevertheless, the change in fiscal policy in 1987 probably played an important role in convincing people, firms (including foreign firms) and financial markets that the government was regaining control of its finances. And the fact remains that the substantial deficit reduction of 1987–1989 was accompanied by a strong output expansion, not by the recession predicted by the basic *IS–LM* model.

Note: For a more detailed discussion, look at Francesco Giavazzi and Marco Pagano, 'Can Severe Fiscal Contractions Be Expansionary? Tales of Two Small European Countries', *NBER Macroeconomics Annual*, 1990, NBER, Cambridge, MA, 75–110.

A survey of what we have learned by looking at programmes of deficit reduction around the world is given in John McDermott and Robert Wescott, 'An Empirical Analysis of Fiscal Adjustments', *IMF Staff Papers*, 1996, **43**(4), 725–753.

---

the current period. In response to the announcement of the deficit reduction, there are now three factors shifting the *IS* curve:

- Current government spending, G, goes down, leading the *IS* curve to shift to the left. At a given interest rate, the decrease in government spending leads to a decrease in total spending and to a decrease in output. This is the standard effect of a reduction in government spending, and it is the only one taken into account in the basic *IS–LM* model.
- Expected future output, Y'^e, goes up, leading the *IS* curve to shift to the right. At a given interest rate, the increase in expected future output leads to an increase in private spending, increasing output.
- The expected future interest rate, r'^e, goes down, leading the *IS* curve to shift to the right. At a given current interest rate, a decrease in the future interest rate stimulates spending and increases output.

What is the net effect of these three shifts in the *IS* curve? Can the effect of expectations on consumption and investment spending offset the decrease in government spending?

Without much more information about the exact form of the *IS* and *LM* relations and about the details of the deficit reduction programme, we cannot tell which shifts will dominate and whether output will go up or down. But our analysis tells us that both cases are possible – that output may go up in response to the deficit reduction. And it gives us a few hints as to when this might happen:

● Note that the smaller the decrease in current government spending, G, the smaller the adverse effect on spending today. Note also that the larger the decrease in expected future government spending, G'^e, the larger the effect on expected future output and interest rates, thus the larger the favourable effect on spending today. This suggests that **back loading** the deficit reduction programme toward the future, with small cuts today and larger cuts in the future, is more likely to lead to an increase in output.

● On the other hand, back loading raises other issues. Announcing the need for painful cuts in spending and then leaving them to the future is likely to decrease the programme's **credibility** – the perceived probability that the government will do what it has promised when the time comes to do it.

● The government must play a delicate balancing act: enough cuts in the current period to show a commitment to deficit reduction and enough cuts left to the future to reduce the adverse effects on the economy in the short run.

More generally, our analysis suggests that anything in a deficit reduction programme that improves expectations of how the future will look is likely to make the short-run effects of deficit reduction less painful. Let us give two examples:

● Measures that are perceived by firms and financial markets as reducing some of the distortions in the economy may improve expectations and make it more likely that output increases in the short run. Take, for example, unemployment benefits. You saw in Chapter 7 that lower unemployment benefits lead to a decline in the natural rate of unemployment, resulting in a higher natural level of output. So, a reform of the social security system, which includes a reduction in the generosity of unemployment benefits, is likely to have two effects on spending and thus on output in the short run:

An adverse effect on the consumption of the unemployed – lower unemployment benefits will reduce their income and their consumption.

A positive effect on spending through expectations – the anticipation of higher output in the future may lead to both higher consumption and higher investment.

If the second effect dominates, the outcome might be an increase in overall spending, increasing output not only in the medium run but also in the short run. (An important caveat: even if a reduction in unemployment benefits increases output, this surely does not imply that unemployment benefits should be eliminated. Even if aggregate income goes up, we must worry about the effects on the distribution of income: the consumption of the unemployed goes down, and the pain associated with being unemployed goes up.)

As you will see in Chapter 22, a very large deficit often leads to very high money creation and, soon after, to very high inflation. Very high inflation leads not only to economic trouble but also to political instability.

● Or take an economy where the government has, in effect, lost control of its budget: government spending is high, tax revenues are low and the deficit is very large. In such an environment, a credible deficit reduction programme is also more likely to increase output in the short run. Before the announcement of the programme, people may have expected major political and economic trouble in the future. The announcement of a programme of deficit reduction may well reassure them that the government has regained control and that the future is less bleak than they anticipated. This decrease in pessimism about the future may lead to an increase in spending and output, even if taxes are increased as part of the deficit reduction programme.

Let's summarise. A programme of deficit reduction may increase output even in the short run. Whether it does depends on many factors, in particular:

- The credibility of the programme – will spending be cut or taxes increased in the future, as announced?
- The timing of the programme – how large are spending cuts in the future relative to current spending cuts?
- The composition of the programme – does the program remove some of the distortions in the economy?
- The state of government finances in the first place – how large is the initial deficit? Is ◄ this a 'last chance' programme? What will happen if it fails?

This gives you a sense of both the importance of expectations in determining the outcome and the complexities involved in the use of fiscal policy in such a context.

> Note how far we have moved from the results of Chapter 3, where, by choosing spending and taxes wisely, the government could achieve any level of output it wanted. Here, even the direction of the effect of a deficit reduction on output is ambiguous.

SUMMARY

- Spending in the goods market depends on current and expected future output and on current and expected future real interest rates.

- Expectations affect demand and, in turn, affect output: changes in expected future output or in the expected future real interest rate lead to changes in spending and in output today.

- By implication, the effects of fiscal and monetary policy on spending and output depend on how the policy affects expectations of future output and real interest rates.

- Rational expectations is the assumption that people, firms and participants in financial markets form expectations of the future by assessing the course of future expected policy and then working out the implications for future output, future interest rates and so on. Although it is clear that most people do not go through this exercise themselves, we can think of them as doing so indirectly by relying on the predictions of public and private forecasters.

- Although there are surely cases in which people, firms or financial investors do not have rational expectations, the assumption of rational expectations seems to be the best benchmark to evaluate the potential effects of alternative policies. Designing a policy on the assumption that people will make systematic mistakes in responding to it would be unwise.

- Changes in the money supply affect the short-term nominal interest rate. Spending depends instead on current and expected future real interest rates. Thus, the effect of monetary policy on activity depends crucially on whether and how changes in the short-run nominal interest rate lead to changes in current and expected future real interest rates.

- A budget deficit reduction may lead to an increase rather than a decrease in output. This is because expectations of higher output and lower interest rates in the future may lead to an increase in spending that more than offsets the reduction in spending coming from the direct effect of the deficit reduction on total spending.

KEY TERMS

QUESTIONS AND PROBLEMS

QUICK CHECK

1. *Using the information in this chapter, label each of the following statements true, false or uncertain. Explain briefly.*

a. Changes in the current one-year real interest rate are likely to have a much larger effect on spending than changes in expected future one-year real interest rates.

b. The introduction of expectations in the goods market model makes the *IS* curve flatter, although it is still downward-sloping.

c. Current money demand depends on current and expected future nominal interest rates.

d. The rational expectations assumption implies that consumers take into account the effects of future fiscal policy on output.

e. Expected future fiscal policy affects expected future economic activity but not current economic activity.

f. Depending on its effect on expectations, a fiscal contraction may actually lead to an economic expansion.

g. Ireland's experience with deficit reduction programmes in 1982 and 1987 provides strong evidence against the hypothesis that deficit reduction can lead to an output expansion.

2. *During the late 1990s, many observers claimed that the USA had transformed into a New Economy, and this justified the very high values for stock prices observed at the time.*

a. Discuss how the belief in the New Economy, combined with the increase in stock prices, affected consumption spending.

b. Stock prices subsequently decreased. Discuss how this might have affected consumption.

3. *For each of the changes in expectations in (a) through (d), determine whether there is a shift in the IS curve, the LM curve, both curves or neither. In each case, assume that expected current and future inflation are equal to zero and that no other exogenous variable is changing.*

a. a decrease in the expected future real interest rate

b. an increase in the current money supply

c. an increase in expected future taxes

d. a decrease in expected future income

4. *Consider the following statement.*

'The rational expectations assumption is unrealistic because, essentially, it amounts to the assumption that every consumer has perfect knowledge of the economy.'

Discuss.

5. *A new head of state, who promised during the campaign that she would cut taxes, has just been elected. People trust that she will keep her promise, but expect that the tax cuts will be implemented only in the future. Determine the impact of the election on current output, the current interest rate, and current private spending under each of the assumptions in (a) through (c). In each case, indicate what you think will happen to Y'^e, r'^e and T'^e, and then how these changes in expectations affect output today.*

a. The central bank will not change its policy.

b. The central bank will act to prevent any change in future output.

c. The central bank will act to prevent any change in the future interest rate.

DIG DEEPER

6. The Clinton deficit reduction package

In 1992, the US deficit was $290 billion. During the presidential campaign, the large deficit emerged as a major issue. When President Clinton won the election, deficit reduction was the first item on the new administration's agenda.

a. What does deficit reduction imply for the medium run and the long run? What are the advantages of reducing the deficit?

In the final version passed by Congress in August 1993, the deficit reduction package included a reduction of $20 billion in its first year, increasing gradually to $131 billion four years later.

b. Why was the deficit reduction package back loaded? What are the advantages and disadvantages of this approach to deficit reduction?

In February 1993, President Clinton presented the budget in his State of the Union address. He asked Alan Greenspan, the Fed chairman, to sit next to First Lady Hillary Clinton during the delivery of the address.

c. What was the purpose of this symbolic gesture? How can the Fed's decision to use expansionary monetary policy in the future affect the short-run response of the economy?

7. A new central bank chairman

Suppose, in a hypothetical economy, that the chairman of the central bank unexpectedly announces that he will retire in one year. At the same time, the head of state announces her nominee to replace the retiring central bank chair. Financial market participants expect the nominee to be confirmed by the government. They also believe that the nominee will conduct a more contractionary monetary policy in the future. In other words, market participants expect the money supply to fall in the future.

a. Consider the present to be the last year of the current central bank chair's term and the future to be the time after that. Given that monetary policy will be more contractionary in the future, what will happen to future interest rates and future output (at least for a while, before output returns to potential GDP)? Given that these changes in future output and future interest rates are predicted, what will happen to output and the interest rate in the present? What will happen to the yield curve on the day of the announcement that the current central bank chair will retire in a year?

Now suppose that instead of making an unexpected announcement, the central bank chair is required by law to retire in one year (there are limits on the term of the central bank chair), and financial market participants have been aware of this for some time. Suppose, as in part (a), that the head of state nominates a replacement who is expected to conduct a more contractionary monetary policy than the current central bank chair.

b. Suppose financial market participants are not surprised by the choice of the head of state. In other words, market participants had correctly predicted who the president would choose as nominee. Under these circumstances, is the announcement of the nominee likely to have any effect on the yield curve?

c. Suppose instead that the identity of the nominee is a surprise and that financial market participants had expected the nominee to be someone who favoured an even more contractionary policy than the actual nominee. Under these circumstances, what is likely to happen to the yield curve on the day of the announcement? (*Hint:* be careful. Compared to what was expected, is the actual nominee expected to follow a more contractionary or more expansionary policy?)

d. On 24 October 2005, Ben Bernanke was nominated to succeed Alan Greenspan as chairman of the Federal Reserve. Do an Internet search and try to learn what happened in financial markets on the day the nomination was announced. Were financial market participants surprised by the choice? If so, was Bernanke believed to favour policies that would lead to higher or lower interest rates (as compared to the expected nominee) over the

next three to five years? (You may also do a yield curve analysis of the kind described in problem 8 for the period around Bernanke's nomination. If you do this, use one-year and five-year interest rates.)

EXPLORE FURTHER

8. Deficits and interest rates

The dramatic increase in the German budget position after 1990 (from a surplus to a large and continuing deficit) has reinvigorated the debate about the effect of fiscal policy on interest rates. This problem asks you to review theory and evidence on this topic.

a. Review what theory predicts about fiscal policy and interest rates. Suppose there is an increase in government spending and a decrease in taxes. Use an *IS–LM* diagram to show what will happen to the nominal interest rate in the short run and the medium run. Assuming that there is no change in monetary policy, what does the *IS–LM* model predict will happen to the yield curve immediately after an increase in government spending and a decrease in taxes?

In the Winter of 1989–1990, following German Reunification, the need to assist residents in the former DDR – thus avoiding mass migration to the West – resulted in a sharp increase in actual and projected federal budget deficits. From a balanced budget in 1989, the deficit was project to increase to 2% of GDP in 1990 and 1991. In the Spring of 1990 these forecasts were revised and the projection for the deficit in 1991 went from 2% to 3% of GDP.

b. Go to the website of the Bundesbank (***http://www.bundesbank.de***) and find the section on 'Statistics'. Go to 'List all Series' and choose 'Interest Rates'. Download the yields on federal securities with annual residual maturity of one and ten years. Get the end-of-month data from 1989–1991.

c. For each month, subtract the one-year yield from the ten-year yield yield to obtain the interest rate spread. What happened to the interest rate spread as the budget picture worsened over the sample period? Is this result consistent with your answer to part (a)?

*We invite you to visit the Blanchard page on the Prentice Hall website, at **www.prenhall.com/blanchard** for this chapter's World Wide Web exercises.*

THE OPEN ECONOMY
EXCHANGE RATES AND POLICY CHOICES

The next two chapters represent the second major extension of the core. They look at more implications of openness – the fact that most economies trade both goods and assets with the rest of the world – than what you already learned in the core.

Chapter 18 Economic policy in an open economy

Chapter 18 characterises the equilibrium of goods and financial markets in an open economy. In other words, it gives an open economy version of the *IS–LM* model we saw in the core. It shows how, under flexible exchange rates, monetary policy affects output not only through its effect on the interest rate but also through its effect on the exchange rate. It shows how fixing the exchange rate also implies giving up the ability to change the interest rate.

Chapter 19 Exchange rate regimes

Chapter 19 looks at the properties of different exchange rate regimes. It first shows how, in the medium run, the real exchange rate can adjust even under a fixed exchange rate regime. It then looks at exchange rate crises under fixed exchange rates and at movements in exchange rates under flexible exchange rates. It ends by discussing the pros and cons of various exchange rate regimes, including the adoption of a common currency such as the euro.

Chapter 18

ECONOMIC POLICY IN AN OPEN ECONOMY

In Chapter 5, we introduced the *IS–LM* model to understand the movements of output and the interest rate in a closed economy. There, we also saw how policy makers can affect the equilibrium levels of output and the interest rate, through fiscal policy, monetary policy or a mix of the two. In Chapter 6, we introduced an open economy version of the *IS–LM* model. That model allows us to characterise the joint movements of output, the interest rate and the exchange rate in an open economy. In this chapter we ask what the effects of fiscal and monetary policies on economic activity are, when both goods and financial markets are open to the rest of the world.

This chapter has five sections:

- Section 18.1 shows the effects of domestic shocks and foreign shocks on the domestic economy's output and trade balance.

- Section 18.2 looks at the effects of a real depreciation on output and the trade balance.

- Section 18.3 gives an alternative description of the equilibrium, which shows the close connection between saving, investment and the trade balance.

- Section 18.4 looks at the role of policy under flexible exchange rates.

- Section 18.5 looks at the role of policy under fixed exchange rates.

18.1 INCREASES IN DEMAND, DOMESTIC OR FOREIGN

How do changes in demand affect output in an open economy? Let's start with an old favourite – an increase in government spending – and then turn to a new exercise, the effects of an increase in foreign demand.

Increases in domestic demand

Suppose the economy is in a recession, and the government decides to increase government spending in order to increase domestic demand and output. What will be the effects on output and on the trade balance?

The answer is given in Figure 18.1. Before the increase in government spending, demand is given by ZZ in Figure 18.1(a), and the equilibrium is at point A, where output equals Y. Let's assume that trade is initially balanced – even though, as we have seen, there is no reason this should be true in general. So, in Figure 18.1(b), $Y = Y_{TB}$.

What happens if the government increases spending by ΔG? At any level of output, demand is higher by ΔG, shifting the demand relation up by ΔG, from ZZ to ZZ'. The equilibrium point moves from A to A', and output increases from Y to Y'. The increase in output is larger than the increase in government spending: there is a multiplier effect.

So far, the story sounds the same as the story for a closed economy in Chapter 3. However, there are two important differences:

- There is now an effect on the trade balance. Because government spending enters neither the exports relation nor the imports relation directly, the relation between net exports and output in Figure 18.1(b) does not shift. So the increase in output from Y to Y' leads to a trade deficit equal to BC: imports go up, and exports do not change. ◄ Starting from trade balance, an increase in government spending leads to a trade deficit.

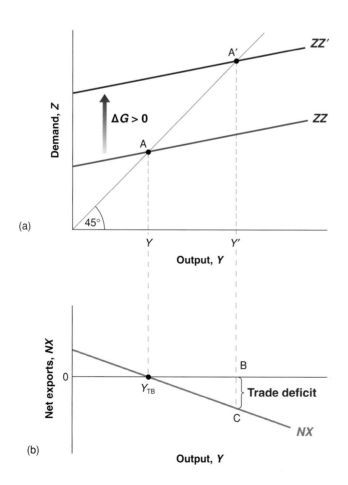

(a)

(b)

Figure 18.1

The effects of an increase in government spending

An increase in government spending leads to an increase in output and to a trade deficit.

An increase in government spending ➤ ● increases output. The multiplier is smaller than in a closed economy.

Not only does government spending now generate a trade deficit, but the effect of government spending on output is smaller than it would be in a closed economy. Recall from Chapter 3 that the smaller the slope of the demand relation, the smaller the multiplier (for example, if ZZ were horizontal, the multiplier would be 1). And recall from Chapter 6 that the demand relation, ZZ, is flatter than the demand relation in a closed economy, DD. This means the *multiplier is smaller in an open economy*.

The smaller multiplier and the trade ➤ deficit have the same cause: some domestic demand falls on foreign goods.

The trade deficit and the smaller multiplier have the same cause: because the economy is open, an increase in demand now falls not only on domestic goods but also on foreign goods. So, when income increases, the effect on the **demand for domestic goods** is smaller than it would be in a closed economy, leading to a smaller multiplier. And, because some of the increase in demand falls on imports – and exports are unchanged – the result is a trade deficit.

These two implications are important. In an open economy, an increase in domestic demand has a smaller effect on output than in a closed economy, and it has an adverse effect on the trade balance. Indeed, the more open the economy, the smaller the effect on output and the larger the adverse effect on the trade balance. Take Belgium, for example. As we saw in Chapter 6, Belgium's ratio of imports to GDP is very high. When domestic demand increases in Belgium, most of the increase in demand is likely to result in an increase in the demand for foreign goods rather than in an increase in the demand for domestic goods. The effect of an increase in government spending is therefore likely to be a large increase in Belgium's trade deficit and only a small increase in its output, making domestic demand expansion a rather unattractive policy for Belgium. Even for the UK, which has a much lower import ratio, an increase in demand will be associated with a worsening of the trade balance.

Increases in foreign demand

Consider now an increase in foreign output – that is, an increase in Y^* – and say we want to analyse its effects on the domestic economy. This could be due to an increase in foreign government spending, G^* – the policy change we just analysed, but now taking place abroad. We will consider this in the next paragraph. Let us start first with the case where we do not know where the increase in Y^* comes from.

Figure 18.2 shows the effects of an increase in foreign activity on domestic output and the trade balance. The initial demand for domestic goods is given by ZZ in Figure 18.2(a). The equilibrium is at point A, with output level Y. Let's again assume that trade is balanced, so that in Figure 18.2(b), the net exports associated with Y equal 0 ($Y = Y_{TB}$).

DD is the domestic demand for goods. ➤ ZZ is the demand for domestic goods. The difference between the two is equal to the trade deficit.

It will be useful here to refer to the line that shows the **domestic demand for goods**, $C + I + G$, as a function of income. This line is drawn as DD. Recall from Section 6.3 that DD is steeper than ZZ. The difference between ZZ and DD equals net exports, so that if trade is balanced at point A, ZZ and DD intersect at point A.

Y^* does not affect either domestic ➤ consumption, domestic investment or domestic government spending directly, and so it does not enter the relation between the domestic demand for goods and output. An increase in Y^* does not shift DD.

Now consider the effects of an increase in foreign output, ΔY^* (for the moment, ignore the line DD; we only need it later). Higher foreign output means higher foreign demand, including higher foreign demand for domestic goods. So the direct effect of the increase in foreign output is an increase in domestic exports by some amount, which we shall denote by ΔX:

● For a given level of output, this increase in exports leads to an increase in the demand for goods by ΔX, so the line showing the demand for domestic goods as a function of output shifts up by ΔX, from ZZ to ZZ′.
● For a given level of output, net exports go up by ΔX. So the line showing net exports as a function of output in Figure 18.2(b) also shifts up by ΔX, from NX to NX′.

The new equilibrium is at point A′ in Figure 18.2(a), with output level Y′. The increase in foreign output leads to an increase in domestic output. The channel is clear: higher foreign

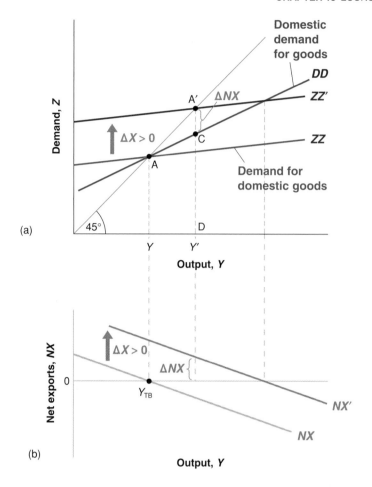

(a)

(b)

Figure 18.2

The effects of an increase in foreign demand

An increase in foreign demand leads to an increase in output and to a trade surplus.

output leads to higher exports of domestic goods, which increases domestic output and the domestic demand for goods through the multiplier.

What happens to the trade balance? We know that exports go up. But could it be that the increase in domestic output leads to such a large increase in imports that the trade balance actually deteriorates? No: the trade balance must improve. To see why, note that when foreign demand increases, the demand for domestic goods shifts up from ZZ to ZZ′; but the line DD, which gives the *domestic demand for goods* as a function of output, does not shift. At the new equilibrium level of output, Y′, domestic demand is given by the distance DC, and the demand for domestic goods is given by DA′. Net exports are therefore given by the distance CA′ – which, because DD is necessarily below ZZ′, is necessarily positive. Thus, while imports increase, the increase does not offset the increase in exports, and the trade balance improves. Y^* directly affects exports and so enters the relation between the demand for domestic goods and output. An increase in Y^* shifts ZZ up.

▸ An increase in foreign output increases domestic output and improves the trade balance.

Fiscal policy revisited

We have derived two basic results so far:

- An increase in domestic demand leads to an increase in domestic output but leads also to a deterioration of the trade balance. (We looked at an increase in government spending, but the results would have been the same for a decrease in taxes, an increase in consumer spending, and so on.)
- An increase in foreign demand (which could come from the same types of changes taking place abroad) leads to an increase in domestic output and an improvement in the trade balance.

These results, in turn, have a number of important implications.

First, and most obviously, they imply that shocks to demand in one country affect all other countries. The stronger the trade links between countries, the stronger the interactions, and the more countries will move together. This implication seems indeed to be consistent with the facts. For example, most OECD countries experienced a strong economic expansion in the second half of the 1990s, followed by a slowdown or an outright recession in the early 2000s. Trade links were probably not the only reason for these common movements. It could be that most countries moved together partly because they were experiencing the same domestic shocks. For example, many countries went through the same 'irrational exuberance' cycle and the same investment boom and bust as the USA. But the available evidence suggests that trade links also played an important role.

Second, these interactions very much complicate the task of policy makers, especially in the case of fiscal policy. Let's explore this argument more closely.

Start with the following observation: governments do not like to run trade deficits, and for good reasons. The main reason is that a country that consistently runs a trade deficit

FOCUS
Fiscal multipliers in an open economy

In this chapter we have shown how an increase in domestic or foreign demand leads to an increase in domestic output. One of the most important implications of these interactions is the impact of fiscal policy, at home and abroad, when countries trade a lot with each other. This is very much the case of European countries, that are heavily open to trade, especially with each other. To understand this, consider a world of two countries, namely Home (a small open economy) and Foreign. Let us write down the components of domestic demand in both countries, based on equation 6.8:

$$Y = C + I + G - \frac{IM}{\varepsilon} + X \qquad (1)$$

$$Y^* = C^* + I^* + G^* - IM^*\varepsilon + X^* \qquad (2)$$

where $X = IM^* = m^*y^*$, with m^* being the proportion of foreign income, y^*, spent on imports (or the foreign propensity to import), i.e. Home's exports are identically equal to Foreign's imports (by definition, as we are describing a world of just two countries), and $X^* = IM = my$, i.e. Foreign's exports are identically equal to Home's imports. By substituting the latter into (1) we get:

$$Y = C + I + G - m\frac{Y}{\varepsilon} + m^*Y^*$$

And, by replacing Consumption, C, with a linear function as in Chapter 5, we get:

$$Y = c_0 + c_1 Y + I + G - m\frac{Y}{\varepsilon} + m^*Y^* = A + \left(c_1 - \frac{m}{\varepsilon}\right)Y + m^*Y^*$$

where $A = (c_0 + I + G)$ is the autonomous spending.

If we solve for the level of real income, Y, we obtain:

$$Y = \frac{1}{1 - c_1 + \dfrac{m}{\varepsilon}}(A + m^*Y^*)$$

Let us now compute the fiscal multiplier, that is the impact on income, Y, of an increase in public spending, G. We can actually compute two fiscal multipliers.

The multiplier of Home's fiscal policy

$$\frac{\delta Y}{\delta G} = \frac{1}{1 - c_1 + \dfrac{m}{\varepsilon}} \qquad (3)$$

Equation (3) shows us two important things.

First, in an open economy (that is, an economy that consumes both domestic goods and imported goods, therefore the propensity to import, m, is positive), the fiscal multiplier is lower than in a closed economy (remember that the fiscal multiplier in a closed economy was equal to $1/(1 - c_1)$).

Second, countries with higher import propensities have lower fiscal multipliers. That is, in countries that demand a relatively high amount of foreign goods (compared to domestic goods), the impact of fiscal policy will be relatively low (compared to countries with a lower import propensity). This is clearly shown in Figure 18.3. Economies with high import propensities such as Belgium, the Czech Republic, Hungary and Ireland have debts from the rest of the world, and therefore has to pay steadily higher interest payments to the rest of the world. Thus, it is no wonder that countries prefer increases in foreign demand (which improve the trade balance) to increases in domestic demand (which worsen the trade balance).

But these preferences can have disastrous implications. Consider a group of countries, all doing a large amount of trade with each other, so that an increase in demand in any one country falls largely on the goods produced in the other countries. Suppose all these countries are in recession, and each has roughly balanced trade to start. In this case, each country might be very reluctant to take measures to increase domestic demand. Were it to do so, the result might be a small increase in output but also a large trade deficit. Instead, each country might just wait for the other countries to increase their demand. This way, it gets the best of both worlds, higher output and an improvement in its trade balance. But if all the countries wait, nothing will happen, and the recession may last a long time (To learn more about the relationship between fiscal multipliers and import propensities across countries, read the Focus box 'Fiscal multipliers in an open economy').

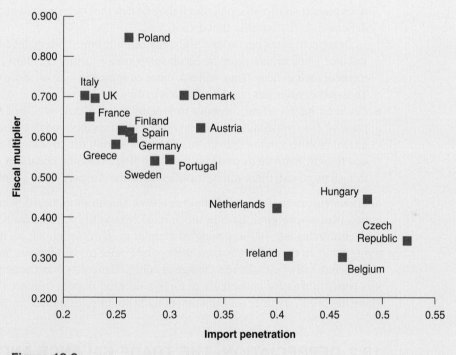

Figure 18.3

Fiscal multipliers and import penetration

Source: Ali Al-Eyd, Ray Barrell and Dawn Holland (2006), *The role of financial markets' openness in the transmission of shocks in Europe*, National Institute of Economic and Social Research, Discussion Paper No. 271, p. 18.

low fiscal multipliers, whereas countries such as France, Italy and the UK have much higher fiscal multipliers.

The multiplier of Foreign's fiscal policy

$$\frac{\delta Y}{\delta G^*} = \frac{m^*}{1 - c_1 + \dfrac{m}{\varepsilon}} \qquad (4)$$

Equation (4) shows another important implications of openness. Fiscal stimuli abroad have expansionary effects also at home. The increase in domestic output following a fiscal expansion abroad is higher the higher the foreign propensity to import, m^*, and the lower the domestic propensity to import, m. In times of widespread recessions, countries with low m may be tempted to just wait for other countries to increase their demand. On the other hand, countries with high m have little incentive to increase demand through public spending because their fiscal multipliers are low. This is very much what happened in 2009, when European countries were largely reluctant to increase public spending to sustain demand.

Is there a way out of this situation? There is – at least in theory. If all countries coordinate their macroeconomic policies so as to increase domestic demand simultaneously, each can increase demand and output without increasing its trade deficit (vis-à-vis the others; their combined trade deficit with respect to the rest of the world will still increase). The reason is clear: the coordinated increase in demand leads to increases in both exports and imports in each country. It is still true that domestic demand expansion leads to larger imports; but this increase in imports is offset by the increase in exports, which comes from the foreign demand expansions.

Coordination is a word governments often invoke. The largest economies of the world – until 2010, the so-called **G8** (the USA, Japan, France, Germany, the UK, Italy, Canada and, since 1996, Russia; the 'G' stands for 'group'), then the G20 (including other emerging and fast growing economies, such as Brazil, China and India) – meet regularly to discuss their economic situation; the communiqué at the end of the meeting rarely fails to mention coordination. But the evidence is that there is in fact very limited macro-coordination among countries. Here are some reasons:

- *Some countries might have to do more than others and may not want to do so.* Suppose that only some countries are in recession. Countries that are not in recession will be reluctant to increase their own demand; but if they do not, the countries that expand will run trade deficits vis-à-vis countries that do not.

  Or suppose some countries are already running large budget deficits. These countries will not want to cut taxes or increase spending further, as doing so would further increase their deficits. They will ask other countries to take on more of the adjustment. Those other countries may be reluctant to do so.

- *Countries have a strong incentive to promise to coordinate and then not deliver on that promise.* Once all countries have agreed, say, to an increase in spending, each country has an incentive not to deliver, so as to benefit from the increase in demand elsewhere and thereby improve its trade position. But if each country cheats, or does not do everything it promised, there will be insufficient demand expansion to get out of the recession.

These reasons are far from abstract concerns. Countries in the EU, which are highly integrated with one another, have in the past 30 years often suffered from such coordination problems. In the late 1970s, a bungled attempt at coordination left most countries wary of trying again. In the early 1980s, an attempt by France to go at it alone led to a large French trade deficit and eventually to a change in policy. Thereafter, most countries decided that it was better to wait for an increase in foreign demand than to increase their own demand. There has been very little coordination of fiscal policy since then in Europe.

18.2 DEPRECIATION, THE TRADE BALANCE AND OUTPUT

Suppose the UK government takes policy measures that lead to a depreciation of the pound – a decrease in the nominal exchange rate. (We shall see in Chapter 24 how it can do this by using monetary policy. For the moment, we will assume the government can simply choose the exchange rate.)

Recall that the real exchange rate is given by

$$\varepsilon \equiv \frac{EP}{P^*}$$

In Chapter 19, we shall look at the effects of a nominal depreciation when we allow the price level to adjust over time. You will see that a nominal depreciation leads to a real depreciation in the short run but not in the medium run.

The real exchange rate, ε (the price of domestic goods in terms of foreign goods), is equal to the nominal exchange rate, E (the price of domestic currency in terms of foreign currency), times the domestic price level, P, divided by the foreign price level, P^*. In the short run, we can take the two price levels, P and P^*, as given. This implies that the nominal depreciation is reflected one-for-one in a real depreciation. More concretely, if the pound depreciates vis-à-vis the euro by 10% (a 10% nominal depreciation), and if the price levels in the euro area and the UK do not change, UK goods will be 10% cheaper compared to European goods (a 10% real depreciation).

How will this real depreciation affect the UK trade balance and UK output?

Depreciation and the trade balance: the Marshall–Lerner condition

Return to the definition of net exports in Chapter 6:

$$NX \equiv X - IM/\varepsilon$$

Replace X and IM by their expressions from equations (6.6) and (6.7):

$$NX = X(Y^*, \varepsilon) - IM(Y, \varepsilon)/\varepsilon$$

Because the real exchange rate, ε, enters the right side of the equation in three places, this makes it clear that the real depreciation affects the trade balance through three separate channels:

- *Exports, X, increase* – the real depreciation makes domestic goods relatively less expensive abroad. This leads to an increase in foreign demand for domestic goods – an increase in domestic exports.
- *Imports, IM, decrease* – the real depreciation makes foreign goods relatively more expensive in the domestic economy (the UK in this case). This leads to a shift in domestic demand toward domestic goods and to a decrease in the quantity of imports.
- *The relative price of foreign goods in terms of domestic goods, 1/ε, increases* – this increases the import bill, IM/ε. The same quantity of imports now costs more to buy (in terms of domestic goods).

> ◀ More concretely, if the pound depreciates vis-à-vis the euro by 10%:
> - UK goods will be cheaper in the euro area, leading to a larger quantity of UK exports to the euro area.
> - European goods will be more expensive in the UK, leading to a smaller quantity of imports of European goods to the UK.
> - European goods will be more expensive, leading to a higher import bill for a given quantity of imports of European goods to the UK.

For the trade balance to improve following a depreciation, exports must increase enough and imports must decrease enough to compensate for the increase in the price of imports. The condition under which a real depreciation leads to an increase in net exports is known as the **Marshall–Lerner condition**. (It is named after the two economists who derived it, Alfred Marshall and Abba Lerner, and is derived formally in the appendix at the end of the chapter.) It turns out – with a complication we will state when we introduce dynamics later in this chapter – that this condition is satisfied in reality. So, for the rest of this book, we shall assume that a real depreciation – a decrease in ε – leads to an increase in net exports – an increase in NX.

The effects of a depreciation

We have looked so far at the *direct* effects of a depreciation on the trade balance – that is, the effects *given domestic and foreign output*. But the effects do not end there. The change in net exports changes domestic output, which affects net exports further.

Because the effects of a real depreciation are very much like those of an increase in foreign output, we can use Figure 18.2, the same figure that we used to show the effects of an increase in foreign output earlier.

Just like an increase in foreign output, a depreciation leads to an increase in net exports (assuming, as we do, that the Marshall–Lerner condition holds), at any level of output. Both the demand relation [ZZ in Figure 18.2(a)] and the net exports relation [NX in Figure 18.2(b)] shift up. The equilibrium moves from A to A', and output increases from Y to Y'. By the same argument we used earlier, the trade balance improves: the increase in imports induced by the increase in output is smaller than the direct improvement in the trade balance induced by the depreciation.

Let's summarise. *The depreciation leads to a shift in demand, both foreign and domestic, toward domestic goods. This shift in demand leads in turn to both an increase in domestic output and an improvement in the trade balance.*

> ◀ Marshall–Lerner condition: given output, a real depreciation leads to an increase in net exports.

There is an alternative to riots – asking ➤ for and obtaining an increase in wages. But, if wages increase, the prices of domestic goods will follow and increase as well, leading to a smaller real depreciation. To discuss this mechanism, we need to look at the supply side in more detail than we have done so far. We return to the dynamics of depreciation, wage and price movements in Chapter 19.

Although a depreciation and an increase in foreign output have the same effect on domestic output and the trade balance, there is a subtle but important difference between the two. A depreciation works by making foreign goods relatively more expensive. But this means that given their income, people – who now have to pay more to buy foreign goods because of the depreciation – are worse off. This mechanism is strongly felt in countries that go through a large depreciation. Governments trying to achieve a large depreciation often find themselves with strikes and riots in the streets, as people react to the much higher prices of imported goods. This was, for example, the case in Mexico, where the large depreciation of the peso in 1994–1995 – from 29 cents per peso in November 1994 to 17 cents per peso in May 1995 – led to a large decline in workers' living standards and to social unrest.

Combining exchange rate and fiscal policies

Suppose output is at its natural level, but the economy is running a large trade deficit. The government would like to reduce the trade deficit while leaving output unchanged. What should it do?

A depreciation alone will not do: it will reduce the trade deficit, but it will also increase output. Nor will a fiscal contraction work: it will reduce the trade deficit, but it will decrease output. What should the government do? The answer: use the right combination of depreciation and fiscal contraction. Figure 18.4 shows what this combination should be.

Suppose the initial equilibrium in Figure 18.4(a) is at A, associated with output Y. At this level of output, there is a trade deficit, given by the distance BC in Figure 18.4(b). If the government wants to eliminate the trade deficit without changing output, it must do two things:

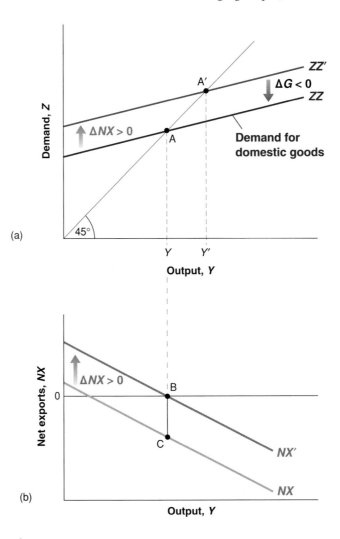

Figure 18.4

The effects of an increase in foreign demand

An increase in foreign demand leads to an increase in output and to a trade surplus.

Table 18.1 Exchange rate and fiscal policy combinations

Initial condition	Trade surplus	Trade deficit
Low output	$\varepsilon ? G\uparrow$	$\varepsilon \downarrow G?$
High output	$\varepsilon \uparrow G?$	$\varepsilon ? G\downarrow$

- It must achieve a depreciation sufficient to eliminate the trade deficit at the initial level of output. The depreciation must be such as to shift the net exports relation from NX to NX' in Figure 18.4(b).

  The problem is that this depreciation, and the associated increase in net exports, also shifts the demand relation in Figure 18.4(a) from ZZ to ZZ'. In the absence of other measures, the equilibrium would move from A to A', and output would increase from Y to Y'.
- In order to avoid the increase in output, the government must reduce government spending so as to shift ZZ' back to ZZ. This combination of a depreciation and a fiscal contraction leads to the same level of output and an improved trade balance.

There is a general point behind this example: to the extent that governments care about *both* the level of output and the trade balance, they have to use *both* fiscal policy and exchange rate policies. We just saw one such combination. Table 18.1 gives some others, depending on the initial output and trade situation. Consider, for example, the top-right corner of the table: initial output is too low (put another way, unemployment is too high), and the economy has a trade deficit. A depreciation will help on both the trade and the output fronts: it reduces the trade deficit and increases output. But there is no reason for the depreciation to achieve both the correct increase in output and the elimination of the trade deficit. Depending on the initial situation and the relative effects of the depreciation on output and the trade balance, the government may need to complement the depreciation with either an increase or a decrease in government spending. This ambiguity is captured by the question mark in the box. Make sure that you understand the logic behind each of the other three cases.

> A general lesson: if you want to achieve two targets (here, output and trade balance), you need two instruments (here, fiscal policy and the exchange rate).

18.3 LOOKING AT DYNAMICS: THE J-CURVE

We have ignored dynamics so far in this chapter. It is time to reintroduce them. The dynamics of consumption, investment, sales and production we discussed in Chapter 3 are as relevant to an open economy as they are to a closed economy. But there are additional dynamic effects as well, which come from the dynamics of exports and imports. We focus on these effects here.

Return to the effects of the exchange rate on the trade balance. We argued earlier that a depreciation leads to an increase in exports and to a decrease in imports. But this does not happen overnight. Think of the dynamic effects of, say, a 10% dollar depreciation.

In the first few months following the depreciation, the effect of the depreciation is likely to be reflected much more in prices than in quantities. The price of imports in the UK goes up, and the price of UK exports abroad goes down. But the quantity of imports and exports is likely to adjust only slowly: it takes a while for consumers to realise that relative prices have changed, it takes a while for firms to shift to less expensive suppliers and so on. So a depreciation may well lead to an initial deterioration of the trade balance; ε decreases, but neither X nor IM adjusts very much initially, leading to a decline in net exports $(X - IM/\varepsilon)$.

As time passes, the effects of the change in the relative prices of both exports and imports become stronger. Less expensive UK goods cause UK consumers and firms to decrease their demand for foreign goods: UK imports decrease. Less expensive UK goods abroad lead foreign consumers and firms to increase their demand for UK goods: UK exports increase. If the Marshall–Lerner condition eventually holds – and we have argued that it does – the response of exports and imports eventually becomes stronger than the adverse price effect, and the eventual effect of the depreciation is an improvement of the trade balance.

> Even these prices may adjust slowly: consider a dollar depreciation. If you are an exporter to the USA, you may want to increase your dollar price less than implied by the exchange rate. In other words, you may decrease your mark-up in order to remain competitive with your US competitors. If you are a US exporter, you may decrease your price in foreign currency abroad by less than implied by the exchange rate. In other words, you may increase your mark-up.

> The response of the trade balance to the real exchange rate:
>
> - Initially: X, IM unchanged, ε decreases $\Rightarrow (X - IM/\varepsilon)$ decreases.
> - Eventually: X increases, IM decreases, ε decreases $(X - IM/\varepsilon)$ increases.

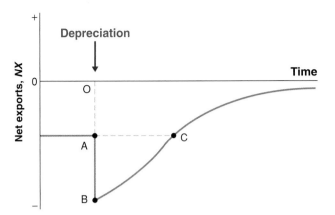

Figure 18.5

The J-curve

A real depreciation leads initially to a deterioration and then to an improvement of the trade balance.

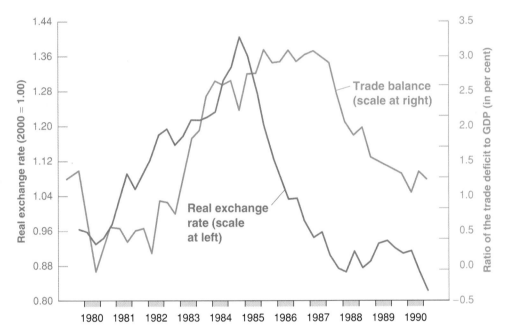

Figure 18.6

The real exchange rate and the ratio of the trade deficit to GDP: USA, 1980–1990

The real appreciation and depreciation of the dollar in the 1980s were reflected in increasing and then decreasing trade deficits. There were, however, substantial lags in the effects of the real exchange rate on the trade balance.

Figure 18.5 captures this adjustment by plotting the evolution of the trade balance against time in response to a real depreciation. The pre-depreciation trade deficit is OA. The depreciation initially *increases* the trade deficit to OB: ε decreases, but neither *IM* nor *X* changes right away. Over time, however, exports increase and imports decrease, reducing the trade deficit. Eventually (if the Marshall–Lerner condition is satisfied), the trade balance improves beyond its initial level; this is what happens from point C on in the figure. Economists refer to this adjustment process as the **J-curve** because – admittedly, with a bit of imagination – the curve in the figure resembles a 'J': first down, then up.

The importance of the dynamic effects of the real exchange rate on the trade balance was seen in the USA in the mid-1980s: Figure 18.6 plots the US trade deficit against the US real exchange rate in the 1980s. As we saw in Chapter 6, the period from 1980–1985 was one of sharp real appreciation, and the period from 1985–1988 one of sharp real depreciation. Turning to the trade deficit, which is expressed as a ratio to GDP, two facts are clear:

1. Movements in the real exchange rate were reflected in parallel movements in net exports. The appreciation was associated with a large increase in the trade deficit, and the later depreciation was associated with a large decrease in the trade balance.

2. There were, however, substantial lags in the response of the trade balance to changes in the real exchange rate. Note how from 1981–1983, the trade deficit remained small while the dollar was appreciating. And note how the steady depreciation of the dollar from 1985 onward was not reflected in an improvement in the trade balance before 1987: the dynamics of the J-curve were very much at work during both episodes.

In general, the econometric evidence on the dynamic relation between exports, imports and the real exchange rate suggests that in all OECD countries, a real depreciation eventually leads to a trade balance improvement. But it also suggests that this process takes some time, typically between six months and a year. These lags have implications not only for the effects of a depreciation on the trade balance but also for the effects of a depreciation on output. If a depreciation initially decreases net exports, it also initially exerts a contractionary effect on output. Thus, if a government relies on a depreciation both to improve the trade balance and to expand domestic output, the effects will go the 'wrong' way for a while.

18.4 SAVING, INVESTMENT AND THE TRADE BALANCE

You saw in Chapter 3 how we could rewrite the condition for equilibrium in the goods market as the condition that investment was equal to saving – the sum of private saving and public saving. We can now derive the corresponding condition for the open economy and show how useful this alternative way of looking at the equilibrium can be.

Start from our equilibrium condition:

$$Y = C + I + G - IM/\varepsilon + X$$

Subtract $C + T$ from both sides and use the fact that private saving is given by $S = Y - C - T$ to get

$$S = I + G - T - IM/\varepsilon + X$$

Use the definition of net exports, $NX \equiv X - IM/\varepsilon$, and reorganise, to get:

$$NX = S + (T - G) - I \qquad [18.1]$$

This condition says that, in equilibrium, the trade balance, NX, must be equal to saving (private saving, S, and public saving, $T - G$) minus investment, I. It follows that *a trade surplus must correspond to an excess of saving over investment; a trade deficit must correspond to an excess of investment over saving.*

One way of getting more intuition for this relation is to go back to the discussion of the current account and the capital account in Chapter 6. There we saw that a trade surplus implies net lending from the country to the rest of the world, and a trade deficit implies net borrowing by the country from the rest of the world. So, consider a country that invests more than it saves, so that $S + (T - G) - 1$ is negative. That country must be borrowing the difference from the rest of the world; it must therefore be running a trade deficit.

Note some of the things that equation (18.1) says:

● An increase in investment must be reflected in either an increase in private saving or public saving, or in a deterioration of the trade balance (a smaller trade surplus or a larger trade deficit).
● An increase in the budget deficit must be reflected in either an increase in private saving, a decrease in investment or a deterioration of the trade balance.
● A country with a high saving rate (private plus public) must have either a high investment rate or a large trade surplus.

Note also, however, what equation (18.1) *does not say*. It does not say, for example, whether a budget deficit will lead to a trade deficit or, instead, to an increase in private saving, or to a decrease in investment. To find out what happens in response to a budget deficit, we must explicitly solve for what happens to output and its components, using the assumptions that we have made about consumption, investment, exports and imports. We can do so using either equation (6.8) – as we have done throughout this chapter – or equation (18.1), as the two are equivalent. However, let me strongly recommend that you use equation (6.8). Using equation (18.1) can, if you are not careful, be very misleading. To see how misleading it can be, consider, for example, the following argument (which is so common that you may have read something similar in newspapers).

It is clear that the USA cannot reduce its large trade deficit (currently around 6% of GDP) through a depreciation. Look at equation (18.1). It shows that the trade deficit is equal to investment minus saving. Why should a depreciation affect either saving or investment? So how can a depreciation affect the trade deficit?

The argument might sound convincing, but we know it is wrong. We showed earlier that a depreciation leads to an improvement in a country's trade position. So what is wrong with the argument? A depreciation actually affects saving and investment: it does so by affecting

FOCUS
The US trade deficit: origins and implications

Since 1996, the ratio of exports to GDP has remained flat, while the ratio of imports to GDP in the USA has rapidly increased. As a result, the trade deficit increased from $104 billion, or 1.2% of US GDP in 1996, to $681 billion, or 4.7% of US GDP in 2008.

The current account deficit (which is equal to the trade deficit minus net income from abroad) was $673 billion in 2008. Put another way, the USA borrowed $673 billion from the rest of the world in 2008. This is a very large amount. It represents about 50% of the world's net saving (saving net of depreciation). And the notion that the world's richest economy is borrowing so much from the rest of the world is quite surprising. It raises two main questions: Where do these deficits come from? And what do they imply for the future? Let's take up each question in turn.

Where does the trade deficit and, by implication, the current account deficit come from?

Three factors appear to have played roughly equal roles in the increase in the current account deficit since the mid-1990s.

The first has been the high US growth rate since the mid-1990s, relative to the growth rates of some of its main trading partners. Table 18.2 gives the average annual growth rate for the USA, the EU and Japan for three periods: 1991–1995, 1996–2000 and 2001–2006. Since 1996, US growth has been much higher than growth in Europe and Japan. The US performance from 1996–2000 reflects the New Economy boom, which we

Table 18.2 Average annual growth rates in the USA, the EU and Japan since 1991 (per cent per year)

	1991–1995	1996–2000	2001–2006
USA	2.5	4.1	3.4
EU	2.1	2.6	1.6
Japan	1.5	1.5	1.6

have discussed at many points in the book. US growth has decreased since 2001 (recall that the USA went through a recession in 2001), but it has remained higher than growth in Europe and Japan.

Higher growth does not necessarily lead to a higher trade deficit. If the main source of the increase in demand and growth in a country is an increase in foreign demand, the country can grow fast and maintain trade balance, or even sustain a trade surplus. In the case of the USA since the mid-1990s, however, the main source of increased demand has been domestic demand, with high consumption demand as the main factor behind the sustained expansion. Thus, higher growth has come with an increasing trade deficit.

The second factor is shifts in the export and import functions – that is, changes in exports or in imports due neither to changes in activity nor to changes in the exchange rate. The evidence is that these shifts have played an important role as well, explaining up to one-third of the increase in the trade deficit. At a given level of income and a given exchange rate, US consumers, for example, buy a higher proportion of foreign goods – say, more foreign cars and fewer domestic cars.

the demand for domestic goods, thereby increasing output. Higher output leads to an increase in saving over investment or, equivalently, to a decrease in the trade deficit.

A good way of making sure that you understand the material in this section is to go back and look at the various cases we have considered, from changes in government spending, to changes in foreign output, to combinations of depreciation and fiscal contraction and so on. Trace what happens in each case to each of the four components of equation (18.1): private saving, public saving (equivalently, the budget surplus), investment and the trade balance. Make sure, as always, that you can tell the story in words.

A good way of making sure you understand the material in the whole chapter is to read the Focus box 'The US trade deficit: origins and implications'. It will show you how the concepts we have developed in this chapter can be used to understand the origins and implications of what is probably, at this point, one of the main issues facing policy makers, not only in the USA but also in the rest of the world.

> Suppose, for example, that the government wants to reduce the trade deficit without changing the level of output, so it uses a combination of depreciation and fiscal contraction. What happens to private saving, public saving and investment?

The third factor has been the evolution of the exchange rate. Even if, at a given real exchange rate, growth leads to an increase in the trade deficit, a real depreciation can help maintain trade balance by making domestic goods more competitive. But just the opposite has happened to the US real exchange rate: from 1996–2002, the USA experienced a large real appreciation, not a real depreciation. Go back to Figure 18.6, which gives the evolution of the US effective real exchange rate. From the second quarter of 1995 to the first quarter of 2002, the real exchange rate index increased from 0.83 to 1.11, a real appreciation of more than 30%. Since then, the dollar has depreciated and, at the end of 2006, the index stood at 0.94, still higher than its 1995 value.

Why was the dollar so strong until 2002, in the face of a large current account deficit? A full discussion will have to wait until the next chapter, when we look at the link between financial decisions and the exchange rate. But, in short, the answer is that there was a very high demand for US assets on the part of foreign investors. This demand was enough to drive the dollar up and, in doing so, to increase the trade and the current account deficits. Since the beginning of 2002, the dollar has depreciated but, because of the two other factors listed – growth differentials and shifts in relative demand for domestic and foreign goods – and because of the lags in the adjustment of exports and imports to the real exchange rate – the J curve – the trade deficit has continued to increase.

This is a good place to make sure we can tell the story in terms of saving and investment. Figure 18.7 gives the evolution of US net saving (that is, US saving net of depreciation) and US net investment (US investment net of depreciation) as ratios to GDP, since 1996, and it tells a clear story: the increase in the trade deficit (which, as you will recall, is equal to the difference between investment and saving) has come primarily from a decrease in the ratio of saving to GDP. And, if one looks closely, it is clear that this decrease in saving has come mostly from a decrease in private saving, S, rather than an increase in the budget deficit, $G - T$: the ratio of the budget deficit to GDP is roughly the same in 2006 as it was in 1996, and the ratio of private saving to GDP is more than 3 percentage points lower in 2006 than it was in 1996. Thus, another way of describing what lies behind the trade deficit is that US consumers are saving substantially less than they were ten years ago. Should they be saving more? We discussed this in Chapter 16. The answer: most of them appear to be saving enough.

What happens next?

Should we expect the large trade deficit and current account deficit to naturally disappear in the future? At an unchanged real exchange rate, the answer is probably no.

If there were good reasons to expect US trading partners to experience much higher growth than the USA over the coming decade, then we could expect to see the same process we saw in the past ten years but this time in reverse: lower growth in the USA than in the rest of the world would lead to a steady reduction in the trade deficit. There are few reasons, however, to expect such a scenario. Although the USA cannot expect to replicate the growth rates of the late 1990s, there is also no reason to expect much lower growth than average over the coming decade. And, while growth has increased in Europe and Japan, sustained higher growth in Europe and Japan than in the USA seems unlikely.

Can we expect the shifts in exports and imports to reverse themselves, leading to an improvement in the trade balance without the need for a depreciation? The source of the shifts is poorly understood, so one must be

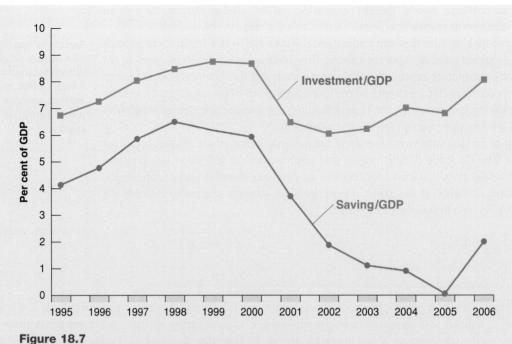

Figure 18.7

US net saving and net investment since 1996 (% of GDP)

careful in predicting what might happen. But there does not appear to be any particular reason to think that, for example, US consumers will shift back from foreign cars to US cars. Put another way, there is no particular reason to expect that the trade deficit will narrow by itself, without a depreciation of the dollar.

Will the dollar depreciate further, leading eventually to a reduction in the trade and current account deficits? The answer is: probably. While financial investors have been willing to lend to the USA until now, there are many reasons to think that they will be reluctant to lend at the current levels of $800 billion or so per year.

These arguments have three implications:

- The US trade and current account deficits will decline in the future.
- This decline is unlikely to happen without a real depreciation. How large a depreciation? Estimates range from 20% to 40% from where we are today – in short, a substantial further real depreciation.
- When will this depreciation take place? This is a hard question to answer. It will take place when foreign investors become reluctant to lend to the USA at the rate of $800 billion or so per year.

Let's go back to the issues discussed in Table 18.1: a depreciation on such a scale will have major effects on the demand for goods both in the USA and abroad.

The depreciation will increase the demand for US goods. If, when the depreciation takes place, US output is already close to its natural level, the risk is that the depreciation will lead to too high a level of demand and too high a level of output. If this happens, it will require a decrease in domestic demand. This may come either from a decrease in spending by consumers or firms or from a reduction in government spending. If the US government succeeds in achieving a smooth depreciation and the decrease in domestic spending, the outcome can be sustained US growth and a reduction of the US trade deficit.

The depreciation will decrease the demand for foreign goods. By the same argument, this may require foreign governments to implement policies to sustain their own demand and output. This would ordinarily call for a fiscal expansion, but it might not be the right solution in this case. A number of countries, such as France and Japan, are already running large budget deficits. For the reasons we saw in Chapter 17, increasing these deficits further may be difficult and even dangerous. If fiscal policy cannot be used to sustain demand and output, a strong dollar depreciation might therefore trigger a recession in those countries.

In short, a smooth reduction of the US trade deficit will require the combination of a dollar depreciation and spending changes both in the USA and abroad. This can be achieved, but it may not be easy.

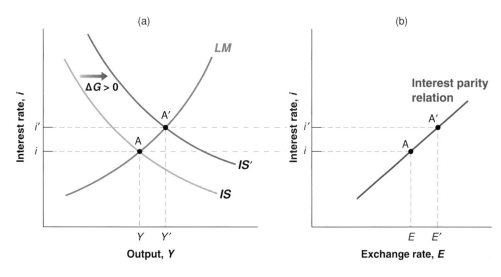

Figure 18.8

The effects of an increase in government spending (2)

An increase in government spending leads to an increase in output, an increase in the interest rate and an appreciation.

18.5 THE EFFECTS OF POLICY IN AN OPEN ECONOMY

Having derived the *IS–LM* model for the open economy, we now put it to use and look at the effects of policy.

The effects of fiscal policy in an open economy

Let's look again at a change in government spending. Suppose that, starting from a balanced budget, the government decides to increase defence spending without raising taxes and so runs a budget deficit. What happens to the level of output? To the composition of output? To the interest rate? To the exchange rate?

The answers are given in Figure 18.8. The economy is initially at point A. The increase in government spending by, say, $\Delta G > 0$ increases output at a given interest rate, shifting the *IS* curve to the right, from *IS* to *IS'* in Figure 18.8(a). Because government spending does not enter the *LM* relation, the *LM* curve does not shift. The new equilibrium is at point A', with a higher level of output and a higher interest rate. In Figure 18.8(b), the higher interest rate leads to an increase in the exchange rate – an appreciation. So *an increase in government spending leads to an increase in output, an increase in the interest rate and an appreciation.*

In words: an increase in government spending leads to an increase in demand, leading to an increase in output. As output increases, so does the demand for money, leading to upward pressure on the interest rate. The increase in the interest rate, which makes domestic bonds more attractive, leads to an appreciation. The higher interest rate and the appreciation both decrease the domestic demand for goods, offsetting some of the effect of government spending on demand and output.

Can we tell what happens to the various components of demand?

● Clearly, consumption and government spending both go up. Consumption goes up because of the increase in income, and government spending goes up by assumption.
● What happens to investment is ambiguous. Recall that investment depends on both output and the interest rate: $I = I(Y, i)$. On the one hand, output goes up, leading to an increase in investment. But on the other, the interest rate also goes up, leading to a decrease in investment. Depending on which of these two effects dominates, investment can go up or down. In short: the effect of government spending on investment is ambiguous in a closed economy; it remains ambiguous in an open economy.
● Recall that net exports depend on domestic output, foreign output and the exchange rate: $NX = NX(Y, Y^*, E)$. Thus, both the increase in output and the appreciation combine

◄ An increase in government spending shifts the *IS* curve to the right. It shifts neither the *LM* curve nor the interest-parity line.

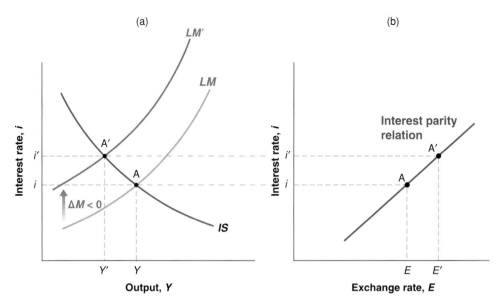

Figure 18.9

The effects of a monetary contraction

A monetary contraction leads to a decrease in output, an increase in the interest rate and an appreciation.

to decrease net exports: the increase in output increases imports, and the appreciation decreases exports and increases imports. As a result, the budget deficit leads to a deterioration of the trade balance. If trade is balanced to start, then the budget deficit leads to a trade deficit. Note that, while an increase in the budget deficit increases the trade deficit, the effect is far from mechanical. It works through the effect of the budget deficit on output and on the exchange rate, and, in turn, on the trade deficit.

The effects of monetary policy in an open economy

> A monetary contraction shifts the *LM* curve up. It shifts neither the *IS* curve nor the interest-parity curve.

Now that we have looked at fiscal policy, we look at our other favourite policy experiment, a monetary contraction. Look at Figure 18.9(a). At a given level of output, a decrease in the money stock by, say, $\Delta M < 0$ leads to an increase in the interest rate: the *LM* curve shifts up,

> Can you tell what happens to consumption, to investment and to net exports?

from *LM* to *LM′*. Because money does not directly enter the *IS* relation, the *IS* curve does not shift. The equilibrium moves from point A to point A′. In Figure 18.9(b), the increase in the interest rate leads to an appreciation.

> As an example, the sharp monetary and fiscal policy changes the US economy went through in the late 1970s and early 1980s produced exactly the same results as predicted by the Mundell–Fleming model.

So *a monetary contraction leads to a decrease in output, an increase in the interest rate and an appreciation*. The story is easy to tell. A monetary contraction leads to an increase in the interest rate, making domestic bonds more attractive and triggering an appreciation. The higher interest rate and the appreciation both decrease demand and output.

This version of the *IS–LM* model for the open economy was first put together in the 1960s

> Robert Mundell was awarded the Nobel Prize in Economics in 1999.

by two economists, Robert Mundell at Columbia University and Marcus Fleming at the International Monetary Fund and is known as the Mundell–Fleming model.

18.6 FIXED EXCHANGE RATES

We have assumed so far that the central bank chose the money supply and let the exchange rate freely adjust in whatever manner was implied by equilibrium in the foreign exchange market. In many countries, this assumption does not reflect reality: central banks act under implicit or explicit exchange rate targets and use monetary policy to achieve those targets. The targets are sometimes implicit, sometimes explicit; they are sometimes specific values, sometimes bands or ranges. These exchange rate arrangements (or *regimes*, as they are called) have many names. Let's first see what the names mean.

Pegs, crawling pegs, bands, the EMS and the euro

At one end of the spectrum are countries with flexible exchange rates, such as the USA or Japan. These countries do not have explicit exchange rate targets. Although their central banks probably do not ignore movements in the exchange rate, they have shown themselves to be quite willing to let their exchange rates fluctuate considerably.

At the other end are countries that operate under *fixed exchange rates*. These countries maintain a fixed exchange rate in terms of some foreign currency. Some peg their currency to the dollar. For example, from 1991–2001, Argentina pegged its currency, the peso, at the highly symbolic exchange rate of 1 dollar for 1 peso (more on this in Chapter 19). Other countries used to peg their currency to the French franc (most of these are former French colonies in Africa); as the French franc has been replaced by the euro, they are now pegged to the euro. Still other countries peg their currency to a basket of foreign currencies, with the weights reflecting the composition of their trade.

The label 'fixed' is a bit misleading: it is not the case that the exchange rate in countries with fixed exchange rates never actually changes. But changes are rare. An extreme case involves the African countries pegged to the French franc. When their exchange rates were readjusted in January 1994, it was the first adjustment in 45 years! Because these changes are rare, economists use specific words to distinguish them from the daily changes that occur under flexible exchange rates. A decrease in the exchange rate under a regime of fixed exchange rates is called a *devaluation* rather than a depreciation, and an increase in the exchange rate under a regime of fixed exchange rates is called a *revaluation* rather than an appreciation.

Between these extremes are countries with various degrees of commitment to an exchange rate target. For example, some countries operate under a **crawling peg**. The name describes it well: these countries typically have inflation rates that exceed the US inflation rate. If they were to peg their nominal exchange rate against the dollar, the more rapid increase in their domestic price level above the US price level would lead to a steady real appreciation and rapidly make their goods uncompetitive. To avoid this effect, these countries choose a predetermined rate of depreciation against the dollar. They choose to 'crawl' (move slowly) vis-à-vis the dollar.

Yet another arrangement is for a group of countries to maintain their bilateral exchange rates (the exchange rate between each pair of countries) within some bands. Perhaps the most prominent example was the **European Monetary System (EMS)**, which determined the movements of exchange rates within the EU from 1978–1998. Under the EMS rules, member countries agreed to maintain their exchange rate vis-à-vis the other currencies in the system within narrow limits, or **bands**, around a **central parity** – a given value for the exchange rate. Changes in the central parity and devaluations or revaluations of specific currencies could occur, but only by common agreement among member countries. After a major crisis in 1992, which led a number of countries to drop out of the EMS altogether, exchange rate adjustments became more and more infrequent, leading a number of countries to move one step further and adopt a common currency, the euro. The conversion from domestic currencies to the euro began on 1 January 1999, and was completed in early 2002. We shall return to the implications of the move to the euro in Chapter 26.

We shall discuss the pros and cons of different exchange regimes in Chapter 19. But first, we must understand how pegging the exchange rate affects monetary policy and fiscal policy. This is what we do in the rest of this section.

Pegging the exchange rate and monetary control

Suppose a country decides to peg its exchange rate at some chosen value, call it $\bar{E}$. How does it actually achieve this? The government cannot just announce the value of the exchange rate and stand there. Rather, it must take measures so that its chosen exchange rate will prevail in the foreign exchange market. Let's look at the implications and mechanics of pegging.

Margin notes:

Like the 'dance of the dollar' in the 1980s (see Chapter 6), there was a 'dance of the yen' in the 1990s. The yen appreciated sharply in the first half of the 1990s, and then depreciated sharply later in the decade.

Recall the definition of the real exchange rate, $\varepsilon = EP/P^*$.
If domestic inflation is higher than foreign inflation:

- P increases faster than P^*
- If E is fixed, EP/P^* steadily increases

Equivalently: there is a steady real appreciation. Domestic goods become steadily more expensive relative to foreign goods.

We will look at the 1992 crisis in Chapter 19.

You can think of countries adopting a common currency as adopting an extreme form of fixed exchange rates: their 'exchange rate' is fixed at one-to-one between any pair of countries.

Pegging or no pegging, the exchange rate and the nominal interest rate must satisfy the interest parity condition:

$$(1 + i_t) = (1 + i_t^*)\left(\frac{E_t}{E_{t+1}^e}\right)$$

Now suppose a country pegs the exchange rate at $E_t = \bar{E}$, so the current exchange rate $E_t = \bar{E}$. If financial and foreign exchange markets believe that the exchange rate will remain pegged at this value, then their expectation of the future exchange rate, E_{t+1}^e, is also equal to $\bar{E}$, and the interest parity relation becomes

$$(1 + i_t) = (1 + i_t^*) \Rightarrow i_t = i_t^*$$

In words: if financial investors expect the exchange rate to remain unchanged, they will require the same nominal interest rate in both countries. *Under a fixed exchange rate and perfect capital mobility, the domestic interest rate must be equal to the foreign interest rate.*

This condition has one further important implication. Return to the equilibrium condition that the supply of money and demand for money be equal. Now that $i = i$, this condition becomes

$$\frac{M}{P} = YL(1^*)$$ [18.2]

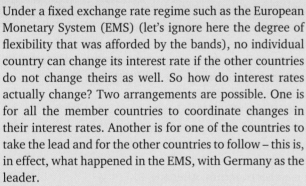

FOCUS
German unification, interest rates and the EMS

Under a fixed exchange rate regime such as the European Monetary System (EMS) (let's ignore here the degree of flexibility that was afforded by the bands), no individual country can change its interest rate if the other countries do not change theirs as well. So how do interest rates actually change? Two arrangements are possible. One is for all the member countries to coordinate changes in their interest rates. Another is for one of the countries to take the lead and for the other countries to follow – this is, in effect, what happened in the EMS, with Germany as the leader.

During the 1980s, most European central banks shared similar goals and were happy to let the Bundesbank (the German central bank) take the lead. But in 1990, German unification led to a sharp divergence in goals between the Bundesbank and the central banks of the other EMS countries. Large budget deficits, triggered by transfers to people and firms in Eastern Germany, together with an investment boom, led to a large increase in demand in Germany. The Bundesbank's fear that this shift would generate too strong an increase in activity led it to adopt a restrictive monetary policy. The result was strong growth in Germany together with a large increase in interest rates.

This may have been the right policy mix for Germany but, for the other European countries, this policy mix was much less appealing. They were not experiencing the same increase in demand but, to stay in the EMS, they had to match German interest rates. The net result was a sharp decrease in demand and output in the other countries. These results are presented in Table 18.3, which gives nominal interest rates, real interest rates, inflation rates and GDP growth from 1990–1992 for Germany and for two of its EMS partners, France and Belgium.

Note first how the high German nominal interest rates were matched by both France and Belgium. In fact, nominal interest rates were actually higher in France than in Germany in all three years! This is because France needed higher interest rates than Germany to maintain the deutschemark/franc parity. The reason is that financial markets were not sure that France would actually keep the parity of the franc vis-à-vis the deutschemark. Worried about a possible devaluation of the franc, financial investors asked for a higher interest rate on French bonds than on German bonds.

Although France and Belgium had to match – or, as we have just seen, more than match – German nominal rates, these two countries had less inflation than Germany. The result was very high real interest rates, much higher than the rate in Germany: in both France and Belgium, average real interest rates from 1990–1992 were close to 7%. And

Suppose an increase in domestic output increases the demand for money. In a closed economy, the central bank could leave the money stock unchanged, leading to an increase in the equilibrium interest rate. In an open economy, and under flexible exchange rates, the central bank can still do the same: the result will be both an increase in the interest rate and an appreciation. But under fixed exchange rates, the central bank cannot keep the money stock unchanged. If it did, the domestic interest rate would increase above the foreign interest rate, leading to an appreciation. To maintain the exchange rate, the central bank must increase the supply of money in line with the increase in the demand for money so the equilibrium interest rate does not change. Given the price level, P, nominal money, M, must adjust so that equation (18.2) holds.

Let's summarise. *Under fixed exchange rates, the central bank gives up monetary policy as a policy instrument.* With a fixed exchange rate, the domestic interest rate must be equal to the foreign interest rate. And the money supply must adjust so as to maintain the interest rate.

Fiscal policy under fixed exchange rates

If monetary policy can no longer be used under fixed exchange rates, what about fiscal policy? To answer this question, we use Figure 18.10.

in both countries, the period 1990–1992 was characterised by slow growth and rising unemployment. Unemployment in France in 1992 was 10.4%, up from 8.9% in 1990. The corresponding numbers for Belgium were 12.1% and 8.7%.

A similar story was unfolding in the other EMS countries. By 1992, average unemployment in the EU, which had been 8.7% in 1990, had increased to 10.3%. The effects of high real interest rates on spending were not the only source of this slowdown, but they were the main one.

By 1992, an increasing number of countries were wondering whether to keep defending their EMS parity or to give it up and lower their interest rates. Worried about the risk of devaluations, financial markets started to ask for higher interest rates in countries where they thought devaluations were more likely. The result was two major exchange rate crises, one in the fall of 1992 and the other in the summer of 1993. By the end of these two crises, two countries, Italy and the UK, had left the EMS. We shall look at these crises, their origins and their implications in Chapter 19.

Table 18.3 Interest rates and output growth: Germany, France and Belgium, 1990–1992

	Nominal interest rates (%)			Inflation (%)		
	1990	1991	1992	1990	1991	1992
Germany	8.05	9.02	9.05	2.07	3.07	4.07
France	10.03	9.06	10.03	2.09	3.00	2.04
Belgium	9.06	9.04	9.04	2.09	2.07	2.04
	Real interest rates (%)			GDP growth (%)		
	1990	1991	1992	1990	1991	1992
Germany	5.07	5.05	4.08	5.07	4.05	2.01
France	7.04	6.06	7.09	2.05	0.07	1.04
Belgium	6.07	6.07	7.00	3.03	2.01	0.08

Note: the nominal interest rate is the short-term nominal interest rate. The real interest rate is the realised real interest rate over the year – that is, the nominal interest rate minus actual inflation over the year. All rates are annual.

Source: OECD *Economic Outlook* database.

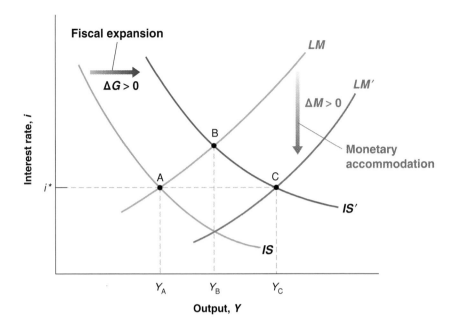

Figure 18.10

The effects of a fiscal expansion under fixed exchange rates

Under flexible exchange rates, a fiscal expansion increases output from Y_A to Y_B. Under fixed exchange rates, output increases from Y_A to Y_C.

Is the effect of fiscal policy stronger in a closed economy or in an open economy with fixed exchange rates?

(*Hint*: the answer is ambiguous.)

Figure 18.10 starts by replicating Figure 18.9(a), which we used earlier to analyse the effects of fiscal policy under flexible exchange rates. In that case, we saw that a fiscal expansion ($\Delta G > 0$) shifted the *IS* curve to the right. Under flexible exchange rates, the money stock remained unchanged, leading to a movement in the equilibrium from point A to point B, with an increase in output from Y_A to Y_B, an increase in the interest rate and an appreciation.

However, under fixed exchange rates, the central bank cannot let the currency appreciate. Because the increase in output leads to an increase in the demand for money, the central bank must accommodate this increased demand for money by increasing the money supply. In terms of Figure 18.10, the central bank must shift the *LM* curve down as the *IS* curve shifts to the right so as to maintain the same interest rate and, thus, the same exchange rate. The equilibrium therefore moves from A to C, with higher output, Y_C, and unchanged interest and exchange rates. So, *under fixed exchange rates, fiscal policy is more powerful than it is under flexible exchange rates. This is because fiscal policy triggers monetary accommodation.*

As this chapter comes to an end, a question should have started to form in your mind: why would a country choose to fix its exchange rate? You have seen a number of reasons why this appears to be a bad idea:

● By fixing the exchange rate, a country gives up a powerful tool for correcting trade imbalances or changing the level of economic activity.
● By committing to a particular exchange rate, a country also gives up control of its interest rate. Not only that, but the country must match movements in the foreign interest rate, at the risk of unwanted effects on its own activity. This is what happened in the early 1990s in Europe. Because of the increase in demand due to the reunification of West and East Germany, Germany felt it had to increase its interest rate. To maintain their parity with the deutschemark, other countries in the European Monetary System were forced to also increase their interest rates, something that they would rather have avoided. (This is the topic of the Focus box 'German unification, interest rates and the EMS'.)
● Although the country retains control of fiscal policy, one policy instrument may not be enough. As you saw in Chapter 6, for example, a fiscal expansion can help the economy get out of a recession, but only at the cost of a larger trade deficit. And a country that wants, for example, to decrease its budget deficit cannot, under fixed exchange rates, use monetary policy to offset the contractionary effect of its fiscal policy on output.

So why do some countries fix their exchange rate? Why have 15 European countries – with more to come – adopted a common currency? To answer these questions, we must do some more work. We must look at what happens not only in the short run – which is what we did in this chapter – but also in the medium run, when the price level can adjust. We must look at the nature of exchange rate crises. Once we have done this, we shall then be able to assess the pros and cons of different exchange rate regimes. These are the topics we take up in Chapter 19.

SUMMARY

- An increase in foreign demand leads, as a result of increased exports, to both an increase in domestic output and an improvement of the trade balance.

- Because increases in foreign demand improve the trade balance and increases in domestic demand worsen the trade balance, countries might be tempted to wait for increases in foreign demand to move them out of a recession. When a group of countries is in recession, coordination can, in principle, help them get out of it.

- If the Marshall–Lerner condition is satisfied – and the empirical evidence indicates that it is – a real depreciation leads to an improvement in net exports.

- A real depreciation leads first to a deterioration of the trade balance and then to an improvement. This adjustment process is known as the J-curve.

- The condition for equilibrium in the goods market can be rewritten as the condition that saving (public and private) minus investment must be equal to the trade balance. A trade surplus corresponds to an excess of saving over investment. A trade deficit corresponds to an excess of investment over saving.

- Under flexible exchange rates, an expansionary fiscal policy leads to an increase in output, an increase in the interest rate and an appreciation.

- Under flexible exchange rates, a contractionary monetary policy leads to a decrease in output, an increase in the interest rate and an appreciation.

KEY TERMS

demand for domestic goods 368	coordination 372	J-curve 376	band 383
domestic demand for goods 368	G8 372	crawling peg 383	central parity 383
	Marshall–Lerner condition 373	European Monetary System (EMS) 383	

QUESTIONS AND PROBLEMS

QUICK CHECK

1. *Using the information in this chapter, label each of the following statements true, false or uncertain. Explain briefly.*

a. The current US trade deficit is the result of unusually high investment, not the result of a decline in national saving.

b. The national income identity implies that budget deficits cause trade deficits.

c. Opening the economy to trade tends to increase the multiplier because an increase in expenditure leads to more exports.

d. If the trade deficit is equal to zero, then the domestic demand for goods and the demand for domestic goods are equal.

e. A real depreciation leads to an immediate improvement in the trade balance.

f. A small open economy can reduce its trade deficit through fiscal contraction at a smaller cost in output than can a large open economy.

g. The current high US trade deficit is solely the result of a real appreciation of US goods between 1995 and 2002.

2. Real and nominal exchange rates and inflation

Using the definition of the real exchange rate (and Propositions 7 and 8 in Appendix 1 at the end of the book), you can show that

$$\frac{(\varepsilon_t - \varepsilon_{t-1})}{\varepsilon_{t-1}} = \frac{(E_t - E_{t-1})}{E_{t-1}} + \pi_t - \pi_t^*$$

In words: the percentage real appreciation equals the percentage nominal appreciation plus the difference between domestic and foreign inflation.

a. If domestic inflation is higher than foreign inflation, but the domestic country has a fixed exchange rate, what happens to the real exchange rate over time? Assume that the Marshall–Lerner condition holds. What happens to the trade balance over time? Explain in words.

b. Suppose the real exchange rate is constant – say, at the level required for net exports (or the current account) to equal zero. In this case, if domestic inflation is higher than foreign inflation, what must happen to the nominal exchange rate over time?

3. *In this chapter, we showed that a monetary expansion in an economy operating under flexible exchange rates leads to an increase in output and a depreciation of the domestic currency.*

a. How does a monetary expansion (in an economy with flexible exchange rates) affect consumption and investment?

b. How does a monetary expansion (in an economy with flexible exchange rates) affect net exports?

4. *Consider an open economy with flexible exchange rates. Suppose output is at the natural level, but there is a trade deficit. What is the appropriate fiscal-monetary policy mix?*

5. Flexible exchange rates and foreign macroeconomic policy

Consider an open economy with flexible exchange rates. Let UIP stand for the uncovered interest parity condition.

a. In an *IS–LM–UIP* diagram, show the effect of an increase in foreign output, Y^*, on domestic output, Y. Explain in words.

b. In an *IS–LM–UIP* diagram, show the effect of an increase in the foreign interest rate, i^*, on domestic output, Y. Explain in words.

c. Given the discussion of the effects of fiscal policy in this chapter, what effect is a foreign fiscal expansion likely to have on foreign output, Y^*, and on the foreign interest rate, i^*? Given the discussion of the effects of monetary policy in this chapter, what effect is a foreign monetary expansion likely to have on Y^* and i^*?

d. Given your answers to parts (a), (b), and (c), how does a foreign fiscal expansion affect domestic output? How does a foreign monetary expansion affect domestic output? (*Hint:* one of these policies has an ambiguous effect on output.)

DIG DEEPER

6. Fixed exchange rates and foreign macroeconomic policy

Consider a fixed exchange rate system, in which a group of countries (called follower countries) peg their currencies to the currency of one country (called the leader country). Since the

currency of the leader country is not fixed against the currencies of countries outside the fixed exchange rate system, the leader country can conduct monetary policy as it wishes. For this problem, consider the domestic country to be a follower country and the foreign country to be the leader country.

a. Redo the analysis of problem 5(a).

b. Redo the analysis of problem 5(b).

c. Using your answers to parts (a) and (b) and problem 5(c), how does a foreign monetary expansion (by the leader country) affect domestic output? How does a foreign fiscal expansion (by the leader country) affect domestic output? (You may assume that the effect of Y^* on domestic output is small.) How do your answers differ from those in 5(d)?

7. Net exports and foreign demand

a. Suppose there is an increase in foreign output. Show the effect on the domestic economy (i.e. replicate Figure 18.2). What is the effect on domestic output? On domestic net exports?

b. If the interest rate remains constant, what will happen to domestic investment? If taxes are fixed, what will happen to the domestic budget deficit?

c. Using equation (18.1), what must happen to private saving? Explain.

d. Foreign output does not appear in equation (18.1), yet it evidently affects net exports. Explain how this is possible.

8. The exchange rate and the labour market

Suppose the domestic currency depreciates (E falls). Assume that P and P* remain constant.

a. How does the nominal depreciation affect the relative price of domestic goods (i.e. the real exchange rate)? Given your answer, what effect would a nominal depreciation likely have on (world) demand for domestic goods? on the domestic unemployment rate?

b. Given the foreign price level, P^*, what is the price of foreign goods in terms of domestic currency? How does a nominal depreciation affect the price of foreign goods in terms of domestic currency? How does a nominal depreciation affect the domestic consumer price index? (*Hint:* remember that domestic consumers buy foreign goods (imports) as well as domestic goods.)

c. If the nominal wage remains constant, how does a nominal depreciation affect the real wage?

d. Comment on the following statement. 'A depreciating currency puts domestic labor on sale.'

9. Eliminating a trade deficit

a. Consider an economy with a trade deficit ($NX < 0$) and with output equal to its natural level. Suppose that, even though output may deviate from its natural level in the short run, it returns to its natural level in the medium run. Assume that the natural level is unaffected by the real exchange rate. What must happen to the real exchange rate over the medium run to eliminate the trade deficit (i.e. to increase NX to 0)?

b. Now write down the national income identity. Assume again that output returns to its natural level in the medium run. If NX increases to 0, what must happen to domestic demand $(C + I + G)$ in the medium run? What government policies are available to reduce domestic demand in the medium run? Identify which components of domestic demand each of these policies affect.

10. Multipliers, openness and fiscal policy

Consider an open economy characterised by the equations below.

$$C = c_0 + c_1(Y - T)$$
$$I = d_0 + d_1 Y$$
$$IM = m_1 Y$$
$$X = x_1 Y^*$$

The parameters m_1 and x_1 are the propensities to import and export. Assume that the real exchange rate is fixed at a value of 1 and treat foreign income, Y^*, as fixed. Also assume that taxes are fixed and that government purchases are exogenous (i.e. decided by the government). We explore the effectiveness of changes in G under alternative assumptions about the propensity to import.

a. Write the equilibrium condition in the market for domestic goods and solve for Y.

b. Suppose government purchases increase by one unit. What is the effect on output? (Assume that $0 < m_1 < c_1 + < 1$. Explain why.)

c. How do net exports change when government purchases increase by one unit?

Now consider two economies, one with $m_1 = 0.5$ and the other with $m_1 = 0.1$. Each economy is characterised by $(c_1 + d_1) = 0.6$.

d. Suppose one of the economies is much larger than the other. Which economy do you expect to have the larger value of m_1? Explain.

e. Calculate your answers to parts (b) and (c) for each economy by substituting the appropriate parameter values.

f. In which economy will fiscal policy have a larger effect on output? In which economy will fiscal policy have a larger effect on net exports?

11. Policy coordination and the world economy

Consider an open economy in which the real exchange rate is fixed and equal to one. Consumption, investment, government spending, and taxes are given by

$$C = 10 + 0.8(Y - T), I = 10, G = 10 \text{ and } T = 10$$

Imports and exports are given by

$$IM = 0.3Y \text{ and } X = 0.3Y^*$$

where Y^* denotes foreign output.

a. Solve for equilibrium output in the domestic economy, given Y^*. What is the multiplier in this economy? If we were to close the economy – so exports and imports were identically equal to zero – what would the multiplier be? Why would the multiplier be different in a closed economy?

b. Assume that the foreign economy is characterised by the same equations as the domestic economy (with asterisks reversed). Use the two sets of equations to solve for the equilibrium output of each country.

[*Hint*: use the equations for the foreign economy to solve for Y^* as a function of Y and substitute this solution for Y^* in part (a).] What is the multiplier for each country now? Why is it different from the open economy multiplier in part (a)?

c. Assume that the domestic government, G, has a target level of output of 125. Assuming that the foreign government does not change G^*, what is the increase in G necessary to achieve the target output in the domestic economy? Solve for net exports and the budget deficit in each country.

d. Suppose each government has a target level of output of 125 and that each government increases government spending by the same amount. What is the common increase in G and G^* necessary to achieve the target output in both countries? Solve for net exports and the budget deficit in each country.

e. Why is fiscal coordination, such as the common increase in G and G^* in part (d), difficult to achieve in practice?

EXPLORE FURTHER

12. The exchange rate as an automatic stabiliser

Consider an economy that suffers a fall in business confidence (which tends to reduce investment). Let UIP stand for the uncovered interest parity condition.

a. Suppose the economy has a flexible exchange rate. In an *IS–LM–UIP* diagram, show the short-run effect of the fall in business confidence on output, the interest rate and the exchange rate. How does the change in the exchange rate, by itself, tend to affect output? Does the change in the exchange rate dampen (make smaller) or amplify (make larger) the effect of the fall in business confidence on output?

b. Suppose instead the economy has a fixed exchange rate. In an *IS–LM–UIP* diagram, show how the economy responds to the fall in business confidence. What must happen to the money supply in order to maintain the fixed exchange rate? How does the effect on output in this economy, with fixed exchange rates, compare to the effect you found for the economy in part (a), with flexible exchange rates?

c. Explain how the exchange rate acts as an automatic stabilizer in an economy with flexible exchange rates.

13. **Demand for US assets, the dollar and the trade deficit**

This question explores how an increase in demand for US assets may have slowed the depreciation of the dollar that many economists believe is warranted by the large US trade deficit. Here, we modify the IS–LM–UIP framework (where UIP stands for uncovered interest parity) to analyse the effects of an increase in demand for US assets. Write the uncovered interest parity condition as

$$(1 + i_t) = (1 + i_t^*) \, E_t / E_{t+1}^e - x$$

where the parameter x represents factors affecting the relative demand for domestic assets. An increase in x means that investors are willing to hold domestic assets at a lower interest rate (given the foreign interest rate, and the current and expected exchange rates).

a. Solve the *UIP* condition for the current exchange rate, E_t.

b. Substitute the result from part (a) in the *IS* curve and construct the *UIP* diagram. As in the text, you may assume that P and P^* are constant and equal to one.

c. Suppose that as a result of a large trade deficit in the domestic economy, financial market participants believe that the domestic currency must depreciate in the future. Therefore, the expected exchange rate, E_{t+1}^e, falls. Show the effect of the fall in the expected exchange rate in the *IS–LM–UIP* diagram. What are the effects on the exchange rate and the trade balance? (*Hint*: in analysing the effect on the trade balance, remember why the *IS* curve shifted in the first place.)

d. Now suppose that the relative demand for domestic assets, *x*, increases. As a benchmark, suppose that the increase in *x* is exactly enough to return the *IS* curve to its original position, before the fall in the expected exchange rate. Show the combined effects of the fall in E_{t+1}^e and the increase in *x* in your *IS–LM–UIP* diagram. What are the ultimate effects on the exchange rate and the trade balance?

e. Based on your analysis, is it possible that an increase in demand for US assets could prevent the dollar from depreciating? Is it possible than an increase in demand for US assets could worsen the US trade balance. Explain your answers.

By the time you read this book, it is possible that relative demand for US assets could be weaker than it is at the time of this writing and that the dollar could be depreciating. Think about how you would use the framework of this problem to assess the current situation.

We invite you to visit the Blanchard page on the Prentice Hall website, at **www.prenhall.com/blanchard** for this chapter's World Wide Web exercises.

FURTHER READING

- A good discussion of the relation among trade deficits, budget deficits, private saving and investment is given in **Barry Bosworth**, *Saving and Investment in a Global Economy*, Brookings Institution, Washington, DC, 1993.

- A good discussion of the US trade deficit and its implications for the future is given in **William Cline**, *The United States as a Debtor Nation*, Peterson Institute, Washington, DC, 2005.

APPENDIX

Derivation of the Marshall–Lerner condition

Start from the definition of net exports:

$$NX \equiv X - IM/\varepsilon$$

Assume trade to be initially balanced, so that $NX = 0$ and $X = IM/\varepsilon$ or, equivalently, $\varepsilon X = IM$. The Marshall–Lerner condition is the condition under which a real depreciation, a decrease in ε, leads to an increase in net exports.

To derive this condition, first multiply both sides of the equation above by ε to get

$$\varepsilon NX = \varepsilon X - IM$$

Now consider a change in the real exchange rate of $\Delta\varepsilon$. The effect of the change in the real exchange rate on the left side of the equation is given by $(\Delta\varepsilon)NX + \varepsilon(\Delta NX)$. Note that, if trade is initially balanced, $NX = 0$, so the first term in this expression is equal to zero, and the effect of the change on the left side is simply given by $\varepsilon(\Delta NX)$. The effect of the change in the real exchange rate on the right side of the equation is given by $(\Delta\varepsilon) X + \varepsilon(\Delta X) - (\Delta IM)$. Putting the two sides together gives

$$\varepsilon(\Delta NX) = (\Delta\varepsilon) X + \varepsilon(\Delta X) - (\Delta IM)$$

Divide both sides by εX to get

$$\frac{\varepsilon(\Delta NX)}{\varepsilon X} = \frac{(\Delta\varepsilon)X}{\varepsilon X} + \frac{\varepsilon(\Delta X)}{\varepsilon X} - \frac{\Delta(IM)}{\varepsilon X}$$

Simplify and use the fact that, if trade is initially balanced, $\varepsilon X = IM$, to replace εX by IM in the last term on the right. This gives

$$\frac{\Delta NX}{X} = \frac{\Delta\varepsilon}{\varepsilon} + \frac{\Delta X}{X} - \frac{\Delta IM}{IM}$$

The change in the trade balance (as a ratio to exports) in response to a real depreciation is equal to the sum of three terms:

- The first term is equal to the proportional change in the real exchange rate. It is negative if there is a real depreciation.
- The second term is equal to the proportional change in exports. It is positive if there is a real depreciation.
- The third term is equal to minus the proportional change in the imports. It is positive if there is a real depreciation.

The Marshall–Lerner condition is the condition that the sum of these three terms be positive. If it is satisfied, a real depreciation leads to an improvement in the trade balance.

A numerical example will help here. Suppose that a 1% depreciation leads to a proportional increase in exports of 0.9% and to a proportional decrease in imports of 0.8%. (Econometric evidence on the relation of exports and imports to the real exchange rate suggest that these are indeed reasonable numbers.) In that case, the right-hand side of the equation is equal to −1% + 0.9% − (−0.8%) = 0.7%. Thus, the trade balance improves: the Marshall–Lerner condition is satisfied.

Chapter 19

EXCHANGE RATE REGIMES

In July 1944, representatives of 44 countries met in Bretton Woods, New Hampshire, to design a new international monetary and exchange rate system. The system they adopted was based on fixed exchange rates, with all member countries other than the USA fixing the price of their currency in terms of dollars. In 1973, a series of exchange rate crises brought an abrupt end to the system – and an end to what is now called 'the Bretton Woods period'. Since then, the world has been characterised by many exchange rate arrangements. Some countries operate under flexible exchange rates, some operate under fixed exchange rates and some go back and forth between regimes. At the end of the 1990s, a major exchange rate agreement was signed in Europe among a group of countries that decided to permanently fix their exchange rates by adopting a single currency, the euro. A few other countries joined the euro area, while others, most notably the UK and Denmark, did not. Which exchange rate regime to choose is one of the most debated issues in macroeconomics, a decision facing every country in the world.

This chapter discusses these issues:

- Section 19.1 looks at the medium run. It shows that, in sharp contrast to the results we derived for the short run in Chapter 18, an economy ends up with the same real exchange rate and output level in the medium run, regardless of whether it operates under fixed exchange rates or flexible exchange rates. This obviously does not make the exchange rate regime irrelevant – the short run matters very much – but it is an important extension and qualification to our previous analysis.

- Section 19.2 takes another look at fixed exchange rates and focuses on exchange rate crises. During a typical exchange rate crisis, a country operating under a fixed exchange rate is forced, often under dramatic conditions, to abandon its parity and to devalue. Such crises were behind the breakdown of the Bretton Woods system. They rocked the European Monetary System in the early 1990s and were a major element of the Asian Crisis of the late 1990s. It is important to understand why they happen and what they imply.

- Section 19.3 takes another look at flexible exchange rates and focuses on the behaviour of exchange rates under a flexible exchange rate regime. It shows that the behaviour of exchange rates and the relation of the exchange rate to monetary policy are, in fact, more complex than we assumed in Chapter 18. Large fluctuations in the exchange rate, and the difficulty of using monetary policy to affect the exchange rate, make a flexible exchange rate regime less attractive than it appeared to be in Chapter 18.

- Section 19.4 puts all these conclusions together and reviews the case for flexible or fixed rates. It discusses two recent and important developments: the move toward a common currency in Europe, and the move toward strong forms of fixed exchange rate regimes, from currency boards to dollarisation.

- Section 19.5 discusses what determines the decision of European countries that are out of the euro area to join or to keep out.

19.1 THE MEDIUM RUN

When we focused on the short run in Chapter 18, we drew a sharp contrast between the behaviour of an economy with flexible exchange rates (in Sections 18.1 to 18.4) and an economy with fixed exchange rates (in Section 8.5):

- Under flexible exchange rates, a country that needed to achieve a real depreciation – for example, to reduce its trade deficit or to get out of a recession – could do so by relying on an expansionary monetary policy to achieve both lower interest and a decrease in the exchange rate – a depreciation.
- Under fixed exchange rates, a country lost both of these instruments: by definition, its nominal exchange rate was fixed and thus could not be adjusted. Moreover, the fixed exchange rate and the interest parity condition implied that the country could not adjust its interest rate; the domestic interest rate had to remain equal to the foreign interest rate.

This appeared to make a flexible exchange rate regime much more attractive than a fixed exchange rate regime: why should a country give up two macroeconomic instruments? As we now shift focus from the short run to the medium run, you shall see that this earlier conclusion needs to be qualified. Although our conclusions about the short run were valid, we shall see that, in the medium run, the difference between the two regimes fades away. More specifically, in the medium run, the economy reaches the same real exchange rate and the same level of output, whether it operates under fixed or under flexible exchange rates.

The intuition for this result is actually easy to give. Recall the definition of the real exchange rate:

$$\varepsilon = \frac{EP}{P*}$$

The real exchange rate, ε, is equal to the nominal exchange rate, E (the price of domestic currency in terms of foreign currency), times the domestic price level, P, divided by the foreign price level, $P*$. There are, therefore, two ways in which the real exchange rate can adjust:

- Through a change in the nominal exchange rate, E – this can be done only under flexible exchange rates. And if we assume that the domestic price level, P, and the foreign price level, $P*$, do not change in the short run, it is the only way to adjust the real exchange rate in the short run.
- Through a change in the domestic price level, P, relative to the foreign price level $P*$ – in the medium run, this option is open even to a country operating under a fixed (nominal) exchange rate. And this is indeed what happens under fixed exchange rates: the adjustment takes place through the price level rather than through the nominal exchange rate.

Let us go through this argument step by step. To begin, let's derive the aggregate demand and aggregate supply relations for an open economy under a fixed exchange rate.

There are three ways in which a UK car can become cheaper relative to a German car: first, through a decrease in the pound price of the UK car. Second, through an increase in the euro price of the German car. Third, through a decrease in the nominal exchange rate – a decrease in the value of the pound in terms of euros.

Aggregate demand under fixed exchange rates

In an open economy with fixed exchange rates, we can write the aggregate demand relation as

$$Y = Y\left(\frac{\bar{E}P}{P^*}, G, T\right) \qquad\qquad [19.1]$$
$$(-, +, -)$$

Recall that the aggregate demand relation captures the effects of the price level on output. It is derived from equilibrium in goods and financial markets.

Output, Y, depends on the real exchange rate, $\bar{E}P/P^*$ ($\bar{E}$ denotes the fixed nominal exchange rate, and P and P^* denote the domestic and foreign price levels, respectively), government spending, G, and taxes, T. An increase in the real exchange rate – a real appreciation – leads to a decrease in output. An increase in government spending leads to an increase in output; an increase in taxes leads to a decrease in output.

The derivation of equation (19.1) is better left to an appendix at the end of this chapter. The intuition behind the equation is straightforward, however:

See equation (8.3).

Recall that, in a closed economy, the aggregate demand relation took the same form as equation (19.1), except for the presence of the real money stock, M/P, instead of the real exchange rate, $\bar{E}P/P^*$.

- The reason for the presence of M/P in a closed economy was the following: by controlling the money supply, the central bank could change the interest rate and affect output. In an open economy, and under fixed exchange rates and perfect capital mobility, the central bank can no longer change the interest rate – which is pinned down by the foreign interest rate. Put another way, under fixed exchange rates, the central bank gives up monetary policy as a policy instrument. This is why the money stock no longer appears in the aggregate demand relation.
- At the same time, the fact that the economy is open implies that we must include a variable that we did not include when we looked at the closed economy earlier: the real exchange rate, $\bar{E}P/P^*$. As we saw in Chapter 18, an increase in the real exchange rate leads to a decrease in the demand for domestic goods and thus a decrease in output. Conversely, a decrease in the real exchange rate leads to an increase in output.

Note that, just as in a closed economy, the aggregate demand relation (19.1) implies a negative relation between the price level and output. But, while the sign of the effect of the price level on output remains the same, the channel is very different:

- In a closed economy, the price level affects output through its effect on the real money stock and, in turn, its effect on the interest rate.

Aggregate demand relation in the open economy under fixed exchange rates: P increases ⇒ $\bar{E}P/P^*$ increases ⇒ Y decreases.

- In an open economy under fixed exchange rates, the price level affects output through its effect on the real exchange rate. Given the fixed nominal exchange rate, $\bar{E}$, and the foreign price level, P^*, an increase in the domestic price level, P, leads to an increase in the real exchange rate, $\bar{E}P/P^*$ – a real appreciation. This real appreciation leads to a decrease in the demand for domestic goods and, in turn, to a decrease in output. Put simply: an increase in the price level makes domestic goods more expensive, thus decreasing the demand for domestic goods and, in turn, decreasing output.

Equilibrium in the short run and in the medium run

The aggregate demand curve associated with equation (19.1) is drawn as the AD curve in Figure 19.1. It is downward-sloping: an increase in the price level decreases output. As always, the relation is drawn for given values of the other variables, in this case for given values of $\bar{E}$, P^*, G and T.

Recall that the aggregate supply relation captures the effects of output on the price level. It is derived from equilibrium in labour markets.

For the aggregate supply curve, we rely on the relation we derived in the core. Going back to the *aggregate supply relation* we derived in Chapter 9, equation (9.2),

$$P = P^e(1 + \mu)F\left(1 - \frac{Y}{L}, z\right) \qquad\qquad [19.2]$$

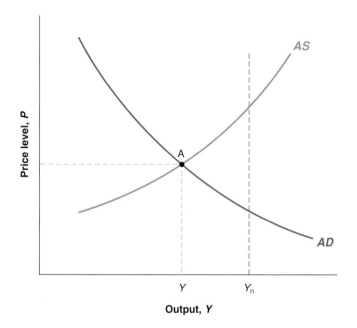

Figure 19.1

Aggregate demand and aggregate supply in an open economy under fixed exchange rates

An increase in the price level leads to a real appreciation and a decrease in output: the aggregate demand curve is downward sloping. An increase in output leads to an increase in the price level: the aggregate supply curve is upward sloping.

The price level, P, depends on the expected price level, P^e, and on the level of output, Y. Recall the two mechanisms at work:

- The expected price level matters because it affects nominal wages, which in turn affect the price level.

  ◄ Aggregate supply relation: Y increases $\Rightarrow P$ increases.

- Higher output matters because it leads to higher employment, which leads to lower unemployment, which leads to higher wages, which leads to a higher price level.

The aggregate supply curve is drawn as the AS curve in Figure 19.1 for a given value of the expected price level. It is upward-sloping: higher output leads to a higher price level.

The short-run equilibrium is given by the intersection of the aggregate demand curve and the aggregate supply curve, point A in Figure 19.1. As is the case in a closed economy, there is no reason why the short-run equilibrium level of output, Y, should be equal to the natural level of output, Y_n. As the figure is drawn, Y is smaller than Y_n, so output is below the natural level of output.

What happens over time? The basic answer is familiar from our earlier look at adjustment in a closed economy, and is shown in Figure 19.2. As long as output remains below the natural level of output, the aggregate supply shifts down. The reason: when output is below the natural level of output, the price level turns out to be lower than was expected. This leads wage setters to revise their expectation of the price level downward, leading to a lower price level at a given level of output – hence, the downward shift of the aggregate supply curve. So, starting from A, the economy moves over time along the aggregate demand curve until it reaches B. At B, output is equal to the natural level of output. The price level is lower than it was at A; by implication, the real exchange rate is lower than it was at A.

◄ Make sure you understand this step. If you need a refresher, return to Section 8.1.

In words: as long as output is below the natural level of output, the price level decreases. The decrease in the price level over time leads to a steady real depreciation. This real depreciation then leads to an increase in output until output has returned to its natural level.

In the medium run, despite the fact that the nominal exchange rate is fixed, the economy still achieves the real depreciation needed to return output to its natural level. This is an important qualification to the conclusions we reached in the previous chapter – where we were focusing only on the short run:

The result that the price level decreases along the path of adjustment comes from our assumption that the foreign price level is constant. If we had assumed instead that the foreign price level was increasing over time, what would be needed would be for the domestic price level to increase less than the foreign price level or, put another way, for domestic inflation to be lower than foreign inflation for some time.

- In the short run, a fixed nominal exchange rate implies a fixed real exchange rate.
- In the medium run, the real exchange rate can adjust even if the nominal exchange rate is fixed. This adjustment is achieved through movements in the price level.

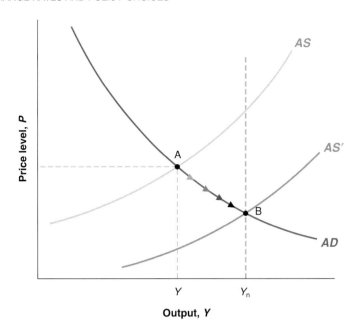

Figure 19.2

Adjustment under fixed exchange rates

The aggregate supply curve shifts down over time, leading to a decrease in the price level, to a real depreciation and to an increase in output. The process ends when output has returned to its natural level.

The case for and against a devaluation

The result that, even under fixed exchange rates, the economy returns to the natural level of output in the medium run is important. But it does not eliminate the fact that the process of adjustment may be long and painful. Output may remain too low and unemployment may remain too high for a long time.

Are there faster and better ways to return output to normal? The answer, within the model we have just developed, is a clear yes.

Suppose that the government decides, while keeping the fixed exchange rate regime, to allow for a one-time devaluation. For a given price level, a devaluation (a decrease in the nominal exchange rate) leads to a real depreciation (a decrease in the real exchange rate) and, therefore, to an increase in output. In other words, a devaluation shifts the aggregate demand curve to the right: output is higher at a given price level.

This has a straightforward implication: a devaluation of the right size can take the economy directly from Y to Y_n. This is shown in Figure 19.3. Suppose the economy is initially at A, the same point A as in Figure 19.2. The right size depreciation shifts the aggregate demand curve from AD to AD', moving the equilibrium from A to C. At C, output is equal to the natural level of output, Y_n, and the real exchange rate is the same as at B. (We know this because output is the same at points B and C. From equation (19.1), and without changes in G or T, this implies that the real exchange rate must also be the same.)

That a devaluation of the 'right size' can return output to the natural level of output right away sounds too good to be true – and, in reality, it is. Achieving the 'right size' devaluation – the devaluation that takes output to Y_n right away – is easier to achieve in a graph than in reality:

- In contrast to our simple aggregate demand relation [see equation (19.1)], the effects of the depreciation on output do not happen right away: as you saw in Chapter 18, the initial effects of a depreciation on output can be contractionary, as people pay more for imports, and the quantities of imports and exports have not adjusted yet.

See Section 18.3 on the J-curve. ➤ - Also, in contrast to our simple aggregate supply relation [see equation (19.2)], there is likely to be a direct effect of the devaluation on the price level. As the price of imported goods increases, the price of a consumption basket increases. This increase is likely to lead workers to ask for higher nominal wages, forcing firms to increase their prices as well.

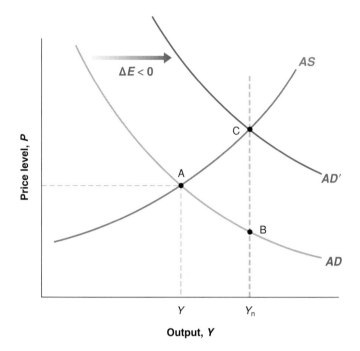

Figure 19.3

Adjustment with a devaluation

A devaluation of the right size can shift aggregate demand to the right, moving the economy to point C. At point C, output is back to the natural level of output.

But these complications do not affect the basic conclusion: a devaluation can hasten the return of output to its natural level. And so, whenever a country under fixed exchange rates faces either a large trade deficit or a severe recession, there is a lot of political pressure either to give up the fixed exchange rate regime altogether, or, at least, to have a one-time devaluation. Perhaps the most forceful presentation of this view was made more than 80 years ago by Keynes, who argued against Winston Churchill's decision to return the British pound in 1925 to its pre–First World War parity with gold. His arguments are presented in the Focus box 'The Return of Britain to the gold standard: Keynes versus Churchill'. Most economic historians believe that history proved Keynes right, and that over-valuation of the pound was one of the main reasons for Britain's poor economic performance after the First World War.

Those who oppose a shift to flexible exchange rates or who oppose a devaluation argue that there are good reasons to choose fixed exchange rates and that too much willingness to devalue defeats the purpose of adopting a fixed exchange rate regime in the first place. They argue that too much willingness on the part of governments to consider devaluations actually leads to an increased likelihood of exchange rate crises. To understand their arguments, we now turn to these crises, what triggers them and what their implications might be.

19.2 EXCHANGE RATE CRISES UNDER FIXED EXCHANGE RATES

Suppose a country has chosen to operate under a fixed exchange rate. Suppose also that financial investors start believing that there may soon be an exchange rate adjustment – either a devaluation or a shift to a flexible exchange rate regime accompanied by a depreciation. We just saw why this might be the case:

- The real exchange rate may be too high. Or, put another way, the domestic currency may be over-valued. In this case, a real depreciation is called for. Although this could be achieved in the medium run without a devaluation, financial investors might conclude that the government will take the quickest way out – and devalue.

Such an overvaluation is likely to happen in a country that pegs its nominal exchange rate to the currency of a country with lower inflation. Higher relative inflation implies a steadily increasing price of domestic goods relative to foreign goods, a steady real appreciation, and so a steady worsening of the trade position. As time passes, the need for an adjustment of the real exchange rate increases, and financial investors become more and more nervous. They start thinking that a devaluation might be coming.

Because it is more convenient, we use the approximation, equation (6.4), rather than the original interest parity condition, equation (6.2).

- Internal conditions may call for a decrease in the domestic interest rate. As we have seen, a decrease in the domestic interest rate cannot be achieved under fixed exchange rates, but it can be achieved if the country is willing to shift to a flexible exchange rate regime. If a country lets the exchange rate float and then decreases its domestic interest rate, we know from Chapter 18 that this will trigger a decrease in the nominal exchange rate – a nominal depreciation.

FOCUS
The return of Britain to the gold standard: Keynes versus Churchill

In 1925, Britain decided to return to the **gold standard**. The gold standard was a system in which each country fixed the price of its currency in terms of gold and stood ready to exchange gold for currency at the stated parity. This system implied fixed exchange rates between countries.

The gold standard had been in place from 1870 until the First World War. Because of the need to finance the war, and to do so in part by money creation, Britain suspended the gold standard in 1914. In 1925, Winston Churchill, then Britain's Chancellor of the Exchequer (the English equivalent of Secretary of the Treasury in the USA), decided to return to the gold standard and to return to it at the pre-war parity – that is, at the pre-war value of the pound in terms of gold. But because prices had increased faster in Britain than in many of its trading partners, returning to the pre-war parity implied a large real appreciation: at the same nominal exchange rate as before the war, British goods were now relatively more expensive relative to foreign goods. (Go back to the definition of the real exchange rate, $\varepsilon = EP/P^*$: the price level in Britain, P, had increased more than the foreign price level, P^*. At a given nominal exchange rate, E, this implied that ε was higher and that Britain suffered from a real appreciation.)

Keynes severely criticised the decision to return to the pre-war parity. In *The Economic Consequences of Mr Churchill*, a book he published in 1925, Keynes argued that if Britain were going to return to the gold standard, it should have done so at a lower price of currency in terms of gold – that is, at a lower nominal exchange rate than the pre-war nominal exchange rate. In a newspaper article, he articulated his views as follows:

There remains, however, the objection to which I have never ceased to attach importance, against the return to gold in actual present conditions in view of the possible consequences on the state of trade and employment. I believe that our price level is too high, if it is converted to gold at the par of exchange, in relation to gold prices elsewhere; and if we consider the prices of those articles only which are not the subject of international trade, and of services, i.e. wages, we shall find that these are materially too high – not less than 5 per cent, and probably 10 per cent. Thus, unless the situation is saved by a rise of prices elsewhere, the Chancellor is committing us to a policy of forcing down money wages by perhaps 2 shillings in the Pound.

I do not believe that this can be achieved without the gravest danger to industrial profits and industrial peace. I would much rather leave the gold value of our currency where it was some months ago than embark on a struggle with every trade union in the country to reduce money wages. It seems wiser and simpler and saner to leave the currency to find its own level for some time longer rather than force a situation where employers are faced with the alternative of closing down or of lowering wages, cost what the struggle may.

For this reason, I remain of the opinion that the Chancellor of the Exchequer has done an ill-judged thing – ill-judged because we are running the risk for no adequate reward if all goes well.

Keynes's prediction turned out to be right. While other countries were growing, Britain remained in recession for the rest of the decade. Most economic historians attribute a good part of the blame to the initial overvaluation.

Source: *The Nation and Athenaeum*, 2 May 1925.

As soon as financial markets believe a devaluation may be coming, maintaining the exchange rate requires an increase – often a large one – in the domestic interest rate. To see this, return to the interest parity condition we derived in Chapter 6:

$$i_t = i_t^* - \frac{(E_{t+1}^e - E_t)}{E_t} \qquad [19.3]$$

In Chapter 6, we interpreted this equation as a relation between the one-year domestic and foreign nominal interest rates, the current exchange rate and the expected exchange rate a year hence, but the choice of one year as the period was arbitrary. The relation holds over a day, a week or a month. If financial markets expect the exchange rate to be 2% lower one month from now, they will hold domestic bonds only if the one-month domestic interest rate exceeds the one-month foreign interest rate by 2% (or, if we express interest rates at an annual rate, if the annual domestic interest rate exceeds the annual foreign interest rate by $2\% \times 12 = 24\%$).

Under fixed exchange rates, the current exchange rate, E_t, is set at some level, say $E_t = \bar{E}$. If markets expect that the parity will be maintained over the period, then $E_{t+1}^e = \bar{E}$, and the interest parity condition simply states that the domestic and the foreign interest rates must be equal.

Suppose, however, that participants in financial markets start anticipating a devaluation – a decrease in the exchange rate. Suppose they believe that, over the coming month, there is a 75% chance the parity will be maintained and a 25% chance there will be a 20% devaluation. The term $(E_{t+1}^e - E_t)/E_t$ in the interest parity equation (19.3), which we assumed equal to 0 earlier, now equals $0.75 \times 0\% + 0.25 \times (-20\%) = -5\%$ (that is, a 75% chance of no change plus a 25% chance of a devaluation of 20%).

This implies that, if the central bank wants to maintain the existing parity, it must now set a monthly interest rate 5% higher than before – 60% higher at an annual rate (12 months $\times$ 5% per month) is the interest differential needed to convince investors to hold domestic bonds rather than foreign bonds! Any smaller interest differential, and investors will not want to hold domestic bonds.

What choices, then, do the government and the central bank have?

- First, the government and the central bank can try to convince markets that they have no intention of devaluing. This is always the first line of defence: communiqués are issued and prime ministers go on TV to reiterate their absolute commitment to the existing parity. But words are cheap, and they rarely convince financial investors.

- Second, the central bank can increase the interest rate but by less than would be needed to satisfy equation (19.3) – in our example, by less than 60%. Although domestic interest rates are high, they are not high enough to fully compensate for the perceived risk of devaluation. This action typically leads to a large capital outflow because financial investors still prefer to get out of domestic bonds into foreign bonds. They sell domestic bonds, getting the proceeds in domestic currency. They then go to the foreign exchange market to sell domestic currency for foreign currency in order to buy foreign bonds. If the central bank did not intervene in the foreign exchange market, the large sales of domestic currency for foreign currency would lead to a depreciation. If it wants to maintain the exchange rate, the central bank must therefore stand ready to buy domestic currency and sell foreign currency at the current exchange rate. In doing so, it often loses most of its reserves of foreign currency.

- Eventually – after a few hours or a few weeks – the choice for the central bank becomes either to increase the interest rate enough to satisfy equation (19.3), or to validate the market's expectations and devalue. Setting a very high short-term domestic interest rate can have a devastating effect on demand and on output – no firm wants to invest and no consumer wants to borrow when interest rates are very high. This course of action makes sense only if (1) the perceived probability of a devaluation is small, so the interest rate does not have to be too high, and (2) the government believes markets will soon become

> ◀ In most countries, the government is formally in charge of choosing the parity, and the central bank is formally in charge of maintaining it. In practice, choosing and maintaining the parity are joint responsibilities of the government and the central bank.

> ◀ In the summer of 1998, Boris Yeltsin announced that the Russian government had no intention of devaluing the rouble. Two weeks later, the rouble collapsed.

FOCUS
The 1992 EMS crisis

An example of the problems we discussed in Section 19.2 is the exchange rate crisis that shook the European Monetary System (EMS) in the early 1990s.

At the start of the 1990s, the EMS appeared to work well. The EMS, which had started in 1979, was an exchange rate system based on fixed parities with bands: each member country (among them, France, Germany, Italy and, beginning in 1990, the UK) had to maintain its exchange rate vis-à-vis all other member countries within narrow bands. The first few years had been rocky, with many realignments – adjustment of parities – among member countries. From 1987–1992, however, there were only two realignments, and there was increasing talk about narrowing the bands further and even moving to the next stage – to the adoption of a common currency.

In 1992, however, financial markets became increasingly convinced that more realignments were soon to come. The reason was one we have already seen in Chapter 18 – namely, the macroeconomic implications of Germany's reunification. Because of the pressure on demand coming from reunification, the Bundesbank (the German central bank) was maintaining high interest rates to avoid too large an increase in output and an increase in inflation in Germany. While Germany's EMS partners needed lower interest rates to reduce the growing unemployment problem, they had to match the German interest rates to maintain their EMS parities. To financial markets, the position of Germany's EMS partners looked increasingly untenable. Lower interest rates outside Germany, and thus devaluations of many currencies vis-à-vis the deutschemark, appeared increasingly likely.

Throughout 1992, the perceived probability of a devaluation forced a number of EMS countries to maintain higher nominal interest rates than even those in Germany. Still, the first major crisis did not come until September 1992.

In early September 1992, the belief that a number of countries were soon going to devalue led to speculative attacks on a number of currencies, with financial investors selling in anticipation of an oncoming devaluation. All the lines of defence described earlier were used by the monetary authorities and the governments of the countries under attack. First, solemn communiqués were issued, but with no discernible effect. Then, interest rates were increased. For example, Sweden's overnight interest rate (the rate for lending and borrowing overnight) increased to 500% (expressed at an annual rate)! But interest rates were not increased by enough to prevent capital outflows and large losses of foreign exchange reserves by the central banks under pressure.

At that point, different countries took different courses of action: Spain devalued its exchange rate. Italy and the UK suspended their participation in the EMS. France decided to tough it out through higher interest rates until the storm was over. Figure 19.4 shows the evolution of the exchange rates vis-à-vis the deutschemark for a number of European countries from January 1992 to December 1993: you can clearly see the effects of the September 1992 crisis and the ensuing depreciations/devaluations.

By the end of September, investors, by and large, believed that no further devaluations were imminent. Some countries were no longer in the EMS. Others had devalued but remained in the EMS, and those that had maintained their parity had shown their determination to stay in the EMS, even if it meant very high interest rates. But the underlying problem – the high German interest rates – was still present, and it was only a matter of time before the next crisis started. In November 1992, further

convinced that no devaluation is coming, allowing domestic interest rates to decrease. Otherwise, the only option is to devalue. (All these steps were very much in evidence during the exchange rate crisis that affected much of Western Europe in 1992. See the Focus box 'The 1992 EMS crisis'.)

To summarise, expectations that a devaluation may be coming can trigger an exchange rate crisis. Faced with such expectations, the government has two options:

● Give in and devalue.
● Fight and maintain the parity, at the cost of very high interest rates and a potential recession. Fighting may not work anyway: the recession may force the government to change policy later on or force the government out of office.

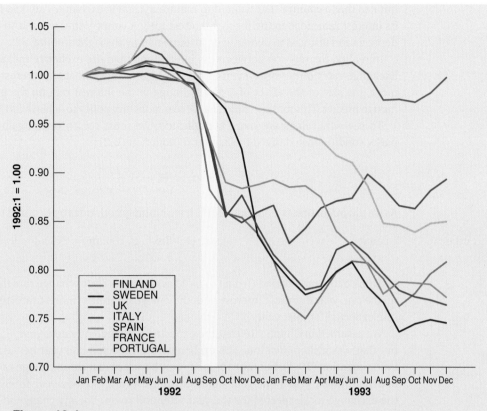

Figure 19.4

Exchange rates of selected European countries relative to the deutschmark, January 1992–December 1993

speculation forced a devaluation of the Spanish peseta, the Portuguese escudo and the Swedish krona. The peseta and the escudo were further devalued in May 1993. In July 1993, after yet another large speculative attack, EMS countries decided to adopt large fluctuation bands ($\pm 15\%$) around central parities, in effect moving to a system that allowed for very large exchange rate fluctuations. This system with wider bands was kept until the adoption of a common currency, the euro, in January 1999.

To summarise: the 1992 EMS crisis resulted from the perception by financial markets that the high interest rates forced by Germany upon its partners under the rules of the EMS were becoming very costly. The belief that some countries might want to devalue or get out of the EMS led investors to ask for even higher interest rates, making it even more costly for those countries to maintain their parity. In the end, some countries could not bear the cost; some devalued and some dropped out. Others remained in the system – but at a substantial cost in terms of output. (For example, average growth in France from 1990–1996 was 1.2%, compared to 2.3% for Germany over the same period.)

An interesting twist here is that a devaluation can occur even if the belief that a devaluation was coming was initially groundless. In other words, even if the government initially has no intention of devaluing, it might be forced to do so if financial markets believe that it will devalue: the cost of maintaining the parity would be a long period of high interest rates and a recession; the government might prefer to devalue instead.

19.3 EXCHANGE RATE MOVEMENTS UNDER FLEXIBLE EXCHANGE RATES

In the model we developed in Chapter 18, there was a simple relation between the interest rate and the exchange rate: the lower the interest rate, the lower the exchange rate. This implied that a country that wanted to maintain a stable exchange rate just had to maintain its interest rate close to the foreign interest rate. A country that wanted to achieve a given depreciation just had to decrease its interest rate by the right amount.

In reality, the relation between the interest rate and the exchange rate is not so simple. Exchange rates often move even in the absence of movements in interest rates. Furthermore, the size of the effect of a given change in the interest rate on the exchange rate is hard to predict. This makes it much harder for monetary policy to achieve its desired outcome.

To see why things are more complicated, we must return once again to the interest parity condition we derived in Chapter 6 [equation (6.2)]:

$$(1 + i_t) = (1 + i_t^*)\left(\frac{E_t}{E_{t+1}^e}\right)$$

As we did in Chapter 6 [equation (6.11)], we multiply both sides by E_{t+1}^e, and reorganise to get

$$E_t = \frac{1 + i_t}{1 + i_t^*} E_{t+1}^e \qquad [19.4]$$

Think of the time period (from t to $t + 1$) as one year. The exchange rate this year depends on the one-year domestic interest rate, the one-year foreign interest rate and the exchange rate expected for next year.

We assumed in Chapter 18 that the expected exchange rate next year, E_{t+1}^e was constant, but that was a simplification. The exchange rate expected one year hence is not constant. Using equation (19.4), but now for next year, it is clear that the exchange rate next year will depend on next year's one-year domestic interest rate, the one-year foreign interest rate, the exchange rate expected for the year after and so on. So, any change in expectations of *current and future* domestic and foreign interest rates, as well as changes in the expected exchange rate in the far future, will affect the exchange rate today.

Let's explore this more closely. Write equation (19.4) for year $t + 1$ rather than for year t:

$$E_{t+1} = \frac{1 + i_{t+1}}{1 + i_{t+1}^*} E_{t+2}^e$$

The exchange rate in year $t + 1$ depends on the domestic interest rate and the foreign interest rate for year $t + 1$, as well as on the expected future exchange rate in year $t + 2$. So, the expectation of the exchange rate in year $t + 1$, held as of year t, is given by

$$E_{t+1}^e = \frac{1 + i_{t+1}^e}{1 + i_{t+1}^{*e}} E_{t+2}^e$$

Replacing E_{t+1}^e in equation (19.4) with this expression gives

$$E_t = \frac{(1 + i_t)(1 + i_{t+1}^e)}{(1 + i_t^*)(1 + i_{t+1}^{*e})} E_{t+2}^e$$

The current exchange rate depends on this year's domestic and foreign interest rates, on next year's expected domestic and foreign interest rates, and on the expected exchange rate two years from now. Continuing to solve forward in time in the same way (by replacing E_{t+2}^e, E_{t+3}^e and so on until, say, year $t + n$) we get

$$E_t = \frac{(1 + i_t)(1 + i_{t+1}^e) \ldots (1 + i_{t+n}^e)}{(1 + i_t^*)(1 + i_{t+1}^{*e}) \ldots (1 + i_{t+1}^{*e})} E_{t+n+1}^e \qquad [19.5]$$

Suppose we take n to be large, say ten years (equation (19.5) holds for any value of n). This relation tells us that the current exchange rate depends on two sets of factors:

● Current and expected domestic and foreign interest rates for each year over the next ten years.
● The expected exchange rate ten years from now.

For some purposes, it is useful to go further and derive a relation between current and expected future domestic and foreign *real* interest rates, the current *real* exchange rate and the expected future *real* exchange rate. This is done in an appendix to this chapter. (The derivation is not much fun, but it is a useful way of brushing up on the relations between real and nominal interest rates and between real and nominal exchange rates.) Equation (19.5) is sufficient, however, to make the three points we want to make here.

Exchange rates and the current account

Any factor that moves the expected future exchange rate, E_{t+n}^e, moves the current exchange rate, E_t. Indeed, if the domestic interest rate and the foreign interest rate are expected to be the same in both countries from t to $t + n$, the fraction on the right in equation (19.5) is equal to 1, so the relation reduces to $E_t = E_{t+n}^e$. In words: the effect of any change in the expected future exchange rate on the current exchange rate is one-for-one.

If we think of n as large (say ten years or more), we can think of E_{t+n}^e as the exchange rate required to achieve current account balance in the medium or long run: countries cannot borrow – run a current account deficit – forever and will not want to lend – run a current account surplus – forever either. Thus, any news that affects forecasts of the current account balance in the future is likely to have an effect on the expected future exchange rate and, in turn, on the exchange rate today. For example, the announcement of a larger-than-expected trade deficit may lead investors to conclude that a depreciation will eventually be needed to reestablish trade balance. Thus, E_{t+n}^e will decrease, leading in turn to a decrease in E_t today.

◄ News about the current account is likely to affect the exchange rate.

Exchange rates and current and future interest rates

Any factor that moves current or expected future domestic or foreign interest rates between year t and year $t + n$ moves the current exchange rate, too. For example, given foreign interest rates, an increase in current or expected future domestic interest rates leads to an increase in E_t – an appreciation.

◄ News about current and future domestic and foreign interest rates is likely to affect the exchange rate.

This implies that any variable which causes investors to change their expectations of future interest rates will lead to a change in the exchange rate today. For example, the 'dance of the dollar' in the 1980s we discussed in earlier chapters – the sharp appreciation of the dollar in the first half of the decade, followed by an equally sharp depreciation later – can be largely explained by the movement in current and expected future US interest rates relative to interest rates in the rest of the world during that period. During the first half of the 1980s, tight monetary policy and expansionary fiscal policy combined to increase US short-term and long-term interest rates, with the increase in long-term rates reflecting anticipations of high short-term interest rates in the future. This increase in both current and expected future interest rates was, in turn, the main cause of the dollar appreciation. Both fiscal and monetary policy were reversed in the second half of the decade, leading to lower US interest rates and a depreciation of the dollar.

◄ For more on the relation between long-term interest rates and current and expected future short-term interest rates, go back to Chapter 15.

Exchange rate volatility

The third implication follows from the first two. In reality, and in contrast to our analysis in Chapter 18, the relation between the interest rate, i_t, and the exchange rate, E_t, is all but mechanical. When the central bank cuts the interest rate, financial markets have to assess whether this action signals a major shift in monetary policy and the cut in the interest rate is just the first of many such cuts, or whether this cut is just a temporary movement in interest rates. Announcements by the central bank may not be very useful: the central bank itself may not even know what it will do in the future. Typically, it will be reacting to early signals, which may be reversed later. Investors also have to assess how foreign central banks will react – whether they will stay put or follow suit and cut their own interest rates. All this makes it difficult to predict what the effect of the change in the interest rate will be on the exchange rate.

Let's be more concrete. Go back to equation (19.5). Assume that $E_{t+n}^e = 1$. Assume that current and expected future domestic interest rates and current and expected future foreign interest rates are all equal to 5%. The current exchange rate is then given by

$$E_t = \frac{(1.05)^n}{(1.05)^n} 1 = 1$$

This may remind you of our discussion ➤ in Chapter 15 of how monetary policy affects stock prices. This is more than a coincidence: like stock prices, the exchange rate depends very much on expectations of variables far into the future. How expectations change in response to a change in a current variable (here, the interest rate) very much determines the outcome.

Now consider a monetary expansion that decreases the current domestic interest rate, i_t, from 5% to 3%. Will this lead to a decrease in E_t – to a depreciation – and if so by how much? The answer: it depends.

Suppose the interest rate is expected to be lower for just one year, so the $n - 1$ expected future interest rates remain unchanged. The current exchange rate then decreases to

$$E_t = \frac{(1.03)(1.05)^{n-1}}{(1.05)^n} = \frac{1.03}{1.05} = 0.98$$

The expansionary monetary policy leads to a decrease in the exchange rate – a depreciation – of only 2%.

Suppose instead that, when the current interest rate declines from 5% to 3%, investors expect the decline to last for five years (so $i_{t+4} = \ldots = i_{t+1} = i_t = 3\%$). The exchange rate then decreases to

$$E_t = \frac{(1.03)^5(1.05)^{n-5}}{(1.05)^n} = \frac{(1.03)^5}{(1.05)^5} = 0.90$$

The expansionary monetary policy now leads to a decrease in the exchange rate – a depreciation – of 10%, a much larger effect.

You can surely think of yet other outcomes. Suppose investors anticipated that the central bank was going to decrease interest rates, and the actual decrease turns out to be smaller than they anticipated. In this case, the investors will revise their expectations of future nominal interest rates *upward*, leading to an appreciation rather than a depreciation of the currency.

When, at the end of the Bretton Woods period, countries moved from fixed exchange rates to flexible exchange rates, most economists had expected that exchange rates would be stable. The large fluctuations in exchange rates that followed – and have continued to this day – came as a surprise. For some time, these fluctuations were thought to be the result of irrational speculation in foreign exchange markets. It was not until the mid-1970s that economists realised that these large movements could be explained, as we have explained them here, by the rational reaction of financial markets to news about future interest rates and the future exchange rate. This has an important implication: a country that decides to operate under flexible exchange rates must accept the fact that it will be exposed to substantial exchange rate fluctuations over time.

19.4 CHOOSING BETWEEN EXCHANGE RATE REGIMES

Let us now return to the question that motivates this chapter: should countries choose flexible exchange rates or fixed exchange rates? Are there circumstances under which flexible rates dominate and others under which fixed rates dominate?

Much of what we have seen in this chapter and Chapter 18 would seem to favour flexible exchange rates:

● Section 19.1 argues that the exchange rate regime may not matter in the medium run. But it does still matter in the short run. In the short run, countries that operate under fixed exchange rates and perfect capital mobility give up two macroeconomic instruments:

the interest rate and the exchange rate. This not only reduces their ability to respond to shocks, but can also lead to exchange rate crises.

- Section 19.2 argues that, in a country with fixed exchange rates, the anticipation of a devaluation leads investors to ask for very high interest rates. This in turn makes the economic situation worse and puts more pressure on the country to devalue. This is another argument against fixed exchange rates.
- Section 19.3 introduces one argument against flexible exchange rates – namely that, under flexible exchange rates, the exchange rate is likely to fluctuate a lot and be difficult to control through monetary policy.

On balance, it would therefore appear that, from a macroeconomic viewpoint, flexible exchange rates dominate fixed exchange rates. This indeed appears to be the consensus that has emerged among economists and policy makers. The consensus goes like this: in general, flexible exchange rates are preferable. There are, however, two exceptions: first, when the central bank cannot be trusted to follow a responsible monetary policy under flexible exchange rates, a strong form of fixed exchange rates, such as a currency board or dollarisation, may provide a solution. Second, when a group of countries is already tightly integrated, a common currency may be the right solution.

Let's discuss in turn each of these two exceptions.

Hard pegs, currency boards and dollarisation

The second case for fixed exchange rates is very different from the first. It is based on the argument that there may be times when a country might want to limit its ability to use monetary policy. We shall look at this argument in more detail in Chapter 22, where we look at the dynamics of hyperinflation, and in Chapter 24, where we look at monetary policy in general. The essence of the argument is simple: look at a country that has had very high inflation in the recent past – perhaps because it was unable to finance its budget deficit by any means other than through money creation, resulting in high money growth and high inflation. Suppose the country decides to reduce money growth and inflation. One way of convincing financial markets that it is serious about doing this is to fix its exchange rate: the need to use the money supply to maintain the parity then ties the hands of the monetary authority.

To the extent that financial markets expect the parity to be maintained, they will stop worrying about money growth being used to finance the budget deficit.

Note the qualifier 'to the extent that financial markets expect the parity to be maintained'. Fixing the exchange rate is not a magic solution. The country also needs to convince financial investors that not only is the exchange rate fixed today, but it will remain fixed in the future. There are two ways it can do so:

- It can make the fixed exchange rate be part of a more general macroeconomic package. Fixing the exchange rate while continuing to run a large budget deficit will only convince financial markets that money growth will start again and that a devaluation is soon to come.

  > When Israel was suffering from high inflation in the 1980s, an Israeli finance minister proposed such a measure as part of a stabilisation programme. His proposal was perceived as an attack on the sovereignty of Israel, and he was quickly fired.

- It can make it symbolically or technically harder to change the parity, an approach known as a **hard peg**.

An extreme form of a hard peg is simply to replace the domestic currency with a foreign currency. Because the foreign currency chosen is typically the dollar, this is known as **dollarisation**. Few countries are willing, however, to give up their currency and adopt the currency of another country. A less extreme way is the use of a **currency board**. Under a currency board, a central bank stands ready to exchange foreign currency for domestic currency at the official exchange rate set by the government; furthermore, the bank cannot engage in open market operations – that is, buy or sell government bonds.

Perhaps the best-known example of a currency board is that adopted by Argentina in 1991, but abandoned in a crisis at the end of 2001. The story is told in the Focus box

FOCUS
Argentina's currency board

When Carlos Menem became president of Argentina in 1989, he inherited an economic mess. Inflation was running at more than 30% per month. Output growth was negative.

Menem and his economy minister, Domingo Cavallo, quickly came to the conclusion that, under these circumstances, the only way to bring money growth – and, by implication, inflation – under control was to peg the peso (Argentina's currency) to the dollar and to do this through a very hard peg. So, in 1991, Cavallo announced that Argentina would adopt a currency board. The central bank would stand ready to exchange pesos for dollars, on demand. Furthermore, it would do so at the highly symbolic rate of 1 dollar for 1 peso.

The creation of a currency board and the choice of a symbolic exchange rate had the same objective: to convince investors that the government was serious about the peg and to make it more difficult for future governments to give up the parity and devalue. By making the fixed exchange rate more credible in this way, the government hoped to decrease the risk of a foreign exchange crisis.

For a while, the currency board appeared to work extremely well. Inflation, which had exceeded 2300% in 1990, was down to 4% by 1994! This was clearly the result of the tight constraints the currency board put on money growth. Even more impressive, this large drop in inflation was accompanied by strong output growth. Output growth averaged 5% per year from 1991–1999.

Beginning in 1999, however, growth turned negative, and Argentina went into a long and deep recession. Was the recession due to the currency board? Yes and no.

- Throughout the second half of the 1990s, the dollar steadily appreciated relative to other major world currencies. Because the peso was pegged to the dollar, the peso also appreciated. By the late 1990s, it was clear that the peso was over-valued, leading to a decrease in demand for goods from Argentina, a decline in output and an increase in the trade deficit.

- Was the currency board fully responsible for the recession? No. There were other causes. But the currency board made it much harder to fight the recession. Lower interest rates and a depreciation of the peso would have helped the economy recover, but under the currency board, this was not an option.

In 2001, the economic crisis turned into a financial and an exchange rate crisis, along the lines described in Section 19.2:

'Argentina's currency board'. Economists differ on what conclusions one should draw from what happened in Argentina. Some conclude that currency boards are not *hard* enough: they do not prevent exchange rate crises. So, if a country decides to adopt a fixed exchange rate, it should go all the way and dollarise. Others conclude that adopting a fixed exchange rate is a bad idea. If currency boards are used at all, they should be used only for a short period of time, until the central bank has re-established its credibility and the country returns to a floating exchange rate regime.

Common currency areas

Looking around the world, one sees many examples of movement toward multinational currencies. In such cases, a group of countries creates a new currency and a new joint central bank. This kind of arrangement applies to the euro zone, where 15 countries have adopted a single currency. There are important arrangement also outside Europe. Six West African states created a new common currency for the region in 2003, and 11 members of the Southern African Development Community are debating whether to adopt the dollar or to create an independent monetary union possibly anchored to the South African rand. Six oil-producing countries (Saudi Arabia, United Arab Emirates, Bahrain, Oman, Qatar and Kuwait) have declared their intention to form a currency union by 2010.

- Because of the recession, Argentina's fiscal deficit had increased, leading to an increase in government debt. Worried that the government might default on its debt, financial investors started asking for very high interest rates on government bonds, making the fiscal deficit even larger and, by doing so, further increasing the risk of default.
- Worried that Argentina would abandon the currency board and devalue in order to fight the recession, investors started asking for very high interest rates in pesos, making it more costly for the government to sustain the parity with the dollar and so making it more likely that the currency board would indeed be abandoned.

In December 2001, the government defaulted on part of its debt. In early 2002, it gave up the currency board and let the peso float. The peso sharply depreciated, reaching 3.75 pesos for 1 dollar by June 2002. Many people and firms, given their earlier confidence in the peg, had borrowed in dollars; they found themselves with a large increase in the value of their dollar debts in terms of pesos. Many firms went bankrupt. The banking system collapsed. Despite the sharp real depreciation, which should have helped exports, GDP in Argentina fell by 11% in 2002, and unemployment increased to nearly 20%. In 2003, output growth turned positive, and it has been consistently high since – exceeding 8% per year – and unemployment has decreased. But it took until 2005 for GDP to reach its 1998 level again.

Does this mean that the currency board was a bad idea? Economists still disagree:

- Some economists argue that it was a good idea but that it did not go far enough. They argue that Argentina should have simply dollarised – that is, adopted the dollar outright as its currency – and eliminated the peso altogether. Eliminating the domestic currency would have eliminated the risk of a devaluation. The lesson, they argue, is that even a currency board does not provide a sufficiently hard peg for the exchange rate. Only dollarisation will do.
- Other (indeed, most) economists argue that the currency board might have been a good idea at the start, but that it should not have been kept in place for so long. Once inflation was under control, Argentina should have moved from a currency board to a floating exchange rate regime. The problem is that Argentina kept the fixed parity with the dollar for too long, to the point where the peso was over-valued, and an exchange rate crisis was inevitable.

The debate is likely to go on. Meanwhile, Argentina is reconstructing its economy.

Note: For a fascinating, fun and strongly opinionated book about Argentina's crisis, read Paul Blustein, *And the Money Kept Rolling In (and Out). Wall Street, the IMF, and the Bankrupting of Argentina*, New York, Public Affairs, 2005.

The Eastern Caribbean Currency Area (ECCA) and the CFA zone in Africa are intermediate between the a currency union and a hard peg. In both cases, the countries have a joint currency and a joint central bank. However, the ECCA currency (Caribbean dollar) has been linked since 1976 to the US dollar (and, before that, to the British pound), and the CFA franc has been tied (except for one devaluation) to the French franc (and now to the euro).

Countries that operate under a fixed exchange rate regime are constrained to all have the same interest rate. But how costly is that constraint? If the countries face roughly the same macroeconomic problems and the same shocks, they will have chosen similar policies in the first place. Forcing them to have the same monetary policy may not be much of a constraint.

This argument was first explored by Robert Mundell, who looked at the conditions under which a set of countries might want to operate under fixed exchange rates or even adopt a common currency. For countries to constitute an **optimal currency area**, Mundell argued, they need to satisfy one of two conditions:

> This is the same Mundell who put together the *IS–LM* model we introduced in Chapter 6 and developed in Chapter 18.

- The countries have to experience similar shocks. We just saw the rationale for this: if they experience similar shocks, then they would have chosen roughly the same monetary policy anyway.
- If the countries experience different shocks, they must have high factor mobility. For example, if workers are willing to move from countries that are doing poorly to countries

that are doing well, factor mobility rather than macroeconomic policy can allow countries to adjust to shocks. When the unemployment rate is high in a country, workers leave that country to take jobs elsewhere, and the unemployment rate in that country decreases back to normal. If the unemployment rate is low, workers come to the country, and the unemployment rate in the country increases back to normal. The exchange rate is not needed.

Each US state could have its own currency that freely floated against other state currencies. But this is not the way things are: the USA is a common currency area, with one currency, the US dollar (whether it is optimal is an issue we will mention in Chapter 26).

Following Mundell's analysis, most economists believe, for example, that the common currency area composed of the 50 states of the USA is close to an optimal currency area. True, the first condition is not satisfied: individual states suffer from different shocks. California is more affected by shifts in demand from Asia than the rest of the USA, Texas is more affected by what happens to the price of oil and so on. But the second condition is largely satisfied. There is considerable labour mobility across states in the USA. When a state does poorly, workers leave that state. When it does well, workers come to that state. State unemployment rates quickly return to normal not because of state-level macroeconomic policy but because of labour mobility.

Clearly, there are also many advantages of using a common currency. For firms and consumers within the USA, the benefits of having a common currency are obvious; imagine how complicated life would be if you had to change currency every time you crossed a state line. The benefits go beyond these lower transaction costs. When prices are quoted in the same currency, it becomes much easier for buyers to compare prices, and competition between firms increases, benefiting consumers. Given these benefits and the limited macroeconomic costs, it makes good sense for the USA to have a single currency.

In adopting the euro, Europe has made the same choice as the USA. When the process of conversion from national currencies to the euro ended in early 2002, the euro became the common currency for 11 European countries. The number of euro countries has now increased to 15. Is the economic argument for this new common currency area as compelling as it is for the USA?

There is little question that a common currency will yield for Europe many of the same benefits that it has for the USA. A report by the European Commission estimates that the elimination of foreign exchange transactions within the euro area led to a reduction in costs of 0.5% of the combined GDP of these countries. There are also clear signs that the use of a common currency has increased competition. When shopping for cars, for example, European consumers now search for the lowest euro price anywhere in the euro area. This has led to a decline in the price of cars in a number of countries.

There is, however, less agreement on whether Europe constitutes an optimal common currency area. This is because neither of the two Mundell conditions appears to be satisfied. Although the future may be different, European countries have experienced very different shocks in the past. Recall our discussion of Germany's reunification and how differently it affected Germany and the other European countries. Furthermore, labour mobility is very low in Europe, and it is likely to remain low. Workers move much less *within* European countries than they do within the USA. Because of language and cultural differences between European countries, mobility *between* countries is even lower.

The risk is, therefore, that one or more euro area members may suffer from a large decline in demand and output but be unable to use either the interest rate or the exchange rate to increase its level of economic activity. As we saw in Section 19.1, the adjustment can still take place in the medium run. But, as we also saw there, this adjustment is likely to be long and painful. At the time of this writing, this is no longer a hypothetical worry: some euro countries, for example Portugal, are suffering from low output and a large trade deficit. Without the option of a devaluation, achieving a real depreciation may require many years of high unemployment and downward pressure on wages and prices in Portugal relative to the rest of the euro area (see Chapters 25 and 26 for further discussion).

SUMMARY

- Even under a fixed exchange rate regime, countries can adjust their *real* exchange rate in the medium run. They can do this by relying on adjustments in the price level. Nevertheless, the adjustment can be long and painful. Exchange rate adjustments can allow the economy to adjust faster and thus reduce the pain that comes from a long adjustment.

- Exchange rate crises typically start when participants in financial markets believe a currency may soon be devalued. Defending the parity then requires very high interest rates, with potentially large adverse macroeconomic effects. These adverse effects may force the country to devalue, even if there were no initial plans for such a devaluation.

- The exchange rate today depends on both (1) the difference between current and expected future domestic interest rates and current and expected future foreign interest rates and (2) the expected future exchange rate.

  Any factor that increases current or expected future domestic interest rates leads to an increase in the exchange rate today.

  Any factor that increases current or expected future foreign interest rates leads to a decrease in the exchange rate today.

  Any factor that increases the expected future exchange rate leads to an increase in the exchange rate today.

- There is wide agreement among economists that flexible exchange rate regimes generally dominate fixed exchange rate regimes, except in two cases:

  1. When a group of countries is highly integrated and forms an optimal currency area (you can think of a common currency for a group of countries as an extreme form of fixed exchange rates among this group of countries). For countries to form an optimal currency area, they must either face largely similar shocks, or there must be high labour mobility across these countries.

  2. When a central bank cannot be trusted to follow a responsible monetary policy under flexible exchange rates. In this case, a strong form of fixed exchange rates, such as dollarisation or a currency board, provides a way of tying the hands of the central bank.

KEY TERMS

gold standard 398
hard peg 405

dollarisation 405

currency board 405

optimal currency area 407

QUESTIONS AND PROBLEMS

QUICK CHECK

1. *Using the information in this chapter, label each of the following statements true, false or uncertain. Explain briefly.*

a. The UK's return to the gold standard caused years of high unemployment.

b. A sudden fear that a country is going to devalue may force an exchange rate crisis, even if the fear initially had no basis.

c. Because economies tend to return to their natural level of output in the medium run, there is a never a reason to devalue.

d. High labour mobility within Europe makes the euro area a good candidate for a common currency.

e. Changes in the expected level of the exchange rate far in the future have little effect on the current level of the exchange rate.

2. *Consider a country operating under fixed exchange rates, with aggregate demand and aggregate supply given by equations (19.1) and (19.2).*

$$AD: Y = Y\left(\frac{\bar{E}P}{P^*}, G, T\right)$$

$$AS: P = P^e(1+\mu)F\left(1-\frac{Y}{L}, z\right)$$

Assume that the economy is initially in medium-run equilibrium, with a constant price level and output equal to the natural level of output. Foreign output, the foreign price level and the foreign interest rate are fixed throughout the problem. Assume that expected (domestic) inflation remains constant throughout the problem.

a. Draw an *AD–AS* diagram for this economy.

b. Now suppose there is an increase in government spending. Show the effects on the *AD–AS* diagram in the short run and the medium run. How do output and the price level change in the medium run?

c. What happens to consumption in the medium run?

d. What happens to the real exchange rate in the medium run? (*Hint*: consider the effect on the price level you identified in part (b).) What happens to net exports in the medium run?

e. Given that the exchange rate is fixed, what is the domestic nominal interest rate? Does the increase in government spending affect the domestic nominal interest rate? What happens to the real interest rate in the medium run? (*Hint*: remember that expected inflation remains constant by assumption.) What happens to investment in the medium run?

f. In a closed economy, how does an increase in government spending affect investment in the medium run? (Refer to Chapter 8 if you need a refresher.)

g. Comment on the following statement. 'In a closed economy, government spending crowds out investment. In an open economy with fixed exchange rates, government spending crowds out net exports.'

3. Nominal and real interest parity

In equation (6.4), we wrote the nominal interest parity condition as

$$i_t \approx i_t^* - \frac{E_{t+1}^e - E_t}{E_t}$$

In the appendix to this chapter, we derive a real interest parity condition. We can write the real interest parity condition in a manner analogous to equation (18.4):

$$r_t \approx r_t^* - \frac{(\varepsilon_{t+1}^e - \varepsilon_t)}{\varepsilon_t}$$

a. Interpret this equation. Under what circumstances will the domestic real interest rate exceed the foreign real interest rate?

Assume that the one-year nominal interest rate is 10% in the domestic economy and 6% in the foreign economy. Also assume that inflation over the coming year is expected to be 6% in the domestic economy and 3% in the foreign economy. Suppose that interest parity holds.

b. What is the expected nominal depreciation of the domestic currency over the coming year?

c. What is the expected real depreciation over the coming year?

d. If you expected a nominal appreciation of the currency over the coming year, should you hold domestic or foreign bonds?

4. Devaluation and interest rates

Consider an open economy with a fixed exchange rate, $\bar{E}$. Throughout the problem, assume that the foreign interest rate, i^*, remains constant.

a. Suppose that financial market participants believe that the government is committed to a fixed exchange rate. What is the expected exchange rate? According to the interest parity condition, what is the domestic interest rate?

b. Suppose that financial market participants do not believe that the government is committed to a fixed exchange rate. Instead, they suspect that the government will either devalue or abandon the fixed exchange rate altogether and adopt a flexible exchange rate. If the government adopts a flexible exchange rate, financial market participants expect the exchange rate to depreciate from its current fixed value, $\bar{E}$. Under these circumstances, how does the expected exchange rate compare to $\bar{E}$? How does the domestic interest rate compare to i^*?

c. Suppose that financial market participants feared a devaluation, as in part (b), and a devaluation actually occurs. The government announces that it will maintain a fixed exchange rate regime but changes the level of the fixed exchange rate to $\bar{E}'$, where $\bar{E}' < \bar{E}$. Suppose that financial market participants believe that the government will remain committed to the new exchange rate, $\bar{E}'$, and that there will be no further devaluations. What happens to the domestic interest rate after the devaluation?

d. Does a devaluation necessarily lead to higher domestic interest rates? Does fear of a devaluation necessarily lead to higher domestic interest rates?

DIG DEEPER

5. Exchange rate overshooting

a. Suppose there is a permanent 10% increase in M in a closed economy. What is the effect on the price level in the medium run? (*Hint*: if you need a refresher, review the analysis in Chapter 8.)

In a closed economy, we said that money was neutral because, in the medium run, a change in the money stock affected only the price level. A change in the money stock did not affect any real variables. A change in the money stock is also neutral in an open economy with flexible exchange rates. In the medium run, a change in the money stock will not affect the real exchange rate, although it will affect the price level and the nominal exchange rate.

b. Consider an open economy with a flexible exchange rate. Write the expression for the real exchange rate. Suppose there is a 10% increase in the money stock and assume that it has the same effect on the price level in the medium run that you found in part (a). If the real exchange rate and the foreign price level are unchanged in the medium run, what must happen to the nominal exchange rate in the medium run?

c. Suppose it takes n years to reach the medium run (and everyone knows this). Given your answer to part (b), what happens to E_{t+n}^e (the expected exchange rate for n periods from now) after a 10% increase in the money stock?

d. Consider equation (19.5). Assume that the foreign interest rate is unchanged for the next n periods. Also assume, for the moment, that the domestic interest rate is unchanged for the next n periods. Given your answer to part (c), what happens to the exchange rate today (at time t) when there is a 10% increase in the money stock?

e. Now assume that after the increase in the money stock, the domestic interest rate falls between time t and time $t + n$. Again, assume that the foreign interest rate is unchanged. As compared to your answer to part (d), what happens to the exchange rate today (at time t)? Does the exchange rate move more in the short run than in the medium run?

The answer to part (e) is yes. In this case, the short-run depreciation is greater than the medium-run depreciation. This phenomenon is called overshooting, and may help to explain why the exchange rate is so variable.

6. Self-fulfilling exchange rate crises

Consider an open economy with a fixed exchange rate, $\bar{E}$. Suppose that, initially, financial market participants believe that the government is committed to the fixed exchange rate. Suddenly, however, financial market participants become fearful that the government will devalue or allow the exchange rate to float (a decision that everyone believes will cause the currency to depreciate).

a. What happens to the expected exchange rate, E^e_{t+1}? (See your answer to problem 4(b).)

Suppose that, despite the change in the expected exchange rate, the government keeps the exchange rate fixed today. Let UIP stand for the uncovered interest parity condition.

b. Draw an *IS–LM–UIP* diagram. How does the change in the expected exchange rate affect the *UIP* curve? As a result, how must the domestic interest rate change to maintain an exchange rate of $\bar{E}$?

c. Given your answer to part (b), what happens to the domestic money supply if the central bank defends the fixed exchange rate? How does the *LM* curve shift?

d. What happens to domestic output and the domestic interest rate? Is it possible that a government that was previously committed to a fixed exchange rate might abandon it when faced with a fear of depreciation (either through devaluation or abandonment of the fixed exchange rate regime)? Is it possible that unfounded fears about a depreciation can create a crisis? Explain your answers.

7. Devaluation and credibility

Consider an open economy with a fixed exchange rate, $\bar{E}$. Suppose that, initially, financial market participants believe that the government is committed to maintaining the fixed exchange rate. Let UIP stand for the uncovered interest parity condition.

Now suppose the central bank announces a devaluation. The exchange rate will remain fixed, but at a new level, $\bar{E}'$, such that $\bar{E}' < \bar{E}$. Suppose that financial market participants believe that there will be no further devaluations and that the government will remain committed to maintaining the exchange rate at $\bar{E}'$.

a. What is the domestic interest rate before the devaluation? If the devaluation is credible, what is the domestic interest rate after the devaluation? (See your answers to problem 4.)

b. Draw an *IS–LM–UIP* diagram for this economy. If the devaluation is credible, how does the expected exchange rate change? How does the change in the expected exchange rate affect the *UIP* curve?

c. How does the devaluation affect the *IS* curve? Given your answer to part (b) and the shift of the *IS* curve, what would happen to the domestic interest rate if there is no change in the domestic money supply?

d. Given your answer to part (c), what must happen to the domestic money supply so that the domestic interest rate achieves the value you identified in part (a)? How does the *LM* curve shift?

e. How is domestic output affected by the devaluation?

f. Suppose that devaluation is not credible in the sense that the devaluation leads financial market participants to expect another devaluation in the future. How does the fear of further devaluation affect the expected exchange rate? How will the expected exchange rate in this case, where devaluation is not credible, compare to your answer to part (b)? Explain in words. Given this effect on the expected exchange rate, what must happen to the domestic interest rate, as compared to your answer to part (a), to maintain the new fixed exchange rate?

EXPLORE FURTHER

8. Exchange rates and expectations

In this chapter, we emphasised that expectations have an important effect on the exchange rate. In this problem, we use data to get a sense of how large a role expectations play. Using the results in Appendix 2 at the end of the chapter, you can show that the uncovered interest parity condition, equation (19.4), can be written as

$$\frac{(E_t - E_{t-1})}{E_{t-1}} \approx (i_t - i^*_t) - (i_{t-1} - i^*_{t-1}) + \frac{(E^e_t - E^e_{t-1})}{E^e_{t-1}}$$

In words, the percentage change in the exchange rate (the appreciation of the domestic currency) is approximately equal to the change in the interest rate differential (between domestic and foreign interest rates) plus the percentage change in exchange rate expectations (the appreciation of the expected domestic currency value). We shall call the interest rate differential the spread.

a. Go to the website of the Bank of England (***www.bankofengland.co.uk***) and obtain data on the three-month Treasury bill rate for the past ten years. Download the data into a spreadsheet. Now go to the website of the European Central Bank (**www.ecb.int**) and download data on the three-month interbank rate (EURIBOR after 1999) for the same time period. For each month, subtract the UK interest rate from the euro interest rate to calculate the spread. Then, for each month, calculate the change in the spread from the preceding month. (Make sure to convert the interest rate data into the proper decimal form.)

b. At the website of the European Central Bank, obtain data on the monthly exchange rate between the euro and the UK pound for the same period as your data from part (a). Again, download the data into a spreadsheet. Calculate the percentage appreciation of the euro for each month. Using the standard deviation function in your software, calculate the standard deviation of the monthly appreciation of the euro. The standard deviation is a measure of the variability of a data series.

c. For each month, subtract the change in the spread (part (a)) from the percentage appreciation of the dollar (part (b)). Call this difference the *change in expectations*. Calculate the standard deviation of the change in expectations. How does it compare to the standard deviation of the monthly appreciation of the dollar?

There are some complications we do not take into account here. Our interest parity condition does not include a variable that measures relative asset demand. We explored the implications of changes in relative asset demands in problem 12 at the end of Chapter 18. In addition, changes in interest rates and expectations may be related. Still, the gist of this analysis survives in more sophisticated work. In the short run, observable economic fundamentals do not account for much of the change in the exchange rate. Much of the difference must be attributed to changing expectations.

We invite you to visit the Blanchard page on the Prentice Hall website, at **www.prenhall.com/blanchard** for this chapter's World Wide Web exercises.

APPENDIX 1

Deriving aggregate demand under fixed exchange rates

To derive the aggregate demand for goods, start from the condition for goods market equilibrium we derived in Chapter 6, equation (6.9):

$$Y = C(Y - T) + I(Y, r) + G + NX(Y, Y^*, \varepsilon)$$

This condition states that, for the goods market to be in equilibrium, output must be equal to the demand for domestic goods – that is, the sum of consumption, investment, government spending and net exports.

Next, recall the following relations:

- The real interest rate, r, is equal to the nominal interest rate, i, minus expected inflation, π^e (see Chapter 14):

$$r = i - \pi^e$$

- The real exchange rate, ε, is defined as (see Chapter 6):

$$\varepsilon = \frac{EP}{P^*}$$

- Under fixed exchange rates, the nominal exchange rate, E, is, by definition, fixed. Denote by $\bar{E}$ the value at which the nominal exchange rate is fixed, so:

$$E = \bar{E}$$

- Under fixed exchange rates and perfect capital mobility, the domestic interest rate, i, must be equal to the foreign interest rate, i^* (see Chapter 6):

$$i = i^*$$

Using these four relations, rewrite equation (19.1) as

$$Y = C(Y - T) + I(Y, i^* - p^e) + G + NX\left(Y, Y^*, \frac{\bar{E}P}{P^*}\right)$$

This is a rich – and complicated – equilibrium condition. It tells us that, in an open economy with fixed exchange rates, equilibrium output (or, more precisely, the level of output implied by equilibrium in the goods, financial and foreign exchange markets) depends on

- Government spending, G, and taxes, T: an increase in government spending increases output. So does a decrease in taxes.

- The foreign nominal interest rate, i^*, minus expected inflation, π^e: an increase in the foreign nominal interest rate requires a parallel increase in the domestic nominal interest rate. Given expected inflation, this increase in the domestic nominal interest rate leads to an increase in the domestic real interest rate and then to lower demand and lower output.

- Foreign output, Y^*: an increase in foreign output increases exports and so increases net exports. The increase in net exports increases domestic output.

- The real exchange rate, ε, is equal to the fixed nominal exchange rate, $\bar{E}$, times the domestic price level, P, divided by the foreign price level, P^*: a decrease in the real exchange rate – equivalently, a real depreciation – leads to an increase in net exports and so to an increase in output.

We focus in the text on the effects of only three of these variables: the real exchange rate, government spending and taxes. We therefore write

$$Y = Y\left(\frac{\bar{E}P}{P^*}, G, T\right)$$
$$(-, +, -)$$

All the other variables that affect demand are taken as given and, to simplify notation, are simply omitted from the relation. This gives us equation (19.1) in the text.

Equation (19.1) gives us the *aggregate demand relation*, the relation between output and the price level implied by equilibrium in the goods market and in financial markets. Note that, in the closed economy, we had to use both the *IS* and the *LM* relations to derive the aggregate demand relation. Under fixed exchange rates, we do not need the *LM* relation. The reason is that the nominal interest rate, rather than being determined jointly by the *IS* and *LM* relations, is determined by the foreign interest rate. (The *LM* relation still holds but, as we saw in Chapter 6, it simply determines the money stock.)

APPENDIX 2

The real exchange rate and domestic and foreign real interest rates

We derived in Section 19.3 a relation between the current nominal exchange rate, the current and expected future domestic and foreign nominal interest rates and the expected future nominal exchange rate (equation (19.5)). This appendix derives a similar relation but in terms of real interest rates and the real exchange rate. It then briefly discusses how this alternative relation can be used to think about movements in the real exchange rate.

Deriving the real interest parity condition

Start from the nominal interest parity condition, equation (6.2):

$$(1 + i_t) = (1 + i_t^*)\frac{E_t}{E_{t+1}^e}$$

Recall the definition of the real interest rate from Chapter 6, equation (6.3):

$$(1 + r_t) \equiv \frac{(1 + i_t)}{(1 + \pi_t^e)}$$

where $\pi_t^e \equiv (P_{t+1}^e - P_t)/P_t$ is the expected rate of inflation. Similarly, the foreign real interest rate is given by:

$$(1 + r_t^*) = \frac{(1 + i_t^*)}{(1 + \pi_t^{*e})}$$

where $\pi_t^{*e} \equiv (P_{t+1}^{*e} - P_t^*)/P_t^*$ is the expected foreign rate of inflation.

Use these two relations to eliminate nominal interest rates in the interest parity condition, so:

$$(1 + r_t) = (1 + r_t^*)\left[\frac{E_t}{E_{t+1}^e}\frac{(1 + \pi_t^{*e})}{(1 + \pi_t^e)}\right] \qquad [19.A1]$$

Note from the definition of inflation that $(1 + \pi_t^e) = P_{t+1}^e/P_t$ and, similarly, $(1 + \pi_t^{*e}) = P_{t+1}^{*e}/P_t^*$.

Using these two relations in the term in brackets gives

$$\frac{E_t}{E_{t+1}^e}\frac{(1 + \pi_t^{*e})}{(1 + \pi_t^e)} = \frac{E_t}{E_{t+1}^e}\frac{P_{t+1}^{*e}P_t}{P_t^*P_{t+1}^e}$$

Reorganising terms, we have

$$\frac{E_t P_{t+1}^{*e} P_t}{E_{t+1}^e P_t^* P_{t+1}^e} = \frac{E_t P_t/P_t^*}{E_{t+1}^e P_{t+1}^e/P_{t+1}^{*e}}$$

Using the definition of the real exchange rate gives

$$\frac{E_t P_t/P_t^*}{E_{t+1}^e P_{t+1}^e/P_{t+1}^{*e}} = \frac{\varepsilon_t}{\varepsilon_{t+1}^e}$$

Replacing in equation (19.A1) gives:

$$(1 + r_t) = (1 + r_t^*)\frac{\varepsilon_t}{\varepsilon_{t+1}^e}$$

Or, equivalently,

$$\varepsilon_t = \frac{1 + r_t}{1 + r_t^*}\varepsilon_{t+1}^e \qquad [19.A2]$$

The real exchange rate today depends on the domestic and foreign real interest rates this year and the expected future real exchange rate next year. This equation corresponds to equation (19.4) in the text but now in terms of the real rather than nominal exchange and interest rates.

Solving the real interest parity condition forward

The next step is to solve equation (19.A2) forward, in the same way as we did it for equation (19.4). Equation (19.A2) implies that the real exchange rate in year $t + 1$ is given by

$$\varepsilon_{t+1} = \frac{1 + r_{t+1}}{1 + r_{t+1}^*}\varepsilon_{t+2}^e$$

Taking expectations, as of year t, gives:

$$\varepsilon_{t+1}^e = \frac{1 + r_{t+1}^e}{1 + r_{t+1}^{*e}}\varepsilon_{t+2}^e$$

Replacing in the previous relation, we have

$$\varepsilon_t = \frac{(1 + r_t)(1 + r_{t+1}^e)}{(1 + r_t^*)(1 + r_{t+1}^{*e})}\varepsilon_{t+2}^e$$

Solving for ε_{t+2}^e, and so on gives

$$\varepsilon_t = \frac{(1 + r_t)(1 + r_{t+1}^e) \ldots (1 + r_{t+n}^e)}{(1 + r_t^*)(1 + r_{t+1}^{*e}) \ldots (1 + r_{t+n}^{*e})}\varepsilon_{t+n+1}^e$$

This relation gives the current real exchange rate as a function of current and expected future domestic real interest rates, of current and expected future foreign real interest rates and of the expected real exchange rate in year $t + n + 1$.

The advantage of this relation over the relation we derived in the text between the nominal exchange rate and nominal interest rates, equation (19.5), is that it is typically easier to predict the future real exchange rate than to predict the future nominal exchange rate. If, for example, the economy suffers from a large trade deficit, we can be fairly confident that there will have to be a real depreciation – that ε_{t+n+1}^e will have to be lower. Whether there will be a nominal depreciation – what happens to E_{t+n+1} – is harder to tell: it depends on what happens to inflation, both at home and abroad over the next n years.

PATHOLOGIES

Sometimes (macroeconomic) things go very wrong: there is a sharp drop in output. Or, instead, government debt become too high. Or inflation increases to very high levels. These pathologies are the focus of the next three chapters.

Chapter 20 The crisis of 2007–2010

Chapter 20 looks at the recent recession of 2007–2010, the worst since the Great Depressions in 1929. The chapter discusses the origin of the financial crisis which started in the USA, how it turned into a full-fledged economic crisis, and how it was that all the world was soon affected. We will try to analyse the basic mechanisms behind the crisis with the tools you have learned in the previous chapters.

Chapter 21 High debt

Chapter 21 looks at the problem of high government debt. Although in principle a high government deficit is neither good nor evil, government deficits can become a problem if they lead to the rapid accumulation of debt. The chapter gives you the tools to analyse whether government debt becomes 'too' high and to understand how a country can stabilise the debt. It also discusses some notable episodes of debt reduction.

Chapter 22 High inflation

Chapter 22 looks at episodes of high inflation, from Germany in the early 1920s to Latin America in the 1980s. It shows the role of both fiscal and monetary policy in generating high inflation. Budget deficits can lead to high nominal money growth, and high nominal money growth leads to high inflation. It then looks at how high inflations end, and at the role and the nature of stabilisation programmes.

Chapter 20

THE CRISIS OF 2007–2010

'If these things were so large, how come everyone missed them?'

Question asked by Her Majesty The Queen to the LSE professors
during a visit to the School in November 2008

In the autumn of 2008, the world entered into the deepest recession experienced since the Second World War. At the time of writing, February 2010, the recovery has already started, especially in Asia and Latin America, the so-called emerging market economies. In the advanced economies, however, unemployment is expected to remain high for quite some time. The origin of this recession was a financial crisis which started in the USA in the summer of 2007, then spread to Europe and eventually affected the entire world. The financial crisis started in the so-called '**sub-prime mortgage**' market. 'Sub-prime' loans are a small part of the US housing mortgage market intended for borrowers with a relatively high probability of eventually not being able to repay their loan. One wonders how it was possible that the difficulties of such a marginal sector of the US mortgage market – sub-prime loans were less than 20% of all housing loans in 2006 – could have shaken financial markets throughout the world. In this chapter we will describe what happened and identify the basic mechanisms at work. We explain how the financial shock was transmitted to the US economy and from there to the rest of the world. We shall then describe the macro-policies that have been put in place to contain the recession and that so far appear to have been successful. Throughout the chapter we rely on what you have learned about macro-economics so far in the book.

The chapter has seven sections:

- Sections 20.1 and 20.2 discuss what happened and what triggered the crisis.

- Section 20.3 discusses banks' 'leverage' and how leverage amplified the initial shocks.

- Section 20.4 goes back to the *IS–LM* model and shows it can be extended to incoporate banks as intermediaries between households and firms.

- Section 20.5 explains how the crisis came to be transmitted to the entire world.

- Section 20.6 discusses how monetary and fiscal policies were used to respond to the crisis.

- Section 20.7 discusses the legacy of the crisis: high public debt.

20.1 WHAT CANNOT KEEP GOING EVENTUALLY STOPS

The best place to begin to understand the origin of the 2007–2010 crisis is Figure 20.1a which shows US house prices since 1890 (the red line). The figure shows two episodes in which house prices rapidly increased. The first, at the end of the 1940s is easy to understand: few houses were built during the Second World War: at the time, the economy was using most of its resources to fight the war. At the end of the conflict, when soldiers returned home, many new families were formed, many new babies were born and the demand for houses shot up. But the supply of houses was small, so prices also shot up.

However, the increase in house prices in the 1940s is small relative to what happened in the first decade of this century. And here there was no obvious reason why prices should shoot up. As the figure shows, neither building costs, which were falling, nor population growth, which did not accelerate, justify such a rapid increase in prices. Yet the boom continued for a decade but then, as nothing can last forever, it stopped and the fall in house

◄ In Figure 20.1, prices are adjusted for inflation, so what the figure really shows is the price of houses relative to all other goods in the economy.

◄ A few economists, most notably Robert Shiller of Yale university (in his now famous book *Irrational Exuberance*, written in 2000) noticed this and repeatedly said that the housing boom could not continue.

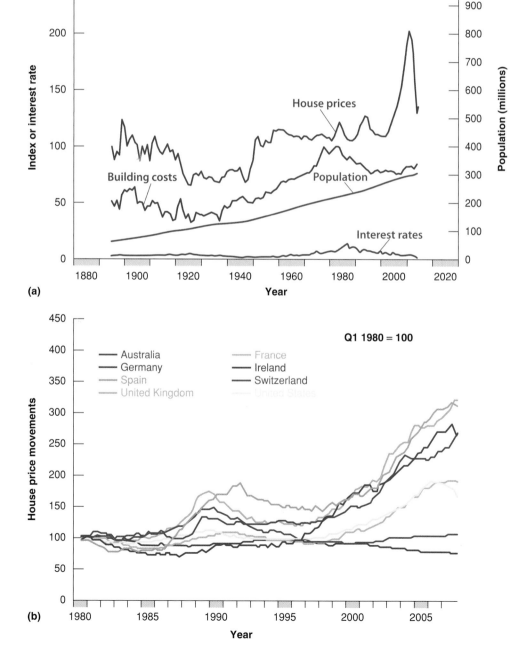

Figure 20.1

House price movements

(a) The price of US houses since 1890 adjusted for inflation.

(b) House prices adjusted for inflation in eight countries since 1980.

Sources: (a) Standard & Poor's, Case-Schiller Index; (b) Bank for International Settlement.

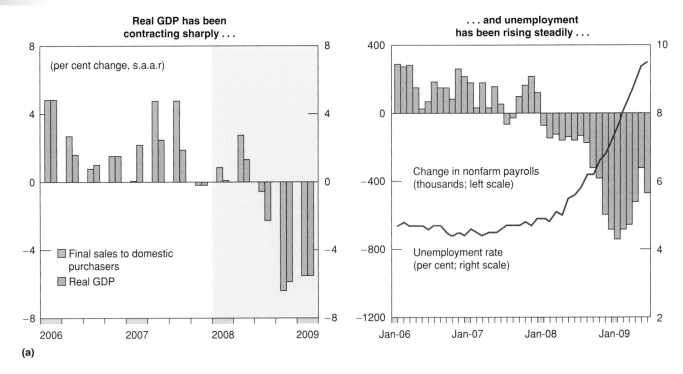

(a)

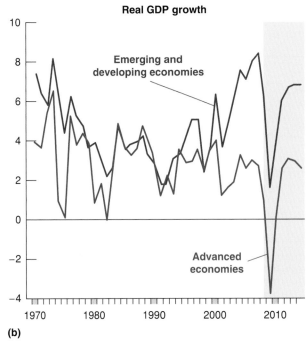

(b)

Figure 20.2

The economic crisis of 2007–2009 and its effect on the global economy

(a) The performance of the US economy in 2007–2009.

(b) The world economy in the crisis.

Source: IMF *World Economic Outlook* 2009.

prices (house prices have fallen about 30% on average in the USA between 2006 and 2009, see Figure 20.1a) swept away the entire economy.

The USA was not the only country where house prices increased a lot. In the UK, Ireland and Spain house prices since 1980 increased even more (Figure 20.1b).

Figure 20.2(a) shows what eventually happened: within a year the unemployment rate in the USA more than doubled, increasing from 4.5% to 9.5%. As shown in Figure 20.2b, soon after the recession hit the entire world.

The value of the houses in which they live counts for about one-third of the total wealth of US families (32% in 2007). It is thus not surprising that a sharp fall in house prices would hit households and induce them to consume less (remember Chapter 5 where we discussed the effects of wealth on consumption.) Still it is surprising that a 30% fall in house prices would have created such a deep recession.

On 19 October 1987, what later came to be called 'Black Monday', Wall Street fell by 20.4% in a single day. Stocks are less important than houses in the wealth of US families: they represent about 20% of the total wealth of US households, a non-negligible amount. Still, the crash of 1987 had almost no effect on consumption and growth. The following year income growth accelerated to 4%, one point more than in 1987.

20.2 HOUSEHOLDS 'UNDER WATER'

The previous section left us with two questions: why did the value of houses shoot up after 2000 and why were the effects of the fall in house price so dramatic? Let us start from the increase in house prices. It is now obvious, looking at Figure 20.1 (but, as we said, it had been obvious to Robert Shiller for some years) that house prices were riding a bubble. 'Housing prices cannot fall!' was a common statement in the years before the crash. As the title of Shiller's book suggests, such exuberance is often irrational.

The increase in house prices was also the effect of a long period of extremely low interest rates which made borrowing to buy a house very attractive – especially if you believed the bubble would continue! The Fed kept interest rates low because inflation was low. House prices were rising fast, but house prices do not enter directly into the index used to compute inflation. What enters is the cost of renting a house, and this did not increase as fast as house prices and, in any case, not fast enough to move the CPI significantly.

So, house prices kept rising due both to irrational exuberance and to very low interest rates. If house prices had been included in the index used to compute inflation, they would have made it rise and the Fed, in the face of rising inflation, would maybe have increased interest rates. The housing bubble would not have grown so much.

Borrowing to buy a house was also encouraged by a change in the rules banks followed to approve a mortgage, which became much less strict. The result was that even families who had a relatively high probability of not being able to pay the mortgage rates, the so-called 'sub-prime' clients, were accorded a loan. Why did banks take on these risks? The point is that they did not, or at least much less than in the past. In the old days, when a bank made a mortgage it kept it on its books till the day it was fully repaid. It thus had a strong incentive to keep an eye on the client and make sure he or she would repay. Today, instead, a bank can pull a large number of mortgages together and sell the financial instrument which contains them to other investors. When an investor, sometimes another bank, buys one of these securities – which contains thousands of mortgages and is called a 'mortgage-backed security' – it cannot check the quality of each individual loan. The quality of the security is certified by a rating agency. But rating agencies too cannot check each individual loan. The result is that quality control became weakened and banks became much less careful when they were making a loan. As we explain in the following Focus box ('Securitisation is a great invention – provided it is done right'), the problem was not securitisation *per se*, but the failure to regulate it appropriately.

If banks are not careful enough when they make a mortgage, it is no surprise that the moment house prices start falling some households go 'under water', meaning that how much they borrowed from the bank exceeds the market value of their house. When this happens households (especially if they think house prices will never bounce back to

◄ That something was wrong in the way banks were extending mortgages to sub-prime clients is clear from Figure 20.3a. The percentage of such clients who defaulted within a year of having received the loan increased from 3% to over 20% from 2004–2007.

◄ Martin Feldstein, an economist at Harvard University, estimated that by the autumn of 2008, that is a year after the start of the crisis, 12 million mortgages had gone under water, this is 10% of all mortgages. See Figure 20.3b.

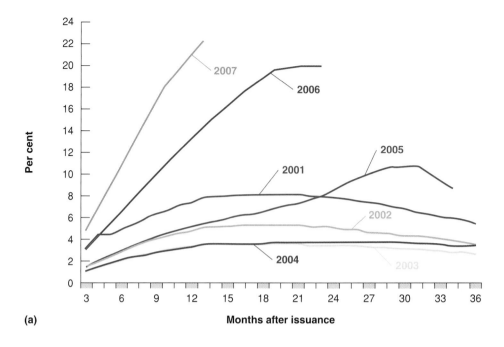

(a)

Months after issuance

(b)

Figure 20.3

Defaults on US sub-prime mortgages

(a) Default rate by year of origination of the mortgage.

Source: Moody's Investors Service.

(b) Homeowners with negative equity (who own more on their mortgages than their homes are worth; millions) (per cent of all homeowners – data are for 2008; thereafter estimates).

Source: IMF *World Economic Outlook* 2009.

A popular website *youwalkaway.com* explains what you should do to walk away from a property whose market value has fallen below the value of the mortgage.

previous levels) have an incentive to 'walk away' from their home. The mortgage then goes into default and the house is 'foreclosed' which means that its property is transferred to the bank. Because the value of the house is smaller than the value of the loan which was originally granted, the bank makes a loss.

However, this is still not enough to explain what happened. Most households do not abandon their home when the price of the house falls below the value of the bank loan (unless they can no longer afford the mortgage payments). Banks did make large losses on foreclosed homes, but not large enough to explain what came close to being a meltdown of the international financial system. And a 30% fall in house prices is not enough, by itself, to explain the sharp fall in household consumption (−3.5% at annual rates for two consecutive quarters) at the end of 2008. Something else must have worked to amplify the shock.

FOCUS
Securitisation is a great invention – provided it is done right

Until the 1970s, US commercial banks could not move beyond the boundaries of the state in which they were incorporated. Banks collected deposits from local customers and made loans locally to households and businesses: out-of state banks were not allowed in. The local concentration of a bank's clients and the very small size of banks (except for a handful in New York) made them particularly weak. Since they could not expand beyond a single state, they were particularly exposed to possible adverse shocks in the region where they were located. In the mid-1980s, for example, when the price of oil collapsed, in Texas – a state whose economy depends mainly on the oil industry – there was a deep recession. As banks in that state made loans almost exclusively to Texan customers, when the latter found themselves in trouble and began to default on their loans, most banks in the state failed.

In the 1980s, two things happened that made US banks more robust. First, banking across state borders was allowed: small local banks were bought by nationwide banks which were large enough not to be exposed to business conditions in a particular state or region. An example is Bank of America, originally a California bank, which in a few years established branches throughout the USA.

Second, the development of new financial instruments allowed banks to diversify their risks without the need to expand beyond the borders of their state. The way a bank can do this is by creating a financial security (hence the name 'securitisation') which contains a large number of loans the bank has made. Such a security can then be sold to other investors. (Figure 20.4 shows how rapidly the issuance of these securities grew precisely in the years house prices were rising.) (Other financial instruments that allow a bank to diversify its risks are 'credit default swaps' (CDS), insurance products that insure against the risk that a customer defaults and fails to repay his or her loan. The bank holds onto the loan but is fully protected in the case of a default.)

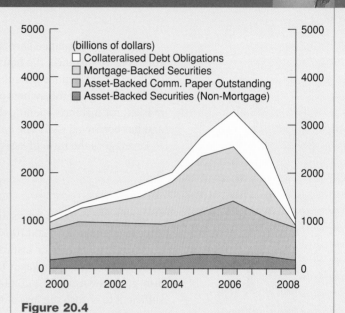

Figure 20.4

The growth of securitisation (annual issues by type of security)

Source: IMF *World Economic Outlook* 2009.

These are all great inventions, but securitisation must be done right. In particular, banks should never lose the incentive to check the quality of their clients. This could easily be done, for instance by allowing a bank to sell only a fraction of each loan it has made (say, no more than 90%), thus remaining exposed to some of the risk. Imposing such rules was the task of regulators – the Fed – but regulators failed to impose them. The crisis is thus, to a large extent, the result of a regulatory failure, not of the creation of new financial instruments. Why regulators failed to impose sound rules is more difficult to understand. One possibility is that they were subject to strong political pressure from an administration whose objective was to accelerate the pace of home ownership in the US, convinced that only when you own a house can you really feel like a citizen.

20.3 LEVERAGE AND AMPLIFICATION

To understand how the effect of the fall in house prices was amplified to the point of inducing a sharp recession, we need to introduce a concept not mentioned so far in the book: 'leverage'. The best way to do it is with an example.

Table 20.1 What is leverage?

	Assets	Liabilities	Capital	Leverage
Bank 1	100	80	20	5
Bank 2	100	95	5	20

Consider the balance sheets of two banks. Both have assets worth €100. These assets could be, for instance, the housing mortgages they issued. The two banks differ in the way their assets are financed: Bank 1 financed the mortgages it had issued with €20 of its own capital (the equity the owners put in when the bank was set up) and borrowed €80 from the market, for instance opening deposits for €80. Bank 2, in contrast, has only €5 of capital and has borrowed €95. The balance sheets of the two banks are shown in Table 20.1.

Leverage is the ratio of assets to capital:

$$\text{Leverage ratio} = \frac{\text{assets}}{\text{capital}}$$

Bank 1 has €100 of assets and €20 of capital: its leverage ratio is 100/20 = 5. For Bank 2 the leverage ratio is 20 (100/5). Now ask yourself what happens if the value of the assets falls from 100 to 80, for instance because house prices fall by 20%. When house prices go down the value of mortgages (which are backed by the value of the houses they financed) also goes down by 20%. Bank 1 remains solvent since the capital of the bank is (just) sufficient to absorb the loss of €20. Bank 2, however, is bankrupt. That is why a high leverage ratio is risky: in the event of a drop in the value of its assets, the bank might become insolvent.

Although it is risky, banks like having a high leverage ratio. Assume that the assets the bank has invested in yield a return of 10%, and forget about costs (assume for simplicity that the bank can borrow paying no interest: this is obviously unrealistic but, in the years before the crisis, interest rates, as we already mentioned, were very low indeed). The owners of Bank 1 will have a return on their capital of 50%: 10/20. The owners of Bank 2 do much better: their return is 10/5, i.e. 200%. There is nothing new here. It's just the 'iron law of finance': you can make higher returns only if you are prepared to run higher risks.

As long as house prices were rising, by keeping their leverage high banks could earn huge profits and none failed. But this long honeymoon did not last and, when it came to an end, many banks found themselves without enough capital to absorb the losses: they were bankrupt.

Why the government did not intervene, imposing a limit on leverage, is a different story. One explanation, as we already mentioned, is that widening the number of US citizens who own a home was a political objective: to achieve it the administration needed to make it attractive for banks to invest in financing housing loans. The way to do it was to allow banks to make these loans with high leverage, i.e. not with their own capital but with cash borrowed cheaply. Bankers were also interested in high leverage because, when things went well, this meant high returns for the bank – and for themselves as well since their bonuses were linked to the profits of the bank. The interest of bankers often translated into campaign contributions to politicians who then lobbied for lax rules on leverage.

Over time the example – and the bad **regulation** – of banks spread to other financial institutions. Table 20.2 shows the average leverage of major financial institutions in the USA in the year before the crisis. The US financial market began to look like an inverted pyramid: a huge volume of risky investments were held on a tiny pedestal of capital. It is not surprising that when the market stopped growing, these institutions turned out to be very fragile. By issuing 'credit default swaps' (the instruments we discussed in the Focus box 'Securitisation is a great invention – provided it is done right'), some insurance companies exposed themselves to the housing market and, when the property market collapsed and the value of mortgages fell, they began to lose without sufficient equity to absorb the losses.

Table 20.2 The leverage of US financial institutions in 2007

Commercial banks	9.08
Cooperative banks	8.07
Financial companies	10.00
Investment banks and hedge funds	27.01
Fannie Mae and Freddie Mac	23.05

Source: Tobias Adrian and Hyun Song Shin, Liquidity, Monetary Policy and Financial Cycles, *Current Issues in Economics and Finance*, 2008, **14**(1), 1–7.

So far, we have understood why leverage is attractive (for bankers) but also risky. What about amplification? Why did high leverage amplify the effects of the fall in house prices on the economy?

When the value of their assets fell, some banks with high leverage went bust. These obviously stopped lending. But also the banks which had enough capital and survived started worrying. In order to survive, they had used almost all their capital and were now alive but weak. In the example above, Bank 2 went bankrupt, but Bank 1 then emerged from the crisis with zero capital and infinite leverage. Banks like Bank 1 strengthened their position in three ways. First, they tried to raise more capital, but this was not easy because a crisis is not a good time to convince people to invest in a bank. Second, they reduced the amount of loans they were holding, which means making fewer new loans and not renewing those that could be stopped. Third, they sold other liquid assets (mostly stocks) at whatever price they could get. The result was a credit freeze (as documented in Figure 20.5) and a fire sale in the stock market. Fire sales happen when investors need to sell their assets fast and prices tumble. These are the main channels through which the financial crisis hit the real economy. The credit squeeze hit investment and the fall in the stock market (coming on top of the fall in house prices) reduced the value of household wealth and thus consumption.

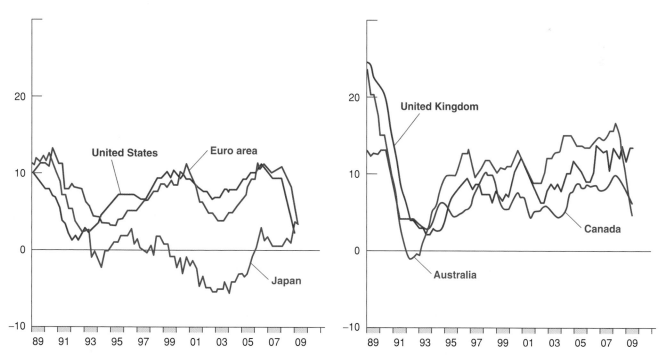

Figure 20.5

Credit to the private non-financial sector

Source: Bank for International Settlements, 2009 Annual Report.

20.4 INVESTMENT DEMAND, WITH BANKS AS INTERMEDIARIES

In the previous section, we argued that an important channel for the transmission of the crisis to the real economy was the balance sheets of banks. As their capital fell, banks started to cut credit, i.e. stopped making loans to firms, and this hit investment. While all of this makes good sense, it is quite far from the simple view of investment from Chapter 5. In this paragraph and in the next, we extend the *IS–LM* model of Chapter 5 to include banks.

In Chapter 5, we considered the case of a firm deciding whether to buy a new machine. We said that the firm must look at *the* interest rate. However, there is no unique interest rate: the interest rate savers receive (the rate on bank deposits, i) is usually lower than the rate at which banks lend to firms (the lending rate). The rate at which banks lend to firms, i.e. the cost of a loan from a bank, ρ, is equal to the rate savers receive plus a spread, x:

$$\rho = i + x$$

Therefore, when a firm has to decide whether to buy a machine, ρ is the interest rate it has to look at. Investment demand therefore depends on the cost of bank loans (and not simply on *the* interest rate as we said in Chapter 4) and can be expressed as:

$$I = I(Y, \rho) \qquad [20.1]$$
$$(+, -)$$

The positive sign under Y in equation (20.1) indicates that an increase in the level of real income leads to an increase in investment (exactly as we discussed in Chapter 4) and the negative sign under ρ indicates that an increase in the cost of bank loans leads to a decrease in investment.

The spread x depends on two factors:

Remember that leverage is the ratio of assets to capital, and the higher is leverage, the riskier is the bank.

- Banks' capital, A^B – As we discussed in the previous section, banks want and often need to maintain a sufficient level of capital: the minimum level of capital may be determined by regulation, or simply by the desire on the part of the bank not to increase its leverage too much. Now assume that a bank's capital falls, for instance because some of the bank's clients fail to pay their loans back. The bank's capital absorbs the loss and reduces by an amount equivalent to the loss in the loans' portfolio (always remember the accounting identity: bank assets = bank liabilities, or loans + other assets = capital + deposits). A fall in the bank's capital increases leverage.

  To face the fall in its capital – in order to restore the original leverage ratio – as we have already seen, the bank has two options: either increase capital or decrease assets. To increase capital, it may look for new investors, willing to bring in fresh capital. Or it can live with the capital that is left, and reduce its assets by reducing the volume of its loans. Both strategies have the effect of reducing the bank's leverage which had increased as a result of the losses on the loans' portfolio.

  As an example, imagine Bank 1, with assets equal to 100 and capital equal to 20, registers a loss equal to 2. Capital goes down to 18. Leverage therefore increases from 5 (= 100/20) to around 5.4 (98/18). To decrease leverage back to the previous level (5), the bank can either increase capital back to 20 (by finding investors willing to put another 2 of their money into the bank's capital), or it must reduce its assets to 90, so that leverage goes down to 5 (= 90/18). Since finding new investors is not immediate, a bank's first reaction to a capital loss is to cut down on assets by reducing the volume of its loans, for instance stopping making new loans. Therefore, when banks' capital is hit, the supply of loans falls.

- Firms' capital A^F – To understand this, consider a firm deciding whether to buy a new machine whose cost is €I. To buy the new equipment the firm asks the bank for a loan of €I. Suppose now that the firm has an amount of capital (the value of its machines and of its plants, the cash in the bank and the financial assets it owns, etc.) equal to A^F. The cost of the bank loan will depend on the difference $(I - A^F)$.

To understand this you should realise that the firm's capital, A^F, can be used as a guarantee for the loan: often a loan contract specifies that if the firm fails to repay $I–A^F$, the bank gets A^F. But loans exceeding A^F cannot be guaranteed by the firm's capital, and thus are riskier for the bank. This is why beyond A^F the bank will charge a spread, x. This spread is called the *external finance premium*, indicating that it is the premium the bank asks for loans that are not guaranteed. (Which of the firm's assets will be accepted as a guarantee, and thus the value of A^F, depends on the bank. Some banks may only accept very liquid assets, cash or government bonds; others may accept even real estate which is riskier because the bank cannot be sure about its value if it were to sell it. What often happens is that the less liquid an asset is the less easy it is to use it as a guarantee.) A firm's own capital, A^F, not only serves as an explicit guarantee for the bank: it also determines the firm's incentives to choose sound investment projects and to carry them out carefully. The larger A^F, the more the firm has to lose if the project fails. This is another reason why the spread, x, depends on $(I - A^F)$.

So, the spread, x, depends on both banks' and firms' capital, therefore we can write:

$$x = x(A^B, A^F)$$
$$(-\ -)$$

The minus signs below A^F and A^B show that when either banks' or firms' capital decreases, the spread, x, increases.

How does a reduction in the capital of firms or banks affect lending? Consider first a fall in firms' capital, A^F (that is, a reduction of the firm's financial assets which reduces the value of the guarantees it can provide). The spread x will increase and so will the cost of credit. Bank lending will fall. Investment, and output, will go down.

Next consider the effect on lending of a fall in the capital of banks, A^B. We have already seen that banks are likely to respond to a fall in A^B by cutting down lending. The effect is the same as that produced by a fall in firms' capital. For any level of the interest rate, i, a fall in A^B will increase the spread, x, and the cost of credit for firms, and therefore will reduce investment, and output.

Now let's go back to the *IS–LM* model. As investment enters the *IS* relation, but not the *LM* relation, all we have to do is to replace, in the *IS* relation, the demand for investment as we described it in Chapter 4, with the new version described above. The 'new' *IS* relation is thus a function of the external finance premium, x, because investment depends on the cost of loans and thus on x: $I\ [Y, i + x(A^B, A^F)]$. Nothing else changes.

Thus, when banks' capital falls – for whatever reason, for instance because the number of families unable to repay their mortgages or their credit card loans increases – the spread, x, increases and the equilibrium cost of bank loans also increases. The result is that the *IS* curve shifts to the left and the new equilibrium level of output decreases, as shown in Figure 20.6.

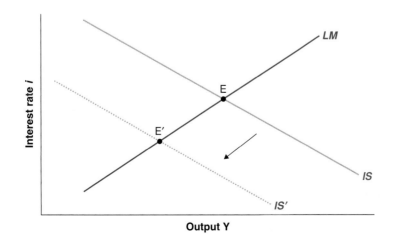

Figure 20.6

Goods and financial market equilibrium following a fall in banks' capital which raises the external finance premium

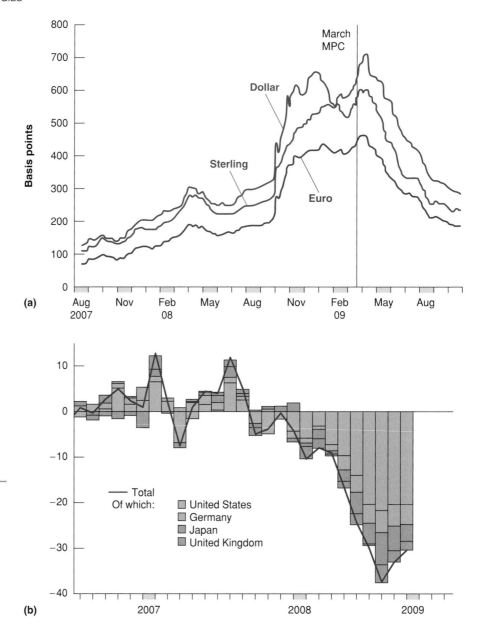

Figure 20.7

The external finance premium and the collapse of investment expenditure

(a) Corporate bonds (investment grade): spreads in the euro area, the UK and the USA.

(b) Capital goods orders.

Sources: IMF and Bank for International Settlements, 2009 Annual Report.

To summarise: any event that affects the value of the assets that sit on the balance sheets of banks (or of firms) – thus any event that changes the capital of banks or firms – will also affect the equilibrium level of output. Moreover, the higher is leverage the larger the effect on output of a given fall in the value of assets. The reason is that the higher is leverage the higher the hit capital takes for any given loss in the value of assets. This is exactly why the financial crisis hit the real economy so hard: a relatively small shock to the value of banks' assets (the losses on sub-prime and other mortgages) was amplified by high leverage and produced large losses in banks' capital. This raised the external finance premium and produced a corresponding fall in investment. Figure 20.7 shows precisely this: the widening of the external finance premium (in the figure this is measured by the corporate bond spread – that is, the difference between the interest rate firms pay on the bonds they issue, ρ, and the lending rate, i) during the crisis in Europe and in the USA and the collapse of investment expenditure in four countries.

20.5 INTERNATIONAL CONTAGION

The financial crisis which started in the USA rapidly affected all major advanced economies and emerging market countries. The main channel of transmission was trade. As you have learned in Chapter 6, openness in goods markets has an important macroeconomic implication: consumers and firms spend part of their disposable income on foreign goods. When disposable income falls, consumption also falls and this reduces both demand for domestic goods and demand for foreign goods, that is imports. During the financial crisis, as US consumers and firms stopped spending, US imports collapsed. Figure 20.8 shows that in just a few months, from July 2008 to February 2009, US imports of goods fell by 46%! As the USA is the single largest importer of goods in the world (US imports account for around 13% of total world imports), such a huge collapse represented a large decrease in exports for countries exporting to the USA. Overall, the contraction of international trade in volume (considering both imports and exports) reached 12% during 2009 (Figure 20.9).

◀ The majority (around 60%) of US imports come from the EU (17%), China (16%), Canada (16%) and Mexico (10%).

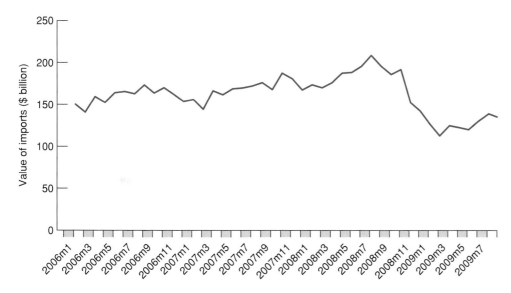

Figure 20.8

The collapse of US merchandise imports in 2009

Source: WTO, Short-term merchandise trade statistics, available at www.wto.org.

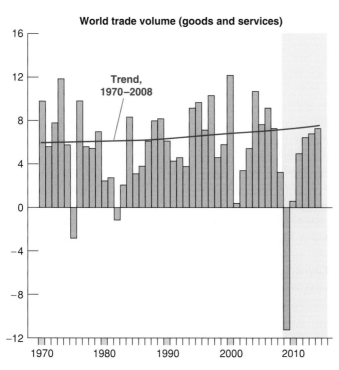

Figure 20.9

The collapse in world trade in 2009

Source: IMF *World Economic Outlook*.

Contagion was larger in countries relatively more dependent on foreign trade – Germany for instance. Among open economies, those with stronger trade ties with the USA – Canada and Mexico above all, but also the EU and China – suffered more. The effects of international contagion were amplified in countries – the UK and Ireland, in particular – where domestic banks suffered problems similar to those of US banks.

20.6 POLICY RESPONSE TO THE CRISIS

In this section, we explain how monetary and fiscal policies were used to respond to the crisis. The basic data are shown in Figure 20.10. Central banks used monetary policy to slash interest rates to close to zero, while governments used fiscal policy to replace private with public demand, trying to replace the fall in private consumption and private investment with higher government spending. Part of the increase in budget deficits was automatic, due to the working of automatic stabilisers (such as higher unemployment benefits) and part was associated with specific actions by governments, such as increases in public investment and reduction in tax rates (see the lower panel of Figure 20.10).

Did policy work, i.e. was the intervention by governments and central banks effective at limiting the effect of the financial crisis on output and employment? Before answering this question, we need to look more closely at monetary policy, since what central banks did was not only to slash interest rates to close to zero. To understand this we need to return to an issue we raised in Chapter 4. There we discussed the possibility of a liquidity trap in the *IS–LM* model. We see this in Figure 20.11. The financial crisis – by reducing banks' capital and, through this channel, investment, as we have seen in Figure 20.7 – shifted the *IS* curve to the left, to *IS'*. Before the crisis, the economy was at full employment at E: the crisis has shifted the equilibrium to E'. Fiscal policy has partly offset the shift in the *IS* curve, bringing it back to *IS''*: the effect is not large, at least in the short run, because, for example, public investment in infrastructure – one of the largest items in the fiscal response package – takes time to put in place and translate into spending.

Monetary policy shifts the *LM* curve, but when it reaches *LM'* the interest rate is zero and 'traditional monetary policy' no longer works because the nominal interest rate cannot fall below zero. Thus the economy is stuck at *Y''* and all monetary policy can do is wait for the effects of fiscal policy to further shift the *IS* curve.

Is there something else the central bank can do? Remember why the *IS* curve shifted in the first place. It was because the fall in their capital induced banks to sell part of their assets, including loans. This raised the cost of borrowing for firms, and the result was lower investment. If the central bank were to step in and buy some of the assets banks wish to get rid of (including some of their loans), the cost of borrowing need not change. For example: assume the bank, following the hit it has taken on its capital, wishes to reduce its lending to the construction industry, and it does so by refusing to provide any new loan to builders. If the central bank is willing to buy a portion of the bank's portfolio of building loans (paying in cash), the bank can keep lending to this industry. In other words, by offering to buy assets from commercial banks, the central bank can undo the original increase in x, the external finance premium, and avoid a contraction of lending. In terms of Figure 20.11, the *LM* curve shifts to the right (because the central bank prints money to buy the banks' assets) but this also shifts the *IS* curve back. The interest rate remains at zero, but output moves back towards Y^*. This is called **quantitative easing**, something we have already seen in Chapter 4.

The Bank of England, for instance, in March 2009 started to buy assets from the private sector. These assets were loans banks had made to firms, or bonds that had been issued

Quantitative easing is a solution when increasing the money supply by cutting interest rates is not working – most obviously when the economy is in a liquidity trap, i.e. interest rates are essentially at zero and it is therefore impossible to cut them further.

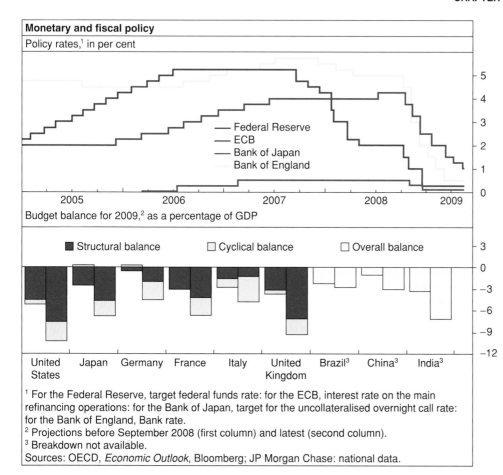

Monetary and fiscal policy

Policy rates,[1] in per cent

Budget balance for 2009,[2] as a percentage of GDP

■ Structural balance □ Cyclical balance □ Overall balance

[1] For the Federal Reserve, target federal funds rate: for the ECB, interest rate on the main refinancing operations: for the Bank of Japan, target for the uncollateralised overnight call rate: for the Bank of England, Bank rate.
[2] Projections before September 2008 (first column) and latest (second column).
[3] Breakdown not available.
Sources: OECD, *Economic Outlook*, Bloomberg; JP Morgan Chase: national data.

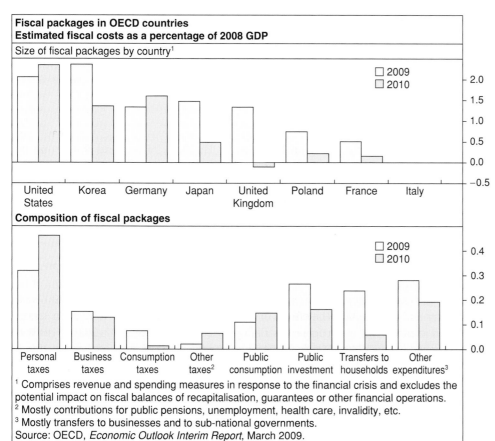

Fiscal packages in OECD countries
Estimated fiscal costs as a percentage of 2008 GDP

Size of fiscal packages by country[1]

Composition of fiscal packages

[1] Comprises revenue and spending measures in response to the financial crisis and excludes the potential impact on fiscal balances of recapitalisation, guarantees or other financial operations.
[2] Mostly contributions for public pensions, unemployment, health care, invalidity, etc.
[3] Mostly transfers to businesses and to sub-national governments.
Source: OECD, *Economic Outlook Interim Report*, March 2009.

Figure 20.10

Policy response to the crisis

Source: Bank for International Settlements, 2009 Annual Report, Graphs VI.1 and VI.7.

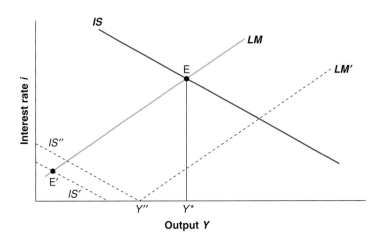

Figure 20.11

Monetary policy in the presence of a liquidity trap

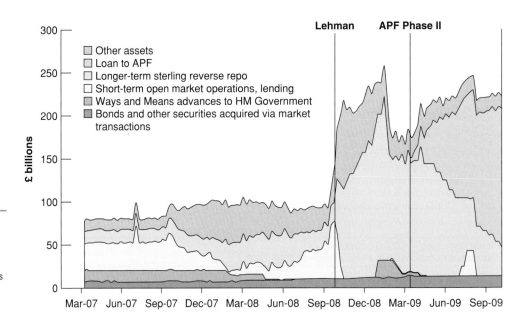

Figure 20.12

Quantitative easing in the UK

Loans to APF are the loans the Bank of England made to the legal entity (the Asset Purchase Facility) in charge of buying assets from the market on behalf of the Bank.

Source: Bank of England.

by firms and bought by banks or other investors. The Bank of England stated that the purpose of these purchase was 'to ease conditions in corporate credit markets and, ultimately, to raise nominal demand', precisely as we have seen in the previous section. By September 2009, these assets accounted for almost all assets held by the Bank of England (Figure 20.12). Because the value of a central bank's assets is equal to the value of its liabilities (namely money), assets bought by banks amounted to almost the entire UK money supply.

At the time of writing, we know that policy intervention did work to avoid a depression. Figure 20.13 shows the path of industrial production and retail sales since the start of the crisis. Although one cannot attribute the turnaround observed in the summer of 2009 only to monetary and fiscal policy, the effects of the financial shock seem to have been serious but limited in time. This is particularly striking if we compare the 2007–2010 crisis with what happened in the 1930s. Figure 20.14 compares the paths of industrial production in the 2007–2010 crisis with what happened after 1929. (We show industrial production, a very imperfect measure of output – industrial production accounts for 15–20% of total output in advanced economies – because this is the only measure of output available for the 1930s.) While output did fall, what happened is nothing like what happened after the financial crisis of 1929.

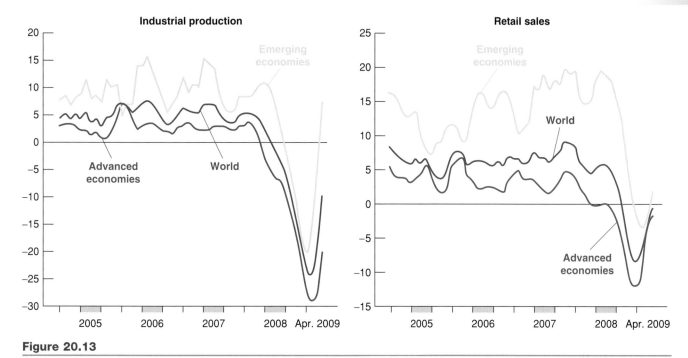

Figure 20.13

Effectiveness of the policy response to the crisis

Source: IMF, *World Economic Outlook*, July 2009 update, Fig. 2.

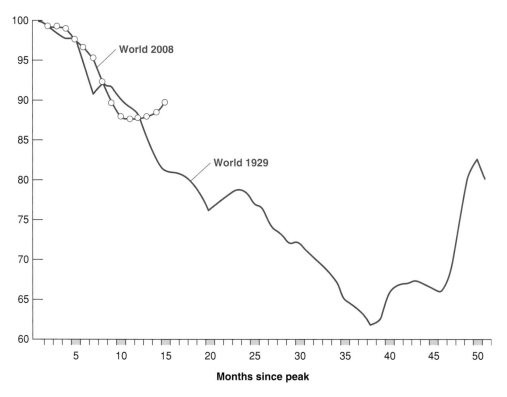

Figure 20.14

The 1930s and the 2007–2010 crisis

Source: Barry Eichengreen, and K. H. O'Rourke, *A Tale of Two Depressions*, Voxeu.org, September 2009.

FOCUS
Why did Poland do so well in the crisis?

Among the EU27, Poland was the only one where in 2009, so far the worst year of the crisis, GDP grew. While output in the EU27 was contracting, on average by 4% (with peaks of –13% in Latvia, –10% in Estonia, –9% in Ireland), Poland grew almost 1%.

Why was Poland different? We look for an answer by comparing Poland (in the table below) with a country which is in many ways relatively similar: Hungary. The difference in macroeconomic outcomes couldn't be sharper. While Poland in the middle of the crisis was growing, Hungary contracted by 6.5%, driven by a sharp fall in households consumption.

Notice first that financial support by the IMF cannot explain the difference. The IMF extended a line of credit to both countries. If anything, the credit Hungary received was larger, as a fraction of its GDP (the ratio of Poland's to Hungary's GDP is 2.5 to 1). The IMF cannot be the explanation. Can the difference in domestic macro-economic policies (both monetary and fiscal policies) be the explanation? The answer is yes.

Poland responded to the crisis with a fiscal expansion: relative to the year the crisis started, the budget deficit widened by 3.4 percentage points of GDP. The fiscal stimulus came in the form of a tax cut that kept consumption growing. But the fiscal stimulus might not have worked had the central bank not accompanied the tax cut with a monetary expansion. The money supply was expanded and the exchange rate depreciated (by 15%). The

exchange rate depreciation was a central part of the policy package. By raising the relative price of imported goods, it shifted demand away from imports toward domestic products. This was important, otherwise the increase in consumption induced by the tax cut would have fallen (at least in part) on imports with little effect on domestic output. Thus a flexible exchange rate regime has served Poland well by facilitating the economy's adjustment to the external shock

Hungary did the opposite: it tightened fiscal policy and kept the exchange rate relatively stable. Consumption collapsed and the fall in consumption translated into a corresponding fall in output because the exchange rate failed to shift whatever demand there was away from imports and toward domestically produced goods.

Why was policy so different? The explanation lies in the conditions the two countries were in when the crisis hit. Because Poland entered the crisis with relatively healthy fundamentals, the government was able to cushion the downturn. This option was not available to Hungary which entered the crisis with a budget deficit as large as 9% of GDP (compared with 2% in Poland) and an 8.5% current account deficit (3% in Poland). Moreover, Hungarian households had borrowed in euros rather than in the domestic currency (the Forint). Following Poland, and letting the Forint depreciate relative to the euro would have increased the burden on those loans, with a depressing effect on consumption.

	GDP growth in 2009	Consumption growth in 2009	Budget deficit 2009 relative to 2007, + indicates a larger budget deficit	Euro exchange rate 2009 relative to 2007, – indicates a depreciation	IMF FCL US$bn
Poland	+1.0%	+2.5%	+3.4%	–15%	20
Hungary	–6.5%	–8.1%	–1.0%	–5%	12

Source: IMF.

Note: FCL are the IMF 'Flexible Credit Lines', a lending facility designed to support countries in the crisis.

20.7 THE LEGACY OF THE CRISIS

Looking forward, what legacy will this crisis leave with us? The main legacy arises from the use of fiscal policy which has resulted in a large increase in public debt (see Figure 20.15): how will this be reduced? The legacy of high debt will be with us for a long time. History shows that periods of debt build-up – for instance during wars – take a long time to be reversed. We shall study some such experiences in Chapter 21. Sometimes high debt goes along with high inflation, as inflation is a way to reduce the real value of debt, as we will learn in Chapter 22.

The concern about inflation also arises from the way monetary policy has been used: not only slashing interest rates to zero, but continuing with quantitative easing, as we have

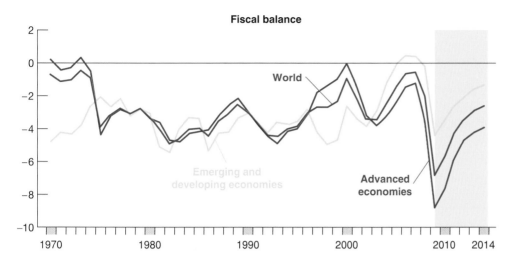

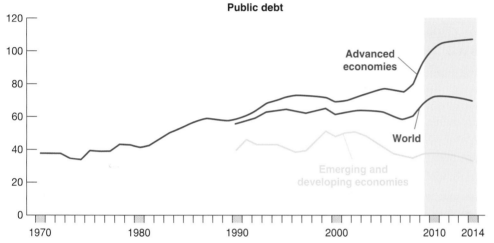

Figure 20.15

Legacies of the crisis: public debt

Source: IMF, *World Economic Outlook*, July 2009 update, Fig. 1.14.

learned in the previous section. In normal times, the central bank would have 'created' additional money buying Treasury bills for the market in a series of open market operations. This time, however, the Fed and the Bank of England (to a lesser extent the ECB) have created money by buying from the market a wide range of securities which, as in the case of the mortgages bought by the Fed, are much less liquid than Treasury bills. When these central banks decide that the time has come to raise interest rates to prevent inflation, they might find that selling such assets back to the market is not easy.

The legacy of high debt and the need to unwind the effects of quantitative easing will shape economic policy in most developed countries for many years to come.

SUMMARY

- In the autumn of 2008, the world entered into the deepest recession experienced since the Second World War. The origin of this recession was a financial crisis which started in the USA in the summer of 2007, then spread to Europe and eventually affected the entire world.

- The crisis of 2007–2010 originated in the US housing market where a sharp fall in house prices hit households and induced them to consume less.

- The effect of the bursting of the housing bubble on consumption was big, but still not enough to explain the

disaster that followed. Within a year of the crisis, the world's financial markets had come to a standstill: credit had stopped flowing even to the best companies, and this translated into a sharp drop in investment.

- The fall in house prices affected banks and was amplified by their response as they tried to limit the impact of house mortgages on their balance sheets.

- The financial crisis which started in the USA rapidly affected all major advanced countries and emerging market countries. One channel of transmission was trade. As

US consumers and firms stopped spending, US imports and world trade collapsed.

● Monetary and fiscal policies were used to reduce the negative impact on the recession. Part of the increase in budget deficits was automatic, due to the working of automatic stabilisers (such as higher unemployment benefits) and part was associated with specific actions by

governments, such as increases in public investment and reduction in tax rates.

● Once the world economy emerges from the recession, two legacies will remain: expansionary monetary policies will translate into higher inflation, and expansionary fiscal policies will cause an increase in government debt across advanced economies.

KEY TERMS

Sub-prime mortgages 416   Regulation 422   Quantitative easing 428

QUESTIONS AND PROBLEMS

QUICK CHECK

1. *Using the information in this chapter, label each of the following statements true, false or uncertain. Explain briefly.*

a. The origins of the recession which began in 2008 can be found in a financial crisis caused by poor functioning of the entire banking system.

b. The boom in house prices since 2000 in the USA did not contribute to the financial crisis because there were sound reasons for the rise in prices.

c. Financial liberalisation was at the origin of the financial crisis; hence a way to prevent another such crisis is strong regulation of the banking system.

d. Banks like to have high leverage because it leads to higher profit, and this is the reason why they expanded lending to subprime borrowers.

e. The main channel of transmission of the financial crisis around the world was the participation of other countries' banks in US financial institutions.

f. The major policy response to the crisis was a severe credit tightening to prevent the banking system from lending to subprime borrowers.

2. Active monetary policy

a. Consider an economy with output below the natural level of output. How could the central bank use monetary policy to return the economy to its natural lever of output? Illustrate your answer in an *IS–LM* diagram.

b. Again suppose that output is below the natural level. This time, however, assume that the central bank does not change monetary policy. Under normal circumstances, how does the economy return to its natural level of output? Illustrate your answer in an *IS–LM* diagram.

c. Considering your answer to part (b), if the central bank does nothing, what is likely to happen to expected inflation? How does this change in expected inflation affect the *IS–LM* diagram? Does output move closer to the natural level?

d. Consider the following policy advice: 'Because the economy always returns to the natural level of output on its own, the central bank does not need to concern itself with recessions.' Do your answers to parts (a) through (c) support this advice?

DIG DEEPER

3. Leverage

Suppose that Bank A has €500 of assets and €80 of capital. Bank B has €400 of assets and €100 of capital.

a. Define and compute the leverage for Bank A and Bank B.

b. Now suppose that the value of the assets falls by 10 for each bank. How does the leverage change for each of the two banks?

c. Suppose neither bank succeeds in restoring capital at the original level. By how much will loans have to decrease if both banks want to maintain the original leverage?

4. Monetary policy in the presence of a liquidity trap

Consider the following IS–LM model:

$$C = 100 + 0.25YD$$
$$T = 200$$
$$G = 350$$
$$I = 150 + 0.25Y - 500i$$
$$(M/P)^d = 2Y - 2000i$$
$$M/P = 2000$$

a. Derive the *IS* relation.

b. Derive the *LM* relation.

c. Solve for the equilibrium real output.

d. Solve for the equilibrium interest rate.

e. Now suppose that autonomous consumption decreases from 100 to 50. Solve for the equilibrium real output and interest rate. Compare the change in the equilibrium level of output with the change in autonomous consumption. Explain briefly.

f. Suppose that the central bank tries to increase the equilibrium real output by increasing the money supply by 10%. Solve for the equilibrium real output and interest rate. Do you think the central bank intervention is effective in increasing the equilibrium real output? Explain briefly.

g. Which alternative measures can the central bank adopt to increase the equilibrium real output?

EXPLORE FURTHER

5. The external finance premium and the cost of bank loans

Consider the following IS–LM model:

$$C = 150 + \tfrac{1}{2}YD$$
$$T = 300$$
$$G = 300$$
$$I = 150 + \tfrac{1}{3}Y - 10\,000\rho$$
$$\rho = i + x$$
$$(M/P)^d = 2Y - 20\,000i$$
$$M/P = 2600$$

a. Imagine the external finance premium (x) is zero. Derive the *IS* relation.

b. Derive the *LM* relation.

c. Solve for the equilibrium real output and interest rate.

d. What is the cost of bank loans and the equilibrium level of investment?

e. Now suppose that firms' capital drops following a severe slump in stock prices and banks charge an external finance premium (x) on loans to firms equal to 0.5%. How does the cost of bank loans change? What is the new equilibrium level of investment? How does this affect the equilibrium real output? Explain briefly.

We invite you to visit the Blanchard page on the Prentice Hall website, at **www.prenhall.com/blanchard** for this chapter's World Wide Web exercises.

FURTHER READING

- For a description of how the financial system created the complex assets that played sach a central role in the crisis, read *Fool's Gold* (New York, Free Press, 2009) by Gillian Tett.

- A blow-by-blow account of how the Fed acted during the crisis is given by David Wessell, in *In FED We Trust: Ben Bernanke's War on the Great Panic* (New York, Crown Business, 2009).

- For a detailed, real-time, history of the crisis, read the series of *World Economic Outlook*, a bi-annual survey of the world economy produced by the International Monetary Fund. The surveys come out in April and October, and are available on the IMF website.

- The legacy of the crisis is analysed in the September (2009) issue of the *World Economic Outlook*.

Chapter 21

HIGH DEBT

Why do economists worry so much when governments run large budget deficits and accumulate debt quickly? In answering this question, they argue that debt slows capital accumulation, puts at risk the stability of the economic system and makes it extremely difficult to conduct monetary policy.

In principle, a high government deficit is neither good nor evil. Deficits (and surpluses) can help to redistribute the burden of taxation over time. Deficits become a problem when they result in rapid accumulation of debt and also because, as we shall discuss, reducing a high debt, once it has been created, can take a long time, often many decades. This is why high debt will turn out to be the most long-lasting consequence of the 2007–2010 financial crisis.

This chapter is in three parts:

- Section 21.1 studies the budget constraint of government – namely the relationship between debt, deficit, government spending and taxes – and examines its consequences.

- Section 21.2 examines which factors determine the evolution over time – the dynamics – of the debt-to-GDP ratio, and what determines debt accumulation.

- Section 21.3 introduces a 'political theory' of debt that will help us understand some historical episodes of large build-ups and subsequent reductions in public debt.

21.1 THE GOVERNMENT'S BUDGET CONSTRAINT

Suppose that the government, starting from a situation of **balanced budget**, decides to cut taxes while keeping public expenditure unchanged, thereby creating a **budget deficit**. What will happen to debt over time? Will the government eventually be forced to increase taxes? If so, by how much: by more than its original cut? To answer these questions, let us start from a definition of the budget deficit. We can write the budget deficit in year t as:

$$deficit_t = rB_{t-1} + G_t - T_t \qquad [21.1]$$

All variables are in real terms, that is measured in units of real output, not in euros or pounds. B_{t-1} is public debt at the end of year $t-1$, i.e. at the beginning of year t. We define B as all the bonds and bills issued by the govrnemnt and held by the private sector (at home or abroad) but excluding those held by the central bank. r is the real interest rate, which for the time being we assume to be constant. rB_{t-1} represents the real interest paid on government bonds in circulation. G_t is government spending on goods and services in year t. T_t are taxes less transfers in year t.

The budget deficit is equal to spending on goods and services, plus interest payments, minus taxes less transfers.

Equation (21.1) has two characteristics.

1. First, we measure interest in real terms – that is not considering the actual interest payments (which are calculated as the **nominal** interest rate times the stock of debt), but *real interest payments*, i.e. the *real* interest rate on existing debt. This is in fact the proper way to measure interest payments. In Brazil, for instance, in the early 1990s, when inflation was running at 50% per year, nominal interest payments were very large because the nominal interest rate was as high as 50%: but the real interest rate (the nominal minus expected inflation) was close to zero: debt was not really a burden for the state. However, the official measures of the deficit are based on actual expenditure and thus on nominal interest payments: as a result, they give a distorted picture of state finances. In Brazil, for instance, the official deficit was extremely high, but the deficit corrected for inflation was not as large. (To see how you can compute the deficit adjusted for inflation starting from the official measure of the deficit, look at the Focus box 'How to compute the budget deficit correct for inflation').

2. To remain consistent with our definition of G as public spending on goods and services, we continue to assume that G includes neither interest payments nor transfers. Transfers are subtracted from T. The official measures of public spending include transfers, and they define revenues as taxes rather than as net taxes. This is simply an accounting convention: adding transfers to expenses or subtracting them from taxes obviously makes a difference when you compute G and T, but it is irrelevant when you compute the deficit.

When a government faces a budget deficit, it may ask the central bank to finance it. In this case, what the government technically does is to sell bonds to the central bank. Alternatively, it may sell the bonds directly to private investors.

In Chapter 22, we will focus on the link between deficits, money creation (what happens when the central bank buys government bonds) and inflation. In this chapter, however, to keep things simple we assume that the only means of **deficit financing** is selling securities to private investors.

In this case, the budget constraint of the government simply says that the increase in government debt in year t must be equal to the deficit in year t:

$$B_t - B_{t-1} = deficit_t$$

So if the government runs a deficit, government debt increases. If the government has a surplus, debt decreases. Using our definition of the deficit, we can write the government budget constraint as:

$$\underbrace{B_t - B_{t-1}}_{} = \underbrace{rB_{t-1}}_{\substack{interest \\ payments}} + \underbrace{(G_t - T_t)}_{\substack{primary \\ deficit}} \qquad [21.2]$$

We do this because what matters, at least for this discussion, are the net sums payed by households to the state, that is the taxes households pay minus the what they receive from the state, such as unemployment benefits and pensions.

Remember there is a (sometimes big) difference between the official deficit and the deficit adusted for inflation.

Recall that in our definition of public debt, this includes only the securities held by private investors, not those purchased by the central bank.

FOCUS
How to compute the budget deficit corrected for inflation

Official measures of the budget deficit are constructed (omitting the time index) as the sum of nominal interest, iB, more government spending on goods and services, G, minus taxes net of transfers, T:

$$\text{official deficit} = iB + G - T$$

This is a measure of the change in *nominal debt*. If it is positive, the government is spending more than it collects, and must therefore issue new debt. If it is negative, the government reimburses part of the existing debt.

But this measure is not suitable to calculate the change in *real debt*, i.e. the variation in what the government will have to pay in terms of goods rather than money.

To understand why, suppose that the official measure of the deficit is equal to zero: the government does not issue or repay any securities. Suppose that inflation is positive and equal to 10%. In this case, at the end of the year, the real value of debt will be reduced by 10%. So, if we define – as we should – the deficit as the change in the real value of debt, the government recorded a budget surplus equal to 10% of the initial value of the debt.

In general: if B is the debt and inflation is π, the official measure of the deficit overstates the correct measure by an amount equal to πB. The correct, inflation-adjusted measure of the deficit is in fact equal to:

$$iB + G - T - \pi B = (i - \pi)B + G - T = rB + G - T$$

where $r = i - \pi$ is the real interest rate.* The correct measure of the deficit is thus equal to the real interest plus government spending minus taxes net of transfers, i.e. the measure that we use in the text.

The difference between the official and the proper measure is equal to πB. This means that the higher the rate of inflation (π) or the level of debt (B), the more imprecise is the official measure of the deficit. In countries where inflation and debt are both very high, the official measure could indicate a very large deficit, even in the presence of a decreasing real debt. For this reason, we should always take inflation into account whenever we derive conclusions on fiscal policy.

Figure 21.1 shows the official measure and the inflation-adjusted deficit for the UK since 1949. Both measures show a strong decline occurring after 1976, an improvement at the end of the 1980s, followed by a sharp deterioration in the mid-1990s, a significant improvement around 2000 and a further deterioration since 2006.

* Note that here r is the nominal interest rate minus actual inflation: it should be called the 'real effective interest rate' to distinguish it from the 'real interest rate' which we defined in Chapter 14 as the nominal interest rate less expected inflation.

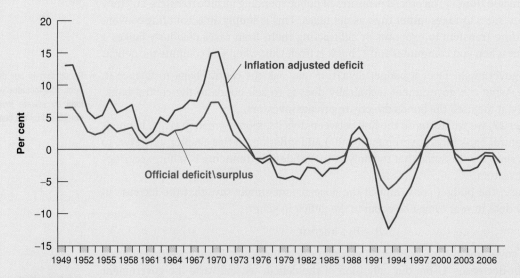

Figure 21.1

Official and inflation adjusted budget deficits for the UK, 1949–2006

Finally, if we move B_{t-1} to the right of the equation and we reorganise the terms, we get:

$$B_t = (1+r)B_{t-1} + G_t - T_t \qquad [21.3]$$

Debt at the end of year t is equal to $(1+r)$ times debt at the end of year $t-1$, plus the **primary deficit**, which is equal to the total defcit minus interst payments, that is $G_t - T_t$. This relation will be very useful in the next sections.

Current and future taxes

We now use equation (21.3) to run an experiment. We want to study the effect on the evolution of debt and future taxes of a tax cut in year 0. We start from a situation in which, up to year 0, the budget had always been in balance, so that debt is zero. In year 0, the government cuts taxes by 1 for one year (the amount is irrelevant, since we are computing everything in real terms; think of the tax cut as a reduction equivalent to 1 unit of output). Then, debt at the end of year 0, B_0, will be equal to 1. What happens next? Let us consider several cases.

- *Repayment in year 1* – suppose the government decides to repay the whole debt in year 1. From equation (21.3), the budget constraint in year 1 is given by:

$$B_1 = (1+r)B_0 + (G_1 - T_1)$$

  If all debt is repaid in year 1 then, at the end of year 1, debt will be equal to zero: $B_1 = 0$. Replacing B_0 with 1 and B_1 with 0, the previous equation becomes:

$$T_1 - G_1 = (1+r)1 = 1 + r$$

  To repay the debt in year 1, the government must therefore create, in year 1, a **primary surplus** equal to $(1+r)$ units of goods. This can happen in two ways: by reducing spending or by increasing taxes. Here we assume that the adjustment is done through taxes, while spending remains unchanged. It follows that a tax cut of 1 in year 0 must be compensated by an increase in taxes by $(1+r)$ in year 1. The path of taxes and debt corresponding to this case is shown in Figure 21.2a (assuming $r = 10\%$). The blue areas represent the deviations of taxes from their initial level, and pink areas represent the debt level.

- *Repayment after t years* – suppose now that the government decides to wait for t years before raising taxes to repay the debt. In this case, from year 1 to year t, the primary deficit will be equal to zero. Let's see what the effects are on the debt level at the beginning of year t (or at the end of year $t-1$). In year 1, the primary deficit is equal to zero. Then, in equation (21.3), debt at the end of year 1 is equal to:

◄ Repayment means that the government buys back securities held by private investors.

$$B_1 = (1+r)B_0 + 0 = 1 + r$$

  where the last equality comes from our initial hypothesis according to which $B_0 = 1$. In year 2, with a primary deficit still equal to zero, debt at the end of the year is:

$$B_2 = (1+r)B_1 + 0 = (1+r)(1+r) = (1+r)^2$$

  Solving for the debt level in year 3 and subsequent years, it is clear that, as long as the government maintains a primary deficit equal to zero, the debt grows at a rate equal to the interest rate, and therefore debt at the end of year $t-1$ is given by:

$$B_{t-1} = (1+r)^{t-1} \qquad [21.4]$$

  Although taxes have been reduced only in year 0, the debt increases continuously from year 0 onwards, at a rate equal to the interest rate. The reason is simple: while the primary deficit is zero, the debt is now positive, as is the interest accruing on the debt itself. Each year, the government must issue more debt to pay interest on existing debt.

  In year t, the year in which the government decides to repay the debt, the budget constraint is given by:

$$B_t = (1+r)B_{t-1} + (G_t - T_t)$$

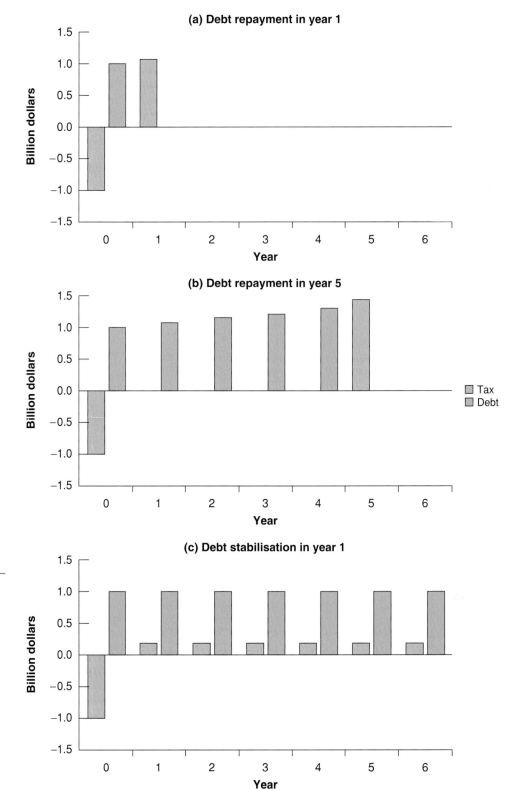

Figure 21.2

Tax reduction, debt repayment and debt stabilisation

(a) If debt is entirely repaid in year 1, a tax reduction equal to 1 in year 0 must be compensated by an increase in taxes by $(1 + r)$ in year 1.

(b) If debt is entirely repaid in year t, a tax reduction equal to 1 in year 0 must be compensated by an increase in taxes by $(1 + r)^t$ in year 1.

(c) If debt is stabilised from year 1 onwards, then taxes must be permanently higher by $(1 + r)$ from year 1 onwards.

If the debt is fully repaid in year t, B_t (the debt at the end of year t) will be equal to zero. Substituting B_t with zero and B_{t-1} with its expression from equation (21.4), we obtain:

$$0 = (1 + r)(1 + r)^{t-1} + (G_t - T_t)$$

By rearranging terms and moving $G_t - T_t$ to the left side, we get:

$$T_t - G_t = (1 + r)^t$$

To repay the debt, the government should produce a primary surplus equal to $(1 + r)^t$ units of goods. If the adjustment is done only through taxation, the initial tax cut of 1 in year 0 implies, after t years and during a single year, a tax increase equal to $(1 + r)^t$. The path of taxes and debt related to this case is shown in Figure 21.2b.

This example allows you to draw a first important conclusion. If government spending remains unchanged, a reduction of taxes today must be offset by an increase in future taxes. The longer the government waits before raising taxes, or the higher the real interest rate, the greater the increase in taxes will have to be.

Debt and primary surpluses

So far we have assumed that the government fully repays its debt. Let us see what happens if the government decides instead to stabilise the debt, i.e. to keep B constant at the level achieved in year 1.

From equation (21.3), the budget constraint in year 1 is given by:

$$B_1 = (1 + r) B_0 + (G_1 - T_1)$$

Debt stabilisation means keeping debt equal to a given level, in our case the level of year 0, so that debt at the end of year 1 will be equal to the debt at the end of year 0, $B_1 = B_0 = 1$. Substituting into the above, we obtain:

$$1 = (1 + r) + (G_1 - T_1)$$

Rearranging terms and moving $G_1 - T_1$ to the left, we get:

$$T_1 - G_1 = (1 + r) - 1 = r$$

To avoid a further increase of debt in year 1, the government must achieve a primary surplus equal to the real interest on existing debt (remember that the level of the debt stabilises at 1). The government must do the same in subsequent years: every year, the primary surplus must be sufficient to cover interest payments, so as to leave the existing level of debt unchanged. The path of taxes and debt is shown in Figure 21.1c: the debt is equal to 1 from year 1 onwards. Taxes are higher from year 1 onwards, by an amount equal to r.

The logic of this argument extends directly to cases where the government decides to wait for t years before stabilising the debt. Since the moment when the government decides to stabilise the debt, it will have to generate primary surpluses sufficient to pay interest payments accrued until then. Of course the longer the government waits to stabilise, the higher the level of debt, the higher the interest payments and the higher the required level of taxes.

This example suggests a second conclusion. The legacy of past deficits is a higher current debt. To stabilise the debt, the government must run a primary surplus equal to the interest on existing debt. The longer the government waits before stabilising the debt, the more painful the stabilisation will be.

> Stabilisation means that the government wants to keep the amount of existing debt constant.

21.2 THE EVOLUTION OF THE DEBT/GDP RATIO

So far we have studied the evolution of the level of public debt in real terms (that is, measured in units of goods). But in an economy where output grows over time, the relevant variable is the ratio of government debt to GDP. By using this, we can tell if the debt is too high, where 'too' must be defined in relation to the ability of the government to repay the debt.

The government budget constraint in terms of GDP

To see how our previous conclusions change, let us move from equation (21.3) to an equation that expresses the evolution of **debt-to-GDP ratio** or **debt ratio**. To do this we need to carry out some further steps. Let's divide both sides of equation (21.3) by real output, Y_t, to get:

$$\frac{B_t}{Y_t} = (1+r)\frac{B_{t-1}}{Y_t} + \frac{G_t - T_t}{Y_t}$$

Rewriting, on the right side, B_{t-1}/Y_t as $(B_t/Y_{t-1})(Y_{t-1}/Y_t)$ (in other words, multiplying the numerator and denominator by Y_{t-1}), the relationship becomes:

$$\frac{B_t}{Y_t} = (1+r)\left(\frac{Y_{t-1}}{Y_t}\right)\frac{B_{t-1}}{Y_{t-1}} + \frac{G_t - T_t}{Y_t}$$

Now that each term is expressed in terms of GDP at time t, we can simplify this expression. By defining g, the growth rate of output, we have $Y_{t-1}/Y_t = 1/(1+g)$. Moreover, by approximating $(1+r)/(1+g)$ with $1 + r - g$ (which is a good enough approximation if the real interest rate and the growth rate of output are relatively small numbers), we can rewrite the previous equation as:

$$\frac{B_t}{Y_t} = (1 + r - g)\frac{B_{t-1}}{Y_{t-1}} + \frac{G_t - T_t}{Y_t} \qquad [21.5]$$

Finally, moving B_{t-1}/Y_{t-1} to the left, we get:

$$\frac{B_t}{Y_t} - \frac{B_{t-1}}{Y_{t-1}} = (r - g)\frac{B_{t-1}}{Y_{t-1}} + \frac{G_t - T_t}{Y_t} \qquad [21.6]$$

This equation tells us that the change in the debt ratio is equal to the sum of two terms:

● The first is the difference between the real interest rate and the rate of growth of GDP, multiplied by the debt ratio at the end of the previous period (and thus at the beginning of the current period). This term refers to interest payments, in real terms, corrected for the growth rate of real GDP. Depending on whether the real interest rate is higher or lower than the growth rate of real GDP, this term is a factor that increases or reduces the debt ratio. Therefore, r and g have opposite effects on the dynamics of the debt ratio.
● The second term is the ratio of the primary deficit to GDP. The primary balance relative to GDP has a positive or negative effect on the growth of debt, respectively, in the case of a deficit ($G_t - T_t > 0$) or a surplus ($G_t - T_t < 0$).

Let's now compare equation (21.6), which describes the evolution of the debt ratio, with equation (21.2), which describes the evolution of the debt level. The difference is the presence of $(r - g)$ in equation (21.6) rather than r in equation (21.2). The reason for this difference is simple. Suppose that the primary deficit is zero. In this case, the debt level will increase at a rate equal to the real interest rate, r. But, if GDP grows, the debt/GDP ratio will grow more slowly; it will grow at a rate equal to real interest rate minus the rate of growth of output, $r - g$. If the rate of growth of the economy is greater than the real interest rate, that is, if $r - g$ is negative, the debt ratio will not only grow more slowly, it will decline from year to year.

The debt ratio in the long run

Equation (21.6) – or, equivalently, equation (21.5) – allows us to analyse the change in the debt ratio from one year to the next. But we can look further ahead and ask if the debt ratio, given all the other variables, will tend to stabilise or will it instead tend to diverge, that is to shoot off to plus infinity or to zero.

Solving a simple differential equation is not difficult, but to keep things simple here we will solve it only graphically. ➤ At this point you could make a small (but very useful) investment by learning the basics of differential equations: read the Focus box 'A qualitative solution of difference equations'. Otherwise you can skip directly to the next section.

FOCUS
A qualitative solution of difference equations

The simplest mathematical tool to study the 'dynamics' of a variable is a difference equation: an expression that relates a variable with its past values. In its simplest form, a difference equation can be written as:

$$y_t = A + \beta y_t - 1 \qquad [1]$$

where y_t is the value that variable y takes at time t. In equation [1] y_t depends on its past values and on an exogenous variable, A. β is, instead, a simple constant, which from now on we will call a parameter.

Since y_t depends on a single lagged value, equation [1] is called a first order difference equation.

We can study the qualitative properties of a difference equation by means of a chart. Equation [1], for example, can be represented graphically on a Cartesian plane, as shown in Figure 21.3.

The vertical axis shows variable y_t and the horizontal axis shows variable $y_t - 1$. The 45° line identifies the points where $y_t = y_t - 1$, whereas curve C represents equation [1] with a slope lower than 1 and a vertical intercept $A > 0$. Point y, the intersection between curve C and the 45° line, is, as we shall see, the equilibrium steady state.

From this graph, we can apply an iterative method. Indeed, if we choose a value of y_0 at time zero, shown on the horizontal axis, we can derive the value of y_1, the vertical axis through the curve C. The value of y_1 can then be shown on the horizontal line through the 45° line (having a slope equal to 1, this line identifies all the points for which

the abscissa is equal to the order). The transfer of y_1 from the vertical to the horizontal axis can be done with the 45° line. Once the value of y_1 on the horizontal axis is identified, we can repeat the same reasoning, finding the value of y_2 on the vertical axis through the curve C. The iteration stops when there is no difference between two successive values of y_t. At this point, there is no more dynamics and the value of y_t coincides with that of steady state, y.

We would reach the same result if we started from an initial value of y greater than y_t such as y_0'. Again, as shown by the arrows in Figure 21.3, the value of y is reached over time. The only difference is that starting from an initial value $y_0 < y$ the dynamic equation [1] generates successively larger values of y_t until you reach stationary equilibrium. Instead, where $y_0' > y$, the dynamic equation generates, moving from one period to another, smaller and smaller values, always leading to the value of y.

So, if the curve C has slope less than 1, the equilibrium point y is reached regardless of the starting value of y_t. A balance that has these characteristics is called a stable equilibrium.

Things are different if the slope is greater than 1, as shown in Figure 21.4. In this case, if we start from a

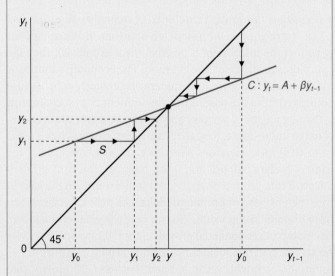

Figure 21.3

A stable equilibrium ($\beta < 1$)

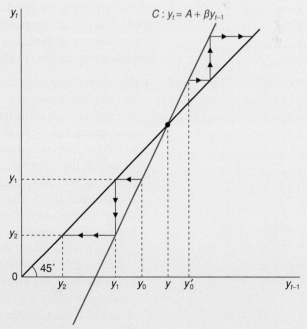

Figure 21.4

The unstable equilibrium ($\beta > 1$)

starting value lower than y, the dynamic equation generates smaller and smaller values over time, gradually moving away from the point of equilibrium.

The same divergent trend occurs if you choose as the initial value $y_0' > y$. In other words, if the slope of the equation [1] is greater than 1 ($\beta > 1$), the steady-state equilibrium is unstable because, starting from different values of y, it gradually moves away from equilibrium.

Equilibrium can be achieved only by choosing a value of y_0 equal to y.

The main rule to be drawn from this analysis is that the dynamic adjustment of a first-order difference equation toward equilibrium steady state is different depending on the value of β and of the initial value of y_t. In particular, the nature of the equilibrium steady state changes according to β: it is stable if $\beta < 1$, unstable if $\beta > 1$.

The Focus box teaches you how to solve this simple difference equation:

$$y_t = \beta y_{t-1} + A$$

where y_t is a generic dynamic variable, β a parameter and A a constant, can be applied to the equation which describes how the debt/GDP ratio evolves through time:

$$\frac{B_t}{Y_t} = (1 + r - g)\frac{B_{t-1}}{Y_{t-1}} + \frac{G_t - T_t}{Y_t}$$

where Y_t is the debt ratio, the parameter β is $1 - r - g$ and the exogenous variable A is $(G_t - T_t)/Y_t$. As we want to study the evolution of the debt ratio, given all other variables, we assume that the government runs primary deficits (or surpluses) in relation to GDP that are constant over time, namely that $(G_t - T_t)/Y_t$ is constant. To keep things simple we also assume that r and g are constant. To analyse the dynamics of the debt ratio a few graphs can help us. First, in Figure 21.5, we rewrite equation (21.5) representing the debt ratio at time t in terms of its value in the previous period. This equation is a line of slope $1 - r - g$ and intercept $(G_t - T_t)/Y_t$ (remember that we are assuming that the primary budget balance is a constant fraction of GDP). On the same figure, we also show the 45° straight line which allows us to project values from the vertical to the horizontal axis, as time goes by.

We have seen that the change in the debt-to-GDP ratio depends on whether the government runs primary surpluses or deficits, and on whether the real interest rate is higher or lower than the growth rate of GDP. Before we solve the equation graphically, you can already guess that two main cases can arise:

- *The normal case* – on most occasions, the growth rate of GDP is smaller than the real interest rate. Equation (21.5) is a straight line with slope greater than 1. What happens to the debt ratio in the long run? If the initial debt is positive (as it usually is), then the government needs primary surpluses to stabilise the debt ratio. The economic intuition is as follows. The interest rate is the rate at which the government accumulates debt because of interest due on the debt inherited from the past. If the government pays such interest by issuing new debt, rather than by means of primary surpluses, the debt ratio will continue to grow at a rate equal to the interest rate. Real GDP, however, grows at rate g – less than r – therefore the debt-to-GDP ratio increases over time. This is true even if the government maintains a primary budget balance and, even more so, if it runs primary deficits. In summary, if the growth rate is lower than the real interest rate, in the case of a positive debt inherited from the past and of primary deficits, the debt ratio increases, gradually diverging away from its equilibrium value. We can now ask what options does a government have if it wishes to stop this exponential growth in the debt ratio. The answer is simple: it must finance the servicing of the debt with adequate primary surpluses.
- *The more exotic case* – although less frequent, it can happen that the GDP growth rate exceeds the real interest rate. Equation (21.5) is then described by a straight line with slope lower than one ($1 + r - g < 1$). The straight line representing equation (21.5) is therefore has a lower slope than the 45° line, which has slope equal to 1. What happens

to the debt ratio in the long run? The debt-to-GDP ratio over time will converge to its steady state value, which we indicate with $\bar{b}$. The economic intuition is as follows: the interest rate determines the speed at which the debt grows if interest payments are financed by issuing new debt. The rate of output growth instead determines the speed at which GDP grows. So, if the primary budget is balanced, and the growth rate exceeds the interest rate, the debt ratio converges to zero. If the government continues running constant primary deficits, the debt ratio continues to converge, but at a value of the debt

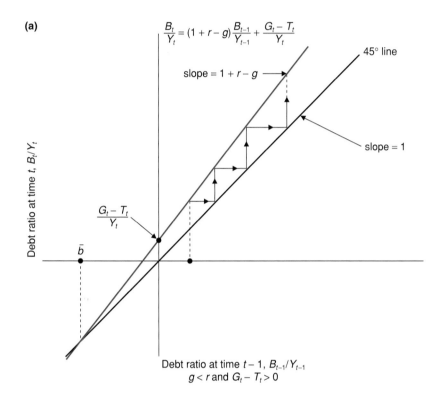

(a)

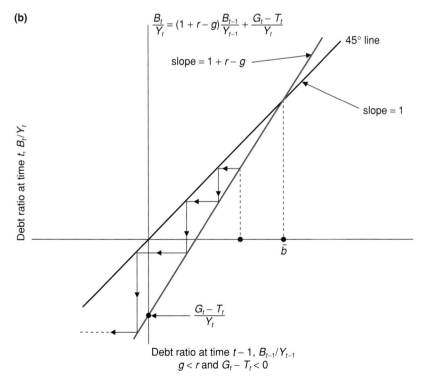

(b)

Figure 21.5

The dynamics of the debt to GDP ratio in the long run

(a) If $g < r$, and if the country has past debt and runs primary deficits $(G_t - T_t > 0)$, then the debt ratio increases going farther away from equilibrium.

(b) Even if $g < r$, and if initial debt is positive, the debt ratio decreases over time if the government runs 'adequate' primary surpluses $(G_t - T_t < 0)$.

(c) If $g > r$, the debt ratio converges to the equilibrium level despite the presence of primary deficits $(G_t - T_t > 0)$.

(d) If $g > r$ and the government runs primary surpluses $(G_t - T_t < 0)$, then the debt ratio always converges to its equilibrium level.

(c)

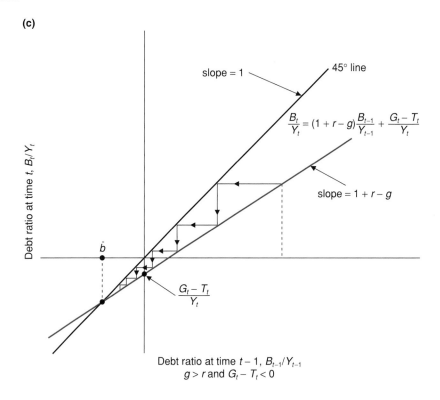

Debt ratio at time $t - 1$, B_{t-1}/Y_{t-1}
$g > r$ and $G_t - T_t < 0$

(d)

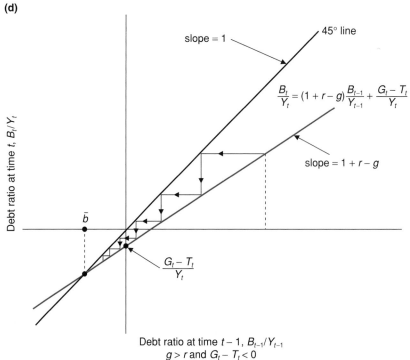

Debt ratio at time $t - 1$, B_{t-1}/Y_{t-1}
$g > r$ and $G_t - T_t < 0$

Figure 21.5

(Cont'd)

such that the reduction in the debt ratio due to the fact that the growth rate is greater than the interest rate exactly offsets the increase in the ratio due to primary deficits. In summary, if the growth rate of output is greater than the interest rate, whatever the value of the debt inherited from the past and even in the presence of primary deficits, the debt ratio always converges to its steady-state value. In the case, therefore, where g exceeds r, the government should not necessarily service the debt using primary surpluses, as constant deficits are compatible with a constant debt-to-GDP ratio.

Since all variables are constant in the steady-state equilibrium, to find B/Y just ask, in equation (21.5), what if $B_t/Y_t = (B_{t-1}/Y_{t-1}) = \bar{b}$, to obtain:

$$\bar{b} = \frac{(G_t - T_t)/Y_t}{g - r}$$

which is positive for $g > r$ and G (sub t) $> T$ (sub t), but also for g, r and G (sub t), T (sub t): in equilibrium the government is a debtor.

In Figure 21.5 we describe all the possible cases arising, those with $g < r$ (cases a and b) and those with $g > r$ (cases c and d).

The evolution of the debt ratio in some European countries

The analysis conducted so far provides a useful guide to analysing the trend in the debt ratio of some European countries. The 1960s were a decade of strong growth in all countries, so strong that the average growth rate exceeded the real interest rate almost everywhere: $r - g$ was negative, and most countries succeeded in reducing the debt ratio without the need to generate large primary surpluses.

The 1970s, in contrast, were a period of much lower growth, but also of very low real interest rates (sometimes negative): $r - g$ on average was still negative, and this further reduced debt ratios. In the early 1980s (after the appointment of Paul Volker as Chairman of the Fed and the resulting shift in US monetary policy) the situation changed dramatically. Real interest rates increased and growth rates slowed down. To avoid an increase in the debt-to-GDP ratio, many countries should have created large surpluses. But this did not happen and the result was a sharp increase in debt ratios.

Table 21.1 shows the dramatic effect on debt and deficits of the use of fiscal policy during the 2007–2010 crisis. The primary balance turned from positive to negative in many European countries between 2008 and 2009 (in the UK, it had already been negative since 2002). The deficit (as a percent of GDP) increased to 11.6% in the USA and to almost 11% in the UK. The worst deterioration of the primary balance happened in Ireland, a country which ran a (modest) surplus in 2007 and, in the next three years, registered a worsening primary deficit up to 12.5% of GDP. As a result, most European countries experienced a dramatic increase in their debt-to-GDP ratios. From 2007–2010, the debt ratio increased by several percentage points, 18% on average in the euro area. In EU27 outside of the euro area, the experiences of individual countries were very varied. The debt ratio increased by 55 percentage points in the UK, up to 82% of GDP, but much less in countries which were less affected by the financial and economic crisis, such as Denmark and Sweden.

The dangers of a very high public debt

We have seen that the higher the level of public debt, the higher the primary surplus (in the normal case $r > g$) needed to keep that debt level stable, i.e. to prevent it from growing. But large primary surpluses require high taxes (remember that so far we are assuming that G remains constant), which introduce distortions in the economy. The recent experience of some European countries with a debt ratio above 100% shows an additional cost: the risk of a vicious circle that can make it difficult or impossible to conduct monetary policy with the only objective being to keep inflation under control.

To understand why, let us return to equation (21.5), which describes the evolution of the debt-to-GDP ratio:

$$\frac{B_t}{Y_t} - \frac{B_{t-1}}{Y_{t-1}} = (r - g)\frac{B_{t-1}}{Y_{t-1}} + \frac{G_t - T_t}{Y_t}$$

Consider a country with a high debt ratio, say 100%. Suppose that the real interest rate is equal to 3%, and that the growth rate is 2%. The first term on the right side of the

Table 21.1 Primary balance, interest expenditure and gross debt in selected advanced countries since 1992

	Primary balance					
	1992–2001	2002–2006	2007	2008	2009	2010
Germany	1.00	−0.4	2.6	2.6	−1.0	−2.9
Ireland	4.50	2.4	1.1	−6.1	−9.8	−12.5
Spain	0.50	2.5	3.8	−2.3	−6.9	−7.8
France	−0.25	−0.5	0.0	−0.6	−3.8	−4.0
Italy	4.05	1.4	3.5	2.4	0.2	0.1
Netherlands	3.25	1.1	2.6	3.2	−0.8	−3.4
Euro area	1.60	0.7	2.3	1.1	−2.3	−3.3
Denmark	4.50	4.8	6.1	5.0	0.1	−2.3
Sweden	1.55	2.6	5.6	4.2	−1.2	−2.5
UK	0.30	−1.0	−0.5	−3.1	−9.4	−10.8
USA	2.40	−0.9	0.2	−3.0	−9.5	−11.6
Japan	−1.40	−3.5	0.0	−0.3	−3.6	−5.2

	Interest expenditure					
	1992–2001	2002–2006	2007	2008	2009	2010
Germany	3.25	2.9	2.8	2.8	2.9	3.0
Ireland	4.15	1.2	1.0	1.1	2.3	3.2
Spain	4.25	2.1	1.6	1.6	1.6	1.9
France	3.25	2.7	2.7	2.8	2.8	3.1
Italy	9.30	4.9	5.0	5.1	4.7	4.8
Netherlands	4.90	2.5	2.2	2.2	2.6	2.7
Euro area	4.95	3.1	2.9	3.0	3.0	3.0
Denmark	5.25	2.3	1.5	1.4	1.7	1.6
Sweden	4.75	2.0	1.8	1.7	1.5	1.4
UK	3.05	2.0	2.2	2.3	2.2	3.0
USA	4.25	2.7	2.9	2.9	2.6	2.6
Japan	3.50	2.6	2.5	2.5	3.0	3.5

	Gross debt						
	2004	2005	2006	2007	2008	2009	2010
Germany	65.6	67.8	67.6	65.1	65.9	73.4	78.7
Ireland	29.4	27.5	24.9	25.0	43.2	61.2	79.7
Spain	46.2	43.0	39.6	36.2	39.5	50.8	62.3
France	64.9	66.4	63.7	63.8	68.0	79.7	86.0
Italy	103.8	105.8	106.5	103.5	105.8	113.0	116.1
Netherlands	52.4	51.8	47.4	45.6	58.2	57.0	63.1
Euro area	69.5	70.0	68.3	66.0	69.3	77.7	83.8
Denmark	44.5	37.1	31.3	26.8	33.3	32.5	33.7
Sweden	51.2	51.0	45.9	40.5	38.0	44.0	47.2
UK	40.6	42.3	43.4	44.2	52.0	68.4	81.7
USA	62.2	62.5	61.9	63.1	70.5	87.0	97.5
Japan	178.1	191.6	191.3	187.7	196.3	217.2	227.4

Notes: values are expressed as a percentage of GDP, 1992–2010; primary balance: net lending/borrowing excluding interest expenditure.

Source: European Commission – Economic Forecast, Spring 2009; IMF, *World Economic Outlook*, April 2009.

equation is equal to (3% − 2%) × 100% = 1% of GDP. Suppose further that the government generates a primary surplus of 1%, a level just sufficient to maintain a constant debt ratio – in this case, the right side of the equation is equal to 1% + (−1%) = 0%.

Suppose now that for some reason – for example, because of a political scandal which increases the perception of risk in the country – investors begin to demand higher returns for holding government bonds denominated in the currency of that country. Suppose further that the central bank wishes to defend the exchange rate (as we have discussed in Chapter 19), and in order to do so increases the interest rate from 3% to 6%. Finally, suppose that the higher interest rate triggers a recession, so that the growth rate falls to 0%. Let us now turn to taxes: $r - g$ is equal to 6% − 0% = 6%. With an increase of $r - g$ to 6%, to maintain a constant debt ratio, the government should increase its primary surplus by five points, from 1% to 6%. It is at this point that the country may enter a vicious circle.

To increase the primary surplus, the government raises taxes, but tax hikes are unpopular; they generate even more political uncertainty and further increase the risk premium and, therefore, interest rates. The fiscal tightening induced by the first increase in interest rates then generates an even deeper recession, further reducing the rate of growth. The increase in the interest rate and the lower growth rate result in higher $r - g$, making it even more difficult to stabilise the debt ratio.

Alternatively, suppose that the government is unable or unwilling to increase the budget surplus by 5% of GDP. Debt increases, and with it the concern of financial markets: if the government was not able to change the primary surplus, the debt-to-GDP ratio would grow indefinitely. The result is that investors will ask for a further interest rate increase. The easiest way in which to exit the vicious circle is by resorting to monetary financing of the deficit (Chapter 23). But once investors realise it, the prospects of higher inflation push up nominal interest rates futher, and so forth. These are not just intellectual speculations. In Italy, in the early 1990s, the 'Tangentopoli' scandals and frequent political crises triggered a series of speculative attacks on the Italian lira, making it necessary to increase interest rates, which resulted in large deficits and a growing debt ratio. The lesson is that countries with high debt should reduce it rapidly.

◀ In Chapter 23 we will see what could happen if the government decided to finance the deficit by printing new money.

How and at what speed should they reduce it? The answer is: through many years, perhaps decades, of primary surpluses. A good example is the UK in the 19th century. At the end of the wars against Napoleon, in the early 1800s, Britain had accumulated a debt ratio in excess of 200%. To reduce that ratio took almost a century: it was only by 1900 that the ratio that had dropped to 30%. The prospect of many decades of fiscal austerity is not encouraging. The result is that, when the level of debt is large, the idea of repudiating it may become attractive. The reasoning is very simple. To repudiate the debt – i.e. to cancel it, in whole or in part – is an attractive solution for the economy. This allows an immediate decrease in taxes, and hence in the distortions associated with them. It also reduces the risk of potential vicious circles. But repudiation carries with it a bigger problem, i.e. the problem of time inconsistency which we will discuss in Chapter 24. If the government fails to honour its promise to repay the debt, it will find it very difficult to borrow again in the future: following a default, financial markets will be very reluctant to buy new government securities. In other words, what seems the best today may not be so in the long term. The repudiation of the debt must be considered a last resort, and probably not a good solution even in situations of extremely high debt, exceeding even those of many countries today. In addition, debt repudation could produce a fall in consumption, as households see the value of their wealth, at least the portion invested in government bonds, reduced. (This is why governments, if they have the choice, prefer to default on securities issued abroad and held by non-resident investors, which of course has other consequences for the international reputation of the country.)

21.3 THE RETURN FROM A HIGH DEBT

At the end of the previous section, we saw that if the stock of public debt, as a ratio to GDP, reaches a very high level, the situation can escalate and lead to a debt crisis: for instance, the government finds it impossible to issue new debt except at extraordinary high interest rates. We can then ask why, in such a case, policy makers wait rather than immediately introducing adequate measures to adjust the budget. One of the reasons why corrective measures are often late and inadequate is that debt crises are largely unpredictable events, and governments tend to be short-sighted: until the crisis hits they are reluctant to admit that a crisis can burst. Therefore governments often do not perceive the urgency of an adjustment.

A second reason is that fiscal stabilisation is often the result of a political struggle between different groups, and between their political representatives. Various economic groups (the young and the old, rentiers and entrepreneurs, etc.) are likely to be affected differently by some of the measures that may be introduced to reduce a high debt. The various groups that make up a society will try to use their political pressure to defend their economic interests. To avoid losing political consensus, and thereby opening social conflicts, governments tend to delay the fiscal correction, allowing debt to grow to the point where it triggers a financial crisis.

How to reduce a high debt?

What are the options open to a government that wants to stabilise or reduce a high and growing debt ratio? There are only three ways (in the normal case $r > g$) to achieve this goal:

- Generate sufficient primary surpluses; to do so the government can cut spending and transfers or increase taxes.
- Resort to monetary financing by the central bank.
- Repudiate the debt, in whole or in part; this means that the government erases, at least in part, the existing debt, or introduces taxes on government securities that were not foreseen when investors had purchased those securities.

Generating primary surpluses is the most virtuous way to reduce a high debt. However, it is also the most difficult way. To cut spending is politically costly, and sometimes it is not socially viable: imposing new and higher taxes is an unpopular choice, and there is a limit to the tax burden beyond which the cost (especially the political cost) of collecting more taxes becomes too high. In this case, a tax plan consistent with the budget constraint becomes unfeasible.

Inflating the debt away can be done in different ways: directly (by issuing money) or indirectly (through a decrease in the real value of debt, if the maturity is long enough).

The government can then convince the central bank to print money by purchasing government bonds. Given the initial level of debt and given the path of public spending, monetary financing reduces the tax levy required for debt relief. However, recourse to the issuing of money is not free of charge because, as we will see in Chapter 23, inflation is also a form, albeit a peculiar one, of taxation. An increase in the money supply increases inflation and reduces the real value of existing nominal debt and of the cash held by citizens. Inflation therefore acts like a tax – the 'inflation tax'. Inflation reduces the disposable income of households because it forces them to spend part of their income just to maintain the real value of the money stock or of the government bonds they wish to hold constant.

Finally, the government may decide to cancel all or part of the debt. Even if, as we have seen, repudiation is in some ways a good solution – it reduces the distortions caused by high tax rates – the result is the breaking up of the relationship of trust between the government and investors, who may no longer be willing to buy public debt. If this happens, the government loses the ability to run deficits in order to distribute over time the burden of an unexpected high expenditure.

Towards a 'political' theory of debt

At first glance, the three ways to finance the budget deficit and reduce debt accumulation – discussed above – may seem very different. In reality, these are different forms of taxation that differ only because they fall on different economic groups. Repudiation, for example, can be treated as a tax on wealth that affects those who hold securities. The inflation tax affects those who hold nominal assets not protected by inflation (money and bonds).

It becomes important, therefore, to take into account the fact that government debt and the economic policy choices needed to reduce it have significant effects on income distribution. This idea has been developed in a recent branch of the economic literature which lies on the border between economics and political science. This literature has proposed a **political theory of government debt**. In particular, some economists argue that the choice of who should 'pay' for the reduction of a high debt is essentially a problem of redistribution of income and wealth between economic groups. When the different economic groups are represented politically it is also possible to establish a relationship between the degree of a country's political stability, distributional conflict and evolution of deficits and debt. Before showing how these ideas can help to understand the different solutions adopted in certain historical episodes of high public debt, we need to take a few more steps.

First, let us distinguish between a stable and an unstable political scenario. A political situation is stable if a political party has a solid majority and controls economic policy decisions. A political situation is unstable if each group has enough power to block a measure that is damaging some groups, but not enough to turn it around. In this case, fiscal adjustment may not be politically feasible. There is no way to resolve the dispute over which items of expenditure should be cut, or which taxes increased, and this prevents the government from reaching a decision, thus undermining its ability to reduce the deficit. In the end, the government must either monetise the debt or repudiate it. As we shall see, this assumption seems a good description of what happened in Germany and France in the first half of the 1920s.

If, instead, the political situation is stable, a political party has enough power to start a fiscal adjustment because it is strong enough to impose the burden of adjustment on others. This was the case in France in the mid-1920s and in the UK in the post-war period. The case of the USA after the Second World War is an example of a reduction in public debt that has not given rise to fights among different social and political groups. But this was only possible because of the high growth rates of income recorded in those years, which contributed to the reduction of the debt ratio.

Suppose that society can be divided into three groups:

- Rentiers (from the French '*rente*' which means annuity) hold wealth in the form of government bonds, i.e. securities which pay an annuity every year.
- Entrepreneurs hold wealth in the form of physical capital that produces profits.
- Workers own human wealth, which produces their salaries.

Each of these interest groups will seek to avoid the burden of adjustment and shift it onto someone else. Rentiers are opposed both to explicit debt repudiation and to an inflation tax, which reduces the real value of debt and, as such, is an implicit from of repudiation. If average debt maturity is short, and hence holders of securities are protected from inflation by the changes in interest rates, then rentiers prefer the inflation tax to debt repudiation. Rentiers also look favourably on various forms of tax increases, whether direct or indirect. Entrepreneurs are opposed to taxes on capital, but not to debt repudiation, nor to monetary financing or to taxes on consumer goods and income. Workers prefer taxes on wealth and capital, and the repudiation of debt, while being opposed to indirect taxes, particularly on consumer goods. They are affected by inflation if wages are not indexed, but they can be made better off by an increase in employment induced by a monetary expansion.

Four episodes of reduction of a high public debt

Historical experiences provide us with illuminating examples of how some countries have emerged from situations of high debt by taking very different solutions. We shall describe the experience of Germany, France and the UK at the end of the First World War and the case of the USA at the end of the Second World War.

Germany in the post-war period

Germany financed military spending during the First World War mainly through borrowing. During the war period, in fact, fiscal revenue accounted for a negligible fraction of overall spending, and the resulting budget deficit was financed by issuing debt, especially short-term debt. But how did Germany plan to repay this debt? Like all the countries that took part in the conflict, it hoped to win the war and shift the debt burden onto the defeated countries. But Germany lost the war and at the end of the conflict found itself with a very high debt stock.

After the war, the German political situation was particularly unstable. Following on from the military defeat, the old nationalistic regime, ruled by aristocrats and the military, collapsed. The Communist Party began to gain broad support but, rather than a communist revolution, what happened was the birth of a new democratic regime, the Weimar Republic. The political situation remained, however, quite unstable. The democratic regime was very weak, threatened both by the workers' unrest linked to the communist movement and, at the other extreme, by the forces of the old regime and new movements of far-right nationalists.

In the first half of the 1920s, the debt problem was aggravated by the high budget deficits accumulated by the Weimar government. In part, these deficits were related to the reparations Germany had to pay to the winners of the war, to France in particular. In reality, reparations accounted for no more than one-third of the deficits in those years. The main reason for the deficits of the years 1920–1923 was a political impasse in fiscal policy. The proposal of drastic tax reforms had further weakened an already weak political situation, making it extremely difficult for the government to collect taxes. For example, the Socialists' proposal to levy an extraordinary tax on firms' capital and profits encountered violent opposition from nationalists and obviously from the entrepreneurs. Similarly, the proposal by entrepreneurs to raise income tax was rejected by the Socialists. The result was that no significant measure was introduced until 1922. The need to strike a compromise between the new and the old regimes had undermined the ability and willingness of the government to increase taxes. The political and fiscal policy impasse of these years left, as the only solution, monetisation which led, as we will see in the next chapter, to hyperinflation. One of effects of the German hyperinflation was the total cancellation of the debt that had existed at the end of the war. By the autumn of 1922, the debt did not exceed 5% of its real value in 1919. This dramatic reduction of wealth struck especially the middle class, which held the largest share of government debt. The reduction of wealth owned by the middle class worsened the income distribution, which is one of the reasons for the subsequent collapse of democratic institutions.

France in the post-war period

In the decade that followed the end of the First World War, the question of who should pay the cost of the debt issued to finance the conflict monopolised the political debate in France. The debt was a particularly difficult problem due both to its size – the public debt represented about 150% of GDP – and its composition – the short-term debt constituted 32% of the total. In the years 1919–1926, in France as well the political situation was very unstable: in a few years, Socialist and Conservative governments alternated one after another. But in the second half of the decade political instability decreased: in 1926 the right won the final fight and was able to form a stable conservative government headed by Raymond Poincaré.

At the beginning of the decade, there seemed to be an easy solution to the French public debt problem: have the Germans pay for it through reparations. It was only at the end of 1922, and after the occupation of the Ruhr, that the French began to understand that German taxpayers would not be able to pay. Then an endless debate began between the opposition, on the one hand, and the conservatives on the other. The left denounced the unfairness of the tax structure, maintaining that, although income taxes were very progressive, only 20% of tax revenue was collected through income taxes. The high incidence of indirect taxes meant that the tax burden fell mostly on the less wealthy. The left, therefore, proposed a unique and progressive tax. At the other extreme, the conservatives opposed progressive income taxes, proposing much more reliance on indirect taxes. The distributional conflict made the political situation increasingly volatile; the French franc was hit by speculation and inflation went up. In fact, the fear of a capital levy made the public unwilling to buy government bonds. As a result, the government had to repay the bonds coming to maturity with monetary financing. In 1926 France was probably on the verge of hyperinflation.

At this point, Raymond Poincaré assumed the leadership of a new Conservative government and announced a drastic stabilisation programme. The element that made this programme different from previous attempts at fiscal adjustment was simply the greater political stability. The programme was credible because the political opponents had been defeated. Inflation ended abruptly, even before the government had started the fiscal adjustment.

◄ Only when Poincaré introduced a bill to shift the tax burden off bondholders did the demand for government bonds recover and inflation stop.

The UK in the post-war period

Even in the UK, the debt was very high at the end of the First World War: the debt-to-GDP ratio had reached 130% in 1919. The policies adopted in the UK, however, were very different from those in Germany and France. What distinguished the UK from Germany and France? The answer is simple: the degree of political stability. As we have seen, both in Germany and in France, the political situation at the end of the conflict was very unstable. In the UK, instead, except for two brief Labour governments, in 1924 and in 1930, the Conservative Party ruled continuously throughout the 1920s and 1930s. Democratic institutions were very solid and, despite very high unemployment, were never really threatened by the risk of a social revolt. This made it possible to introduce fiscal and monetary contractions, whose main objective was the stability of sterling and its return to its pre-war value – thus allowing a return to the gold standard. At the same time, the government produced budget surpluses in order to reduce the high public debt. The UK was one of the very few European countries where no expansionary fiscal policies were implemented to promote economic recovery.

Throughout the 1920s, and until the second half of the 1930s, fiscal surpluses, however, were not sufficient to reduce public debt. In this period, interest rates greatly exceeded the rate of growth of GDP. In 1923, the debt reached 170% of GDP and remained above 150% up to 1936. The debt-to-GDP ratio only started to decline in the second half of the 1930s, 15 years after the war.

Who bore the burden of debt reduction in the UK? Certainly not those who had bought government securities, since there was no form of repudiation, either explicit or implicitly through inflation. The burden of adjustment was borne primarily by taxpayers. Among them, those in the less wealthy classes were especially affected, because of an increasingly regressive tax system. For example, the introduction of taxes on specific products (tea, sugar, tobacco, milk, etc.) had a significant regressive effect.

The USA after the Second World War

The debt accumulated by the USA at the end of the Second World War was very close, in relation to GDP, to the debt ratio in the UK after the First World War. In both cases, moreover, the political situation was relatively stable. That is why both the UK and the US governments were able to start a fiscal adjustment without being forced to resort to repudiation. The USA, however, had greater success than the UK: 15 years after the end of the Second World War, the debt-to-GDP ratio was halved; in the UK, in contrast, 15 years passed before the debt ratio began to fall. So what distinguished the USA in the 1950s from the UK in the 1920s? During the period 1948–1968, the average growth rate of GDP in the USA was 4%, while real interest rates did not exceed 0.5%. Unlike the case of the UK, in the USA budget surpluses were accompanied by rapid output growth that exceeded the level of real interest rates. There is a simple but important lesson: it is easier to reduce a high debt when the economy is growing.

SUMMARY

- Governments, like households and individuals, can spend less or more than the amount of their revenues. When public spending exceeds taxes, a government runs a budget deficit. When public spending is lower than taxes, a government runs a budget surplus.

- In principle, a high government deficit is neither good nor evil. Deficits (and surpluses) can actually help to redistribute the burder of taxation over time. But deficits become a problem when they result in rapid accumulation of debt.

- To tell whether government debt is 'too' high, the relevant variable to look at is the ratio of government debt-to-GDP. Whether debt is 'too' high must be defined in relation to the ability of government to repay the debt.

- To stabilise the debt, the government must run a primay surplus equal to the interest on existing debt. The longer the government waits before stabilising the debt, the more painful the stabilisation wiil be.

- When $r > g$, the reduction of the debt ratio requires primary surpluses. When $r < g$, a country can reduce the debt ratio without the need to generate primary surpluses.

- The massive use of fiscal policy to help the economies of many European countries to face the recession of 2007–2010 resulted in a significant deterioration of primary balances that turned from positive to negative in most cases. These large budget deficits caused a dramatic increase in the debt ratio, which doubled in several countries.

KEY TERMS

balanced budget 437

budget deficit 437

nominal and real interest payments 437

deficit financing 437

primary deficit 439

primary surplus 439

debt stabilisation 441

debt-to-GDP ratio, or debt ratio 441

debt repudiation 449

political theory of government debt 451

QUESTIONS AND PROBLEMS

QUICK CHECK

1. *Using the information in this chapter, label each of the following statements true, false or uncertain. Explain briefly.*

a. The seigniorage (the profit that results from the difference in the cost of printing money and the face value of that money) is equal to real money balances multiplied by the nominal interest rate.

b. During a hyperinflation, individuals increase the use of currency.

c. Given money balances, an increase in money growth causes an increase in seigniorage.

d. The net effect of money growth on seigniorage is certain and positive.

e. In the short term, increased rates of money growth cause a decrease of seigniorage through real money balances.

f. In the medium term, increasing rates of money growth generate a decrease in real money balances and an increase in seigniorage (at a decreasing rate).

g. In the long term, the government may finance the deficit with constant money growth rates.

h. A higher money growth leads to a steady increase in production.

i. A simple programme to stabilise prices and wages can stop a process of hyperinflation.

j. The Olivera–Tanzi effect is the improvement in the deficit in the presence of high inflation.

2. *Consider an economy in which the official budget deficit is 4% of GDP, the debt-to-GDP ratio is 100%, the nominal interest rate is 10% and the inflation rate is 7%.*

a. What is the relationship between the primary balance and GDP?

b. What is the balance adjusted for inflation as a percentage of GDP?

c. Suppose that production is down 2% compared to natural levels. What is the cyclically adjusted balance ratio to GDP adjusted for inflation and balance/GDP?

d. Suppose instead that production is initially at its natural level, and that output growth remains constant at the normal rate of 2%. Does the debt ratio increase or decrease?

3. *Suppose that in a country's public debt, inflation and the rate of GDP growth are all equal to zero, and that the interest rate is 5%. In year t, the country recorded a deficit of 10% of GDP, and in year t + 1 onwards eliminates the primary deficit.*

Calculate the deficit (as percentage of GDP) in years $t + 1$ and $t + 2$.

DIG DEEPER

4. *Consider the economy described in problem 2 and assume that there is a fixed exchange rate. Suppose further that financial investors fear that the debt level is too high, and that the government may have to devalue to stimulate production (and thus tax revenues) and reduce debt. Financial investors expect a devaluation of 10%. In other words, the expected exchange rate, E^e_{t+1}, decreases by 10% from its previous value.*

a. We recall the uncovered interest parity condition: if the foreign interest rate is and remains equal to 10%, what happens when the domestic interest rate decreases by 10%?

b. Suppose that domestic inflation remains unchanged. What happens to the real interest rate nationally? What will happen to the rate of growth?

c. What happens to the official budget deficit and to the deficit adjusted for inflation?

d. Suppose that the growth rate declines from 2% to 0%. What happens to the change in the debt/GDP? (We assume that the primary balance ratio to GDP remains unchanged, although the decrease in growth rate may reduce tax revenues.)

e. Were investors' fears justified?

5. *Consider the data of the previous year but assume that the country has primary surpluses of less than 2% of GDP instead of 1% of GDP.*

a. Calculate the debt ratio in 2006, 2007 and 2008.

b. In light of the results, do you think that primary surpluses of 1% should be considered 'good' with a view to reducing the debt ratio.

EXPLORE FURTHER

6. *Consider an economy where the ratio of debt to GDP is 40%, the primary deficit is 4% of GDP, the rate of growth is 3% and the real interest rate is 3%.*

a. Using a spreadsheet, calculate the debt ratio after ten years, assuming that the primary deficit remains at 4% of GDP each year as the economy grows at the normal rate of growth each year and that the real interest rate remains constant at 2%.

b. Suppose that the real interest rate increases to 5%, but that everything else remains as in part (a). Calculate the debt ratio after ten years.

c. Suppose that the rate of growth falls to 1% and that the economy will grow at the normal rate each year. Everything else remains as in part (a). Calculate the debt ratio after ten years. Compare your answer with that in (b).

d. Returning to the assumptions of part (a), suppose that the policy makers decide that a debt ratio above 50% is dangerous. Check that the immediate reduction of the primary deficit of 1% retained for ten years will lead to a debt ratio of 50% after ten years. What level of primary deficit will be necessary to maintain a debt ratio of 50%?

e. Following on from (d), suppose that policy makers wait five years before changing the tax policy. For five years, the primary deficit remains at 4% of GDP. What is the debt ratio after five years? Suppose that after five years economic policy makers decide to reduce the debt ratio to 50%. From year 6 to year 10, what is the constant primary deficit level which will lead to a debt ratio of 50% at the end of 10?

f. Suppose that the policy makers decide to enact the policy in part (d) or part (e). If these policies lead to a reduction in the rate of output growth for a time, how will they affect the level of primary deficit needed to achieve a debt ratio of 50% after ten years?

g. What policy – the one in part (d) or the one in part (e) – do you think is more dangerous for the stability of the economy?

*We invite you to visit the Blanchard page on the Prentice Hall website, at **www.prenhall.com/blanchard** for this chapter's World Wide Web exercises.*

FURTHER READING

● Chapter 13 of the volume by **R. Farmer**, *Macroeconomics*, **Cincinnati, OH, South-Western College Publishing, 1998**, analyses the dynamics of debt and deficits in line with the discussion of this chapter.

● For an illuminating analysis of how various countries have emerged from situations of high debt, you can read **A. Alesina**, 'The End of Large Public Debts', in *High Public Debt: The Italian Experience*, **edited by F. Giavazzi and L. Spaventa, Cambridge, Cambridge University Press, 1988**.

Chapter 22

HIGH INFLATION

In Chapter 20, we argued that one of the legacies of the 2007–2010 crisis is the risk that it might be followed by a period of high inflation. Inflation could be the result of the failure by central banks to draw from the economy the large amount of money injected during the crisis through open market purchases of bonds and other assets. We discussed the 'Quantitative Easing' and the 'Credit Easing' in Chapter 20. But it could also be the result of the political incentive to reduce the real value of public debt (another legacy of the crisis) through a brief period of unexpected inflation that raises the price level.

Episodes of high inflation have been frequent in history. They have typically occurred in situations more extreme than, but not fundamentally different from, the current circumstances. Often inflation has been the result of printing large amounts of money to finance a large budget deficit; on other occasions – for example in Italy at the end of the Second World War – a bout of inflation has been deliberately induced by the government and the central bank to lower the real value of the public debt. Why is high inflation costly? How can prices stabilise once the economy has entered a high-inflation period? These are the issues addressed in this chapter.

In 1913, the value of all currency circulating in Germany was 6 billion marks. Ten years later, in October 1923, 6 billion marks was barely enough to buy a 1-kilo loaf of rye bread in Berlin. A month later, the price of the same loaf of bread had increased to 428 billion marks.

The German **hyperinflation** of the early 1920s is probably the most famous hyperinflation. (Hyperinflation simply means very high inflation.) But it is not the only one. Table 22.1 summarises the seven major hyperinflations that followed the First and Second World Wars. They share a number of features. They were all short (lasting a year or so) but intense, with inflation running at 50% per month or more. In all cases, the increases in price levels were staggering. As you can see, the largest price increase actually occured not in Germany, but in Hungary after the Second World War. What cost 1 Hungarian pengö in August 1945 cost 3800 trillions of trillions of pengös less than a year later.

Table 22.1 Seven hyperinflations of the 1920s and 1940s

	Beginning	End	P_T/P_0	Average monthly inflation rate, %	Average monthly money growth (%)
Austria	Oct. 1921	Aug. 1922	70	47	31
Germany	Aug. 1922	Nov. 1923	1.0×10^{10}	322	314
Greece	Nov. 1943	Nov. 1944	4.7×10^6	365	220
Hungary 1	Mar. 1923	Feb. 1924	44	46	33
Hungary 2	Aug. 1945	Jul. 1946	3.8×10^{27}	19.8	12.2
Poland	Jan. 1923	Jan. 1924	699	82	72
Russia	Dec. 1921	Jan. 1924	1.2×10^5	57	49

Note: P_T/P_0 is the price level in the last month of hyperinflation divided by the price level in the first month.

Source: Philip Cagan, 'The Monetary Dynamics of Hyperinflation', in Milton Friedman, ed., *Studies in the Quantity Theory of Money*, University of Chicago Press, Chicago, IL, 1956, Table 1.

Such rates of inflation had not been seen before, nor have they been seen since. The closest in the recent past occured in Bolivia in 1984 and 1985. From January 1984 to September 1985, Bolivian inflation averaged 40% per month – a roughly 1000-fold increase in the price level over 21 months. (With an inflation rate of 40% per month, the price level at the end of 21 months is $(1 + 0.4)^{21} = 1171$ times the price level at the beginning.) But many countries, especially in Latin America, have struggled with prolonged bouts of high inflation. Table 22.2 gives the average monthly inflation rates for four Latin American countries from 1976–2000. All four had at least five years with average monthly inflation running above 20% per month. Both Argentina and Brazil had monthly inflation rates in excess of 10% per month for more than a decade. All four countries have now returned to low inflation. Today, inflation is low in nearly all countries, the only exception being Zimbabwe where, as of mid-2007, the monthly inflation rate was around 25%.

Table 22.2 High inflation in Latin America, 1976–2000

	Average monthly inflation rate, %				
	1976–1980	1981–1985	1986–1990	1991–1995	1996–2000
Argentina	9.03	12.07	20.00	20.30	0.00
Brazil	3.04	7.09	20.07	19.00	0.06
Nicaragua	1.04	3.06	35.06	8.05	0.08
Peru	3.04	6.00	23.07	4.08	0.08

Source: *International Financial Statistics*, IMF, various issues.

What causes hyperinflations? You saw in Chapter 11 that inflation ultimately comes from nominal money growth. The relation between nominal money growth and inflation is confirmed by the last two columns of Table 22.1. Note how, in each country, high inflation was associated with correspondingly high nominal money growth. Why was nominal money growth so high? The answer turns out to be common to all hyperinflations: nominal money growth is high because the budget deficit is high. The budget deficit is high because the economy is affected by major shocks that make it difficult or impossible for the government to finance its expenditures in any way other than by money creation.

In this chapter, we look at this answer in more detail, relying on examples from various hyperinflations:

- Section 22.1 looks at the relation between the budget deficit and money creation.

- Section 22.2 looks at the relation between inflation and real money balances.

- Section 22.3 puts the two together and shows how a large budget deficit can lead to high and increasing inflation.

- Section 22.4 looks at how hyperinflations end.

- Section 22.5 draws conclusions from our two chapters on pathologies – depressions and slumps in Chapter 20, and high inflation in this chapter.

22.1 BUDGET DEFICITS AND MONEY CREATION

A government can finance its budget deficit in one of two ways:

- It can borrow, the way you or I would. We borrow by taking out a loan. Governments borrow by issuing bonds.
- It can do something that neither you nor I can do: it can, in effect, finance the deficit by creating money. I say 'in effect' because, as you remember from Chapter 4, governments do not create money; the central bank creates money. But, with the central bank's cooperation, the government can, in effect, finance itself through money creation: it can issue bonds and ask the central bank to buy them. The central bank then pays the government with money it creates, and the government uses that money to finance its deficit. This process is called **debt monetisation.**

Most of the time and in most countries, deficits are financed primarily through borrowing rather than through money creation. But at the start of hyperinflations, two changes usually take place:

- There is a budget crisis. The source is typically a major social or economic upheaval.

  It may be a civil war or a revolution that destroys the state's ability to collect taxes. This was the case, for example, in Nicaragua in the 1980s.

  It may come from the aftermath of a war that leaves the government with both smaller tax revenues and the large expenditures needed for reconstruction. This is what happened in Germany in 1922 and 1923. Burdened with payments for the war (called *war reparations*) it had to pay to Allied forces, Germany had a budget deficit equal to more than two-thirds of its expenditures.

  It may come from a large adverse economic shock – for example, a large decline in the price of a raw material that is both the country's major export and its main source of revenues. As you will see in the Focus box ('The Bolivian hyperinflation of the 1980s'), this is what happened in Bolivia in the 1980s. The decline in the price of tin, Bolivia's principal export, was one of the main causes of the Bolivian hyperinflation.

  It may come from a bad policy decision. This is the case for Zimbabwe, where the decision to redistribute land away from white farmers in 2000 led to a catastrophic decline in agricultural output and, in turn, a large fall of GDP and a large increase in the budget deficit. (To know what happened in Zimbabwe after 2000 until today, read the Focus box 'Hyperinflation in Zimbabwe' on page 469.)

We are taking a shortcut here. What ➤ should be on the right side of equation (22.1) is *H*, the monetary base – that's the money created by the central bank – not *M*, the money stock (which includes both currency and chequable deposits). We ignore the distinction here.

- The government becomes increasingly unable to borrow from the public or from abroad to finance its deficit. The reason is the size of the deficit itself. Worried that the government might not be able to repay the debt in the future, potential lenders start asking the government for higher and higher interest rates. Sometimes, foreign lenders decide to stop lending to the government altogether. As a result, the government increasingly turns to the other source of finance – money creation. Eventually, most of the deficit is financed through money creation.

How large is the rate of nominal money growth needed to finance a given amount of revenues?

- Let M be the nominal money stock, measured, say, at the end of each month. (In the case of hyperinflation, things change so quickly that it is useful to look at what happens from month to month rather than from quarter to quarter or from year to year.) Let ΔM be the change in the nominal money stock from the end of last month to the end of this month – nominal money creation during the month.
- The revenue, in real terms (that is, in terms of goods), that the government generates by creating an amount of money equal to ΔM is therefore $\Delta M/P$ – nominal money creation during the month divided by the price level. This real revenue from money creation is

called **seignorage**. The word is revealing: the right to issue money was a precious source of revenue for the 'seigneurs' of the past: they could buy the goods they wanted by issuing their own money and using it to pay for the goods.

We can summarise this as follows:

$$\text{Seignorage} = \frac{\Delta M}{P} \qquad [22.1]$$

Seignorage is equal to money creation divided by the price level. To see what rate of nominal money growth is required to generate a given amount of seignorage, note that we can rewrite $\Delta M/P$ as

$$\frac{\Delta M}{P} = \frac{\Delta M}{M}\frac{M}{P}$$

In words: we can think of seignorage, $\Delta M/P$, as the product of the rate of nominal money growth, $\Delta M/M$, and real money balances, M/P. The larger the real money balances held in the economy, the larger the amount of seignorage corresponding to a given rate of nominal money growth. Replacing this expression in equation (22.1) gives

◄ 'Real money balances' is just another name for the real money stock.

$$\text{Seignorage} = \frac{\Delta M}{M}\frac{M}{P} \qquad [22.2]$$

This gives us the relation we wanted between seignorage, the rate of nominal money growth and real money balances. To think about relevant magnitudes, it is convenient to divide both sides of equation (22.2) by real income (measured at a monthly rate):

◄ Remember: income is a flow. Y here is real income per month.

$$\frac{\text{Seignorage}}{Y} = \frac{\Delta M}{M}\left(\frac{M/P}{Y}\right) \qquad [22.3]$$

Suppose the government is running a budget deficit equal to 10% of real income and decides to finance it through seignorage, so deficit/Y = seignorage/Y = 0.1. Suppose people hold real balances equal to two months of income, so $(M/P)/Y = 2$. This implies that nominal money growth must satisfy

$$\frac{\Delta M}{M} \times 2 = 0.1 \Rightarrow \frac{\Delta M}{M} = 0.05$$

To finance a deficit of 10% of real income through seignorage, the monthly growth rate of nominal money must be equal to 5%.

Does this mean that the government can finance a deficit equal to 20% of real income through a rate of nominal money growth of 10%, a deficit of 40% of real income through a rate of nominal money growth of 20% and so on? No. As nominal money growth increases, so does inflation. And as inflation increases, the opportunity cost of holding money increases, leading people to reduce their real money balances. In terms of equation (22.2), an increase in nominal money growth, $\Delta M/M$, leads to a decrease in real money balances, M/P, so that an increase in nominal money growth will generate a less-than-proportional increase in seignorage. What is crucial here is how much people adjust their real money balances in response to inflation, and it is the issue to which we turn next.

Before we do, let's summarise what we learned in this section. *Seignorage – the amount of revenues the government gets from money creation – is equal to the product of the rate of nominal money growth and real money balances.*

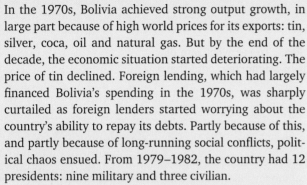

FOCUS
The Bolivian hyperinflation of the 1980s

In the 1970s, Bolivia achieved strong output growth, in large part because of high world prices for its exports: tin, silver, coca, oil and natural gas. But by the end of the decade, the economic situation started deteriorating. The price of tin declined. Foreign lending, which had largely financed Bolivia's spending in the 1970s, was sharply curtailed as foreign lenders started worrying about the country's ability to repay its debts. Partly because of this, and partly because of long-running social conflicts, political chaos ensued. From 1979–1982, the country had 12 presidents: nine military and three civilian.

When the first freely elected president in 18 years came to power in 1982, he faced a nearly impossible task. US commercial banks and other foreign lenders were running scared. They did not want to make new loans to Bolivia, and they wanted the previous loans to be repaid. Net private (medium-term and long-term) foreign lending to the Bolivian government had fallen from 3.5% of GDP in 1980 to 20.3% in 1982 and to −0.3% in 1982 and to −1.0% in 1983. Because the government had no other choice, it resorted to money creation to finance the budget deficit.

Inflation and budget deficits

The next three years were characterised by the interaction of steadily increasing inflation and steadily increasing budget deficits.

Table 22.3 gives the budget numbers for the period 1981–1986. Because of the lags in tax collection, the effect of rising inflation was a sharp reduction in real tax revenues. In addition, the government's attempt to maintain low prices for public services generated large deficits for state-run firms. As these deficits were financed by

subsidies from the state, the result was a further increase in Bolivia's budget deficit. In 1984, it reached a staggering 31.6% of GDP.

The result of higher budget deficits and the need for higher seignorage was an increase in nominal money growth and inflation. Inflation, which averaged 2.5% per month in 1981, increased to 7% in 1982 and to 11% in 1983. As shown in Figure 22.1, which shows Bolivia's monthly inflation rate from January 1984 to April 1986 (the vertical line indicates the beginning of stabilisation), inflation kept increasing in 1984 and 1985, reaching 182% in February 1985.

Stabilisation

There were many attempts at stabilisation in Bolivia along the way. Stabilisation programmes were launched in November 1982, November 1983, April 1984, August 1984 and February 1985. The April 1984 package was an orthodox programme involving a large devaluation, the announcement of a tax reform and an increase in public-sector prices. But the opposition from trade unions was too strong, and the programme was abandoned.

After the election of a new president, yet another attempt at stabilisation was made in September 1985. This one proved successful. The stabilisation plan was organised around the elimination of the budget deficit. Its main features were:

- *Fiscal policy* – public-sector prices were increased; food and energy prices were increased; public-sector wages were frozen; and a tax reform, aimed at re-establishing and broadening the tax base, was announced.

Table 22.3 Central government revenues, expenditures and the deficit as a percentage of Bolivian GDP

	1981	1982	1983	1984	1985	1986
Revenues	9.4	4.6	2.6	2.6	1.3	10.3
Expenditures	15.1	26.9	20.1	33.2	6.1	7.7
Budget balance (−: deficit)	−5.7	−22.3	−17.5	−30.6	−4.8	−2.6

Source: Jeffrey Sachs, *The Bolivian Hyperinflation and Stabilization*, NBER working paper no. 2073, November 1986, Table 3, NBER, Cambridge, MA.

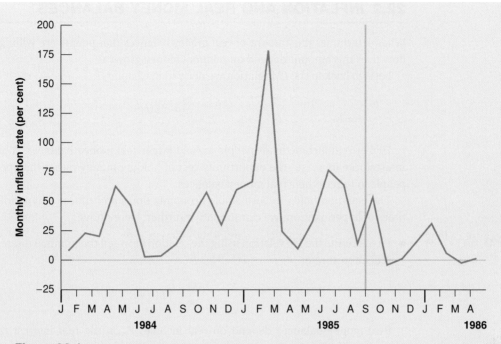

Figure 22.1

Bolivian monthly inflation rate, January 1984–April 1986

- *Monetary policy* – the official exchange rate of the peso was adjusted to what the black market rate (the actual exchange rate at which one could exchange pesos for dollars before the stabilisation programme) had been pre-stabilisation. The exchange rate was set at 1.1 million pesos to the dollar, up from 67 000 pesos to the dollar the month before (a 1600% devaluation). The exchange rate was then left to float, within limits.
- *Re-establish international creditworthiness* – negotiations were begun with international organisations and commercial banks to restructure Bolivia's debt. An agreement with its foreign creditors and the IMF was reached nine months later, in June 1986.

As they had in the previous attempt at stabilisation, the unions called a general strike. In response, the government declared a state of siege, and the strike ended. After hyperinflation and so many failed attempts to control it, public opinion was clearly in favour of stabilisation.

The effects of stabilisation plan on inflation were dramatic. By the second week of September, the inflation rate was actually negative! Inflation did not remain negative for very long, but the average monthly rate of inflation was below 2% from 1986–1989. As Table 22.4 shows, the budget deficit was drastically reduced in 1986, and the average deficit was below 5% of GNP for the rest of the decade.

Did stabilisation have a negative effect on output? It probably did. Real interest rates remained very high for more than a year after stabilisation. The full effect of these high real interest rates on output is hard to establish because, at the same time as stabilisation was implemented, Bolivia was hit with further large declines in the prices of tin and natural gas. In addition, a major campaign against narcotics had the effect of disrupting cocoa production. How much of the Bolivian recession of 1986 was due to stabilisation and how much was due to these other factors is difficult to assess. The recession lasted a year. Since 1986, output has grown at an average rate of 3% per year, and average inflation has remained under 10%.

Source: The material in this box draws largely from Jeffrey Sachs, *The Bolivian Hyperinflation and Stabilization*, NBER working paper no. 2073, November 1986, NBER, Cambridge, MA. Sachs was one of the architects of the stabilisation programme. See also Juan Antonio Morales, 'The Transition from Stabilization to Sustained Growth in Bolivia', in Michael Bruno, et al., eds, *Lessons of Economic Stabilization and Its Aftermath*, MIT Press, Cambridge, MA, 1991.

22.2 INFLATION AND REAL MONEY BALANCES

What determines the amount of real money balances that people are willing to hold? And how does this amount depend on nominal money growth?

Let's go back to the *LM* relation we derived in Chapter 5:

$$\frac{M}{P} = YL(i)$$
$$(-)$$

Higher real income leads people to hold larger real money balances. A higher nominal interest rate increases the opportunity cost of holding money rather than bonds and leads people to reduce their real money balances.

The equation holds in both stable economic times and times of hyperinflation, but, in times of hyperinflation, we can simplify it further. Here's how:

Recall, from Chapter 14, that $r = i - \pi^e$. Equivalently, $i = r + \pi^e$.

● First, rewrite the *LM* relation using the relation between the nominal interest rate and the real interest rate:

$$\frac{M}{P} = YL(r + \pi^e)$$

Real money balances depend on real income, Y, on the real interest rate, r, and on expected inflation, π^e.

● Second, note that, while all three variables (Y, r and π^e) vary over time during a hyperinflation, expected inflation is likely to move much more than the other two variables: during a typical hyperinflation, actual inflation – and presumably expected inflation – may move by 20% per month or more from one month to the next.

So it is not a bad approximation to assume that both income and the real interest rate are constant and focus on just the movements in expected inflation. So we write

$$\frac{M}{P} = \bar{Y}L(\bar{r} + \pi^e) \qquad [22.4]$$
$$(-)$$

where the bars over Y and r mean that we now take both income and the real interest rate as constant. In times of hyperinflation, equation (22.4) tells us we can think of real money balances as depending primarily on the expected rate of inflation. As expected inflation increases and it becomes more and more costly to hold money, people will reduce their real money balances.

In describing the Austrian hyperinflation of the 1920s, Keynes noted: 'In Vienna, during the period of collapse, mushroom exchange banks sprang up at every street corner, where you could change your krone into Zurich francs within a few minutes of receiving them, and so avoid the risk of loss during the time it would take you to reach your usual bank.'

During a hyperinflation, people indeed find many ways to reduce their real money balances. When the monthly rate of inflation is 100%, for example, currency kept for a month will lose half of its real value (because things cost twice as much a month later). **Barter**, the exchange of goods for other goods rather than for money, increases. Payments for wages become much more frequent – often twice weekly. When people are paid, they rush to stores to buy goods. Despite the fact that the government often makes it illegal for its citizens to use currencies other than the one it is printing, people shift to foreign currencies as stores of value. And even if it is illegal, an increasing number of transactions take place in foreign currency. During the Latin American hyperinflations of the 1980s, people shifted to US dollars. The shift to dollars has become so widespread in the world that it has a name: **dollarisation** (that is, the use of dollars in another country's domestic transactions).

One of the hopes of the EU is that the euro may replace the dollar as the foreign currency of choice. (Why would the EU want this to happen?) If it happens, we may have to speak of 'euro-isation' rather than of 'dollarisation.'

By how much do real money balances actually decrease as inflation increases? Figure 22.2 examines the evidence from the Hungarian hyperinflation of the early 1920s and provides some insights:

● Figure 22.2(a) plots real money balances and the monthly inflation rate from November 1922 to February 1924. Note how movements in inflation are reflected in opposite movements in real money balances. The short-lived decline in Hungarian inflation from July

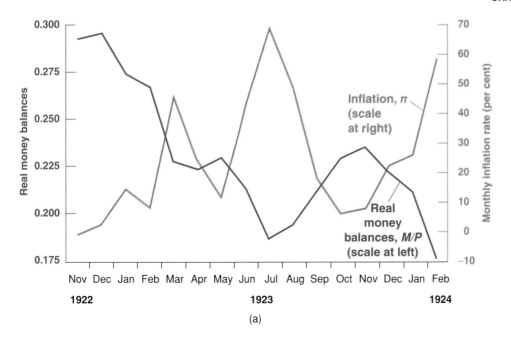

(a)

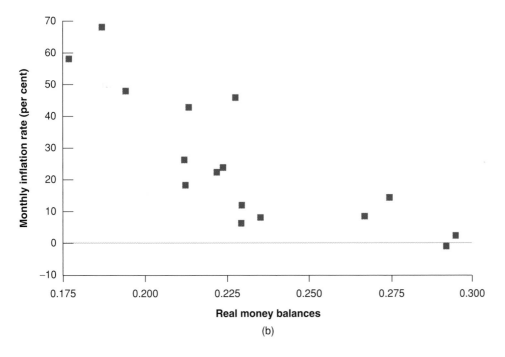

(b)

Figure 22.2

Inflation and real money balances in Hungary, November 1922– February 1924

At the end of the Hungarian hyperinflation, real money balances stood at roughly half their pre-hyperinflation level.

to October 1923 is reflected in an equally short-lived increase in real money balances. At the end of the hyperinflation in February 1924, real money balances were roughly half what they had been at the beginning.

- Figure 22.2(b) presents the same information as Figure 22.2(a), but in the form of a scatter diagram. It plots monthly real money balances on the horizontal axis against inflation on the vertical axis. (We do not observe expected inflation, which is the variable we would like to plot, so we use actual inflation instead.) Note how the points nicely describe a downward-sloping demand for money: as actual inflation – and presumably, expected inflation as well – increases, the demand for money strongly decreases.

Let's summarise what we learned in this section. *Increases in expected inflation lead people to decrease their use of money and to decrease their real money balances.*

◄ This decrease in real money balances explains why, in Table 22.1, average inflation is higher-than-average nominal money growth during each of the seven post-war hyperinflations: that real money balances, *M/P*, decrease during a hyperinflation implies that prices, *P*, must increase more than *M*. In other words, average inflation must be higher than average nominal money growth.

22.3 DEFICITS, SEIGNORAGE AND INFLATION

We have derived two relations:

- The relation between seignorage, nominal money growth and real money balances [equation (22.2)]. Seignorage is equal to the product of nominal money growth and real money balances.
- The relation between real money balances and expected inflation [equation (22.4)]. An increase in expected inflation leads people to decrease their real money balances.

Combining the two equations gives

$$\text{Seignorage} = \left(\frac{\Delta M}{M}\right)\left(\frac{M}{P}\right)$$

$$= \left(\frac{\Delta M}{M}\right)[\bar{Y}L(\bar{r} + \pi^e)] \tag{22.5}$$

The first line repeats equation (22.2). The second line replaces real money balances by their expression in terms of expected inflation, from equation (22.4).

Equation (22.5) gives us what we need to show how the need to finance a large budget deficit through seignorage can lead not only to *high inflation* but also, as is the case during hyperinflations, to *high and increasing inflation*.

The case of constant nominal money growth

Suppose the government chooses a *constant* rate of nominal money growth and maintains that rate forever. (Clearly, this is not what happens during hyperinflations, where the rate of nominal money growth typically increases over the course of the hyperinflation; we shall get more realistic later.) How much seignorage will this constant rate of nominal money growth generate?

Recall: in the medium run [equation ➤ (10.8)]:

$\pi = g_m - \bar{g}y$
$\bar{g}_y = 0 \Rightarrow \pi = g_m$

If nominal money growth is constant forever, then inflation and expected inflation must eventually be constant as well. Assume, for simplicity, that output growth equals zero. Then, actual inflation and expected inflation must both equal nominal money growth:

$$\pi^e = \pi = \frac{\Delta M}{M}$$

Replacing π^e with $\Delta M/M$ in equation (22.5) gives

$$\text{Seignorage} = \frac{\Delta M}{M}\left[\bar{Y}L\left(\bar{r} + \frac{\Delta M}{M}\right)\right] \tag{22.6}$$

$\Delta M/M$ increases ➤ Seignorage increases.

Note that nominal money growth, $\Delta M/M$, enters the equation in two places and has two opposite effects on seignorage:

- Given real money balances, nominal money growth increases seignorage. This effect is captured by the first term in $\Delta M/M$ in equation (22.6).

$\Delta M/M$ increases $\Rightarrow \pi$ increases $\Rightarrow$ ➤ π^e increases $\Rightarrow L(\bar{r} + \pi^e)$ decreases $\Rightarrow M/P$ decreases $\Rightarrow$ Seignorage decreases.

- An increase in nominal money growth increases inflation and therefore decreases real money balances. This effect is captured by $\Delta M/M$ in the second term on the right in equation (22.6).

So the net effect of nominal money growth on seignorage is ambiguous. The empirical evidence is that the relation between seignorage and nominal money growth looks as shown in Figure 22.3.

The relation is hump shaped. When nominal money growth is low – the situation in Europe or the USA at the time of writing – an increase in nominal money growth leads to a small reduction in real money balances. Thus, higher money growth leads to an increase in seignorage.

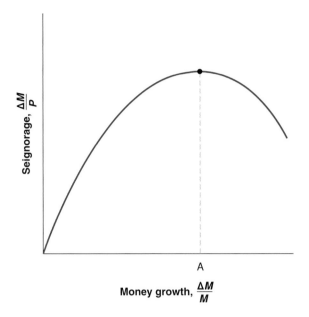

Figure 22.3

Seignorage and nominal money growth

Seignorage is first an increasing function, then a decreasing function of nominal money growth.

When nominal money growth (and therefore inflation) is very high, however, the reduction in real money balances induced by higher nominal money growth becomes larger and larger. Eventually, there is a rate of nominal money growth – point A in Figure 22.3 – beyond which further increases in nominal money growth *decrease* seignorage.

The shape of the relation in Figure 22.3 may look familiar to those of you who have studied the economics of taxation. Income tax revenues equal the *tax rate on income* times income – the *tax base*. At low tax rates, the tax rate has little influence on how much people work, and tax revenues increase with the tax rate. But as tax rates increase further, some people start working less – or stop declaring part of their income – and the tax base decreases. As the income tax reaches very high levels, increases in the tax rate lead to a decline in tax revenues. Obviously, tax rates of 100% lead to no tax revenue at all: why work if the government takes all your income?

This relation between tax revenues and the tax rate is often called the **Laffer curve**, after the economist Arthur Laffer, who argued in the early 1980s that a cut in US tax rates would lead to more tax revenues. He was clearly wrong about where the USA was on the curve: tax revenues went down, not up. But the general point still stands: when tax rates are high enough, a further increase in the tax rate can lead to a decrease in tax revenues.

There is more than a simple analogy here. Inflation can be thought of as a tax on money balances. The tax rate is the rate of inflation, π, which reduces the real value of money holdings. The tax base is real money balances, M/P The product of these two variables, $\pi(M/P)$, is called the **inflation tax**. There is a subtle difference with other forms of ◀ If the inflation rate is 5%, you lose taxation: what the government receives from money creation at any point in time is not the 5% of the value of your real money inflation tax but rather seignorage $(\Delta M/M)(M/P)$. However, the two are closely related. balances. It is as if you were paying When nominal money growth is constant, inflation must eventually be equal to nominal a tax of 5% on these balances. money growth, so that

$$\text{Inflation tax} = \pi\left(\frac{M}{P}\right)$$

$$= \left(\frac{\Delta M}{M}\right)\left(\frac{M}{P}\right)$$

$$= \text{Seignorage}$$

What rate of nominal money growth leads to the *most seignorage*, and how much seignorage does it generate? These are the questions that Philip Cagan asked in a classic paper on hyperinflation written in 1956. In one of the earliest uses of econometrics, Cagan estimated

Table 22.4 Nominal money growth and seignorage

	Rate of money growth maximising seignorage (% per month)	Implied seignorage (% of output)	Actual rate of money growth (% per month)
Austria	12	13	31
Germany	20	14	314
Greece	28	11	220
Hungary 1	12	19	33
Hungary 2	32	6	12.2
Poland	54	4.6	72
Russia	39	0.5	49

Note: monthly rate of nominal money growth, in per cent.

Source: Philip Cagan, 'The Monetary Dynamics of Hyperinflation', in Milton Friedman, ed., *Studies in the Quantity Theory of Money*, University of Chicago Press, Chicago, IL, 1956.

the relation between the demand for money and expected inflation [equation (22.4)] during each of the hyperinflations in Table 22.1. Then, using equation (22.6), he computed the rate of nominal money growth that maximised seignorage and the resulting amount of seignorage. The answers he obtained are given in the first two columns of Table 22.3. The third column repeats the actual nominal money growth numbers from Table 22.1.

Table 22.4 shows something very interesting: in all seven hyperinflations, actual average nominal money growth (column 3) far exceeded the rate of nominal money growth that maximises seignorage (column 1). Compare the actual rate of nominal money growth in Hungary after the Second World War, 12 200% per month, to the rate of nominal money growth that would have maximised seignorage, 32% per month. This would seem to be a serious problem for the story we have developed so far. If the reason for money creation was to finance the budget deficit, why was the actual rate of nominal money growth so much higher than the number that maximises seignorage? The answer lies in the dynamics of the economy's adjustment to high nominal money growth. We now turn to that.

Dynamics and increasing inflation

Let's return to the argument we just developed: *if maintained forever*, a higher rate of nominal money growth will *eventually* lead to a proportional increase in both actual inflation and expected inflation and, therefore, to a decrease in real money balances. If nominal money growth is higher than the amount that maximises seignorage, the increase in nominal money growth will lead to a decrease in seignorage.

The crucial words in the argument are *if maintained forever* and *eventually*. Consider a government that needs to finance a suddenly much larger deficit and decides to do so by creating money. As the rate of money growth increases, it may take a while for inflation and expected inflation to adjust. Even as expected inflation increases, it will take a while longer for people to fully adjust their real money balances: creating barter arrangements takes time, the use of foreign currencies in transactions develops slowly, and so on.

Let's explore this argument more formally. Recall our equation for seignorage:

$$\text{Seignorage} = \left(\frac{\Delta M}{M}\right)\left(\frac{M}{P}\right)$$

● In the short run, an increase in the rate of nominal money growth, $\Delta M/M$, may lead to little change in real money balances, M/P. Put another way, if it is willing to increase nominal money growth sufficiently, a government will be able to generate nearly any amount of seignorage that it wants *in the short run*, far in excess of the numbers in the second column of Table 22.4.

- Over time, as prices adjust and real money balances decrease, the government will find that the same rate of nominal money growth yields less and less seignorage. M/P will decrease, leading to lower seignorage for a given rate of nominal money growth, $\Delta M/M$.
- So, if the government keeps trying to finance a deficit larger than the deficit shown in the second column of Table 22.4 (for example, if Austria tries to finance a deficit that is more than 13% of GDP), it will find that it cannot do so with a constant rate of nominal money growth. The only way it can succeed is by continually *increasing* the rate of nominal money growth. This is why actual nominal money growth exceeds the numbers in the first column, and why hyperinflations are nearly always characterised by increasing nominal money growth and inflation.

There is also another effect at work, which we have ignored until now. We have taken the deficit as given. But as the inflation rate becomes very high, the budget deficit typically becomes larger as well. Part of the reason has to do with lags in tax collection. This effect is known as the **Tanzi–Olivera effect**, for Vito Tanzi and Julio Olivera, two economists who have emphasised its importance. As taxes are collected on past nominal income, their real value goes down with inflation. For example, if income taxes are paid this year on income received last year, and if the price level this year is ten times higher than last year's price level, the actual tax rate is only one-tenth of the official tax rate. Thus, high inflation typically decreases real government revenues, making the deficit problem worse.

The problem is often compounded by other effects on the expenditure side: governments often try to slow inflation by prohibiting firms under state control from increasing their prices, despite the fact that their costs are increasing with inflation. The direct effect on inflation is small at best, but the firms then run a deficit that must in turn be financed by subsidies from the government, which further increases the budget deficit. As the budget deficit increases, so does the need for more seignorage, and so does the need for even higher nominal money growth.

Hyperinflations and economic activity

We have focused so far on movements in nominal money growth and inflation – which clearly dominate the economic scene during a hyperinflation. But hyperinflations affect the economy in many other ways.

Initially, higher nominal money growth may lead to an *increase* in output. It takes some time for increases in nominal money growth to be reflected in inflation and, during that time, the effects of higher nominal money growth are expansionary. As you saw in Chapter 14, an increase in nominal money growth initially *decreases* nominal interest rates and real interest rates, leading to an increase in demand and an increase in output.

This is an 'other things being equal' statement. Other things may not be equal. For example, if what is behind the budget deficits and higher money growth is a bad agricultural shock, output is more likely to go down than up.

But as inflation becomes very high, the adverse effects of inflation dominate:

In the short run: g_m increases $\Rightarrow i$ decreases. Also, g_m increases g_m increases $\Rightarrow i$ increases. So $r = i - \pi^e$ decreases for both reasons.

- The transaction system works less and less well. One famous example of inefficient exchange occurred in Germany at the end of its hyperinflation: people actually had to use wheelbarrows to cart around the huge amounts of currency they needed for their daily transactions.

A joke heard in Israel during the high inflation of the 1980s:

- Price signals become less and less useful: because prices change so often, it is difficult for consumers and producers to assess the relative prices of goods and to make informed decisions. The evidence shows that the higher the rate of inflation, the higher the variation in the relative prices of different goods. Thus the price system, which is crucial to the functioning of a market economy, also becomes less and less efficient.

'Why is it cheaper to take a taxi rather than the bus? Because in the bus, you have to pay the fare at the beginning of the ride. In the taxi, you pay only at the end.'

- Swings in the inflation rate become larger. It becomes harder to predict what inflation will be in the near future, whether it will be, say, 500% or 1000% over the next year. Borrowing at a given nominal interest rate becomes more and more a gamble. If you borrow at, say, 1000% for a year, you may end up paying a real interest rate of 500% or 0%: a large difference! The result is that borrowing and lending typically come to a near stop in the final months of hyperinflation, leading to a large decline in investment.

We have discussed here the costs of very high inflation. The discussion at the time of writing in OECD countries is about the costs of, say, 4% inflation versus 0%. The issues are quite different in that case, and we return to it in Chapter 24.

So, as inflation increases and its costs become larger, there is typically an increasing consensus that it should be stopped. This takes us to the next section, how hyperinflations actually end.

22.4 HOW DO HYPERINFLATIONS END?

Hyperinflations do not die a natural death. Rather, they have to be stopped through a **stabilisation programme**.

The elements of a stabilisation programme

What needs to be done to end a hyperinflation follows from our analysis of the causes of hyperinflation:

- There must be a fiscal reform and a credible reduction of the government's budget deficit. This reform must take place on both the expenditure side and the revenue side of the budget.

    On the expenditure side, reform typically implies reducing the government subsidies that have often mushroomed during the hyperinflation. Obtaining a temporary suspension of interest payments on foreign debt also helps to decrease expenditures. An important component of stabilisation in Germany in 1922 was the reduction in its 'reparation payments' – precisely those payments that had triggered the hyperinflation in the first place.

    On the revenue side, what is required is not so much an increase in overall taxation but rather a change in the composition of taxation. This is an important point: as you saw, during a hyperinflation, people are in effect paying a tax – the inflation tax. Stabilisation involves replacing the inflation tax with other taxes. The challenge is to put in place and collect these other taxes. This cannot be done overnight, but it is essential that people become convinced that it will be done and that the budget deficit will be reduced.

- The central bank must make a credible commitment that it will no longer automatically monetise the government debt. This credibility can be achieved in a number of ways. The central bank can be prohibited, by decree, from buying any government debt, so that no monetisation of the debt is possible. Or the central bank can peg the exchange rate to the currency of a country with low inflation. An even more drastic step is to officially adopt dollarisation – that is, making a foreign currency the country's official currency. This step is drastic because it implies giving up seignorage altogether, and it is often perceived as a decrease in the country's independence.

- Are other measures needed as well? Some economists argue that **incomes policies** – that is, wage and/or price guidelines or controls – should be used, in addition to fiscal and monetary measures, to help the economy reach a new lower rate of inflation. Incomes policies, they argue, help coordinate expectations around a new lower rate of inflation. If firms know wages will not increase, they will not increase their prices. If workers know prices will not increase, they will not ask for wage increases, and inflation will be eliminated more easily. Others argue that a credible deficit reduction and central bank independence are all that is required. They argue that the appropriate policy changes, if credible, can lead to dramatic changes in expectations and therefore lead to the elimination of expected and actual inflation nearly overnight. They point to the potential dangers of wage and price controls: the government might end up relying on the controls, and not take the painful but needed fiscal and policy measures to end the hyperinflation. Also, if the structure of relative prices is distorted to begin with, price controls run the risk of maintaining these distortions.

    Stabilisation programmes that do not include incomes policies are called **orthodox**; those that do are called **heterodox** (because they rely on both monetary-fiscal changes and incomes policies). The hyperinflations in Table 22.1 were all ended through orthodox programmes. Many of the Latin American stabilisations of the 1980s and 1990s relied instead on heterodox programmes.

This is what Argentina did in 1991. It adopted a currency board and fixed the exchange rate at 1 dollar for 1 peso. See Chapter 19's discussion of currency boards, and of the evolution of the Argentinian economy since 1991.

This argument was particularly relevant in the stabilisations in Eastern Europe in the early 1990s, where, because of central planning, the initial structure of relative prices was very different from the structure of relative prices in a market economy. Imposing wage or price controls would have prevented relative prices from adjusting to their appropriate market value.

FOCUS
Hyperinflation in Zimbabwe

On 18 April 1980, when the new sovereign independent republic of Zimbabwe was born from the former British colony of Rhodesia, the Rhodesian Dollar was replaced by the Zimbabwe dollar at par. The Zimbabwean dollar was once worth about 1.59 US dollars.

Hyperinflation in Zimbabwe began in the early 2000s, shortly after Zimbabwe's confiscation of white-owned farmland and its repudiation of debt owed to the International Monetary Fund. In February 2006, the governor of the Reserve Bank of Zimbabwe, Dr Gideon Gono, announced that the government had printed 21 trillion Zimbabwean dollars in order to buy foreign currency to pay off IMF arrears. In early May 2006, Zimbabwe's government began printing money again to produce about 60 trillion Zimbabwean dollars. The additional currency was required to finance the recent 300% increase in salaries for soldiers and policemen and 200% for other civil servants. The money was not budgeted for the current fiscal year, and the government did not say where it would come from.

In February 2007, the central bank of Zimbabwe declared inflation 'illegal', outlawing any rise in prices on certain commodities between 1 March and 30 June 2007.

Figures from November 2008 estimated Zimbabwe's annual inflation rate at 89.7 sextillion 10^{21}%. Zimbabwe's central bank stopped posting inflation figures in January, when it stood at a relatively modest 100 580%. A loaf of bread then cost 30 billion Zimbabwean dollars.

Banknotes in Zimbabwe rarely lasted more than a few weeks because they lost their value so quickly. A 500 000 Zimbabwe dollar bill issued in late 2008 was already out of circulation in 2009: it was worth just 0.00004 US cents at the official exchange rate.

A family-owned Bavarian company – the same that once provided blank notes for the Weimar Republic in the 1920s – has sent tonnes of blank notes to the Zimbabwean capital Harare. The company, which has been doing business with the African nation since before Mr Mugabe took power in 1980, is one of the few sources in the world for the specialised paper that is so important in an age when computers and laser printers have made forgery so easy. However, in July 2008 the company, under pressure from the German government, stopped sending notes to Zimbabwe.

Although the paper shortage made printing more money difficult for Zimbabwe, this would have hardly been enough to end hyperinflation in the country, unless it decided to adopt an entirely different monetary system.

In late December 2008 and early January 2009, the use of foreign currency as a common medium of exchange has become increasingly popular as fewer goods and services were being sold and bought in local currency. In April 2009, Zimbabwe abandoned printing of the Zimbabwean dollar, and the South African rand and US dollar became the standard currencies for exchange. The government has said it does not intend to reintroduce the currency until 2010.

Source: Marcus Walker and Andrew Higgins, Zimbabwe Can't Paper Over Its Million-Percent Inflation Anymore, *Wall Street Journal*, 2 July 2008, page A1.

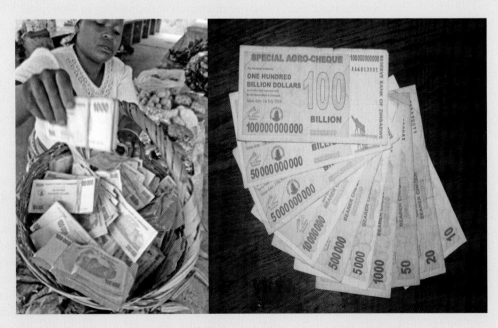

Can stabilisation programs fail?

As we saw in Chapter 19, the instrument used to stabilise inflation in Argentina, a currency board, led to another major macroeconomic crisis ten years later.

Can stabilisation programs fail? Yes. They can fail, and they often do. Argentina went through five stabilisation plans from 1984–1989 before succeeding in the early 1990s. Brazil succeeded only in 1995, in its sixth attempt in 12 years.

Sometimes failure comes from a botched or half-hearted effort at stabilisation. A government puts wage controls in place but does not take the measures needed to reduce the deficit and nominal money growth. Wage controls cannot work if nominal money growth continues, and the stabilisation program eventually fails.

An example is the failed stabilisation attempt in April 1984 in Bolivia described in the first Focus box in this chapter. Remember: the rate of real money growth equals the rate of nominal money growth minus the rate of inflation. If inflation decreases by less than nominal money growth, this implies negative real money growth – a decrease in the real money stock. This decrease in the real money stock then leads to high interest rates, which can trigger a recession.

Sometimes failure comes from political opposition. If social conflict was one of the causes of the initial budget deficit and thus was at the root of the hyperinflation, it may still be present and just as hard to resolve at the time of stabilisation. Those who stand to lose from the fiscal reform needed to reduce the deficit will oppose the stabilisation programme. Often, workers who perceive an increase in the price of public services or an increase in taxation, but who do not fully perceive the decrease in the inflation tax, will go on strike or even riot, and the stabilisation plan will fail.

Failure can also come from the anticipation of failure. Suppose the exchange rate is fixed to the dollar as part of the stabilisation programme. Also suppose participants in financial markets anticipate that the government will soon be forced to devalue. To compensate for the risk of devaluation, they require very high interest rates to hold domestic bonds rather than US bonds. These very high interest rates then lead to a recession, and the recession forces the government to devalue, validating the markets' initial fears. If, instead, investors believe that the government will maintain the exchange rate, the risk of devaluation will be lower, interest rates will be lower and the government will be able to proceed with stabilisation. To many economists, the successes and failures of stabilisation plans often appear to have an element of self-fulfilling prophecy. Even well-conceived plans work only if they are expected to work. In other words, skill, luck and good public relations all play a role.

This is a variation on the theme of self-fulfilling exchange rate crises developed in Chapter 19.

The costs of stabilisation

You saw in Chapter 10 how the US disinflation of the early 1980s was associated with a recession and a large increase in unemployment. Similarly, disinflation in Europe in the 1980s was also associated with a large increase in unemployment. We might therefore expect the much larger disinflations associated with the end of a hyperinflation to be associated with very large recessions or even depressions. This is typically not the case.

To understand why, recall our discussion of disinflation in Section 10.3. We argued that there are three reasons inflation might not decrease as fast as nominal money growth, leading to a recession:

- Wages are typically set in nominal terms for some period of time (up to three years in the USA) and, as a result, many of them are already determined when the decision to disinflate is made.
- Wage contracts are typically staggered, making it difficult to implement a slowdown in all wages at the same time.
- The change in monetary policy may not be fully and instantaneously credible.

Hyperinflation eliminates the first two problems. During hyperinflation, wages and prices are adjusted so often that both nominal rigidities and the staggering of wage decisions become nearly irrelevant.

But the issue of credibility remains. The fact that even coherent programmes might not succeed implies that no programme is fully credible from the start. If, for example, the government decides to fix the exchange rate, a high interest rate may be needed initially to maintain the parity. Those programmes that turn out to be successful are ones where increased credibility leads to lower interest rates over time. But even when credibility is eventually achieved, the initial high interest rate often leads to a recession. Overall, the evidence is that most, but not all, hyperinflations involve some decline in output.

How should a stabilisation package be designed in order to reduce this output cost? Should the stabilisation programme be orthodox or heterodox? Should there be restrictions on nominal money growth, or should the exchange rate be fixed? At this point, few countries are experiencing high inflation, so these questions are not at the top of policy makers' agendas. But, if history is any guide, some countries will again lose control of their budgets, finance the budget deficit through money creation and experience high inflation, if not hyperinflation. These questions will then surely resurface.

All rich and most middle-income countries in the world have low inflation rates at this point. A few, such as Japan, have deflation. The two middle-income countries with the highest inflation rates as of mid-2007 are Venezuela, with an inflation rate of 20%, and Turkey, with an inflation rate of 13%.

22.5 CONCLUSIONS

An underlying theme of the core of this book is that, although output fluctuates around its natural level in the short run, it tends to return to this natural level in the medium run. If the adjustment is too slow, fiscal and monetary policy can be used to help and shape the adjustment. Most of the time, this is indeed what happens. But, as this chapter and Chapter 20 tell us, it does not always happen.

- Sometimes, the adjustment mechanism that is supposed to return the economy to its natural level of output breaks down. An economy in a slump or in a depression experiences deflation, and deflation makes things worse rather than better.
- Monetary and fiscal policies may prove unable to help. In a slump, monetary policy may be constrained by the liquidity trap – the fact that nominal interest rates cannot be negative. Expansionary fiscal policy might not be an option because the budget deficit is very high to start with: the increase in government debt triggered by the high deficits might become a problem in and of itself.
- Governments may lose control of both fiscal policy and monetary policy. Faced with major adverse shocks – war, civil war, a collapse of exports, a social explosion – a government might lose control of its budget, run a large budget deficit and have no other choice but to finance the deficit through money creation. The result of this loss of control might be high inflation or even hyperinflation.

SUMMARY

- Hyperinflations are periods of high inflation. The most extreme hyperinflations took place after the First and Second World Wars in Europe. But Latin America has experienced episodes of high inflation as recently as the early 1990s.

- High inflation comes from high nominal money growth. High nominal money growth comes from the combination of large budget deficits and the inability to finance these large budget deficits through borrowing, either from the public or from abroad.

- The revenues from money creation are called seignorage. Seignorage is equal to the product of nominal money growth and real money balances. The smaller real money balances, the higher the required rate of nominal money growth, and therefore the higher the rate of inflation required to generate a given amount of seignorage.

- Hyperinflations are typically characterised by increasing inflation. There are two reasons for this. One is that higher nominal money growth leads to higher inflation, inducing people to reduce their real money balances, and requiring even higher nominal money growth (and thus leading to even higher inflation) to finance the same real deficit. The other reason is that higher inflation often increases the deficit, which requires higher nominal money growth, and even higher inflation.

- Hyperinflations are ended through stabilisation programmes. To be successful, stabilisation programmes must include fiscal measures aimed at reducing the deficit, and monetary measures aimed at reducing or eliminating money creation as a way of financing of the deficit. Some stabilisation plans also include wage and price guidelines or controls.

- A stabilisation programme that imposes wage and price controls without changes in fiscal policy and monetary policy will ultimately fail. But even well-conceived programmes do not always succeed. Anticipations of failure may lead to the failure of even a well-conceived plan.

KEY TERMS

QUESTIONS AND PROBLEMS

QUICK CHECK

1. *Using the information in this chapter, label each of the following statements true, false or uncertain. Explain briefly.*

a. In the short run, governments can finance a deficit of any size through money growth.

b. The inflation tax is always equal to seignorage.

c. Hyperinflations may distort prices, but they have no effect on real output.

d. The solution to ending a hyperinflation is to institute a wage and price freeze.

e. Because inflation is generally good for those who borrow money, hyperinflations are the best times to take out large loans.

f. Budget deficits usually shrink during hyperinflations.

2. *Assume that money demand takes the form*

$$\frac{M}{P} = Y[1 - (r + \pi^e)]$$

where Y = 1000 and r = 0.1.

a. Assume that, in the short run, π^e is constant and equal to 25%. Calculate the amount of seignorage for each rate of money growth, $\Delta M/M$, listed below.

  i.   25%

  ii. 50%

  iii. 75%

b. In the medium run, $\pi^e = \pi = \Delta M/M$. Compute the amount of seignorage associated with the three rates of money growth in part (a). Explain why the answers differ from those in part (a).

3. *How would each of the policies listed in parts (a) through (b) change the Tanzi–Olivera effect?*

a. requiring monthly instead of yearly income tax payments by households

b. assessing greater penalties for under-withholding of taxes from monthly paychecks

c. decreasing the income tax and increasing the sales tax

DIG DEEPER

4. *You are the economic adviser to a country experiencing a hyperinflation. Politicians debating the proper course of stabilisation have advocated various positions, listed in statements (a) through (e). Discuss each statement in turn.*

a. 'This crisis will not end until workers begin to pay their fair share of taxes.'

b. 'The central bank has demonstrated that it cannot responsibly wield its power to create money, so we have no choice but to adopt a currency board.'

c. 'Price controls are necessary to end this madness.'

d. 'Stabilisation will be successful only if there is a large recession and if there is a substantial increase in unemployment.'

e. 'Let's not blame the central bank. The problem is fiscal policy, not monetary policy.'

5. *What is the rate of money growth that maximises seignorage in the economy described in problem 2(b)?*

(*Hint:* you learned in problem 2(b) that seignorage, in the medium run, is greater at money growth of 50% than at money growth of 25% or 75%. Start by calculating seignorage for money growth rates near 50%. Increase and then decrease money growth rates by one percentage point until you find the answer.)

EXPLORE FURTHER

6. High inflation around the world

a. Go to the website of the IMF (*www.imf.org*) and find the current issue of the *World Economic Outlook*. In the Statistical Appendix, look at the table that lists inflation rates. Find countries that have inflation rates of 10% or higher. Which country has the highest inflation rate, and what is the rate?

b. Find Venezuela in the inflation table. How long has Venezuela had an inflation rate of more than 10%? Look at the projected inflation rates for the current year and the next year. Does inflation show any signs of slowing in Venezuela?

c. Venezuela is an oil producer, so its economy fluctuates with oil prices. Government tax revenues, in particular, depend heavily on the prosperity of the oil industry. With oil prices rising, Venezuela has increased government spending dramatically in recent years. Suppose oil prices fall in the future, but Venezuela does not reduce government spending. How would a fall in oil prices affect the budget deficit in Venezuela? Given the effect on the budget deficit, and following the logic of this chapter, how would a fall in oil prices make a hyperinflation possible in Venezuela?

> We invite you to visit the Blanchard page on the Prentice Hall website, at **www.prenhall.com/blanchard** for this chapter's World Wide Web exercises.

FURTHER READING

- For more on the German hyperinflation, read **Steven Webb**, *Hyperinflation and Stabilization in the Weimar Republic*, **Oxford University Press, New York, 1989**.

Two good reviews of what economists know and don't know about hyperinflation are:

- **Rudiger Dornbusch, Federico Sturzenegger and Holger Wolf, 'Extreme Inflation: Dynamics and Stabilization',** *Brookings Papers on Economic Activity*, **21, 1990–2, 1–84**.

- **Pierre Richard Agenor and Peter Montiel,** *Development Macroeconomics*, **Princeton University Press, Princeton, NJ, 1995**, Chapters 8–11. Chapter 8 is easy to read; the other chapters are more difficult.

- The experience of Israel, which went through high inflation and stabilisation in the 1980s, is described in **Michael Bruno's** *Crisis, Stabilization and Economic Reform*, **Oxford University Press, New York, 1993**, especially Chapters 2–5. Bruno was the head of Israel's central bank for most of that period.

- One of the classic articles on how to end hyperinflation is **Thomas Sargent, 'The Ends of Four Big Inflations', in Robert Hall, ed.,** *Inflation: Causes and Effects*, **NBER and the University of Chicago, Chicago, IL, 1982, 41–97**. In that article, Sargent argues that a credible programme can lead to stabilisation at little or no cost in terms of activity.

- **Rudiger Dornbusch and Stanley Fischer, 'Stopping Hyperinflations, Past and Present', in** *Weltwirtschaftlichers Archiv*, **122 (1), 1986, 1–47**, gives a very readable description of the end of hyperinflations in Germany, Austria, Poland and Italy in 1947; Israel in 1985; and Argentina in 1985.

SHOULD POLICY MAKERS BE RESTRAINED?

Nearly every chapter of this book has looked at the role of policy. The next two chapters put it all together.

Chapter 23 Policy and policy makers: what do we know?

Chapter 23 asks two questions: given the uncertainty about the effects of macroeconomic policy, wouldn't it be better not to use policy at all? And, even if policy can in principle be useful, can we trust policy makers to carry out the right policy? The bottom lines: uncertainty limits the role of policy. Policy makers do not always do the right thing. But, with the right institutions, policy can help and should be used.

Chapter 24 Monetary and fiscal policy rules and constraints

Chapter 24 looks at monetary and fiscal policies. It reviews what we have learned, chapter by chapter, and then focuses on two issues. The first is the optimal rate of inflation: high inflation is bad, but how low a rate of inflation should the central bank aim for? The second is the design of policy: should the central bank target money growth or should it target inflation? What rule should the central bank use to adjust the interest rate? The final part looks at fiscal policy, reviewing more closely what we have learned and then looking more closely at the implications of the government budget constraint for the relation between debt, spending and taxes. Next, it considers several issues, from how wars should be financed, to the dangers of accumulating too high a level of debt, before ending with a description of the current budget situation in the USA and a discussion of the problems on the horizon.

Chapter 23

POLICY AND POLICY MAKERS: WHAT DO WE KNOW?

At many points in this book, we have seen how the right mix of fiscal and monetary policy can help a country out of a recession, improve its trade position without increasing activity and igniting inflation, slow down an overheating economy, stimulate investment and capital accumulation and so on.

These conclusions, however, appear to be at odds with frequent demands that policy makers be tightly restrained: in Europe, the countries that adopted the euro signed the 'Stability and Growth Pact,' which requires them to keep their budget deficit under 3% of GDP or else face large fines. Monetary policy is also under fire. For example, the charter of the central bank of New Zealand, written in 1989, defines monetary policy's sole role as the maintenance of price stability, to the exclusion of any other macroeconomic goal.

This chapter discusses the arguments for restraining macroeconomic policy:

- Sections 23.1 and 23.2 look at one line of argument, namely that policy makers may have good intentions, but they end up doing more harm than good.

- Section 23.3 looks at another – more cynical – line, that policy makers do what is best for them, which is not necessarily what is best for the country.

On 15 January 2004, the German cartoonist, Horst Haitzinger, took an ironic look ('It was self-defence, honest!') at the uncomfortable position of Hans Eichel, German Finance Minister, who was attempting to justify the position of the Federal Republic of Germany (FRG) before the Court of Justice of the European Communities regarding its failure to comply with the Stability and Growth Pact.

Source: Haitzinger, Horst. Haitzinger Karikaturen 2004. München: Bruckmann, 2004, p. 9. *http://www.ena.lu?lang=2&doc=23469.*

23.1 UNCERTAINTY AND POLICY

A blunt way of stating the first argument in favour of policy restraints is that those who know little should do little (and the 2009–10 crisis that so few economists had anticipated is a humbling reminder of how little most of us know). The argument has two parts: macroeconomists, and by implication the policy makers who rely on their advice, know little; they should therefore do little. Let's look at each part separately.

How much do macroeconomists actually know?

Macroeconomists are like doctors treating cancer. They know a lot, but there is a lot they don't know.

Take an economy with high unemployment, where the central bank is considering the use of monetary policy to increase economic activity. Think of the sequence of links between an increase in money and an increase in output – all the questions the central bank faces when deciding whether and by how much to increase the money supply:

- Is the current high rate of unemployment above the natural rate of unemployment, or has the natural rate of unemployment itself increased (Chapters 9 and 10)?
- If the unemployment rate is close to the natural rate of unemployment, isn't there a risk that monetary expansion will lead to a decrease in unemployment below the natural rate of unemployment and cause an increase in inflation (Chapters 9 and 10)?
- By how much will the change in the money supply decrease the short-term interest rate (Chapter 4)? What will be the effect of the decrease in the short-term interest rate on the long-term interest rate (Chapter 15)? By how much will stock prices increase (Chapter 15)? By how much will the currency depreciate (Chapter 18)?
- How long will it take for lower long-term interest rates and higher stock prices to affect investment and consumption spending (Chapter 16)? How long will it take for the J-curve effects to work themselves out and for the trade balance to improve (Chapter 18)? What is the danger that the effects come too late, when the economy has already recovered?

When assessing these questions, central banks – or macroeconomic policy makers in general – do not operate in a vacuum. They rely in particular on macroeconometric models. The equations in these models show how these individual links have looked in the past. But different models yield different answers. This is because they have different structures, different lists of equations and different lists of variables.

We will consider two cases. A fiscal policy and a monetary policy shock. Let us start first with a monetary policy shock.

Consider a case where the euro area economy is growing at its normal growth rate; call this the *baseline* case. Suppose now, that over the period of a year, the ECB increases the nominal short-term interest rate by a 1% point. What will happen to the output in the euro area?

Table 23.1 shows the deviation of output from the baseline predicted by each of four macroeconomic models available for the euro area (the characteristics of these models are

Table 23.1 The response of output to a monetary shock: predictions from four models

Year	AWM	MULTIMOD III	NIGEM	QUEST
1	−0.19	−0.20	−0.16	−0.57
2	−0.30	−0.14	−0.22	−0.10
3	−0.28	−0.02	−0.11	−0.03
5	−0.17	−0.02	−0.04	−0.02
10	−0.01	0.02	0.0	−0.01

Note: the first-year monetary policy multipliers are greater in QUEST than in the other three models.

Source: Kenneth F. Wallis, 'Comparing economic models of the euro economy', *Economic Modeling*, **21**, 735–758, 2004.

described in the Focus box 'Four macroeconometric models'. All four models predict that output decreases for some time after the increase in the short-term nominal interest rate. What is reported in the table is the value of the monetary policy multipliers you have learned in Chapter 5. The four models predict different impacts of the increase in the short-term interest rate on output. After one year, the average deviation of output from the baseline is negative. The range of answers goes from nearly no change (−0.16% in the NIGEM model) to −0.57%, a range of 0.41%. Two years out, the average deviation is −0.19%; the range is

FOCUS
Four macroeconometric models

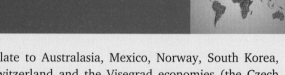

There are four major macro models for the euro area:

- the Area-Wide Model (AWM) of the European Central Bank (Fagan *et al.*, 2001). The AWM treats the euro area as a single economy. It corresponds to a conventional national economy macro model, with the rest of the world treated as exogenous. Although this includes the three EU members that have not adopted the single currency, and Greece, which did not join the third stage of EMU until 1 January 2001, in the current model the rest of the world is proxied by a four-country aggregate, comprising the USA, Japan, the UK and Switzerland.

and three well-established multicountry models, namely:

- MULTIMOD Mark III, developed in the Research Department of the IMF in Washington, DC (Laxton *et al.*, 1998). This model contains separate models for each of the Group of Seven (G7) countries – the USA, Canada, Japan, France, Germany, Italy and the UK – and for an aggregate grouping of 14 smaller industrial countries. The remaining economies of the world are then aggregated into two separate blocks of developing and transition economies. Each of the industrial country models has the structure of a complete national-economy model, whereas the two remaining blocks are modelled in much less detail.

The following two models – NIGEM and QUEST – are more disaggregated, each having complete country models for each EU member (taking the Belgium–Luxembourg Economic Union as a single entity) and a finer division of the rest of the world.

- NIGEM, developed at the National Institute of Economic and Social Research, London (Barrell *et al.*, 2001). NIGEM has six intermediate-size models consisting of a very basic description of the domestic economy (output and prices) together with trade volume and price equations and the balance of payments; these

relate to Australasia, Mexico, Norway, South Korea, Switzerland and the Visegrad economies (the Czech Republic, Hungary, Poland). Finally, there are seven simpler trade-and-payments models for China, OPEC, Developing Europe, Africa, Latin America, other LDCs and the rest of East Asia.

- The QUEST model of the European Commission (Roeger and in't Veld, 1997) separately models the USA and Japan, then describes the rest of the world by 11 trade-and-payments models. Four of these relate to the larger remaining OECD countries (Australia, Canada, Norway, Switzerland) and seven to various groups of countries, very much as above (Central and Eastern Europe, the rest of the OECD, OPEC, the former Soviet Union, 'dynamic' Asian economies, the rest of Asia and the rest of Africa and Latin America).

All the models describe the economy as you have learned in the previous chapters: the economy tends to its medium-run equilibrium with output equal to the natural level of output and employment at the level consistent with unemployment being at the natural level. All the models incorporate what you have learned about the behaviour of economic agents, that is they suppose that financial markets, firms and households take their economic decisions based on their 'rational' expectations about the future.

References:

Fagan, G., Henry, J., Mestre, R., *An Area-Wide Model (AWM) for the Euro Area*, Working Paper No.42, European Central Bank, Frankfurt, 2001.

Laxton, D., Isard, P., Faruqee, H., Prasad, E., Turtelboom, B., *MULTIMOD Mark III: the core dynamic and steady-state models*, Occasional Paper No.164, International Monetary Fund, Washington DC, 1998.

Barrell, R., Dury, K., Hurst, I., Pain, N., *Modelling the World Economy: the National Institute Global Economic Model*. Presented at an ENEPRI workshop on Simulation Properties of Macroeconometric Models, CEPII, Paris, 2001.

Roeger, W. and in't Veld, J., *QUEST II: a multi country business cycle and growth model*, Working paper, European Commission DGII, Brussels, 1997.

Source: This box is taken from an article by Kenneth F. Wallis 'Comparing economic models of the euro economy', in *Economic Modeling*, **21**, 735–758, 2004.

Table 23.2 The response of output to a fiscal shock
(a reduction in G equivalent to 1% of euro area GDP):
predictions from two models

Year	AWM	MULTIMOD III
1	−1.35	−1.48
2	−0.52	0.23
3	0.09	0.24
5	0.22	0.11
10	0.03	0.00

Note: the first-year fiscal policy multipliers are well above 1 in both models.

Source: Kenneth F. Wallis, 'Comparing economic models of the euro economy',
Economic Modeling, 21, 735–758, 2004.

down to 0.20%. But two models (AWM and NIGEM) predict a higher second-year monetary policy multiplier compared to the first-year multiplier; that is they predict that the largest negative impact on output of an increase in the short-term interest rate happens after two years. On the other hand, QUEST and MULTIMOD III predict that the largest impact on output happen in the first year. Five years out, the average deviation is −0.06%, but the answers range from −0.02% to −0.17%. Ten years out, the average deviation is 0%, but the answers range from −0.01% to 0.02%. Admittedly, the range of answers is not as large as is was in macroeconometric models used in the1980s, where the range of answers was much larger than it is now. But still, if we measure uncertainty by the range of answers from this set of models, there is a certain amount of uncertainty about the effects of policy.

Now consider a case where the euro area economy is growing at its normal growth rate; call this the *baseline* case. Suppose now, that over the period of a year, government spending is reduced by 1% of GDP, area-wide. What will happen to the output in the euro area?

Table 23.2 shows the effect on GDP of the fiscal contraction. Only two models are included in the table, AWM and MULTIMOD III, which can provide area-wide results. The responses of GDP to the fiscal contraction show wide variation, with impact multipliers well in excess of 1 on AWM and MULTIMOD III, 1.35 and 1.48, respectively. In both cases, the change in investment accounts for most of the reduction in GDP.

Should uncertainty lead policy makers to do less?

Should uncertainty about the effects of policy lead policy makers to do less? In general, the answer is yes. Consider the following example, which builds on the simulations we just looked at.

Suppose the euro area economy is in recession. The ECB is considering using monetary policy to expand output. To concentrate on uncertainty about the effects of policy, let's assume that the ECB knows everything else for sure. By how much should the ECB decrease the short-term nominal interest rate?

Taking the average of the responses from the different models in Table 23.1 (but with the opposite sign), a decrease in short-term nominal interest rate of 1% leads to a 0.28% increase in output in the first year. Suppose the ECB takes this average relation as holding with *certainty*. What it should then do is straightforward. To achieve 1% more output growth requires the ECB to decrease the short-term interest rate by 1%/0.28 = 3.6%. The ECB should therefore decrease the interest rate by 3.6%. This is clearly impossible, as nominal interest rates in the euro area have been much lower than that for a long time. But our example here serves to make another point. If the economy's response is equal to the *average* response from the four models, this decrease in interest rates will achieve 1% higher output growth at the end of the year.

Suppose the ECB actually decreases rates by 3.6%. But let's now take into account uncertainty, as measured by the *range* of responses of the different models in Table 23.2. Recall that the range of responses of output to a 1% decrease in interest rates after one year varies from −0.16% to −0.57%; equivalently, a 1% decrease in interest rates leads to a range of increases in output from 0.16% to 0.57%. These ranges imply that a decrease in interest rates of 3.6% leads, across models, to an output response anywhere between 0.58% and 2%.

This example relies on the notion of *multiplicative uncertainty* – that because the effects of policy are uncertain, more active policies lead to more uncertainty. See William Brainard, 'Uncertainty and the Effectiveness of Policy', *American Economic Review*, 1967, **57**, 411–425.

The conclusion is clear: given the range of uncertainty about the effects of monetary policy on output, decreasing interest rates by 3.6% would be irresponsible. If the effects of interest rates on output are as weak as suggested by one of the four models, output growth at the end of the year would increase by just around half percentage point. Given this uncertainty, the ECB should consider carefully whether and by how much to decrease the short-term interest rate. (In fact, as the short-term interest rate is much lower than 3.6% in the euro area, the ECB, to help the economy out of the recession of 2007–2010, did not have the option to reduce rates by as much as 3.6%, and had to resort to other forms of monetary policy, i.e. quantitative easing, as you learned in Chapter 20).

Uncertainty and restraints on policy makers

Let's summarise: there is substantial uncertainty about the effects of macroeconomic policy. This uncertainty should lead policy makers to be more cautious and to use less active policy. Policies should be broadly aimed at avoiding prolonged recessions, slowing down booms and avoiding inflationary pressure. The higher unemployment or the higher inflation, the more active the policies should be. But they should stop well short of **fine-tuning**, of trying to achieve constant unemployment or constant output growth.

Friedman and Modigliani are the same two economists who independently developed the modern theory of consumption we saw in Chapter 16.

These conclusions would have been controversial 20 years ago. Back then, there was a heated debate between two groups of economists. One group, headed by Milton Friedman from the University of Chicago, argued that because of long and variable lags, activist policy is likely to do more harm than good. The other group, headed by Franco Modigliani from MIT, had just built the first generation of large macroeconometric models and believed that economists' knowledge was becoming good enough to allow for increasing fine-tuning of the economy. Today, most economists recognise that there is substantial uncertainty about the effects of policy. They also accept the implication that this uncertainty should lead to less active policies.

Differences of opinion are more pronounced on the effects of fiscal than monetary policy. During the financial crisis of 2007–2010 there was widespread agreement on the need to use monetary policy both to offset the shock to aggregate demand and to compensate the shift in the demand for money (the crisis induced people to hold more money and fewer bonds for any given level of the interest rate). Whether to use government spending to offset the shock to aggregate demand was more controversial. In the USA, the UK and Ireland, governments relied extensively on fiscal policy: in the USA the budget deficit increased from 2.2% of GDP in 2006 to 13.6% in 2009; in the UK from 2.7% to 15.5%, in Ireland the budget shifted from a 3% surplus in 2006 to a 12% deficit in 2009. Continental Europe did much less: Germany for instance increased the deficit from 1.5% of GDP in 2006 to 4% in 2009. Underlying these differences in policies lie differences in views about the effects of a fiscal stimulus, with the Europeans less convinced than the Anglo-Saxons that an increase in public spending translates into higher GDP growth.

Note, however, that what we have developed so far is an argument for *self-restraint by* policy makers, not for *restraints on* policy makers. If policy makers understand the implications of uncertainty – and there is no particular reason to think they don't – they will, on their own, follow less active policies. There is no reason to impose further restraints, such as the requirement that money growth be constant or that the budget be balanced. Let's now turn to arguments for restraints *on* policy makers.

23.2 EXPECTATIONS AND POLICY

One of the reasons why the effects of macroeconomic policy are uncertain is the interaction of policy and expectations. How a policy works, and sometimes whether it works at all, depends not only on how it affects current variables but also on how it affects expectations about the future. (This was the main theme of Chapter 17.) The importance of expectations for policy, however, goes beyond uncertainty about the effects of policy. This brings us to a discussion of *games*.

Until 30 years ago, macroeconomic policy was seen in the same way as the control of a complicated machine. Methods of **optimal control**, developed initially to control and guide rockets, were being increasingly used to design macroeconomic policy. Economists no longer think this way. It has become clear that the economy is fundamentally different from a machine, even a very complicated one. Unlike a machine, the economy is composed of people and firms who try to anticipate what policy makers will do, and who react not only to current policy but also to expectations of future policy. Hence, macroeconomic policy must be thought of as a **game** between the policy makers and 'the economy' – more concretely, the people and the firms in the economy. So, when thinking about policy, what we need is not **optimal control theory** but rather **game theory**.

Warning: when economists say *game*, they do not mean 'entertainment'; they mean **strategic interactions** between **players**. In the context of macroeconomic policy, the players are the policy makers on one side, and people and firms on the other. The strategic interactions are clear: what people and firms do depends on what they expect policy makers to do. In turn, what policy makers do depends on what is happening in the economy.

Game theory has become an important tool in all branches of economics. Both the 1994 and the 2005 Nobel Prizes in Economics were awarded to game theorists. In 1994, it was awarded to John Nash, from Princeton; John Harsanyi, from Berkeley; and Reinhard Selten, from Germany (John Nash's life is portrayed in the movie *A Beautiful Mind*). In 2005, it was awarded to Robert Aumann, from Israel, and Tom Schelling, from Harvard.

> Game theory has given economists many insights, often explaining how some apparently strange behaviour makes sense when one understands the nature of the game being played. One of these insights is particularly important for our discussion of restraints here: sometimes you can do better in a game by giving up some of your options. To see why, let's start with an example from outside economics – governments' policies toward hostage takers.

Hostage takings and negotiations

Most governments have stated policies that they will not negotiate with hostage takers. The reason for this stated policy is clear: to deter hostage taking by making it unattractive to take hostages.

Suppose that, despite the stated policy, somebody is taken hostage. Now that the hostage taking has taken place anyway, why not negotiate? Whatever compensation the hostage takers demand is likely to be less costly than the alternative – the likelihood that the hostage will be killed. So the best policy would appear to be to announce that you will not negotiate but, if somebody is taken hostage, negotiate.

Upon reflection, it is clear that this would in fact be a very bad policy. Hostage takers' decisions do not depend on the stated policy but on what they expect will actually happen if they take a hostage. If they know that negotiations will actually take place, they will rightly consider the stated policy as irrelevant. And hostage takings will take place.

So what is the best policy? Despite the fact that once hostage takings have taken place, negotiations typically lead to a better outcome, the best policy is for governments to commit *not* to negotiate. By giving up the option to negotiate, they are likely to prevent hostage takings in the first place.

Let's now turn to a macroeconomic example, based on the relation between inflation and unemployment. As you will see, exactly the same logic is involved.

> This example was developed by Finn Kydland, from Carnegie Mellon, and Edward Prescott, then from Minnesota and now at Arizona State University, in 'Rules Rather than Discretion: the Inconsistency of Optimal Plans', *Journal of Political Economy*, 1977, 3 85. Kydland and Prescott were awarded the Nobel Prize in Economics in 2004.

Inflation and unemployment revisited

Recall the relation between inflation and unemployment we derived in Chapter 9 [equation (9.9), with the time indexes omitted here for simplicity]:

$$\pi = \pi^e - \alpha(u - u_n) \quad [23.1]$$

Inflation, π, depends on expected inflation, π^e, and on the difference between the actual unemployment rate, u, and the natural unemployment rate, u_n. The coefficient α captures the effect of unemployment on inflation, given expected inflation: when unemployment is above the natural rate, inflation is lower than expected; when unemployment is below the natural rate, inflation is higher than expected.

Suppose the central bank announces that it will follow a monetary policy consistent with zero inflation. On the assumption that people believe the announcement, expected inflation, π^e, as embodied in wage contracts, is equal to zero, and the central bank faces the following relation between unemployment and inflation:

$$\pi = -\alpha(u - u_n) \qquad [23.2]$$

A refresher:
Given labour market conditions, and given their expectations of what prices will be, firms and workers set nominal wages. Given the nominal wages firms have to pay, firms then set prices. So, prices depend on expected prices and labour market conditions. Equivalently, price inflation depends on expected price inflation and labour market conditions. This is what is captured in equation (23.1).

If the central bank follows through with its announced policy, it will choose an unemployment rate equal to the natural rate; from equation (23.2), inflation will be equal to zero, just as the central bank announced and people expected.

Achieving zero inflation and an unemployment rate equal to the natural rate is not a bad outcome. But it would seem that the central bank can actually do even better: for simplicity, we assume that the central bank can choose the unemployment rate – and, by implication, the inflation rate – exactly. In doing so, we ignore the uncertainty about the effects of policy. This was the topic of Section 23.1, but it is not central here.

If $\alpha = 1$, equation (23.2) implies $\pi = (u - u_n)$. If $\pi = 1\%$, then $(u - u_n) = -1\%$.

- Recall from Chapter 9 that in the USA, α is roughly equal to 1. So equation (23.2) implies that, by accepting just 1% inflation, the central bank can achieve an unemployment rate of 1% below the natural rate of unemployment. Suppose the central bank – and everybody else in the economy – finds the trade-off attractive and decides to decrease unemployment by 1% in exchange for an inflation rate of 1%. This incentive to deviate from the announced policy once the other player has made his move – in this case, once wage setters have set the wage – is known in game theory as the **time inconsistency** of optimal policy. In our example, the central bank can improve the outcome this period by deviating from its announced policy of zero inflation: by accepting some inflation, it can achieve a substantial reduction in unemployment.

Remember that the natural rate of unemployment is neither natural nor best in any sense (see Chapters 7 and 9). It may be reasonable for the central bank and everyone else in the economy to prefer an unemployment rate lower than the natural rate of unemployment.

- Unfortunately, this is not the end of the story. Seeing that the central bank has increased money by more than it announced it would, wage setters are likely to begin to expect positive inflation of 1%. If the central bank still wants to achieve an unemployment rate 1% below the natural rate, it will have to achieve 2% inflation. However, if it does achieve 2% inflation, wage setters are likely to increase their expectations of inflation further, and so on.

- The eventual outcome is likely to be high inflation. Because wage setters understand the central bank's motives, expected inflation catches up with actual inflation, and the central bank will eventually be unsuccessful in its attempt to achieve an unemployment rate below the natural rate. In short, attempts by the central bank to make things better lead in the end to things being worse. The economy ends up with the *same unemployment rate* that would have prevailed if the central bank had followed its announced policy, but with *much higher inflation*.

How relevant is this example? Very relevant. Go back to Chapter 9: we can read the history of the Phillips curve and the increase in inflation in the 1970s as coming precisely from the central bank's attempts to keep unemployment below the natural rate of unemployment, leading to higher and higher expected inflation, and higher and higher actual inflation. In that light, the shift of the original Phillips curve can be seen as the adjustment of wage setters' expectations to the central bank's behaviour.

So what is the best policy for the central bank to follow in this case? It is to make a credible commitment that it will not try to decrease unemployment below the natural rate. By giving up the option of deviating from its announced policy, the central bank can achieve unemployment equal to the natural rate of unemployment and zero inflation. The analogy with the hostage taking example is clear: by credibly committing not to do something that would appear desirable at the time, policy makers can achieve a better outcome: no hostage takings in our earlier example, no inflation here.

Establishing credibility

How can a central bank credibly commit not to deviate from its announced policy?

One way to establish its credibility is for a central bank to give up – or to be stripped by law of – its policy making power. For example, the mandate of the central bank can be defined by law in terms of a simple rule, such as setting money growth at 0% forever. (An alternative, which we discussed in Chapter 19, is to adopt a hard peg, such as a currency board or even dollarisation: in this case, instead of giving up its ability to use money growth, the central bank gives up its ability to use the exchange rate and the interest rate.)

Such a law surely takes care of the problem of time inconsistency. But the tight restraint it creates comes close to throwing out the baby with the bathwater. We want to prevent the central bank from pursuing too high a rate of money growth in an attempt to lower unemployment below the natural unemployment rate. But – subject to the restrictions discussed in Section 23.1 – we still want the central bank to be able to expand the money supply when unemployment is far above the natural rate, and contract the money supply when unemployment is far below the natural rate. Such actions become impossible under a constant-money-growth rule. There are indeed better ways to deal with time inconsistency. In the case of monetary policy, our discussion suggests various ways of dealing with the problem.

A first step is to make the central bank independent. Politicians, who face frequent re-elections, are likely to want lower unemployment now, even if it leads to inflation later. Making the central bank independent, and making it difficult for politicians to fire the central banker, makes it easier for the central bank to resist the political pressure to decrease unemployment below the natural rate of unemployment.

This may not be enough, however. Even if it is not subject to political pressure, the central bank will still be tempted to decrease unemployment below the natural rate: doing so leads to a better outcome in the short run. So, a second step is to give incentives to central bankers to take the long view – that is, to take into account the long-run costs from higher inflation. One way of doing so is to give them long terms in office, so they have a long horizon and have an incentive to build credibility.

A third step may be to appoint a 'conservative' central banker, somebody who dislikes inflation very much and is therefore less willing to accept more inflation in exchange for less unemployment when unemployment is at the natural rate. When the economy is at the natural rate, such a central banker will be less tempted to embark on a monetary expansion. Thus, the problem of time inconsistency will be reduced.

These are the steps many countries have taken over the past two decades. Central banks have been given more independence. Central bankers have been given long terms in office. And governments typically have appointed central bankers who are more 'conservative' than the governments themselves – central bankers who appear to care more about inflation and less about unemployment than the government. (See the Focus box 'Was Alan Blinder wrong in speaking the truth?')

Figure 23.1 suggests that this approach has been successful. The vertical axis gives the average annual inflation rates in 18 OECD countries for the period 1960–1990. The horizontal axis gives the value of an index of 'central bank independence,' constructed by looking at a number of legal provisions in the bank's charter – for example, whether and how the government can remove the head of the bank. There is a striking inverse relation between the two variables, as summarised by the regression line: more central bank independence appears to be systematically associated with lower inflation.

Time consistency and restraints on policy makers

Let's summarise what we have learned in this section.

We have examined arguments for putting restraints on policymakers, based on the issue of time inconsistency.

A warning:

Figure 23.1 shows correlation, not necessarily causality. It may be that countries that dislike inflation tend both to give more independence to their central bankers and have lower inflation. (This is another example of the difference between correlation and causality – discussed in Appendix 2 at the end of the book.)

Figure 23.1

Inflation and central bank independence

Across OECD countries, the higher the degree of central bank independence, the lower the rate of inflation.

Source: Vittorio Grilli, Donato Masciandar, and Guido Tabellini, 'Political and Monetary Institutions and Public Financial Policies in the Industrial Countries', *Economic Policy*, October 1991, 341–392.

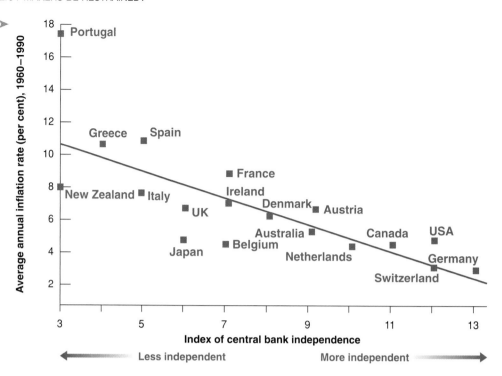

FOCUS
Was Alan Blinder wrong in speaking the truth?

In the summer of 1994, President Clinton appointed Alan Blinder, an economist from Princeton, Vice-Chairman (in effect, second in command) of the Federal Reserve Board. A few weeks later, Blinder, speaking at an economic conference, indicated his belief that the Fed has both the responsibility and the ability, when unemployment is high, to use monetary policy to help the economy recover. This statement was badly received. Bond prices fell, and most newspapers ran editorials critical of Blinder.

Why was the reaction of markets and newspapers so negative? It was surely not that Blinder was wrong. There is no doubt that monetary policy can and should help the economy out of a recession. Indeed, the Federal Reserve Bank Act of 1978 requires the Fed to pursue full employment as well as low inflation.

The reaction was negative because, in terms of the argument we developed in the text, Blinder revealed by

his words that he was not a conservative central banker, that he cared about unemployment as well as inflation. With the unemployment rate at the time equal to 6.1%, close to what was thought to be the natural rate of unemployment at the time, markets interpreted Blinder's statements as suggesting that he might want to decrease unemployment below the natural rate. Interest rates increased because of higher expected inflation – bond prices decreased.

The moral of the story: whatever views central bankers may hold, they should try to look and sound conservative. This is why many heads of central banks are reluctant to admit, at least in public, the existence of any trade-off between unemployment and inflation, even in the short run.

We have looked at the case of monetary policy. But similar issues arise in the context of fiscal policy. For instance, we discussed in Chapter 21 the issue of debt repudiation – the option for the government to cancel its debt obligations – and see that the conclusions there are very similar to those in the case of monetary policy.

When issues of time inconsistency are relevant, tight restraints on policy makers – such as a fixed-money-growth rule in the case of monetary policy, or a balanced budget rule in the case of fiscal policy – can provide a rough solution. But the solution has large costs because it prevents the use of macroeconomic policy altogether. Better solutions typically involve designing better institutions (such as an independent central bank or a better budget process) that can reduce the problem of time inconsistency while, at the same time, allowing the use of policy for the stabilisation of output.

23.3 POLITICS AND POLICY

We have assumed so far that policy makers are *benevolent* – that they try to do what is best for the economy. However, much public discussion challenges that assumption: politicians or policy makers, the argument goes, do what is best for themselves, and this is not always what is best for the country.

You have heard the arguments: politicians avoid the hard decisions, they pander to the electorate, partisan politics leads to gridlock and nothing ever gets done. Discussing the flaws of democracy goes far beyond the scope of this book. What we can do here is to briefly review how these arguments apply to macroeconomic policy and then look at the empirical evidence and see what light it sheds on the issue of policy restraints.

Games between policy makers and voters

Many macroeconomic policy decisions involve trading off short-run losses against long-run gains – or, conversely, short-run gains against long-run losses.

Take, for example, tax cuts. By definition, tax cuts lead to lower taxes today. They are also likely to lead to an increase in activity and, therefore, to an increase in pre-tax income, for some time. But unless they are matched by equal decreases in government spending, they lead to a larger budget deficit and to the need for an increase in taxes in the future. If voters are short-sighted, the temptation for politicians to cut taxes may prove irresistible. Politics may lead to systematic deficits, at least until the level of government debt has become so high that politicians are scared into action.

Now move on from taxes to macroeconomic policy in general. Again suppose that voters are short-sighted. If the politicians' main goal is to please voters and get re-elected, what better policy than to expand aggregate demand before an election, leading to higher growth and lower unemployment? True, growth in excess of the normal growth rate cannot be sustained, and eventually the economy must return to the natural level of output: higher growth now must be followed by lower growth later. But with the right timing and short-sighted voters, higher growth can win elections. Thus, we might expect a clear **political business cycle**, with higher growth on average before elections than after elections.

> From Okun's law, we know that output growth in excess of normal growth leads to a decline in the unemployment rate below the natural rate of unemployment. In the medium run, we know that the unemployment rate must increase back to the natural rate of unemployment. This in turn requires output growth below normal for some time. See Chapter 10.

The arguments we have just laid out are familiar; you have heard them before, in one form or another. And their logic is convincing. The question is: how well do they fit the facts?

Take first deficits and debt. The argument above would lead you to expect that budget deficits and high government debt have always been and always will be there. Figure 23.2, which gives the evolution of the ratio of government debt to GDP in the UK since 1900, shows that the reality is more complex.

Look first at the evolution of the ratio of debt to GDP from 1900–1980. Note that each of the three build-ups in debt was associated with special circumstances: the First World War for the first build-up, the Great Depression for the second and the Second World War for the third. These were times of unusually high military spending or unusual declines in output. Adverse circumstances – not pandering to voters – were clearly behind the large deficit and the resulting increase in debt during each of these three episodes. Note also how, in each case, the build-up was followed by a steady decrease in debt. In particular, note how the ratio of debt to GDP, which was as high as 250% around 1950, was steadily reduced to a post-war low below 50% in the early 1990s.

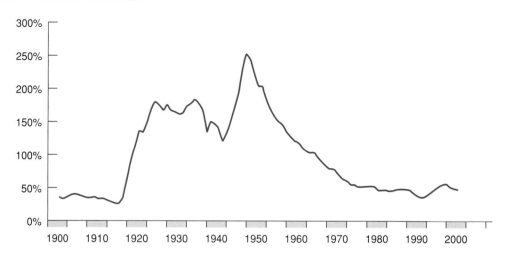

Figure 23.2

The evolution of the ratio of UK debt-to-GDP since 1900

The three major build-ups of debt since 1900 have been associated with the First World War, the Great Depression and the Second World War.

Source: *Bank of England Statistical Abstract,* Part 1, 2000 edition, Table 15.2 (cited in HM Treasury, *Public Finances Databank,* October 2001).

Table 23.3 Average growth during Labour and Conservative administrations in the UK (per cent per year)

	Year of				
	First	**Second**	**Third**	**Fourth**	**Average**
Conservative Party	1.48	1.26	1.29	1.39	1.35
Labour Party	1.34	1.65	1.89	0.82	1.50
Average	1.40	1.47	1.59	1.16	1.43

Let us now return to the political-business-cycle argument, that policy makers try to get high output growth before the elections so they will be re-elected. If the political business cycle were important, we would expect to see faster growth before elections than after. Table 23.3 gives average output growth rates for each of the first four years of each UK government from the second Wilson administration in 1974, until the third Blair administration ended in 2007, distinguishing between Conservative and Labour governments. Look at the last line: growth has not been highest on average in the last year of a ministry; actually, average growth in the fourth years of a ministry was the lowest compared to average growth in previous years. Moreover, the average difference across years is small: 1.16% in the fourth year of an administration versus 1.40% in the first year. (We shall return later in this chapter to the other interesting feature in the table – the difference between Conservative and Labour governments.) However, if you look at Conservative and Labour governments separately, you will notice that the former achieved on average higher growth in the fourth year of a ministry with respect to the second and third years, which is not the case with Labour governments. It would seem that the Conservatives, unlike their opponents, tried to stimulate the economy towards the end of their ministries to win elections. Overall, there is still little evidence of manipulation – or at least of successful manipulation – of the economy to win elections.

Games between policy makers

Another line of argument shifts the focus from games between politicians and voters to games between policy makers.

Suppose, for example, that the party in power wants to reduce spending but faces opposition to spending cuts in Parliament. One way of putting pressure both on Parliament and on the future parties in power is to cut taxes and create deficits. As debt increases over time, the increasing pressure to reduce deficits may in turn force Parliament and the future parties in power to reduce spending – something they would not have been willing to do otherwise.

Or suppose that, either for the reason we just saw or for any other reason, the country is facing large budget deficits. Both parties want to reduce the deficit, but they disagree about the way to do it: one party wants to reduce deficits primarily through an increase in taxes; the other wants to reduce deficits primarily through a decrease in spending. Both parties may hold out on the hope that the other side will give in first. Only when debt has increased sufficiently, and it becomes urgent to reduce deficits, will one party give up. Game theorists refer to these situations as **wars of attrition**. The hope that the other side will give in leads to long and often costly delays. Such wars of attrition happen often in the context of fiscal policy, and deficit reduction occurs long after it should.

Wars of attrition arise in other macroeconomic contexts, such as during episodes of hyperinflation. As you saw in Chapter 22, hyperinflations come from the use of money creation to finance large budget deficits. Although the need to reduce those deficits is usually recognised early on, support for stabilisation programmes – which include the elimination of those deficits – typically comes only after inflation has reached such high levels that economic activity is severely affected.

Another example of games between political parties is the movements in economic activity brought about by the alternation of parties in power. Conservatives typically worry more than Labour about inflation. They worry less than Labour about unemployment. So we would expect Labour governments to show stronger growth – and thus less unemployment and more inflation – than Conservative governments. This prediction appears to fit the facts quite well. Look at Table 23.3 again. Average growth has been 1.50% during Labour governments, compared to 1.35% during Conservative governments. The most striking contrast is in the third year, 1.89% during Labour governments, compared to 1.29% during Conservative governments.

This raises an intriguing question: why is the effect so much stronger in the administration's *third* year? The theory of unemployment and inflation we developed in Chapter 10 suggests a possible hypothesis: there are lags in the effects of policy, so it takes more than two years for a new government to affect the economy. And sustaining higher growth than normal for too long would lead to increasing inflation, so even a Labour government would not want to sustain higher growth throughout its term. Thus, differences in growth rates tend to decline in the fourth year of Labour and Conservative governments and to be much closer to each other towards the end of a ministry – more so than in the third year. In fact, during Labour governments, growth actually declined in the fourth year compared to the first three years.

SUMMARY

- The effects of macroeconomic policies are always uncertain. This uncertainty should lead policy makers to be more cautious and to use less active policies. Policies must be broadly aimed at avoiding prolonged recessions, slowing down booms and avoiding inflationary pressure. The higher the level of unemployment or inflation, the more active the policies should be. But they should stop short of fine-tuning, of trying to maintain constant unemployment or constant output growth.

- Using macroeconomic policy to control the economy is fundamentally different from controlling a machine. Unlike a machine, the economy is composed of people and firms who try to anticipate what policy makers will do, and who react not only to current policy but also to expectations of future policy. In this sense, macroeconomic policy can be thought of as a game between policy makers and people in the economy.

- When playing a game, it is sometimes better for a player to give up some of his or her options. For example, when a hostage taking occurs, it is better to negotiate with the hostage takers than not to negotiate. But a government that credibly commits to not negotiating with hostage takers – a government that gives up the option of negotiation – is actually more likely to deter hostage takings from occurring.

- The same argument applies to various aspects of macroeconomic policy. By credibly committing not to using monetary policy to decrease unemployment below the natural rate of unemployment, a central bank can alleviate fears that money growth will be high and, in the process, decrease both expected and actual inflation. When issues of time inconsistency are relevant, tight restraints on policy makers – such as a fixed-money-growth rule in the case of monetary policy – can provide a rough solution. But the solution can have large costs if it prevents the use of macroeconomic policy altogether. Better methods typically involve designing better institutions (such as an independent central bank) that can reduce the problem of time inconsistency without eliminating monetary policy as a macroeconomic policy tool.

- Another argument for putting restraints on policy makers is that policy makers may play games either with the public or among themselves, and these games may lead to undesirable outcomes. Politicians may try to fool a short-sighted electorate by choosing policies with short-run benefits but large long-term costs – for example, large budget deficits. Political parties may delay painful decisions, hoping that the other party will make the adjustment and take the blame. In cases like this, tight restraints on policy, such as a constitutional amendment to balance the budget, again provide a rough solution. Better ways typically involve better institutions and better ways of designing the process through which policy and decisions are made.

KEY TERMS

QUESTIONS AND PROBLEMS

QUICK CHECK

1. *Using the information in this chapter, label each of the following statements true, false or uncertain. Explain briefly.*

a. There is so much uncertainty about the effects of monetary policy that we would be better off not using it.

b. Elect a Labour government if you want low unemployment.

c. There is clear evidence of political business cycles in the UK: low unemployment during election campaigns and higher unemployment the rest of the time.

d. Rules are ineffective in reducing budget deficits.

e. Governments would be wise to announce a no-negotiation policy with hostage takers.

f. If hostages are taken, it is clearly wise for governments to negotiate with hostage takers, even if the government has announced a no-negotiation policy.

g. When a central bank announces a target inflation rate, it has no incentive to deviate from the target.

2. Implementing a political business cycle

You are the economic adviser to a newly elected prime minister. In four years she will face another election. Voters want a low unemployment rate and a low inflation rate. However, you believe that voting decisions are influenced heavily by the values of unemployment and inflation in the last year before the election, and that the economy's performance in the first three years of a prime minister's administration has little effect on voting behaviour.

Assume that inflation last year was 10%, and that the unemployment rate was equal to the natural rate. The Phillips curve is given by

$$\pi_t = \pi_{t-1} - \alpha(u_t - u_n)$$

Assume that you can use fiscal and monetary policy to achieve any unemployment rate you want for each of the next four years. Your task is to help the prime minister achieve low unemployment and low inflation in the last year of her administration.

a. Suppose you want to achieve a low unemployment rate (i.e. an unemployment rate below the natural rate) in the year before the next election (four years from today). What will happen to inflation in the fourth year?

b. Given the effect on inflation you identified in part (a), what would you advise the prime minister to do in the early years of her administration to achieve low inflation in the fourth year?

c. Now suppose the Phillips curve is given by

$$\pi_t = \pi_t^e - \alpha(u_t - u_n)$$

In addition, assume that people form inflation expectations, π_t^e, based on consideration of the future (as opposed to looking only at inflation last year), and are aware that the prime minister has an incentive to carry out the policies you identified in parts (a) and (b). Are the policies you described in parts (a) and (b) likely to be successful? Why or why not?

3. *Suppose the government amends the constitution to prevent government officials from negotiating with terrorists.*

What are the advantages of such a policy? What are the disadvantages?

4. *New Zealand rewrote the charter of its central bank in the early 1990s to make low inflation its only goal.*

Why would New Zealand want to do this?

DIG DEEPER

5. Political expectations, inflation and unemployment

Consider a country with two political parties, Labour and Conservative. Labour care more about unemployment than Conservative, and Conservative care more about inflation than Labour. When Labour are in power, they choose an inflation rate of π_L, and when the Conservatives are in power, they choose an inflation rate of π_C. We assume that $\pi_L > \pi_C$.

The Phillips curve is given by

$$\pi_t = \pi_t^e - \alpha(u_t - u_n)$$

An election is about to be held. Assume that expectations about inflation for the coming year (represented by π_t^e) are formed before the election. (Essentially, this assumption means that wages for the coming year are set before the election.) Moreover, Labour and Conservative have an equal chance of winning the election.

a. Solve for expected inflation, in terms of π_L and π_C.

b. Suppose Labour win the election and implement their target inflation rate, π_L. Given your solution for expected inflation in part (a), how will the unemployment rate compare to the natural rate of unemployment?

c. Suppose the Conservatives win the election and implement their target inflation rate, π_C. Given your solution for expected inflation in part (a), how will the unemployment rate compare to the natural rate of unemployment?

d. Do these results fit the evidence in Table 23.3? Why or why not?

e. Now suppose that everybody expects Labour to win the election, and Labour indeed win. If Labour implement their target inflation rate, how will the unemployment rate compare to the natural rate?

6. Deficit reduction as a prisoner's dilemma game

Suppose there is a budget deficit. It can be reduced by cutting military spending, by cutting social security, or by cutting both. Labour have to decide whether to support cuts in social security. The Conservatives have to decide whether to support cuts in military spending.

The possible outcomes are represented in the following table:

		Social security cuts	
		Yes	**No**
Defence cuts	Yes	(R = 1, D = –2)	(R = –2, D = 3)
	No	(R = 3, D = –2)	(R = –1, D = –1)

The table presents payoffs to each party under the various outcomes. Think of a payoff as a measure of happiness for a given party under a given outcome. If Labour vote for social security cuts and the Conservatives vote against cuts in military spending, the Conservatives receive a payoff of 3 and Labour receive a payoff of 22.

a. If the Conservatives decide to cut military spending, what is the best response of Labour? Given this response, what is the payoff for the Conservatives?

b. If the Conservatives decide not to cut military spending, what is the best response of Labour? Given this response, what is the payoff for the Conservatives?

c. What will the Conservatives do? What will Labour do? Will the budget deficit be reduced? Why or why not? (A game with a payoff structure like the one in this problem, and which produces the outcome you have just described, is known as a *prisoner's dilemma*.) Is there a way to improve the outcome?

EXPLORE FURTHER

7. Games, pre-commitment and time inconsistency in the news

Current events offer abundant examples of disputes in which the parties are involved in a game, try to commit themselves to lines of action in advance and face issues of time inconsistency. Examples arise in the domestic political process, international affairs and labour–management relations.

a. Choose a current dispute (or one resolved recently) to investigate. Do an Internet search to learn the issues involved in the dispute, the actions taken by the parties to date and the current state of play.

b. In what ways have the parties tried to pre-commit to certain actions in the future? Do they face issues of time inconsistency? Have the parties failed to carry out any of their threatened actions?

c. Does the dispute resemble a prisoner's dilemma game (a game with a payoff structure like the one described in problem 6)? In other words, does it seem likely (or did it actually happen) that the individual incentives of the parties will lead them to an unfavourable outcome – one that could be improved for both parties through cooperation? Is there a deal to be made? What attempts have the parties made to negotiate?

d. How do you think the dispute will be resolved (or how has it been resolved)?

*We invite you to visit the Blanchard page on the Prentice Hall website, at **www.prenhall.com/blanchard** for this chapter's World Wide Web exercises.*

FURTHER READING

- If you want to learn more on these issues, a very useful reference is **Alan Drazen**, *Political Economy in Macroeconomics*, **Princeton University Press, Princeton, NJ, 2000**.

- A leading proponent of the view that governments misbehave and should be tightly restrained is **James Buchanan**, from George Mason University. Buchanan received the Nobel Prize in 1986 for his work on public choice. Read, for example, his book with **Richard Wagner**, *Democracy in*

Deficit: The Political Legacy of Lord Keynes, **Academic Press, New York, 1977**.

- For an interpretation of the increase in inflation in the 1970s as a result of time inconsistency, see **Henry Chappell and Rob McGregor, 'Did Time Consistency Contribute to the Great Inflation?'** *Economics & Politics*, 2004, 16, 233–251.

Chapter 24

MONETARY AND FISCAL POLICY RULES AND CONSTRAINTS

Nearly every chapter has said something about monetary and fiscal policies. This chapter puts all these things together and ties up the remaining loose ends.

Let's first briefly review what you have learned about monetary policy:

- In the short run, monetary policy affects the level of output as well as its composition:
  - An increase in money leads to a decrease in interest rates and a depreciation of the currency.
  - Both of these lead to an increase in the demand for goods and an increase in output.

- In the medium run and the long run, monetary policy is neutral:
  - Changes in either the level or the rate of growth of money have no effect on output or unemployment.
  - Changes in the level of money lead to proportional increases in prices.
  - Changes in the rate of nominal money growth lead to corresponding changes in the inflation rate.

Let's also review what you have learned about fiscal policy:

- In the short run, a budget deficit (triggered, say, by a increase in government spending) increases demand and output. What happens to investment spending is ambiguous.

- In the medium run, output returns to the natural level of output. The interest rate and the composition of spending are different, however. The interest rate is higher, and investment spending is lower.

- In the long run, lower investment leads to a lower capital stock and, therefore, a lower level of output.

With these effects in mind, this chapter looks at the goals and methods of monetary and fiscal policies today. The chapter is divided in three sections.

The first two sections deal with monetary policy rules:

- Section 24.1 discusses what inflation rate central banks should try to achieve in the medium run and the long run, in other words what is the optimal inflation rate.

- Section 24.2 discusses how monetary policy should be designed both to achieve this inflation rate in the medium run and the long run, and to reduce output fluctuations in the short run.

The last section deals with fiscal policy rules and constraints:

● Section 24.3 examines a number of fiscal policy issues where the government budget constraint plays a central role, from the proposition that deficits do not really matter, to tax distortions. It then describes some notable cases of fiscal policy rules around the world: the rules imposed by the Stability and Growth Pact on the members of the European Monetary Union, the Golden Rule recently introduced in the UK and the balanced budget rule in the USA.

24.1 THE OPTIMAL INFLATION RATE

At this stage, the debate in OECD countries is largely between those who think some inflation (say 3%) is fine and those who want to achieve price stability – that is, 0% inflation.

Those who want an inflation rate around 3% emphasise that the costs of 3% versus 0% inflation are small and that the benefits of inflation are worth keeping. They argue that some of the costs of inflation could be avoided by indexing the tax system and issuing more indexed bonds. They also argue that getting inflation down from its current rate to zero would require some increase in unemployment for some time, and that this transition cost may well exceed the eventual benefits.

Those who want to aim for 0% make the point that 0% is a very different target rate from all others: it corresponds to price stability. This is desirable in itself. Knowing that the price level will be roughly the same in ten or 20 years as it is today simplifies a number of complicated decisions and eliminates the scope for money illusion. Also, given the time consistency problem facing central banks (discussed in Chapter 23), credibility and simplicity of the target inflation rate are important. Proponents of 0% inflation believe price stability can achieve these goals better than a target inflation rate of 3%.

The debate is not settled. For the time being, most central banks appear to be aiming for low but positive inflation – that is, inflation rates between 2% and 3%.

The costs of inflation

We saw in Chapter 22 how very high inflation, say a rate of 30% per month or more, can disrupt economic activity. The debate in OECD countries today, however, is not about the costs of inflation rates of 30% per month or more. Rather, it centres on the advantages of, say, 0% versus 3% inflation per year. Within that range, economists identify four main costs of inflation: (1) shoe-leather costs, (2) tax distortions, (3) money illusion and (4) inflation variability.

Shoe-leather costs

From Chapter 14: in the medium run, the real interest rate is not affected by inflation. The increase in inflation is reflected one-for-one in an increase in the nominal interest rate. This is called the Fisher effect.

➤ In the medium run, a higher inflation rate leads to a higher nominal interest rate and so to a higher opportunity cost of holding money. As a result, people decrease their money balances by making more trips to the bank – thus the expression **shoe-leather costs**. These trips would be avoided if inflation were lower and people could be doing other things instead, such as working more or enjoying leisure.

During hyperinflations, shoe-leather costs can become quite large. But their importance in times of moderate inflation is limited. If an inflation rate of 3% leads people to go to the bank say one more time every month, or to do one more transaction between their money market fund and their current account every month, this hardly qualifies as a major cost of inflation.

Tax distortions

The second cost of inflation comes from the interaction between the tax system and inflation.

Consider, for example, the taxation of capital gains. Taxes on capital gains are typically based on the change in the price of an asset between the time it is purchased and the time it is sold. This implies that the higher the rate of inflation, the higher the tax. An example will make this clear:

- Suppose inflation has been running at $\pi\%$ per year for the past ten years.
- Suppose you bought your house for €50 000 ten years ago, and you are selling it today for €50 000 $\times (1 + \pi\%)^{10}$ – so its real value is unchanged.

- If the capital gains tax is 30%, the *effective tax rate* on the sale of your house – defined as the ratio of the tax you pay to the price for which you sell your house – is

$$(30\%)\frac{50\ 000(1 + \pi\%)^{10} - 50\ 000}{50\ 000(1 + \pi\%)^{10}}$$

◄ The numerator of the fraction equals the sale price minus the purchase price. The denominator is the sale price.

- Because you are selling your house for the same real price at which you bought it, your real capital gain is zero, so you should not be paying any tax. Indeed, if $\pi = 0$ – if there has been no inflation – then the effective tax rate is 0%. But if $\pi = 3\%$, then the effective tax rate is 7.6%: despite the fact that your real capital gain is zero, you end up paying a high tax.

The problems created by the interactions between taxation and inflation extend beyond capital gains taxes. Although we know that the real rate of return on an asset is the real interest rate, not the nominal interest rate, income for the purpose of income taxation includes nominal interest payments, not real interest payments. Or, to take yet another example, until the early 1980s in the USA, the income levels corresponding to different income tax rates were not increased automatically with inflation. As a result, people were pushed into higher tax brackets as their nominal income – but not necessarily their real income – increased over time, an effect known as *bracket creep*.

You might argue that this cost is not a cost of inflation *per se*, but rather the result of a badly designed tax system. In the house example we just discussed, the government could eliminate the problem if it *indexed* the purchase price to the price level – that is, if it adjusted the purchase price for inflation since the time of purchase – and computed the tax on the difference between the sale price and the adjusted purchase price. Under that computation, there would be no capital gains and therefore no capital gains tax to pay. But because tax codes rarely allow for such systematic adjustment, the inflation rate matters and leads to distortions.

Money illusion

The third cost of inflation comes from **money illusion** – the notion that people appear to make systematic mistakes in assessing nominal versus real changes. A number of computations that would be simple when prices are stable become more complicated when there is inflation. When they compare their income this year to their income in previous years, people have to keep track of the history of inflation. When they choose between different assets or when they decide how much to consume or save, they have to keep track of the difference between the real interest rate and the nominal interest rate. Casual evidence suggests that many people find these computations difficult and often fail to make the relevant distinctions. Economists and psychologists have gathered more formal evidence, and it suggests that inflation often leads people and firms to make incorrect decisions (see the Focus box 'Money illusion'). If this is the case, then a simple solution is to have zero inflation.

Inflation variability

The fourth cost comes from the fact that higher inflation is typically associated with *more variable inflation*. And more variable inflation means financial assets such as bonds, which promise fixed nominal payments in the future, become riskier.

Take a bond that pays €1000 in ten years. With constant inflation over the next ten years, not only the nominal value but also the real value of the bond in ten years is known with certainty – we can compute exactly how much a euro will be worth in ten years. But with variable inflation, the real value of €1000 in ten years becomes uncertain. The more variability there is, the more uncertainty it creates. Saving for retirement becomes more difficult. For those who have invested in bonds, lower inflation than they expected means a better retirement; but higher inflation may mean poverty. This is one of the reasons retirees, for whom part of their income is fixed in money terms, typically worry more about inflation than other groups in the population.

A good and sad movie about surviving ➤ on a fixed pension in Italy after the Second World War is *Umberto D*, made by Vittorio de Sica in 1952.

You might argue, as in the case of taxes, that these costs are not due to inflation *per se*, but rather to the financial markets' inability to provide assets that protect their holders against inflation. Rather than issuing only nominal bonds (bonds that promise a fixed nominal amount in the future), governments or firms could also issue *indexed bonds* – bonds that promise a nominal amount adjusted for inflation, so people do not have to worry about the real value of the bond when they retire. Indeed, as we saw in Chapter 15, a number of countries, including the UK, France and Sweden, have now introduced such bonds, so people can better protect themselves against movements in inflation.

FOCUS
Money illusion

There is a lot of anecdotal evidence that many people fail to adjust properly for inflation in their financial computations. Recently, economists and psychologists have started looking at money illusion more closely. In a recent study, two psychologists, Eldar Shafir from Princeton University and Amos Tversky from Stanford University, and one economist, Peter Diamond from MIT, designed a survey aimed at finding how prevalent money illusion is and what causes it. Among the many questions they asked of people in various groups (people at Newark International Airport, people at two New Jersey shopping malls and a group of Princeton undergraduates) is the following.

Suppose Adam, Ben and Carl each received an inheritance of $200 000 and each used it immediately to purchase a house. Suppose each sold his house one year after buying it. Economic conditions were, however, different in each case:

- During the time Adam owned the house, there was a 25% deflation – the prices of all goods and services decreased by approximately 25%. A year after Adam bought the house, he sold it for $154 000 (23% less than what he had paid).
- During the time Ben owned the house, there was no inflation or deflation – the prices of all goods and services did not change significantly during the year. A year after Ben bought the house, he sold it for $198 000 (1% less than what he had paid).

- During the time Carl owned the house, there was a 25% inflation – the prices of all goods and services increased by approximately 25%. A year after Carl bought the house, he sold it for $246 000 (23% more than what he had paid).

Please rank Adam, Ben and Carl in terms of the success of their house transactions. Assign '1' to the person who made the best deal and '3' to the person who made the worst deal.

In nominal terms, Carl clearly made the best deal, followed by Ben, followed by Adam. But what is relevant is how they did in real terms – adjusting for inflation. In real terms, the ranking is reversed: Adam, with a 2% real gain, made the best deal, followed by Ben (with a 1% loss), followed by Carl (with a 2% loss).

The survey's answers were as follows:

Rank	Adam	Ben	Carl
1st	37%	15%	48%
2nd	10%	74%	16%
3rd	53%	11%	36%

Carl was ranked first by 48% of the respondents, and Adam was ranked third by 53% of the respondents. These answers suggest that money illusion is very prevalent. In other words, people (even Princeton undergraduates) have a hard time adjusting for inflation.

The benefits of inflation

Inflation is actually not all bad. One can identify three benefits of inflation: (1) seignorage, (2) the option of negative real interest rates for macroeconomic policy and (3) (somewhat paradoxically) the use of the interaction between money illusion and inflation in facilitating real wage adjustments.

Seignorage

Money creation – the ultimate source of inflation – is one of the ways in which the government can finance its spending. Put another way, money creation is an alternative to borrowing from the public or raising taxes.

As you saw in Chapter 22, the government typically does not 'create' money to pay for its spending. Rather, the government issues and sells bonds and spends the proceeds. But if the bonds are bought by the central bank, which then creates money to pay for them, the result is the same: other things being equal, the revenues from money creation – that is, *seignorage* – allow the government to borrow less from the public or to lower taxes.

How large is seignorage in practice? When looking at hyperinflations in Chapter 22, you saw that seignorage is often an important source of government finance in countries with very high inflation rates. But its importance in OECD economies today, and for the range of inflation rates we are considering, is much more limited. Take the case of the USA. The ratio of the monetary base – the money issued by the ECB (see Chapter 4) – to GDP is about 6%. An increase in nominal money growth of 3% per year (which eventually leads to a 3% increase in inflation) would lead therefore to an increase in seignorage of 3% × 6%, or 0.18% of GDP. This is a small amount of revenues to get in exchange for 3% more inflation.

Therefore, while the seignorage argument is sometimes relevant (for example, in economies that do not yet have a good fiscal system in place), it hardly seems relevant in the discussion of whether OECD countries today should have, say, 0% versus 3% inflation.

> Let H denote the monetary base – the money issued by the central bank. Then
>
> $$\frac{Seignorage}{Y} = \frac{\Delta H}{PY} = \frac{\Delta H}{H} \frac{H}{PY}$$
>
> where $\Delta H/H$ is the rate of growth of the monetary base, and H/PY is the ratio of the monetary base to nominal GDP.

The option of negative real interest rates

The seignorage argument follows from our discussion of the liquidity trap and its macroeconomic implications in Chapter 5. A numerical example will help here. Consider two economies, both with a natural real interest rate equal to 2%.

> From Chapter 14: the natural real interest rate is the real interest rate implied by equilibrium in the goods market when output is equal to its natural level.

- In the first economy, the central bank maintains an average inflation rate of 3%, so the nominal interest rate is, on average, equal to 2% + 3% = 5%.
- In the second economy, the central bank maintains an average inflation rate of 0%, so the nominal interest rate is, on average, equal to 2% + 3% = 5%.
- Suppose both economies are hit by a similar adverse shock, which leads, at a given interest rate, to a decrease in spending and a decrease in output in the short run.
- In the first economy, the central bank can decrease the nominal interest rate from 5% to 0%, a decrease of 5%. Under the assumption that expected inflation does not change immediately and remains equal to 3%, the real interest rate decreases from 2% to –3%. This is likely to have a strong positive effect on spending and help the economy recover.
- In the second economy, the central bank can only decrease the nominal interest rate from 2% to 0%, a decrease of 2%. Under the assumption that expected inflation does not change right away and remains equal to 0%, the real interest rate decreases only by 2%, from 2% to 0%. This small decrease in the real interest rate may not increase spending by very much.

In short, an economy with a higher average inflation rate has more scope to use monetary policy to fight a recession. An economy with a low average inflation rate may find itself unable to use monetary policy to return output to the natural level of output. This possibility is far from being just theoretical. Japan faced precisely such a limit on monetary policy, and its recession turned into a slump. In the early 2000s, many economists worried that other countries may also be at risk. Many countries, including the USA, had low inflation and low nominal interest rates. When, during the financial crisis of 2007–2010, these countries were faced with adverse shocks to spending, the room for monetary policy to help avoid a decline in output was clearly limited. As a consequence, monetary policy was introduced in the form of quantitative easing, that is an increase in the amount of money circulating in the economy rather than a decrease in interest rates, which were already too close to zero.

Money illusion revisited

Paradoxically, the presence of money illusion provides at least one argument *for* having a positive inflation rate.

To see why, consider two situations. In the first, inflation is 3%, and your wage goes up by 1% in nominal terms – in euros. In the second, inflation is 0%, and your wage goes down by 2% in nominal terms. Both lead to the same 2% decrease in your real wage, so you should be indifferent. The evidence, however, shows that many people will accept the real wage cut more easily in the first case than in the second case.

Why is this example relevant to our discussion? Because, as you saw in Chapter 12, the constant process of change that characterises modern economies means some workers must sometimes take real pay cuts. Thus, the argument goes, the presence of inflation allows for these downward real-wage adjustments more easily than when there is no inflation. This argument is plausible. Economists have not established its importance; but because so many economies now have very low inflation, we may soon be in a position to test it.

> See, for example, the results of a survey of managers by Alan Blinder and Don Choi, in 'A Shred of Evidence on Theories of Wage Rigidity', *Quarterly Journal of Economics*, 1990, **105**(4), 1003–1015.

> A conflict of metaphors: because inflation makes these real wage adjustments easier to achieve, some economists say inflation 'greases the wheels' of the economy. Others, emphasising the adverse effects of inflation on relative prices, say that inflation 'puts sand' in the economy.

24.2 MONETARY POLICY RULES

Until the 1990s, the design of monetary policy typically centred around nominal money growth. Central banks chose a nominal money growth target for the medium run. And they thought about short-run monetary policy in terms of deviations of nominal money growth from that target. In the past decade, however, this design has evolved. Most central banks have adopted an inflation rate target rather than a nominal money growth rate target. And they think about short-run monetary policy in terms of movements in the nominal interest rate, rather than in terms of movements in the rate of nominal money growth. Let's first look at what they did earlier, before turning to what they do now.

Money growth targets and target ranges

Until the 1990s, monetary policy in OECD countries was typically conducted as follows:

- The central bank chose a target rate for nominal money growth corresponding to the inflation rate it wanted to achieve in the medium run. If, for example, it wanted to achieve an inflation rate of 4% and the normal rate of growth of output (the rate of growth implied by the rate of technological progress and the rate of population growth) was 3%, the central bank chose a target rate of nominal money growth of 7%.
- In the short run, the central bank allowed for deviations of nominal money growth from the target. If, for example, the economy was in a recession, the central bank increased nominal money growth above the target value to allow for a decrease in the interest rate and a faster recovery of output. In an expansion, it might do the reverse to slow down output growth.
- To communicate to the public both what it wanted to achieve in the medium run and what it intended to do in the short run, the central bank announced a range for the rate of nominal money growth it intended to achieve. Sometimes, this range was presented as a commitment from the central bank; sometimes, it was presented simply as a forecast rather than as a commitment.

Over time, central banks became disenchanted with this way of conducting monetary policy. Let's now look at why.

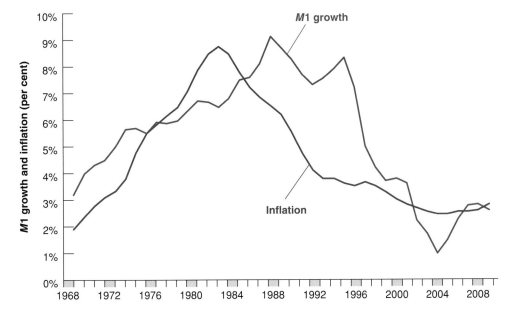

Figure 24.1

M1 growth and inflation in the UK: ten-year averages since 1968

There is no tight relation between M1 growth and inflation – not even in the medium run.

Money growth and inflation revisited

The design of monetary policy around nominal money growth is based on the assumption that there is a close relation between inflation and nominal money growth in the medium run. The problem is that, in practice, this relation is not very tight. If nominal money growth is high, inflation will also be high; and if nominal money growth is low, inflation will be low. But the relation is not tight enough that, by choosing a rate of nominal money growth, the central bank can achieve precisely its desired rate of inflation – not even in the medium run.

    The relation between inflation and nominal money growth is shown in Figure 24.1, which plots ten-year averages of the inflation rate against ten-year averages of the growth rate of the money stock since 1968 (so the numbers for inflation and for money growth for 2000, for example, are the average inflation rate and the average growth rate of money from 1991 to 2000) in the UK. The inflation rate is constructed using the CPI as the price index. The growth rate of nominal money is constructed using M1 as the measure for the money stock. The reason for using ten-year averages should be clear: in the short run, changes in nominal money growth affect mostly output, not inflation. It is only in the medium run that a relation between nominal money growth and inflation should emerge. Taking ten-year averages of both nominal money growth and inflation is a way of detecting such a medium-run relation.

    Figure 24.1 shows that, for the UK since 1968, the relation between M1 growth and inflation has not been very tight. True, both went up at the beginning of the period, and both have come down since. But note how inflation started declining in the early 1980s, while nominal money growth remained high for another decade and came down only in the 1990s. Average inflation from 1982–1992 was down to 3.8%, while average money growth over the same period was still running at 7.5%. Since 2006, average inflation and average money growth have remained closer, around 0.2%.

    Why is the relation between M1 growth and inflation not tighter? Because of *shifts in the demand for money.* An example will help. Suppose, as the result of the introduction of credit cards, people decide to hold only half the amount of money they held before; in other words, the real demand for money decreases by half. In the medium run, the real money stock must also decrease by half. For a given nominal money stock, the price level must double. Even if the nominal money stock remains constant, there is still a period of inflation

    ◄ Recall that inflation and nominal money growth move together during episodes of hyperinflation (Chapter 22).

    ◄ From Chapter 4: M1 measures the amount of money in the economy and is constructed as the sum of currency and deposits. The central bank does not directly control M1. What it controls is H, the monetary base; but it can choose H to achieve any value of M1 it wants. It is therefore reasonable to think that the central bank controls M1.

FOCUS
The unsuccessful search for the right monetary aggregate

The reason the demand for money shifts over time goes beyond the introduction of credit cards. To understand why, we must challenge an assumption we have maintained until now – namely that there is a sharp distinction between money and other assets. In fact, there are many financial assets that are close to money. They cannot be used for transactions – at least not without restrictions – but they can be exchanged for money at little cost. In other words, these assets are very **liquid**; this makes them attractive substitutes for money. Shifts between money and these assets are the main factor behind shifts in the demand for money.

Take, for example, money market fund shares. Money market funds are financial intermediaries that hold as assets short-maturity securities (typically Treasury bills in the USA or BTS in the UK) and have deposits (or shares, as they are called) as liabilities. The funds pay depositors an interest rate close to the T-bill rate minus the administrative costs of running the fund. Deposits can be exchanged for money on notice and at little cost. Most money market funds allow depositors to write cheques but only above a certain amount, typically $500. Because of this restriction, money market funds are not included in **M1**. When these funds were introduced in the mid-1970s, people were able for the first time to hold a very liquid asset while receiving an interest rate close to that on T-bills. Money market funds quickly became very attractive, increasing from nothing in 1973 to $321 billion in 1989. (In comparison, chequeable deposits were $280 billion in 1989.) Many people reduced their bank account balances and moved to money market funds. In other words, there was a large negative shift in the demand for money.

The presence of such shifts between money and other liquid assets led central banks to construct and report measures that include not only money but also other liquid assets. These measures are called **monetary aggregates** and come under the names M2, M3 and so on. The narrowest definition of money supply in common use is M0. The definition of M0 used in the UK is bank notes and coins in circulation, plus banks' deposits with the Bank of England. M0 is also known as the wide monetary base. This term refers to the fact that the money measured by M0 supplies the base on which other forms of money (such as bank deposits) are based.

In the UK, M2 includes notes and coins in circulation with the public; *plus*, UK private sector's non-interest-bearing sterling sight deposits with banks in the UK; *plus* UK private sector's interest-bearing retail sterling deposits with banks in the UK. In the USA M2 – which is also sometimes called **broad money** – includes M1 (currency and chequeable deposits) plus money market mutual fund shares, money market deposit accounts (the same as money market shares, but issued by banks rather than money market funds) and time deposits (deposits with an explicit maturity of a few months to a few years and with a penalty for early withdrawal).

The construction of M2 and other monetary aggregates would appear to offer a solution to our earlier problem: if most of the shifts in the demand for money are between M1 and other assets within M2, the demand for M2 should be more stable than the demand for M1, and so there should be a tighter relation between M2 growth and inflation than between M1 growth and inflation. If so, the central bank could choose targets for M2 growth rather than for M1 growth. This is indeed the solution that many central banks adopted. But it did not work well, for two reasons:

- The relation between M2 growth and inflation is no tighter than the relation between M1 growth and inflation and the same conclusions apply to **M3** growth.
- More importantly, while the central bank controls M1, it does not control M2. If people shift from government securities to money market funds, this will increase M2 – which includes money market funds but does not include government securities. There is little the central bank can do about this increase in M2. Thus, M2 is a strange target: it is neither under the direct control of the central bank nor what the central bank ultimately cares about.

In short, the relation between inflation and the growth of monetary aggregates such as M2 and M3 is no tighter than the relation between inflation and the growth rate of M1. And the central bank has little control over the growth of these monetary aggregates anyway. This is why, in most countries, monetary policy has shifted its focus from monetary aggregates – whether it is M1, M2, or M3 – to inflation.

as the price level doubles. During this period, there is no tight relation between nominal money growth (which is zero) and inflation (which is positive).

Frequent and large shifts in money demand created serious problems for central banks. They found themselves torn between trying to keep a stable target for money growth and staying within announced bands (in order to maintain credibility), or adjusting to shifts in money demand (in order to stabilise output in the short run and inflation in the medium run). Starting in the early 1990s, a dramatic rethinking of monetary policy took place, based instead on **inflation targeting** (see pp. 501–2) rather than money growth targeting, and the use of interest rate rules. Let's look at the way monetary policy is conducted today.

From equation (5.3) (the *LM* equation): the real money supply (the left side) must be equal to the real demand for money (the right side):

$$\frac{M}{P} = YL(i)$$

If, as a result of the introduction of credit cards, the real demand for money halves, then

$$\frac{M}{P} = \frac{1}{2}YL(i)$$

For a given level of output and a given interest rate, M/P must also halve. Given M, this implies that P must double.

Interest rate rules

Given the discussion so far, the next question is how to achieve the inflation target. In answer to this question, John Taylor from Stanford University argued that, because the central bank affects spending through the interest rate, the central bank should think directly in terms of the choice of an interest rate rather than a rate of nominal money growth. He then suggested a rule that the central bank should follow to set the interest rate. This rule, which is now known as the **Taylor rule**, goes as follows:

- Let π_t be the rate of inflation and π^* be the target rate of inflation.
- Let i_t be the nominal interest rate and i^* be the target nominal interest rate – the nominal interest rate associated with the target rate of inflation, π^*, in the medium run.
- Let u_t be the unemployment rate and u_n be the natural unemployment rate.

From Chapter 14: in the medium run, the real interest rate is equal to the natural real interest rate, r_n, so the nominal interest rate moves one-for-one with the inflation rate: if $r_n = 2\%$ and the target inflation rate, $\pi^* = 3\%$, then the target nominal interest rate, $i^* = 2\% + 3\% = 5\%$. If the target inflation rate π^*, is 0%, then $i^* = 2\% + 0\% = 2\%$.

Think of the central bank as choosing the nominal interest rate, i. (Recall from Chapter 4 that, through open market operations, the central bank can achieve any short-term nominal interest rate that it wants.) Then, Taylor argued, the central bank should adopt the following rule:

$$i_t = i^* + a(\pi_t - \pi^*) - b(u_t - u_n)$$

where a and b are positive coefficients.

Let's look at what the rule says:

- If inflation is equal to target inflation ($\pi_t = \pi^*$) and the unemployment rate is equal to the natural rate of unemployment ($u_t = u_n$), then the central bank should set the nominal interest rate, i_t, equal to its target value, i^*. This way, the economy can stay on the same path, with inflation equal to the target inflation rate and unemployment equal to the natural rate of unemployment.
- If inflation is higher than the target ($\pi_t > \pi^*$), the central bank should increase the nominal interest rate, i_t, above i^*. This higher interest rate will increase unemployment, and this increase in unemployment will lead to a decrease in inflation.

  The coefficient a should therefore reflect how much the central bank cares about unemployment versus inflation. The higher a, the more the central bank will increase the interest rate in response to inflation, the more the economy will slow down, the more unemployment will increase, and the faster inflation will return to the target inflation rate.

  In any case, Taylor pointed out, a should be larger than 1. Why? Because what matters for spending is the real interest rate, not the nominal interest rate. When inflation increases, the central bank, if it wants to decrease spending and output, must increase the *real* interest rate. In other words, it must increase the nominal interest rate more than one-for-one with inflation.
- If unemployment is higher than the natural rate of unemployment ($u > u_n$) the central bank should decrease the nominal interest rate. The lower nominal interest rate will increase output, leading to a decrease in unemployment. Like the coefficient a,

the coefficient b should reflect how much the central bank cares about unemployment relative to inflation. The higher b, the more the central bank will be willing to deviate from target inflation to keep unemployment close to the natural rate of unemployment.

In stating this rule, Taylor did not argue that it should be followed blindly: many other events, such as an exchange rate crisis, or the need to change the composition of spending, and thus the mix between monetary policy and fiscal policy, justify changing the nominal interest rate for reasons other than those included in the rule. But, he argued, the rule provided a useful way of thinking about monetary policy: once the central bank has chosen a target rate of inflation, it should try to achieve it by adjusting the nominal interest rate. The rule it should follow should take into account not only current inflation but also current unemployment.

Since it was first introduced, the Taylor rule has generated a lot of interest, both from researchers and from central banks:

- Interestingly, researchers looking at the behaviour of both the Fed in the USA and the ECB in the euro area have found that, although neither of these two central banks thought of itself as following a Taylor rule, this rule actually describes their behaviour over the past 15 to 20 years quite well.
- Other researchers have explored whether it is possible to improve on this simple rule – for example, whether the nominal interest rate should be allowed to respond not only to current inflation but also to expected future inflation.
- Yet other researchers have discussed whether central banks should adopt an explicit interest rate rule and follow it closely, or whether they should use the rule more informally and feel free to deviate from the rule when appropriate. We shall return to this issue in discussing the behaviour of the ECB in the next section.
- In general, most central banks have now shifted from thinking in terms of nominal money growth to thinking in terms of an interest rate rule. Whatever happens to nominal money growth as a result of following such a nominal interest rate rule is increasingly seen as unimportant by both the central banks and financial markets.

The instruments of monetary policy

Recall from Chapter 4 that we can think of the determination of the interest rate in three equivalent ways:

- The supply of central bank money must be equal to the demand for central bank money.
- The supply of reserves, equal to central bank money minus the currency held by people, must be equal to the demand for reserves by banks.
- The supply of money (currency and deposit accounts) must be equal to the demand for money.

You saw in Chapter 4 that we can think of the interest rate as being determined by the demand for and the supply of central bank money. Recall that the equilibrium condition [equation (4.11)] is given by

$$H = [c + \theta(1 - c)]€YL(i) \qquad [24.1]$$

On the left side is H, the supply of central bank money – equivalently, the monetary base. On the right side is the demand for central bank money – the sum of the demand for currency by people, $c€YL(i)$, and the demand for reserves by banks, $\theta(1 - c)€YL(i)$. Think of it this way:

- Start with $€YL(i)$, the overall demand for money (currency and deposit accounts, $M1$). This demand depends on income and the opportunity cost of holding money – the interest rate on bonds.
- The parameter c is the proportion of money people want to hold in the form of currency. So $c€YL(i)$ is the demand for currency by people. See Chapter 4 for a review.
- What people do not hold in currency, they hold in the form of deposit accounts. Deposit accounts are therefore a fraction $(1 - c)$ of the overall demand for money, so deposit accounts are equal to $(1 - c)€YL(i)$. The parameter θ denotes the ratio of reserves held by banks to deposit accounts. So the demand for reserves by banks is $\theta(1 - c)€YL(i)$.

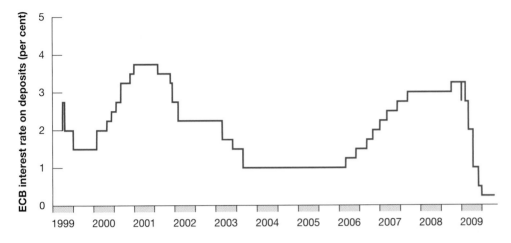

Figure 24.2

The ECB interest rate since 1999

In 2001–2002, and again in 2009, the ECB dramatically decreased the interest rate to reduce the depth and length of the recession.

Source: ECB.

- Adding the demand for currency, $c€YL(i)$, and the demand for reserves by banks, $\theta(1 - c)€YL(i)$, gives the total demand for central bank money – which is the right side of the equation.

The equilibrium interest rate is then the interest rate at which the supply of, and the demand for, central bank money are equal (you will know more about the instruments the ECB has at its disposal to affect this interest rate in Chapter 25).

Over its first ten years of experience, the ECB has shown a willingness to use the nominal interest rate to stabilise activity when it was needed. Figure 24.2 shows the evolution of the ECB interest rate on interbank deposits since 1999. In 2001–2002, the ECB aggressively cut interest rates, overall by almost 3 percentage points, down to 1%. Again, in 2009, to help the euro area economy out of the recession following the financial crisis started in 2007, the ECB dramatically cut interest rates, much more rapidly than in the first case, and almost down to zero.

Inflation targeting

In many countries, central banks have defined as their primary goal the achievement of a low inflation rate, both in the short run and in the medium run. This is known as inflation targeting:

- Trying to achieve a given inflation target *in the medium run* would seem, and indeed is, a clear improvement over trying to achieve a nominal money growth target. After all, in the medium run, the primary goal of monetary policy is to achieve a given rate of inflation. Better to have an inflation rate as the target than a nominal money growth target which, as we have seen, may not lead to the desired rate of inflation.
- Trying to achieve a given inflation target *in the short run* would appear to be much more controversial. Focusing exclusively on inflation would seem to eliminate any role monetary policy could play in reducing output fluctuations. But, in fact, this is not the case. To see why, return to the Phillips curve relation between inflation, p_t, lagged inflation, p_{t-1}, and the deviation of the unemployment rate, u_t, from the natural rate of unemployment, u_n [equation (9.10)]:

$$\pi_t = \pi_{t-1} - \alpha(u_t - u_n)$$

Let the inflation rate target be π^*. Suppose the central bank could achieve its inflation target exactly in every period. Then the relation would become

$$\pi^* = \pi^* - \alpha(u_t - u_n)$$

$0 = -\alpha(u_t - u_n) \Rightarrow u_t = u_n$

➤ The unemployment rate, u_t, would always equal u_n, the natural rate of unemployment; by implication, output would always be equal to the natural level of output. In effect, inflation targeting would lead the central bank to act in such a way as to eliminate all deviations of output from its natural level.

The intuition: if the central bank saw that an adverse demand shock were going to lead to a recession, it would know that, without a monetary expansion, the economy would experience a decline in inflation below the target rate of inflation. To maintain stable inflation, the central bank would then rely on a monetary expansion to avoid the recession. The converse would apply to a favourable demand shock: fearing an increase in inflation above the target rate, the central bank would rely on a monetary contraction to slow down the economy and keep output at the natural level of output. As a result of this active monetary policy, output would remain at the natural level of output all the time.

The result we have just derived – that inflation targeting eliminates deviations of output from its natural level – is too strong, however, for two reasons:

- The central bank cannot always achieve the rate of inflation it wants in the short run. So suppose that, for example, the central bank was not able to achieve its desired rate of inflation last year, so π_{t-1} is higher than π^*. Then it is not clear that the central bank should try to hit its target this year and achieve $\pi_t = \pi^*$: the Phillips curve relation implies that such a decrease in inflation would require a potentially large increase in unemployment. We return to this issue shortly.
- Like all other macroeconomic relations, the Phillips curve relation above does not hold exactly. It will happen that, for example, inflation increases even when unemployment is at the natural rate of unemployment. In this case, the central bank will face a more difficult choice: whether to keep unemployment at the natural rate and allow inflation to increase, or to increase unemployment above the natural rate to keep inflation in check.

These qualifications are important, but the basic point remains: inflation targeting makes good sense in the medium run and allows monetary policy to stabilise output around its natural level in the short run.

The countries with inflation above 5%: Czech Republic, with 6.3%; Hungary, with 6%; Iceland, with 12.6%; Mexico, with 5.1%; and Turkey, with 10.4%.

➤ Table 24.1 shows how inflation has steadily gone down in rich countries since the early 1980s. In 1981, average inflation in OECD countries was 11.9%; in 2008, it was down to 3.6%. In 1981, two countries (out of 30) had inflation rates below 5%; in 2008, the number had increased to 25.

Does this mean that most central banks have now achieved their goal? Or should they aim for an even lower inflation rate, perhaps 0%? The answer depends on the costs and benefits of inflation.

Table 24.1 Inflation rates in OECD countries since 1981

Year	1981	1985	1990	1995	2000	2005	2008	2009 Q1
OECD average[a]	11.9%	7.3%	7.0%	6.1%	4.1%	2.6%	3.6%	1.2%
Number of countries with inflation below 5%[b]	2	11	11	22	23	29	25	27

[a] Average Consumer Price Index inflation rates, country weights are based on the previous year's household private final consumption expenditure and relevant purchasing power parity (PPP).
[b] Out of 30 countries (27 countries before 1990).

Source: OECD *Economic Outlook* database.

FOCUS
Inflation targeting in Sweden

Sweden started the transition to a new monetary regime in January 1993. Two months before (on 19 November 1992), the fixed exchange rate regime had been abandoned and the krona – following a very costly but failed attempt to defend the parity – had been allowed to float. Soon thereafter (on 14 January 1993) the Riksbank announced that monetary policy would be run based on an inflation targeting regime, and the first prototype *Inflation Report* was published in June of that year. The inflation target was set at 2%.

The Riksbank Act of 1999 greatly increased the independence of the central bank along several dimensions, in particular by creating an independent Executive Board with long-term appointments that are protected from severance from employment and that can neither 'seek nor take instructions when fulfilling their monetary policy duties'.

This Focus box analyses how Swedish monetary policy has been run. In evaluating Swedish monetary policy over the past decade, we examine several questions: (1) whether it produced good economic performance in the long run; (2) were policy rates set appropriately; and (3) what has been the relationship between monetary policy and the exchange rate?

IT and Sweden's overall economic performance

Monetary policy is unable to affect a country's level of potential output. What it can and should do is try to minimise fluctuations of actual around potential output but, as we argued in this chapter, the best way to do this is not by focusing on output or employment targets, but rather on the path of inflation. One way to evaluate whether the Swedish monetary policy regime during the past ten years has been successful thus consists in looking at the volatility of output along with the behaviour of inflation and inflation expectations.

Output gaps are difficult to measure and, not surprisingly, one is presented with a rich variety of different techniques for measuring such a gap. Based on our experience we decided to choose the output gap constructed using a statistical technique (the Hodrick–Prescott filter) that defines such a gap as the difference between actual output and an estimate of the underlying trend in output.

Figure 24.3 computes the volatility of the output gap over four sub-periods: 1980–1989, the years preceding the banking crisis; 1990–1994, the period characterised by the banking and subsequently the exchange rate crises; 1995–1998, the early years of the new monetary policy regime, before the Riksbank had gained full

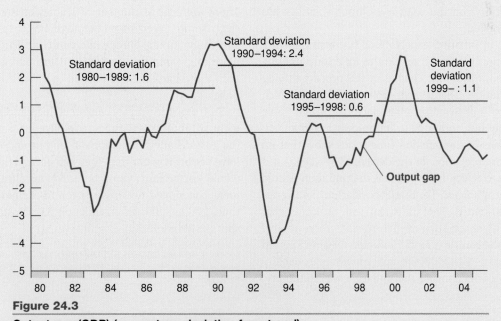

Figure 24.3

Output gap (GDP) (percentage deviation from trend)

Source: Francesco Giavazzi and Frederic S. Mishkin, *An Evaluation of Swedish Monetary Policy Between 1995 and 2005*, Finance Committee, Swedish Parliament.

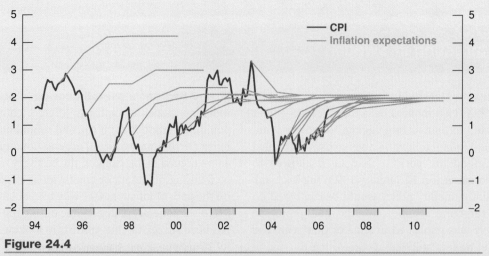

Figure 24.4

CPI and money market inflation expectations (annual percentage change)

Source: Francesco Giavazzi and Frederic S. Mishkin, *An Evaluation of Swedish Monetary Policy Between 1995 and 2005*, Finance Committee, Swedish Parliament.

independence; and finally 1999–2005. The volatility of the output gap is lower since 1999, compared with its level in the 1980s: the standard deviation is 1.1 in the more recent period, compared with 1.6 in the 1980s. This means a 30% reduction in output volatility.

Figure 24.4 shows inflation expectations at various horizons. For each year the grey lines show inflation expectations at 1, 2, 3, 4 and 5-years horizons. The message from Figures 24.3 and 24.4 is very clear: the new monetary policy regime has allowed Sweden to stabilise inflation expectations with no loss in terms of higher output volatility: on the contrary, output volatility has also been reduced.

The shift in inflation expectations is consistent with the observation that the transition to inflation targeting has produced a dramatic change in the process driving Swedish inflation. This is clear from Figure 24.5 which shows the path of Swedish inflation. Inflation has come down sharply but, in addition, its process has changed. Statistical tests of the inflation time-series show that up to 1993 (more precisely, for the decade 1984–1993) it is not possible to reject the hypothesis that inflation drifted without a firm anchor, i.e. that the inflation time series was non-stationary. The statistical test indicates that there is a 43% chance that over the decade there was *no* anchor. On the contrary, for the inflation targeting period over the years 1994–2003, the corresponding probability is just 0.27%, which means that inflation was stationary.

Inflation targeting has succeeded in establishing a solid nominal anchor.

What have been the effects on unemployment? Unemployment in Sweden has been higher in the past 15 years than it had been before the crisis of the early 1990s (Figure 24.6): it was fluctuating between 1.5% and 3.5%, and has now shifted to a range about 3 points higher. As we have argued in Chapter 9, however, because there is no long-run trade-off between inflation and employment, there was little that monetary policy could do to shift unemployment back to the old range. There are a large number of studies of the reasons for the rise in Swedish unemployment, a phenomenon shared by other European countries. This is not the place to get into this discussion. Our point is simply that such a rise cannot be attributed to the shift in monetary policy.

Still, monetary policy can affect fluctuations of employment within the new range. We have just seen that over the past decade fluctuations in output and employment have not been wider than they had been in the past, but it would not be fair to stop here. For instance, unemployment has moved towards the top of the new range at a time, 2002–2005, when inflation has constantly undershot the 2% target.

Source: Francesco Giavazzi and Frederic S. Mishkin, *An Evaluation of Swedish Monetary Policy Between 1995 and 2005*, Finance Committee, Swedish Parliament.

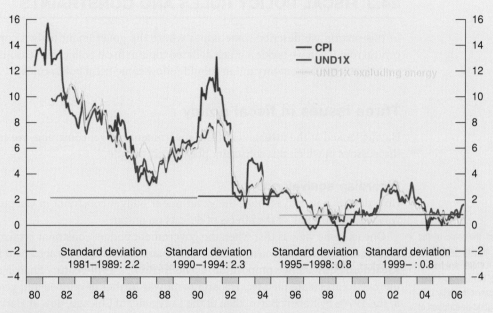

Figure 24.5

Swedish inflation assessed using different measures (annual percentage change)

Source: Francesco Giavazzi and Frederic S. Mishkin, *An Evaluation of Swedish Monetary Policy Between 1995 and 2005*, Finance Committee, Swedish Parliament.

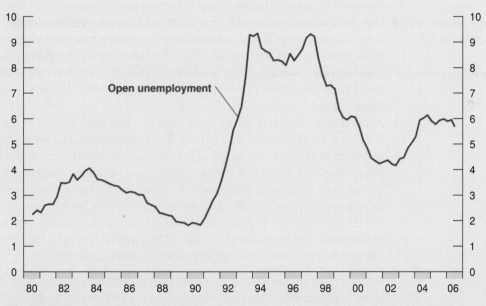

Figure 24.6

Open unemployment in Sweden (per cent of the labour force), seasonally adjusted

Source: Francesco Giavazzi and Frederic S. Mishkin, *An Evaluation of Swedish Monetary Policy Between 1995 and 2005*, Finance Committee, Swedish Parliament.

24.3 FISCAL POLICY RULES AND CONSTRAINTS

In this section we describe some issues where the government budget constraint plays a central role. Then we tackle a much debated topic in fiscal policy: the reasons why countries participating in a monetary union should follow some fiscal policy rules.

Three issues in fiscal policy

Having looked at the mechanics of the government budget constraint, we can now take up three issues in which this constraint plays a central role.

Ricardian equivalence

How does taking into account the government budget constraint in Chapter 21 affect the way we should think of the effects of deficits on output?

One extreme view is that when the government budget constraint is taken into account, neither deficits nor debt have an effect on economic activity! This argument is known as the **Ricardian equivalence** proposition. David Ricardo, a 19th-century English economist, was the first to articulate its logic. His argument was further developed and given prominence in the 1970s by Robert Barro, then at the University of Chicago, now at Harvard University. For this reason, the argument is also known as the **Ricardo–Barro proposition**.

> While Ricardo stated the logic of the argument, he also argued that there were many reasons it would not hold in practice. In contrast, Barro argues that not only is the argument logically correct, but it is also a good description of reality.

The best way to understand the logic of the proposition is to use the example of tax changes.

- Suppose that the government decreases taxes by 1 (again think 1 billion euros) this year. As it does so, it announces that, to repay the debt, it will increase taxes by $1 + r$ next year. What will be the effect of the initial tax cut on consumption?

> See Chapter 16 for a definition of human wealth and a discussion of its role in consumption.

- One possible answer is: no effect at all. Why? Because consumers realise that the tax cut is not much of a gift: lower taxes this year are exactly offset, in present value, by higher taxes next year. Put another way, their human wealth – the present value of after-tax labur income – is unaffected. Current taxes go down by 1, but the present value of next year's taxes goes up by $(1 + r)/(1 + r)$, and the net effect of the two changes is exactly equal to zero.

- Another way of coming to the same answer – this time looking at saving rather than looking at consumption – is as follows. To say that consumers do not change their consumption in response to the tax cut is the same as saying that *private saving increases one-for-one with the deficit*. So the Ricardian equivalence proposition says that, if a government finances a given path of spending through deficits, private saving will increase one-for-one with the decrease in public saving, leaving total saving unchanged. The total amount left for investment will not be affected. Over time, the mechanics of the government budget constraint imply that government debt will increase. But this increase will not come at the expense of capital accumulation.

Under the Ricardian equivalence proposition, the long sequence of deficits and the increase in government debt that characterised the OECD until the late 1990s are no cause for worry. As governments were dissaving, the argument goes, people were saving more in anticipation of the higher taxes to come. The decrease in public saving was offset by an equal increase in private saving. Total saving was therefore unaffected, and so was investment. OECD economies have the same capital stock today that they would have had if there had been no increase in debt. High debt is no cause for concern.

How seriously should you take the Ricardian equivalence proposition? Most economists would answer: 'Seriously, but not seriously enough to think that deficits and debt are irrelevant.' A major theme of this book has been that expectations matter, that consumption decisions depend not only on current income but also on expected future income. If it were widely believed that a tax cut this year is going to be followed by an offsetting increase in taxes *next year*, the effect on consumption would indeed probably be small. Many consumers

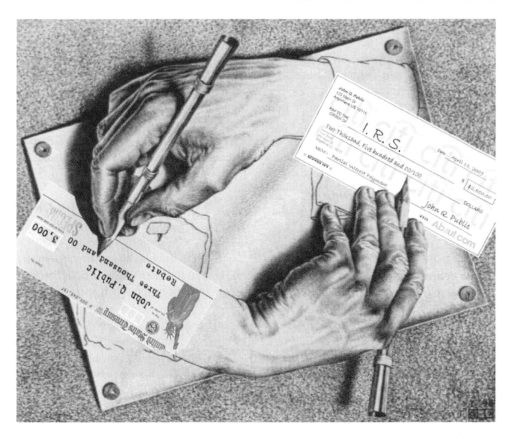

Figure 24.7

Ricardian equivalence illustrated

Source: Monk McHugh, Across the Street Blog, M. C. Escher Economist, 21 February 2009.

would save most or all of the tax cut in anticipation of higher taxes next year. (Replace 'year' with 'month' or 'week,' and the argument becomes even more convincing.)

Of course, tax cuts rarely come with the announcement of corresponding tax increases a year later. Consumers have to guess when and how taxes will eventually be increased. This fact does not by itself invalidate the Ricardian equivalence argument: no matter when taxes will be increased, the government budget constraint still implies that the present value of future tax increases must always be equal to the decrease in taxes today. Take the second example we looked at in Chapter 23 in which the government waits t years to increase taxes, and so increases taxes by $(1 + r)^{t-1}$. The present value in year 0 of this expected tax increase is $(1 + r)^{t-1}/(1 + r)^{t-1} = 1$; exactly equal to the original tax cut. The change in human wealth from the tax cut is still zero.

> The increase in taxes in t years is $(1 + r)^{t-1}$. The discount factor for a euro t years from now is $1/(1 + r)^{t-1}$. So the value of the increase in taxes t years from now as of today is $(1 + r)^{t-1}/(1 + r)^{t-1} = 1$.

But insofar as future tax increases appear more distant and their timing more uncertain, consumers are in fact more likely to ignore them. This may be the case because they expect to die before taxes go up or, more likely, because they just do not think that far into the future. In either case, Ricardian equivalence is likely to fail.

So, it is safe to conclude that budget deficits have an important effect on activity – although perhaps a smaller effect than we thought before going through the Ricardian equivalence argument. In the short run, larger deficits are likely to lead to higher demand and to higher output. In the long run, higher government debt lowers capital accumulation and, as a result, lowers output.

Deficits, output stabilisation and the cyclically adjusted deficit

The fact that budget deficits do, indeed, have long-run adverse effects on capital accumulation and, in turn, on output, does not imply that fiscal policy should not be used to reduce output fluctuations. Rather, it implies that deficits during recessions should be offset by surpluses during booms, so as not to lead to a steady increase in debt.

> Note the analogy with monetary policy: the fact that higher money growth leads in the long run to more inflation does not imply that monetary policy should not be used for output stabilisation.

Ignore output growth in this section, ➤ and so ignore the distinction between stabilising the debt and stabilising the debt-to-GDP ratio. (Verify that the argument extends to the case where output is growing.)

To help assess whether fiscal policy is on track, economists have constructed deficit measures that tell what the deficit would be, under existing tax and spending rules, if output were at the natural level of output. Such measures come under many names, ranging from the **full-employment deficit**, to the **mid-cycle deficit**, to the **standardised employment deficit**, to the **structural deficit** (the term used by the OECD). We shall use **cyclically adjusted deficit**, the term we find the most intuitive.

The cyclically adjusted deficit gives a simple benchmark against which to judge the direction of fiscal policy: if the actual deficit is large but the cyclically adjusted deficit is zero, then current fiscal policy is consistent with no systematic increase in debt over time. The debt will increase as long as output is below the natural level of output; but as output returns to its natural level, the deficit will disappear and the debt will stabilise.

It does not follow that the goal of fiscal policy should be to maintain a cyclically adjusted deficit equal to zero at all times. In a recession, the government may want to run a deficit large enough that even the cyclically adjusted deficit is positive. In that case, the fact that the cyclically adjusted deficit is positive provides a useful warning. The warning is that the return of output to its natural level will not be enough to stabilise the debt: the government will have to take specific measures, from tax increases to cuts in spending, to decrease the deficit at some point in the future.

The theory underlying the concept of cyclically adjusted deficit is simple; the practice of it has proven tricky. To see why, we need to look at how measures of the cyclically adjusted deficit are constructed. Construction requires two steps. First, establish how much lower the deficit would be if output were, say, 1% higher. Second, assess how far output is from its natural level:

● The first step is straightforward. A reliable rule of thumb is that a 1% decrease in output leads automatically to an increase in the deficit of 0.5% of GDP. This increase occurs because most taxes are proportional to output, whereas most government spending does not depend on the level of output. This means that a decrease in output, which leads to a decrease in revenues and not much change in spending, naturally leads to a larger deficit.

  If output is, say, 5% below its natural level, the deficit as a ratio to GDP will therefore be about 2.5% larger than it would be if output were at the natural level of output. (This effect of activity on the deficit has been called an **automatic stabiliser**: a recession naturally generates a deficit, and therefore a fiscal expansion, which partly counteracts the recession.)

● The second step is more difficult. Recall from Chapter 7 that the natural level of output is the output level that would be produced if the economy were operating at the natural rate of unemployment. Too low an estimate of the natural rate of unemployment will lead to too high an estimate of the natural level of output, and therefore to too optimistic a measure of the cyclically adjusted deficit.

See our discussion of high European ➤ unemployment in Chapter 9.

  This difficulty explains in part what happened in Europe in the 1980s. Based on the assumption of an unchanged natural unemployment rate, the cyclically adjusted deficits of the 1980s did not look that bad: if European unemployment had returned to its level of the 1970s, the associated increase in output would have been sufficient to re-establish budget balance in most countries. But, it turned out, much of the increase in unemployment reflected an increase in the natural unemployment rate, and unemployment remained very high during the 1980s. As a result, the decade was characterised by high deficits and large increases in debt ratios in most countries.

Wars and deficits

Look at the two peaks associated ➤ with the First and Second World War in Figure 23.4.

Wars typically bring about large budget deficits. As you saw in Chapter 23, the two largest increases in US government debt in the 20th century took place during the First and Second World Wars.

Is it right for governments to rely so much on deficits to finance wars? After all, war economies are usually operating at low unemployment, so the output stabilisation reasons for running deficits we examined earlier are irrelevant. The answer, nevertheless, is yes. In fact, there are two good reasons to run deficits during wars:

- The first is distributional – Deficit finance is a way to pass some of the burden of the war to those alive after the war, and it seems only fair for future generations to share in the sacrifices the war requires.
- The second is more narrowly economic – Deficit spending helps reduce tax distortions.

Let's look at each reason in turn.

1. *Passing on the burden of the war*

Wars lead to large increases in government spending. Consider the implications of financing this increased spending either through increased taxes or through debt. To distinguish this case from our earlier discussion of output stabilisation, let's also assume that output is fixed at the natural level of output:

- Suppose the government relies on deficit finance. With government spending sharply up, there will be a very large increase in the demand for goods. Given our assumption that output stays the same, the interest rate will have to increase enough to maintain equilibrium. Investment, which depends on the interest rate, will decrease sharply.
- Suppose instead that the government finances the spending increase through an increase in taxes – say, income taxes. Consumption will decline sharply. Exactly how much depends on consumers' expectations: the longer they expect the war to last, the longer they will expect higher taxes to last, and the more they will decrease their consumption. In any case, the increase in government spending will be partly offset by a decrease in consumption. Interest rates will increase by less than they would have increased under deficit spending, and investment will therefore decrease by less.

In short, for a given output, the increase in government spending requires either a decrease in consumption and/or a decrease in investment. Whether the government relies on tax increases or deficits determines whether consumption or investment does more of the adjustment when government spending goes up.

How does this affect who bears the burden of the war? The more the government relies on deficits, the smaller the decrease in consumption during the war and the larger the decrease in investment. Lower investment means a lower capital stock after the war and, therefore, lower output after the war. By reducing capital accumulation, deficits become a way of passing some of the burden of the war on to future generations.

> ◀ Assume that the economy is closed, so that $Y = C + I + G$. Suppose that G goes up and Y remains the same. Then, $C + I$ must go down. If taxes are not increased, most of the decrease will come from a decrease in I. If taxes are increased, most of the decrease will come from a decrease in C.

2. *Reducing tax distortions*

There is another argument for running deficits, not only during wars but, more generally, in times when government spending is exceptionally high. Think, for example, of reconstruction after an earthquake, or the costs involved in the reunification of Germany in the early 1990s. See the Focus box 'German unification, interest rates and the EMS' in Chapter 18.

The argument is as follows: if the government were to increase taxes in order to finance the increase in spending, tax rates would have to be very high. Very high tax rates can lead to very high economic distortions: faced with very high income tax rates, people work less or engage in illegal, untaxed activities. Rather than moving the tax rate up and down to always balance the budget, it is better (from the point of view of reducing distortions) to maintain a relatively constant tax rate – to *smooth taxes*. **Tax smoothing** implies running large deficits when government spending is exceptionally high and small surpluses the rest of the time.

Politics and fiscal restraints

We saw in Chapter 23 (Games between policy makers) that politics can sometimes lead to long and lasting budget deficits. Can rules be put in place to limit these adverse effects?

One approach tried in the USA is to use a constitutional amendment to balance the budget, such as the amendment proposed by the Republicans in 1994, would surely eliminate the problem of deficits. But, just like a constant money growth rule in the case of monetary policy, it would eliminate the use of fiscal policy as a macroeconomic instrument altogether. This is just too high a price to pay.

A better approach is to put in place rules that put limits on either deficits or debt. This is harder than it sounds. Rules such as limits on the ratio of the deficit to GDP or the ratio of debt to GDP are more flexible than a balanced budget requirement; but they may still not be flexible enough if the economy is affected by particularly bad shocks. This has been made clear by the problems faced by the Stability and Growth Pact; these problems are discussed at more length in Chapter 26. More flexible or more complex rules, such as rules that allow for special circumstances, or rules that take into account the state of the economy, are harder to design and, especially, harder to enforce. For example, allowing the deficit to be higher if the unemployment rate is higher than the natural rate requires having a simple and unambiguous way of computing the natural rate – a nearly impossible task.

A complementary approach is to put in place mechanisms to reduce deficits, were such deficits to arise. Consider, for example, a mechanism that triggers automatic spending cuts when the deficit gets too large. Suppose the budget deficit is too large, and it is desirable to cut spending across the board by 5%. Members of Parliament will find it difficult to explain to their constituency why their favourite spending programme was cut by 5%. Now suppose the deficit triggers automatic across-the-board spending cuts of 5% without any government action. Knowing that other programmes will be cut, Members of Parliament will accept cuts in their favourite programmes more easily. They will also be better able to deflect the blame for the cuts: members of Parliament who succeed in limiting the cuts to their favourite programme to, say, 4% (by convincing Parliament to make deeper cuts in some other programmes in order to maintain the lower overall level of spending) can then return to their constituents and claim that they successfully prevented even larger cuts.

This was indeed the approach which is used in the UK. The UK government specifies two key fiscal rules that provide benchmarks against which the performance of fiscal policy can be judged. These are:

● *The golden rule* – over the economic cycle, the government will borrow only to invest and not to fund current spending; this rule was officially adopted by former Chancellor of the Exchequer, Prime Minister Gordon Brown. The government will meet the golden rule if, on average over a complete economic cycle, the current budget is in balance or surplus.

● *The sustainable investment rule* – public sector net debt as a proportion of GDP will be held over the economic cycle at a stable and prudent level. The Chancellor has stated that, other things equal, net debt will be maintained below 40% of GDP over the current economic cycle, in accordance with the sustainable investment rule.

This was also the approach which was used to reduce deficits in the USA in the 1990s. The Budget Enforcement Act, passed in 1990 and extended by new legislation in 1993 and 1997, introduced two main rules:

● It imposed constraints on spending. Spending was divided into two categories: discretionary spending (roughly: spending on goods and services, including defence) and mandatory spending (roughly: transfer payments to individuals). Constraints, called *spending caps*, were set on discretionary spending for the following five years. These caps were set in such a way as to require a small but steady decrease in discretionary spending (in real terms). Explicit provisions were made for emergencies. For example, spending on Operation Desert Storm during the Gulf War in 1991 was not subject to the caps.

● It required that a new transfer programme could be adopted only if it could be shown that it would not increase deficits in the future (either by raising new revenues or by decreasing spending on an existing programme). This rule is known as the pay-as-you-go rule, or the PAYGO rule.

The focus on spending rather than on the deficit itself had one important implication. If there was a recession, hence a decrease in revenues, the deficit could increase without triggering a decrease in spending. This happened in 1991 and 1992 when, because of the recession, the deficit increased – despite the fact that spending satisfied the constraints imposed by the caps. This focus on spending had two desirable effects: it allowed for a larger fiscal deficit during a recession – a good thing from the point of view of macro-economic policy; and it decreased the pressure to break the rules during a recession – a good thing from a political point of view.

By 1998, deficits were gone and, for the first time in 20 years, the federal budget was in surplus. Not all of the deficit reduction was due to the Budget Enforcement Act rules: a decrease in defence spending due to the end of the Cold War and a large increase in tax revenues due to the strong expansion of the second half of the 1990s were important factors. But there is wide agreement that the rules played an important role in making sure that decreases in defence spending and increases in tax revenues were used for deficit reduction rather than for increases in other spending programmes.

Once budget surpluses appeared, however, Congress became increasingly willing to break its own rules. Spending caps were systematically broken, and the PAYGO rule was allowed to expire in 2002. At the time of this writing, deficits are large and predicted to remain so for many years to come. It is clear that, although spending caps and PAYGO rules were essential in reducing deficits in the 1990s, they did not prevent large deficits from reappearing in the 2000s. This is leading some economists and policy makers to conclude that, in the end, nothing short of a constitutional amendment can do the job of avoiding deficits. The issue is likely to rise again to the forefront of discussions of fiscal policy in the future.

We now return to the euro area and ask why have the members of the monetary union thought it necessary to accompany it with the fiscal rules.

Why impose fiscal rules on countries participating in a monetary union?

There are two reasons why it is appropriate that the member countries of a monetary union are subject to constraints on their fiscal policies:

1. *To correct the incentive to pass on the costs of fiscal expansion.*
In a closed economy, when the government increases the budget deficit, by cutting taxes or by increasing government spending, income growth is compensated by the increase in interest rates – the *IS* curve moves to the right, but the *LM* curve does not move, the new equilibrium income is higher, but interest rates are also higher, slightly reducing private demand. In an open economy with a fixed exchange rate – the case of a monetary union – the smaller the size of the country which increases the deficit relative to the area to which the exchange rate is anchored, the smaller will be the increase in the interest rate. If the country is very small, the interest rate of the 'rest of the world' does not move, whatever the small country does.

EMU is an intermediate case. Consider, for example, the effect of fiscal expansion in France. First, income will grow, not only in France, but also in the rest of the EMU, though the indirect effect of the increase in French imports (see the Focus box 'Fiscal multipliers in an open economy' in Chapter 18). So the demand for money grows in EMU. If the ECB keeps the supply of money unchanged, euro interest rates increase. This, similarly to what happens in a closed economy, crowds out private demand and reduces the positive impact of fiscal expansion. How much interest rates increase depends, of course, on the size of the French economy compared to the rest of EMU. If it were not France but, for example, Slovenia to increase the budget deficit, the effect on total demand in the euro area would be negligible and euro interest rates would not move, just as in the case of a 'small open economy' with fixed exchange rates. But if France increases its deficit, euro interest rates will rise.

Let us now consider the position of the various countries in EMU. What happens in France is exactly what would have happened in a system of fixed exchange rates: an increase in demand, partly mitigated by an increase in international interest rates. The other countries suffer from higher interest rates without the benefit of an expansionary fiscal policy, or at least without a direct benefit: they have a small benefit indirectly through the increase in French imports. So while in France, despite rising interest rates, income certainly grows, the effect in the rest of the EMU is ambiguous: income might also fall. And there is also another effect. Since the EMU as a whole has a flexible exchange rate with the rest of the world, the euro exchange rate will appreciate, for example against the dollar. The larger the country that has increased its budget deficit (France in our example), the larger this appreciation will be. An appreciation of the exchange rate reduces exports of all euro area countries, not only French exports.

What can other countries do? As they are members of a monetary union, they cannot control the supply of money; they can choose between putting up with the effect of the French fiscal expansion, which for them could be negative, or also implementing a fiscal expansion. This example suggests why the member countries of a monetary union wish to agree on the type of fiscal policy that each of them will implement, that is, adopt common fiscal rules.

2. *To prevent financial crisis in one country spreading to all other members.*
Suppose that in a certain month financial markets were unwilling to buy all the bonds that the Greek government wished to issue to finance the deficit in that month and, above all, to pay for the bonds that reach maturity in that month. Before the monetary union was formed, what would have happened is probably an intervention by the Bank of Greece: to prevent the government from going bankrupt, the Bank of Greece would have purchased the unsold securities – or rather, those unsold at the interest rate above which the government was unwilling to go. The supply of money would be increased, but this was basically a lesser evil than bankruptcy.

What other countries fear is that the ECB would have to do the same, with the effect of increasing the supply of money across the euro area. This explains why both the Maastricht Treaty and the criteria for admission to EMU, as well as the rules of the Stability and Growth Pact, state that high-debt countries must quickly reduce their stocks of public debt. But there is another concern. EMU speeds up financial integration among member countries: this means that financial assets move more easily between member countries because they are now all denominated in the same currency and there is no longer a foreign exchange risk. Consequently, Greek government securities are held, to a greater extent than before the euro, by banks and insurance companies in France and Germany and also by households in those countries. A bankruptcy of the Greek government would hit the other countries to a greater extent, compared to the years before the euro. This explains why EMU increases concern over countries with high public debt and also why, to avoid bankruptcy in a member state, the ECB would be forced to increase the supply of money to protect savers throughout the whole EMU. (What happened in Greece – a euro country – in 2010 is a vivid reminder of their problems.)

SUMMARY

On the optimal rate of inflation:

- Inflation is down to very low levels in most OECD countries. One question facing central banks is whether they should try to achieve price stability – that is, zero inflation.

- The main arguments for zero inflation are:
  1. Inflation, together with an imperfectly indexed tax system, leads to tax distortions.
  2. Because of money illusion, inflation leads people and firms to make incorrect decisions.

3. Higher inflation typically comes with higher inflation variability, creating more uncertainty and making it more difficult for people and firms to make decisions.

4. As a target, price stability has a simplicity and a credibility that a positive inflation target does not have.

- There are also arguments for maintaining low but positive inflation:

  1. Positive revenues from nominal money growth – seignorage – allow for decreases in taxes elsewhere in the budget. However, this argument is quantitatively unimportant when comparing inflation rates of 0% versus, say, 3%.

  2. Positive actual and expected inflation allow the central bank to achieve negative real interest rates, an option that can be useful when fighting a recession.

  3. Positive inflation allows firms to achieve real wage cuts when needed without requiring nominal wage cuts.

  4. Further decreasing inflation from its current rate to zero would require an increase in unemployment for some time, and this transition cost might exceed whatever benefits come from zero inflation.

On the design of monetary policy:

- Traditionally, the design of monetary policy was focused on nominal money growth. But because of the poor relation between inflation and nominal money growth, this approach has been abandoned by most central banks.

- Central banks now typically focus on an inflation rate target rather than a nominal money growth rate target. And they think about monetary policy in terms of determining the nominal interest rate rather than in terms of determining the rate of nominal money growth.

- The Taylor rule gives a useful way of thinking about the choice of the nominal interest rate. The rule states that the central bank should move its interest rate in response to two main factors: the deviation of the inflation rate from the target rate of inflation, and the deviation of the unemployment rate from the natural rate of unemployment. A central bank that follows this rule will stabilise activity and achieve its target inflation rate in the medium run.

- The government budget constraint gives the evolution of government debt as a function of spending and taxes. One way of expressing the constraint is that the change in debt (the deficit) is equal to the primary deficit plus interest payments on the debt. The primary deficit is the difference between government spending on goods and services, G, and taxes net of transfers, T.

- If government spending is unchanged, a decrease in taxes must eventually be offset by an increase in taxes in the future. The longer the government waits to increase taxes or the higher the real interest rate, the higher the eventual increase in taxes.

- The legacy of past deficits is higher debt. To stabilise the debt, the government must eliminate the deficit. To eliminate the deficit, it must run a primary surplus equal to the interest payments on the existing debt.

- Under the Ricardian equivalence proposition, a larger deficit is offset by an equal increase in private saving. Deficits have no effect on demand and on output. The accumulation of debt does not affect capital accumulation. When Ricardian equivalence fails, larger deficits lead to higher demand and higher output in the short run. The accumulation of debt leads to lower capital accumulation and thus to lower output in the long run.

- Member countries of a monetary union should impose constraints on their fiscal policy for two reasons: to correct the incentive of small countries to pass on the cost of a fiscal expansion to other member countries, and to prevent that a financial crisis in a country spreads to all other members.

KEY TERMS

QUESTIONS AND PROBLEMS

QUICK CHECK

1. *Using the information in this chapter, label each of the following statements true, false or uncertain. Explain briefly.*

a. The most important argument in favour of a positive rate of inflation in OECD countries is seignorage.

b. The ECB should target $M2$ growth because it moves quite closely with inflation.

c. Fighting inflation should be the ECB's only purpose.

d. Because most people have little trouble distinguishing between nominal and real values, inflation does not distort decision-making.

e. The ECB uses **reserve requirements** as its primary instrument of monetary policy.

f. The higher the inflation rate, the higher the effective tax rate on capital gains.

g. If Ricardian equivalence holds, then an increase in income taxes will affect neither consumption nor saving.

h. Tax smoothing and deficit finance help spread the burden of war across generations.

2. *Explain how each of the developments listed in (a) through (d) would affect the demand for M1 and M2.*

a. Banks reduce penalties on early withdrawal from time deposits.

b. The government forbids the use of money market funds for cheque-writing purposes.

c. The government legislates a tax on all ATM transactions.

d. The government decides to impose a tax on all transactions involving government securities with maturities more than one year.

3. Taxes, inflation and home ownership

In this chapter, we discussed the effect of inflation on the effective capital-gains tax rate on the sale of a home. In this question, we explore the effect of inflation on another feature of the tax code – the deductibility of mortgage interest.

Suppose you have a mortgage of €50 000. Expected inflation is p^e, and the nominal interest rate on your mortgage is i. Consider two cases.

i. $\pi^e = 0\%$; $i = 4\%$
ii. $\pi^e = 10\%$; $i = 14\%$

a. What is the real interest rate you are paying on your mortgage in each case?

b. Suppose you can deduct nominal mortgage interest payments from your income before paying income tax. Assume that the tax rate is 25%. So, for each euro you pay in mortgage interest, you pay 25 cents less in taxes, in effect getting a subsidy from the government for your mortgage costs. Compute, in each case, the real interest rate you are paying on your mortgage, taking into account this subsidy.

c. Considering only the deductibility of mortgage interest (and not capital-gains taxation), is inflation good for homeowners?

4. Inflation targets

Consider a central bank that has an inflation target, p^*. The Phillips curve is given by

$$\pi_t - \pi_{t-1} = -\alpha(u_t - u_n)$$

a. If the central bank is able to keep the inflation rate equal to the target inflation rate every period, will there be dramatic fluctuations in unemployment?

b. Is the central bank likely to be able to hit its inflation target every period?

c. Suppose the natural rate of unemployment, u_n, changes frequently. How will these changes affect the central bank's ability to hit its inflation target? Explain.

DIG DEEPER

5. *Suppose you have been elected to Parliament. One day, one of your colleagues makes the following statement:*

The central bank chair is the most powerful economic policy maker in our country. We should not turn over the keys to the economy to someone who was not elected and therefore has no accountability. Parliament should impose an explicit Taylor rule on the central bank. Parliament should choose not only the target inflation rate but the relative weight on the inflation and unemployment targets. Why should the preferences of an individual substitute for the will of the people, as expressed through the democratic and legislative processes?

Do you agree with your colleague? Discuss the advantages and disadvantages of imposing an explicit Taylor rule on the central bank.

6. Inflation targeting and the Taylor rule in the *IS–LM* model

*This problem is based on David Romer's 'Short-Run Fluctuations,' which is available on his website (**emlab.berkeley. edu/users/dromer/index.shtml**). Consider a closed economy in which the central bank follows an interest rate rule. The IS relation is given by*

$$Y = C(Y - T) + I(Y, r) + G$$

where r is the real interest rate.

The central bank sets the nominal interest rate according to the rule

$$i = i^* + a(\pi^e - \pi^*) + b(Y - Y_n)$$

where π^e is expected inflation, π^* is the target rate of inflation and Y_n is the natural level of output. Assume that $a > 1$ and $b > 0$. The symbol i^* is the interest rate the central bank chooses when expected inflation equals the target rate and output equals the natural level. The central bank will increase the nominal interest rate when expected inflation rises above the target or when output rises above the natural level.

(Note that the Taylor rule described in this chapter uses actual inflation instead of expected inflation, and it uses unemployment instead of output. The interest rate rule we use in this problem simplifies the analysis and does not change the basic results.)

Real and nominal interest rates are related by

$$r = i - \pi^e$$

a. Define the variable r^* as $r^* = i^* - \pi^*$. Use the definition of the real interest rate to express the interest rate rule as

$$r = r^* + (a - 1)(\pi^e - \pi^*) + b(Y - Y_n)$$

(*Hint*: subtract p^* from each side of the nominal interest rate rule and rearrange the right-hand side of the equation.)

b. Graph the *IS* relation in a diagram, with r on the vertical axis and Y on the horizontal axis. In the same diagram, graph the interest rate rule (in terms of the real interest rate) you derived in part (a) for given values of p^e, p^* and Y_n. Call the interest rate rule the monetary policy (*MP*) relation.

c. Using the diagram you drew in part (b), show that an increase in government spending leads to an increase in output and the real interest rate in the short run.

d. Now consider a change in the monetary policy rule. Suppose the central bank reduces its target inflation rate, p^*. How does the fall in p^* affect the *MP* relation? (Remember that $a > 1$.) What happens to output and the real interest rate in the short run?

7. *Consider the economy described in problem 6.*

a. Suppose the economy starts with $Y - Y_n$ and $\pi^e = \pi^*$.

b. Now suppose there is an increase in π^e. Assume that Y_n does not change. Using the diagram you drew in problem 6(b), show how the increase in p^e affects the *MP* relation. (Again, remember that $a > 1$.) What happens to output and the real interest rate in the short run?

c. Without attempting to model the dynamics of inflation explicitly, assume that inflation and expected inflation will increase over time if $Y > Y_n$, and that they will decrease over time if $Y < Y_n$. Given the effect on output you found in part (a), will π^e tend to return to the target rate of inflation, π^*, over time?

d. Redo part (a), but assuming this time that $a < 1$. How does the increase in π^e affect the *MP* relation when $a < 1$?

What happens to output and the real interest rate in the short run?

e. Again assume that inflation and expected inflation will increase over time if $Y > Y_n$ and that they will decrease over time if $Y > Y_n$. Given the effect on output you found in part (c), will π^e tend to return to the target rate of inflation, π^*, over time? Is it sensible for the parameter a (in the interest rate rule) to take values less than one?

8. *Consider an economy characterised by the following facts.*

   i.   *The official budget deficit is 3% of GDP.*
   ii. *The debt-to-GDP ratio is 100%.*
   iii. *The nominal interest rate is 8%.*
   iv. *The inflation rate is 6%.*

a. What is the primary deficit/surplus ratio to GDP?

b. What is the inflation-adjusted deficit/surplus ratio to GDP?

c. Suppose that output is 2% below its natural level. What is the cyclically adjusted, inflation-adjusted deficit/surplus ratio to GDP?

d. Suppose instead that output begins at its natural level and that output growth remains constant at the normal rate of 2%. How will the debt-to-GDP ratio change over time?

DIG DEEPER

9. Ricardian equivalence and fiscal policy

First consider an economy in which Ricardian equivalence does not hold (i.e. an economy like the one we have described in this book).

a. Suppose the government starts with a balanced budget. Then, there is an increase in government spending, but there is no change in taxes. Show in an *IS–LM* diagram the effect of this policy on output in the short run. How will the government finance the increase in government spending?

b. Suppose, as in part (a), that the government starts with a balanced budget and then increases government spending. This time, however, assume that taxes increase by the same amount as government spending. Show in an *IS–LM* diagram the effect of this policy on output in the short run. (It may help to recall the discussion of the multiplier in Chapter 3. Does government spending or tax policy have a bigger multiplier?) How does the output effect compare with the effect in part (a)?

Now suppose Ricardian equivalence holds in this economy. [Parts (c) and (d) do not require use of diagrams.]

c. Consider again an increase in government spending with no change in taxes. How does the output effect compare to the output effects in parts (a) and (b)?

d. Consider again an increase in government spending combined with an increase in taxes of the same amount. How does this output effect compare to the output effects in parts (a) and (b)?

e. Comment on each of the following statements:

  i. 'Under Ricardian equivalence, government spending has no effect on output.'

  ii. 'Under Ricardian equivalence, changes in taxes have no effect no output.'

10. Current monetary policy

Problem 10 in Chapter 4 asked you to consider the current stance of monetary policy. Here, you are asked to do so again, but with the additional understanding of monetary policy you have gained in this and previous chapters.

Go to the website of the ECB and download either the press release you considered in Chapter 4 (if you did problem 10) or the most recent press release of the Governing Council.

a. What is the stance of monetary policy, as described in the press release?

b. Is there evidence that the GC considers both inflation and unemployment in setting interest rate policy, as would be implied by the Taylor rule?

c. Does any of the language of the press release seem to be aimed at increasing the credibility of the ECB (as committed to low inflation) or at affecting inflation expectations?

> *We invite you to visit the Blanchard page on the Prentice Hall website, at* **www.prenhall.com/blanchard** *for this chapter's World Wide Web exercises.*

FURTHER READING

- 'Modern Central Banking', written by Stanley Fischer for the 300th anniversary of the Bank of England (published in Forrest Capie, Stanley Fischer, Charles Goodhart and Norbert Schnadt eds, *The Future of Central Banking*, Cambridge University Press, Cambridge, UK, 1995), provides a nice discussion of the current issues in central banking. (Stanley Fischer is now governor of the Central Bank of Israel.) Read also 'What Central Bankers Could Learn from Academics – and Vice Versa', by Alan Blinder, *Journal of Economic Perspectives*, 1997, 11(2), 3–19.

- On inflation targeting, read Ben Bernanke and Frederic Mishkin, 'Inflation Targeting: A New Framework for Monetary Policy?' *Journal of Economic Perspectives*, 1997, 11(2), 97–116. (This article was written by Ben Bernanke before he became chairman of the ECB. Frederic Mishkin, on leave from Columbia University, is currently a member of the Board of Governors of the Federal Reserve.)

- For more detail on how the ECB operates, read Glenn Hubbard, *Money, the Financial System, and the Economy*, 5th ed., Addison-Wesley, Reading, MA, 2004.

- For more on monetary policy under Alan Greenspan, read N. Gregory Mankiw, 'U.S. Monetary Policy During the 1990s', in *American Economic Policy in the 1990s*, MIT Press, Cambridge, MA, 2001.

- For a more relaxing read, see Bob Woodward, *Maestro; Greenspan's Fed and the American Boom*, Simon & Schuster, New York, 2001.

- The modern statement of the Ricardian equivalence proposition is Robert Barro's 'Are Government Bonds Net Wealth?' *Journal of Political Economy*, December 1974, 1095–117.

EUROPE IN PROGRESS

Since 1957, when six European countries (Belgium, the Federal Republic of Germany, France, Italy, Luxembourg and the Netherlands) decided to build a European Economic Community (EEC) based on a common market covering a whole range of goods and services, European economic integration has gone a long way. It now includes 27 countries, 16 of which have also formed a monetary union. Many others have already applied for euro membership, and the few who initially decided to opt out might change their minds in the future.

Chapter 25 European economic and monetary integration

Chapter 25 describes the monetary history of Europe, the early experiments with the system of fixed exchange rates to the European Monetary System (EMS), until the signing of the Maastricht Treaty in 1991, when 12 European countries formally decided to adopt a common currency. It also describes the European Central Bank (ECB), its institutional structure, goals and strategies.

Chapter 26 The euro: the ins and the outs

Chapter 26 discusses the economic reasons for a monetary union and whether the euro area meets them, i.e. whether it is an optimal currency area. It then reviews the first ten years of the euro (1999–2009) and asks why did some European countries decide to opt out of the single currency, and whether the recent financial and economic turmoil has altered the incentives to join EMU.

Source: Cartoonstock.com.

Chapter 25

EUROPEAN ECONOMIC AND MONETARY INTEGRATION

On 1 January 1999 12 countries of the European Union abandoned their national currencies to use a common currency, the euro. During the first three years the old national currencies continued to circulate, although linked by fixed exchange rates. From 1 January 2002 the euro replaced national currencies, which were quickly withdrawn from circulation. The birth of the euro is the most significant currency phenomenon of the 20th century, with important consequences for the future of European citizens. This chapter is entirely devoted to the **European Economic and Monetary Union (EMU)**, its history and the functioning of its institutions. We also try to study and evaluate the first ten years of the European Central Bank (ECB), the supranational institution which is responsible for conducting monetary policy in the EMU. Finally, we ask whether EMU will, besides centralising the conduct of monetary policy, also cause a change in the way that countries conduct fiscal policy.

The chapter consists of four sections:

- Section 25.1 tells the story of how it was that 12 countries decided, voluntarily, to abandon monetary sovereignty and delegate the management of monetary policy to a common central bank.

- Sections 25.2 and 25.3 review the monetary history of Europe, the early experiments with the system of fixed exchange rates, and the **European Monetary System (EMS)**, until the signing of the Maastricht Treaty in 1991, when European countries formally decided to adopt a common currency.

- Section 25.4 describes the ECB, its institutional structure, its goals and strategies. We will also try to assess the behaviour of the ECB during its first ten years of life.

25.1 WHY HAVE EUROPEANS ALWAYS BEEN SO ADVERSE TO EXCHANGE RATE VOLATILITY?

The decision to adopt a common currency represents the ultimate attempt to fix exchange rates between different countries. As we saw in Chapter 19, a system of fixed exchange rates is always subject to the risk of a devaluation, whereas a common currency rules this possibility out, setting the parities in a definitive way. How can such a choice be explained from an economic perspective? It is difficult to understand the process that led to the creation of the EMU if you do not understand why Europeans have always tried to limit fluctuations between their currencies.

◄ If financial markets start anticipating a devaluation, that is a decrease in the exchange rate, then the central bank must set a higher interest rate if the existing parity is to be maintained. However, the central bank might not be able to convince the markets that there will be no devaluation and, eventually, might have to devalue.

There are three reasons why Europeans have always been so concerned about the volatility of exchange rates between their currencies – more worried than, for example, the Americans or the Japanese.

- First, they live in very open economies, where international trade is a particularly important component of national income. As we saw in Chapter 14, the higher the share of exports or imports in total income, the greater the effect, on the same income, of a change in the exchange rate. Therefore, exchange rate volatility among European currencies has a big impact on the national income of European countries.
- Second, Europeans believe that the wide **exchange rate fluctuations** in Europe in the 1920s and 1930s contributed decisively to the crisis of national economies in the period between the wars, and had no small part in determining the collapse of European democracies and the outbreak of the Second World War.
- A final factor is the common agricultural market. For many years, until the early 1980s, the common agricultural market was the only tangible activity of the EU (at that time called the EEC, the European Economic Community): if the common agricultural market had ceased working, perhaps the union would have lost its reason to exist. But the common agricultural market needed stable exchange rates: it could hardly have survived with high exchange rate volatility within Europe.

The degree of openness of European economies

As we saw in Chapter 14, a devaluation reduces the relative price of domestic goods, and thus increases the demand for exports and reduces the demand for imports. The higher the share of imports and exports on total income (that is, the greater the '**degree of openness**' of the economy) the greater the macroeconomic effect of a devaluation – and the same will happen in the event of a revaluation. The exchange rate is a macroeconomic variable whose importance is greater the higher the degree of openness of the economy.

The economies of EU countries are very open. Table 25.1 shows the degree of openness – measured as the sum of exports and imports on total income – of European economies. The sum of exports and imports on total income is around 50% in larger countries like France, Spain, Italy and the UK (slightly higher in Germany) and much higher, even higher than 100%, in small countries like Belgium, Luxembourg and the Netherlands. Compared to large non-European countries like Japan or the USA, European economies are much more open. However, most European countries trade mainly with each other, and less with countries outside of Europe. In fact, if we do not consider intra-European trade – that is, bilateral trade flows between any two European countries – and calculate the degree of openness of the EU to the rest of the world, we see that this is less than the degree of openness of the USA or Japan (26% compared to, respectively, 27 and 31%). So when Europeans say they are concerned about fluctuations in exchange rates, their concern is primarily with exchange rate fluctuations within Europe.

◄ The degree of openness of an economy can be measured as the ratio of exports to GDP or the ratio of imports to GDP: when the trade balance is zero, the two measures are clearly the same. In Table 25.1 we consider a measure that takes into account the fact that trade is usually not balanced: the sum of exports and imports.

Table 25.1 The degree of openness of European economies
(exports + imports/GDP), 2005–2007

Austria	107.2	Norway	74.7
Belgium	172.0	Netherlands	133.5
Cyprus	96.8	Portugal	70.7
Denmark	98.6	Slovenia	136.9
Finland	84.2	Spain	59.1
France	54.7	Sweden	94.6
Germany	83.6	UK	57.7
Greece	44.3		
Ireland	149.4		
Italy	55.8	UE-27	26.4*
Luxembourg	285.2	USA	27.3
Malta	167.4*	Japan	31.5

* 2004–2006

Source: WTO Trade Statistics.

The legacy of the competitive devaluations of the 1920s and 1930s

There is a book that describes in an illuminating way why, since the 1950s, Europeans have been so worried by exchange rate fluctuations: *International Currency Experience: Lessons from the Inter-War Period*, written in 1944 by Ragnar Nurske, an Estonian economist who, during the Second World War, worked at the Economic Department of the League of Nations, the institution that preceded the United Nations.

In the post-war period, exchange rate fluctuations, instead of facilitating the adjustment of the balance of payments, intensified initial imbalances, giving rise to even higher economic instability. (One particularly instructive example of the effects of uncontrolled changes in exchange rates, is the story of the French franc between 1922 and 1926.) In fact, the large exchange rate fluctuations in that period were largely due to the attempt of various countries to use the exchange rate as a macroeconomic instrument to exit from the deep recession of the 1930s. But a devaluation increases a country's competitiveness only to the extent that it reduces the competitiveness of its trading partners. A devaluation then immediately gives rise to retaliation by other countries which also have a motive to devalue. Eventually competitive devaluation leads to higher inflation everywhere. This is precisely what happened in the 1930s. But there is more: when countries realised that devaluations were not effective, some began to defend their products with tariffs and duties. The end result of such **competitive devaluation** was the collapse of free trade.

Politicians who worked in the 1950s for the creation of the first supranational European institutions (in particular, France's Robert Schuman, Germany's Konrad Adenauer and Italy's Alcide De Gasperi) had in mind the experience of the 1930s. They were convinced that inflation and the end of free trade were in no small measure responsible for the crisis of European democracies and the emergence of authoritarian regimes in the period between the two world wars. They believed that one of the main tasks of the new institutions was the creation of a monetary system that could avoid exchange rate fluctuations within Europe.

Exchange rate fluctuations and the Common Agricultural Market

1 ECU = $\Sigma_i \alpha_i M_i$ where $\alpha_i M_i$ are the quantities of the various currencies included in the basket: 10 deutschemarks, 1000 Italian lire, etc. The value of an ECU in terms of say, Italian lire or French francs, varied with bilateral exchange rates between European currencies.

Since the start of the **Common Agricultural Policy** in the 1960s, the price of agricultural products, such as wheat, was been the same in all European countries. Until 1999 the price was expressed in ECU. The ECU was simply a unit of account, and was used as numeral in transactions within the EU. One ECU corresponded to a fixed amount of each of its component currencies – the currencies of the EU.

Consider what happened when a currency, say the French franc, devalued against the ECU, for example because the franc was devalued relative to all other European currencies. The price of an ECU in terms of marks or lire fell, that is the mark and the lira were revalued against the ECU – this is because an ECU was now worth less because it contained a currency, the franc, which was worth less. If the ECU price of wheat remained unchanged, it was supposed to increase in francs and decrease in marks, to the extent that it had to reflect the devaluation of the franc against the mark.

However, whenever a country devalued, the government in that country tried to prevent the domestic price of agricultural products from increasing: in our example, the French did not allow the domestic price of wheat to increase, as they feared this would increase inflation. At the same time, Germany tried to prevent its domestic price from falling, so as not to damage German farmers. The end result was a change in relative prices. At this point, it was worth buying wheat in France where, after the devaluation, the price expressed in marks had fallen, and selling it in Germany, where the price in marks had remained unchanged.

To avoid a situation where all the French wheat went to Germany, any variation in exchange rates within the EU was accompanied by the introduction of import duties and tariffs, that is, instruments that removed the incentive to transfer all the French wheat to Germany. But import duties and tariffs were the very negation of the common market from which it all started.

Therefore, it is easily understandable why Europeans, since the 1960s, have been so much worried by exchange rate fluctuations within Europe. Frequent changes in exchange rates would have destroyed the common agricultural market that for many years – from the Treaty of Rome of 1958 until the Single Act of 1985 – was the only tangible activity of the EU. If the common agricultural market had failed, the very survival of the union would have been in danger – as the European Commission would have been left with little to do – and European integration would probably have stopped.

25.2 THE MONETARY HISTORY OF EUROPE FROM POST-WAR TO THE PRESENT DAY

From Bretton Woods to the European Monetary System

From the early years immediately after the end of the Second World War and until 1971, bilateral exchange rate volatility within Europe was limited by a common peg to the dollar. During those years, the international monetary system functioned as envisaged by the **Bretton Woods** agreements. The latter, in 1945, had created the International Monetary Fund, the institution responsible for overseeing the international monetary system. In the Bretton Woods system, each currency could not deviate from the dollar by more than 0.75% (below or above), so that the fluctuation band had a width of 1.50% around a central rate. Any changes in the central rate against the dollar had to be negotiated with and authorised by the IMF. Bilateral exchange rate fluctuations between pairs of European currencies were therefore limited within a band of 3%. With few exceptions – the revaluation of the central parity for the German mark in 1961, the devaluation of the parity for the French franc in 1969 – bilateral exchange rates in Europe remained stable for a long time.

In the early 1970s, however, the Bretton Woods system collapsed. The reason was, essentially, the incompatibility between economic policy goals in Germany and in the USA. The USA had to fund the Vietnam war, and to do so they needed an accommodating monetary policy, allowing the Fed to finance the federal deficit. However, this would increase inflation. But in a system of essentially fixed exchange rates, inflation may not be very different between countries: countries with relatively higher inflation become gradually less competitive, their trade balances deteriorate and, eventually, they need to devalue to restore trade balance. To devalue means to abandon the fixed exchange rate. Germany was then forced, if she wanted to save the fixed parity between the deutschemark and the US dollar, to accept the US inflation rate, even if it was higher than the Bundesbank target. In 1971, the Germans decided to exit from the system. The exit of the mark, then the second most important currency in the world, caused the end of the Bretton Woods system.

The way in which the Germans did this was by raising their domestic interest rates in order to prevent an increase in inflation. With German interest rates higher than US rates, capital flowed from the USA to Germany, as investors sold dollars to buy marks and bought German bonds that paid a higher yield than US bonds. The Fed, worried about US domestic economic goals, did not follow suit – that is they did not increase interest rates – the only action that would have enabled them to prevent a devaluation of the dollar. Eventually the dollar devalued.

In a first phase the band around the dollar was simply enlarged; then, as from March 1973, exchange rates began to fluctuate freely. Within Europe, the mark increased rapidly vis-à-vis the dollar; the Italian lira and the French franc were revalued, but to a lesser extent, and therefore depreciated against the mark. The end of fixed exchange rates was therefore accompanied by wide fluctuations in the relative competitiveness of European countries.

Initially, the devaluations of the Italian lira and French franc, against the mark, benefited French and Italian products to the detriment of German goods. But the advantage was short-lived: the devaluations were soon accompanied by an increase in inflation that eroded the initial competitive advantage. Once again, the Europeans clashed with the ineffectiveness of the exchange rate as an instrument of economic policy: in the late 1970s inflation in Italy and the UK exceeded 20%, and in France it was close to 15%.

The European Monetary System

A return to stable exchange rates was the main reason that prompted European governments to create, in 1978, the European Monetary System (EMS), an exchange rate agreement that substantially reproduced a small Bretton Woods system limited to European countries and in which the mark served as an anchor as it had been for the dollar during the years of Bretton Woods. In September 1992, the EMS also collapsed for reasons similar to those which, 20 years before, had led to the end of Bretton Woods: the incompatibility between German monetary policy goals, dictated by the needs of Germany's reunification, and those of other European countries. The end of the EMS was accompanied once again by wide fluctuations in exchange rates: between September 1992 and March 1995 the Italian lira was devalued against the mark by almost 50%. This experience finally convinced the Europeans that only the adoption of a single currency would eliminate exchange rate fluctuations in Europe. Six years after the euro was born.

As we have seen, the EMS was the European response to the end of the Bretton Woods system and the high exchange rate volatility of the 1970s. The EMS allowed a period of relatively stable exchange rates, but did not eliminate devaluations. Between 1979 and 1992 there were ten devaluations: in each case, the central parity of one or more European currencies were devalued against the mark. These devaluations were necessary because the EMS was not accompanied by a complete convergence of inflation: inflation in Germany remained consistently lower than in the rest of Europe. As long as exchange rates against the mark remained fixed, countries with relatively higher inflation gradually lost their competitiveness and trade balances deteriorated. Then a devaluation was the way to restore equilibrium in the balance of payments. Within the EMS, however, devaluations were not unilateral, but collegial decisions. The decision to change the central parity against the mark required agreement by all the countries participating in the system – as with the Bretton Woods system, when a devaluation required the approval of the IMF. A country could not unilaterally decide when to devalue, and the amount of the devaluation must also be agreed. This collective decision-making allowed countries with high inflation to be 'regulated': if a country did not reduce its inflation rate, it could be 'punished' by delaying the devaluation of its currency and by reducing the size of the devaluation when it happened.

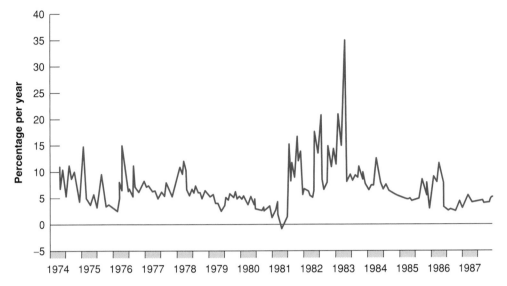

Figure 25.1

Differential between French and German three-month interest rates

When the interest rate differential widens, as at the beginning of 1983, this means that the market expects a devaluation of the French franc.

The result was that inflation gradually declined towards the German level. Italy, for example, entered the EMS with an inflation rate above 20%, which decreased gradually to 5%.

All this was possible only because monetary authorities were able to decide when to devalue. Central banks, not the market, made decisions on devaluations. How was this possible? And why do we now believe that markets should instead decide when a currency should devalue, not central banks (think about the devaluation of Southeast Asian currencies in 1997). To answer this question we must first better understand how the EMS worked.

How did the EMS work?

When a currency reached the top margin of the fluctuation band – the maximum allowable devaluation against the deutschemark (DM) – the central bank of that country had two options: raise interest rates in order to defend the exchange rate, or ask for a 'realignment', i.e. a devaluation of the central parity that implied the shift of the fluctuation band upwards. Figure 25.1 shows an example for the French franc (FF). The increases in interest rates in francs above interest rates in marks signal moments of weakness of the franc. In some cases, the interest rate differential vanishes because markets are convinced that there will not be a realignment; in other cases, the gap is closed after the realignment takes place – as in March 1983, when the central parity of the franc was devalued by 8% compared to the DM.

To understand the relationship between expectations of a devaluation and interest rate differential, take the arbitrage condition between the returns on assets denominated in different currencies that we have seen in Chapter 6 – equation [6.4] – and rewrite it as:

$$i^{FF} - i^{DM} \approx \frac{(FF/DM)^e_{t+1} - (FF/DM)_t}{(FF/DM)_t} = px + (1-p)0 = px$$

◀ Remember what the interest parity condition says: arbitrage by investors implies that the domestic interest rate must be equal to the foreign interest rate minus the expected appreciation rate of the domestic currency.

which corresponds to eq. 6.4 if you replace:

$$i^{FF} = i_t, \; i^{DM} = i^*_t, \; (FF/DM)^e_{t+1} = E^e_{t+1} \text{ and } (FF/DM)_t = E_t$$

Consider first the first two terms of this equation. Investors will continue to hold securities denominated in French francs, even when they expect a devaluation of the franc (when the right term in the first equality is positive) if their yield, i^{FF}, grows enough, compared to the performance of similar securities denominated in marks (i.e. i^{DM}), thereby compensating for the losses they would suffer if the franc eventually devalues.

Now consider the second equality. The expected franc–mark exchange rate devaluation can be expressed as the sum of two terms: the probability, p, that the devaluation occurs, multiplied by the amount of the devaluation, in the event it occurs – which we indicated

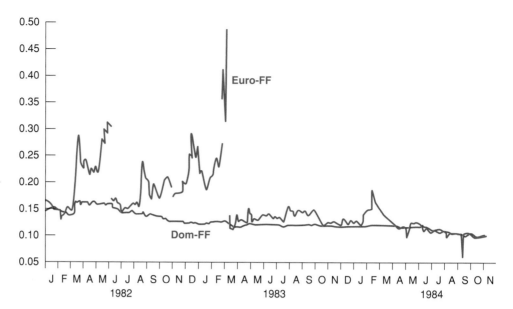

Figure 25.2

France: on-shore and off-shore three-month interest rates

Controls on capital flows allowed France to separate the internal financial market from the international market, especially in times preceding realignments.

with $x + (1 - p)$, the probability that no devaluation occurs, multiplied by zero. This expression shows how the ratio between the two interest rates fluctuates with changing market expectations about a devaluation.

The relationship between the French and the German rates shown in Figure 25.1 is a measure of market expectations regarding the devaluation of the French franc. Figure 25.1 shows that when a spread emerges between French and German interest rates, this is because it is the French rate that moves, while the German rate is unchanged. This is a characteristic of exchange rate regimes built around a 'central' currency, as the dollar in Bretton Woods and the deutschemark in the EMS. If the system is under pressure – for example, because markets expect a devaluation – all of the adjustment will be taken by peripheral countries, like France in our example. The core country never modifies its monetary policy to cope with the tensions of the system. For this reason, the country of the central currency is called the **anchor of the system**.

Controls on capital flows

Figure 25.2 shows two series of interest rates in francs. The series called 'Euro-FF' shows the interest rates on securities denominated in French francs, but held outside of France, for example in London. The series called 'Dom-FF' indicates similar interest rates on securities held in France. The emergence of a differential (sometimes large, as in March 1983) between the two interest rates is due to **controls on capital flows** – also known as foreign exchange controls. These are laws that prevent citizens from holding financial assets abroad, even if denominated in the national currency. In 1983, for example, a French citizen could not hold securities in London – even if denominated in French francs. In this way, the French authorities, like those of other European countries, ensured that the defence of the exchange rate did not cause sharp increases in domestic rates.

Foreign exchange controls are limitations imposed by governments on the purchase or sale of domestic currency by foreigners and/or of foreign currency by residents.

As long as there were foreign exchange controls, the defence of the exchange rate was relatively inexpensive for the peripheral countries. Consider, for example, the case of Italy: the rate on lira-denominated securities held in London could remain relatively high even for long periods, without any cost for Italy; the Italian public deficit continued to be financed at much lower rates. Capital controls worked then as a 'hidden tax' because they actually forced savers to invest at lower rates than those that they would have obtained had they been allowed to purchase securities abroad.

Controls on capital flows allowed governments to defend the exchange rate even when the market believed that this should be devalued. They did not eliminate the need, sooner or later, to devalue – as they did not eliminate the inflation differentials – but allowed monetary authorities to delay the size and the timing of devaluations.

This autonomy disappeared on the day when foreign exchange controls – that had become incompatible with the integration of European financial market were lifted. At that moment the EMS was doomed.

Fixed exchange rates and free capital flows

When there are no foreign exchange controls and a country can no longer endure the costs of high interest rates – for example, because the level of public debt is high – there are apparently two options:

1. The market is convinced that the exchange rate is sustainable, i.e. that the economic policy of the country is consistent with a fixed exchange rate. In this case, investors do not expect a devaluation ($p = 0$), so interest rates remain the same as rates in the central country and defending the exchange rate involves no cost: the exchange rate remains fixed.
2. The market expects a devaluation ($p > 0$). In this case, the domestic interest rates rise and domestic monetary authorities have no choice but to raise the white flag and devalue.

Solution (1) is unstable, however. Think about what happens at time t if policy is consistent with a fixed exchange rate, but investors expect that in future, at time $t + 1$, economic policy will change – for example with a new government – thus making a devaluation possible: p becomes positive and the domestic interest rates rise. If the fear of a future devaluation is sufficiently widespread and increasing interest rates is too expensive for the government, for example, because public debt is high, a country may be forced to devalue even before it experiences the change of government and even if this does not occur. Fears of a devaluation can then self-fulfil, even if economic policy remains consistent with the fixed exchange rate.

With foreign exchange controls removed because they were incompatible with the single market, only two options were thus open to Europe:

1. To abandon any attempt to stabilise exchange rates and move to a flexible exchange rate regime, that is leaving it to the market to determine exchange rates between European currencies.
2. To abandon exchange rates, adopting a common currency.

It is for this reason that European financial integration, combined with the old dislike by Europeans for flexible exchange rates, led as a natural consequence to monetary union.

The Maastricht Treaty

Although the crisis of the EMS has probably accelerated the timetable for the creation of the euro, the decision to adopt a single currency came long before, and was taken with the signing of the **Maastricht Treaty** in February 1992. The Maastricht Treaty, which in reality is called the Treaty of the European Union, is a key document for the history of European integration and for the birth of the euro. In particular, the Treaty created a new suprana-tional institution, the European Central Bank, the institution responsible for conducting monetary policy in the EMU.

The Maastricht Treaty also established some convergence criteria that countries aspiring to enter the EMU had to meet. In the early 1990s, European countries, in fact, showed large macroeconomic differences: in particular, with regard to inflation and public deficits. Precisely because the single currency makes it obviously impossible to devalue, a condition for starting the EMU was therefore the convergence of macroeconomic variables, beginning with inflation.

The criteria adopted by the Treaty, which are described in the following Focus box, related in particular to exchange rate stability, convergence of interest rates in the long run, inflation rates and two indicators of public finance: deficit/GDP and debt/GDP ratios.

FOCUS
Criteria for admissions to the EMU set by the Maastricht Treaty

Inflation rate. The rate of inflation in the year preceding accession must not be more than 1.5 percentage points above that of the three best-performing member states in terms of price stability.

Public debt and deficits. The ratio of the government deficit to GDP must not exceed 3% unless:

● either the ratio has declined substantially and continuously and reached a level that comes close to the reference value; or, alternatively,
● the excess over the reference value is only exceptional and temporary and the ratio remains close to the reference value.

The ratio of government debt to GDP must not exceed 60% of GDP, unless the ratio is sufficiently diminishing and approaching the reference value at a satisfactory pace.

Exchange rate. Exchange rate movements must have been within the normal fluctuation margins provided for by the exchange-rate mechanism of the EMS, for at least two years, without devaluing against the currency of any other member state.

Long-term interest rate. Observed over a period of one year before the examination, a member state has had an average nominal long-term interest rate that does not exceed by more than 2 percentage points that of, at most, the three best performing member states in terms of price stability. Interest rates shall be measured on the basis of long-term government bonds or comparable securities, taking into account differences in national definitions.

The decision to name the new currency 'euro' was adopted in December 1995 by the European Council. On the same occasion, the Council confirmed that EMU would definitely start on 1 January 1999: at that time, the exchange rate between the participating currencies would be irrevocably fixed (Table 25.2) while the new coins and notes were to be introduced on 1 January 2002.

The latest step on the way towards EMU was on 3 May 1998, when the Council of Heads of State and Government agreed on which of the member states met the admission criteria and therefore could enter EMU. There were 11 countries: Belgium, Germany, Spain, France, Ireland, Italy, Luxembourg, the Netherlands, Austria, Portugal and Finland. The months preceding the final decision on which countries would participate in EMU were particularly uncertain, especially as regards Italy, the country that started out more distant with regard to the convergence criteria imposed by the Maastricht Treaty. Greece was not allowed to

Table 25.2 Euro conversion rates

		1 euro =
Austria	ATS	13.7603
Belgium	BEF	40.3399
Cyprus	CTP	0.585274
Finland	FIM	5.94573
France	FRF	6.55957
Germany	DEM	1.95583
Greece	GRD	340.750
Ireland	IEP	0.787564
Italy	ITL	1936.27
Luxembourg	LUF	40.3399
Malta	MTL	0.429300
Netherlands	NLG	2.20371
Portugal	PTE	200.482
Slovenia	SIT	239.640
Spain	ESP	166.386

enter in the first place because it did not comply with all the convergence criteria, and Sweden was not allowed because it has decided not to participate in the EMS (and being a member of the EMS for at least two years was a condition for admission to EMU). As regards the UK and Denmark, they were in special circumstances at that time. The UK, despite having ratified the Maastricht Treaty, had asked to postpone to a later date the choice of whether or not to join (the clause of 'opting-out'), while Denmark had linked the ratification of the Treaty to holding a new referendum, after one in July 1992 in which the Danes had rejected the euro. So far the referendum has not yet taken place.

To member states that did not participate from the beginning (called 'states with a derogation'), the Treaty guarantees the possibility of adopting the single currency at a later date. Article 109k of the Treaty provides that 'at least once every two years or at the request of a Member State with a derogation' on the basis of a report from the Commission and the ECB on the degree of convergence achieved, the European Council shall decide which Member States with a derogation satisfy the necessary conditions to join the euro. Greece did not qualify initially and did not join until 1 January 2001. When the euro was introduced in 1999, 11 countries made up the euro area. Sixteen countries now belong, the most recent members being Slovakia, Slovenia, Cyprus and Malta.

25.3 THE EUROPEAN SYSTEM OF CENTRAL BANKS: STRUCTURE AND OBJECTIVES

After examining the most significant stages of the process that led to the creation of the ECB, we now consider its organisational structure, responsibilities and some elements of the monetary policy strategy that it pursues.

Monetary policy in the euro area is managed by the ECB, which, along with the 27 national central banks of all EU member states (regardless of whether they have adopted the euro), form the **European System of Central Banks (ESCB)**. One key feature of the ESCB is its independence with respect both to other European institutions and to the national governments of the countries that are part of the euro area. Article 7 of the Maastrict Treaty stresses independence unequivocally, arguing that 'neither a national bank, nor any member of their decision-making bodies shall seek or take instructions from Community institutions or bodies, nor from the governments of the Member States'. The division of tasks between the ECB and national central banks is carried out as follows. Monetary policy decisions are centralised at the ECB, so that monetary policy at European level is unique, but its implementation decentralised to the national banks, which are responsible for carrying out open market operations in the individual countries.

- Decision-making bodies of the ECB are the Governing Council and the Executive Board. There is also a third body, called the General Council, which has no decision-making powers but acts only in an advisory capacity.
- The Governing Council is composed of the six members of the Executive Board and the governors of national central banks of countries that are part of the euro area. This body is responsible for formulating monetary policy and establishing guidelines for its implementation. The Council normally meets twice a month (on Thursdays).
- The Executive Board comprises the President, the Vice-President and four other members 'selected from among persons of recognised reputation and experience in banking and money' by the Heads of State and Government of the EU. The Executive Board implements monetary policy in accordance with the guidelines and decisions laid down by the Governing Council, giving instructions to national central banks. The Executive Board may be delegated certain powers when the Governing Council so decides.
- The General Council is composed of the President, the Vice-President and the governors of national central banks of all 27 countries that are part of the EU (the 16 countries

which belong to the euro and the 11 which do not). This body has no decision-making capacity in the field of monetary policy but has some monitoring activities and may act in an advisory capacity. The groundwork for establishing the irrevocable conversion rates to be applied when the states that currently are not part of EMU are allowed to join is also among the responsibilities of the General Council.

An important aspect of the mode of operation of the governing bodies of the ECB concerns the process by which decisions are made. Both the Governing Council and the Executive Committee reach agreement by means of votes taken on the basis of two fundamental rules. The first rule is that each member holds one vote and the second is that decisions are taken by simple majority.

The first rule is particularly important: governors of central banks all have the same weight, regardless of the economic importance of the country of origin. Governors have not been assigned a weight proportional to the size of the economy of their country, such as in the IMF and World Bank, because such an arrangement would have suggested that the governors represent specific national interests.

Although the Treaty stipulates that central banks' (NCB) governors sit on the Governing Council in a personal capacity, the reality is that they end up representing their respective countries. And, since NCB governors have 16 out of 22 seats on the Council, this makes decision making complicated particularly when economic conditions across the EMU members diverge. Decision making will become even more complicated when EMU membership is extended to all 27 EU countries. For further discussion of these problems, see the end of this chapter. If we compare the structure of the ECB with that of another federal central bank, the Fed, we can see that the Fed's Federal Open Market Committee consists of seven members appointed by the centre and only five members belonging to the regional Federal Reserve Banks.

The objectives of monetary policy

The basic task of the ECB is to conduct monetary policy in EMU. To understand how the ECB carries out its mission, we must first define the objectives of monetary policy, and then identify the strategies and methods used to achieve them.

Without prejudice to the objective of price stability, the ESCB shall support the objectives of the EU: a high level of employment and sustainable and non-inflationary growth.

Article 105.1 of the Maastricht Treaty gives absolute priority to the objective of price stability. Other goals, namely to support the economic policies of the EU, are formulated in a rather vague way and can be pursued only if they are compatible with price stability. In contrast to the position held in other institutional contexts, especially in the US Federal Reserve System, the ECB held that the objective of price stability was sufficiently important to require a precise definition. Consequently, the ECB has stated that 'price stability is defined as a situation in which the one-year increase in the consumer price index for the euro area is less than 2%'.

First, note that the definition of inflation refers to the euro area as a whole. This is another sign that the decisions of the ECB will be based on assessments covering only the area as a whole and not specific situations in individual countries. It should also be noted that the term 'increase . . . less than 2%' means that price stability is considered compatible with a rate of change that must take place with in the range 0–2%. It follows that a deflation, that is, a prolonged decline in the price level, would not be considered compatible with the objective of price stability.

The basic question remains about the wisdom of adopting such a strict definition of price stability. It has been noted that the approach taken by the ECB is probably too ambitious. There are no recent examples of countries that have managed to keep inflation below 2% for long periods of time: just remember that between 1950 and 1997 the rate of inflation in Germany remained under 2% in only in 15 out of those 48 years (see the Focus box on the Riksbanken in Chapter 24).

Monetary policy strategies and behaviour of the ECB

In recent years, there has been an extensive debate on the various 'strategies' that monetary authorities can pursue to reach the objective of price stability. Two basic approaches have been compared, as discussed in Chapter 24: monetary targeting and inflation targeting. As we will see, the ECB's strategy does not identify with either of those alternatives. To understand why, it is useful to first review the main features distinguishing the two approaches.

- The monetary targeting strategy is based on the announcement by the central bank of a rate of money growth. The action of the central bank focuses on the achievement of that growth rate: as soon as money growth differs from the expected growth 'path', the central bank intervenes by making the appropriate corrections. Several studies show that the monetary targeting approach is optimal only in special circumstances: it requires, in particular, a remarkable stability of the currency demand function. The monetary targeting strategy has been used for many years by the Bundesbank, which however has followed that strategy in a rather flexible and pragmatic way.

- 'Inflation targeting' refers to a strategy based on the announcement by the central bank of a desired path for future inflation. In this case, the central bank decides its corrective actions on the basis of deviations of expected inflation from the desired path. (Note that the relevant deviation is between expected and desired inflation: this reflects the fact that monetary policy has no immediate impact on inflation.) The advantage of inflation targeting is that the aim of the central bank is very clearly stated, since it refers directly to the objective of price stability. The main drawback is that the inflation rate is not directly controllable by the central bank. Inflation targeting has been successfully used in recent years in a number of countries including Canada, New Zealand, the UK and Sweden. This approach is quite recent and the good results achieved should be evaluated taking into account the fact that, with low inflation such as has been seen in recent years, the objective of price stability was certainly easier to achieve. (See Focus box on the Riksbank in Chapter 24.)

According to the ECB, both the theoretical debate and the empirical evidence make it impossible to identify clearly the superiority of one approach over another. In this situation, the ECB has decided to pursue an approach that has officially been called the 'stability-oriented monetary policy strategy' which includes elements of the two different strategies briefly described above. The choice in favour of an 'intermediate approach' finds its main justification in the opinion of the ECB, according to which, at present, the available empirical evidence on the process of monetary policy transmission in the euro area is not yet sufficiently reliable. In other words, we do not yet know how much impact a change in interest rates has on inflation, nor how long it takes to occur. In this regard, the problem of the so-called 'structural break' is likely to play a role, in the sense that the empirical evidence relating to the period in which the monetary union did not yet exist may no longer be valid now that the union is in place.

To achieve the objective of price stability the ECB therefore adopts a **'two-pillar'** **strategy**. Figure 25.3 shows the two pillars of the ECB's monetary policy strategy. The first pillar of the strategy relates to the money supply and is referred to as 'monetary analysis'. The Governing Council of the ECB announces a reference value for money growth: the value is not considered a binding target (as it is in the case of monetary targeting) and there is, therefore, no commitment to correct deviations of strict monetary growth from the reference value in the short term. Despite the fact that it does not pursue a monetary targeting strategy, the ECB attaches great importance to controlling the amount of money

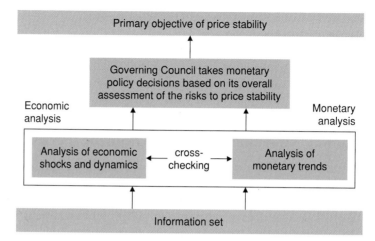

Figure 25.3

The two pillars of the ECB's monetary policy strategy

Source: European Central Bank, *Monthly Bulletin*, 10th Anniversary of the ECB, June 2008, p. 39.

in order to pursue the objective of price stability. In this regard, the following statements in an official document of the ECB are noteworthy: 'Inflation is ultimately a monetary phenomenon. [. . .] For a monetary policy aimed at maintaining price stability, money is a natural anchor, robust and reliable.'

The ECB believes however that reference to the money supply, although extremely important, is not sufficient to implement a monetary policy that can achieve the objective of price stability. A second pillar is therefore needed, i.e.what is referred to as 'economic analysis'. An official document of the ECB states: 'In parallel to the analysis of monetary growth in relation to the reference value, a comprehensive evaluation of the forecasts on the trends of prices in the euro area and the threats to their stability will play a key role in the strategy of the Eurosystem. This assessment will be accomplished by referring to a broad range of economic indicators. The main indicators that the ECB notes include, *inter alia*, various measures of real economic activity, labour costs, exchange rates, prices of financial assets and details on the expectations of firms and consumers taken from surveys.'

However, beyond the rethoric of official documents, it is now generally accepted, at least within financial markets, that the ECB is acting as a *de facto* inflation targeter and that it decides the level of interest rates based on its inflation forecast for the euro area. Any efforts to evaluate the behaviour of the new central bank in its first ten years of life should thus be based on this assumption. Before doing this, however, in the next section we briefly describe the operational modalities of the ECB, namely the tools and procedures for implementing monetary policy in the Eurosystem.

25.4 HOW DOES THE ECB WORK IN PRACTICE?

As we have seen at the beginning of this section, the implementation of monetary policy is delegated to the Executive Board of the ECB, according to the decisions and guidelines laid down by the Governing Council. The primary objective of the ECB is guarenteeing price stability. To achieve its objective, the ECB has at its disposal three instruments of monetary policy: **open market operations, the standing facilities of NCB and minimum reserve requirements.**

Open market operations

Open market operations – the purchase or sale of bonds by the Eurosystem (i.e. the ECB and the NCBs) – have the purpose of controlling interest rates and the liquidity in the market and signalling the stance of monetary policy.

There are four types of open market operations in the Eurosystem:

- **Main refinancing operations** are regular transactions with a frequency and maturity of one week with the aim of providing liquidity to the financial sector. They are executed by the national central banks according to a pre-specified calendar. The main refinancing operations provide the bulk of the liquidity of the financial sector.
- **Longer-term refinancing operations (LTROs)** are liquidity-providing transactions conducted monthly and having a maturity of three months. Longer-term refinancing operations that are conduced at irregular intervals or with other maturities are also possible. They are executed by the national central banks according to a pre-specified calendar. These operations aim to provide banks with additional longer-term liquidity.
- **Fine-tuning operations** can be executed on an *ad hoc* basis to manage the liquidity situation in the market and to steer interest rates. In particular, they aim to smooth the effects on interest rates caused by unexpected liquidity fluctuations. Fine-tuning operations will normally be executed by the national central banks.
- **Structural operations** are executed whenever the ECB wishes to adjust the structural position of the Eurosystem vis-à-vis the financial sector (on a regular or non-regular basis).

The standing facilities

Standing facilities are those operations, managed by the national central banks in a decentralised manner, that aim to provide and absorb overnight liquidity; signaling the general stance of monetary policy and place a limit on overnight fluctuations in market interest rates. Banks have access on their own initiative to two types of lending:

- The marginal lending facility to obtain overnight liquidity from national central banks, against assets given as a guarantee. Under normal circumstances, there are no credit limits provided that banks post acceptable collateral (the list of assets accepted as collateral is drawn up by the ECB). The interest rate on the marginal lending facility normally provides a *ceiling* for the overnight market interest rate.
- The facility to make overnight deposits with the national central banks. Under normal circumstances, there are no limits or other restrictions on access. The interest rate on deposits at the central bank is usually a *floor* for the market interest rate overnight.

Minimum reserves

Minimum reserves are an integral part of the operational framework for the monetary policy in the euro area. The purpose of the minimum reserve system is to pursue the aim of stabilising money market interest rates. The minimum reserve requirement of each institution is determined in relation to its balance sheet. To satisfy their minimum reserve requirements banks must, on average, over one month, hold a sufficient amount of reserves. This implies that compliance with the reserve requirement is determined on the basis of the institutions' average daily reserve holdings over a maintenance period of one month. The required reserve holdings are remunerated at a level corresponding to the average interest rate of the main refinancing operations of the Eurosystem over the maintenance period.

The first ten years of the ECB: a tentative assessment

Assessing the behaviour of the ECB after only one decade of its life is not easy. Ten years is not long enough to be able to extrapolate from ECB decisions the rule that it followed, and to understand if the bank has really adopted the two-pillar strategy, or whether, as

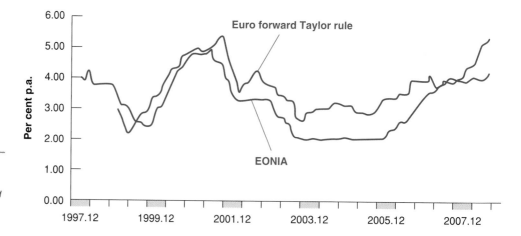

Figure 25.4

How different is the ECB from the Bundesbank?

Source: D.J.C. Smant, *ECB Interest Rate and Money Growth Rules*, Rotterdam, Erasmus University, mimeo.

financial markets believe, it was more worried about expected inflation forgetting the evolution of monetary aggregates.

One criticism often made is the claim that the ECB simply transposed to the whole of Europe the monetary policy rule formerly followed by the German central bank, the Bundesbank. To understand whether this is a sound criticism, let us look at Figure 25.4. To understand it, go back to the concept of the 'Taylor rule' presented in Chapter 24. This simple rule for reading the behaviour of monetary authorities has proved a very successful tool in interpreting and predicting the behaviour of central banks. The rule clearly does not match the first pillar of the ECB, as monetary aggregates do not enter there. But the Taylor rule does not even coincide with pure inflation targeting, that is, the assumption that the central bank has only one objective, inflation.

Using a simple formula, if we denote the interest rate set by the central bank at time t as i_t, the Taylor rule says that monetary authorities will set the interest rate based on the following formula:

$$i_t = a_0 + a_1(\pi^e_{t+1} - \pi^*) + a_2 Y^t / Y^* \qquad [25.1]$$

where π^e_{t+1} indicates expected inflation for time $t + 1$, π^* is the inflation target, Y_t is GDP at time t, Y^* is potential GDP, i.e. the level corresponding to full employment. Equation [25.1] includes expected inflation, since the central bank can do nothing to change current inflation: by changing interest rates it can only hope to influence future inflation (where the term 'future' means one or two years from now) because of the time it takes for a change in interest rates to affect inflation. Using historical data on real GDP and expected inflation, econometrics allows us to estimate the values of the coefficients a_0, a_1 and a_2 in equation [25.1]. In general, the higher the coefficient a_1 with respect to a_2, the greater is the concern of the central bank for inflation. When studying the behaviour of the Bundesbank until 1998, one finds values of $a_1 = 1.3$ and $a_2 = 0.3$.

Figure 25.4 shows first the overnight interest rates set by the ECB since January 1999, the month the ECB came into existence (this overnight rate is called EONIA, ECB Overnight Interest Rate Average). To give a little perspective, the chart reconstructs a theoretical rate for EONIA before January 1999, using the overnight rates of the countries adopting the euro: this is the blue line. The pink line shows the rate that the ECB would have to set if it had behaved exactly like the Bundesbank – clearly a Bundesbank that had to face the same euro area variables, inflation and growth, which the ECB has faced. As you can see, after an initial period during which the ECB has actually shadowed the Bundesbank, the bank seems to have 'freed itself' from the German experience. Interst rates from 2001 onwards are significantly different (lower) than what the Bundesbank would have chosen if it were facing similar conditions for growth and inflation.

It is obviously still too early to write a history of the ECB. These exercises are used primarily to make the point that what matters for evaluating a central bank are the facts, not the words written in the treaties or the announcements made by monetary authorities. If we were to take the exercise illustrated in Figure 25.3 seriously, we should conclude that the ECB, in its first four years of life, did not behave as it said it would, that is, it never took the first pillar seriously into account. In fact, the Taylor rule does not give any weight to monetary variables. Moreover, it probably gave more weight to real variables, namely GDP, than the statute itself requires.

Eventually, the market is the best test of the effectiveness of a central bank's monetary policy when its ultimate objective by statute is to keep inflation under control. What does the market expect? Do financial operators expect that inflation will remain below the limit set by the ECB (2%) or do they think that it will exceed that limit? Figure 25.5 shows two measures of long-term inflation expectations. These are the measures the ECB itself uses to gain insights into the expectations of the private sector. As you will remember from Chapter 15, there are two types of measures: measures based on surveys of private sector inflation expectations and measures based on comparisons between inflation-indexed bonds' yields and nominal bonds' yields. The Focus box 'Measures of euro area expectations of future inflation' summarises all the available measures of euro area inflation expectations.

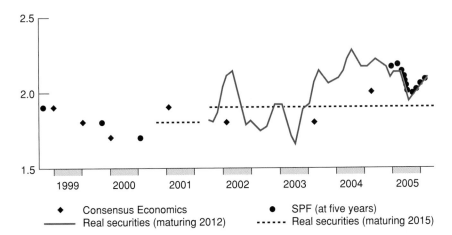

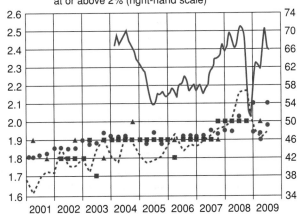

Sources: Consensus Economics, Euro Zone Barometer, Reuters and ECB calculations.

Figure 25.5

The ECB and expected inflation

Source: ECB, *Monthly Bulletin*, August 2009.

FOCUS
Measures of euro area expectations of future inflation

There are several available measures of inflation expectations in the euro area (see Table 25.3).

Survey-based measures

Survey-based measures provide direct measures of inflation expectations. There are several available surveys of private sector inflation expectations in the euro area.

1. *The European Commission Consumer Survey on Inflation Expectations*. Every month since 1985, the European Commission has reported on consumers' expectations for consumer price trends over the following 12 months on the basis of a survey of nearly 20 000 consumers in the euro area. These consumer surveys are conducted at the national level and the results for the euro area are compiled by aggregating the country data.

2. *The ECB Survey of Professional Forecasters (SPF)*. The SPF corresponds to the ECB Survey of Professional Forecasters, a survey the ECB has carried out every quarter since the beginning of 1999. The SPF collects information on expectations for euro area inflation, as well as for other relevant variables (mainly GDP growth and the unemployment rate) from a panel of more than 70 expert forecasters from financial or non-financial institutions that are based in the EU.

3. *Euro Zone Barometer*. Since 2002, MJEconomics, a London-based consultancy, has been publishing its 'Euro Zone Barometer', which contains forecasts for euro area HICP inflation one and two years ahead, based on a panel of professional forecasters.

4. *Consensus Economics' forecast*. Consensus Economics Inc., a private company, has published monthly average forecasts for major economic variables for several countries since 1989. It publishes the forecast averages of professional forecasters for the euro area's consumer prices for the year in question and for the following year based on a panel of around 30 participants.

Financial-market based measures

1. *Break-even inflation rates*. The difference between the yield on a nominal bond and that on an index-linked bond of the same maturity is often referred to as the 'break-even' inflation rate, as it would be the

Figure 25.5 shows projections from two different groups of professional analysts (SPF and Consensus Economics) and from the Euro Zone Barometer, and the probability, calculated from the SPF projections, that future inflation will be at or above 2%. Finally, the blue line refers to the predictions that are implicit in the interest rates of 'real' securities, i.e. the return on material assets that are protected from inflation, which is a market-based measure of inflation expectations five years ahead. As you learned in Chapter 17, by comparing the yield spread between nominal and inflation-linked (or 'real') bonds, you can derive the implicit inflation expectations among financial market participants. These expectations are a little 'more volatile' than the survey-based measures. In particular, notice the significant increase in market-based inflation expectations since mid-2007, i.e. the beginning of the financial crisis which began in the USA. Until that time, financial markets were confident that the ECB would be able to keep inflation at least close to 2% (in any case no more than 2.2%) for many years. Moreover, market-based measures were largely in line with survey-based measures. In 2008, financial markets expected that inflation would sharply decline in the near future due to the widespread recession. However, since September of that year, market-based expectations have become more erratic and are no longer in line with survey-based measures. In fact, they seem to point to a significant increase in expected inflation in the near future. Actually, such an increase does not suggest that financial markets expect a recovery in the near future, but is largely due to an increase in real yields – i.e. yields of inflation-indexed bonds – compared to nominal bonds' yields. As you learned in Chapter 15, higher bond yields imply lower bond prices, as the price of a bond varies inversely with the

Table 25.3 Summary of available measures of euro area inflation more than 12 months ahead

Source	Agents	Frequency	Horizons
Survey-based measures			
European Commission consumer survey	Consumers	Monthly	Twelve months ahead
ECB Survey of Professional Forecasters	Professional forecasters	Quarterly	– Current and next calendar years (and rolling horizons one and two years ahead) – Five years ahead
Consensus Economics	Professional forecasters	Monthly Biannual	– Current and next calendar years – Six to ten years ahead
Euro Zone Barometer	Professional forecasters	Monthly Quarterly	– Current and next calendar years – Four years ahead
Financial market-based measures			
Break-even inflation rates	Financial market participants	Intra-day	At present, between two and around 30 years ahead
Inflation-linked swap rates	Financial market participants	Intra-day	Two to 30 years ahead

hypothetical rate of inflation at which the expected real – i.e. inflation-adjusted – return on the two bonds would be the same if both were held until maturity (as you learned in Chapter 15).

2. *Inflation-linked swap rates.* Inflation-linked swap rates can be used as an additional source of information about market expectations of future inflation. In an inflation-linked swap agreement, an investor commits to a single payment on the basis of a fixed rate agreed at the beginning and, in return, receives payments based on realised inflation over the life of the contract.

Source: 'Measures of Inflations Expectations in the euro area', in *European Central Bank, Monthly Bulletin*, July 2006.

nominal interest rate. Following the massive financial transactions carried out by several investors who wanted or needed to sell their bonds in the autumn of 2008, bond prices fell and real yields increased.

The ECB and the enlargement of the EU

Scarcely had the EU grown to 15 members when preparations began for a new enlargement on an unprecedented scale. In the mid-1990s, the former Soviet-bloc countries (Bulgaria, the Czech Republic, Hungary, Poland, Romania and Slovakia), the three Baltic states that had been part of the Soviet Union (Estonia, Latvia and Lithuania), one of the republics of former Yugoslavia (Slovenia) and two Mediterranean countries (Cyprus and Malta) began knocking at the EU's door.

The EU welcomed this chance to help stabilise the European continent and to extend the benefits of European integration to these young democracies. Negotiations on future membership opened in December 1997. The EU enlargement to 25 countries took place on 1 May 2004 when ten of the 12 candidates joined. Bulgaria and Romania followed on 1 January 2007. It is expected that, in the years after enlargement, a few of the new members will join the monetary union, partly because the euro is not an option but an integral part of the European constitution (and indeed the UK, Sweden and Denmark have had to obtain a waiver to stay temporarily outside the euro), and partly because one of the reasons why the countries of Central and Eastern Europe wanted to enter the EU is to adopt the euro as their currency.

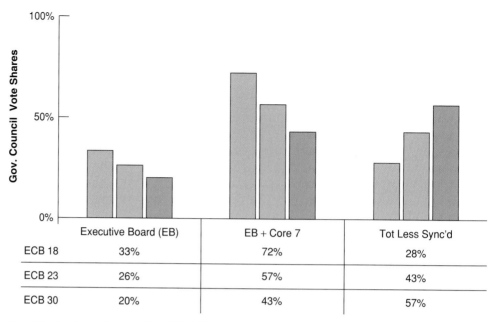

Figure 25.6

Possible coalitions in the Governing Council of the ECB

Source: Twelve is Company, Twenty-seven is a Crowd: Preparing the ECB for Enlargement, *CEPR*, 09/2001, Giavazzi Francesco with R. Balwin, E. Berglof and M. Widgrén.

	Executive Board (EB)	EB + Core 7	Tot Less Sync'd
ECB 18	33%	72%	28%
ECB 23	26%	57%	43%
ECB 30	20%	43%	57%

Note: The last two columns add to 100%. The 1st bar is the ECB18, 2nd bar is ECB23 and 3rd ECB30. Core 7 = D, F, I, NL, B, L, A.
Less Synchronised = Ire, P, E, Fin, Gr and Entrants in ECB23 and 30

How would the ECB work if the number of countries adopting the euro should increase to include all EU members? The answer is pretty badly. Monetary policy cannot be decided by an assembly of 31 members: the governors of the 24 national central banks, plus the six members of the Executive Board of the ECB. Such a large assembly is not suitable for taking swift and efficient decisions on interest rates. Furthermore, since each member of the Governing Council has one vote, and decisions require a simple majority, coalitions of countries could emerge that represent a relatively small fraction of the GDP of the EMU, but could have the majority of the Council.

Figure 25.6 shows the possible majorities that could arise in an enlarged Governing Council voting with the current rules. Note first that the relative weight of the Executive Committee – the six members of the Council that do not come from the national central banks – decreases with the size of the Council. Remember that in the case of the Fed, the Executive Committee has a majority in the Open Market Committee, the committee which decides monetary policy. In the figure, we take into account the ECB before the accession of Cyprus, Malta, Slovakia and Slovenia to EMU (12 countries + six members of the Executive Committee, a total of 18), an EMU enlarged to 17 countries (the first 12, plus the UK, Denmark and Sweden, and two countries from Central Europe) and finally an EMU which coincides with the union enlarged to 25 countries and in which the Board is composed of 31 people. Note that in the larger configuration (25 countries and 31 members of the Council) the Executive Board plus the governors of seven countries that represent the heart of the EMU (Germany, France, Italy, Belgium, Holland, Austria and Luxembourg) are no longer a majority. Instead, a coalition of countries 'not synchronised', that is, whose economies are less correlated with the heart of the EMU (Ireland, Portugal, Greece, Spain, Finland and the countries of Central and Eastern Europe), would have a majority in the Governing Council.

SUMMARY

- The Europeans have always been concerned about the volatility of the exchange rate between their currencies. First, they live in very open economies, where international trade is an important component of national income. Second, the wide fluctuations in exchange rates in Europe in the 1920s and 1930s are seen as having contributed to the crisis of national economies in the period between the wars. A final factor is the Common Agricultural Market, which needs stable exchange rates to operate properly. After the collapse of the Bretton Woods system, the response of Europeans to the high volatility of exchange rates that had occurred in the 1970s was the EMS, an agreement of exchange limited to European countries where the mark acted as the anchor of the system. The EMS allowed a period of relatively stable exchange rates, but between 1979 and 1992 there were ten devaluations: in each case the central parity of one or more European currencies were devalued against the mark.

- In the EMS devaluations were not unilateral decisions, but collegial; when a currency reached the top margin of fluctuation, the central bank of that country had two options: raise interest rates in order to defend the exchange or request a realignment, that is, a devaluation of the central parity.

- The Maastricht Treaty is a fundamental document for the history of European integration and for the birth of the euro. It established some convergence criteria that countries aspiring to enter the EMU were obliged to meet. The criteria adopted by the treaty concerned in particular: exchange rate stability, convergence of interest rates in the long run, inflation rates and two indicators of public finance: the deficit / GDP ratio and debt ratio.

- Monetary policy in the euro area is managed by the European Central Bank (ECB) which, together with national central banks, forms the European System of Central Banks (ESCB).

- The basic task of the ECB is to conduct monetary policy in the EMU. Article 105.1 of the Maastricht Treaty gives absolute priority to the objective of price stability.

- While the formulation of monetary policy is the responsibility of the ECB Governing Council, the implementation of monetary policy is given to the Executive Board of the ECB, according to the decisions and guidelines established by the Governing Council.

- In order to achieve its objectives, the Eurosystem has at its disposal a set of instruments of monetary policy: open market operations, and the standing facilities of the institutions subject to the ESCB's minimum reserve system (known as counterparties); it also requires banks to hold minimum reserves on accounts with the Eurosystem.

KEY TERMS

European Economic and Monetary Union (EMU) 518	competitive devaluation 520	Maastricht Treaty 525	longer-term refinancing operations (LTROs) 531
European Monetary System (EMS) 518	Common Agricultural Policy 520	European System of Central Banks (ESCB) 527	fine-tuning operations 531
exchange rate fluctuations 519	Bretton Woods 521	two pillar strategy 529	structural operations 531
degree of openness 519	controls on capital flows 524	open market operation 530	standing facilities 531
		main refinancing operations 531	minimum reserves 531

QUESTIONS AND PROBLEMS

QUICK CHECK

1. *Using the information in this chapter, label each of the following statements true, false or uncertain. Explain briefly.*

a. European countries have always been negatively affected by exchange rate volatility among their currencies (prior to Euro adoption) because their economies are heavily integrated with one another.

b. A system of fixed exchange rates and a common currency are perfect substitutes.

c. Countries that form a monetary union have to set rules for their fiscal policies to maintain the stability of their exchange rate.

d. To be admitted to the European Monetary Union, countries must satisfy a set of minimum requirements based on a set of macroeconomic variables.

e. The European Central Bank pursues as its main objective the goal of price stability.

f. During its first ten years of life, the European Central Bank has *de facto* behaved as the Bundesbank would have done.

2. *Describe why the European Monetary System was not an efficient mechanism to limit exchange rate volatility among European countries.*

DIG DEEPER

3. The ECB open market operations

Describe the main open market operations carried out by the European Central Bank and their objectives. Visit the website of the European Central Bank and find the section on 'Open Market Operations'. Read the most recent 'Weekly Financial Statement' (the section about 'Items related to monetary policy operations') and collect the data about the Eurosystem's transactions during that week. Explain briefly what might be the reasons for the difference compared to the preceding week.

4. Import propensity and exchange rate changes

In Chapter 7 you learned that the higher the share of exports or imports in total income, the greater the effect, on the same income, of a change in the exchange rate. In this problem you will compare two economies with different propensities to import.

Suppose that exports and imports of country A and country B are described by the following relations:

$$X = X(Y^*, \varepsilon) = aY^* - b\varepsilon$$

$$IM = IM(Y, \varepsilon) = \alpha Y + \beta\varepsilon$$

$$NX = X - IM/\varepsilon$$

where the two countries differ only in terms of import propensity. Country A has a higher import propensity than country B ($\alpha_A > \alpha_B$).

a. Draw net exports as a function of output for each country in the same graph.

b. What is the slope of the net export function?

c. Is the relation between import propensity and Y_{TB} positive or negative? Explain briefly.

d. Does the import propensity impact on the sensitivity of net exports to changes in the exchange rate? (*Hint:* derive the net export function with respect to the exchange rate and see what happens to that derivative following a change in the exchange rate.)

e. How does this relates to the discussion about European countries being adverse to exchange rate volatility?

EXPLORE FURTHER

5. The Taylor rule

In this chapter you learned that the way monetary authorities set interest rates can be described by the following formula, which is know as Taylor rule (from the name of an economist, John Taylor, who was observing the US economy in the 1980s):

$$R_t = a_0 + a_1(p^e_{t+1} - p^*) + a_2(y_t + y^*)$$

Go to the website of your country's central bank (the ECB if you are in the EMU), and download the data about potential GDP, real GDP, the rate of inflation and the short term interest rate for the past ten years. Copy and paste them in your favourite spreadsheet.

a. Compute the average inflation for each year.

b. Assuming there is a target inflation of 2%, say what the real interest rate should have been if monetary authorities had followed the Taylor rule written above.

c. How would your answer change if the difference between potential output and actual output was bigger? Explain briefly.

We invite you to visit the Blanchard page on the Prentice Hall website, at **www.prenhall.com/blanchard** for this chapter's World Wide Web exercises.

FURTHER READING

- For an analysis of the role of the EMS in countries with high inflation you can read **F. Giavazzi and M. Pagano, 'The Advantage of Tying One's Hands: EMS Discipline and Central Bank Credibility'**, *European Economic Review*, 32, 1055–1075, 1988.

- If you want to know about European countries which tried to limit exchange rate flexibility before eventually deciding to adopt the euro, you should read F. Giavazzi and A. Giovannini, *Limiting Exchange Rate Flexibility: The European Monetary System*, MIT Press, 1989.

Chapter 26

THE EURO: THE INS AND THE OUTS

In the previous chapter we described the European Economic and Monetary Union, its history and the functioning of its institutions. In this chapter we focus on the single European currency, the euro.

Before the 2007–2010 crisis, the question often posed was whether there was a chance that the euro area might fall apart. Many observers worried that countries like Greece, Italy and Portugal were doing so poorly that they could have succumbed to the temptation to exit the euro in order to regain the ability to use the exchange rate as a policy instrument (that is, to be able to devalue the exchange rate in order to increase competitiveness and to escape from a recession). Inside the euro, these countries would have needed large real wage adjustments to restore a balance between nominal wage growth, productivity and inflation. A devaluation, as we have seen in Chapter 19, is a way to reduce – albeit only temporarily – real wages without cutting nominal wages. However, the possibility of either country abandoning the euro today seems rather remote. At the beginning the crisis – paradoxically perhaps – strengthened the euro area. Countries with traditionally 'weak' currencies have realised that, without the anchor of the euro, they would have experienced a loop similar to the one that hit Iceland or Hungary (and, to a lesser extent, also the UK): a speculative attack and a balance of payments crisis. At the time of writing, February 2010, the difficulty of adjusting real wages when a devaluation is impossible has come back to haunt the euro area, most notably in Greece.

This chapter tackles a number of issues, some involving the euro area member countries and others involving countries that decided to opt out or not to join EMU:

- Section 26.1 discusses the economic reasons for a monetary union and whether the euro area meets them, i.e. whether it is an **optimal currency area**.

- Section 26.2 reviews the first ten years of the euro (1999–2009).

- Section 26.3 asks why some European countries decided to opt out of the single currency, and whether the recent financial and economic turmoil has altered the incentives to join EMU.

26.1 IS EUROPE AN OPTIMAL CURRENCY AREA?

In Chapter 25 we outlined the main stages of monetary integration among the EU countries. At this point, we pause to reflect on the purely economic reasons for monetary union, highlighting the advantages and disadvantages that may result from the decision to create a currency union. Recall that in the previous chapter we listed the advantages for the European common market of a fixed exchange rate regime without currency oscillations. However, we have never discussed the possible costs associated with that choice. Only with an analysis of costs and benefits it is possible to judge the welfare implications of monetary union for European citizens. In fact, a group of countries is said to constitute an 'optimal currency area' only if the (macroeconomic and microeconomic) benefits from having just one currency outweigh the costs.

Robert Mundell, Nobel Prize for economics in 1999, was the first economist to suggest, back in the late 1960s, that European countries might form an optimal currency area, pointing out the costs and benefits arising from the choice to abandon exchange rate flexibility forever. If we are to know whether the EU (or a group of countries in general) is an optimal currency area, the various benefits of forming a monetary union have to be compared to the costs which arise when countries give away exchange rate flexibility for ever. In various chapters of the book, we have come across some of the advantages of adopting a common currency. We summarise the costs and benefits of a monetary union in the focus box below.

We are now ready to start answering our initial question: is the euro area an optimal currency area? To answer this question we need to understand to what extent European economies are likely to face asymmetric shocks. (However, before answering, make sure you have read the Focus box below.)

FOCUS
Costs and benefits of a monetary union

The major benefits of joining a monetary union are both macroeconomic and microeconomic. As we mentioned in Chapter 25, the microeconomic benefits of a monetary union are:

- *Reduced uncertainty*. For example, the elimination of exchange rate fluctuations removes the uncertainty about interest rate differentials among member countries and hence the uncertainty about discounted present value of future profits (as you learned in Chapter 14).
- *Reduced transaction costs*. Before monetary union, in a round-trip through all European countries, the conversion costs from one currency to the next one cost 47% of the initial sum. The European commission estimated such costs at 0.25–0.5% of EU GDP per year.
- *Price transparency*. Before monetary union, prices for identical goods (e.g. a given brand of car) differed substantially across European countries. A common currency, by easing price comparisons, has reduced price differentials (although price differences still exist due to transport costs and tax differences).

The main macroeconomic benefits of a monetary union are:

- *Anti-inflationary reputation*. As we saw in Chapter 25, a country with a pro-inflationary reputation (e.g. Italy), may dramatically improve its reputation by forming a monetary union with a country with a very good reputation (e.g. Germany). Compared to a peg, a monetary union is more credible as it is irreversible (see Chapter 19). Notice, however, that a country could achieve the same outcome, while at the same time maintaining monetary independence, by simply making the central bank independent (e.g. the UK or Sweden).
- **Monetary policy** coordination. As we saw in Chapter 18, in the short run, a monetary expansion under flexible exchange rates leads to a depreciation and increases output at home at the expense of foreign output ('beggar-thy-neighbour policy'). Governments usually ignore negative effects on other countries ('negative externalities'), and all countries might eventually lose

One way to quantify the importance of asymmetric shocks in Europe is to study how the level of economic activity in the different regions of a European country fluctuates relative to other regions of the same country. In fact, if economic activity (i.e. output) in a given region of a country is highly correlated to economic activity in the other regions of the same country, this means that the country does not experience idiosyncratic shocks within its borders. If, instead, output in a given region of a country is not highly correlated with output in the other regions of the same country, this means that the country faces asymmetric shocks within its borders. In other words, regions within the same country display asymmetric business cycles when their level of economic activity fluctuates relative to other regions in the same country. These asymmetric business cycles may have their origin in differences in the pattern of specialisation – that is, of the mix of goods being produced – in different regions of the same country and this may lead to asymmetric shocks within a country to the extent that different sectors may face different demand and/or supply conditions. (Instead, regions of a single country generally share the same economic policy and therefore policy differences should not be responsible for regional fluctuations at a country level.)

After ten years of monetary union, data are available which can be analysed to see to what extent member countries did face asymmetric shocks. In Table 26.1, we look at the correlation between the growth of GDP of the regions within a same country and the growth of national GDP for the decade 1996–2006 (which covers the transition from individual country currencies to the euro). The data suggest that the process of European integration is going in the right direction: overall, the regions of each country are becoming more European and less national. Indeed, in each of the four largest European economies, economic activity in the regions of a same country has become less correlated (after 2001, compared to the second half of the 1990s) with what happens in the other regions of that

if everybody tries to depreciate with no gain. (The 1930s were an example of the dramatic costs of such policies.) A common currency eliminates such externalities.

- *European seignorage.* As we described in the Focus box 'Euro vs US dollar as a leading international reserve currency' in Chapter 4, as the euro starts playing the role of a reserve currency, its share in world reserves will increase, and so will European seignorage. An increase of the share in world reserves from 20% to 30% is worth 0.5% of GDP.
- *Trade effects.* Last but not least, currency unions have positive effects on trade among member countries. According to the recent empirical literature on the trade effects of the euro, the common currency did boost intra-euro area trade by something between 5% and 10% on average (but divergent estimates exist, suggesting that the euro's trade effects might be even larger).

The main cost of sacrificing exchange rate flexibility between different regions, in the presence of rigidities in prices and wages, depends upon the magnitude of **asymmetric shocks** that affect these regions. Economists define *asymmetric shocks* as those unexpected changes in demand and/or in aggregate supply that hit one country but not its main trading partners. A violent and sudden fall in demand for French wine, which has no effect on aggregate demand in Ireland, is an example of an asymmetric shock. Aggregate demand falls in France, but not in Ireland. To return to goods market equilibrium, the real exchange rate has to adjust, and this is easier under flexible than under fixed exchange rates.

To understand why this is the case, let us go back to our discussion of adjustment in Chapter 19. If the nominal exchange rate is fixed, a decrease of aggregate demand in France reduces output (if prices/wages are sticky in the short run and the real exchange rate is also sticky). If the exchange rate between France and Ireland cannot be changed, the adjustment to such a shock will require lower prices, and thus lower wages, in France, relative to Ireland. Under flexible exchange rates, the nominal exchange rate would change to bring about the necessary change in the real exchange rate (automatic stabilisation). So a major cost of a monetary union is the loss of the exchange rate as an automatic stabiliser in the event of asymmetric shocks.

Table 26.1 Correlation between regional and aggregate GDP growth

	1996–2000		2001–2006	
	National	**EA12**	**National**	**EA12**
France (22 regions)	0.78	0.60	0.57	0.55
Germany (39 regions)	0.82	0.62	0.58	0.57
Italy (21 regions)	0.98	0.11	0.50	0.35
UK (37 regions)	0.94	−0.66	0.87	0.61

Source: A. Fatàs, 'EMU, Countries or Regions? Lessons from the EMS Experience, *European Economic Review*, 41, 1997, 207–247.

country than it does with the whole euro area. This is especially true for the three countries that joined the euro, and to a lesser extent for the UK; but also in the UK the growth of GDP at the regional level has become more correlated with what happens in the whole euro area than with what happens across the UK. In particular, notice how the correlation between GDP growth in UK regions and GDP growth in the euro area was negative in the second half of the 1990s, and became positive after 2001. This suggests that UK regions are becoming (much) more European and (a little) less British. Notice also that French and German regions, on the contrary, seem to have been subject to (slightly) more asymmetric shocks after 2001 than in the second half of the 1990s.

What can we learn from these data? If the national components of business cycles become less and less important, then having a common currency must be considered superior (in terms of dealing with asymmetric shocks) than maintaining national currencies. If, instead, the differences between regional fluctuations and aggregate fluctuations had remained large, suggesting that asymmetric shocks have remained important, this could have been a problem for the functioning of monetary union.

Intra-industry trade occurs when a country imports and exports the same good or, more generally, goods belonging to the same sector, for example cars versus cars.

Inter-industry trade occurs when a country imports and exports different goods, or goods belonging to different sectors, that is cars versus umbrellas.

What about Europe? Are differences between regional fluctuations and aggregate fluctuations large or small? Remember from Chapter 25 that European countries show a great diversity among them, in terms of per capita income, unemployment levels, sectoral specialisation and productive structure. Asymmetric shocks are more likely between countries which produce different products, because different sectors are likely to face different demand and supply conditions. Therefore, European countries whose imports and exports are largely dominated by products belonging to the same sectors, i.e. where trade is largely intra-industry, should face less asymmetric shocks than countries whose trade flows mainly consist of different products (inter-industry trade).

As we have discussed in this section, for many European regions the possibility of facing asymmetric shocks has decreased as economic integration within Europe has proceeded, but the same might not be true for all member countries. In fact, some regions outside the core EU countries and those with less diversified production structure and concentrated specialisation patterns still might have to face changes in supply and/or demand conditions which do not hit the other regions of the same country. In such cases, participating in a monetary union could be rather costly. However, there are factors that may reduce the costs of a monetary union (and therefore of the choice of giving up exchange rate flexibility) even when asymmetric shocks are large.

A major factor that could reduce the costs of a monetary union in the presence of asymmetric shocks among member countries is high labour mobility between regions. A favourite argument in the debate on how to deal with potential asymmetric shocks in Europe is to say that, if labour was mobile, the loss of exchange rate flexibility would not be crucial. Labour mobility implies that if aggregate demand fell, in our example, in France, labour would migrate from France to other European countries, thus reducing the natural level of output in France and increasing the natural level of output in Ireland, and so re-establishing equilibrium without a change in the real exchange rate.

Table 26.2 Growth rate of interregional migration (percentage of total population, annual average)

	Canada	United States	Germany	Italy	UK
1970–79	0.43	1.20	0.27	0.37	0.47
1980–89	0.44	0.58	0.34	0.33	0.26
1990–95	0.52	0.06	0.31	0.40	0.20

Source: M. Obstfeld and G. Peri, Regional Non-Adjustment and Fiscal Policy, *Economic Policy*, 1999, 26, 207–247.

How mobile are workers among European countries? Table 26.2 shows the percentage of annual net migration between regions (or states) of five countries. It shows how interregional mobility in Italy and Germany is between one third and a half that of mobility within the USA or Canada. In conclusion, considering simultaneously the importance of asymmetric shocks and low labour mobility, it is difficult to argue that the euro area is an optimal monetary area. (In truth, if we consider Canada and the USA jointly, it is not necessarily true that the optimal currency area would match the *political* borders. Mundell, in a famous 1961 article, stated that, from an economic point of view, it would have been more efficient to divide North America in a longitudinal direction between East and West, rather than between north (Canada) and south (USA) as it has been historically divided.)

However, this argument is purely theoretical: prices adjust more quickly than labour moves. Therefore, even a high degree of labour mobility between regions would not be enough to avoid the impact that asymmetric shocks might have on different regions. This is true even in the USA, which has no linguistic barriers and where there is a great deal of cross-state migration.

Based on the evidence described above, some economists argue that not only is Europe *not* an optimal monetary union, but not even individual European countries are. There is, however, a huge difference between the EU and a nation state. Nation states, unlike the EU, have a mechanism to deal with asymmetric shocks: a common fiscal policy which allows the use of transfers from one region to another (between the south and the north of the UK, for instance) to offset the effects of asymmetric shocks. The use of fiscal policy as a mechanism for redistribution between regions in order to protect against asymmetric shocks has been studied by several economists, and various studies have concluded that this role is extremely important. Between 20% and 30% of the effects of asymmetric shocks to the income of US states is compensated for by fiscal policy, i.e. by transfers from the Federal Government in Washington. Similar results apply to Canada and the UK. In the EU, fiscal policy cannot work because there are virtually no Europe-wide taxes, and therefore this means of adjusting to asymmetric shocks is precluded.

In the euro area, not only is there no common fiscal policy (and hence the possibility of fiscal transfers among countries) but also national governments might not be allowed to use their fiscal policies as a means to maintain EU stability in the face of asymmetric shocks. In fact, as we have seen in Chapter 25, the process that led to the birth of a single European currency has requested, through the Maastricht criteria, that member countries accept some constraint on their fiscal policies. In 1997, these conditions became permanent and were included in the so-called Stability and Growth Pact. One interesting question about the effects of the Pact is whether it has limited the ability to use automatic stabilisers, thereby contributing to making recessions more severe.

◁ Remember the Maastrict criteria explained in the Focus box in Chapter 25.

26.2 THE FIRST TEN YEARS OF THE EURO (1999–2009)

Ten years into the euro experience we can evaluate the extent to which the single currency has fulfilled its promises. To provide an assessment of the effects of the euro on member countries, let us first recall what these promises were.

Business cycle convergence

A major debate took place while the euro was being designed over whether the single currency would induce convergence or divergence in the economic performance of member countries. The argument in favour of convergence was simple: a single monetary policy means no more idiosyncratic (i.e. country-specific) nominal shocks, and thus one less reason for divergent economic cycles. The fiscal rules introduced with the Stability and Growth Pact added to this argument by limiting the ability to use fiscal policy as a stabilising tool. At the same time, increased economic integration (reduced transport costs, harmonised regulation, higher mobility of capital and labour) would induce specialisation. As countries, or regions, specialise in specific industries they would be subject to industry-specific shocks: this would result in more, not less macroeconomic divergence. The two mechanisms may refer to different time horizons: specialisation takes time, while more synchronised nominal shocks happen almost instantaneously once a monetary union is formed. A lot has been written on **business cycle convergence** within the euro area and how it has been affected by the EMU, but the literature is far from being consensual.

Recent studies show that member countries which had similar levels of per capita GDP in the 1970s (the core group) have also experienced similar business cycles since then, and no significant change is associated with the EMU. For the other countries, there is a lot of uncertainty and not many generalisations can be made: but in this group as well, no clear change since the EMU can be identified. It is interesting to note that the countries in the core group have remained homogeneous over time while countries that started further away from the average have shown no tendency to become closer to the euro area. Differences in levels of economic activity remain persistent. Some countries seem to have converged, like Spain; others do not seem to have caught up, like Greece. Ireland, on the other hand, has caught up very fast. But overall, the evidence shows that in the first ten years business cycles have hardly changed.

The loss of exchange rate flexibility and monetary policy has had almost no effect on output co-movements across countries even if, as has been emphasised by many observers, EMU member states have differed from one another with respect to degree of competitiveness, real interest rates and other economic characteristics. Although the differences in output growth across the euro area countries are not large, differences in output growth remain persistent and reflect differences in structural and institutional features across countries. This is what we turn to in the next section.

Growth

Growth has not been uniform within the monetary union, nor was it uniform before monetary union. As shown in Figure 26.1, the 12 countries participating in the original euro area have grown at very different rates since 1970 and continued to grow at very different rates after 1999.

One possible explanation for output growth differentials is that they may partly reflect the catch-up of lower-income countries. In fact, as you learned in Chapter 11, countries with a level of capital per worker much lower than the steady-state level will grow faster than those with a level of capital per worker closer to their steady-state. The left-hand panel of Figure 26.1 indicates that among the low-income group of countries of the 1970s – Ireland, Greece, Spain and Portugal – some limited catching up occurred in Ireland and Portugal during the 1970s and 1980s. However, these four countries were still well below the euro area average in 1989. Ireland, Greece and Spain subsequently made considerable progress, and Ireland has even been able to reach and then substantially overtake the euro area average in recent years (see the right-hand panel of the figure). By contrast, per capita GDP in Portugal relative to the euro area average has declined slightly since 2000.

Also, compared to an overall average cumulative growth of 9.3% over the period 2001–2010, Finland, Greece, Ireland and Spain have grown much more, twice or three times as much, while Austria, Belgium, France and the Netherlands have grown closer to

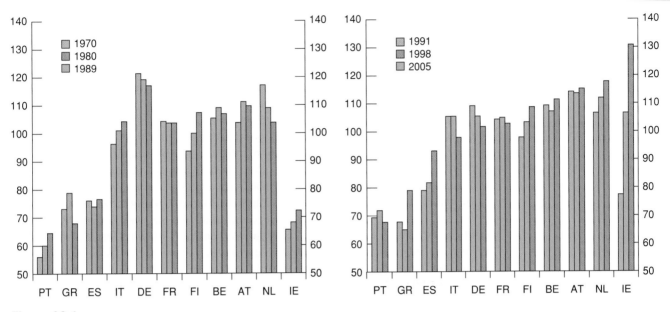

Figure 26.1

Per capita GDP in euro area economies since 1970

Source: European Central Bank, *Monthly Bulletin*, April 2007.

the average. On the other hand, Italy and Portugal and, to a lesser extent Germany, have grown less than average.

Apart from initial conditions, supply-side factors are behind these growth differentials: as you learned in Chapter 11, demand factors affect growth in the short run while in the medium run growth is likely to depend more on supply-side factors, such as structural and institutional factors.

Looking at the supply side, let us go back to the growth accounting exercise we presented in Chapter 11. In that chapter, we saw that real output growth per capita can be broken down into changes in hourly labour productivity (real GDP/total hours worked), changes in hours worked per worker and changes in the participation to the labour force (labour force/population). By applying this decomposition to the growth of real output per capita of euro member countries since 1999, we can shed some light on the output growth differentials among them.

Table 26.3 suggests that the factors behind real GDP growth – labour productivity, hours per worker and labour force participation – played different roles across countries. In particular, with regard to labour productivity, it is worth noting that some euro area countries,

Table 26.3 The sources of growth differentials across euro area economies since 1999

	Real GDP per capita	Labour productivity	Hours per worker	Participation
Austria	1.5	1.6	0.2	−0.2
Belgium	1.7	1.4	0.3	0.0
Finland	2.8	2.1	0.7	−0.1
France	1.5	2.1	−0.6	0.0
Germany	1.1	1.5	0.1	−0.5
Greece	4.0	3.7	−0.4	0.7
Ireland	5.2	3.8	0.9	0.4
Italy	0.8	0.4	−0.9	1.3
Luxembourg	3.6	1.7	−0.1	1.9
Netherlands	1.6	1.5	0.3	−0.3
Portugal	1.0	1.0	0.3	−0.4
Spain	2.5	0.5	0.4	1.5
Euro area	1.4	1.2	0.0	0.2

Source: calculated on data from European Central Bank and Groningen Growth and Development Centre.

such as Italy, Portugal and Spain, lagged far behind the euro area average (1.2% per year). On the other hand, Greece and Ireland registered a large improvement in labour productivity, which is the major factor explaining their high growth rates since 1999. Secondly, euro area economies behaved very differently in terms of hours worked: hours per worker declined in France, Greece, Italy and Luxembourg while they increased in the other countries, especially in Ireland and Finland. Finally, changes in labour force participation were very different across countries: it increased between 1.5 and 2 percentage points per year in Luxembourg and Spain, as a result of positive demographic developments (including immigration flows). However, in a certain number of countries labour force participation declined, most notably in Germany and Portugal. This is the most important factor explaining why these two countries grew less than average after 1999.

Overall, the greatest differences across European countries are rooted in diverse levels of labour productivity: the successful economic performance of Ireland since 1999 is largely due to improvement of labour productivity (whereas in Spain, growth of real GDP per capita has been mainly due to increased participation). Productivity performance has also been higher than average in three small European countries: Austria, Belgium and the Netherlands. Finland and France also have labour productivity which is almost twice the euro area average; here, the divergent trends in the number of hours worked – increasing in Finland, decreasing in France – is at the root of the significant difference in economic performance since 1999.

But how can differences in labour productivity be explained? As you learned in Chapter 11, labour productivity depends on total factor productivity and the capital stock available for the working population. It has been shown that the high levels of productivity in some member countries come from differences in total productivity growth which, in turn, have benefited from decreased product market regulation in the goods sector and, even more so, in the services sectors, as well as in labour and capital markets. On the other hand, regulations limiting competition in such markets have a negative impact on technological progress, and thus on productivity growth. There is also growing evidence that different degrees of efficiency in the financial system can explain differences in total productivity across countries. On some of these issues, European countries have converged to similar levels, as in the case of product market regulations (as you saw in Chapter 7); but on many other issues, there is still a long way to go before member countries can (if ever) reach similar conditions.

So, how has the euro affected member countries in terms of convergence of income per capita? Apparently not too much. Again, as for business cycle convergence, despite the loss of exchange rate flexibility and monetary policy independence, member states still show large differences in growth rates due to structural differences in the underlying sources of growth: labour productivity, hours worked and labour force participation.

26.3 SHOULD THE OUTS JOIN?

Remember from Chapter 25 that the clause of 'opting out' refers to the choice to postpone the decision of whether or not to join at a later date.

Since its beginning, when the euro area consisted of 12 countries, four more have joined: Cyprus, Malta and Slovakia. Yet major countries are still reluctant to do so, most notably Denmark, Sweden and the UK. In this section, we will briefly summarise the motivations and the political and economic events that accompanied the decision not to join EMU by two countries: Sweden, which did not opt out of EMU, but has not yet decided to join; and the UK which, like Denmark, explicitly postponed to a later date the decision whether to adopt the euro or not.

When the Swedish government negotiated its entry into the EU in 1993–1994, the negotiations did not include an exemption from adopting the euro. In contrast to Denmark and the UK, which did obtain such an exemption, Sweden is therefore required by EU law to join EMU and adopt the euro as soon as the convergence criteria specified in the Maastricht Treaty are fulfilled. Nevertheless, the Swedish Parliament (the Riksdag) decided in 1997 that Sweden would not join the Exchange Rate Mechanism (ERM) of the EMS, and the

Swedish central bank (Sveriges Riksbank) has followed a policy of inflation targeting with a flexible exchange rate since 1993.

As a consequence, in the assessments made by the European Commission prior to the launch of EMU in 1999 and every two years since 2000, Sweden has been judged not to fulfil the criterion regarding exchange rate stability, which requires the member state to participate in the ERM. Sweden therefore is a member state with derogation but not exempted from participating in the EMU. A national referendum on Swedish participation in EMU was held in September 2003, and the result was a rejection of membership with 56% of the electorate voting against and 42% voting in favour. As a consequence, the Riksdag decision of 1997 remains in force, and Sweden remains outside EMU.

How should one consider the decision by a country not to join, from a purely economic point of view? In the case of Sweden, a recent study by Ulf Söderström (an economist at the Riksbank) looks at whether or not participation in the monetary union would be advantageous for the country. On the one hand, the business cycle since the mid-1990s has been closely correlated with the euro area economies: this would suggest that Sweden has overall been subject to similar shocks to those that hit the euro area. But the study also showed that the exchange rate has acted to destabilise, rather than stabilise, the Swedish economy: this suggests that an independent monetary policy with a flexible exchange rate could be rather costly for Sweden. The evidence thus is inconclusive. Finally, counterfactual simulations of a model of the Swedish economy suggest that Swedish inflation and GDP growth might have been slightly higher if Sweden had been a member of EMU since the launch in 1999, but also that GDP growth might have been more volatile.

In the UK, the euro has been a long-standing part of the debate about the implications of the country's integration into the EU. The UK affirmed its commitment to eventually adopting the euro in repeated official statements: in 1972, 1974, 1985 and 1989. But since 1974, UK policy makers have expressed reservations about economic and monetary union, which were finally made official with the securing of an 'opt-out' clause in 1991 that was executed in 1997.

A major element of the opposition to euro membership has taken the form of opposition to the perceived loss of political sovereignty, and some adherents to that argument regard it as a sufficient condition for rejecting the monetary union even if euro membership could be shown to be desirable on economic grounds. This seemed to be the stance taken by several members of the Conservative governments over the 1990s, but that position was decisively renounced as government policy when in 1997 the Blair Government stated that economic merits would be the only criteria for entry.

Shortly after its election in 1997, the Blair Government 'committed the UK to the principle of joining the single currency', but made any recommendation about actual entry conditional on *five economic tests* being passed. The five economic tests are:

1. Are business cycles and economic structures compatible so that we and others could live with euro interest rates on a permanent basis?
2. If problems emerge, is there sufficient flexibility to deal with them
3. Would joining EMU create better conditions for firms making long-term decisions to invest in Britain?
4. What impact would entry into EMU have on the financial services industry?
5. In summary, will joining EMU promote higher growth, stability and a lasting increase in jobs?

The UK Government determined in 1997 and 2003 that these tests had not yet been satisfied, and so did not proceed to a referendum on UK membership of the euro area. Until the recent financial crisis of 2007–2010, the prospects of the UK becoming a member of the euro area seemed remote. Its continuing good macroeconomic performance over

1997–2007, the success of the inflation targeting regime and the move to even greater seniority within the UK government of critics of membership (most notably Gordon Brown's move from Chancellor of the Exchequer to Prime Minister) have all been factors reducing the likelihood of euro adoption.

Today, after the first ten years of the euro experience, we can compare the monetary policy regimes followed by the European Central Bank and Bank of England since 1999, and thus we can try to assess the likely effect that monetary union would have on UK economic performance. Economists studying the UK experience found that interest-rate variability would decline if the UK were to join EMU. Thus embracing the euro would appear to confer on the UK more stable interest rates.

Moreover, some economists suggest that the 'strong pound' period starting in 1996 and continuing during nearly a decade of the euro existence is a strong argument in favour of euro adoption. Proponents of UK participation contend that the strong pound shifted UK employment from the exchange-rate-sensitive manufacturing sector to the financial services sector, and that the increase in employment in the latter has proved to be ephemeral. The recent sudden reversal of the pound's appreciation (remember from Chapter 14 the collapse of the pound/euro exchange rate in 2009), at a time of worldwide contraction in the financial services sector, is said by advocates of euro membership to demonstrate further the disadvantage of the UK's exercise of its opt-out from euro participation.

Still, using only economic arguments, it is difficult to come to an unambiguous answer about the pros and cons of euro membership. One must accept that an important factor in the decision to join the euro is political. Countries such as the UK, which fear that the euro might be a step toward political integration and thus a threat to national sovereignty, are unlikely to join, at least until such concerns have been set aside.

Has the crisis altered the incentive to join EMU?

Throughout this chapter we have considered the various benefits arising from membership in the euro area. And we have admitted that there are also important challenges which member countries have to face, especially in the design of fiscal policy. So far, we have considered 'tranquil' times. But in a crisis, the benefits appear to be magnified. For instance, compare two otherwise similar countries (in terms of information technologies, productivity, good policies, etc.): Sweden, which decided not to join, and Finland, which joined. It is hard to tell which of the two did better over the decade preceding the crisis.

Since the start of EMU, the exchange between the Swedish currency (the krona) and the euro had remained remarkably stable – so stable that one could have argued that the Riksbank was really targeting the exchange rate rather than setting its monetary policy based on an inflation target and with a flexible exchange rate. But since the crisis erupted, the krona in a few months has depreciated by almost 10% against the euro. This has confronted Sweden with a difficult policy choice: raise interest rates to stabilise the krona–euro exchange rate or lower them to address the effects of the crisis and also a possible recession. The Swedish experience during the crisis suggests that when the times get rough euro membership becomes a clear plus.

It is interesting that Denmark, Sweden and the UK reacted to the crisis by moving in opposite directions. Sweden and the UK have given up on exchange rate stability and have lowered rates; the Danish central bank has intervened heavily in the foreign exchange market and has raised interest rates from 5% to 5.5% – to try to stabilise the exchange rate. As a result, a renewed debate about the benefits of euro membership has opened up in Denmark: some argue that the country should hold a new referendum on the euro. Even Iceland has recently applied for EU membership with a view to being able eventually to adopt the euro.

Iceland is only an extreme case of a more general phenomenon – that of a small country with its own currency, and banking sectors too large to be bailed out (should they go bankrupt) by national authorities. Others are Denmark, Sweden and Switzerland. The UK is larger but some of the arguments apply to the UK as well. And in fact a renewed debate about euro area membership has recently started in the UK.

Similar problems have manifested themselves in Central and Eastern Europe. In Hungary, almost all mortgages were denominated in Swiss francs or euros: a currency depreciation would trigger a series of personal and banking failures. Thus the country is struggling between the desire to stabilise the exchange rate and the need to expand the money supply (thus weakening the exchange rate) to provide liquidity to the economy. Thus there is no doubt in our mind that the crisis of 2007–2010 has altered the incentives to join the euro. It has also provided the countries that are already members with reasons to be more cautious about enlargement. The euro's second decade promises plenty of interesting developments.

FOCUS
How Iceland suddenly realised the potential benefits of euro membership

Iceland is a small open economy – with a population of just 300 000 – and a trade-to-GDP ratio around 80%. It has its own currency, the Icelandic króna.

In 2008, when the financial crisis started to spread around the world, Iceland was one of its first (and smaller) victims. To understand why, we have to start from the privatisation of the banking sector in Iceland which was completed in 2003. Since then, the banking system has grown enormously compared to the relatively small size of the country's GDP. Icelandic banks increased their assets from being worth slightly more than 100% of the country's GDP to being worth close to 1000% of GDP (i.e. ten times bigger than the size of the economy!).

In 2008, when the market suddenly realised that the banking system had become far too big for the national government to be able to intervene to prevent bankruptcy in case of troubles, foreign investors started to escape from the country. Massive capital outflows caused a huge depreciation of the Icelandic króna. Within a week, the three major banks collapsed, the króna's value dropped by more than 70% and the stock market lost more than 80% of its value.

For a small economy that is totally dependent on imports, such a huge depreciation caused a large increase in the cost of imported goods (with very little opportunity on the part of Icelandic consumers to switch from imported to domestic goods, as the country produces domestically a very limited range of goods).

Moreover, because of the banking crisis, Iceland has gone overnight from being one of the lowest indebted countries in Europe, to being among the highest indebted: the public sector debt increased as a result of the budgetary cost of recapitalising the banking system in order to fulfil the deposit insurance obligations. Some of the debt is denominated in foreign currency. As the króna depreciated, the interest rate on the debt servicing became much more expensive.

In response, Iceland formulated a comprehensive programme to tackle the consequences of the crisis, for which it requested a loan from the IMF. In the short run, the programme used monetary and exchange rate policies to stabilise the króna. First of all, to prevent large capital outflows from causing a further sharp drop in the króna, Iceland introduced restrictions on capital flows.

During the first year of the programme, automatic fiscal stabilisers were also allowed to work. As you learned in Chapter 23, tax revenues tend to fall during recessions and the opposite is true for public spending. Therefore, the primary fiscal deficit increased from about ½% of GDP in 2008 to about 8½% of GDP in 2009 to a predicted to reach 13% of GDP in 2010. As you learned in Chapter 21, excessive deficits are a source of concern to the extent that they translate into higher government debt.

Iceland now already has a debt-to-GDP ratio higher than 100%. There are only three other European countries (and only one OECD country outside Europe, Japan) that surpassed that threshold – Belgium, Greece and Italy. But, unlike these three countries, Iceland does not have the shelter of euro membership. Such a high debt is a source of major concern for a small open economy, even more so as it is denominated in foreign currency. In fact, to be able to borrow from abroad such a huge amount of money, relative to the size of its domestic economy, Iceland will have to pay high interest rates. This will mean a high burden on future generations.

There is no easy way out for Iceland. As you learned in Chapter 21, when the debt service increases more rapidly then the size of the economy (that is, when $i > g$), primary surpluses are needed to stabilise the debt. Instead, Iceland has been running rapidly increasing primary deficits. All the conditions are set for an exploding debt-to-GDP ratio. Inflating the debt away and defaulting are possible options, but would probably cause even more problems than they would solve.

In these circumstances, Iceland discovered that if the country were a member of EMU, it would not have experienced such a huge currency devaluation and would be better off. In fact, a weak króna does not help to boost exports, as Iceland's export basket is very limited, but only inflates the import bill.

In July 2009, Iceland applied for EU membership in order to eventually become a member of EMU. Even if the application is set on a fast-track, it will be at least a couple of years before the country will be able to join. And even then, unlike before the banking crisis, the country might not be able to fulfil the criteria to join EMU.

SUMMARY

- What are the advantages and disadvantages of a monetary union? Among the microeconomic benefits are reduced uncertainty, reduced transaction costs, price transparency; the main macroeconomic benefits are stabilisation in the face of financial market shocks, anti-inflationary reputation, monetary policy coordination, European seignorage and positive trade effects.

- The main cost of sacrificing flexibility of the exchange between different regions, in the presence of rigidities in prices and wages, depends upon the magnitude of asymmetric shocks that affect these regions. Considering the importance of asymmetric shocks and low labour mobility, it is difficult to argue that the euro is an optimal monetary union.

- Two factors reduce the costs of a monetary union for member countries in the presence of asymmetric shocks: high labour mobility between regions and high degree of openness to trade between regions.

- During the first ten years of the euro, the dynamics of economic activity in member countries hardly changed, i.e. the loss of exchange rate flexibility and monetary policy independence for individual member countries had almost no effect on output co-movements across countries.

- There are still large output growth differentials among member countries which depend largely on differences in labour productivity, on hours worked per worker and on labour participation. Trends over these variables still differ across member countries, although a catch-up process has increased output growth in some of the (once) poorest member countries.

- After a decade of existence of the euro, it is possible to compare the performance of non-member and member countries, and thus to re-assess the decision by some countries not to join. The evidence shows that there are incentives for some of them to join, although there is no consensus on how much weight should be given to the costs side. But a debate has already started on whether it would be desirable to adopt the euro, especially after the crisis of 2007–2010, which has had the effect of strengthening the euro area vis à vis non-member countries.

KEY TERMS

QUESTIONS AND PROBLEMS

QUICK CHECK

1. *Using the information in this chapter, label each of the following statements true, false or uncertain. Explain briefly.*

a. A group of countries is said to form an 'optimal currency area' only if the macroeconomic benefits from having just one currency outweigh the costs.

b. Since the introduction of the euro, price differentials have completely disappeared between euro member countries.

c. There exist divergent estimates about the positive trade effects of the euro on member countries, but all of them point to a significant increase in trade flows among member countries.

d. There is no cost of sacrificing exchange rate flexibility between different regions if wages and prices are perfectly flexible.

e. If wages and prices are not flexible, the main cost of sacrificing exchange rate flexibility between different regions depends on whether these regions face asymmetric shocks to aggregate demand.

f. Euro member countries have faced no asymmetric shocks in the first ten years of the euro; therefore the euro area can be considered an 'optimal currency area'.

2. *Describe which are the main benefits and costs of a monetary union.*

DIG DEEPER

3. Monetary policy coordination

Among the benefits of a monetary union, the need for member countries to have monetary policy coordination prevents each member country from using monetary policy in an arbitrary manner. Illustrate in a graph the advantage, with respect to aggregate welfare, of member countries not being able to use expansionary monetary policies to increase domestic output at the expense of other members' output.

4. Monetary union vs exchange rate peg

Compare the pros and cons of a monetary union with those of an exchange rate peg.

EXPLORE FURTHER

5. Correlation between regional and aggregate GDP growth

In this problem you are asked to compute the correlation between regional and aggregate EA12 GDP growth for your country (or for another country of your choice), as in Table 26.1 (which reports only a few European countries).

a. Go to the Eurostat website (***http://epp.eurostat.ec. europa.eu/portal/page/portal/eurostat/home/***) and go to the section on Statistics and then to the section on Regions and Cities. In the Regional Economic Accounts, download the regional GDP growth for the regions of your country (NUTS 2 or 3 level) for the past ten years. Now download, from the main Statistics section, the aggregate GDP growth for the Euro Area 12 (EA12) for the same years.

b. Compute the correlation between regional and national GDP growth for the two sub-periods, as in Table 26.1. Are regions in your country more or less similar to each other in terms of growth?

c. Now compute the correlation between regional and aggregate EA12 GDP growth for the two sub-periods, as in Table 26.1. Are the regions in your country more or less similar to the evolution of GDP in the EA12?

> We invite you to visit the Blanchard page on the Prentice Hall website, at **www.prenhall.com/blanchard** for this chapter's World Wide Web exercises.

FURTHER READING

- This chapter has reported some of the recent results of the empirical literature on the macroeconomic effects of the euro on member countries and on the incentives for non-members to join, most of which are inspired from *Europe and the Euro* **by Alberto Alesina and Francesco Giavazzi (eds), Chicago University Press, Chicago, IL.**

- If you want to know more about the empirical literature that studied the trade effects of the euro for member countries, read the excellent (and also short) *The Euro's trade effects* **by Richard Baldwin, ECB Working Paper No. 594, ECB, Frankfurt.**

APPENDIX 1 A maths refresher

This appendix presents the mathematical tools and the mathematical results that are used in this book.

Geometric series

Definition:

A geometric series is a sum of numbers of the form

$$1 + x + x^2 + \ldots + x^n$$

where x is a number that may be greater or smaller than 1 and x^n denotes x to the power n, that is x times itself n times.
Examples of such series are:

- The sum of spending in each round of the multiplier (Chapter 3). If c is the marginal propensity to consume, then the sum of increases in spending after $n + 1$ rounds is given by

$$1 + c + c^2 + \ldots + c^n$$

- The present discounted value of a sequence of payments of €1 each year for n years (Chapter 13), when the interest rate is equal to i:

$$1 + \frac{1}{1+i} + \frac{1}{(1+i)^2} + \ldots + \frac{1}{(1+i)^{n-1}}$$

We usually have two questions we want to answer when encountering such a series:

1. What is the sum?
2. Does the sum explode as we let n increase, decrease or does it reach a finite limit? If so, what is that limit?

The following propositions tell you what you need to know to answer these questions.

Proposition 1 tells you how to compute the sum.

Proposition 1:

$$1 + x + x^2 + \ldots + x^n = \frac{1 - x^{n+1}}{1 - x} \qquad [\text{A1.1}]$$

Here is the proof: multiply the sum by $(1 - x)$, and use the fact that $x^a x^b = x^{a+b}$ (that is, add exponents when multiplying):

$$
\begin{aligned}
(1 + x + x^2 + \ldots + x^n)(1 - x) &= 1 + x + x^2 + \ldots + x^n \\
&\quad - x - x^2 \ldots - x^n - x^{n+1} \\
&= 1 \qquad\qquad\qquad - x^{n+1}
\end{aligned}
$$

All the terms on the right except for the first and the last cancel. Dividing both sides by $(1 - x)$ gives equation (A1.1).

This formula can be used for any x and any n. If, for example, x is 0.9 and n is 10, then the sum is equal to 6.86. If x is 1.2 and n is 10, then the sum is 32.15.

Proposition 2 tells you what happens as n gets large.

Proposition 2:

If x is less than 1, the sum goes to $1/(1 - x)$ as n gets large. If x is equal to or greater than 1, the sum explodes as n gets large.

Here is the proof: if x is less than 1, then x^n goes to 0 as n gets large. Thus, from equation (A1.1), the sum goes to $1/(1 - x)$. If x is greater than 1, then x^n becomes larger and larger as n increases, $1 - x^n$ becomes a larger and larger negative number, and the ratio $(1 - x^n)/(1 - x)$ becomes a larger and larger positive number. Thus, the sum explodes as n gets large.

Application from Chapter 14:

Consider the present value of a payment of €1 forever, starting next year, when the interest rate is i. The present value is given by

$$\frac{1}{(1+i)} + \frac{1}{(1+i)^2} + \ldots \qquad [\text{A1.2}]$$

Factoring out $1/(1 + i)$, rewrite this present value as

$$\frac{1}{(1+i)}\left[1 + \frac{1}{(1+i)} + \ldots\right]$$

The term in brackets is a geometric series, with $x = 1/(1 + i)$. As the interest rate, i, is positive, x is less than 1. Applying Proposition 2, when n gets large, the term in brackets equals

$$\frac{1}{1 - \dfrac{1}{(1+i)}} = \frac{(1+i)}{(1+i-1)} = \frac{(1+i)}{i}$$

Replacing the term in brackets in the previous equation with $(1 + i)/i$ gives:

$$\frac{1}{(1+i)}\left[\frac{(1+i)}{i}\right] = \frac{1}{i}$$

The present value of a sequence of payments of €1 per year forever, starting next year, is equal to €1 divided by the interest rate. If i is equal to 5% per year, the present value equals €1/0.05 = €20.

Useful approximations

Throughout this book, we use a number of approximations that make computations easier. These approximations are most reliable when the variables x, y, z are small, say between 0% and 10%. The numerical examples in Propositions 3–10 are based on the values $x = 0.05$ and $y = 0.03$.

Proposition 3:

$$(1 + x)(1 + y) \approx (1 + x + y) \qquad [A1.3]$$

Here is the proof: Expanding $(1 + x)(1 + y)$ gives $(1 + x)(1 + y) = 1 + x + y + xy$. If x and y are small, then the product xy is very small and can be ignored as an approximation (for example, if $x = 0.05$ and $y = 0.03$, then $xy = 0.0015$). So $(1 + x)(1 + y)$ is approximately equal to $(1 + x + y)$.

For the values x and y above, for example, the approximation gives 1.08 compared to an exact value of 1.0815.

Proposition 4:

$$(1 + x)^2 \approx 1 + 2x \qquad [A1.4]$$

The proof follows directly from Proposition 3, with $y = x$. For the value of $x = 0.05$, the approximation gives 1.10, compared to an exact value of 1.1025.

Application from Chapter 15:

From arbitrage, the relation between the two-year interest rate and the current and the expected one-year interest rates is given by

$$(1 + i_{2t})^2 = (1 + i_{1t})(1 + i_{1t+1}^e)$$

Using Proposition 4 for the left side of the equation gives

$$(1 + i_{2t})^2 \approx 1 + 2i_{2t}$$

Using Proposition 3 for the right side of the equation gives

$$(1 + i_{1t})(1 + i_{1t+1}^e) \approx 1 + i_{1t} + i_{1t+1}^e$$

Using this expression to replace $(1 + i_{1t})(1 + i_{1t+1}^e)$ in the original arbitrage relation gives

$$1 + 2i_{2t} = 1 + i_{1t} + i_{1t+1}^e$$

Or, reorganising,

$$i_{2t} = \frac{(i_{1t} + i_{1t+1}^e)}{2}$$

The two-year interest rate is approximately equal to the average of the current and the expected one-year interest rates.

Proposition 5:

$$(1 + x)^n \approx 1 + nx \qquad [A1.5]$$

The proof follows by repeated application of Propositions 3 and 4. For example, $(1 + x)^3 = (1 + x)^2(1 + x) \approx (1 + 2x)(1 + x)$ by Proposition 4, $\approx (1 + 2x + x) = 1 + 3x$ by Proposition 3.

The approximation becomes worse as n increases, however. For example, for $x = 0.05$ and $n = 5$, the approximation gives 1.25, compared to an exact value of 1.2763. For $n = 10$, the approximation gives 1.50, compared to an exact value of 1.63.

Proposition 6:

$$\frac{(1 + x)}{(1 + y)} \approx (1 + x - y) \qquad [A1.6]$$

Here is the proof. Consider the product $(1 + x - y)(1 + y)$. Expanding this product gives $(1 + x - y)(1 + y) = 1 + x + xy - y^2$. If both x and y are small, then xy and y^2 are very small, so $(1 + x - y)(1 + y) \approx (1 + x)$. Dividing both sides of this approximation by $(1 + y)$ gives the proposition above.

For the values of $x = 0.05$ and $y = 0.03$, the approximation gives 1.02, while the correct value is 1.019.

Application from Chapter 14:

The real interest rate is defined by

$$(1 + r_t) = \frac{(1 + i_t)}{(1 + \pi_t^e)}$$

Using Proposition 6 gives

$$(1 + r_t) \approx (1 + i_t - \pi_t^e)$$

Simplifying,

$$r_t \approx i_t - \pi_t^e$$

This gives us the approximation we use at many points in this book: the real interest rate is approximately equal to the nominal interest rate minus expected inflation.

These approximations are also very convenient when dealing with growth rates. Define the rate of growth of x by $g_x = \Delta x / x$, and similarly for z, g_z, y and g_y. The following numerical examples are based on the values $g_x = 0.05$ and $g_y = 0.03$.

Proposition 7:

If $z = xy$, then

$$g_z \approx g_x + g_y \qquad [A1.7]$$

Here is the proof. Let Δz be the increase in z when x increases by Δx and y increases by Δy. Then, by definition:

$$z + \Delta z = (x + \Delta x)(y + \Delta y)$$

Divide both sides by z. The left side becomes

$$\frac{z + \Delta z}{z} = \left(1 + \frac{\Delta z}{z}\right)$$

The right side becomes

$$\frac{(x + \Delta x)(y + \Delta y)}{z} = \frac{(x + \Delta x)(y + \Delta y)}{x \qquad y}$$

$$= \left(1 + \frac{\Delta x}{x}\right)\left(1 + \frac{\Delta y}{y}\right)$$

where the first equality follows from the fact that $z = xy$, the second equality from simplifying each of the two fractions.

Using the expressions for the left and right sides gives

$$\left(1 + \frac{\Delta z}{z}\right) = \left(1 + \frac{\Delta x}{x}\right)\left(1 + \frac{\Delta y}{y}\right)$$

Or, equivalently,

$$(1 + g_z) = (1 + g_x)(1 + g_y)$$

From Proposition 3, $(1 + g_z) \approx (1 + g_x + g_y)$, or, equivalently,

$$g_z \approx g_x + g_y$$

For $g_x = 0.05$ and $g_y = 0.03$, the approximation gives $g_z = 8\%$, while the correct value is 8.15%.

Application from Chapter 13:

Let the production function be of the form $Y = NA$, where Y is production, N is employment and A is productivity. Denoting the growth rates of Y, N and A by g_Y, g_N and g_A, respectively, Proposition 7 implies

$$g_Y \approx g_N + g_A$$

The rate of output growth is approximately equal to the rate of employment growth plus the rate of productivity growth.

Proposition 8:

If $z = x/y$, then

$$g_z \approx g_x - g_y \qquad \text{[A1.8]}$$

Here is the proof. Let Δz be the increase in z, when x increases by Δx and y increases by Δy. Then, by definition:

$$x + \Delta z = \frac{x + \Delta x}{y + \Delta y}$$

Divide both sides by z. The left side becomes

$$\frac{(z + \Delta z)}{z} = \left(1 + \frac{\Delta z}{z}\right)$$

The right side becomes

$$\frac{(x + \Delta x)}{(y + \Delta y)}\frac{1}{z} = \frac{(x + \Delta x)y}{(y + \Delta y)x} = \frac{(x + \Delta x)/x}{(y + \Delta y)/y} = \frac{1 + (\Delta x/x)}{1 + (\Delta y/y)}$$

where the first equality comes from the fact that $z = x/y$, the second equality comes from rearranging terms and the third equality comes from simplifying.

Using the expressions for the left and right sides gives:

$$1 + \Delta z/z = \frac{1 + (\Delta x/x)}{1 + (\Delta y/y)}$$

Or, substituting,

$$1 + g_z = \frac{1 + g_x}{1 + g_y}$$

From Proposition 6, $(1 + g_z) \approx (1 + g_x - g_y)$, or, equivalently,

$$g_z \approx g_x - g_y$$

For $g_x = 0.05$ and $g_y = 0.03$, the approximation gives $g_z = 2\%$, while the correct value is 1.9%.

Application from Chapter 10:

Let aggregate demand be given by $Y = \gamma M/P$, where Y is output, M is nominal money, P is the price level and γ is a constant. It follows from Propositions 7 and 8 that:

$$g_Y \approx g_\gamma + g_M - \pi$$

where π is the rate of growth of prices, equivalently the rate of inflation. As γ is constant, g_γ is equal to zero. Thus,

$$g_Y \approx g_M - \pi$$

The rate of output growth is approximately equal to the rate of growth of nominal money minus the rate of inflation.

Functions

We use functions informally in this book, as a way of denoting how a variable depends on one or more other variables.

In some cases, we look at how a variable Y moves with a variable X. We write this relation as

$$Y = f(X)$$
$$(+)$$

A plus sign below X indicates a positive relation: an increase in X leads to an increase in Y. A minus sign below X indicates a negative relation: an increase in X leads to a decrease in Y.

In some cases, we allow the variable Y to depend on more than one variable. For example, we allow Y to depend on X and Z:

$$Y = f(X, Z)$$
$$(+, -)$$

The signs indicate that an increase in X leads to an increase in Y, and that an increase in Z leads to a decrease in Y.

An example of such a function is the investment function (5.1) in Chapter 5:

$$I = I(Y, i)$$
$$(+, -)$$

This equation says that investment, I, increases with production, Y, and decreases with the interest rate, i.

In some cases, it is reasonable to assume that the relation between two or more variables is a **linear relation**. A given increase in X always leads to the same increase in Y. In that case, the function is given by:

$$Y = a + bX$$

This relation can be represented by a line giving Y for any value of X.

The parameter a gives the value of Y when X is equal to zero. It is called the **intercept** because it gives the value of Y when the line representing the relation 'intercepts' (crosses) the vertical axis.

The parameter b tells us by how much Y increases when X increases by 1. It is called the **slope** because it is equal to the slope of the line representing the relation.

A simple linear relation is the relation $Y = X$, which is represented by the 45° line and has a slope of 1. Another example of a linear relation is the consumption function (3.2) in Chapter 3:

$$C = c_0 + c_1 Y_D$$

where C is consumption and Y_D is disposable income. c_0 tells us what consumption would be if disposable income were equal to zero. c_1 tells us by how much consumption increases when income increases by 1 unit; c_1 is called the marginal propensity to consume.

Logarithmic scales

A variable that grows at a constant growth rate increases by larger and larger increments over time. Take a variable X that grows over time at a constant growth rate, say at 3% per year:

- Start in year 0 and assume that $X = 2$. So a 3% increase in X represents an increase of $0.06 (0.03 \times 2)$.
- Go to year 20. X is now equal to $2(1.03)^{20} = 3.61$. A 3% increase now represents an increase of $0.11 (0.03 \times 3.61)$.
- Go to year 100. X is equal to $2(1.03)^{100} = 38.4$. A 3% increase represents an increase of $1.15 (0.03 \times 38.4)$, so an increase about 20 times larger than in year 0.

If we plot X against time using a standard (linear) vertical scale, the plot looks like Figure A1.1(a). The increases in X become larger and larger over time (0.06 in year 0, 0.11 in year 20 and 1.15 in year 100). The curve representing X against time becomes steeper and steeper.

Another way of representing the evolution of X is to use a *logarithmic scale* to measure X on the vertical axis. The property of a logarithmic scale is that the same *proportional* increase in this variable is represented by the same vertical distance on the scale. So the behaviour of a variable such as X, which increases by the same proportional increase (3%) each year, is now represented by a line. Figure A1.1(b) represents the behaviour of X, this time using a logarithmic scale on the vertical axis. The fact that the relation is represented by a line indicates that X is growing at a constant rate over time. The higher the rate of growth, the steeper the line.

In contrast to X, economic variables such as GDP do not grow at a constant growth rate every year. Their growth rate may be higher in some decades and lower in others. A recession may lead to a few years of negative growth. Yet, when looking at their evolution over time, it is often more informative to use a logarithmic scale than a linear scale. Let's see why.

Figure A1.2(a) plots real US GDP from 1890–2006 using a standard (linear) scale. Because real US GDP is about 46 times bigger in 2006 than in 1890, the same proportional increase in GDP is 46 times bigger in 2006 than in 1890. So the curve representing the evolution of GDP over time becomes steeper and steeper over time. It is very difficult to see from the figure whether the US economy is growing faster or slower than it was 50 years ago or 100 years ago.

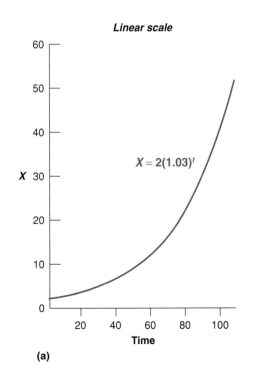

Linear scale

(a)

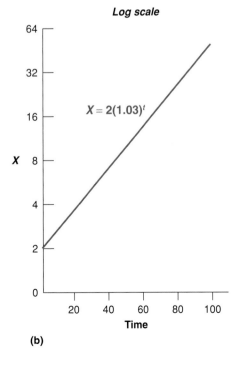

Log scale

$X = 2(1.03)^t$

(b)

Figure A1.1

(a) The evolution of X using a linear scale.

(b) The evolution of X using a logarithmic scale.

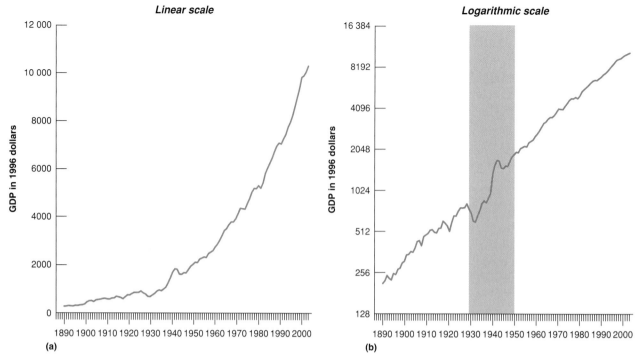

Figure A1.2

(a) US GDP since 1890 using a linear scale.

(b) US GDP since 1890 using a logarithmic scale.

Figure A1.2(b) plots US GDP from 1890–2006, now using a logarithmic scale. If the growth rate of GDP was the same every year – so the proportional increase in GDP was the same every year – the evolution of GDP would be represented by a line – the same way as the evolution of X was represented by a line in Figure A1.1(b). Because the growth rate of GDP is not constant from year to year – so the proportional increase in GDP is not the same every year – the evolution of GDP is no longer represented by a line. Unlike in Figure A1.2(a), GDP does not explode over time, and the graph is more informative. Here are two examples:

● If, in Figure A1.2(b), we were to draw a line to fit the curve from 1890–1929 and another line to fit the curve from 1950–2003 (the two periods are separated by the shaded area in Figure A1.2(b)), the two lines would have roughly the same slope. What this tells us is that the average growth rate was roughly the same during the two periods.

● The decline in output from 1929–1933 is very visible in Figure A1.2(b). So is the strong recovery of output that follows. By the 1950s, output appears to be back to its old trend line. This suggests that the Great Depression was not associated with a permanently lower level of output.

Note, in both cases, that you could not have derived these conclusions by looking at Figure A1.2(a), but you can derive them by looking at Figure A1.2(b). This shows the usefulness of using a logarithmic scale.

KEY TERMS

How do we know that consumption depends on disposable income? How do we know the value of the propensity to consume?

To answer these questions, and more generally, to estimate behavioural relations and find out the values of the relevant parameters, economists use *econometrics* – the set of statistical techniques designed for use in economics. Econometrics can get very technical, but the basic principles behind it are simple.

Our purpose in this appendix is to show you these basic principles. We shall do so using as an example the consumption function introduced in Chapter 3, and we shall concentrate on estimating c_1, the propensity to consume out of disposable income.

Changes in consumption and changes in disposable income

The propensity to consume tells us by how much consumption changes for a given change in disposable income. A natural first step is simply to plot changes in consumption versus changes in disposable income and see how the relation between the two looks. You can see this in Figure A2.1.

The vertical axis in Figure A2.1 measures the annual change in consumption minus the average annual change in consumption, for each year from 1970–2006. More precisely, let C_t denote consumption in year t. Let ΔC_t denote $C_t - C_{t-1}$, the change in consumption from year $t-1$ to year t. Let ΔC denote the average annual change in consumption since 1970. The variable measured on the vertical axis is constructed as $\Delta C_t - \overline{\Delta C}$. A positive value of the variable represents an increase in consumption larger than average, while a negative value represents an increase in consumption smaller than average.

Similarly, the horizontal axis measures the annual change in disposable income, minus the average annual change in disposable income since 1970, $\Delta Y_{Dt} - \overline{\Delta Y_D}$.

A particular square in the figure gives the deviations of the change in consumption and disposable income from their respective means for a particular year between 1970 and 2006. In 2006 for example, the change in consumption was higher than average by $50 billion; the change in disposable income was higher than average by $67 billion. (For our purposes, it is not important to know which year each square refers to, just what the set of points in the diagram looks like. So, except for 2006, the years are not indicated on Figure A2.1.)

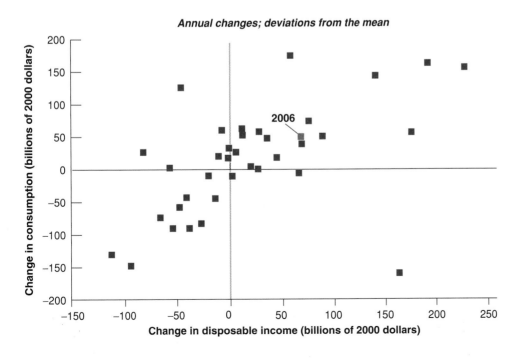

Annual changes; deviations from the mean

Figure A2.1

Changes in consumption vs changes in disposable income, since 1970

There is a clear positive relation between changes in consumption and changes in disposable income.

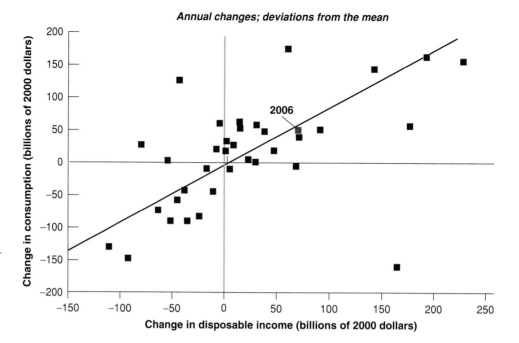

Figure A2.2

Changes in consumption and changes in disposable income: the regression line

The regression line is the line that fits the scatter of points best.

Figure A2.1 suggests two main conclusions:

- There is a clear positive relation between changes in consumption and changes in disposable income. Most of the points lie in the upper-right and lower-left quadrants of the figure: when disposable income increases by less than average, so typically does consumption.

- The relation between the two variables is good but not perfect. In particular, some points lie in the upper-left quadrant: these points correspond to years when smaller-than-average changes in disposable income were associated with higher-than-average changes in consumption.

Econometrics allows us to state these two conclusions more precisely and to get an estimate of the propensity to consume. Using an econometrics software package, we can find the line that fits the cloud of points in Figure A2.1 best. This line-fitting process is called **ordinary least squares (OLS)**. The estimated equation corresponding to the line is called a **regression** and the line itself is called the **regression line**. The term *least squares* comes from the fact that the line has the property that it minimises the sum of the squared distances of the points to the line – thus gives the 'least' 'squares'. The word *ordinary* comes from the fact that this is the simplest method used in econometrics.

In our case, the estimated equation is given by

$$(\Delta C_t - \overline{\Delta C}) = 0.77(\Delta Y_{Dt} - \overline{\Delta Y_D}) = \text{residual} \qquad \text{[A2.1]}$$
$$\bar{R} = 0.58$$

The regression line corresponding to this estimated equation is drawn in Figure A2.2. Equation (A2.1) reports two important numbers (econometrics packages give more

information than those reported here; a typical printout, together with further explanations, is given in the Focus box 'A guide to understanding econometric results'):

- The first important number is the estimated propensity to consume. The equation tells us that an increase in disposable income of $1 billion above normal is typically associated with an increase in consumption of $0.77 billion above normal. In other words, the estimated propensity to consume is 0.77. It is positive but smaller than 1.

- The second important number is $\bar{R}^2$, which is a measure of how well the regression line fits:

  Having estimated the effect of disposable income on consumption, we can decompose the change in consumption for each year into that part that is due to the change in disposable income – the first term on the right in equation (A2.1) – and the rest, which is called the **residual**. For example, the residual for 2006 is indicated in Figure A2.2 by the vertical distance from the point representing 2006 to the regression line. (The point representing 2006 happens to be nearly on the regression line, so the vertical distance is very small.)

  If all the points in Figure A2.2 were exactly on the estimated line, all residuals would be 0; all changes in consumption would be explained by changes in disposable income. As you can see, however, this is not the case. $\bar{R}^2$ is a statistic that tells us how well the line fits. $\bar{R}^2$ is always between 0 and 1. A value of 1 would imply that the relation between the two variables is perfect, that all points are exactly on the regression line. A value of 0 would imply that the computer can see no relation between the two variables. The value of $\bar{R}^2$ of 0.58 in

FOCUS
A guide to understanding econometric results

In your readings, you may run across results of estimation using econometrics. Here is a guide, which uses the slightly simplified, but otherwise untouched computer output for equation (A2.1):

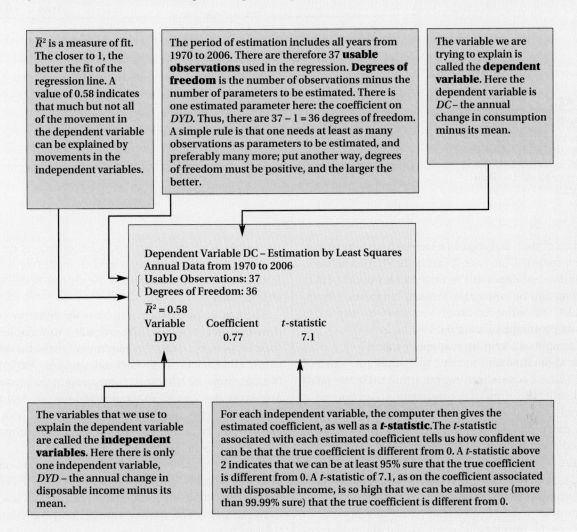

$\overline{R}^2$ is a measure of fit. The closer to 1, the better the fit of the regression line. A value of 0.58 indicates that much but not all of the movement in the dependent variable can be explained by movements in the independent variables.

The period of estimation includes all years from 1970 to 2006. There are therefore 37 **usable observations** used in the regression. **Degrees of freedom** is the number of observations minus the number of parameters to be estimated. There is one estimated parameter here: the coefficient on *DYD*. Thus, there are 37 − 1 = 36 degrees of freedom. A simple rule is that one needs at least as many observations as parameters to be estimated, and preferably many more; put another way, degrees of freedom must be positive, and the larger the better.

The variable we are trying to explain is called the **dependent variable**. Here the dependent variable is *DC* – the annual change in consumption minus its mean.

Dependent Variable DC – Estimation by Least Squares
Annual Data from 1970 to 2006
Usable Observations: 37
Degrees of Freedom: 36

$\overline{R}^2 = 0.58$

Variable	Coefficient	*t*-statistic
DYD	0.77	7.1

The variables that we use to explain the dependent variable are called the **independent variables**. Here there is only one independent variable, *DYD* – the annual change in disposable income minus its mean.

For each independent variable, the computer then gives the estimated coefficient, as well as a **t-statistic**. The *t*-statistic associated with each estimated coefficient tells us how confident we can be that the true coefficient is different from 0. A *t*-statistic above 2 indicates that we can be at least 95% sure that the true coefficient is different from 0. A *t*-statistic of 7.1, as on the coefficient associated with disposable income, is so high that we can be almost sure (more than 99.99% sure) that the true coefficient is different from 0.

equation (A2.1) is high, but not very high. It confirms the message from Figure A2.2: movements in disposable income clearly affect consumption, but there is still quite a bit of movement in consumption that cannot be explained by movements in disposable income.

Correlation versus causality

We have established so far that consumption and disposable income typically move together. More formally, we have seen that there is a positive **correlation** – the technical term for 'co-relation' – between annual changes in consumption and annual changes in disposable income. And we have interpreted this relation as showing **causality** – that an increase in disposable income causes an increase in consumption.

We need to think again about this interpretation. A positive relation between consumption and disposable income may reflect the effect of disposable income on consumption. But it may also reflect the effect of consumption on disposable income. Indeed, the model we developed in Chapter 3 tells us that if, for any reason, consumers decide to spend

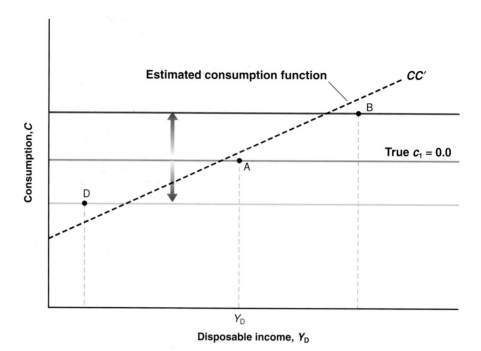

Figure A2.3

A misleading regression

The relation between disposable income and consumption comes from the effect of consumption on income rather than from the effect of income on consumption.

more, then output, and therefore income and, in turn, disposable income will increase. If part of the relation between consumption and disposable income comes from the effect of consumption on disposable income, interpreting equation (A2.1) as telling us about the effect of disposable income on consumption is not right.

An example will help here: suppose consumption does not depend on disposable income, so that the true value of c_1 is 0. (This is not very realistic, but it will make the point most clearly.) So draw the consumption function as a horizontal line (a line with a 0 slope) in Figure A2.3. Next, suppose that disposable income equals Y_D, so that the initial combination of consumption and disposable income is given by point A.

Now suppose that, because of improved confidence, consumers increase their consumption, so the consumption line shifts up. If demand affects output, then income and, in turn, disposable income, increase, so that the new combination of consumption and disposable income will be given by, say, point B. If, instead, consumers become more pessimistic, the consumption line shifts down, and so does output, leading to a combination of consumption and disposable income given by point D.

If we look at that economy, we observe points A, B and D. If, as we did earlier, we draw the best-fitting line through these points, we estimate an upward-sloping line, such as CC', and so estimate a positive value for propensity to consume, c_1. Remember, however, that the true value of c_1 is 0. Why do we get the wrong answer – a positive value for c_1 when the true value is 0? Because we interpret the positive relation between disposable income and consumption as showing the effect of disposable income on

consumption when, in fact, the relation reflects the effect of consumption on disposable income: higher consumption leads to higher demand, higher output and higher disposable income.

There is an important lesson here: *the difference between correlation and causality*. The fact that two variables move together does not imply that movements in the first variable cause movements in the second variable. Perhaps the causality runs the other way: movements in the second variable cause movements in the first variable. Or perhaps, as is likely to be the case here, the causality runs both ways: disposable income affects consumption, *and* consumption affects disposable income.

Is there a way out of the correlation-versus-causality problem? If we are interested – and we are – in the effect of disposable income on consumption, can we still learn that from the data? The answer yes, but only by using more information.

Suppose we *knew* that a specific change in disposable income was not caused by a change in consumption. Then, by looking at the reaction of consumption to *this* change in disposable income, we could learn how consumption responds to disposable income; we could estimate the propensity to consume.

This answer would seem to simply assume away the problem: how can we tell that a change in disposable income is not due to a change in consumption? In fact, sometimes we can tell. Suppose, for example, that the government embarks on a major increase in defence spending, leading to an increase in demand and, in turn, an increase in output. In that case, if we see both disposable income and consumption increase, we can safely assume that the movement in consumption reflects the effect of disposable income on consumption, and thus estimate the propensity to consume.

This example suggests a general strategy:

- Find exogenous variables – that is, variables that affect disposable income but are not in turn affected by it.
- Look at the change in consumption in response not to all changes in disposable income – as we did in our earlier regression – but in response to those changes in disposable income that can be explained by changes in these exogenous variables.

By following this strategy, we can be confident that what we are estimating is the effect of disposable income on consumption, and not the other way around.

The problem of finding such exogenous variables is known as the **identification problem** in econometrics. These exogenous variables, when they can be found, are called **instruments**. Methods of estimation that rely on the use of such instruments are called **instrumental variable methods**.

When equation (A2.1) is estimated using an instrumental variable method – using current and past changes in government defence spending as the instruments – rather than ordinary least squares, as we did earlier, the estimated equation becomes

$$(\Delta C_t - \overline{\Delta C}) = 0.62(\Delta Y_{Dt} - \overline{\Delta Y_D})$$

Note that the coefficient on disposable income, 0.62, is smaller than 0.77 in equation (A2.1). This decrease in the estimated propensity to consume is exactly what we would expect: our earlier estimate in equation (A2.1) reflected not only the effect of disposable income on consumption, but also the effect of consumption on disposable income. The use of instruments eliminates this second effect, which is why we find a smaller estimated effect of disposable income on consumption.

This short introduction to econometrics is no substitute for a course in econometrics. But it gives you a sense of how economists use data to estimate relations and parameters, and to identify causal relations between economic variables.

KEY TERMS

GLOSSARY

above the line, below the line In the balance of payments, the items in the *current account* are above the line drawn to divide them from the items in the *capital account*, which appear below the line.

accelerationist Phillips curve See *modified Phillips curve.*

adaptive expectations A backward-looking method of forming expectations by adjusting for past mistakes.

adjusted nominal money growth Nominal money growth minus normal output growth.

aggregate demand relation The demand for output at a given price level. It is derived from equilibrium in goods and financial markets.

aggregate output The total amount of output produced in the economy.

aggregate private spending The sum of all nongovernment spending. Also called *private spending.*

aggregate production function The relation between the quantity of aggregate output produced and the quantities of inputs used in production.

aggregate supply relation The price level at which firms are willing to supply a given level of output. It is derived from equilibrium in the labour market.

animal spirits A term introduced by Keynes to refer to movements in investment that could not be explained by movements in current variables.

appreciation (nominal) An increase in the price of domestic currency in terms of foreign currency. Corresponds to an increase in the exchange rate.

appropriability of research The extent to which firms benefit from the results of their research and development efforts.

arbitrage The proposition that the expected rates of return on two financial assets must be equal. Also called *risky arbitrage* to distinguish it from *riskless arbitrage*, the proposition that the actual

rates of return on two financial assets must be the same.

asymmetric shocks Shifts in demand which hit two different countries in opposiste ways.

automatic stabiliser The fact that a decrease in output leads, under given tax and spending rules, to an increase in the budget deficit. This increase in the budget deficit in turn increases demand and thus stabilises output.

autonomous spending The component of the demand for goods that does not depend on the level of output.

back loading Deferring the payment until specified conditions have been implemented.

balance of payments A set of accounts that summarise a country's transactions with the rest of the world.

balanced budget A budget in which taxes are equal to government spending.

balanced growth The situation in which output, capital and effective labour all grow at the same rate.

band (for exchange rates) The limits within which the exchange rate is allowed to move under a fixed exchange rate system.

bank reserves Holdings of central bank money by banks. The difference between what banks receive from depositors and what they lend to firms or hold as bonds.

bank run Simultaneous attempts by depositors to withdraw their funds from a bank.

bargaining power The relative strength of each side in a negotiation or a dispute.

barter The exchange of goods for other goods rather than for money.

base year When constructing real GDP by evaluating quantities in different years using a given set of prices, the year to which this given set of prices corresponds.

behavioural equation An equation that captures some aspect of behaviour.

bilateral exchange rate The real exchange rate between two countries.

bond A financial asset that promises a stream of known payments over some period of time.

bond rating The assessment of a bond based on its default risk.

broad money See *M2.*

Bretton Woods System of monetary management that established the rules for commercial and financial relations among the world's major industrial states in the mid-20th century. It included an obligation for each country to adopt a monetary policy that maintained the exchange rate of its currency within a fixed value – plus or minus one percent – in terms of gold.

BRICs (or 'the BRIC countries') Acronym – first coined by Goldman Sachs in 2001 – that refers to the fast-growing developing economies of Brazil, Russia, India and China.

budget deficit The excess of government expenditures over government revenues.

budget surplus The excess of government revenues over government expenditures.

business cycle convergence Close relationship between economy-wide fluctuations in production or economic activity in different countries.

business cycles See *output fluctuations.*

capital account In the balance of payments, a summary of a country's asset transactions with the rest of the world.

capital account balance The net result of public and private international investment flowing in and out of a country. This includes foreign direct investment, portfolio investment (such as changes in holdings of stocks and bonds) and other investments (such as changes in holdings in loans, bank accounts, and currencies).

capital account deficit An imbalance in a nation's balance of payments capital account in which payments made by the country for purchasing foreign assets exceed payments received by the country for selling domestic assets. In other words, investment by the domestic economy in foreign assets is less than foreign investment in domestic assets.

capital account surplus An imbalance in a nation's balance of payments capital account in which payments received by the country for selling domestic assets exceed payments made by the country for purchasing foreign assets. In other words, investment by the domestic economy in foreign assets is greater than foreign investment in domestic assets.

capital accumulation Increase in the capital stock.

capital controls Restrictions on the foreign assets domestic residents can hold, and on the domestic assets foreigners can hold.

cash flow The net flow of cash a firm is receiving.

causality A relation between cause and effect.

central bank money Money issued by the central bank. Also known as the *monetary base* and *high-powered money*.

central parity The reference value of the exchange rate around which the exchange rate is allowed to move under a fixed exchange rate system. The centre of the *band*.

Cobb–Douglas production function A standard production function which is applied to describe how much output two inputs into a production process make, with the hypothesis of constant returns to scale.

collective bargaining Wage bargaining between unions and firms.

Common Agricultural Policy (CAP) System of European Union agricultural subsidies and programs. The CAP combines a direct subsidy payment for crops and land which may be cultivated with price support mechanisms, including guaranteed minimum prices, import tariffs and quotas on certain goods from outside the EU.

competitive devaluation In a fixed exchange rate system, an official lowering of the value of a country's currency, by which the monetary authority formally sets a new fixed rate with respect to a foreign reference currency, done with the aim to improve domestic growth by shifting demand away from imports onto domestically produced goods.

confidence band When estimating the dynamic effect of one variable on another, the range of values where we can be confident the true dynamic effect lies.

constant returns to scale The proposition that a proportional increase (or decrease) of all inputs leads to the same proportional increase (or decrease) in output.

consumption (C) Goods and services purchased by consumers.

consumption function A function that relates consumption to its determinants.

consumption smoothing Preference for a consumption path that is constant over time.

contractionary open market operation An open-market operation in which the central bank sells bonds to decrease the money supply.

controls on capital flows Regulations preventing residents of a country from holding foreign denominated assets or currency and non-residents from holding domestic denominated assets or currency.

convergence The tendency for countries with lower output per capita to grow faster, leading to convergence of output per capita across countries.

coordination (of macroeconomic policies between two countries) The joint design of macroeconomic policies to improve the economic situation in the two countries.

corporate bond A bond issued by a corporation.

correlation A measure of the way two variables move together. A positive correlation indicates that the two variables tend to move in the same direction. A negative correlation indicates that the two variables tend to move in opposite directions. A correlation of zero indicates that there is no apparent relation between the two variables.

cost of living The cost of maintaining a certain standard of living in a certain region or country.

coupon bond A bond that promises multiple payments before maturity and one payment at maturity.

coupon payments The payments before maturity on a coupon bond.

coupon rate The ratio of the coupon payment to the face value of a coupon bond.

crawling peg An exchange rate mechanism in which the exchange rate is allowed to move over time according to a pre-specified formula.

credibility The degree to which people and markets believe that a policy announcement will actually be implemented and followed through.

currency Coins and notes.

currency board An exchange rate system in which: (i) the central bank stands ready to buy or sell foreign currency at the official exchange rate; (ii) the central bank cannot engage in open-market operations, that is buy or sell government bonds.

current account In the balance of payments, the summary of a country's payments to and from the rest of the world.

current account balance The net revenues that arise from a country's international sales and purchases of goods and services plus net international transfers.

current account deficit An excess of expenditure over receipts on current account in a country's balance of payments. See also *current account balance*.

current account surplus Excess of receipts over expenditure on current account in a country's balance of payments. See also *current account balance*.

current yield The ratio of the coupon payment to the price of a coupon bond.

cyclically adjusted deficit A measure of what the government deficit would be under existing tax and spending rules, if output were at its natural level. Also called a *full-employment deficit*, *midcycle deficit*, *standardised employment deficit*, or *structural deficit*.

debt finance Financing based on loans or the issuance of bonds.

debt monetisation The printing of money to finance a deficit.

debt ratio See *debt-to-GDP ratio*.

debt repudiation A unilateral decision by a debtor not to repay its debt.

debt stabilisation Convergence of the debt ratio to a steady-state level.

debt-to-GDP ratio The ratio of debt to gross domestic product. Also called simply the *debt ratio*.

decreasing returns to capital The property that increases in capital lead to smaller and smaller increases in output as the level of capital increases.

decreasing returns to labour The property that increases in labour lead to smaller and smaller increases in output as the level of labour increases.

default risk (or credit risk) The risk of loss due to a debtor's non-payment of a loan or other line of credit (either the principal or interest (coupon) or both).

deficit financing (or **deficit spending)** Deficit spending is the amount by which a government spending exceeds income over a particular period of time, also called simply 'deficit', or 'budget deficit', the opposite of budget surplus.

deflation Negative inflation.

degree of openness Ratio of exports (and/or imports) to GDP.

degrees of freedom The number of usable observations in a *regression* minus the number of parameters to be estimated.

demand for domestic goods The demand for domestic goods by people, firms and governments, both domestic and foreign. Equal to the domestic demand for goods plus net exports.

dependent variable A variable whose value is determined by one or more other variables.

deposit account A current account, savings account or other type of bank account that allows money to be deposited and withdrawn by the account holder.

deposit insurance Measure implemented in many countries to protect bank depositors, in full or in part, from losses caused by a bank's inability to pay its debts when due.

depreciation (nominal) A decrease in the price of domestic currency in terms of a foreign currency. Corresponds to a decrease in the exchange rate.

devaluation A decrease in the exchange rate in a fixed exchange rate system.

discount bond A bond that promises a single payment at maturity.

discount factor The value today of a (euro other national currency unit) at some time in the future.

discount rate (i) The interest rate used to discount a sequence of future payments. Equal to the nominal interest rate when discounting future nominal payments and

to the real interest rate when discounting future real payments. (ii) The interest rate at which the central bank lends to banks. (iii) In the context of intertemporal consumption decisions, it is the rate at which an individual discounts future consumption.

discouraged worker A person who has given up looking for employment.

disinflation A decrease in inflation.

disposable income (Y_D), The income that remains once consumers have received transfers from the government and paid their taxes.

dividends The portion of a corporation's profits that the firm pays out each period to its shareholders.

dollarisation The use of dollars in domestic transactions in a country other than the USA.

domestic demand for goods The sum of consumption, investment and government spending.

duration of unemployment The period of time during which a worker is unemployed.

dynamics Movements of one or more economic variables over time.

effective labour The number of workers in an economy times the state of technology.

effective real exchange rate See *multilateral exchange rate.*

efficiency wage The wage at which a worker is performing a job most efficiently or productively.

efficiency wage theories Economists call the theories that link the *productivity* or the *efficiency* of workers to the wage they are paid efficiency wage theories.

emerging economies Countries with low output per person, and high growth.

employment Total number of individuals who are employed.

employment protection Employment protection refers both to regulations concerning hiring (e.g. rules favouring disadvantaged groups, conditions for using temporary or fixed-term contracts, training requirements) and firing (e.g. redundancy procedures, mandated prenotification periods and severance payments, special requirements for collective dismissals and short-time work schemes).

endogenous variable A variable that depends on other variables in a model and is thus explained within the model.

endowment Amount of goods owned by an individual.

EONIA Acronym for Euro Overnight Index Average – a rate used as a benchmark for the markets in the European system of central banks. It is calucalte by taking the weighted average of all the overnight offer rates in the market.

equilibrium The equality between demand and supply.

equilibrium condition The condition that supply be equal to demand.

equilibrium in the goods market The condition that the supply of goods be equal to the demand for goods.

equity finance Financing based on the issuance of shares.

equity premium Risk premium required by investors to hold stocks rather than short-term bonds.

EU15 The original group of 15 countries that formed the European Union including the three new member countries that joined in 1995 (Austria, Finland and Sweden).

EU27 The group of 27 countries that joined the European Union until 2007. It included the 15 members of EU15 plus Cyprus, Czech Republic, Estonia, Hungary, Latvia, Lithuania, Malta, Poland, Slovakia and Slovenia that joined in 2004, and Bulgaria and Romania that joined in 2007.

European Central Bank (ECB) One of the world's most important central banks, responsible for monetary policy covering the 16 member States of the Eurozone. It was established by the European Union in 1998 with its headquarters in Frankfurt, Germany.

European Economic and Monetary Union (EMU) Consists of three stages coordinating economic policy, achieving economic convergence and culminating with the adoption of the euro, the EU's single currency. All member states of the European Union are expected to participate in the EMU. All member states, except Denmark and the UK, have committed themselves by treaty to join EMU. Sixteen member states of the European Union have entered the third stage and have adopted the euro as their currency. Denmark, Estonia, Latvia, and Lithuania are the current participants in the exchange rate mechanism. Of the pre-2004 members, the UK and Sweden have not joined ERM II and Denmark remains in ERM without proceeding to the third stage

European Monetary System (EMS) Arrangement established in 1979 under the Jenkins European Commission where most nations of the European Economic Community (EEC) linked their currencies to prevent large fluctuations relative to one another.

European System of Central Banks (ESCB) The European Central Bank (ECB) and the national central banks (NCBs) of all the 27 European Union (EU) Member States.

exchange rate fluctuation In a flexible exchange rate system, the free movement of the exchange rate.

exogenous variable A variable that is not explained within a model but, rather, is taken as given.

expansion A period of positive GDP growth.

expansionary open market operation An open-market operation in which the central bank buys bonds to increase the money supply.

expectations hypothesis The hypothesis that financial investors are risk neutral, which implies that expected returns on all financial assets have to be equal.

expectations-augmented Phillips curve See *modified Phillips curve*.

expected present discounted value The value today of an expected sequence of future payments. Also called *present discounted value* or *present value*.

exports (*X*) The purchases of domestic goods and services by foreigners.

face value (on a bond) The single payment at maturity promised by a discount bond.

fad A period of time during which, for reasons of fashion or over-optimism, financial investors are willing to pay more for a stock than its fundamental value.

fertility of research The degree to which spending on research and development translates into new ideas and new products.

final good Goods that are ultimately consumed rather than used in the production of another good.

finance theory Field that deals with investment making decisions.

financial intermediary A financial institution that receives funds from people, firms or other financial institutions, and uses these funds to make loans or buy financial assets.

financial investment The purchase of financial assets.

financial markets The markets in which financial assets are bought and sold.

financial wealth The value of all of one's financial assets minus all financial liabilities. Sometimes called *wealth*, for short.

fine-tuning A macroeconomic policy aimed at precisely hitting a given target, such as constant unemployment or constant output growth.

fine-tuning operations – A non-regular open market operation executed by the Eurosystem, mainly to deal with unexpected liquidity fluctuations in the market.

fiscal consolidation See *fiscal contraction*.

fiscal contraction A policy aimed at reducing the budget deficit through a decrease in government spending or an increase in taxation. Also called *fiscal consolidation*.

fiscal expansion An increase in government spending or a decrease in taxation, which leads to an increase in the budget deficit.

fiscal policy A government's choice of taxes and spending.

fiscal policy multiplier The increase in aggregate demand following a €1 increase in government spending (or following increases in other components of autonomous demand of the same amount).

Fisher effect or Fisher hypothesis The proposition that, in the long run, an increase in nominal money growth is reflected in an identical increase in both the nominal interest rate and the inflation rate, leaving the real interest rate unchanged.

fixed exchange rate An exchange rate between the currencies of two or more countries that is fixed at some level and adjusted only infrequently.

fixed investment See *investment (I)*.

flow A variable that can be expressed as a quantity per unit of time (such as income).

foreign exchange Foreign currency; all currencies other than the domestic currency of a given country.

four tigers The four Asian economies of Singapore, Taiwan, Hong Kong and South Korea.

full-employment deficit See *cyclically adjusted deficit*.

fully funded system A retirement system in which the contributions of current workers are invested in financial assets, with the proceeds (principal and interest) given back to the workers when they retire.

fundamental value (of a stock) The present value of expected dividends.

G8 The seven major economic powers in the world: the USA, Japan, France, Germany, the UK, Italy and Canada.

game *Strategic interactions* between *players*.

game theory The prediction of outcomes from *games*.

GDP adjusted for inflation See *real GDP*.

GDP at constant prices See *real GDP*.

GDP at current prices See *nominal GDP*.

GDP deflator The ratio of nominal GDP to real GDP; a measure of the overall price level. Gives the average price of the final goods produced in the economy.

GDP growth The growth rate of real GDP in year t; equal to $(Y_t - Y_{t-1})/Y_{t-1}$.

GDP in terms of goods See *real GDP*.

geometric series A mathematical sequence in which the ratio of one term to the preceding term remains the same. A sequence of the form $1 + c + c^2 + \ldots + c^n$.

gold standard A system in which a country fixed the price of its currency in terms of gold and stood ready to exchange gold for currency at the stated parity.

golden-rule level of capital The level of capital at which steady-state consumption is maximised.

government bond A bond issued by a government or a government agency.

government spending (*G*) The goods and services purchased by regional, and local governments.

government transfers Payments made by the government to individuals that are not in exchange for goods or services. Example: social security payments.

gross domestic product (GDP) A measure of aggregate output in the national income accounts.

gross national product (GNP) A measure of aggregate output in the national income accounts.

growth The steady increase in aggregate output over time.

hard peg The exchange rate to which a country commits under a fixed exchange rate system.

Harmonised Index of Consumer Prices (HICP) An indicator of inflation and price stability for the European Central Bank (ECB). It is a consumer price index which is compiled according to a methodology that has been harmonised across EU countries. The euro area HICP is a weighted average of price indices of member states who have adopted the euro.

hedonic pricing An approach to calculating real GDP that treats goods as providing a collection of characteristics, each with an implicit price.

heterodox stabilisation programme A stabilization programme that includes incomes policies.

high-powered money See *central bank money*.

hires Workers newly employed by firms.

housing wealth The value of the housing stock.

human capital The set of skills possessed by the workers in an economy.

human wealth The labour-income component of wealth.

hyperinflation Very high inflation.

identification problem In econometrics, the problem of finding whether correlation between variables X and Y indicates a causal relation from X to Y, or from Y to X, or both. This problem is solved by finding exogenous variables, called *instruments*, that affect X and do not affect Y directly, or affect Y and do not affect X directly.

identity An equation that holds by definition, denoted by the sign ≡.

imports (IM) The purchases of foreign goods and services by domestic consumers, firms and the government.

income The flow of revenue from work, rental income, interest and dividends.

incomes policies Government policies that set up wage and/or price guidelines or controls.

independent variable A variable that is taken as given in a relation or in a model.

index number A number, such as the GDP deflator, that has no natural level and is thus set to equal some value (typically 1 or 100) in a given period.

indexed bond A bond that promises payments adjusted for inflation.

inflation A sustained rise in the general level of prices.

inflation rate The rate at which the price level increases over time.

inflation targeting The conduct of monetary policy to achieve a given inflation rate over time.

inflation tax The product of the rate of inflation and real money balances.

information technology revolution The booming software industry and the widespread use of personal computers in firms, governments and households.

instrumental variable methods In econometrics, methods of estimation that use *instruments* to estimate causal relations between different variables.

instruments In econometrics, the exogenous variables that allow the identification problem to be solved.

interbank market Foreign exchange market where banks exchange different currencies. The interbank market is an important segment of the foreign exchange market.

intercept In a linear relation between two variables, the value of the first variable when the second variable is equal to zero.

interest parity condition See *uncovered interest parity*.

interest rate rule Rule follwed by the central bank to determine the desired level of the interest rate.

intermediate good A good used in the production of a final good.

International Monetary Fund (IMF) The principal international economic organization. Publishes the *World Economic Outlook* annually and the *International Financial Statistics (IFS)* monthly.

intertemporal budget constraint Budget constraint that applies to consumption choices over subsequent periods of time.

inventory investment The difference between production and sales.

investment (I) Purchases of new houses and apartments by people, and purchases of new capital goods (machines and plants) by firms.

investment income In the current account, income received by domestic residents from their holdings of foreign assets.

IS curve A downward-sloping curve relating output to the interest rate. The curve corresponding to the *IS relation*, the equilibrium condition for the goods market.

IS relation An equilibrium condition stating that the demand for goods must be equal to the supply of goods, or equivalently that investment must be equal to saving. The equilibrium condition for the goods market.

J-curve A curve depicting the initial deterioration in the trade balance caused by a real depreciation, followed by an improvement in the trade balance.

junk bond A bond with a high risk of default.

labour force The sum of those employed and those unemployed.

Labour Force Survey (LFS) Statistical survey conducted in EU member countries annually designed to capture data about the labour market.

labour hoarding The practice of retaining workers during a period of low product demand rather than laying them off.

labour in efficiency units See *effective labour*.

labour productivity The ratio of output to the number of workers.

Laffer curve A curve showing the relation between tax revenues and the tax rate.

layoffs Workers who lose their jobs either temporarily or permanently.

leavers Workers who leave their jobs for better alternatives.

life (of a bond) See *maturity*.

life cycle theory of consumption The theory of consumption, developed initially by Franco Modigliani, which emphasises that the planning horizon of consumers is their lifetime.

linear relation A relation between two variables such that a one-unit increase in one variable always leads to an increase of n units in the other variable.

liquid asset An asset that can be sold easily and at little cost.

liquidity trap The case where nominal interest rates are equal to zero, and monetary policy cannot, therefore, decrease them further.

LM curve An upward-sloping curve relating the interest rate to output. The curve corresponding to the *LM relation,* the equilibrium condition for financial markets.

LM relation An equilibrium condition stating that the demand for money must be equal to the supply of money. The equilibrium condition for financial markets.

logarithmic scale A scale in which the same proportional increase is represented by the same distance on the scale, so that a variable that grows at a constant rate is represented by a straight line.

long run A period of time extending over decades.

Longer-term refinancing operations (LTRO) Monthly open market operations carried out by the European Central Bank (ECB) as an instrument for the implementation of monetary policy. Although the Main Refinancing Operations (MRO) conducte (bi)weekly are the ECB's primary policy instrument, LTROs are far from negligible.

Lucas critique The proposition, put forth by Robert Lucas, that existing relations between economic variables may change when policy changes. An example is the apparent trade-off between inflation and unemployment, which may disappear if policy makers try to exploit it.

M1 A 'narrow' money aggregate that comprises currency in circulation and overnight deposits.

M2 An 'intermediate' monetary aggregate that comprises *M*1 plus deposits with an agreed maturity of up to two years and deposits redeemable at notice of up to three months.

M3 A 'broad' monetary aggregate that comprises *M*2 plus repurchase agreements, money market fund shares and units as well as debt securities with a maturity of up to two years.

Maastricht Treaty (formally, the **Treaty on European Union**, **TEU**) Treaty signed in 1992 in Maastricht, the Netherlands between the members of the European Community and entered into force in 1993. It created the European Union and led to the creation of the euro. The treaty led to the creation of the euro currency, and created what is commonly referred to as the pillar structure of the European Union. This conception of the Union divides it into the European Community (EC) pillar, the Common Foreign and Security Policy (CFSP) pillar, and the Justice and Home Affairs (JHA) pillar.

main refinancing operation (MRO) in the European System of Central Banks, the MRO provides the bulk of liquidity to the banking system.

Malthusian trap Following Malthus' theory that population increase would outpace increases in the means of subsistence, indicates a steady decrease in the amount of resources available to each individual over time.

marginal propensity to consume (c_1) The effect on consumption of an additional euro disposable income.

marginal propensity to save ($1 - c_1$) The effect on saving of an additional dollar of disposable income. (Equal to one minus the marginal propensity to consume.)

mark-up The ratio of price to marginal cost. It is a measure of market power across firms or industries.

Marshall–Lerner condition The condition under which a real depreciation leads to an increase in net exports.

maturity The length of time over which a financial asset (typically a bond) promises to make payments to the holder.

medium run A period of time between the *short run* and the *long run.*

mid-cycle deficit See *cyclically adjusted deficit.*

minimum reserves The minimum amount of reserves a credit institution is required to hold with a central bank. In the minimum reserve framework of the Eurosystem, the reserve requirement of a credit institution is calculated by multiplying the reserve ratio for each category of items in the reserve base by the amount of those items on the institution's balance sheet.

minimum wage Lowest hourly rate an employer can pay an employee. In some countries (such as the US) the minimum wage is set by a statute while in others (such as the UK) it is set by the wage council of each industry.

models of endogenous growth Models in which accumulation of physical and human capital can sustain growth even in the absence of technological progress.

modified Phillips curve The curve that plots the change in the inflation rate against the unemployment rate. Also called an *expectations-augmented Phillips curve* or an *accelerationist Phillips curve.*

monetary aggregate The market value of a sum of liquid assets. *M*1 is a monetary aggregate that includes only the most liquid assets.

monetary base See *central bank money.*

monetary contraction A change in monetary policy, which leads to an increase in the interest rate. Also called *monetary tightening.*

monetary expansion A change in monetary policy, which leads to a decrease in the interest rate.

monetary policy The use of the money stock by the central bank to affect interest rates and, by implication, economic activity and inflation.

monetary–fiscal policy mix The combination of monetary and fiscal policies in effect at a given time.

monetary tightening See *monetary contraction.*

money Those financial assets that can be used directly to buy goods.

money illusion The proposition that people make systematic mistakes in assessing nominal versus real changes.

money market funds Financial institutions that receive funds from people and use them to buy short-term bonds.

money multiplier The increase in the money supply resulting from a one-euro increase in central bank money.

Moore's law Describes a long-term trend in the history of compcuting hardware, in which the number of transistors that can be placed inexpensively on an integrated circuit has doubled approximately every two years.

multilateral exchange rate (multilateral real exchange rate) The real exchange rate between a country and its trading partners, computed as a weighted average of bilateral real exchange rates. Also called the *trade-weighted real exchange rate* or *effective real exchange rate.*

multiplier The ratio of the change in an *endogenous variable* to the change in an *exogenous variable* (for example, the ratio of the change in output to a change in autonomous spending).

Mundell–Fleming model A model of simultaneous equilibrium in both goods and financial markets for an open economy.

narrow banking Restrictions on banks that would require them to hold only short-term government bonds.

natural level of employment The level of employment that prevails when unemployment is equal to its natural rate.

natural level of output The level of production that prevails when employment is equal to its natural level.

natural rate of unemployment The unemployment rate at which price and wage decisions are consistent.

net capital flows Capital flows from the rest of the world to the domestic economy, minus capital flows to the rest of the world from the domestic economy.

net exports (X–IM) The difference between exports and imports. Also called the *trade balance.*

net transfers received In the current account, the net value of foreign aid received minus foreign aid given.

neutrality of money The proposition that an increase in nominal money has no effect on output or the interest rate, but is reflected entirely in a proportional increase in the price level.

nominal exchange rate The price of domestic currency in terms of foreign currency. The number of units of foreign currency you can get for one unit of domestic currency.

nominal GDP The sum of the quantities of final goods produced in an economy times their current price.

nominal interest rate The interest rate in terms of the national currency. It tells us how many euros (for example) one has to repay in the future in exchange for borrowing €1 today.

nominal rigidities The slow adjustment of nominal wages and prices to changes in economic activity.

non-accelerating inflation rate of unemployment (NAIRU) The unemployment rate at which inflation neither decreases nor increases. See *natural rate of unemployment.*

non-employment rate The ratio of population minus employment, to population.

non-human wealth The financial and housing component of wealth.

non-residential investment The purchase of new capital goods by firms: *structures* and *producer durable equipment.*

normal growth rate The rate of output growth needed to maintain a constant unemployment rate.

not in the labour force The number of people who are neither employed nor looking for employment.

***n*-year interest rate** See *yield to maturity.*

Okun's law The relation between GDP growth and the change in the unemployment rate.

open market operation The purchase or sale of government bonds by the central bank for the purpose of increasing or decreasing the money supply.

openness in factor markets The opportunity for firms to choose where to locate production, and for workers to choose where to work and whether or not to migrate.

openness in financial markets The opportunity for financial investors to choose between domestic and foreign financial assets.

openness in goods markets The opportunity for consumers and firms to choose between domestic and foreign goods.

optimal control The control of a system (a machine, a rocket, an economy) by means of mathematical methods.

optimal control theory The set of mathematical methods used for *optimal control.*

optimal currency area Also known as optimum currency area, it is a geographical region in which it would maximise economic efficiency to have the entire region share a single currency.

ordinary least squares A statistical method to find the best-fitting relation between two or more variables.

Organisation for Economic Cooperation and Development (OECD) An international organisation that collects and studies economic data for many countries. Most of the world's rich countries belong to the OECD.

orthodox stabilisation programme A stabilisation programme that does not include incomes policies.

out of the labour force Individuals who do not have a job but are not looking for one.

output fluctuations Movements in output around its trend. Also called *business cycles.*

output per person A country's gross domestic product divided by its population.

panel data set A data set that gives the values of one or more variables for many individuals or many firms over some period of time.

paradox of saving The result that an attempt by people to save more may lead both to a decline in output and to unchanged saving.

parameter A coefficient in a behavioural equation.

participation rate The ratio of the labour force to the non-institutional civilian population.

patent The legal right granted to a person or firm to exclude anyone else from the production or use of a new product or technique for a certain period of time.

pay-as-you-go system A retirement system in which the contributions of current workers are used to pay benefits to current retirees.

permanent income theory of consumption The theory of consumption, developed by Milton Friedman, that emphasises that people make consumption decisions based not on current income, but on their notion of permanent income.

Phillips curve The curve that plots the relation between movements in inflation and unemployment. The original Phillips curve captured the relation between the inflation rate and the unemployment rate. The *modified Phillips curve* captures the relation between (i) the change in the inflation rate and (ii) the unemployment rate.

players The participants in a *game*. Depending on the context, players may be people, firms, governments and so on.

point-year of excess employment A difference between the actual unemployment rate and the natural unemployment rate of one percentage point for one year.

policy mix See *monetary-fiscal policy mix*.

political business cycle Fluctuations in economic activity caused by the manipulation of the economy for electoral gain.

political theory of government debt A theory about the political process through which the level of government debt is decided.

population in working age Population aged between 15 and 64 years.

present discounted value See *expected present discounted value*.

present value See *expected present discounted value*.

price level The general level of prices in an economy.

price-setting relation The relation between the price chosen by firms, the nominal wage and the mark-up.

primary deficit Government spending, excluding interest payments on the debt, minus government revenues. (The negative of the *primary surplus*.)

primary surplus Government revenues minus government spending, excluding interest payments on the debt.

private saving (S) Saving by the private sector. The value of consumers' disposable income minus their consumption.

private spending See *aggregate private spending*.

profitability The expected present discounted value of profits.

propagation mechanism The dynamic effects of a *shock* on output and its components.

public saving (T – G) Saving by the government; equal to government revenues minus government spending. Also called the *budget surplus*. (A *budget deficit* represents public dissaving.)

purchasing power Income in terms of goods.

purchasing power parity (PPP) A method of adjustment used to allow for international comparisons of GDP.

quantitative easing An extreme form of monetary policy used to stimulate an economy where interest rates are either at, or close to, zero. Normally, a central bank stimulates the economy indirectly by lowering interest rates but when it cannot lower them any further it can purchases financial assets (mostly short-term), including government paper and corporate bonds, from financial institutions (such as banks) using money it has created out of nothing.

quotas Restrictions on the quantities of goods that can be imported.

$\bar{R}^2$ A measure of fit, between zero and one, from a *regression*. An $\bar{R}^2$ of zero implies that there is no apparent relation between the variables under consideration. An $\bar{R}^2$ of 1 implies a perfect fit: all the *residuals* are equal to zero.

random walk The path of a variable whose changes over time are unpredictable.

rate of growth of multifactor productivity See *Solow residual*.

rational expectations The formation of expectations based on rational forecasts, rather than on simple extrapolations of the past.

rational speculative bubble An increase in stock prices based on the rational expectation of further increases in prices in the future.

real appreciation An increase in the relative price of domestic goods in terms of foreign goods. An increase in the real exchange rate.

real depreciation A decrease in the relative price of domestic goods in terms of foreign goods. An increase in the real exchange rate.

real exchange rate The relative price of domestic goods in terms of foreign goods.

real GDP A measure of aggregate output. The sum of quantities produced in an economy times their price in a base year. Also known as *GDP in terms of goods, GDP in constant dollars* or *GDP adjusted for inflation*.

real GDP per capita Real GDP divided by population.

real interest rate The interest rate in terms of goods. It tells us how many goods one has to repay in the future in exchange for borrowing the equivalent one good today.

recession A period of negative GDP growth. Usually refers to at least two consecutive quarters of negative GDP growth.

regression The output of *ordinary least squares*. Gives the equation corresponding to the estimated relation between variables, together with information about the degree of fit and the relative importance of the different variables.

regression line The best-fitting line corresponding to the equation obtained by using *ordinary least squares*.

regulation In the context of the banking sector, regulations are a form of government regulation which subjects banks to certain requirements, restrictions and guidelines.

rental cost of capital See *user cost*.

representative consumer The representative consumer hypothesis assumes that all individuals are identical, or that there is only one (representative) individual.

research and development (R&D) Spending aimed at discovering and developing new ideas and products.

reservation wage The wage that would make a worker indifferent between working and being unemployed.

reserve ratio The ratio of bank reserves to chequeable deposits.

reserve requirements The minimum amount of reserves that banks must hold in proportion to chequeable deposits.

residential investment The purchase of new homes and apartments by people.

residual The difference between the actual value of a variable and the value implied by the *regression line*. Small residuals indicate a good fit.

revaluation An increase in the exchange rate in a fixed exchange rate system.

Ricardian equivalence The proposition that neither government deficits nor government debt have an effect on economic activity. Also called the *Ricardo-Barro proposition*.

Ricardo–Barro proposition See *Ricardian equivalence.*

risk averse A person is risk averse if he/she prefers to receive a given amount for sure to an uncertain amount with the same expected value.

risk neutral A person is risk neutral if he/she is indifferent between receiving a given amount for sure or an uncertain amount with the same expected value.

risk premium The difference between the interest rate paid on a given bond and the interest rate paid on a bond with the highest rating.

sacrifice ratio The number of point-years of excess unemployment needed to achieve a decrease in inflation of 1%.

saving The sum of private and public saving, denoted by *S*.

saving rate The proportion of income that is saved.

savings The accumulated value of past saving. Also called *wealth.*

seignorage The revenues from the creation of money.

separations Workers who are leaving or losing their jobs.

share A financial asset issued by a firm that promises to pay a sequence of payments, called dividends, in the future. Also called *stock.*

shocks Movements in the factors that affect aggregate demand and/or aggregate supply.

shoe-leather costs The costs of going to the bank to take money out of a chequeing account.

short run A period of time extending over a few years at most.

slope In a linear relation between two variables, the amount by which the first variable increases when the second increases by one unit.

Solow residual The excess of actual output growth over what can be accounted for by the growth in capital and labour.

stabilisation programme A government program aimed at stabilising the economy (typically stopping high inflation).

stagflation The combination of stagnation and inflation.

staggering of wage decisions The fact that different wages are adjusted at different times, making it impossible to achieve a synchronised decrease in nominal wage inflation.

standard of living Level of material comfort as measured by the goods and services available to an individual, group or country.

standardised employment deficit See *cyclically adjusted deficit.*

standing facilities Facilities offered by the Eurosystem to credit institutions. There are two standing facilities: (i) marginal lending facility in order to obtain overnight liquidity from the central bank against the presentation of sufficient eligible assets; (ii) deposit facility in order to make overnight deposits with the central bank.

state of technology The degree of technological development in a country or industry.

static expectations See *adaptive expectations.*

statistical discrepancy A difference between two numbers that should be equal, coming from differences in sources or methods of construction for the two numbers.

steady state In an economy without technological progress, the state of the economy where output and capital per worker are no longer changing. In an economy with technological progress, the state of the economy where output and capital per effective worker are no longer changing.

stock A variable that can be expressed as a quantity at a point in time (such as wealth). Also a synonym for *share.*

stocks An alternative term for inventories. Also, an alternative term for shares.

strategic interactions An environment in which the actions of one player depend on and affect the actions of another player.

structural deficit See *cyclically adjusted deficit.*

structural operation An open market operation executed by the Eurosystem, mainly in order to adjust the structural liquidity position of the financial sector vis-à-vis the Eurosystem.

structural rate of unemployment See *natural rate of unemployment.*

sub-prime mortgages Mortgages accorded to borrowers with weakened credit histories including payment delinquencies, and possibly more severe problems such as charge-offs, judgments, and bankruptcies. These borrowers have reduced repayment capacity as measured by credit scores or debt-to-income ratios.

System of National Accounts (SNA) The System of National Accounts (SNA) consists of a coherent, consistent and integrated set of macroeconomic accounts, balance sheets and tables based on a set of internationally agreed concepts, definitions, classifications and accounting rules. (SNA 1.1) The System of National Accounts 1993 (SNA) has been prepared under the joint responsibility of the United Nations, the International Monetary Fund, the Commission of the European Communities, the OECD and the World Bank.

Tanzi–Olivera effect The adverse effect of inflation on tax revenues and in turn on the budget deficit.

tariffs Taxes on imported goods.

tax smoothing The principle of keeping tax rates roughly constant, so that the government runs large deficits when government spending is exceptionally high and small surpluses the rest of the time.

Taylor rule A rule, suggested by John Taylor, telling a central bank how to adjust the nominal interest rate in response to deviations of inflation from its target, and of the unemployment rate from the natural rate.

technological catch-up The process through which countries or firms come near to the technology frontier over time.

technology frontier The highest level reached upon a technological path.

technological progress An improvement in the state of technology.

technology gap The differences between states of technology across countries.

term structure of interest rates See *yield curve.*

time inconsistency In game theory, the incentive for one player to deviate from his previously announced course of action once the other player has moved.

Tobin's q The ratio of the value of the capital stock, computed by adding the stock market value of firms and the debt of firms, to the replacement cost of capital.

total wealth The sum of human wealth and non-human wealth.

tradable goods Goods that compete with foreign goods in domestic or foreign markets.

trade balance The difference between exports and imports. Also called *net exports.*

trade deficit A negative trade balance, that is, imports exceed exports.

trade surplus A positive trade balance, that is, exports exceed imports.

two pillar strategy The European Central Bank's strategy for managing monetary policy. One pillar is the control of the growth of monetary supply in the medium and long term. The other pillar is the monitoring of inflation expectations.

t-**statistic** A statistic associated with an estimated coefficient in a regression that indicates how confident one can be that the true coefficient differs from zero.

uncovered interest parity An arbitrage relation stating that domestic and foreign bonds must have the same expected rate of return, expressed in terms of a common currency.

underground economy That part of a nation's economic activity that is not measured in official statistics, either because the activity is illegal or because people and firms are seeking to avoid paying taxes.

unemployment Total number of individuals who are not employed and are looking for a job.

unemployment rate The ratio of the number of unemployed to the labour force.

usable observation An observation for which the values of all the variables under consideration are available for *regression* purposes.

user cost of capital The cost of using capital over a year, or a given period of time. The sum of the real interest rate and the depreciation rate. Also called the *rental cost of capital.*

value added The value a firm adds in the production process, equal to the value of its production minus the value of the intermediate inputs it uses in production.

wage indexation A rule that automatically increases wages in response to an increase in prices.

wage–price spiral The mechanism by which increases in wages lead to increases in prices, which lead in turn to further increases in wages, and so on.

wage-setting relation The relation between the wage chosen by wage setters, the price level, and the unemployment rate.

war of attrition When both parties to an argument hold their grounds, hoping that the other party will give in.

yield curve The relation between yield and maturity for bonds of different maturities. Also called the *term structure of interest rates.*

yield to maturity The constant interest rate that makes the price of an *n*-year bond today equal to the present value of future payments. Also called the *n-year interest rate.*

SYMBOLS USED IN THIS BOOK

m	Propensity to import	18
μ	Markup of prices over wages	7
N	Employment	2
N_n	Natural level of employment	7
NX	Net exports	6
P	GDP deflator/CPI/price level	2
P^*	Foreign price level	6
π	Inflation	2
Π	Profit per unit of capital	16
Q	Real stock price	15
$€Q$	Nominal stock price	15
R	Bank reserves	4
r	Real interest rate	14
S	Private saving	3
s	Private saving rate	12
T	Net taxes (taxes paid by consumers minus transfers)	3
θ	Reserve ratio of banks	4
U	Unemployment	2
u	Unemployment rate	2
u_n	Natural rate of unemployment	7
V	Present value of a sequence of real payments z	13
$€V$	Present value of a sequence of nominal payments $£z$	13
W	Nominal wage/wealth	7, 16
Y	Real GDP/output/production	2
$€Y$	Nominal GDP	2
Y_D	Disposable income	3
Y_L	Labour income	16
Y_n	Natural level of output	14
Y^*	Foreign output	6
X	Exports	3
Z	Demand for goods	3
z	Factors that affect the wage, given unemployment	14
z	Real payment	14
$€z$	Nominal payment	14

INDEX